# 100 MASTERS OF MYSTERY AND DETECTIVE FICTION

# 100 MASTERS OF MYSTERY AND DETECTIVE FICTION

**Volume 2**
Baynard H. Kendrick — Israel Zangwill
375 – 757
Appendices

*edited by*
**Fiona Kelleghan**
University of Miami

SALEM PRESS, INC.
Pasadena, California          Hackensack, New Jersey

Essays originally appeared in *Critical Survey of Mystery and Detective Fiction*, 1988; new material has been added

∞ The paper used in these volumes conforms to the American National Standard for Permanence of Paper for Printed Library Materials, Z39.48-1992 (R1997).

**Library of Congress Cataloging-in-Publication Data**
100 masters of mystery and detective fiction / edited by Fiona Kelleghan.
    p. cm. — (Magill's choice)
    Essays taken from Salem Press's Critical survey of mystery and detective fiction, published in 1988.
    Includes bibliographical references and index.
    Contents: v. 1. Margery Allingham—Harry Kemelman — v. 2. Baynard H. Kendrick—Israel Zangwill.
    ISBN 0-89356-958-5 (set : alk. paper) — ISBN 0-89356-973-9 (v. 1 : alk. paper) — ISBN 0-89356-977-1 (v. 2 : alk. paper)
    1. Detective and mystery stories—History and criticism. 2. Detective and mystery stories—Bio-bibliography. 3. Detective and mystery stories—Stories, plots, etc. I. Title: One hundred masters of mystery and detective fiction. II. Kelleghan, Fiona, 1965 - . III. Critical survey of mystery and detective fiction. IV. Series.

PN3448.D4 A16 2001
809.3′872—dc21

                        2001032834

First Printing

# Contents – Volume 2

# 100 Masters of Mystery and Detective Fiction

# Baynard H. Kendrick

**Born:** Philadelphia, Pennsylvania; April 8, 1894
**Died:** Ocala, Florida; March 22, 1977

**Also wrote as** • Richard Hayward

**Types of plot** • Private investigator • police procedural

**Principal series** • Miles Standish Rice, 1936-1938 • Captain Duncan Maclain, 1937-1962.

**Principal series characters** • MILES STANDISH RICE, a tall, lanky deputy sheriff from Florida, is chiefly remembered for his famous self-introduction: "I'm Miles Standish Rice—the Hungry!" His cases reveal the author's interest in the landscape and varied traditions of his adopted state.
• DUNCAN MACLAIN, a private investigator, is blind. Adaptation to his visual disability has heightened the awareness of his other senses to an extraordinary degree, but it is his sensitivity to others and their emotional handicaps which is memorable.

**Contribution** • The first six of the thirteen Maclain novels have been described as "outstanding," ranking with the best detective fiction done in the late 1930's and early 1940's by an American. Out of his personal experience working with blinded veterans, Baynard H. Kendrick created the character of Captain Duncan Maclain. Kendrick wanted to prove that the disadvantages associated with lack of sight could be overcome, and that the blind need not be treated as dependent children. Consequently, he deliberately placed his blind investigator in the most harrowing of situations. Maclain is not, however, superhuman in the mold of Ernest Bramah's Max Carrados. Kendrick could invent puzzles and twisting plots as well as the best of his contemporaries, but his unique contribution is his portrait of a believable disabled person in a dangerous occupation. Kendrick was one of the founders of the Mystery Writers of America, served as its first president, and received the organization's Grand Masters Award in 1967.

**Biography** • Baynard Hardwick Kendrick was born on April 8, 1894, the son of John Ryland Kendrick and Juliana Lawton Kendrick. Graduated from the Episcopal Academy in 1912, he later became the first American to join the Canadian army, enlisting in the infantry only one hour after the declaration of war. He was on active duty in France and Salonika and was decorated by the British and Canadian governments. His association with World War I convalescent homes led to a lifelong interest in the training of the blind. On May 2, 1919, he married Edythe Stevens; they had three children, Baynard, Edith, and Julia. After Edythe's death, he married Jean Morris in 1971. During the years between the end of the war and the publication of his first novel, *Blood on Lake Louisa* (1934), Kendrick traveled widely, lived in almost every corner of the United States, and tried almost every job imaginable, including that of lawyer, certified public accountant, hotel manager, publisher, and secretary to a door company.

Kendrick considered Florida his home and was a member of the editorial board of the *Florida Historical Quarterly* and director of the Florida Historical Society; he wrote the column "Florida's Fabulous Past" for the *Tampa Sunday Tribune* (1961-1964). His best-selling novel *The Flames of Time* (1948) deals with the state's turbulent past.

Kendrick was the organizer of the Blinded Veteran's Association and served as chairman of the board of directors and as its only sighted consultant. In honor of his work in the training and rehabilitation of blinded veterans, Kendrick received a plaque from General Omar Bradley. The film *Bright Victory* (1951), an adaptation of his novel *Lights Out* (1945), which concerns the trauma of the blinded soldier, earned for him the Screen Writers Guild's Robert Meltzer Award and the Spearhead Medal of the Third Armored Division. It is no surprise that all of his works have been transcribed into Braille.

In addition to *Lights Out*, Kendrick has had other works adapted for film, and the 1971 television series *Longstreet* was based partly on the character of Duncan Maclain. Suffering from ill health during the last ten years of his life, Kendrick wrote his last mystery, *Flight from a Firing Wall*, in 1966, but he remained an active fund-raiser for the Blinded Veterans' Association until his death in 1977.

**Analysis** • In *The Last Express* (1937), Baynard H. Kendrick introduced the figure of Captain Duncan Maclain, the tall, handsome war hero turned private investigator who is blessed with the gift of analytic reasoning and a flair for the dramatic. This description is typical of many detectives of the 1930's. The plots of the early Maclain books, in their love of the bizarre and the complex, are also representative of the era. What separates the Maclain novels from the rest is a marked shift in emphasis.

In many classic novels of detection, the sleuth, even though he may be endowed with a variety of affectations and idiosyncrasies, is a subordinate figure. The star attraction is generally the plot, upon whose intricacy and brilliance the success of the novel depends. Therefore, even if the reader cannot tolerate the detective, the ingenuity of the problem and its resolution can still be admired. In a Duncan Maclain novel, however, the opposite is true. The work stands or falls on the credibility of the characterization of Maclain himself, for he is blind. Consequently, the things that a nonhandicapped detective takes for granted become magnified in importance and, in some cases, must be explained in great detail. For example, a sighted detective may explain why he shot at a fleeing criminal and missed. Maclain must explain why he did not–he shoots at first sound.

It is essential to point out that Kendrick's choice of a blind detective is not a gimmick. Supposedly based on a friend of Kendrick who was blinded in World War I, Maclain is not blind simply to be different. Passionate in his support for the disabled and an authority on the training and rehabilitation of the blind, Kendrick deliberately created a detective who could stand as a symbol not only for the sightless but also for those who could not accept the blind as valuable members of society. Kendrick admitted that he wanted his novels to be used as propaganda in the fight for the understanding and the mainstreaming of the handicapped. Therein lies the artistic problem inherent in the portrayal of Duncan Maclain. It is very difficult to be a propagandistic symbol and, at the same time, an interesting and credible human being. Yet Maclain must be interesting and credible because of his complete domination of the novels in which he appears. The plot is secondary to the man and the detective. How does one portray the vulnerability and humanity of the man when one also wants to emphasize his invulnerability to the accidents of fate?

Kendrick's solution was to surround Maclain with an array of secondary characters, both friends and servants, who function as his own personal support group. Unfortunately, too often they are just that: merely members of a group with little or no individuality. At times they are stereotypes such as Cappo, Maclain's manservant-chauffeur. As chorus characters, they exist simply to provide transportation for the captain or to comment on his brillance. Even his wife is a vague, shadowy figure. The only memorable auxiliary figures are his Seeing Eye dogs, Driest and Schnucke, who generally seem more human than the humans themselves. Schnucke acts as the detective's guide, and Driest, an attack dog, is his bodyguard. The two are lovingly described in the novels, and when they are wounded trying to protect their master, the reader feels more sympathy for them than for any of the human victims, including perhaps Maclain.

This stance seems to be a deliberate decision on the author's part–he wants no sympathy for his blind detective. He wants Maclain to be judged according to his skill and intelligence as a detective. In the understandable desire to prove that Maclain can compete and even excel in his dangerous career, however, Kendrick sacrifices the human credibility for the professional and surrounds Maclain with an aura of rigid perfection. Kendrick was aware of this difficulty and frequently has his characters comment on their reactions to the captain's personality or lack of it. The typical response is one of awe:

> She returned to her apartment feeling a little awed. There was a quality of frightening perfection about Duncan Maclain. She knew he was engaged, but sometimes Bonnie wondered. Was Maclain's fiancée in love with the handsome, virile man, or fascinated by the cold perfection of the disembodied human machine?

The second reaction to Maclain is usually one of disbelief on discovering that he is actually blind. Here again, given the didactic motives underlying the creation of Maclain, Kendrick was faced with an almost unsolvable dilemma. On one hand, he was adamant in his belief that the blind are not different from others and should not be set apart or perceived as special in any way. In fact, Maclain does not even agree that he is blind in the accepted sense of the word:

> "I'm not blind, though," said Duncan Maclain. "I merely lost the use of my eyes in the last World War. There are many definitions of the word *blind* in the dictionary, Miss Vreeland. There are even more of the verb to see. Only one definition of each applies to impression through the eyes."

On the other hand, proud of the accomplishments of the blind and anxious to prove their worth, Kendrick wants to demonstrate what they can achieve. Therefore, the reader has the paradoxical portrait of a blind man who is never happier than when people forget that he is blind, but who also delights in displaying what he, without sight, can do. Maclain loves to show off; his favorite parlor tricks are doing jigsaw puzzles and his famous Sherlock Holmes routine. The following sequence, with variations, is repeated at the beginning of all Maclain novels and short stories.

> He sank down farther in his chair and clasped his long, sensitive fingers together. "You're five foot six, Miss Vreeland—a couple of inches taller than your cousin. You weigh—I trust I won't offend you—about fifteen pounds more. One hundred and thirty to her hundred and fifteen. You are older than she is—." "Wait," said Katherine, "You must have made inquiries about us. Why, Captain Maclain?"
> "My only inquiries were made through my senses." The captain sat erect, holding her with a sightless stare from his perfect eyes. "Your height is unmistakable from the length of your stride. I've walked with both you and Bonnie across this hall. Weight can be judged unerringly by the feel of anyone's arm. Every fair has weight guessers who make a living from this knowledge. The voice betrays one's age, and many other things—sorrow, pleasure, and pain."

The impression gathered about Maclain is always one of superiority, which is not atypical. Great detectives are great detectives because they are superior, and most of them love to demonstrate the scope of their intellects. What is different is that Maclain and his creator continuously feel compelled to vaunt the detective's talents. Clearly, to a great extent, this showboating is a result of the blind person's position in society. Kendrick's novels are treatises on the treatment afforded the blind. One of the successes of his work is his artful and sardonic capturing of the various nuances of society's ignorance and prejudices. This skill is especially manifest in the novels which describe the closed society of the upper class—for example, *Make Mine Maclain* (1947). The Beautiful People simply do not know how to treat someone who is less than physically perfect, and although they can pretend that the less fortunate and the disabled do not exist, they cannot overlook Duncan Maclain. Criminals are at an even greater disadvantage when they are confronted by the captain. Scornful of the sighted representatives of law and order, they find the idea of a blind investigator laughable—until they fail and he succeeds. Good examples of Kendrick's richest irony can be found in his analysis of the three-layered prejudice of upper-class criminals who, being Nazis, view Maclain as a type of freak. They, like much of society, take it for granted that since Maclain is physically handicapped, he must also be mentally deficient, a fact that the detective exploits to the fullest. In many of these cases, his success is a direct result of his blindness. His adversaries continually underestimate their foe.

It is also certainly true that the success of Duncan Maclain, literary character, is a result of his blindness. Although Kendrick won critical acclaim for his earlier Miles Standish Rice novels (for example, *The Iron Spiders*, 1936, in which a serial killer leaves behind black spiders as his calling card), they evoked little popular response. With the introduction of the blind captain, however, Kendrick's stock as a mystery writer soared. (It did not hurt that most of the Maclain novels, especially those written during the war years, were serialized in many of the most popular magazines of the time.) Readers were fascinated by the tall, enigmatic Maclain and the necessary paraphernalia of his life—his dogs, his Braille watch, his Dictaphones and recording devices. They loved seeing him triumph in situations that would have made a sighted superathlete cringe. Such public approval, in addition to the enthusiastic support of organizations for the blind and the disabled, led to a change in direction for Kendrick.

In his earlier work, the puzzle and its solution had always dominated. Buoyed by the public response to the exploits of his blind investigator, however, Kendrick gradually turned away from the classic novel of deduction to the world of espionage and the thriller. In these later works, Maclain is confronted by ever more dangerous situations; this harried leaping from one escapade to another robs the blind man of some of his credibility, the quality which is of most value to him as a literary figure. Maclain had been at his best in novels such as *The Odor of Violets* (1941), perhaps the major work of this series. *The Odor of Violets*, even though it deals with spies and saboteurs, is still essentially a novel of deduction set in the closed world of a private house. The critics, impressed by the skilled maneuvering of the intricate plotting, compared Maclain favorably to Bramah's Max Carrados, the first blind detective in fiction. Increasingly, however, as Kendrick puts Maclain through his paces, the novels begin to emphasize violence and frantic pursuit. *Out of Control* (1945), the last important Maclain novel, is one long chase scene. There is no mystery as the detective trails a psychopathic murderess through the wilds of the mountains of Tennessee. After 1945, the quality of Kendrick's work suffers a marked decline. Kendrick did make a minor comeback with his last work, *Flight from a Firing Wall*, a novel of suspense centered on the author's firsthand knowledge of intrigue and espionage in the Cuban refugee enclaves of Southern Florida.

Kendrick considered his support of the blind to be his profession. His creation of Duncan Maclain was only one aspect of that lifelong advocacy. When speaking of the Maclain novels, Kendrick never mentioned the artistic nature of his work but instead always stressed the technical detail required for the depiction of a blind hero. He was most proud of the fact that "the accuracy with which I attempted to portray the character . . . caused me to be called in for consultation on the training of the blinded veterans by the U.S. Army in World War II."

Although he was a writer of popular fiction, Kendrick espoused a classical theory of literature: He believed that art should teach while it entertained. One adjective that could be used to describe his fiction, however, is very modern: Kendrick's work was nothing if not committed.

## Principal mystery and detective fiction

SERIES: Captain Duncan Maclain: *The Last Express*, 1937; *The Whistling Hangman*, 1937; *The Odor of Violets*, 1941 (also as *Eyes in the Night*); *Blind Man's Bluff*, 1943; *Out of Control*, 1945; *Death Knell*, 1945; *Make Mine Maclain*, 1947 (also as *The Murderer Who Wanted More*); *You Die Today*, 1952; *Blind Allies*, 1954; *Reservations for Death*, 1957; *Clear and Present Danger*, 1958; *The Aluminum Turtle*, 1960 (also as *The Spear Gun Murders*); *Frankincense and Murder*, 1961. Miles Standish Rice: *The Iron Spiders*, 1936; *The Eleven of Diamonds*, 1936; *Death Beyond the Go-Thru*, 1938.

OTHER NOVELS: *Blood on Lake Louisa*, 1934; *The Tunnel*, 1949; *Trapped*, 1952; *The Soft Arms of Death*, 1955; *Hot Red Money*, 1959; *Flight from a Firing Wall*, 1966.

## Other major works

NOVELS: *Lights Out*, 1945; *The Flames of Time*, 1948.

NONFICTION: *The Never Talk Back*, 1954 (with Henry Trefflick); *Florida Trails to Turnpikes*, 1964; *Orlando: A Century Plus*, 1976.

## Bibliography

Kendrick, Baynard. "It's a Mystery to Me." *Writer* 60 (September, 1947): 324-326.

*The New Yorker*. Review of *Death Beyond the Go-Thru*, by Baynard H. Kendrick. 14 (November 19, 1938): 116.

_____. Review of *Out of Control*, by Baynard H. Kendrick. 21 (August 25, 1945): 64.

"Portrait." *The Saturday Review of Literature* 31 (July 3, 1948): 14.

"Portrait." *Time* 51 (June 14, 1948): 107.

*The Saturday Review of Literature*. Review of *The Last Express*, by Baynard H. Kendrick. 16 (June 5, 1937): 16.

_____. Review of *The Whistling Hangman*, by Baynard H. Kendrick. 17 (January 1, 1938): 24.

*Time*. Review of *Blind Man's Bluff*, by Baynard H. Kendrick. 41 (February 1, 1943): 88.

*Charlene E. Suscavage*

# John le Carré

## David John Moore Cornwell

**Born:** Poole, Dorset, England; October 19, 1931

**Type of plot** • Espionage

**Principal series** • George Smiley, 1961-1980.

**Principal series character** • GEORGE SMILEY is a master spy and holder of various official and unofficial posts in Great Britain's Secret Intelligence Service; he is separated from his unfaithful wife. Middle-aged, short, plump, and bespectacled, the waddling, owlish, Pickwickian Smiley is a most unlikely hero. Vaguely idealistic, he lives for his work.

**Contribution** • John le Carré began writing espionage novels in the early 1960's, when the major figure in the field was Ian Fleming, creator of the cartoonishly superhuman James Bond. Le Carré's fiction stands in sharp contrast, emphasizing the drudgery, boredom, and moral ambiguity in the decidedly unglamorous world of the real-life agent, who is more often a bureaucrat than an adventurer. Although many credit him with inventing the realistic espionage tale, le Carré denies such an achievement, acknowledging such predecessors as W. Somerset Maugham with his Ashenden stories. By creating some of the most believable characters and plausible situations in the genre, le Carré has perhaps had the most influence on the development of espionage fiction. In addition to being the best-selling espionage novelist, he has been acclaimed for turning a form of entertainment into an art form, for finding the poetry in the labyrinthine machinations of his plots. He has been judged more than a genre writer by many critics, deserving of inclusion in such serious company as Iris Murdoch and John Fowles. According to Andrew Rutherford, Le Carré offers "exciting, disturbing, therapeutic fantasies of action and intrigue; but in his best work he also engages with political, moral and psychological complexities, demonstrating the capacity of entertainment art to transcend its own self-imposed limitations."

**Biography** • David John Moore Cornwell was born October 19, 1931, in Poole, Dorset, England, the son of Ronald Thomas Archibald Cornwell and Olive Glassy Cornwell. His father was an extravagant businessman who ran for Parliament as a Liberal, and as *A Perfect Spy* (1986), le Carré's most autobiographical novel, makes clear, he was also a confidence trickster who went to prison for fraud. Because his parents divorced when he was five, young David

*John le Carré.* (The Douglas Brothers)

experienced no consistent family life: He did not see his mother from the time he began school until he was twenty-one. "I think a great part of one's adult life," he has said, "is concerned with getting even for the slights one suffered as a child."

The lonely little boy sought an outlet for his frustrations in writing. Although his literary efforts were discouraged at Sherborne School in Dorset, Cornwell won the school's prize for English verse. He attended Berne University in Switzerland for a year and served in the Army Intelligence Corps in Vienna before reading German at Lincoln College, Oxford University. He married Alison Ann Veronica Sharp in 1954 and received a first-class honors degree from the University of Oxford in 1956. After teaching for two dismal years at Eton College and trying unsuccessfully to become a free-lance illustrator of children's books, he found a position in the Foreign Service in 1959.

While commuting by train from Buckinghamshire to the Foreign Office in London, he wrote his first novel, *Call for the Dead* (1961). Since Foreign Service officials were not supposed to publish novels under their own names, he acquired his pseudonym, le Carré, which means "the square" in French. From 1960 to 1963, he served, officially, as second secretary in the British embassy in Bonn while following Germany's internal politics for British intelligence; during that time, he also wrote his second novel, *A Murder of Quality* (1962).

After the modest successes of his first two books, le Carré's initial bestseller came in 1963 with *The Spy Who Came In from the Cold*, written while he commuted to work in Bonn. In addition to selling more than twenty million copies, the novel won several awards, including the Edgar Allan Poe Award of the Mystery Writers of America. It also enabled le Carré to quit his job and write full time.

Le Carré has three sons, Simon, Stephen, and Timothy, by his first marriage. After his 1971 divorce, he married Valerie Jane Eustace, an editor for his English publisher, in 1972, and they have one son, Nicholas, and homes in Cornwall, London, and Switzerland.

**Analysis** • John le Carré's agents are tired, bitter, and lonely men desperately trying to hold on to the vestiges of their ideals and illusions, to keep away from the abyss of cynicism and despair. Alec Leamas, the protagonist of *The Spy Who Came In from the Cold*, has been in the field too long but allows himself to be talked into undertaking one last assignment, only to be deceived by his masters, spiritually destroyed, and killed. There are no heroes or villains on le Carré's Cold War battlefields: Everyone uses everyone, and conspiracies lie everywhere, like mines.

In a 1974 interview with the British Broadcasting Corporation, Le Carré said that his novels differ from most thrillers in which the plot is imposed upon the characters. He said that he writes the kind of book in which "you take one character, you take another character and you put them into collision, and the collision arrives because they have different appetites, and you begin to get the essence of drama." When bringing about these collisions, le Carré is less interested in the events than in how the characters respond, that is, their moral behavior.

Le Carré's novels reflect his belief that people barely know themselves, that in human relations "we frequently affect attitudes to which we subscribe perhaps intellectually, but not emotionally." He considers such relations "fraught with a nerve-wracking tension." Such a view of life in which this tension leads to conspiracies is appropriate for a writer of espionage fiction. The espionage novel, according to le Carré, becomes "a kind of fable about forces we do believe in the West are stacked against us."

George Smiley is the perfect le Carré protagonist because of his ability to see conspiracies of which others are unaware. In *Call for the Dead*, his suspicions about the suicide of a Foreign Office clerk lead to unmasking the duplicities of one of his closest friends. (Betrayal of one's friends is a major le Carré theme.) In *A Murder of Quality*, a straightforward mystery, Smiley enters the closed world of the public school—an institution le Carré finds almost as fascinating and corrupt as the intelligence establishment—to solve the murder of a schoolmaster's wife. After appearing as a minor character in *The Spy Who Came In from the Cold* and *The Looking-Glass War* (1965), Smiley reaches his fullest development in the trilogy that pits him against his Soviet opposite number, known as Karla. *Tinker, Tailor, Soldier, Spy* (1974), *The Honourable Schoolboy* (1977), and *Smiley's People* (1980), which were published together in 1982 as *The Quest for Karla*, show le Carré working on a much larger canvas than before with dozens of characters serving as the chess pieces that Karla and Smiley deploy all over Europe and Asia in their deadly battle of wits.

Smiley is forced to accomplish his goals not only without the help of his superiors but also often despite their interference. In *Tinker, Tailor, Soldier, Spy*, Control, the longtime head of the Secret Intelligence Service (always referred to as the Circus, for the location of its offices in the Cambridge Circus section of London), has died and is replaced by the unctuous Percy Alleline. Control had suspected that the Soviets had placed a double agent, or mole, in the higher echelons of the Circus. (Le Carré is credited with making this use of "mole" popular.) He had therefore sent Jim Prideaux, one of the Circus's best agents, to Czechoslovakia to uncover evidence about the mole's identity, but a trap is laid, resulting in the wounding and torture of Prideaux.

After Control's death, Smiley, with the help of the delightfully colorful Connie Sachs, head of Russian research, slowly and painstakingly tracks the mole through the records of intelligence operations. This procedure is hampered by the lack of cooperation from Alleline, whom the mole cleverly manipulates. Smiley learns more and more about the head of Moscow Centre, Karla, the man behind the mole, the then-unknown agent Smiley once had in his grasp. He discovers that the mole is Bill Haydon–the Circus's golden boy, the lover of Ann Smiley, and the best friend of Jim Prideaux. (Haydon clearly suggests the infamous double agent Kim Philby; le Carré wrote the introduction to a 1968 study of Philby.) Before Haydon can be swapped to the Soviets, the shocked, disillusioned Prideaux kills him. Since *Tinker, Tailor, Soldier, Spy* centers on the quest for Karla's mole, it more closely resembles traditional mystery fiction than any of le Carré's other espionage novels.

*The Honourable Schoolboy*, which won the James Tait Black Memorial Prize and the Gold Dagger of the Crime Writers' Association, focuses on Smiley's efforts to restore the credibility of the Circus. Again with the help of Connie Sachs, he backtracks through the files to attempt to learn what information Haydon has covered up or destroyed, discovering that Karla has made large gold payments to a Hong Kong trust account. Smiley's legman, Jerry Westerby, a dissolute, aristocratic journalist, goes to Hong Kong to help unravel the strands of the multilayered plot.

The trust proves to be controlled by Drake Ko, a Hong Kong millionaire, whose supposedly dead brother, Nelson, is Karla's double agent in China. Nelson Ko intends to sneak into Hong Kong to be reunited with Drake, but Saul Enderby, Smiley's new boss, has been working behind his back and has arranged for the Central Intelligence Agency (CIA) to reap the rewards, including details of China's military capabilities. Westerby has fallen for Drake's beautiful English mistress and attempts to disrupt Nelson's capture and is killed.

In *Smiley's People*, the now-retired Smiley learns that Soviet agents in Paris are attempting to establish a new identity for a Russian girl. Piecing together bits of seemingly unrelated information, he, with the assistance of Connie Sachs and other old friends, discovers that Karla has a disturbed daughter in a Swiss sanatorium. Smiley is his own legman this time as he travels to Hamburg, Paris, and Berne to ferret out the facts and obtain satisfaction from his nemesis. By detecting that Karla has illegally used public funds to care for his daughter, Smiley forces the Soviet superspy to defect. As with Jerry Westerby, Karla's downfall results from love, a particularly dangerous emotion throughout le Carré's works, as Smiley's feelings for his adulterous Ann particularly attest.

Le Carré's writing style is primarily simple, with heavy reliance on dialogue. His descriptive passages usually focus on the actions of his characters and only occasionally delineate places and things. When presenting a complex idea, personage, or situation, however, his style can become more ornate, with meandering, parenthetical sentences resembling those of Henry James and William Faulkner. Le Carré has been criticized for creating excessively intertwined, difficult-to-follow plots. While this charge has some validity, he is trying to present his stories in the same way his characters see them: as fragments of a puzzle, the outline of which will be clear once its components finally begin to connect. The reader trusts le Carré as a guide through this moral miasma, since his close attention to detail indicates that he truly knows the minutiae of espionage.

Like Graham Greene (who called *The Spy Who Came In from the Cold* the best espionage story he had ever read), le Carré is a moralist who uses the conventions of espionage to convey his views of society. His is a devious world in which the best intentions have little effect. In 1966, le Carré wrote, "There is no victory and no virtue in the Cold War, only a condition of human illness and a political misery." The Cold War espionage in his novels is a morally ambiguous undertaking full of fear, deceit, betrayal, and disillusionment. The unmasking of Haydon destroys Prideaux's illusions about friendship, loyalty, and love. (Le Carré has said that he cannot believe in "constancy, group values, [or] obligations.")

Le Carré's spies are generally weak, decent men manipulated by cynical bureaucrats who rarely take any risks. These spies are uncertain whether the values they defend are more endangered by the enemy or by their employers. Those in power see their work as a form of gamesmanship, with these particular games played to create the impression that Great Britain remains a world power, while the realities only underscore the decay of the lost Empire, especially in the Hong Kong scenes of *The Honourable Schoolboy* and the ironic first names of the Ko brothers.

Distrust of institutions and those who run them appears throughout le Carré's fiction. In an interview with the French monthly *Lire*, he admits,

> I probably took refuge in the world of espionage to escape my father.... To understand, explain and justify my father's betrayal of his milieu, class and society, one has to blame the institutions and the men behind them as well as the respectability in which I found temporary refuge when I fled.

He sees the institutions taking on lives of their own contrary to their creators' intentions. This lack of control is clearly evident in Great Britain, where the social system produces an administrative elite, personified by Saul Enderby, who can be affable and charming while remaining morally sterile. When someone such as Westerby attempts to make a stand as an individual, he is destroyed. Le Carré considers Western institutions arrogant for attempting to transform the rest of the world in their image. As Westerby, with his suggestive name, travels through Thailand, Laos, Cambodia, and Vietnam in 1975, he witnesses the decadence and degradation brought on by the failure of the West to understand the East.

The Karla trilogy is crammed with allusions to the myth of the Holy Grail: The Soviet disinformation in *Tinker, Tailor, Soldier, Spy* comes from an imaginary agent known as Source Merlin. Smiley is both a Percival pursuing the Grail—Ann refers to her husband's obsession with Karla as the "black Grail"—and an aged King Arthur attempting to restore harmony in his land. The Circus is in disarray because the members of the inner circle, abetted by Haydon's treachery, have, like the knights of the Round Table, broken their vows of loyalty and obedience. Le Carré evokes this myth to emphasize the loss of ideals in an England where everything is shrouded in ambiguity.

Le Carré has said that each of his novels begins with the image of a character, and his skill at creating enthralling protagonists and scores of believable secondary characters is perhaps the greatest strength of his stories. He juggles his Whitehall officials, police, journalists, schoolmasters, CIA agents, prostitutes, and drug smugglers with the finesse of Charles Dickens. Characterization is so prominent in a le Carré novel that a reviewer for *The Times Literary Supplement* criticized *A Murder of Quality* for paying it excessive attention.

Westerby and Smiley, the most captivating characters in the Karla trilogy, clearly illustrate their creator's skills. Westerby has long been called "the schoolboy" because of his ever-present bag of books. On his journey through Southeast Asia, he reads works by Joseph Conrad, Ford Madox Ford, T. E. Lawrence, and Graham Greene, writers who explore the failures of romantic idealism and discover the heart of darkness. He is particularly reminiscent of the doomed romantic hero of Conrad's *Lord Jim* (1900) and is pathetic for failing to see that he is repeating the errors of the characters about whom he is reading. Despite being a journalist and would-be novelist, Westerby is essentially a man of action, often taking unnecessary risks: "Jerry at heart was a soldier and voted with his feet. . . . What a man thinks is his own business. What matters is what he does." Last in a line of English aristocrats, Westerby represents the best of those believing in honor and good intentions as well as their inevitable failure. In a world of Karlas, Allelines, Enderbys, and Haydons, Westerby stands out for his admirable, if foolish, belief that romantic heroism has a place in a world of Cold War tensions.

Le Carré's most remarkable achievement with George Smiley is that, over seven novels and twenty years, he grows into an almost mythic figure while remaining all too human. Clumsy, meek, and short-sighted, he is both extremely specific and quite enigmatic. Peter Guillam, his protégé, assistant, and most devoted supporter, never truly understands him. His name is doubly ironic since Smiley wears an emotionless mask, and George is the name of England's dragon-slaying patron saint and of the kings who were heads of state during the two world wars. Westerby is surprised to learn that such a seemingly ordinary man served three years undercover in Germany during World War II.

Like his creator, Smiley interprets all of life in terms of conspiracy. He keeps a photograph of Karla in his office to remind him that at least one conspiracy has a human face. Since spying should be an impersonal business, his superiors reprimand him for always saying "Karla" when he means "Moscow Centre." They also believe that he wastes time on menial matters when he should delegate responsibility to his subordinates. Nevertheless, his need for control compels him to involve himself in all aspects of an operation.

Smiley has enough self-knowledge to realize that because he is obsessed by his work he cannot blame Ann for her infidelity. He is also possessed by self-doubt, wondering "whether Ann was right and his striving had become nothing other than a private journey among the beasts and villains of his own insufficiency." Le Carré ensures some distance between the reader and Smiley by having reliable characters question his actions. Westerby is perturbed by the "failed priest" side of Smiley, who seems to assume "that the whole blasted Western world shared his worries and had to be talked round to a proper way of thinking." In a 1985 speech at The Johns Hopkins University, le Carré criticized his creation for being the kind of man who "would sacrifice his own morality on the altar of national necessity." Westerby is finally a more admirable character for daring, however hopelessly, to assert the dignity of the individual over that of the institution.

At the end of *Smiley's People*, Peter Guillam tells Smiley that he has won, but his master is not so certain. What exactly has been won, and at what cost? If, in le Carré's ambiguous world, there are no heroes or villains, neither can there be any victories.

In addition to the renowned Smiley, le Carré created a host of other memorable characters. In the third and fourth decades of his writing career came Charlie, his first female protagonist, in *The Little Drummer Girl* (1983), who is initiated into the violent and illusory world of espionage; Magnus Pym of *A Perfect Spy* (1986) who suffers the humiliation of his father's betrayals, only to turn his own duplicitous behavior into art form; Jonathan Pine from *The Night Manager* (1993), who was as close as le Carré ever came to a James Bond-type superspy; and Nat Brock of *Single and Single* (1999), whom many likened to a spiffed up and modernized George Smiley.

As le Carré's literary dominance entered its fifth decade, it remained important to note that his tales of espionage have also been adapted to film. Worthy of note are *The Spy Who Came in from the Cold* (1965, starring Richard Burton) and *The Russia House* (1990, starring Sean Connery) and television versions of *A Perfect Spy* from Masterpiece Theatre and the extraordinary BBC miniseries of *Tinker, Tailor, Sailor, Spy*. which starred Alec Guinness as George Smiley. Though le Carré characterized Guinness's performance as "brilliant," it nevertheless had a negative impact on the author; he had imagined his most famous creation rather differently. Yet Guinness so inhabited the role and had so firmly imprinted his image in le Carré's mind that the author chose to abandon Smiley in favor of newer protagonists, such as Charlie, Magnus, Ned Palfrey (who was prominent in both *The Russia House* and *The Secret Pilgrim*), Jonathan, and finally Nat, who appeared ready to carry on where Smiley left off.

**Principal mystery and detective fiction**
SERIES: George Smiley: *Call for the Dead,* 1961 (also as *The Deadly Affair*); *A Murder of Quality,* 1962; *The Spy Who Came In from the Cold,* 1963; *The Looking-Glass War,* 1965; *Tinker, Tailor, Soldier, Spy,* 1974; *The Honourable Schoolboy,* 1977; *Smiley's People,* 1980.

OTHER NOVELS: *A Small Town in Germany,* 1968; *The Little Drummer Girl,* 1983; *A Perfect Spy,* 1986; *The Russia House,* 1989; *The Secret Pilgrim,* 1991; *The Night Manager,* 1993; *Our Game,* 1995; *The Tailor of Panama,* 1996; *Single and Single,* 1999; *The Constant Gardener,* 2000.

**Other major works**
NOVEL: *The Naive and Sentimental Lover,* 1971.
SCREENPLAYS: *Dare I Weep, Dare I Mourn,* 1966; *The End of the Line,* 1970.
TELEPLAY: *Smiley's People,* 1982 (with John Hopkins).
NONFICTION: *The Clandestine Muse: The G. Harry Pouder Memorial Lecture Delivered at Johns Hopkins University on May the 20th, 1986,* 1986; *Vanishing England,* 1987 (with Gareth H. Davies); *Nervous Times: An Address Given at the Savoy Hotel at the Annual Dinner of the Anglo-Israel Association,* 1998.

**Bibliography**

Aronoff, Myron J. *The Spy Novels of John le Carré: Balancing Ethics and Politics.* New York: St. Martin's Press, 1999.

Barley, Tony. *Taking Sides: The Fiction of John le Carré.* Philadelphia: Open University Press, 1986.

Beene, Lynn Dianne. *John le Carré.* New York: Twayne, 1992.

Bloom, Clive, ed. *Spy Thrillers: From Buchan to le Carré.* New York: St. Martin's Press, 1990.

Bold, Alan, ed., *The Quest for John le Carré.* New York: St. Martin's Press, 1988.

Bradbury, Richard. "Reading John Le Carré." In *Spy Thrillers: From Buchan to Le Carré,* edited by Clive Bloom. New York: St. Martin's Press, 1990.

Cawelti, John G., and Bruce A. Rosenberg. *The Spy Story.* Chicago: University of Chicago Press, 1987.

Cobbs, John L. *Understanding John le Carré.* Columbia: University of South Carolina Press, 1998.

Hayes, Michael J. "Are You Telling Me Lies, David?: The Work of John Le Carré." In *Spy Thrillers: From Buchan to Le Carré,* edited by Clive Bloom. New York: St. Martin's Press, 1990.

"Le Carré, John." In *Mystery and Suspense Writers: The Literature of Crime, Detection, and Espionage,* edited by Robin W. Winks and Maureen Corrigan. New York: Charles Scribner's Sons, 1998.

Monaghan, David. *The Novels of John le Carré: The Art of Survival.* New York: Basil Blackwell, 1985.

Monaghan, David. *Smiley's Circus: A Guide to the Secret World of John le Carré.* New York: St. Martin's Press, 1986.

Sauerberg, Lars O. *Secret Agents in Fiction: Ian Fleming, John le Carré, and Len Deighton.* New York: St. Martin's Press, 1984.

Symons, Julian. *Bloody Murder: From the Detective Story to the Crime Novel: A History.* Rev. ed. New York: Viking, 1985.

*Michael Adams*
*Updated by Fiona Kelleghan and Taryn Benbow-Pfalzgraf*

# Elmore Leonard

**Born:** New Orleans, Louisiana; October 11, 1925

**Also wrote as** • Emmett Long

**Type of plot** • Thriller

**Contribution** • Elmore Leonard's stylistic distinctions, which have evolved amply, if not uniformly, in the thrillers that he has published since 1953, constitute his chief literary contribution. He describes these works as novels. Without being epigrammatic or memorable for intellectual substance, his prose is singularly spare and athletic. Yet the plausible and linguistically permissive realism of his writing style brilliantly suits his characters, evoking in uncommon circumstances the cadences of twentieth century American common speech.

Leonard's growing body of work and, beginning with *Get Shorty* (1990), the multiplying and celebrated film adaptations of his novels, gained the momentum of a cultural phenomenon all their own, a fractured urban mythos of the interestingly bent antihero, warmly quixotic and chillingly cool at the same time.

Leonard has successfully structured suspenseful plots by developing seemingly limited, unattractive, and apparently unheroic characters. Indeed, protagonists and villains, even in their own settings, are usually marginal people whom Leonard makes surprisingly compelling. Similarly, his settings are evocative rather than abundantly descriptive of peripheral locales: Detroit's grim urban decay; Miami's sun-drenched tawdriness; Kentucky's, Michigan's, and the Southwest's mean stoop-labor country. Thus, Leonard's thriller novels, more than those of Dashiell Hammett, Raymond Chandler, or Ross Macdonald, center on the depiction of socially and morally marginal people in marginal settings. His villains are eminently menacing, while his protagonists become suprisingly moral, even heroic. Consequently, his understated realism is transformed into a redemptive romanticism, which emphasizes even the so-called loser's capacities for proceeding to the showdown and for functioning briefly at life's extremities.

**Biography** • The son of Elmore John and Flora Amelia (Rivé) Leonard, Elmore Leonard was born on October 11, 1925, in New Orleans, Louisiana. For a time, his father's affiliation with General Motors meant frequent moves, until eventually the family settled in Detroit. Subsequently, Leonard has done much of his writing there, and the very unsuburban portions of the city have been the principal scenes of several of his thrillers—notably, *Fifty-two Pickup*

(1974), *Swag* (1976), *Unknown Man No. 89* (1977), *City Primeval* (1980), *Touch* (1987), and *Freaky Deaky* (1988).

After having served in the navy as a Seabee and aboard ship in the Pacific from 1943 to 1946, Leonard returned to Detroit. He married Beverly Claire Cline in 1949, starting a family that eventually included five children. Divorced in 1977, he married Joan Leanne Lancaster two years later. Meanwhile, majoring in English, he earned his bachelor's degree at the University of Detroit in 1950 and soon began working for a Detroit advertising agency.

A self-disciplined author, Leonard, despite his economic obligations, nourished his writing at home during the early 1950's. For pennies a word he

*Elmore Leonard.* (Marc Hauser)

sold his initial work to *Argosy*, then to other Western magazines, until in 1953 he published his first novel, *The Bounty Hunters*, followed by seven other Westerns, including *Escape from Five Shadows* (1955), *Valdez Is Coming* (1969), and *Hombre* (1961), the latter honored by the Western Writers of America as one of the twenty-five best Western novels of all time.

In the mid-1970's, Leonard abandoned Westerns for crime and suspense thrillers, *Fifty-two Pickup* being among the first. Professional recognition from other writers was soon forthcoming: *The Switch* (1978) was nominated for the Mystery Writers of America's Edgar Allan Poe Award, which in 1983 he won with his novel *LaBrava*. The award not only confirmed Leonard's earlier cult following but also brought literary success and a more general appreciation of his craftsmanship.

Despite a productive career—he averaged a novel about every two years between 1953 and 1983—Leonard was slow to catch on with general audiences until the appearance of *LaBrava* in 1983. Through those years he relied heavily upon screenwriting for financial support. He wrote *Joe Kidd* (1972), a Clint Eastwood vehicle, for example, as well as the screenplays for several of his own stories. During that period only two of his novels, *Hombre* and *Stick*, were made into films. Things changed dramatically during the 1990's. The film version of *Get Shorty* (1995), with John Travolta, from a novel that seems to have been written to be filmed, catalyzed a a whole younger generation of directors' interest in his work. After that film's success, most of Leonard's novels were optioned to be made into films. Other acclaimed films made of his work include Steven Soderbergh's adaptation of *Out of Sight* (1996) and Quentin Tarantino's *Jackie Brown* (1997), adapted from Leonard's novel *Rum Punch* (1992). Undoubtedly, circumstances encouraged his exploration of several forms of writing; he nevertheless remained substantially within the bounds of the thriller novel and has demonstrated almost all of his impressive growth as an author within that genre.

**Analysis** • Since the publication of *LaBrava*, Leonard's writings have undergone a number of facile, if perhaps inevitable, comparisons with the work of classic thriller authors such as Dashiell Hammett and Raymond Chandler, as well as with more recently recognized masters in the genre: John D. MacDonald, Ross Macdonald, and George V. Higgins. At best, such associations are superficial. Leonard himself acknowledges the influences of James M. Cain, Ernest Hemingway, John O'Hara, and John Steinbeck upon his narrative style, while denying significant indebtedness to the deans of the thriller.

Leonard qualifies, like those whom he credits with influencing him, as a realist. Nevertheless, he is his own kind. Unlike Hemingway's protagonists, whose tragedies, unalleviated by the humor of the trivial, die in the high passes or bear the cruel limits of their physical and psychological infirmities to the bitter end, Leonard's protagonists evade or outwit their outrageous fortunes. Whatever mare's nests they fall into as a consequence of chance, bad luck, excessive greed, or cleverness, in the end, they sally forth into their futures avenged—or little the worse for the experience. To be sure, friends, lovers, and the wicked die violently as Leonard's stories unfold; the protagonists, however, cheat Fate. Leonard is true to the constraints of his specialty; consequently, for both the author and the reader an ordinary, plausible kind of justice is done. Matter-of-factly and in an apparently unsentimental way, Leonard therefore successfully blends the stark realism accentuated by his prose and characterizations with the romantic.

Because of his productivity, Leonard has fielded an impressive array of characters. Without losing their individuation they do, however, tend to fall into two broad categories. His villains are compelling reminders of the efficient, monstrous animality of the slayings that are the stuff of most modern societies' daily news. In *Unknown Man No. 89*, when Virgil Royal, a petty hired assassin, cold-bloodedly shotguns Robert Leary—himself an insane multiple killer—in a hairdressing salon, Virgil's sole reflection on the incident is that he was too stupid to pick the till on the way out. When Virgil later employs his reptilian brain to plan a barroom ambush—but not before wanting to cool his mark with a bit of conversation—his genial, redneck target readily foils the attempt by simply walking into the bar and shooting Virgil and his luckless partner on sight. In *Split Images* (1982), Robbie Daniels, a young Miami multimillionaire and gun enthusiast with a frightening sense of invulnerability, shoots people for fun, while Frank Renda, the monomaniacal mob hit man in *Mr. Majestyk* (1974), calmly allows his cronies to be slain in order to winkle out and kill the eponymous hero. Teddy Magyk of *Glitz* (1985), another graduate of Raiford Prison, is a mother-dependent rapist who murders in pursuit of vengeance. In *Freaky Deaky*, Robin and Skip, a pair of amoral, acid-dropping wastrels from the 1960's who pool talents to extort money from one of their repulsive, former Yippie-turned-Yuppie pals, are made menacing because they are mental dropouts with infantile emotions.

Rum Punch (1992) brings back Ordell and Louis Gara from *The Switch*, amoral losers who still manage to be appealing, and *Pronto's* (1993) Tommy (the Zip) Bucks is a syndicate boss's cast-iron Sicilian hitman. Leonard's villains flourish in the 1898 Cuba of *Cuba Libre* (1998). Gambler Warren Ganz of *Riding the Rap* decides that taking kidnap victims and treating them as he saw them treated on television in the hostage crisis in Lebanon is a good career move. In *Be Cool* (1999) someone who appears safely humorous turns quite suddenly into a pitiless and violent murderer.

Yet Leonard lends each of these characters verisimilitude. They speak in the American idiom and, in a world whose media convince one of the omnipresence of perverts, delinquents, terrorists, and serial killers, and of the inherent and unpredictable brutality of the streets, they become credible. Moreover, through Leonard's handling, in which all characters' motives and behaviors merit attention—his villains are distinct and authentic, however improbable they might seem. To paraphrase the author: In real life terrible things happen, without much in the way of warning.

Similarly, Leonard's varied protagonists are either lower-middle class or equally marginal denizens of the criminal world. Jack Ryan, the Texan and reformed alcoholic hero of *Unknown Man No. 89*, is a free-lance Detroit process server. Calvin A. Maguire of *Gold Coast* (1980) is an experienced petty thief and former convict. Though he thinks that he is going straight, so too is Jack Delaney of *Bandits* (1987), while his female companion, Lucy Nichols, is a former nun and the errant daughter of an oilman. Among Leonard's heroes, low-ranked but veteran (mostly homicide) detectives figure prominently: Clement Cruz in *City Primeval*, Lieutenant Bryan Hurd in *Split Images*, and Chris Mankowski in *Freaky Deaky*. On the other hand, outside the law, though within the local mores, is Son Martin, the Kentuckian and veteran of World War I, who, during Prohibition, stakes his life on preserving his inherited moonshine cache in *The Moonshine War* (1969). There are *Cuba Libre's* American cowboy running guns to Cuban rebels and flight attendant Jackie Burke of *Rum Punch*, arguably Leonard's best realized female character. The missionary priest of *Pagan Babies* (2000), "Father" Terry Dunn, starts out the book avenging the deaths of his Rwandan flock, and Debbie Dewey, the woman he later hooks up with, is an ex-con turned stand-up commedienne.

Not least in this gallery is Ernest Stickley, Jr.–the dubious hero of *Swag* and *Stick*–an experienced car thief and armed robber who fails to avoid returning to prison but against the odds manages a vengeful sting and an escape from a murder charge. Others include Raylan Givens and Harry Arno of *Pronto* and *Riding the Rap*, a Kentucky cowboy and U.S. deputy marshal whose sturdy fa-

talism balances the criminal burlesque unfolding around him, and an aging
bookmaker who gets on the wrong side of syndicate heavies. There is also the
basically decent, though nonetheless criminal, loan-shark-turned-film-pro-
ducer Chili Palmer of *Get Shorty* and *Be Cool*. Collectively, such protagonists
are an ordinary lot. Nevertheless, Leonard, placing them under pressure, ex-
tracts the most from their inherent qualities. They are durable, resilient, brief
of speech, and shrewd within the range of their experience. Whether homicide
detectives, loan sharks, con artists, marshals, melon growers, or moonshiners,
they like, or are accustomed to, what they do—and they do it rather well.

Leonard's characters are engaged neither by abstractions nor by learned
intellection. They live by their own rules: Like John Russell, the Western
hero of Leonard's *Hombre*, Detroit's Lieutenant Cruz in *City Primeval* is able
to dispose of the murderous Clement Mansell coldly and impersonally—just
as Russell could have slain bad-man Frank Baden—but he seems more natural, and dramatic, in intensely personal face-to-face showdowns. Thus, while
the setting for Leonard's heroes—since he stopped writing Westerns in the
early 1960's—is usually an urban "frontier," they nevertheless bear distinct resemblances to his Western protagonists. Leonard, in short, has helped to ur-
banize rudimentary Western fiction.

His taut prose, however, is distinctly urban. It is reflective of America's acquies-
cence to a broader range of what years ago were the manners and speech chiefly of
its subcultures. Generally, Leonard has avoided using the language of explicit sexual allusion or four-letter expletives merely for the sake of titillating his readers. He
accurately replicates the manner in which such terms have supplanted what formerly passed for clean speech among "respectable" people, so much so that it has
become clichéd—and thereby harmless—among all classes since World War II. Yet he
has not simply transcribed the newly accepted American vernacular. The familiar,
fragmented voice of even the descriptions, through omission of articles, adjectives, and
pronouns, and the shifting of verbs into participle form creates a language that is
hyperrealistic—sounding more real than a straight recording ever could. He has given
the vernacular a rhythm, a cadence, of his own which removes it from its essentially
boring banality and makes for pithy reading.

Leonard's settings, like many of his characters, have persistently been peripheral
to the mainstream: Offices, corporate boardrooms, production plants, churches, and
schools are off the beats of his heroes and villains. The desert way-stations and abandoned mining town of *Hombre* are replaced by counterparts in the melon fields north
of Phoenix; in the vacuous mansions of suburban Detroit and Miami; in the glitzy sea-
sides, motels, and casinos of Atlantic City and South Florida; or in the back reaches of
Appalachia.

While these are marginal runs for marginal people, Leonard nevertheless
appreciates that struggles between good and evil are just as compelling there
as elsewhere and that the ambit for sharp wits, experience, tenacity, resil-
ience, bravery, and the search for approximate justice is equally broad. In the
best sense, he has written one kind of genuine popular literature, which if it is
to be read in that context, almost necessarily substitutes a democratized and

romanticized realism for high diction, "fine" writing, or classic tragedy. Because of those substitutions, it is all the more entertaining.

**Principal mystery and detective fiction**

NOVELS: *The Big Bounce*, 1969; *The Moonshine War*, 1969; *Valdez Is Coming*, 1970; *Mr. Majestyk*, 1974; *Fifty-two Pickup*, 1974; *Swag*, 1976 (also as *Ryan's Rules*); *The Hunted*, 1977; *Unknown Man No. 89*, 1977; *The Switch*, 1978; *City Primeval*, 1980; *Gold Coast*, 1980; *Cat Chaser*, 1982; *Split Images*, 1982; *LaBrava*, 1983; *Stick*, 1983; *Glitz*, 1985; *Bandits*, 1987; *Touch*, 1987; *Freaky Deaky*, 1988; *Killshot*, 1989; *Get Shorty*, 1990; *Maximum Bob*, 1991; *Rum Punch*, 1992 (also as *Jackie Brown*); *Pronto*, 1993; *Riding the Rap*, 1995; *Out of Sight*, 1996; *Cuba Libre*, 1998; *Be Cool*, 1999; *Pagan Babies*, 2000.

**Other major works**

NOVELS: *The Bounty Hunters*, 1953; *Escape from Five Shadows*, 1955; *The Law at Randado*, 1955; *Last Stand at Saber River*, 1959 (also as *Lawless River* and *Stand on the Saber*); *Hombre*, 1961; *Valdez Is Coming*, 1969; *Forty Lashes Less One*, 1972; *Gunsights*, 1979; *Elmore Leonard's Western Roundup #1*, 1998; *Elmore Leonard's Western Roundup #2*, 1998.

SHORT FICTION: *The Tonto Woman and Other Western Stories*, 1998.

SCREENPLAYS: *The Moonshine War*, 1970; *Joe Kidd*, 1972; *Mr. Majestyk*, 1974; *Stick*, 1984.

NONFICTION: *Notebooks*, 1991.

**Bibliography**

Callendar, Newgate. "Decent Men in Trouble." *The New York Times Book Review* 82 (May 22, 1977): 13.

Challen, Paul C. *Get Dutch!: A Biography of Elmore Leonard*. Toronto: ECW Press, 2000.

Devlin, James E. *Elmore Leonard*. New York: Twayne, 1999.

Geherin, David. *Elmore Leonard*. New York: Continuum, 1989.

"Leonard, Elmore." In *Mystery and Suspense Writers: The Literature of Crime, Detection, and Espionage*, edited by Robin W. Winks and Maureen Corrigan. New York: Charles Scribner's Sons, 1998.

Mitgang, Herbert. "Novelist Discovered After Twenty-three Books." *The New York Times*, October 1, 1983, sec. 1, p. 17.

Stade, George. "Villains Have the Fun." *The New York Times Book Review*, 88 (March 6, 1983): 11.

Tucker, Ken. "The Author Vanishes: Elmore Leonard's Quiet Thrillers." *The Village Voice*, February 23, 1982, sec. 8, p. 41.

Yardley, Jonathan. "Elmore Leonard: Making Crime Pay in Miami." *The Washington Post Book World*, February 20, 1983, p. 3.

*Clifton K. Yearley*
*Updated by Fiona Kelleghan and Jessica Reisman*

# Gaston Leroux

**Born:** Paris, France; May 6, 1868
**Died:** Nice, France; April 16, 1927

**Types of plot** • Amateur sleuth • thriller • horror

**Principal series** • Joseph Rouletabille, 1907-1923 • Chéri-Bibi, 1913-1925.

**Principal series characters** • JOSEPH ROULETABILLE, an investigative reporter and amateur sleuth, is employed by the Paris daily *L'Èpoque.* A prodigy, he displayed his mathematical genius at the age of nine. As a child, he was accused of a theft of which he was innocent and ran away from his boarding school in Eu. He lived on the street until age eighteen, when he became a reporter on the Paris paper. Soon Rouletabille's editor assigned him to investigate "the mystery of the yellow room." The brilliance which Rouletabille displays in solving this and later mysteries brings him world renown as a detective. Although a rationalist, he is not a worshiper of reason. He holds that it is incorrect to apply logical processes to external signs without first having grasped them intuitively. In his thinking, therefore, Rouletabille is as much a philosopher as a mathematician.

• CHÉRI-BIBI, whose real name is Jean Mascart, is regarded by the public as the king of criminals. Growing up in Puys, near Dieppe, he was a butcher's apprentice when he was mistakenly convicted for the murder of M. Bourrelier, a wealthy shipowner and the father of Cécily, the beautiful girl whom the poor butcher's boy loved. Although Chéri-Bibi's life was spared, he was sentenced to a long term in prison. His life then became a series of escapes and repeated imprisonments as he committed various crimes in his efforts to survive and to remain free. As an innocent man to whom society has meted out injustice, he blames his difficulties on fate. At the same time, he is a man who knows how to laugh.

**Contribution** • Gaston Leroux, a journalist by profession, proved himself an outstanding author of two different kinds of popular fiction: what the French term the *roman policier* and the *roman d'adventure.* Both these terms are broad and ambiguous: the first embraces more specifically the detective mystery, the police procedural, and the crime story. The second term embraces such vague categories as thriller, novel of suspense, and horror story as well as the more specific espionage story, gothic romance, Western, fantasy, and science fiction.

Leroux's first novel in his famous Joseph Rouletabille series, *Le Mystère de la chambre jaune* (1907; *The Mystery of the Yellow Room,* 1908), is a detective mystery. It focuses on the solution of a mysterious crime by an unofficial detective whose method is opposed and superior to that of the police. In composing this novel, Leroux followed his predecessor Edgar Allan Poe, who in inventing the detective mystery had reacted negatively to the police-procedural narrative emerging in François-Eugène Vidocq's work. Leroux also sought to go Poe one better, by using a locked room which, unlike Poe's in "The Murders in the Rue Morgue," is hermetically sealed.

In following Poe rather than his important French predecessor Émile Gaboriau—who was the first after Poe to focus on the process of criminal detection, in his *L'Affaire Lerouge* (1866; *The Widow Lerouge*, 1873)—Leroux composed a contrapolice narrative (Gaboriau's detective, M. Lecoq, is an *agent de police*, and hence his novel is a police procedural and not a detective mystery). In trying to do something different from both Poe and Gaboriau, Leroux created with *The Mystery of the Yellow Room* a detective mystery that became a landmark in the history of this genre. Indeed, it remains a valued classic of the form.

Although his second Rouletabille novel, *Le Parfum de la dame en noir* (1908; *The Perfume of the Lady in Black*, 1909), proved less successful than his first, it is more important than the rest of the series. After 1909, the series becomes focused less on detective mysteries and more on adventures that hew closely to the political realities of the time.

Leroux's legend of Chéri-Bibi begins with *Chéri-Bibi* (1913), a play. It continues with five novels, the last published in 1925. The books in this series belong to the subgenre of the crime novel, but they are concerned with mythic crime, with crime against the order of things as well as crime against the body and soul of man. At the same time their style is baroque, with an intertextuality showing the traces of archaeological myths, social codes, and literary techniques. They declare themselves immediately as something artificial, a matter of artistry.

Their Rabelaisian excess suggests that the Chéri-Bibi novels are not to be taken seriously; it would, however, be wrong to conclude that they are ridiculous melodrama. They are extraordinary books, whose texts are stuffed with signs of political, ethical, and aesthetic importance precursive of the age of modernity, of the primitive, repressed drives within man's unconscious that underlie class prejudice and legal judgments, of the later developments of existentialist philosophy and negative theology, and of the poststructuralist view that literary texts are not products of innocence but laden with hidden meaning. The legend of Chéri-Bibi as told by Leroux amounts to tragicomedy of modernist proportions, although its *fons et origo* is archaeological and archetypal.

**Biography** • Gaston Leroux, a lawyer, journalist, and writer of fiction, was born in Paris on May 6, 1868, two years before the formation of the Third Republic. He was the son of a building contractor. Although Paris-born, Leroux always thought of himself as a *Normande*, as his mother was from Normandy. He lived for some years at Eu, inland from Le Tréport, while his father was engaged in the restoration of a castle. Leroux attended a school in Eu for a time; later, he was graduated from secondary school in Caen, Normandy.

Leroux removed himself to Paris, where he took up residence in the Latin Quarter and began the study of law, which he later practiced upon completion of his studies. A description of his physique about this time by a contemporary indicates that he was a plump man with a curly, chestnut beard. From behind his spectacles, his dark eyes sparkled with malice, his countenance suggesting repressed irreverence. He overflowed with life and energy, and he seemed to have in him something of the street Arab and the Bacchic reveler. The whole judicial system frustrated and irritated him. Eventually, he quit. Leroux remained cynical about the judicial system the rest of his life, and this attitude pervades his fiction. His Rouletabille redresses the errors of human justice, and Chéri-Bibi, for a time at least, is both the victim of judicial error and the instrument of supreme justice.

After his stint as a lawyer, Leroux decided to enter the world of journalism. In 1892, he worked for the *Ècho de Paris*, first as a law reporter, then as a theater critic. Soon leaving the *Ècho de Paris*, he became a reporter on the *Matin*. It was not long before Leroux became one of the greatest journalists of his time. He interviewed illustrious persons, he covered the Dreyfus affair, and he became a foreign correspondent. He followed the peripatetics of the Otto Nordenskjöld expedition to Antarctica (1901-1903). He covered the Russian Revolution of 1905 and later interviewed the admiral who had quelled the rebellion in Moscow. In 1907, Leroux spent some time in Morocco and covered the eruption of Vesuvius in Italy. Too old to be mobilized at the outbreak of World War I, he covered the Armenian massacre by the Turks in 1915. At that point, Leroux decided that he had had enough of traveling to foreign places and terminated his career as a journalist.

Having to find another way to earn a living, Leroux hit upon the writing of novels of adventure, including the *roman policier*. After several months of writing, he produced the manuscript of his first novel, *The Mystery of the Yellow Room*. This story was first published in the September 7, 1907, issue of the magazine *L'Illustration*. It proved an immediate success and was succeeded the following year by *The Perfume of the Lady in Black*, which was almost as successful as his first novel. With these two books, Leroux became a world-famous author, and he was to continue to write many more successful novels until his death in Nice on April 16, 1927. As a skilled writer of fiction he has not been forgotten. Apart from the fine study of him by Antoinette Peské and Pierre Marty in their *Les Terribles* of 1951, the journal *Bizarre* devoted its first issue to him in 1953, and the journal *Europe* paid tribute to him in its June/July, 1981, issue.

**Analysis** • The first two volumes of the Rouletabille series, *The Mystery of the Yellow Room* and *The Perfume of the Lady in Black*, are Gaston Leroux's masterpieces. These novels complement each other by rounding out the character and personality of their hero, the reporter-detective Joseph Rouletabille. They also involve Rouletabille's confidant Sainclair (who also serves as the narrator), Mathilde Stangerson (the Lady in Black), Robert Darzac, and the notorious criminal Ballmeyer (alias Jean Roussel and Frédéric Larsan). Both stories involve the attempted murder of Mathilde Stangerson by the same persistent criminal whose identity is hidden from the rest of the characters until uncovered by Rouletabille, and both concern the mystery of how the criminal entered a hermetically sealed room to make such attempts and escaped thereafter.

The two novels differ in the times and places in which their stories occur in France. *The Mystery of the Yellow Room* takes place in 1892, principally at the Château du Glandier, located on the edge of the forest of Sainte-Genevieve, just above Èpinay-sur-Orge. It is the residence of the famous American-French chemist Professor Stangerson and his beautiful daughter Mathilde, who assists her father in his experiments regarding his theory of the "dissociation of matter" by electrical action that contradicted the law of the "conservation of matter." Her bedroom, abutting her father's laboratory, is the sealed "yellow room" in which she is viciously attacked and seriously injured by the unknown criminal. The narrative of *The Perfume of the Lady in Black* takes place in 1895–although flashbacks take the reader to earlier times in the lives of Rouletabille, Stangerson, and Larsan. The main events take place at the Fort of Hercules, located at Roches Rouges, near Menton on the Côte d'Azur, the home of Arthur and Edith Rance. In *The Perfume of the Lady in Black*, Mathilde Stangerson and Robert Darzac are married. As husband and wife, they occupy adjoining bedrooms in the Square Tower of the fort, and these apartments are hermetically sealed when an attempt on the life of Darzac takes place inside, thus constituting another locked-room mystery. In addition, there are mysteries concerning the identification of Larsan and the one "body too many."

What is not so plain about these two novels, among a number of subordinate matters, is their underlying mythical structures, which are hidden, particularly in *The Mystery of the Yellow Room*, by the technical device of displacement or the adaptation of myth to realistic criteria. In *The Mystery of the Yellow Room*, Rouletabille says of Mathilde Stangerson: "I saw her. . . . I breathed *her*–I inhaled the perfume of the lady in black. . . . How the memory of that perfume–felt by me alone–carries me back to the days of my childhood." Although ignorant at this time that she is his mother, he–and he alone–senses the fragrance, one might say the aura, of the mother he knew as a child. *The Perfume of the Lady in Black* reveals that Rouletabille was separated from his mother at age nine. When he applied for the job of reporter in *The Mystery of the Yellow Room*, its editor in chief asked him his name. He replied "Joseph Josephine." The editor remarked, "That's not a name," but added that it made no difference. Like Odysseus, Rouletabille has no name because he does not know the identity of his parents. His fellow reporters gave him the nickname Rouletabille because of his marble-shaped head.

Endowed with an Oedipus complex, Rouletabille–as it turns out–seeks to protect his mother from her male attacker and to identify him. Hence, from a mythical point of view, the plot of *The Mystery of the Yellow Room* amounts to a "search for the father," although Rouletabille does not learn the identity of his father until *The Perfume of the Lady in Black*. Nevertheless, Rouletabille is powerfully intuitive; he is a psychic before he is a mathematician or a logician. He may seem a Telemachus and in a way he is. Not only does he search for his father but also, having learned of his father's identity, Rouletabille cannot help admiring him for his bravery, wisdom, and cunning, which are the chief qualities of Odysseus. At the end of *The Mystery of the Yellow Room*, he allows Larsan (who is revealed as his father) to escape the law, ostensibly to protect his mother's secret, but one suspects that his psychic feeling would not allow for both his father's capture and the protection of his mother.

The *Perfume of the Lady in Black* begins by asking the question: Who is Rouletabille? In answering this question, the novel is more frank than *The Mystery of the Yellow Room*. It soon discloses that its plot is, in essence, a "search for the mother," the father being found by accident, or, more likely from Leroux's point of view, the finding of the father being the result of fate or destiny. Toward the conclusion of *The Perfume of the Lady in Black*, Oedipus-Rouletabille is prepared to kill Laius-Larsan if need be to protect Jocasta-Mathilde, but he does not have to because Larsan kills himself. After the reunion of the real Robert Darzac and Mathilde, Rouletabille resolves his Oedipus complex (he is now twenty-one and has become an adult) by contentedly leaving his mother in the protection of her new husband. He returns to Paris in favor of his journalistic responsibilities and a proposed trip to Russia.

If the two novels taken together have an overriding theme, it is an attack of pure empiricism: Presumptions based on what is seen alone may prove false if the reality lies in what has not been seen. Rouletabille is suspicious of appearances because they may be illusory. Hypotheses based on the intuitive and creative power of the imagination must form a circle within whose circumference reason and logic must be confined. Reasoning has both good and bad ends. Observations must be instinctive, and logic must not be twisted in favor of preconceived ideas. Rouletabille says to Larsan: "It's dangerous, very dangerous, Monsieur Fred, to go from a preconceived idea to find the proofs to fit it." Facts are empty sacks which will not stand upright until filled with correct interpretations.

*The Mystery of the Yellow Room* and *The Perfume of the Lady in Black* differ considerably in style and treatment. The style of the former is plain, factual, largely unemotional. Descriptions are sparse, and little or no use is made of simile. Nevertheless, the style is interesting–indeed, it is absorbing–from beginning to end. On the other hand, *The Perfume of the Lady in Black* is more complicated and lavish. It contains more elaborate descriptions and more imaginative speculations. Leroux's treatment of his subject in *The Perfume of the Lady in Black* is far more emotional than that in *The Mystery of the Yellow Room*. For example, he remarks of Larsan's attack on the Square Tower:

> In a siege as mysterious as this, the attack may be in everything or in nothing. . . .
> The assailant is as still as the grave . . . and the enemy approaches the walls walking
> in his stocking feet. . . . It is, perhaps, in the very stillness itself, but again, it may, per-
> haps, be in the spoken word. It is in a tone, in a sigh, in a breath. It is a gesture. . . . It
> may be in all which is hidden . . . all that is revealed—in everything which one sees
> and which one does not see.

In *The Perfume of the Lady in Black* Rouletabille is continually losing control of
his emotions, then regaining his concentration. As a result, the narrator,
Sainclair, is sometimes required to sustain the story line. This frenetic seesaw-
ing between emotionalism and calmness veils from the reader the novel's development and its unity.

While Leroux's work is rooted in nineteenth century melodrama and the
prototypical detective fiction of Poe and his followers, it also anticipates the
post-World War II vogue for serious fiction that appropriates the conventions
of the detective novel only to subvert them. The difference is that, while in the
works of contemporary writers such as Alain Robbe-Grillet and Leonardo
Sciascia the subversion is intentional, in Leroux's baroque fictions it may have
been unconscious.

### Principal mystery and detective fiction

SERIES: Chéri-Bibi: *Chéri-Bibi*, 1913 (with Alévy and Marcel Nadaud); *Les
Cages flottantes*, 1921 (*The Floating Prison*, 1922; also as *Wolves of the Sea*); *Chéri-
Bibi et Cécily*, 1921 (*Chéri-Bibi and Cécily*, 1923; also as *Missing Men*); *Palas et
Chéri-Bibi*, 1921; *Fatalitas!*, 1921 (*Chéri-Bibi, Mystery Man*, 1924; also as *The
Dark Road*); *Le Coup d'état de Chéri-Bibi*, 1925 (*The New Idol*, 1928). Joseph
Rouletabille: *Le Mystère de la chambre jaune*, 1907 (*The Mystery of the Yellow Room*,
1908; also as *Murder in the Bedroom*); *Le Parfum de la dame en noir*, 1908 (*The Per-
fume of the Lady in Black*, 1909); *Rouletabille chez le tsar*, 1913 (*The Secret of the
Night*, 1914); *Le Château noir*, 1916; *Les Ètranges noces de Rouletabille*, 1916;
*Rouletabille chez Krupp*, 1920; *Le Crime de Rouletabille*, 1922 (*The Slave Bangle*,
1925; also as *The Phantom Clue*); *Rouletabille chez les Bohémians*, 1923 (*The Sleuth
Hound*, 1926; also as *The Octopus of Paris*).

OTHER NOVELS: *La Double Vie de Theophraste Longuet*, 1904 (*The Double Life*,
1909); *Fantôme de l'opéra*, 1910 (*The Phantom of the Opera*, 1911); *Le Fauteuil
hanté*, 1911 (*The Haunted Chair*, 1931); *Balaoo*, 1912 (English translation, 1913);
*L'Èpouse du soleil*, 1913 (*The Bride of the Sun*, 1915); *L'Homme qui revient de loin*,
1917 (*The Man Who Came Back from the Dead*, 1918); *Le Capitaine Hyx*, 1920 (*The
Amazing Adventures of Carolus Herbert*, 1922); *Le Cœur cambriolé*, 1922 (*The Bur-
gled Heart*, 1925; also as *The New Terror*); *La Machine à assassiner*, 1923 (*The Machine to Kill*, 1935); *La Poupée sanglante*, 1924 (*The Kiss That Killed*, 1934); *Le Fils
de trois pères*, 1926 (*The Son of Three Fathers*, 1927); *Mister Flow*, 1927 (*The Man of
a Hundred Masks*, 1930; also as *The Queen of Crime*); *Lady Helena*, 1929 (*Lady
Helena: Or, The Mysterious Lady*, 1931).

**Other major works**

PLAYS: *La Maison des juges,* 1906 (with Pierre Wolff); *Le Lys,* 1909 (with Wolff); *L'Homme qui a vu diable,* 1911; *Le Mystère de la chambre jaune,* 1912; *Alsace,* 1913 (with Lucien Camille).

NONFICTION: *L'Agonie de la Russie blanche,* 1928.

## Bibliography

Flynn, John L. *Phantoms of the Opera: The Face Behind the Mask.* East Meadow, N.Y.: Image Publications, 1993.

Murch, A. *The Development of the Detective Novel.* New York: Philosophical Library, 1958.

*The New York Times.* Review of *The Mystery of the Yellow Room,* by Gaston Leroux. 13 (August 1, 1908): 426.

Symons, Julian. *Mortal Consequences: A History from the Detective Story to the Crime Novel.* London: Faber & Faber, 1972.

Thomson, H. Douglas. *Masters of Mystery: A Study of the Detective Story.* London: W. Collins Sons, 1931.

*Richard P. Benton*

# Richard Lockridge and Frances Lockridge

## Richard Lockridge

**Born:** St. Joseph, Missouri; September 25, 1898
**Died:** Tryon, North Carolina; June 19, 1982

## Frances Lockridge

**Born:** Kansas City, Missouri; January 10, 1896
**Died:** Norwalk, Connecticut; February 17, 1963

**Also wrote as** • Francis Richards

**Types of plot** • Amateur sleuth • police procedural

**Principal series** • Mr. and Mrs. North, 1940-1963 • Merton Heimrich, 1947-1976 • Nathan Shapiro, 1956-1980 • Bernie Simmons, 1962-1974.

**Principal series characters** • PAM NORTH, a slim, attractive woman who charms and bewilders her listeners with her elliptical conversations. She is very fond of cats, often talking to them. Intelligent and curious, Pam often takes the lead in walking inadvertently into dangerous situations which lead to the murderer.

• GERALD (JERRY) NORTH, a publisher. Devoted to his wife and accustomed to her style, he understands her and acts the role of a straight man. Like his wife, he favors dry martinis and good companionship at elegant meals. Jerry and Pam are both compassionate, a quality that motivates them to become involved in detection.

• BILL WEIGAND appears frequently in the North series. As an officer in the homicide squad, Weigand and his assistant, DETECTIVE SERGEANT ALOYSIUS CLARENCE MULLINS, work closely with the Norths on cases. Weigand is a likable character, a kind and effective professional.

• MERTON HEIMRICH, of the New York State Police, rises steadily in rank in the series devoted to his adventures, from lieutenant to captain to inspector. He also meets and marries SUSAN FAYE, a widow with a ten-year-old son, MICHAEL. Heimrich's gradual success in his professional and personal life does not much change his kind nature and rather gloomy outlook.

• NATHAN SHAPIRO, a lieutenant in the homicide squad, is a self-doubting but most competent investigator. He normally works with Captain Weigand, but in one novel he is teamed with Merton Heimrich. Unlike the other North principals, he prefers sweet sherry to a dry martini. Some readers have compared him to the television detective Columbo.

• BERNARD SIMMONS, the tall, red-haired assistant district attorney of New York City. When not working on cases, he is working on a relationship with his girlfriend, NORA CURRAN, hoping that she will marry him.

• WALTER BRINKLEY, a white-haired, pudgy professor of English, retired from Dykeman University, is a recurring Lockridge character, though he does not have his own series.

**Contribution** • With the creation of their husband-and-wife team, Pam and Gerald North, Richard and Frances Lockridge added to the small number of mystery novels featuring couples. Theirs was an immensely popular team, leading to a radio and television series, a play, and a motion picture. The Mystery Writers Association awarded the Lockridges the first Edgar Allan Poe Award for the best radio mystery program in 1945.

Both journalists, Frances and Richard Lockridge produced novels at a steady rate, drawing upon their own experiences. Even the series about law-enforcement detectives emphasizes the characters' personal lives and their relationships with their spouses or lovers, creating a comfortable air of stability and family strength. Although the novels feature a variety of detective figures, the Lockridge novels as a whole create a miniature world of their own, in that characters sometimes overlap series. Lockridge readers are thus provided with the pleasure of entry into a familiar world in most of the novels.

While the Lockridges' plotting was seldom intricate, they created a series of personable characters and picked interesting subjects as backgrounds. Simply and clearly written, their novels have been admired for the civilized tone, the gentle humor, and the glimpses they afford of American life.

**Biography** • Richard Orson Lockridge was born on September 25, 1898, in St. Joseph, Missouri, the son of Ralph David L. Lockridge and Mary Olive (Notson) Lockridge. He attended Kansas City Junior College and the University of Missouri at Columbia before his education was interrupted by navy service in 1918. After the war, he held a variety of jobs, including stints at the United States Census Bureau, as a wholesale grocer, at a carnival, and in a printing shop. He studied journalism briefly before he started his journalistic career as a reporter for the *Kansas City Kansan* in 1921. In New York, he became the drama critic at the *New York Sun* and contributed frequently to *The New Yorker*. He served as a public relations officer for the navy in World War II. Returning to journalism after the war, he acquired a reputation as a fast, reliable rewrite man in his newspaper work.

Frances Louise Davis, born on January 10, 1896, in Kansas City, Missouri, also became a journalist. She attended the University of Kansas and worked for four years at the *Kansas City Post* as a reporter and feature writer. In New York City, she wrote for *The New York Times*'s "Hundred Neediest" section, continuing her role as a "sob sister." Her long experience as a publicist for the State Charities Aid Association (1922-1942) led to an interest in the problems of child adoption and a book, *How to Adopt a Child* (1928).

Davis and Lockridge met and married in 1922. Their first move to New York City was not successful; they returned to Kansas, but decided to try again. Their second attempt succeeded, though they lived precariously, never having enough money. It was during these lean times that Richard wrote about some of their experiences in short humorous pieces which led to the Pam and Jerry North characters. Both avid readers of mysteries, together they created three long-running series, keeping up on other writing as well. They were elected co-presidents of the Mystery Writers Association in 1960.

Two years after Frances's death in 1963, Richard married Hildegarde Dolson, also a writer, and continued to write prolifically. Richard Lockridge died in 1982, after a series of strokes, in Tryon, North Carolina.

**Analysis** • Frances Lockridge's and Richard Lockridge's most popular characters, Pam and Jerry North, appeared in nonmystery genres before they became amateur sleuths. Richard Lockridge first wrote of the experiences of a couple similar to his wife and himself in a series of short pieces for the *New York Sun*. Later, the Norths resurfaced in the short domestic comedies which he wrote for *The New Yorker*. Their surname, their creator said, "was merely lifted from the somewhat amorphous, and frequently inept, people who played the North hands in bridge problems." In their initial existence, the couple did not have first names, and neither had an occupation.

The Norths' final passage to amateur-sleuth status came when Frances Lockridge decided to write a mystery during one summer vacation. Her husband became interested, and together they worked out a story. Because the Norths were well-established characters by then, the Lockridges kept them as the main characters and retained the humorous tone previously used in North stories. According to Frances, her own role was to contribute interesting characters and her husband's was to kill them off. After their story conferences and the joint preparation of outlines and summaries, Richard did all the writing.

When Richard continued writing other series after the death of Frances, reviewers suggested that his style had changed, a claim that seemed to baffle and amuse him. The style of the collaborative Lockridge books, praised as quiet, understated, graceful, and easy to read, certainly is consistent, though the novels featuring characters other than the Norths seem more serious in tone. The North novels were initially admired for their infectious humor. They are a delightful blend of urbane chic (somewhat reminiscent of the tone of motion-picture screwball comedies) and an attention to social issues, a legacy of the authors' journalistic training.

The Lockridges fall into the category of detective-fiction writers who consider it their job to play fair with the reader in producing interesting puzzles to solve. Among his rules, Richard Lockridge said, were that butlers and detectives are never the criminals, that there is only one murderer, and that the detective must disclose all the clues. It is this last requirement that occasions the frequent meals and dry martinis in the North series. Pam and Jerry, often with their police-officer friend Bill Weigand and his wife, Dorian, discuss cases over meals at elegant restaurants or at home. A whimsical fascination with the activities of cats adds to the comic charm of the novels. Pam's thought processes are sometimes relayed in her conversations with the assorted cats which appear throughout the series. These monologues, like the scenes of socializing, serve a dual purpose, adding a warm, sometimes comic touch of characterization and deftly passing on information to the reader.

Another unwavering source of amusement for the reader is the ire the Norths arouse in Inspector O'Malley, Bill Weigand's superior. "Those Norths!" he sputters whenever he discovers that they are in the thick of the latest homicide. A running gag is the obligatory suspicion that falls on the Norths themselves: Why do they so often find the bodies? the inspector wonders. Though on an intensive diet of the North books this comic touch becomes rather wearying, it is nevertheless true that, as with characters in a situation comedy or any other kind of series, these predictable touches are part of the appeal.

Though Richard Lockridge found the casting of Gracie Allen as Pam North in the film featuring the Norths a "triumph of miscasting," there is a distinct aura of the daffy charm of George Burns and Gracie Allen about Pam and Jerry North. Like Gracie Allen, Pam is much given to elliptical dialogue which bewilders everyone unaccustomed to her thought processes; Jerry, like George Burns, is the straight man who can practically foretell the confusion that Pam is about to spread. Jerry's publishing career, which presumably supports their elegant life-style, comes in handy as a source of cases. In *Murder Within Murder* (1946), for example, one of his free-lance researchers is murdered; in *The Long Skeleton* (1958), one of Jerry's best-selling authors becomes centrally involved in the murder, and *Murder Has Its Points* (1961) similarly revolves around one of Jerry's authors. Pam is the one who solves the mystery, however, because of her intuitive intelligence, a quality described by Richard Lockridge as a "superior mental alacrity." She is so often caught up in a dangerous situation in the final scenes of a novel that the predictability moved Howard Haycraft, by 1946, to complain: "Someday I'd like to read a North story in which Mrs. North does not wander alone and unprotected into the murderer's parlor in the last chapter."

Though Pam is also sometimes described as scatterbrained, and though the structure of the North novels themselves leaves an impression of flighty formula fiction, the Lockridge novels as a whole tackle interesting political and social issues. Hildegarde Dolson, Richard Lockridge's second wife, noted that a reviewer had once said that her husband did more good for liberal causes than polemics do, to which Richard responded that his social theories intentionally spilled out in the novels. *Murder Is Suggested* (1959) gives an interesting account of the view of hypnosis at that period; the sobering responsibilities of medical practice are taken up in *Murder by the Book* (1963). In *Twice Retired* (1970), a Bernie Simmons mystery, there is a touching portrayal of the evil effects of Fascism on families: The egocentric behavior of a general in the armed forces, recklessly deploying forces for his own glory, brings about tragedy for his nephew.

The Lockridges were skillful in incorporating their own experiences into their novels; thus, the early novels in particular have been praised for their mirroring of specific elements of American life. The atmosphere of prewar Greenwich Village, for example, is rendered faithfully in *The Norths Meet Murder* (1940). *Death on the Aisle* (1942) is set in a theater, a milieu with which Richard Lockridge was familiar from his years as a drama critic. The Merton Heimrich novels are often set in suburban Westchester, Putnam, and Dutchess counties, in all of which the Lockridges lived for a while. The Lockridges' experience with a friend who bred Angus cattle is reflected in *Death and the Gentle Bull* (1954), a novel featuring Captain Heimrich. Frances Lockridge's experiences as a publicist with a private committee for the placement and adoption of children underlies *A Pinch of Poison* (1941) and *Quest for the Bogeyman* (1964), both of which have an adoption theme.

The Lockridges' own life also accounts for another characteristic of their novels: In marked contrast to the American tradition of the lone detective, the Lockridge detectives, as Chris and Jane Filstrup observe, have stable relationships. In addition to the compatible marriage of Pam and Jerry North, there are Bill Weigand and his wife, Dorian, Merton Heimrich and his wife, Susan, Bernie Simmons and his girlfriend, Nora Curran.

These touches of personal and social realities, however, contribute only to the variety of milieu in the Lockridge novels. While these novels do provide realistic glimpses of American life, in other respects they follow the murder-mystery convention of a closed circle of people. A distinguishing Lockridge extension of this convention is the overlapping in the series. Captain Bill Weigand, the family friend in the North series, appears in the Nathan Shapiro series as the main character's superior. Even fictional settings reappear: For example, the imaginary Dyckman University (based on Columbia University, where Richard Lockridge taught briefly) appears in *Murder Is Suggested*, a North mystery, and is the home institution of Professor Emeritus Walter Brinkley in *Twice Retired*, a Bernie Simmons novel. This familiarity of recurring characters and settings extends the family atmosphere of the North series to the other novels as well.

As a reporter, Richard Lockridge had covered crime stories and many important trials, while Frances had specialized in human-interest articles. Nevertheless, though New York City appears frequently as a locale, and law enforcement officials—Heimrich, Shapiro, Weigand, Simmons—outnumber the amateur sleuths as principal characters in the Lockridge novels, there is little of the grim, the sordid, or the violent. Far from depicting the harsh realities of big-city life or exploring the complexities of police politics, the Lockridges created their own version of the cozy English village murder mystery. Indeed, asked to which writers he was often compared, Richard Lockridge said, "They identify me as a writer of the old-fashioned mystery, which I am. Which I prefer to the bang-bang school, the private eye who is slugged, knocked unconscious, and is up without a bruise the next day."

The Lockridge novels—charming, humorous, interesting for their treatment of a variety of social issues—are in the tradition of well-crafted novels of entertainment. The Norths' long fictional lives—more than forty books, a radio series that lasted thirteen years, a television series that ran for two years, a Broadway play with 162 performances, and a film—are a testament to the ability of their creators to intrigue and amuse. The Lockridges are rightly admired for their ability to sketch comically endearing characters. For the Lockridge fan there is great comfort in the sheer quantity of the Lockridge output. With a combined total of more than eighty titles to their credit, the Lockridges have produced for readers the pleasure of many engrossing reads.

### Principal mystery and detective fiction

SERIES: Merton Heimrich: *Think of Death*, 1947; *I Want to Go Home*, 1948; *Spin Your Web, Lady!*, 1949; *Foggy, Foggy Death*, 1950; *A Client Is Cancelled*, 1951; *Death by Association*, 1952 (also as *Trial by Terror*); *Stand Up and Die*, 1953; *Death and the Gentle Bull*, 1954 (also as *Killer in the Straw*); *Burnt Offering*, 1955; *Let Dead Enough Alone*, 1956; *Practice to Deceive*, 1957; *Accent on Murder*, 1958; *Show Red for Danger*, 1960; *With One Stone*, 1961 (also as *No Dignity in Death*); *First Come, First Kill*, 1962; *The Distant Clue*, 1963; *Murder Roundabout*, 1966 (by Richard Lockridge); *With Option to Die*, 1967 (by Richard Lockridge); *A Risky Way to Kill*, 1969 (by Richard Lockridge); *Inspector's Holiday*, 1971 (by Richard Lockridge); *Not I, Said the Sparrow*, 1973 (by Richard Lockridge); *Dead Run*, 1976 (by Richard Lockridge); *The Tenth Life*, 1977 (by Richard Lockridge). Paul Lane: *Night of Shadows*, 1962; *Quest for the Bogeyman*, 1964. Mr. and Mrs. North: *The Norths Meet Murder*, 1940; *Murder out of Turn*, 1941; *A Pinch of Poison*, 1941; *Death on the Aisle*, 1942; *Hanged for a Sheep*, 1942; *Death Takes a Bow*, 1943; *Killing the Goose*, 1944; *Payoff for the Banker*, 1945; *Death of a Tall Man*, 1946; *Murder Within Murder*, 1946; *Untidy Murder*, 1947; *Murder Is Served*, 1948; *The Dishonest Murderer*, 1949; *Murder in a Hurry*, 1950; *Murder Comes First*, 1951; *Dead as a Dinosaur*, 1952; *Death Has a Small Voice*, 1953; *Curtain for a Jester*, 1953; *A Key to Death*, 1954; *Death of An Angel*, 1955 (also as *Mr. and Mrs. North and the Poisoned Playboy*); *Voyage into Violence*, 1956; *The Long Skeleton*, 1958; *Murder Is Suggested*, 1959; *The Judge Is Reversed*, 1960; *Murder Has Its Points*, 1961; *Murder by the Book*, 1963. Nathan Shapiro: *The Faceless Adversary*, 1956 (also as *Case of the Murdered Redhead*); *Murder and Blueberry Pie*, 1959 (also as *Call It Coincidence*); *The Drill Is Death*, 1961; *Murder Can't Wait*, 1964 (by Richard Lockridge); *Murder for Art's Sake*, 1967 (by Richard Lockridge); *Die Laughing*, 1969 (by Richard Lockridge); *Preach No More*, 1971; *Write Murder Down*, 1972; *Or Was He Pushed?*, 1975; *A Streak of Light*, 1976; *The Old Die Young*, 1980. Bernie Simmons: *And Left for Dead*, 1962; *The Devious Ones*, 1964 (also as *Four Hours to Fear*); *Squire of Death*, 1965 (by Richard Lockridge); *A Plate of Red Herrings*, 1968 (by Richard

Lockridge); *Twice Retired,* 1970 (by Richard Lockridge); *Something up a Sleeve,* 1972 (by Richard Lockridge); *Death on the Hour,* 1974 (by Richard Lockridge).

OTHER NOVELS: *Death in the Mind,* 1945 (by Richard Lockridge with G. H. Estabrooks); *Sgt. Mickey and General Ike,* 1946 (by Richard Lockridge with Michael McKeogh); *A Matter of Taste,* 1949 (by Richard Lockridge); *Catch as Catch Can,* 1958; *The Innocent House,* 1959; *The Golden Man,* 1960; *The Ticking Clock,* 1962; *Murder in False-Face,* 1968 (by Richard Lockridge); *Troubled Journey,* 1970 (by Richard Lockridge); *Death in a Sunny Place,* 1972 (by Richard Lockridge).

## Other major works

NOVELS: *The Empty Day,* 1965 (by Richard Lockridge); *Encounter in Key West,* 1966 (by Richard Lockridge).

SHORT FICTION: *Mr. and Mrs. North,* 1936 (by Richard Lockridge).

RADIO PLAY: *Mr. and Mrs. North,* 1945.

NONFICTION: *How to Adopt a Child,* 1928 (by Frances Lockridge; revised as *Adopting a Child,* 1950); *Darling of Misfortune: Edwin Booth,* 1932 (by Richard Lockridge); *Cats and People,* 1950 (by Richard Lockridge).

CHILDREN'S LITERATURE: *The Proud Cat,* 1951; *The Lucky Cat,* 1953; *The Nameless Cat,* 1954; *The Cat Who Rode Cows,* 1955; *One Lady, Two Cats,* 1967 (by Richard Lockridge).

EDITED TEXT: *Crime for Two,* 1955.

## Bibliography

Banks, R. Jeff. "Mr. and Mrs. North." *The Armchair Detective* 9 (June, 1976): 182-183.

Fraser, C. Gerald. "Richard Lockridge, Writer of North Mysteries." *The New York Times,* June 21, 1982, p. D9.

Lockridge, Richard. Interview by Chris Filstrup and Jane Filstrup. *The Armchair Detective* 11 (October, 1978): 382-393.

Penzler, Otto, ed. *The Great Detectives.* Boston: Little, Brown, 1978.

Townsend, Guy M. "Richard and Frances Lockridge." In *Twentieth-Century Crime and Mystery Writers,* edited by John M. Reilly. 2d ed. New York: St. Martin's Press, 1985.

*Shakuntala Jayaswal*

# Marie Belloc Lowndes

**Born:** Marylebone, London, England; 1868
**Died:** Eversly Cross, Hampshire, England; November 14, 1947

**Also wrote as** • Philip Curtin

**Types of plot** • Psychological • historical

**Principal series** • Hercules Popeau, 1913-1940.

**Principal series character** • HERCULES POPEAU, an elderly French detective, represents Lowndes's attempt at traditional detective fiction. Perhaps because of the author's own French heritage, Popeau is never given to the histrionics and idiosyncrasies so typical of his many French and Belgian detective contemporaries.

**Contribution** • Marie Belloc Lowndes was one of the first novelists to base her work on historical criminal cases, at times utilizing actual courtroom testimony. This innovation, however, presented her with a dilemma: If the reader knows the outcome of the problem, where is the suspense? Lowndes's solution was to focus attention not on the crime but on the underlying motives and, above all, on the reactions of those affected by its consequences. Most of her characters, whether murderers, accomplices, or bystanders, are ordinary people who, to their horror, become gradually enmeshed in circumstances beyond their control. Lowndes, unique in her day, was particularly adept at portraying the psychology of women who not only shielded criminals but also could be cold-blooded killers. It is to one extraordinary, even mythical, figure in criminal lore, however, that Lowndes owes her place of honor in the mystery Hall of Fame. In *The Lodger* (1913), she was the first to seize on the rich material latent in the Jack the Ripper murders. She also was the first to participate in the game of guessing the Ripper's identity. Her assumption that the hierarchy of the Metropolitan Police knew and covered up the identity of the murderer has formed the basis of many subsequent theories concerning the notorious serial killer.

**Biography** • Marie Belloc Lowndes was born in the summer of 1868 into a family renowned for its literary, social, and scientific achievements. Her parents, both nearing forty at the time of her birth, had already distinguished themselves in their respective careers, her French father, Louis Belloc, in law, and her English mother, Bessie Raynor Parkes, as a leader in the fight for women's rights. Bessie Parkes was also the editor of one of the first women's magazines in Great Britain. Lowndes's French grandmother had translated Harriet Beecher Stowe's *Uncle Tom's Cabin* (1882), and her maternal great-great-grandfather was Joseph Priestley, the discoverer of oxygen. Her younger brother, Hilaire Belloc, was the well-known novelist and poet.

The bilingual Lowndes considered herself to be French, even though she was born and later died in England, wrote in English, and lost her French father during her early childhood. She had little formal schooling, except for two years in a convent school, but claimed to have begun writing at the age of sixteen. Her familial connections brought her in contact with the important figures of the day, and her literary career began with sketches of famous writers such as Jules Verne which were published in magazines such as *The Strand*. In 1896, she married the journalist and writer Frederic Sawrey Lowndes. They had two daughters and a son.

At the beginning of her literary career, Lowndes was primarily known as a writer of witty and satirical sketches of upper- and middle-class society. After the publication of her first novel of suspense, *When No Man Pursueth* (1910), however, her works increasingly began to focus on the psychological motivation of crime. Since 1926, numerous versions of her suspense novels have been adapted to the screen. The most famous have clearly been the various reworkings of *The Lodger*, starting with the Alfred Hitchcock classic *The Lodger* (1926), with Ivor Novello as the mysterious upstairs tenant.

During the 1930's, Lowndes concentrated her energies on writing for the stage, adapting many of her own works. Her expertise in the manipulation of dialogue served her well in her account of another famous murder case, that of Lizzie Borden. In *Lizzie Borden: A Study in Conjecture* (1939), Lowndes offers her own solution to the crime. Lowndes wrote four biographical volumes: *"I, Too, Have Lived in Arcadia": A Record of Love and of Childhood* (1941), *Where Love and Friendship Dwelt* (1943), *The Merry Wives of Westminster* (1946), and *A Passing World* (1948). *Where Love and Friendship Dwelt* contains fascinating glimpses into the lives of important literary and political figures of the early twentieth century. During World War II, the Lowndeses' house in London was destroyed in a bombing raid, and Lowndes retired to her country house in Hampshire, where she died on November 14, 1947.

**Analysis** • Marie Belloc Lowndes subtitled her first attempt at suspense fiction, *When No Man Pursueth,* as "An Everyday Story." Its setting is not the gothic castle, the lonely moor, or the Chinese opium den, so beloved of her generation, but a tiny, common English village filled with pleasant, ordinary English people living pleasant, ordinary lives—except for the fact that one man is slowly murdering his wife in quite a vile manner. The protagonist is a country doctor who, to his own amazement, begins to realize the truth. He has no direct proof, and another doctor does not agree with his suspicions, but slowly and reluctantly he is drawn into action. The focus of the novel is neither on the victim nor the murderer but on the workings of the young doctor's mind. This careful delineation of the psychology of an ordinary person confronted by extraordinary circumstances was to become the linchpin of all Lowndes's later work. What interested Lowndes was not the "who" but the "why." In fact, her trademark was the revelation of the criminal's identity at the beginning of the novel rather than at the end. Bereft of the value of the dramatic denouement, Lowndes experimented with different narrators and narrative techniques. In *The Chink in the Armour* (1912), which somewhat resembles the much later *Before the Fact* (1932) by Francis Iles, the story is told from the point of view of the intended victim.

Victims were not, however, psychologically interesting to Lowndes. Her emphasis on motivation enabled her to break away from many of the stereotypes of her time. Although her writing does have its share of pathetic heroines, more common are the strong, amoral women whose straying from the path of accepted behavior is painstakingly depicted. Lowndes was particularly intrigued by the psychology of the woman poisoner. Two of her most popular works, *The Story of Ivy* (1927) and *Letty Lynton* (1931), analyze two such women who ruthlessly try to rid themselves of all obstacles that block their path to monetary gain or sexual satisfaction. Interest in these novels is maintained in the revelation of the protagonist's true identity as layer after layer of psychological camouflage is painfully stripped away. Both works contain courtroom scenes, and Lowndes's skill at dialogue is evident in her adroit maneuvering of the verbal give-and-take of a trial. In 1939, Lowndes united this expertise to her concentration on psychological motivation in her acclaimed tour de force, *Lizzie Borden*.

Lowndes had long used actual criminal cases as background for her suspense novels, and she is principally remembered for these fictional reconstructions. The Borden case fascinated her—not only was it one of the most controversial cases in United States criminal history, but also the notorious Borden seemed to be the real-life counterpart of Lowndes's own fictional murderesses. In 1893, the New York jury, although apparently presented with incontrovertible evidence of guilt, voted to acquit Borden. In Lowndes's reconstruction of the case, Borden's guilt or innocence is never an issue. She wholeheartedly accepts Edmund Pearson's 1924 analysis of the trial which ridiculed the acquittal. For Lowndes, the interesting question is the motive underlying the guilt, which she defines as destructive love. Controlled by a tyrannical father and dominated by passions that she could not control, the quiet, repressed Borden visualized murder as a logical step in her quest for sexual liberation. Although no shred of evidence has ever arisen to substantiate Lowndes's claim, her psychological insights and masterful setting of the scene lend a credibility which is further reinforced by its insertion between the factual prologue and epilogue. Unfortunately, the technical skill of the novel has at times been obscured by the prevailing theories about the Borden case. In 1971, both Pearson's and Lowndes's work were caustically attacked by the journalist Edmund Radin, who, decrying the bias of Pearson's assertions, named the Borden servant, Bridget, as the culprit. Since the publication of Radin's own book, *Lizzie Borden: The Untold Story* (1971), opinion generally has been divided between the Lowndes-Pearson and Radin camps. Another theory, rapidly gaining a following, deals with reputed epilepsy and concomitant temporary insanity in the Borden family.

The Lowndes work which is considered a classic of its kind concerns another famous criminal, Jack the Ripper. *The Lodger* is a complex weaving of Lowndes's preoccupation with criminal history, feminine psychology, and obsessive motivation. It also represents a milestone as the first fictional treatment of a subject that has continued to fascinate connoisseurs of crime; many consider it to be not only the first but still the best fictional reworking of the Jack the Ripper story.

In 1913, Lowndes was still wary of using actual names. Her murderer is called "The Avenger," and all of her references to historical names and details are veiled. So well did she execute this deliberate vagueness that upon publication of the work, many critics did not even mention its similarity to the Ripper case. Instead, labeling it a psychological study, they congratulated her for her clinical impartiality.

Rather than focusing on the murderer himself, Lowndes centers her attention on an impoverished former servant named Ellen Bunting. The tale is set in a shabby street near Marylebone Road, London, in an old house whose tenants, in order to survive, have had to rent their upstairs rooms to lodgers. (Lowndes herself was born in a lodging house in Marylebone, although in a far better section.) The beginning of the novel is a microcosm of Lowndes's art in suspense writing. The reader is presented with detailed descriptions of an ordinary, middle-aged couple and their house and its furnishings, typical of their class and period. Everything is in order and nothing attracts attention. The thick damask curtains are drawn against the dampness and intrusions from the street. Suddenly, however, the outside world enters with the echoing shout of newsboys crying the late edition of the day's paper. Only one word stands out—murder.

Reading about the series of brutal murders committed during the past fortnight has been Mr. Bunting's only diversion from his financial woes. Slipping out into the street, he guiltily buys the paper and reads it under the streetlamp, afraid to return home with his purchase. Remorsefully, he realizes not only that it was wasteful to have spent the sorely needed money, but also that his wife, Ellen, is angered by any reference to immorality or physical violence. Decent people, in her opinion, should be above such morbid curiosity. It is cold and foggy outside, however, and Bunting slowly enters the house with his paper and sits down to read about the most recent murder. Absorbed in the fiction, he does not respond to the sudden knock, and so it is his wife who slowly opens the front door.

> On the top of the three steps which led up to the door, there stood the long, lanky figure of a man, clad in an Inverness cape and an old-fashioned top hat. He waited for a few seconds blinking at her, perhaps dazzled by the light of the gas in the passage. . . .

"Is it not a fact that you let lodgings?" he asked, and there was something shrill, unbalanced, hesitating, in his voice. . . .

And then, for the first time, Mrs. Bunting noticed that he held a narrow bag in his left hand. It was quite a new bag, made of strong brown leather.

"I am looking for some quiet rooms," he said. Ellen Bunting, knowing instinctively that this man is a gentleman, smilingly invites Mr. Sleuth into her home. The Buntings are overjoyed. Financial disaster has been temporarily postponed with the arrival of this most-generous stranger. His oddities do not concern them, for after a lifetime spent in servitude, the Buntings are tolerant of, and even amused by, the eccentricities of the upper classes.

A decrease in suspense and surprise generally accompanies any familiarity with the subject, but, paradoxically, it is the modern reader's detailed knowledge of the Whitechapel murders which increase the drama in *The Lodger*. In 1913, unaware of many of the facts or theories surrounding the case, few readers recognized Lowndes's skill in weaving historical detail or surmise into her fictional pattern. By 1944, the year of the remake of the film *The Lodger*, starring Laird Cregar, the audience was immersed in Ripper lore and thrilled at the first close-up of the small leather bag surrounded by swirling fog. Consequently, the modern reader is well ahead of Ellen Bunting in her discovery of the truth. Such prescience, however, in no way diminishes the novel's impact. The true center of interest has always been Ellen Bunting, and it is soon made clear that what the reader knows Ellen would give anything to hide.

Their lodger quite literally represents hope for the Buntings. Without the rent money, they would starve. Moreover, Mr. Sleuth is Ellen's lodger; he trusts her. In a famous passage, Lowndes analyzes the psychological motivation underlying this protective instinct:

> In the long history of crime it has very, very seldom happened that a woman has betrayed one who has taken refuge with her. The timorous and cautious woman has not infrequently hunted a human being fleeing from his pursuer from her door, but she has not revealed the fact that he was ever there. In fact, it may almost be said that such betrayal has never taken place unless the betrayer has been actuated by love of gain, or by a longing for revenge. So far, perhaps because she is subject rather than citizen, her duty as a component part of civilised society weights but lightly on woman's shoulders.

Ellen Bunting feels no obligation to the forces of law and order. As a respectable, nineteenth century woman of her class, she would consider it a mark of shame to be associated with the police. The fact that the beau of her stepdaughter Daisy is a policeman makes no difference. One can have a policeman as an acquaintance or even as a member of the family, but one must not be soiled by his sordid occupation. It is indeed fortunate that this particular policeman, besotted by Daisy, shows no curiosity in the lodger or his odd comings and goings. Ellen is also typical of the psychology of her class and time in her feelings toward the victims. One reason that she can shield the real murderer is that she is not sympathetic toward the dead women. Contemptuous of their class and morality, she believes that they deserve what they get.

It is clear why Lowndes's portrait of Ellen Bunting surprised many critics. The taciturn, prejudiced, unlovely landlady is a far cry from the usual lady in distress. Lowndes has justly been praised by writers such as Ernest Hemingway for psychological insights into the mind of this woman, who slowly becomes a prisoner of her own fear. It is not physical fear; Ellen is afraid not of her lodger but of social ostracism. Lying in bed at night listening for the sounds of Mr. Sleuth's footsteps, Ellen has visions of being identified as the woman who harbored the criminal, which would mean that she and her husband would never get another lodger. Although differing from most of Lowndes's women protagonists in age and class, Ellen, who considers herself to be an extremely decent, religious woman, is nevertheless like the others in her amoral approach to her problem. Ellen sees no inherent ethical dilemma in sheltering a homicidal maniac. On the contrary, self-interest demands that she keep him safe.

There are times, however, when her resolution wanes. For example, spurred by a need to know if the police are any closer to the truth, she attends the inquest on one of The Avenger's victims. For the first time, a victim becomes human to her, and the enormity of the crimes hits home. Hearing the gruesome details, Ellen becomes physically ill but still cannot bring herself to betray Mr. Sleuth. In fact, she never does. It is not her fault that in a final ironic twist of fate, her loyalty becomes meaningless. At the end, Mr. Sleuth believes that she has betrayed him.

In the best of Marie Lowndes's fiction, suspense lies in the unraveling of an ordinary mind and spirit confronted by unusual circumstances. Lowndes resented being called a crime writer and would have been amazed to discover her name indelibly linked with that of an extraordinary criminal.

## Principal mystery and detective fiction

SERIES: Hercules Popeau: *A Labor of Hercules,* 1943.

OTHER NOVELS: *When No Man Pursueth: An Everyday Story,* 1910; *Jane Oglander,* 1911; *The Chink in the Armour,* 1912 (also as *The House of Peril*); *Mary Pechell,* 1912; *The Lodger,* 1913; *The End of Her Honeymoon,* 1913; *Good Old Anna,* 1915; *The Price of Admiralty,* 1915; *The Red Cross Barge,* 1916; *Lilla: A Part of Her Life,* 1916; *Love and Hatred,* 1917; *Out of the War?,* 1918 (also as *The Gentleman Anonymous*); *From the Vasty Deep,* 1920 (also as *From out the Vasty Deep*); *The Lonely House,* 1920; *What Timmy Did,* 1922; *The Terriford Mystery,* 1924; *What Really Happened,* 1926; *The Story of Ivy,* 1927; *Thou Shalt Not Kill,* 1927; *Cressida: No Mystery,* 1928; *Duchess Laura: Certain Days of Her Life,* 1929 (also as *The Duchess Intervenes*); *Love's Revenge,* 1929; *One of Those Ways,* 1929; *Letty Lynton,* 1931; *Vanderlyn's Adventure,* 1931 (also as *The House by the Sea*); *Jenny Newstead,* 1932; *Love Is a Flame,* 1932; *The Reason Why,* 1932; *Duchess Laura—Further Days from Her Life,* 1933; *Another Man's Wife,* 1934; *The Chianti Flask,* 1934; *Who Rides on a Tiger,* 1935; *And Call It Accident,* 1936; *The Second Key,* 1936 (also as *The Injured Lover*); *The Marriage-Broker,* 1937 (also as *The Fortune of Bridget*

*Malone)*; *Motive*, 1938; *Lizzie Borden: A Study in Conjecture*, 1939; *Reckless Anger*, 1939; *The Christine Diamond*, 1940; *Before the Storm*, 1941.

OTHER SHORT FICTION: *Studies in Love and Terror*, 1913; *Why They Married*, 1923; *Bread of Deceit*, 1925 (also as *Afterwards*); *Some Men and Women*, 1925; *What of the Night?*, 1943.

PLAYS: *The Lonely House*, 1924 (with Charles Randolph); *What Really Happened*, 1932; *Her Last Adventure*, 1936.

### Other major works

NOVELS: *The Philosophy of the Marquise*, 1899; *The Heart of Penelope*, 1904; *Barbara Rebell*, 1905; *The Pulse of Life*, 1908; *The Uttermost Farthing*, 1908; *She Dwelt with Beauty*, 1949.

PLAYS: *The Key: A Love Drama*, 1930 (also as *The Second Key*); *With All John's Love*, 1930; *Why Be Lonely?*, 1931 (with F. S. A. Lowndes); *The Empress Eugenie*, 1938.

NONFICTION: *H. R. H. the Prince of Wales: An Account of His Career*, 1898 (revised as *His Most Gracious Majesty King Edward VII*, 1901); *The Philosophy of the Marquise*, 1899; *T. R. H. the Prince and Princess of Wales*, 1902; *Noted Murder Mysteries*, 1914; *"I, Too, Have Lived in Arcadia": A Record of Love and of Childhood*, 1941; *Where Love and Friendship Dwelt*, 1943; *The Merry Wives of Westminster*, 1946; *A Passing World*, 1948; *The Young Hilaire Belloc*, 1956; *Letters and Diaries of Marie Bellow Lowndes, 1911-1947*, 1971 (edited by Susan Lowndes).

CHILDREN'S LITERATURE: *Told in Gallant Deeds: A Child's History of the War*, 1914.

TRANSLATION: *Edmund and Jules de Goncourt, with Letters and Leaves from Their Journals*, 1895 (with M. Shedlock).

### Bibliography

Murch, Alma E. *The Development of the Detective Novel.* New York: Philosophical Library, 1958.

*The Nation.* Review of *The Lodger*, by Marie Belloc Lowndes. 908 (April 2, 1914): 363.

Odell, Robin. *Jack the Ripper in Fact and Fiction.* London: Harrap, 1965.

*Saturday Review.* Review of *When No Man Pursueth*, by Marie Belloc Lowndes. 109 (February 26, 1910): 274.

Sherwood, Margaret. "The Makers of Plots." *The Atlantic Monthly* 107 (October, 1911): 557-568.

*The Spectator.* Review of *When No Man Pursueth*, by Marie Belloc Lowndes. 104 (March 5, 1910): 387.

*Charlene E. Suscavage*

# Robert Ludlum

**Born:** New York, New York; May 25, 1927
**Died:** Naples, Florida; March 12, 2001

**Also wrote as** • Jonathan Ryder • Michael Shepherd

**Types of plot** • Thriller • espionage

**Contribution** • Each of Robert Ludlum's novels typically features a middle-class American in his mid-thirties, well-educated and often financially secure, who can be said to represent a type of twentieth century Everyman. This individual unwittingly and unwillingly faces a Dantesque mid-life crisis, becoming involved in events which transcend his own experiences and demand that he respond and react to a life-threatening, often world-threatening challenge as the result of an all-encompassing conspiracy. The particular conspiracy faced by a Ludlum protagonist varies between such disparate entities as international big business, organized crime, Fascism, Communism, Middle Eastern terrorists, and religious fanatics, but it always threatens to destroy the ideals and institutions of a way of life.

Ludlum's heroes battle against power, particularly absolute power; monopolistic institutions, whether political, ideological, economic, or criminal, threaten the acceptable status quo that they strive to maintain. In Ludlum's fast-paced writing, with its convoluted plots and its international settings, the confrontation between good and evil is complex but ultimately clear-cut, and the conclusion generally manifests itself in graphic violence. Power and evil, however, are not always permanently defeated; like the phoenix, they rise from the ashes only to be faced again by the hero.

**Biography** • Robert Ludlum was born on May 25, 1927, in New York City, the son of George Hartford Ludlum and Margaret Wadsworth. His family was from the upper middle class, and although his father died when Ludlum was still young, he attended a series of private schools. He became enamored of acting and the theater, and on his own initiative he obtained a part in a Broadway show. Before finishing school, he attempted to enlist in the Royal Canadian Air Force but was rejected because he was underage. He later served in the United States Marine Corps. After leaving the service, he enrolled in Wesleyan University in Middletown, Connecticut, as a theater major. At college he met his future wife, Mary Ryducha, with whom he later had three children. Ludlum was graduated with honors in 1951.

For the next several years Ludlum pursued an acting career. He was moderately successful, playing a number of parts in regional theater, on Broadway, and particularly in television. He became a featured player but never achieved stardom, often playing, he said, a murderer or a lawyer. In the late 1950's he turned to producing plays rather than acting in them, and he established a financially successful theater in a New Jersey suburban shopping center; he later complained that although he personally wished to produce more avant-garde plays, they inevitably were financial failures. By 1970, at the age of forty-three, he was ready for a new beginning.

Ludlum had considered becoming a writer for many years. He took the plot for his first novel from a short-story outline which he had begun years before. After numerous rejections, *The Scarlatti Inheritance* was published in 1971. He continued to supplement his income by doing voice-overs for television and radio advertisements, but by the mid-1970's his novels had become so successful that he was able to write full-time. From their home in a two-hundred-year-old farmhouse in suburban Connecticut, Ludlum and his wife traveled widely. Many notes and photographs from their travels served as research for his novels. On March 12, 2001, he died in his Naples, Florida, home after suffering a massive heart attack.

**Analysis** • Robert Ludlum established both his writing style and his literary themes in his first book, *The Scarlatti Inheritance*; although they were to be subsequently refined, what he discovered then has proved to be successful in his later novels. Long an avid reader of history, Ludlum considered the question of how the Nazis came to power in Germany. His answer, in fiction, was that they were supported by a small number of ruthless and ambitious international financiers, including Americans, who hoped to create an economic superpower. The conspiracy was discovered by a lone American intelligence officer who successfully dealt with the threat in an equally ruthless and violent manner. As with his later books, no reviewers praised Ludlum's style, but most were captivated by the energy and entertainment of the fast-moving story. The plot was convoluted and improbable and the writing melodramatic, but the formula worked. Various themes in his first novel would reappear in later ones: the relatively powerless individual who accidentally stumbles across a larger-than-life conspiracy to do evil, historical issues regarding the Nazi movement, and various international settings.

His next two novels saw Ludlum restrict his locale to the United States. He possibly perceived that in spite of the success of his first book, he was not yet ready to deal fully with such broad historical and international topics, even through his imaginative fiction. *The Osterman Weekend* (1972) continued the precedent established by his first novel of a three-word title (which was followed in all the novels published under his own name), but instead of ranging over years and countries, the story is played out in only a few days in a New Jersey suburb. Four couples are invited to the home of John Tanner, but just prior to the party Tanner is approached by a supposed Central Intelligence Agency (CIA) agent who warns Tanner about an international conspiracy of financial fanatics known as "Omega" and tells Tanner that it is likely that at least some of the invited guests are members of that secret order. Over the course of a few hours, tension and paranoia become paramount, violence occurs, the CIA fails to protect the innocent, and Tanner is forced to save the day himself. Ludlum, who has identified himself as a political liberal of the 1950's, has stated that "What I don't like in the world is largeness–large corporations, large governments." His moral anger at such conglomerations of power is a recurring theme in his novels.

In his third novel, *The Matlock Paper* (1973), Ludlum keeps his scenes in the northeastern United States. James Barbour Matlock, a young English professor at Carlyle University (possibly modeled on Ludlum's own Wesleyan), becomes involved in a conspiracy, known as Nimrod, which aims to control the narcotics trade in New England. Both college officials and students have been sucked into the corrupt maelstrom of Nimrod.

The basic plots of Ludlum's earliest books were improbable but compelling. If professional historians remained doubtful about the existence, much less the efficacy, of the various conspiracies that Ludlum proposed, nevertheless he had succeeded in touching deep chords in many modern readers. Since the end of World War II, questions concerning the rise of Communism in China, the acquisition of atomic secrets by the Russians, the assassination of John F. Kennedy, the motives for American involvement in Vietnam, and the Watergate conspiracy have puzzled Americans. Most persons refused to believe that these situations were the result of mere chance, accident, bad luck, long-term historical trends, or abstract forces. Instead, they were seen as the result of conscious human actions inspired by alien ideologies, immoral ambitions, superhuman greed, or fanatic commitments. In the bureaucratic world of the mid- and late twentieth century, the antagonist was not merely a single individual but a group of dedicated fanatics, acting together, secretly, with unlimited goals and demands aiming toward total power. Ludlum understood these fears: "We're living in a time when you can't take things at face value anymore. This is no longer the age of Aquarius–it's the age of conspiracy." To that insight he added fast-paced writing, complex plots, exotic locations, and considerable violence. His books became international best-sellers.

After the success of his first three novels, Ludlum, for some unexplained reason, published two novels, *Trevayne* (1973) and *The Cry of the Halidon* (1974), under the pseudonym Jonathan Ryder, a variation on one of his wife's acting names. Both novels concerned conspiracies engendered by international finance, and both were set on the exotic Caribbean island of Jamaica. In an interesting if not entirely successful change of pace, during that same period he also published *The Road to Gandolfo* (1975), under the pseudonym Michael Shepherd, in which he seems to be spoofing his own work, or at least his chosen genre. The plot revolves around the kidnapping of a pope by a military figure aiming at financial and political power, but the typical Ludlum theme is handled humorously and satirically. Under his own name, Ludlum always presents his conspiracies with great seriousness: "I take my work very seriously, and I generally write about something that outrages me as a man."

*The Gemini Contenders* (1976) was one of Ludlum's most ambitious and successful novels. The story begins in the early days of World War II but only secondarily concerns one of his perennial *bêtes noires*, German Fascism. The plot progresses to the waning days of the Vietnam War, but one of the most significant events in the novel occurred almost two thousand years before. No Ludlum novel has covered so many centuries. Less uniquely but still impressively, the story travels around the globe, from its beginnings in Greece and Italy, to England, to the United States—Washington, New England, and New York City—to Vietnam, and back to Europe. As is usual in Ludlum's books, the background detail adds considerably to the veracity of the plot, but the geographical and historical information never detracts from the story line and the dynamic energy of the writing. Ludlum has observed, "As Shaw once said, if you want to convince somebody, entertain him. That's what I try to do. In the theater you can't bore people. They'll walk out." Ludlum rarely bores the reader.

Ludlum generally begins his novels with the hypothetical question "What if?" In *The Chancellor Manuscript* (1977), the author asks what if J. Edgar Hoover had been assassinated instead of dying of natural causes? In *The Gemini Contenders*, Ludlum poses to the reader the possibility that a long-secret document concerning the origins of Christianity exists from the first century A.D. For many centuries the document has been kept in total secrecy by a fanatical order of Greek monks, but in the early days of World War II it was deemed too dangerous for it to remain in its traditional place of hiding. In the event of a Nazi invasion of Greece, the document might be discovered and then used by the German government to create religious differences within the Christian community and thus weaken the allied cause, facilitating Adolf Hitler's dream of establishing his Third Reich for a thousand years.

As usual in Ludlum's plots, the story's resolution involves a secret and corrupt conspiracy that entangles the hero; in *The Gemini Contenders*, however, the heroes are twin brothers, grandsons of the only man who knew the hiding place of the secret document. One twin, Andrew, is a professional soldier and a war hero in Vietnam; the other, Adrian, more reflective, has become a lawyer. Like Cain and Abel, the brothers become antagonists. Both, however, are committed to rooting out corruption—Andrew in the military, Adrian in government and business. Ludlum has claimed, "I have one true loathing—for fanatics of all persuasions, right or left," and in his desire to cleanse the military, Andrew has become a fanatic. He and several of his comrades have formed a secret organization known as Eye Corps. It is a typical example of one of Ludlum's conspiracies: Secret and elitist, it follows its own rules, and regardless of its initial beneficial goals, it has become seduced by the vision of power and aims at taking over the United States Defense Department and, in effect, the country itself. In *The Chancellor Manuscript*, the secret elite group dedicated to preservation and betterment of the country is a small cadre of elder statesmen known as Inver Brass. In time, individual members of the secret organization also turn from the light to the darkness. Ludlum is consistent throughout his novels in portraying the corrupting effects of power, and secret power is the most dangerous.

In most Ludlum stories, issues and confrontations are resolved only through violence, and *The Gemini Contenders* is no different. When accused of glamorizing mayhem, Ludlum responds to his critics: "Have they read Sophocles? What about Aeschylus? C'mon, this century has not exactly been all roses. I use violence because it is realistic to my plots, but I do not romanticize it." Ludlum's use and description of violence not only furthered his plots but also undoubtedly contributed to his great popularity. By the time of the final battle between Andrew and Adrian, literally scores of characters—men, women, and children, the young and the old—have been most graphically maimed and murdered. Ludlum describes Andrew's death in the following manner:

> The soldier's hand was in the grave. He whipped it out. In his grip was a rope; he lurched off the ground, swinging the rope violently. Tied to the end was a grappling hook, its three prongs slashing through the air.
>
> Adrian sprang to his left, firing the enormous weapon at the crazed killer from Eye Corps.
>
> The soldier's chest exploded. The rope, held in a grip of steel, swung in a circle—the grappling hook spinning like an insanely off-course gyroscope—around the soldier's head. The body shot forward, over the sheet of rock, and plummeted down, its scream echoing, filling the mountains with its pitch of horror.
>
> With a sudden, sickening vibration the rope sprang taut, quivering in the thin layer of disturbed snow. . . .
>
> . . . He [Adrian] limped to the edge of the plateau and looked over the sheet of rock.
>
> Suspended below was the soldier's body, the grappling hook imbedded in his neck. A prong had been plunged up through Andrew's throat, its point protruding from the gaping mouth.

Thus Ludlum's originally unwilling and unwitting individual triumphs over fanatics and conspiracies; Abel/Adrian kills Cain/Andrew. Yet in Ludlum's novels, the triumph is not necessarily permanent or clear-cut. At the end of *The Gemini Contenders*, Adrian has finally discovered the message of the secret document, the message which could threaten the world's stability: It was not Christ who died on the Cross but an impostor, and Christ Himself committed suicide three days after the Crucifixion. The novel ends with Adrian neither releasing the document to the public nor permanently ensuring its secrecy by destroying it; he decides instead to keep it secret for the present, bearing the burdens of it himself, an existential act which perhaps represents Ludlum's ideal human quality.

In the second decade of his prolific writing career, Ludlum began to carry characters from one book to the next. Jason Bourne, the American suffering from amnesia in *The Bourne Identity* (1980), was brought back for further conspiratorial adventures in both *The Bourne Supremacy* (1986) and *The Bourne Ultimatum* (1990). The secret group Inver Brass, introduced in *The Chancellor Manuscript*, reappeared in *The Icarus Agenda* (1988), and Sam and The Hawk, from Ludlum's satirical *The Road to Gandolfo* (written under the Shepherd pseudonym and republished in 1982 under Ludlum) were revisited in the similarly humorous *The Road to Omaha* (1992), while rowdy Brandon Scofield from *The Matarese Circle* returned in *The Matarese Countdown* (1997) to once again battle maniacal Matarese members intent on dominating the world.

After five more bestsellers in the 1990's, Ludlum decided to try something different—a paperback original, *The Hades Factor* (2000), as the first in a series called *Covert-One*, similar to Tom Clancy's hugely popular *OpCenter* and *Net Force* books. Cowritten with Gayle Lynds, the thriller followed Ludlum's usual tenets of terrorism and conspiracy, this time involving biological warfare.

Ludlum's characters and plots also gained wider exposure through film adaptations: *The Scarlatti Inheritance*, *The Osterman Weekend*, and *The Holcroft Covenant* were made into major motion pictures and later released on video; *The Rhinemann Exchange*, *The Bourne Identity*, and *The Apocalypse Watch* were transformed into television miniseries. Though critics greeted the films in much the same way reviewers did the books—lamenting the overwrought plots filled to capacity with ultra violence—audiences were willing to overlook contrivance for a chance to see a Ludlum adventure on celluloid. In 2000 Ludlum's film reputation improved when Universal Pictures announced its intention to create a big-screen adaptation of *The Bourne Identity* starring Hollywood golden boy Brad Pitt as Jason Bourne.

## Principal mystery and detective fiction

NOVELS: *The Scarlatti Inheritance*, 1971; *The Osterman Weekend*, 1972; *The Matlock Paper*, 1973; *Trevayne*, 1973; *The Cry of the Halidon*, 1974; *The Rhinemann Exchange*, 1974; *The Road to Gandolfo*, 1975; *The Gemini Contenders*, 1976; *The Chancellor Manuscript*, 1977; *The Holcroft Covenant*, 1978; *The Matarese Circle*, 1979; *The Bourne Identity*, 1980; *The Parsifal Mosaic*, 1982; *The Aquitaine Progression*, 1984; *The Bourne Supremacy*, 1986; *The Icarus Agenda*, 1988; *The Bourne Ultimatum*, 1990; *The Road to Omaha*, 1992; *The Scorpio Illusion*, 1993; *Three Complete Novels: The Ludlum Triad*, 1994; *The Apocalypse Watch*, 1995; *The Matarese Countdown*, 1997; *The Hades Factor* (with Gayle Lynds) 2000; *The Prometheus Deception*, 2000; *The Compact Cassandra: A Covert One Novel*, 2001 (with Philip Shelby).

## Bibliography

Adler, Jerry. "The Ludlum Enigma." *Newsweek* 119 (April 19, 1982): 99.

Baxter, Susan, and Mark Nichols. "Robert Ludlum and the Realm of Evil." *Maclean's* 97 (April 9, 1984): 50-52.

Block, Lawrence. "The Ludlum Conspiracy." *Writer's Digest* 62 (September, 1977): 25-26.

Brandt, Bruce E. "Reflections of 'The Paranoid Style' in the Current Suspense Novel." *Clues: A Journal of Detection* 3 (Spring/Summer, 1982): 62-69.

Donaldson-Evans, Lance K. "Conspiracy, Betrayal, and the Popularity of a Genre: Ludlum, Forsyth, Gerárd de Villiers, and the Spy Novel Format." *Clues: A Journal of Detection* 4 (Fall/Winter, 1983): 92-114.

Greenberg, Martin H., ed. *The Robert Ludlum Companion.* New York: Bantam Books, 1993.

Klemesrud, Judy. "Behind the Best Sellers: Robert Ludlum." *The New York Times Book Review* 82 (July 10, 1977): 38.

"Ludlum, Robert." In *Mystery and Suspense Writers: The Literature of Crime, Detection, and Espionage,* edited by Robin W. Winks and Maureen Corrigan. New York: Charles Scribner's Sons, 1998.

Macdonald, Gina. *Robert Ludlum: A Critical Companion.* Westport, Conn.: Greenwood Press, 1997.

Merry, Bruce. *Anatomy of the Spy Thriller.* Montreal: McGill-Queen's University Press, 1977.

Skarda, Patricia L. "Robert Ludlum." In *Dictionary of Literary Biography Yearbook: 1982.* Detroit, Mich.: Gale Research, 1983.

*Eugene S. Larson*
*Updated by Fiona Kelleghan and Taryn Benbow-Pfalzgraf*

# Ed McBain

## Evan Hunter

**Born:** New York, New York; October 15, 1926

**Also wrote as** • Curt Cannon • Hunt Collins • Ezra Hannon • Richard Marsten

**Types of plot** • Police procedural • thriller

**Principal series** • 87th Precinct, 1956-        .

**Principal series characters** • STEVEN LOUIS CARELLA, the 87th Precinct's senior police detective, is between thirty-five and forty years old. Tall, athletic, and of Italian descent, he is intensely devoted to his wife, a beautiful deaf-mute, and to their twin children. Honest, intelligent, tenacious, and experienced, Carella is humanized by his humor, temporary defeats, and unsentimental concern for denizens of his hard world.
  • THE DEAF MAN, who periodically appears in the series, is a cunning, big-city superhood who delights in challenging the police. Often Carella's nemesis, he is a ruthless, streetwise variation of Sir Arthur Conan Doyle's Professor Moriarty.
  • COTTON HAWES, an 87th Precinct detective who often works with Carella. Named for Cotton Mather, Hawes loves the cop's existence, looking up at society's underbelly. He has a sense of outrage and is one of the few characters allowed brief bursts of social commentary, particularly on the degradations of slum street-life.
  • MEYER MEYER, a veteran, middle-aged 87th Precinct detective. He is a source of humor and commonsensical morality.
  • ARTHUR (BIG BAD LEROY) BROWN, a huge, experienced, thoughtful black detective. When teamed with Teddy Carella, understated musing on race relations attends their conversation and interactions.
  • BERT KLING, a white, Midwestern hayseed. Self-conscious about his relative inexperience as a cop in earlier volumes, he matures somewhat as the series does.
  • TEDDY CARELLA, Steve's wife and a source of tenderness, intrepidity, and insightful intelligence; she provides her husband with his emotional compass.
  • EILEEN BURKE, a female detective and past paramour of Kling's, whose presence and secondary storyline recurs in later volumes.

**Contribution** • Ed McBain's fifty-plus 87th Precinct novels rank him among the most prolific authors of police procedurals. Acclaimed the best in this genre by, among others, the Mystery Writers of America, winning an Edgar Allan Poe Award in 1957 and a Grand Masters Award in 1986. His knowledge of police methods is thorough and convincing; the 87th Precinct novels focus upon them with a ruthless economy that adds to their excitement, information, and entertainment. In spite of this singular concentration, McBain has nevertheless managed to present his readers with several plausible, three-dimensional–though never complex, profound, or overpowering–characters who operate in an otherwise largely implied, lightly sketched, and labeled urban landscape. McBain's special skill lies in his keen depiction of these characters as trackers and the unwavering quality of his narrative gaze. A major contribution of the 87th Precinct series to the genre has been to establish the ensemble detectives scenario in the popular consciousness. Long before the television series *Hill Street Blues*–which many readers believe was based on McBain's series–the detectives of the 87th Precinct set the standard for intelligent police procedural featuring a group cast. In addition, his Matthew Hope series, begun in 1978 and concluded in 1998, as well as suspense and mystery novels written outside the two series, furnish the genre with many compelling, complex, and involving works.

**Biography** • Evan Hunter (who writes in the mystery/detective genre as Ed McBain) was born Salvatore A. Lombino, the son of Charles and Marie Lombino, in New York City on October 15, 1926, and reared during the first dozen years of his life in an Italian slum. He attended Evander Childs High School in the Bronx, where his family had moved in 1938. Following graduation, he went to New York City's Art Students' League on scholarship and from there to Cooper Union Art School. Hunter's own self-estimate, however, was that his artistic talents ranged well below those of his fellow students. He had enjoyed writing for his high school literary magazine, and when he joined the navy in 1944 he started once again. After more than a year of service on a destroyer in the Pacific, he left the navy and entered Hunter College. In 1950, he was graduated Phi Beta Kappa with his bachelor's degree in English. In 1949, he had been married to Anita Melnick, a classmate at Hunter College; they had three sons. The marriage eventually ended in divorce, and Hunter married Mary Vann Finley in 1973.

Until 1954, Hunter held various jobs: He was a substitute teacher in New York vocational schools, worked for a literary agency, answered the night phone at the American Automobile Club, and sold lobsters for a wholesale firm. Although by 1954 he had published nearly one hundred short stories and had written several novels, *The Blackboard Jungle* (1954) was the first to bring him success. Hunter also wrote the screenplay for Hitchcock's late masterpiece *The Birds*, and a number of television movies of the 87th Precinct novels have been made.

**Analysis** • Ed McBain is a serious, versatile, prolific, and successful writer. His 87th Precinct police procedurals are usually written in about a month, yet they have been appreciated by large audiences, who are more familiar with Ed McBain than with Evan Hunter. Indeed, McBain's works effectively replaced those of Erle Stanley Gardner and Georges Simenon, among others, as a standard on the bookstores' mystery/detective-fiction shelves.

*Glenn Ford (left) and Sidney Poitier in the film adaptation of Ed McBain's* Blackboard Jungle. (Museum of Modern Art/Film Stills Archives)

McBain's appeal—in the 87th Precinct stories—is explicable in several ways. Clearly, he intends to entertain with swiftly moving, dramatic stories. In addition, he clearly entertains himself in the sense that he is free to explore any subject matter so long as it relates to the precinct's criminal investigations. This freedom allows him considerable range. Indeed, his work offers glimpses of a Dickensian array of characters: junkies, medical examiners, prostitutes, actors, patrolmen, psychologists, lawyers, businessmen, burglars and arsonists, psychopaths, gang members, housewives, social workers, clergy, district attorneys, female cops, and politicians. The list, if not inexhaustible, is extensive.

Considerable appeal also stems from McBain's clinical concentration upon the crime. A corpse is discovered—hanged, beaten, shot, dismembered, poisoned, drowned, or overdosed—and everything subsequently concentrates upon how it came to be where and what it was. Kept distinct are whatever effects the corpse and the crime may have on shaping those who are involved with it or are enmeshed in the crime. The detailing of violence is employed not to titillate or to provoke but to underscore the fact that violence, senseless and otherwise, is part of a cop's daily reality. Nauseating situations are normal.

The precinct's professional survival—and sanity—thus depends upon the extent to which its individuals understand, have mastered, and have a feel for certain unvarying procedures "as disciplined as the pattern of a bull fight." McBain holds his readers because his knowledge of those procedures (learned from the New York and Florida police) has a professional imprimatur. It is the application of procedures, authoritatively unfolded by McBain, that is central to every novel.

Descriptive background in the 87th Precinct stories is minimal. New York City is called simply Isola; it is divided into five sections, as dissimilar as foreign countries. There are the River Harb and the River Dix (Styx), which surround the city; Calm's Point (ironically, a dangerous section); West Riverhead; Lower Isola; the Gold Coast; and Cloak City (a garment center, in later books Coke City) are self-defining names.

Principal characters in the 87th Precinct stories are also sketchily described. Detective Steve Carella is merely a tall, athletic man in his late thirties or early forties with somewhat slanted, Oriental eyes. Yet Carella, as much as anyone, is the central figure. So it is with the other precinct detectives. McBain's rough characterization reflects his view of the police and the nature of their work. Like an army, Isola's police force is a vast, hierarchical organization, and detectives are only organization men. He has compared them to account executives, a notoriously cutthroat profession, yet detectives have a singular difference: They view the myriad forms of death daily. In McBain's corpus, cops witness the slow, individual decay of the slums' inhabitants. Each day, they witness the death in the addicts' search for heroin; the death by confinement for burglars, thieves, pimps, hustlers, muggers, and killers; the death of the whore's honor and integrity under repeated sexual stabbings; the death of street gangs, which live in fear and use violence to banish it; and the death of love in ordinary and deadly domestic violence. McBain's detectives focus upon the case, probe for information with their tested methods, in the hope that "another one" can be filed. Nevertheless, McBain registers their recognition that their procedures are often intrinsically inadequate, that with nothing to go on the police often have little chance of solving many murders, and that chance and coincidence, as much as the skillful adherence to procedure, frequently illuminate and resolve the crime.

Given this setting, in which organization and procedure are paramount, the detectives, not without passion, are pushed toward functioning as emotionally uninvolved trackers and observers. Consequently, while McBain certainly does not treat the precinct's detectives as interchangeable parts, he realistically depicts them as a unit. When Carella is not on center stage, Cotton Hawes, Meyer Meyer, Arthur Brown, and Bert Kling, among others, carry on. In such a context, McBain uses situations—rather than lengthy descriptions, extended conversations, stream-of-consciousness ruminations, or one character's analysis of another—to define them as individuals.

In this sense, his 87th Precinct detectives are relatively dull and unimaginative fellows—relative, that is, to the people whom they encounter and pursue. McBain merely illustrates something that every newspaper reporter and his readers accept: Crimes and criminals, as a rule, are perceived as intrinsically more interesting than the badge-numbered organization men (and women) who try to stop them. McBain, who ably recounts what the police do and how they do it, copes with this perception in two ways. He gives a third dimension to the detectives: Carella's devotion to his family and his belated recognition in high school that he was not only an Italian but an Italian Jew as well; Cotton Hawes's continual embarrassment, on and off the job, because of his name (and as far as readers are concerned, because of the fact that he is puritanical); Meyer Meyer's unblinking defense of his ridiculously apparent toupee, his avuncular insistence on lecturing a junkie, and his delight in discovering a murder victim whom he knew—so that for once there is a name for the detectives to use; and Bert Kling's horror, when, turning over a murder victim, he discovers that it was his fiancée and his delight in marrying a gorgeous model, only to be cuckolded within months—all of these touches humanize most of the precinct's seventeen detectives.

Further plays of imagination and injections of color come from those whom detectives interview, interrogate, and pursue, although none of these characters rises to the stature of the Deaf Man. A quintessential villain, the Deaf Man is also the quintessential embodiment of criminality. He taunts and challenges Carella and the precinct with clues to past or impending crimes; he flaunts his disguises, changes his appearance and name; he apparently dies a number of deaths but phoenixlike rises again; he recruits and when necessary abandons his dupes; he is a virtuoso murderer, thief, arsonist, con man, and layer of false trails; he is to the precinct a perpetual reminder that crime always pays for some, that criminality is perpetual and elusive.

The 87th Precinct books have matured and deepened over the years. Entries such as *Lullaby* (1989), *Mischief* (1993), which features the return of the Deaf man, *Nocturne* (1997), *The Last Best Hope* (1998), which brings together the principals of the Matthew Hope series with the 87th Precinct detectives, and *The Last Dance* (2000) have the strength and freshness of true virtuosity. Violence, emotion, sex, insights and musings on the fraught and continual decay of urban life, bad jokes, and black humor blend together with McBain's trademark procedural and forensic veracity, understated characterizations, well-realized, tautly paced plots into cogent stories with essentially American, urban hearts. His detectives—brave as they can be—mostly are neither heroes nor antiheroes. They persistently, humorously, at times foolishly, and sometimes successfully, proceed against the worst human products of those values and environs inimical to the American self-image.

### Principal mystery and detective fiction

SERIES: 87th Precinct: *Cop Hater*, 1956; *The Mugger*, 1956; *The Pusher*, 1956; *The Con Man*, 1957; *Killer's Choice*, 1958; *Killer's Payoff*, 1958; *Lady Killer*, 1958;

*Killer's Wedge,* 1959; *'Til Death,* 1959; *King's Ransom,* 1959; *Give the Boys a Great Big Hand,* 1960; *The Heckler,* 1960; *See Them Die,* 1960; *Lady, Lady, I Did It!,* 1961; *Like Love,* 1962; *The Empty Hours,* 1962; *Ten Plus One,* 1963; *Ax,* 1964; *He Who Hesitates,* 1965; *Doll,* 1965; *Eighty Million Eyes,* 1966; *Fuzz,* 1968; *Shotgun,* 1969; *Jigsaw,* 1970; *Hail, Hail, the Gang's All Here!,* 1971; *Sadie When She Died,* 1972; *Let's Hear It for the Deaf Man,* 1972; *Hail to the Chief,* 1973; *Bread,* 1974; *Blood Relatives,* 1975; *Where There's Smoke,* 1975; *So Long As You Both Shall Live,* 1976; *Guns,* 1976; *Long Time No See,* 1977; *Calypso,* 1979; *Ghosts,* 1980; *Heat,* 1981; *Ice,* 1983; *Lightning,* 1984; *Eight Black Horses,* 1985; *Poison,* 1987; *Tricks,* 1987. Matthew Hope: *Goldilocks,* 1977; *And All Through the House,* 1984; *Rumpelstiltskin,* 1981; *Beauty and the Beast,* 1982; *Jack and the Beanstalk,* 1984; *Snow White and Red Rose,* 1985; *Cinderella,* 1986; *Puss in Boots,* 1987; *Tricks,* 1987; *The Heckler,* 1988; *McBain's Ladies: The Women of the 87th Precinct,* 1988; *Lullaby,* 1989; *McBain's Ladies, Too: More Women of the 87th Precinct,* 1989; *Vespers,* 1990; *Widows,* 1991; *Kiss,* 1992; *Mischief,* 1993; *Romance,* 1995; *Nocturne,* 1997; *The Big Bad City,* 1999; *The Last Dance,* 1999; *Money, Money, Money,* 2001.

OTHER NOVELS: *The Evil Sleep!,* 1952; *The Big Fix,* 1952 (also as *So Nude, So Dead*); *Don't Crowd Me,* 1953 (also as *The Paradise Party*); *The Blackboard Jungle,* 1954; *Runaway Black,* 1954; *Murder in the Navy,* 1955 (also as *Death of a Nurse*); *The Spiked Heel,* 1956; *Vanishing Ladies,* 1957; *Even the Wicked,* 1958; *A Matter of Conviction,* 1959 (also as *The Young Savages*); *Big Man,* 1959; *The Sentries,* 1965; *A Horse's Head,* 1967; *Nobody Knew They Were There,* 1971; *Every Little Crook and Nanny,* 1972; *Doors,* 1975; *Lizzie,* 1984; *Another Part of the City,* 1986.

OTHER SHORT FICTION: *The Jungle Kids,* 1956; *I Like 'Em Tough,* 1958; *The Last Spin and Other Stories,* 1960; *Happy New Year, Herbie, and Other Stories,* 1963; *The McBain Brief,* 1982.

## Other major works

NOVELS: *Tomorrow's World,* 1956; *Second Ending,* 1956 (also as *Quartet in H*); *Strangers When We Meet,* 1958; *Mothers and Daughters,* 1961; *Buddwing,* 1964; *The Paper Dragon,* 1966; *Last Summer,* 1968; *Sons,* 1969; *Come Winter,* 1973; *Streets of Gold,* 1974; *The Chisholms: A Novel of the Journey West,* 1976; *Walk Proud,* 1979 (also as *Gangs!*); *Love, Dad,* 1981; *Far from the Sea,* 1983; *Downtown,* 1989; *Driving Lessons,* 1999; *Candyland: A Novel in Two Parts,* 2001.

SHORT FICTION: *The Beheading and Other Stories,* 1971; *Running from Legs and Other Stories,* 2000.

PLAYS: *The Easter Man,* 1964 (also as *A Race of Hairy Men*); *The Conjuror,* 1969.

SCREENPLAYS: *Strangers When We Meet,* 1960; *The Birds,* 1963; *Fuzz,* 1972; *Walk Proud,* 1979.

TELEPLAYS: *Appointment at Eleven,* 1955-1961; *The Chisholms,* 1978-1979.

NONFICTION: *McBain's Ladies: The Women of the 87th Precinct,* 1988.

CHILDREN'S LITERATURE: *Find the Feathered Serpent,* 1952; *Rocket to Luna,* 1952; *Danger: Dinosaurs!,* 1953; *The Remarkable Harry,* 1961; *The Wonderful Button,* 1961; *Me and Mr. Stenner,* 1976.

EDITED TEXTS: *Crime Squad,* 1968; *Homicide Department,* 1968; *Downpour,* 1969; *Ticket to Death,* 1969; *The Best American Mystery Stories,* 1999.

MISCELLANEOUS: *The Easter Man (a Play) and Six Stories,* 1972 (also as *Seven*).

## Bibliography

Boucher, Anthony. Introduction to *The 87th Precinct.* New York: Simon & Schuster, 1959.

Dove, George N. *The Boys from Grover Avenue: Ed McBain's 87th Precinct Novels.* Bowling Green, Ohio: Bowling Green State University Popular Press,1985.

Dove, George N. "Ed McBain." In *The Police Procedural.* Bowling Green, Ohio: Bowling Green State University Popular Press, 1982.

Hamill, Pete. "The Poet of Pulp." *The New Yorker* 75 (January 10, 2000): 62.

"Hunter, Evan." In *Mystery and Suspense Writers: The Literature of Crime, Detection, and Espionage,* edited by Robin W. Winks and Maureen Corrigan. New York: Charles Scribner's Sons, 1998.

Knight, Stephen. "'. . . A Deceptive Coolness': Ed McBain's Police Novels." In *Form and Ideology in Crime Fiction.* Bloomington: Indiana University Press, 1980.

McBain, Ed. Interview. *The Writer* 82 (April, 1969): 11-14.

Podhoretz, John. "On the McBain Beat." *Weekly Standard* 5, no. 19 (January 31, 2000): 4.

Pronzini, Bill. "The 'Mystery' Career of Evan Hunter." *The Armchair Detective* 5 (April, 1972): 129-132.

*Clifton K. Yearley*
*Updated by Fiona Kelleghan and Jessica Reisman*

# James McClure

**Born:** Johannesburg, South Africa; October 9, 1939

**Type of plot** • Police procedural

**Principal series** • Tromp Kramer/Mickey Zondi, 1971-　.

**Principal series characters** • TROMP KRAMER, a lieutenant on the Trekkersburg Murder and Robbery Squad, South African Central Intelligence Division (CID), is an unmarried Afrikaner. As the series progresses, from his youthful lustiness, irreverence, and independence, he matures into a more introspective, sympathetic detective. He retains his compassionate but antisocial stance, observing quietly the vagaries of South African apartheid. Kramer's observations in detection are astute, but he depends on others for information on which he can speculate, using wit, luck, and an uncanny intuition in order to develop leads and to solve cases.

• DETECTIVE SERGEANT MICKEY ZONDI, Kramer's assistant, partner, and friend. A Zulu from a rural village who worked as a houseboy for a year before joining the CID and who was educated by missionaries, Zondi lives in the Trekkersburg township of Zwela Village. He thus has insights that Kramer can only discern intuitively or have reported to him. Gifted with a photographic memory, Zondi frequently contributes as much to a crime's solution as Kramer does, often using recall and logic while Kramer relies on experience and intuition.

• THE WIDOW FOURIE, Kramer's slightly younger lover, who despite her sense of propriety agrees to live with Kramer on a small farm, Blue Haze, just outside the city. Supportive and attentive to Kramer's domestic needs, Fourie is not only his sexual companion but also his confidante, providing refuge from his hectic job; her questions often provoke Kramer to further insights into the case at hand.

• DR. CHRISTIAAN STRYDOM, the district surgeon, is a pathologist for the Trekkersburg CID. A man of relatively liberal views, Strydom craves data, often being so thorough in researching background information that he misses the obvious conclusions at which Kramer arrives. Whether by uncovering the constrictive powers of a python or by discovering a little-known treatise on the hangman's art, Strydom provides an exotic technology of death in the series.

**Contribution** • With the procedurals which develop the Kramer-Zondi partnership, James McClure fashions a neutral portrayal of South African apartheid society as seen from within. Amassing much historical and cultural information in the course of his exposition, characterization, and plot, McClure nevertheless maintains a carefully guarded distance from any direct, judgmental commentary. Indeed, McClure claims that "the *neutrality* of the crime story" is the primary appeal of the genre. Of the South African novel, he says, "Every novel . . . that I'd come across . . . had been self-limiting . . . in that its antiapartheid slant made it appeal only to the 'converted.'" By guarding the neutrality of his novels, he believes that he can "leave people to make their own moral judgments." Seeking to appeal universally to his readers, McClure considers his first obligation to be entertainment, "leaving graver matters–which [can] be included, but obliquely–to those with the time, money, and intellectual capacity to indulge them."

Although conscious of his craftsmanship and the psychological complexity of his characters, McClure makes his procedurals hew closely to the facts of daily existence under apartheid, so that the culture and place, evoked even descriptively, are integral to his success as a crime novelist. That McClure's readership includes not only mystery devotees but also international antiapartheid activists and academic literati as well as the South African police attests his achievement of neutrality without compromising the serious, socially significant framework of his novels. McClure's Kramer and Zondi novels are taught in creative writing courses at the college level in the United States.

**Biography** • Born on October 9, 1939, in Johannesburg, South Africa, the son of a military intelligence officer, James McClure was, from his earliest years, witness to the violence and compassion of the paradoxical South African lifestyle. During the years of World War II, while the family was living at military headquarters near Pretoria, antiaircraft guns were installed in the family garden. When the family moved to Pietermaritzburg, the capital of Natal and the hometown model for Trekkersburg, the violence shifted from international war to domestic but bloody strife among the servants and workers. McClure's mother was able to temper that violence, however, through her close, compassionate relationship with Miriam Makhatini, the family's Zulu nanny whom McClure considers a second mother. Along with his natural mother's relative openness within apartheid, the boy received, from his father–an avid reader, occasional writer, and master of seven languages–a respect for books, languages, and people that kept him reading actively, despite his marginal interest in formal education.

Growing up and remaining in Pietermaritzburg, McClure developed interests in art and photography, working for a commercial studio in 1958-1959 after his graduation from high school. He then taught art and English at a boys' preparatory school until 1963. Although he had written stories, plays, and a young adult novel, McClure did not yet think of himself as a writer, preferring instead to hone his editing skills, to practice photography, and to develop a new career in journalism. From 1963 to 1965, he worked for Natal newspapers, often in regular contact with the police and the courts as a reporter. The paradoxes of such an inside look at law enforcement under apartheid, however, led to his working long hours; during that time, he "saw too much."

In 1965, McClure, his American wife, Lorly, whom he had wed in 1962, and the first of his three children left South Africa for Edinburgh, Scotland, where he worked for a year as a subeditor. During the following three years, the McClure family lived in a small apartment in Oxford while he worked for the *Oxford Mail*. After a momentary triumph when he sold a script, "The Hole," about an American in Vietnam, to Granada Television and could then afford a modest house, a television directors' strike left that play and another, "Coach to Vahalla," without hope of production. Feeling that success depended on more than his writing, McClure stopped working for television drama, and in 1969 he switched employers, intent on developing a features department for the *Oxford Times*. Then, encouraged by the success of a fellow subeditor, facing a vacation during which he could not afford to travel, and bored with television for entertainment, McClure began his first Kramer-Zondi novel, *The Steam Pig* (1971). Ten days after he submitted the typescript, he had a contract–and *The Steam Pig* went on to be named the Best Crime Novel of 1971 and to win the Crime Writers' Association Gold Dagger Award.

With the success of this first novel and the continued favorable reviews and critical acclaim of those that followed, McClure turned to writing professionally in 1974, winning the Silver Dagger Award for his spy thriller *Rogue Eagle* (1976). He has continued to garner praise not only for his series but also for his nonfiction studies of police departments in Liverpool and San Diego.

**Analysis** • Rather than emphasize the obvious political contexts of his South African crime novels, James McClure focuses on providing his readers with the straightforward entertainment of detection. Clues are not withheld, but the rationale for the solutions to which they lead is so deeply enmeshed in apartheid that one leaves the resolution of a case knowing who committed the crime but pondering circumstance and motive in an effort to understand why it was committed–even when a superficial answer is readily apparent. Weaving observations of daily survival, the historical background, and the social tensions of life in South Africa into exposition, dialogue, and description, McClure, like murder victim and antiapartheid novelist Naomi Stride in *The Artful Egg* (1984), keeps the political undertones oblique. Consequently, the polemical themes of much South African fiction are muted, and the novels are not so much subversive as they are compassionate toward all races suffering from the bleakness of a rigidly racist society.

McClure maintains his neutral stance by means of a shifting point of view controlled by the perspective of his characters. While he avoids explicit judgment of the society he describes, he nevertheless shows so much of South African life that, once having been offered the material, his readers are virtually compelled to arrive at their own moral judgments. Scene shifts are rapid and diverse; Kramer and Zondi often pursue parallel and sometimes related cases that take them into the country as well as through various sections of the city, bringing them into contact with blacks and whites, rich and poor. Besides describing the center of these diverse scenes, CID headquarters, McClure, throughout the series, develops portraits of a rural Zulu village, a library, an illicit township drinking house (*shebeen*), the city council chambers, a liberal's mansion, a white nationalist's farm, a township shack, a zoological institute, a prostitute's bungalow, a forensic laboratory, a prison gallows, an apartheid hospital, and a decaying resort, among many other locales. His precise details and evocative images are interspersed so carefully among plot development, characterization, and exposition that readers are never distracted from Kramer and Zondi's detective work, yet each scene, upon reflection, reveals the subtle effects of apartheid.

McClure's knack for shifting the point of view in his scenes permits his characters, even minor ones, to express their values through dialogue and in the contextual narration that reflects attitudes varying from crude, overt racism to blind revolutionary zeal. Many of Kramer's fellow white policemen are proponents of Afrikaner nationalism, yet McClure refrains from stereotyping his characters. He allows his African characters, too, the same extended range of responses to conditions under apartheid. Zondi, in *The Gooseberry Fool* (1974), is nearly killed by a rioting crowd of people evicted from their homes by the Security Forces–the crowd believes that all policemen, whatever the branch, are racist murderers. Lenny Francis, in *The Steam Pig*, arranges his own sister's murder, in part because of his envy of her ability to pass as white. Mario Da Gama and Ruru, in *Snake* (1975), use apartheid's blindness to shape a white-black alliance in crime, certain that such a partnership is beyond suspicion. Because the viewpoints and values expressed by McClure's characters embody such a range of sensibilities, he deters readers from easy, snap judgments about South Africa and its peoples.

In the rapid exchanges between Kramer and Zondi and in more extended dialogues, McClure suggests that the messy search for clarity not only in solving the case but also in understanding apartheid will not come easily. Ethnic pride and linguistic heritage permeate the dialogue, both directly and subtly. Spiked with humor, yet provoking consistently a sense of doubt, hostility, or fear, his dialogue includes occasional Afrikaans and Zulu words and phrases even as his characters find bemusement in the irregularities of English. While McClure's dialogue models the process of detection, it also illustrates the fragility and tension both within a racial group and across racial lines. Characters, as a result, seem tentative and fearful of speaking their minds. Just as Kramer and Zondi probe and push to crack the alibis of their suspects, so McClure's dialogue probes and pushes his readers to crack their narrow views of South Africa.

The exotic plotting of McClure's novels is so integral to their South African setting that even this basic element of the procedural provokes thought long after the entertainment has faded. In *The Steam Pig*, the Zulu murderer uses a sharpened bicycle spoke as a weapon, seeking to make the death appear to have resulted from heart failure. The murder itself, however, is one of the disastrous consequences of an arbitrary reclassification of a family's race. In *The Sunday Hangman* (1977), a group of Boer farmers become obsessed with the technical lore of hanging in their self-righteous sentencing of criminals who have escaped the courts through legal loopholes; these vigilantes undermine the authority of the very laws on which their privileges depend. McClure's plots suggest through their surface construction the deeper, psychological turmoil of apartheid. In *Snake*, a wealthy white liberal, son of a Supreme Court justice, strangles an exotic dancer, making it appear that her own pet python was the culprit. His motive is an obsessive desire for illicit sex with a black woman, but his victim is instead a darkly tanned, racist white. In no other setting but South Africa would such complex ironies and the thematic possibilities they raise be possible.

The essence of McClure's novels, however, is found in the complicated relationship between Kramer and Zondi. Despite their growing affection and understanding, they must present the mask of master and slave to others around them: Everyone expects the conventions of apartheid, especially the police. Consequently, Kramer must feign racism and Zondi must act subservient. Only when they are alone can they tease each other with racial humor or comment on the blindness of others. They may save each other's lives while on the job, but neither can inhabit the social world of the other, however well they may know and understand it. McClure illustrates the stark contrast in their personal lives in each novel. In *The Sunday Hangman*, the Widow Fourie suggests to Kramer that, should Zondi lose his job as the result of a lingering leg injury, he might work for them as their gardener. Zondi's family dwells in a two-room, dirt-floor shack while Kramer and Fourie live in Blue Haze, a sprawling old farmhouse. The white couple's admiration for Zondi, even Fourie's charity in *The Gooseberry Fool*, cannot change the circumstances of his life. In the same novel, Kramer waits while Zondi lies in a coma and grapples with his anguish because he cannot show his compassion for fear of being perceived as a black sympathizer, thereby losing his authority as a detective among his white assistants.

Kramer and Zondi, however, work so well as partners that they serve as a symbol of not only the failures but also the hopes of South African culture. While they demonstrate the limiting effects of historical and cultural racism upon their individual lives and friendship, they also testify to the potential of individuals to overcome those dehumanizing constraints.

*The Song Dog* (1991) is a "prequel" to the Kramer/Zondi series, in that it reveals how they first met in the early 1960's. Kramer is still new to Natal and appears more uncouth, more Afrikaner and hard-line, than he is in the later works. The book was inspired by the arrest of the African National Congress leader Nelson Mandela in Howick, which McClure heard about when he was visiting the police station that very afternoon. McClure told an interviewer that he intended the book to be the last in the series as well as the first, and to dramatize the relationship between Kramer and Zondi as they get to know each other and to "get it right."

McClure's allusions to previous books in the series suggest that, on the whole, the series itself seeks to fulfill that potential of an identity based on personal qualities and capabilities rather than on race and class. These books offer no definitive, absolute answers to the questions they raise; just as Kramer notes his reluctance to confront the truth in *Snake,* McClure's fictions provide a limited truth, "having solved a problem without supplying any real answers." Readers, however, find that beneath the surface of entertaining detection they must confront the turmoil of apartheid in South Africa. McClure's vivid material, well-crafted writing, and neutral stance provide just that opportunity for his readers' own cultural detective work–if they so choose.

## Principal mystery and detective fiction

SERIES: Tromp Kramer/Mickey Zondi: *The Steam Pig,* 1971; *The Caterpillar Cop,* 1972; *The Gooseberry Fool,* 1974; *Snake,* 1975; *The Sunday Hangman,* 1977; *The Blood of an Englishman,* 1980; *The Artful Egg,* 1984; *Imago: A Modern Comedy of Manners,* 1988; *The Song Dog,* 1991.

OTHER NOVELS: *The Hanging of the Angels,* 1968; *Four and Twenty Virgins,* 1973; *Rogue Eagle,* 1976.

## Other major works

NONFICTION: *Killers,* 1976; *Spike Island,* 1980; *Cop World,* 1984.

## Bibliography

Dove, George N. *The Police Procedural.* Bowling Green, Ohio: Bowling Green State University Popular Press, 1982.

Gordimer, Nadine. "English-Language Literature and Politics in South Africa." *Journal of South African Studies* 2 (1975): 131-150.

Lockwood, Bert B. Jr. "A Study in Black and White: The South Africa of James McClure." *Human Rights Quarterly* 440 (1983).

McClure, James. Interview by Donald Wall. *Clues: A Journal of Detection* 6 (Spring/Summer, 1985): 7-25.

_____. "A Bright Grey." In *Colloquium on Crime: Eleven Renowned Mystery Writers Discuss Their Work,* edited by Robin W. Winks. New York: Scribner, 1986.

Peck, Richard. *A Morbid Fascination: White Prose and Politics in Apartheid South Africa.* Westport, Conn.: Greenwood Press, 1997.

_____. "The Mystery of McClure's Trekkersburg Mysteries: Text and Non-reception in South Africa." *English in Africa* 22, no. 1 (May, 1995): 48-71.

Schleh, Eugene. "Spotlight on South Africa: The Novels of James McClure." *Clues: A Journal of Detection* 7 (Fall/Winter, 1986): 99-107.

Wall, Donald. "Apartheid in the Novels of James McClure." *The Armchair Detective* 10 (October, 1977): 348-351.

*Michael Loudon*

# John D. MacDonald

**Born:** Sharon, Pennsylvania; July 24, 1916
**Died:** Milwaukee, Wisconsin; December 28, 1986

**Type of plot** • Hard-boiled

**Principal series** • Travis McGee, 1964-1985.

**Principal series character** • TRAVIS McGEE is a self-described "salvage expert," specializing in recovering stolen goods for clients who are helpless, hapless, and innocent victims of confidence men. He is a tough, independent man with a romantic streak and a moral code.

**Contribution** • John D. MacDonald takes the hard-boiled detective and fashions him into the modern version of a knight-errant. McGee usually gets involved in helping young women who have been bilked of their money by charming male swindlers. In McGee's code of honor, the worst crime is taking advantage of the innocent and the naïve. He couples his fiercely moral views with strong convictions about the nature of modern society, which he deplores for its rapacious violation of the environment and its greedy exploitation of human beings. Knowing he cannot change the structure of society fundamentally, McGee opts for living on its fringes and for doing battle with the hucksters and cheats who thrive on fooling women—and sometimes gullible men—by deceit and trickery. Although he is a fierce individualist, McGee is remarkable for having such a well-developed social consciousness. He is a man who realizes that his way of life is in itself a statement, a challenge to the status quo.

**Biography** • John Dann MacDonald was born on July 24, 1916, the only son of Andrew and Marguerite MacDonald, in Sharon, Pennsylvania. When he was ten years old, his family moved to Utica, New York, where he attended the Utica Free Academy. Two years later he contracted mastoiditis and scarlet fever and almost died. His sickness changed his life, making him an avid reader and a deeply reflective person.

MacDonald's father wanted his son to be a businessman, and MacDonald obliged his father by attending business schools in Philadelphia and Syracuse, where he was graduated with a B.S. in business administration in 1936. After his marriage in 1938, graduation from the Harvard Graduate Business Administration School in 1939, and a series of unsatisfactory jobs, he enlisted in the navy in 1940. It was a relief to him to have a sure means of supporting his family (his son was born in 1939) and not to worry about his place in the competitive business world. Soon he began to write—although his first short story was not published until 1946. His work for the navy and for the Office of Strategic Services (the precursor of the Central Intelligence Agency) gave him valuable background and experience for his fiction.

After World War II, MacDonald began to make a modest living from selling stories to magazines. He published his first full-length novel in 1950 and went on to produce books about a wide range of subjects, including science fiction. In 1952, he began living in Florida, the setting for all the Travis McGee novels. Although he is best known for the Travis McGee series, it makes up less than half of his total output as a writer. *Condominium* (1977), for example, was a best-seller and earned significant praise for the fineness of its moral and aesthetic vision.

**Analysis** • As John D. MacDonald freely admitted on many occasions, Travis McGee was his mouthpiece for the expression of opinions on a wide range of contemporary issues. MacDonald was a mature writer when he created McGee in 1964, so he knew how to create the detective as a full-fledged character interacting in complex ways with other characters. Although MacDonald showed that he could cleverly manipulate detective story plots, he always emphasized the significance of themes and characterization. He was not overly concerned with the whodunit form or with the mysteries the detective solves, but instead stressed the detective's moral nature and intelligence. How McGee goes about his job is at least as important as his discovery and apprehension of the murderers he pursues.

Since McGee is always the first-person narrator of the novels, his consciousness is of paramount interest. He works for himself and the people who hire him. He owns and lives on a boat, *The Busted Flush*, named in memory of a winning hand in a poker game. McGee had been losing hand after hand and then finally won one by bluffing a flush. His luck turned, and he won enough to take possession of the boat. The name of the boat points to the basic situation in which McGee usually finds himself. Fate usually deals him what looks like a losing hand, but somehow he manages to pull out or "salvage" something of value.

McGee is no unmarked hero. Indeed, the McGee series is remarkable for the many wounds and broken bones the detective suffers. He has been shot in the head and has endured all manner of injuries to his face, his ribs, and his legs. He is a rugged six feet, four inches tall and weighs more than two hundred pounds (although his opponents often mistake him for being a good twenty pounds lighter). McGee always manages to escape with his life because of his mental and physical agility. He can duck and dance away from blows, and he can fall out of a hot air balloon from a height of about four stories, landing so that only his knee needs surgery. Yet he recognizes that no matter how good he is, sooner or later he will be nailed. One of the finer pleasures of the McGee series is reading his analyses of fights, his calculations as to when to take blows on his forearms and elbows and when to penetrate his opponent's defense.

McGee never comes away from any of his cases with a clean victory. Sometimes one of his clients dies. Many times innocent people who get in the way of McGee's investigations die. For example, McGee understands that in order to catch up with Boone Waxwell in *Bright Orange for the Shroud* (1965), he has to use a woman whom Waxwell is stalking as bait. McGee's timing is off, however, and Boone gets hold of the woman and rapes her before McGee's plan of entrapment gets under way. Characteristically, the vicious Waxwell eventually manages to impale himself in a way that is just retribution for the many women he has violated. A rough, crude sort of justice—a kind of symmetry—does operate in the McGee novels, but it is at the expense of the guilty and the innocent alike.

Waxwell is also a particularly good example of MacDonald's deftness at creating complex characters. Boone talks like an easygoing country boy. He does not seem particularly bright. Yet McGee finds that this is a façade, that Waxwell hides his cunning, murderous nature with a mild-mannered, good-natured style. Knowing this, and even after being warned, McGee still underestimates Waxwell.

One of the most fascinating aspects of the Travis McGee series is his patient piecing together of plots and human characters. In *Free Fall in Crimson* (1981), a terminally ill millionaire is beaten to death. He had, at most, another six months to live. Why was he murdered? Is there any connection between his daughter's fatal accident on a bicycle, his death, and the fact that she was due to inherit his fortune? In order to trace the chain of events, to understand who had the most to profit from the millionaire's death, McGee calls on his friend Meyer, an economist among other things, who has a gift for seeing the "big picture" in ways that are beyond Travis, who is better as a painstaking collector of details. Since virtually every McGee case revolves around money, he needs a knowledgeable consultant who can explain or speculate upon the many ways money can be extorted and conned from people, or how it can find its way into various enterprises that conceal the source of revenue.

McGee and Meyer often work as a team. MacDonald found it necessary to invent Meyer because of the limitations of the first-person point of view. With McGee as narrator, everything is seen or reported from his perspective. Dialogue sometimes allows other points of view to intrude, but only a true collaborator could widen and extend McGee's consciousness. Like Sherlock Holmes and Dr. Watson, or Nero Wolfe and Archie Goodwin, McGee and Meyer complement each other and compensate for what the other lacks. Meyer is certainly no man of action—as is proved in *Free Fall in Crimson*, where he buckles under pressure and almost causes McGee's death.

MacDonald also introduced Meyer to give his detective series a tension and variety that is often lacking in formula fiction. As MacDonald notes, Meyer helped to solve a technical problem:

> I have to keep the plot the same without allowing it to look as if it is the same. Little Orphan Annie gets into a horrible situation and Travis—Daddy Warbucks—comes

and saves her. Every time. So . . . you become a little bit wary of a plot structure which is going to leave too many doors closed as you're writing it. I brought in Meyer about the fourth book because there were getting to be too many interior monologues.

If McGee is a Daddy Warbucks helping vulnerable young girls who have been swindled and molested, he is also a romantic who falls in love with some of the women he saves. McGee's cases take an emotional toll on him. Like Dashiell Hammett's Sam Spade, McGee has a tough-guy exterior which hides a streak of sentimentality. He knows better than to indulge himself, yet he never completes a case unscarred by mental trauma. Compared to most fictional detectives, McGee is a feminist—in the sense that he is deeply aware of women's feelings. He often rejects women who invite him to engage in recreational sex. He is not above using manipulative women sexually to solve a case, but such women are his equals. He does not condescend to them. He also likes to describe love play. Sex scenes in the MacDonald series are as evocative as the fight sequences.

In Travis McGee, John D. MacDonald created a character with a temper—if not a background—like his own. MacDonald hated working for business firms. He did not find himself as a man or as a writer until he decided to abandon the competition of the business world. Similarly, Travis McGee turns his back on the corporate enterprise. He has contempt—as did MacDonald—for the industries that are ruining Florida's environment. The McGee novels are full of laments for the spoilage of the state's lovely land and sea refuges. Neither MacDonald nor McGee sees a way to change the world, but both the author and his character elaborate on a consciousness of exquisite, discriminating taste.

Travis McGee is a rough-hewn version—perhaps it would be better to say an inversion—of Rex Stout's Nero Wolfe. Wolfe never left home; McGee is rarely at home. He travels the state of Florida—and sometime beyond it to Iowa, Illinois, and other states—to solve his cases. His home is a boat, and he is always in motion. Whereas Wolfe is sedentary and fat, McGee watches his diet. For all of their differences, however, each detective is admired for the way he savors and measures experience. McGee, the poor man's Nero Wolfe, the proletarian amateur, is the upholder of public and private standards.

In medieval literature the knight went forth to save a damsel in distress or to vindicate a lady's honor. In *The Deep Blue Good-by* (1964), the first McGee novel, in *A Purple Place for Dying* (which was published the same year), and in *The Green Ripper* (1979), McGee explicitly refers to himself as a kind of worn-out, yet indefatigable knight, ready to tilt his lance at dragons. He realizes that the odds are against him, but he cannot live with himself if he does not set forth. The imperative is moral. A seasoned veteran who knows how to spell himself, who waits for his second wind, McGee is the resilient hero and the modern anti-hero, making no great claims for his prowess yet surviving precisely because he knows his limitations. In a Florida fast being overtaken by developers, confidence men, and greedy corporations, McGee remains a voice of conscience, acting upon his own principles and pointing out the damage caused by a world that ignores ethical and ecological concerns.

## Principal mystery and detective fiction

SERIES: Travis McGee: *The Deep Blue Good-by*, 1964; *Nightmare in Pink*, 1964; *A Purple Place for Dying*, 1964; *The Quick Red Fox*, 1964; *A Deadly Shade of Gold*, 1965; *Bright Orange for the Shroud*, 1965; *Darker Than Amber*, 1966; *One Fearful Yellow Eye*, 1966; *Pale Gray for Guilt*, 1968; *The Girl in the Plain Brown Wrapper*, 1968; *Dress Her in Indigo*, 1969; *The Long Lavender Look*, 1970; *A Tan and Sandy Silence*, 1972; *The Turquoise Lament*, 1973; *The Scarlet Ruse*, 1973; *The Dreadful Lemon Sky*, 1975; *The Empty Copper Sea*, 1978; *The Green Ripper*, 1979; *Free Fall in Crimson*, 1981; *Cinnamon Skin*, 1982; *The Lonely Silver Rain*, 1985.

OTHER NOVELS: *The Brass Cupcake*, 1950; *Judge Me Not*, 1951; *Murder for the Bride*, 1951; *Weep for Me*, 1951; *The Damned*, 1952; *Dead Low Tide*, 1953; *The Neon Jungle*, 1953; *All These Condemned*, 1954; *Area of Suspicion*, 1954, revised 1961; *A Bullet for Cinderella*, 1955 (also as *On the Make*); *Cry Hard, Cry Fast*, 1955; *You Live Once*, 1956 (also as *You Kill Me*); *April Evil*, 1956; *Murder in the Wind*, 1956; *Border Town Girl*, 1956 (also as *Five Star Fugitive*); *Death Trap*, 1957; *The Empty Trap*, 1957; *A Man of Affairs*, 1957; *The Price of Murder*, 1957; *The Deceivers*, 1958; *Soft Touch*, 1958 (also as *Man-Trap*); *Clemmie*, 1958; *The Executioners*, 1958 (also as *Cape Fear*); *The Beach Girls*, 1959; *The Crossroads*, 1959; *Deadly Welcome*, 1959; *The End of the Night*, 1960; *Slam the Big Door*, 1960; *The Only Girl in the Game*, 1960; *Where Is Janet Gantry?*, 1961; *One Monday We Killed Them All*, 1961; *A Flash of Green*, 1962; *A Key to the Suite*, 1962; *The Girl, the Gold Watch, and Everything*, 1962; *The Drowner*, 1963; *On the Run*, 1963; *The Last One Left*, 1967; *One More Sunday*, 1984; *Barrier Island*, 1986.

OTHER SHORT FICTION: *End of the Tiger and Other Stories*, 1966; *Seven*, 1971; *The Good Old Stuff: Thirteen Early Stories*, 1982; *Two*, 1983; *More Good Old Stuff*, 1984.

## Other major works

NOVELS: *Wine of the Dreamers*, 1951 (also as *Planet of the Dreamers*); *Ballroom of the Skies*, 1952; *Cancel All Our Vows*, 1953; *Contrary Pleasure*, 1954; *Please Write for Details*, 1959; *I Could Go On Singing*, 1963; *Condominium*, 1977.

SHORT FICTION: *Other Times, Other Worlds*, 1978.

NONFICTION: *The House Guests*, 1965; *No Deadly Drug*, 1968; *Nothing Can Go Wrong*, 1981 (with John H. Kilpack).

EDITED TEXT: *The Lethal Sex*, 1959.

## Bibliography

Campbell, Frank D., Jr. *John D. MacDonald and the Colorful World of Travis McGee*. San Bernardino, Calif.: Borgo Press, 1977.

Geherin, David. *John D. MacDonald*. New York: Frederick Ungar, 1982.

Hirshberg, Edgar. *John D. MacDonald*. Boston: Twayne, 1985.

"MacDonald, John D." In *Mystery and Suspense Writers: The Literature of Crime*,

*Detection, and Espionage,* edited by Robin W. Winks and Maureen Corrigan. New York: Charles Scribner's Sons, 1998.

Merrill, Hugh. *The Red Hot Typewriter: The Life and Times of John D. MacDonald.* New York: St. Martin's, 2000.

Moore, Lewis D. *Meditations on America: John D. MacDonald's Travis McGee Series and Other Fiction.* Bowling Green, Ohio: Bowling Green State University Popular Press, 1994.

Shine, Walter, and Jean Shine. *A Bibliography of the Published Works of John D. MacDonald with Selected Biographical Materials and Critical Essays.* Gainesville: Patrons of the Libraries, University of Florida, 1980.

*Carl Rollyson*

# Ross Macdonald

## Kenneth Millar

**Born:** Los Gatos, California; December 13, 1915
**Died:** Santa Barbara, California; July 11, 1983

**Also wrote as** • John Macdonald • John Ross Macdonald

**Type of plot** • Private investigator

**Principal series** • Lew Archer, 1949-1976.

**Principal series character** • LEW ARCHER, a private investigator, formerly on the Long Beach police force, divorced. About thirty-five years old when he first appears, he ages in the course of the series to fifty or so, remaining unmarried. A tough but caring man, he is sustained by his conviction that "everything matters"– that every human life has a meaning which awaits discovery and understanding.

**Contribution** • Ross Macdonald's eighteen novels featuring Lew Archer, the compassionate private eye who serves as their narrator and central intelligence, have been described as "the finest series of detective novels ever written by an American." Working in the tradition of Dashiell Hammett and Raymond Chandler, masters of the hard-boiled detective novel, Macdonald surpassed them in craftsmanship and psychological depth. He saw in popular fiction the promise of "democratic prose," fashioned from the American vernacular. His language is economical, deceptively simple, capable of poetry. For the most part, his characters are ordinary people, neither heroes nor villains, rendered with full justice to the moral complexity of their experience. His books are also a composite portrait of a particular place and its society; few novelists, whether inside or outside the mystery genre, have achieved the accuracy, the social range, and the insight of Macdonald's anatomy of California.

**Biography** • Ross Macdonald was born Kenneth Millar on December 13, 1915, in Los Gatos, California, the son of John Macdonald Millar and Annie Moyer Millar. ("Ross Macdonald" was a pen name which he adopted after having published several books; in private life he remained Kenneth Millar.) Macdonald was an only child; his parents, both forty years old at his birth, were Canadian. When Macdonald was still an infant, the family moved to Vancouver, British Columbia, where Macdonald's father, an amateur writer, worked as a harbor pilot. When Macdonald was three years old, his father abandoned the family.

Macdonald spent most of his childhood and youth in the homes of relatives all across Canada. In Kitchener, Ontario, he attended the Kitchener-Waterloo Collegiate and Vocational School, from which he was graduated in 1932. There, he met his future wife, Margaret Ellis Sturm; his first publication, a Sherlock Holmes parody, appeared in an issue of the school magazine which also included her first published story.

In 1932, Macdonald's father died, leaving an insurance policy of twenty-five hundred dollars. On the strength of that modest legacy, Macdonald was able to enter the University of Western Ontario. Following his graduation in 1938, he married Margaret Sturm; their only child, Linda Jane Millar, was born a year later.

In 1941, Millar began graduate study in English literature at the University of Michigan in Ann Arbor. (He received his Ph.D. in 1952 upon completion of his dissertation, "The Inward Eye: A Revaluation of Coleridge's Psychological Criticism.") In the same year, Margaret Millar published her first novel, *The Invisible Worm*; she was to enjoy a productive and successful career as a mystery writer. Macdonald's own first novel, *The Dark Tunnel*, was published in 1944, by which time he was an ensign in the United States Naval Reserve, serving as a communications officer on an escort carrier. After the war, Macdonald joined his wife and daughter in Santa Barbara. With the exception of a year spent in Menlo Park, 1956-1957, during which time he underwent psychotherapy, Macdonald lived in Santa Barbara for the remainder of his life.

Between 1946 and 1976, Macdonald published twenty-three novels. In 1974, he was awarded the Grand Master Award of the Mystery Writers of America. In 1981, he was diagnosed as having Alzheimer's disease. He died on July 11, 1983.

**Analysis** • Ross Macdonald began his career with two spy novels: *The Dark Tunnel*, written in only one month while he was taking courses for his doctorate, and *Trouble Follows Me* (1946), which he completed on board ship while serving in the navy. His third and fourth books, *Blue City* (1947) and *The Three Roads* (1948), in which he turned to the hard-boiled style, were written in Santa Barbara in a nine-month span after his discharge. Together, these four novels constitute Macdonald's apprenticeship. They are marred by overwriting and other flaws, but they served their purpose, allowing him to establish himself as a professional writer.

Macdonald found his voice with his fifth novel, *The Moving Target* (1949). It is no accident that this key book was the first to feature private investigator Lew Archer: With Archer as narrator, Macdonald was able to deepen and humanize the form he had inherited from Hammett and Chandler. In his analytical awareness of what he was doing as a writer and how he was doing it, Macdonald was quite exceptional, and his essays and occasional pieces, collected in *Self-Portrait: Ceaselessly into the Past* (1981), remain the best guide to his work. In his essay "The Writer as Detective Hero," he sketches the history of the detective story and discusses his contribution to the genre via the character of Archer.

The focus of the essay, as its title suggests, is on the relationship between fictional detectives and their creators, from Edgar Allan Poe's C. Auguste Dupin and Arthur Conan Doyle's Sherlock Holmes to Hammett's Sam Spade and Chandler's Philip Marlowe. In Macdonald's view, the central purpose of the detective story is to provide an "imaginative arena" in which troubling realities can be confronted "safely, under artistic controls." The fictional detective, Macdonald suggests, is a projection of the author, a mediating figure by means of which the writer is able to

*Ross Macdonald.* (Hal Boucher)

"handle dangerous emotional material." Early detectives such as Dupin and Holmes enact the triumph of reason over the "nightmare forces of the mind" (although in Poe's stories, Macdonald notes, there remains a "residue of horror"). Sam Spade, the archetypal hard-boiled detective, is a much more realistic character, yet his creator deprives him of the ability to make sense of his experience—and thereby denies him full humanity. Marlowe is gifted with a richer sensibility, at once ironic and lyrical, yet there is a strong vein of romanticism in his portrayal.

Macdonald's Lew Archer has something in common with all these predecessors, yet he differs from them as well:

> Archer is a hero who sometimes verges on being an antihero. While he is a man of action, his actions are largely directed to putting together the stories of other people's lives and discovering their significance. He is less a doer than a questioner, a consciousness in which the meanings of other lives emerge. This gradually developed conception of the detective hero as the mind of the novel is not wholly new, but it is probably my main contribution to this special branch of fiction.

With this passage, Macdonald's title, "The Writer as Detective Hero," gains added resonance. Macdonald, the writer, is a kind of private investigator; Archer, the detective, is a poet, perceiving hidden connections. Both writer and detective are in the business of "putting together the stories of other people's lives and discovering their significance." Indeed, in many of the novels, Archer explicitly identifies the impulse that keeps him going, nowhere more forcefully than in *The Far Side of the Dollar* (1965), when, in response to a skeptical question ("Why does it matter?"), he states his credo: "Life hangs together in one piece. Everything is connected with everything else. The problem is to find the connections."

As Macdonald acknowledges, this altered conception of the detective hero (and, thereby, the detective novel) developed gradually. The early Archer books, while unmistakably individual, nevertheless retain many features of the traditional hard-boiled novel; like Chandler's Marlowe, Archer trades insults with gangsters, is repeatedly embroiled in violent, melodramatic confrontations, and encounters the requisite complement of dangerous and seductive women: "The full red lips were parted and the black eyes dreamed downward heavily. . . . I had to remind myself that a man was dead" (*The Way Some People Die*, 1951). The texture of the later books is subtler; Archer is less cynical, more introspective. It is easy to exaggerate the contrast, as many critics have done; after all, every one of the Archer books follows the conventions of the detective novel—a form as artificial, Macdonald remarked, as the sonnet. Still, it is undeniable that Macdonald's novels following *The Galton Case* (1959), the book he regarded as marking his breakthrough, reveal his increasing mastery of those familiar conventions and his ability to employ them in a highly original fashion.

That mastery is particularly apparent in *The Underground Man* (1971), the sixteenth Archer novel and one of the best. The title echoes Fyodor Dostoevski; Macdonald thus claims for his own a tradition that includes *Crime and Punishment* and *The Brothers Karamazov*. The point is that the heritage of the crime novel is much richer than is generally acknowledged. Macdonald was not seeking to add a literary cachet to his work; rather, he was passionately committed to the value of popular literature. His experience of poverty and the humiliation that went with it made him a lifelong partisan of the underclass and an enemy of privilege. Those attitudes are reflected in the social commentary that threads through his books; more important, they helped to shape the language of his fiction.

The opening sentences of *The Underground Man* are typical: "A rattle of leaves woke me some time before dawn. A hot wind was breathing in at the bedroom window. I got up and closed the window and lay in bed and listened to the wind." The language is economical and direct; the sentences follow one another with compelling speed. Macdonald's apparently simple language is in fact highly stylized; to achieve the effect of simplicity—without falling into self-parody—requires great art. Macdonald based his style on the spoken language, "the carrier of our social and cultural meanings." A genuinely democratic society, he believed, needs a vital popular literature written in a language accessible to all its members: "A book which can be read by everyone, a convention which is widely used and understood in all its variations, holds a civilization together as nothing else can."

It is just such a convention which permits readers to accept a private eye who (to borrow Macdonald's tribute to Chandler's style) writes "like a slumming angel." Here is Lew Archer on the first page of *The Underground Man*: "It was a bright September morning. The edges of the sky had a yellowish tinge like cheap paper darkening in the sunlight." The marvelous similes that are Macdonald's trademark do not serve a merely decorative purpose; they create patterns of imagery which are integral to the structure of his novels. Here, there is a hint of the forest fire that will dominate the narrative.

On that bright morning, Archer is feeding peanuts to jays on the lawn of his apartment building in West Los Angeles. An anxious little boy emerges from an apartment usually occupied by an older couple; soon the boy, whose name is Ronny Broadhurst, is having a good time with Archer, catching peanuts in his mouth. The fun is interrupted by the arrival of the boy's father, Stanley Broadhurst, who has come to take Ronny to Santa Teresa (a fictitious town modeled on Santa Barbara) to visit his grandmother. The boy's mother, Jean Broadhurst, comes out of the apartment and an ugly scene ensues, initiated by Stanley. Eventually he leaves with his son and a young blonde woman, evidently eighteen or nineteen, who has been waiting out of sight in his car.

The reader may be grumbling that Archer's entry into the Broadhursts' troubles is a little too conveniently arranged. Does not Archer himself say (in this book and in others as well), "I don't believe in coincidences"? Indeed, there is no coincidence here, for Macdonald has a reversal in store. Several hours after Stanley leaves, Jean Broadhurst comes to Archer's apartment. A forest fire has started in Santa Teresa, near Stanley's mother's ranch. Jean asks Archer to take her there; she is worried about Ronny. On the way, she admits that the Wallers, the couple whose apartment she is borrowing, have told her about Archer and his profession, and that, under the pressure of her trouble with her husband, this knowledge may have prompted her to stay in the Wallers' place.

The deftness of this opening is sustained throughout the novel. Everything fits, yet nothing is contrived. Stanley's father has not been seen for fifteen years, having apparently left his wife and son for another woman. Stanley has become obsessed with tracing his father, increasingly neglecting his own family. At the Broadhurst ranch in Santa Teresa, Archer meets a Forest Service investigator who has discovered Stanley's hastily buried body. The fire, now raging out of control, was started by his cigarillo, dropped in the tinderlike grass when he was murdered. Ronny and the teenage girl have disappeared.

With no forcing, Macdonald draws a parallel between the fire and the ramifying Broadhurst case, which proves to involve many people in a tangle of guilt, deception, and murder. The consequences of the fire are enormous—completely out of scale, it would seem, with the tiny flame that started it. So it is, Macdonald suggests, with human affairs.

Such a conclusion, baldly stated, is little more than a cliché. Macdonald's novels, however, are not statements: They are stories that unfold in time with the inevitability of tragedy, and their revelations, even on a second or third reading, move the reader to pity and wonder.

## Principal mystery and detective fiction

SERIES: Lew Archer: *The Moving Target*, 1949; *The Drowning Pool*, 1950 (also as *Harper*); *The Way Some People Die*, 1951; *The Ivory Grin*, 1952 (also as *Marked for Murder*); *Find a Victim*, 1954; *The Name Is Archer*, 1955; *The Barbarous Coast*, 1956; *The Doomsters*, 1958; *The Galton Case*, 1959; *The Wycherly Woman*, 1961; *The Zebra-Striped Hearse*, 1962; *The Chill*, 1964; *The Far Side of the Dollar*, 1965; *Black Money*, 1966; *The Instant Enemy*, 1968; *The Goodbye Look*, 1969; *The Underground Man*, 1971; *Sleeping Beauty*, 1973; *The Blue Hammer*, 1976; *Lew Archer, Private Investigator*, 1977.

OTHER NOVELS: *The Dark Tunnel*, 1944 (also as *I Die Slowly*); *Trouble Follows Me*, 1946 (also as *Night Train*); *Blue City*, 1947; *The Three Roads*, 1948; *Meet Me at the Morgue*, 1953 (also as *Experience with Evil*); *The Ferguson Affair*, 1960.

## Other major works

NONFICTION: *On Crime Writing*, 1973; *Self-Portrait: Ceaselessly into the Past*, 1981.

## Bibliography

Bruccoli, Matthew J. *Ross Macdonald*. San Diego: Harcourt Brace Jovanovich, 1984.

_____. *Ross Macdonald/Kenneth Millar: A Descriptive Bibliography*. Pittsburgh, Penn.: University of Pittsburgh Press, 1983.

Bruccoli, Matthew J. and Richard Layman, eds. *Hardboiled Mystery Writers: Raymond Chandler, Dashiell Hammett, Ross Macdonald*. Detroit: Gale Research, 1989.

"Macdonald, Ross." In *Mystery and Suspense Writers: The Literature of Crime, Detection, and Espionage*, edited by Robin W. Winks and Maureen Corrigan. New York: Charles Scribner's Sons, 1998.

Mahan, Jeffrey H. *A Long Way from Solving That One: Psycho/Social and Ethical Implications of Ross Macdonald's Lew Archer Tales*. Lanham, Md.: University Press of America, 1990.

Nolan, Tom. *Ross Macdonald: A Biography*. New York: Scribner, 1999.

Schopen, Bernard. *Ross Macdonald*. Boston: Twayne, 1990.

Sipper, Ralph B., ed. *Inward Journey: Ross Macdonald*. Santa Barbara, Calif.: Cordelia Editions, 1984.

Skinner, Robert E. *The Hard-Boiled Explicator: A Guide to the Study of Dashiell Hammett, Raymond Chandler, and Ross Macdonald*. Metuchen, N.J.: Scarecrow Press, 1985.

Speir, Jerry. *Ross Macdonald*. New York: Frederick Ungar, 1978.

Weinkauf, Mary S. *Hard-Boiled Heretic: The Lew Archer Novels of Ross Macdonald*. New York: Gramercy Books, 1994.

Wolfe, Peter. *Dreamers Who Live Their Dreams: The World of Ross Macdonald's Novels*. Bowling Green, Ohio: Bowling Green State University Popular Press, 1976.

*John Wilson*

# William P. McGivern

**Born:** Chicago, Illinois; December 6, 1922
**Died:** Palm Desert, California; November 18, 1982

**Types of plot** • Police procedural • thriller

**Also wrote as** • Bill Peters

**Contribution** • William P. McGivern's work differs considerably from the general run of crime fiction of the 1940's and 1950's, the years when the author did his best work. While much of the writing of his contemporaries during this period presented protagonists with fixed, relatively stable personalities, McGivern's work generally took another direction. His novels on crime are particularly notable for their depth and sensitivity in the portrayal of the central character and for their trenchant analysis of the moral and psychological effects of the corruption that surrounds him in the netherworld of big-city politics and public service.

{Although formidable and independent in his interaction with others, the McGivern protagonist struggles with an inner world of psychological complexity and moral peril. He is consistently engaged in reluctant self-analysis and introspection, following a path that inevitably leads to self-discovery.

McGivern also brings to his writing a thorough knowledge of police work. In a subtle blend of casuistry and objective analysis, he examines the implications of its pressures and scant rewards, its frequent inability to meet the high and often-unrealistic expectations of the public, with an insight achieved by few of his contemporaries in the genre of crime fiction.

**Biography** • William Peter McGivern was born in Chicago, Illinois, on December 6, 1922, the second son of Peter Francis McGivern and Julia Costello McGivern. His father was a banker and businessman, his mother a dress designer who catered to a fashionable clientele in her shop on Michigan Boulevard. For a time, his father's business interests brought the family to Mobile, Alabama, where McGivern was reared.

In 1937, McGivern quit high school and returned to Chicago, where he worked as a laborer for the Pullman Company in the Pennsylvania Railroad yards. During this time, he read widely and eclectically, particularly the works of American authors such as Nathaniel Hawthorne, Thomas Wolfe, Ernest Hemingway, and F. Scott Fitzgerald. He also discovered the prose of G. K. Chesterton and the poetry of Robert Burns. In addition to his wide reading, he had begun to write. By 1940, he was publishing in the pulp-fiction market, particularly in science fiction and fantasy magazines.

During World War II, McGivern served three and one-half years in the United States Army and was decorated for service in the European campaign. He would later draw on these experiences in an autobiographical novel, *Soldiers of '44* (1979), based on his experiences as a sergeant in charge of a fifteen-man gun section during the Battle of the Bulge. At war's end, he was stationed in England, where, for a period of four months, he attended the University of Birmingham. McGivern was discharged from the army in January, 1946.

In December, 1948, McGivern married Maureen Daly, also a writer. They had two children, a son and a daughter. From 1949 to 1951, McGivern worked as a reporter and book reviewer for the *Philadelphia Evening Bulletin*. As a police reporter, he became interested in policemen and detectives and how they function in an environment of big-city corruption. The experience provided the details and factual basis for several of his crime novels.

In a long and distinguished career, McGivern published some twenty-five crime novels and an array of short stories, screenplays, and television scripts. In 1980, he was elected president of the Mystery Writers of America, which had given him its Edgar Allan Poe Award for his novel *The Big Heat* in 1952, the year it was published. McGivern died on November 18, 1982.

**Analysis** • William P. McGivern began his career as a conventional crime fiction writer, submitting to pulp magazines the formula fiction that was their mainstay through the 1920's and 1930's. He continued this formula approach into the late 1940's, when he turned from the short story to the crime novel with the publication of his first book, *But Death Runs Faster* (1948). His brief tenure as a crime reporter in Philadelphia gave him both factual material and psychological insight into the daily, behind-the-scenes operations of big-city police, a combination which brought considerable authenticity to his writing. In the early 1950's, McGivern experimented with other forms of writing, including fantasy and science fiction. More notably, in his writing about crime he experimented with a Mickey Spillane-style plot and protagonist, exemplified in his fifth novel, *Blondes Die Young* (1952). Apparently, he had some misgivings about the Spillane approach to plot and characterization, for he published the novel under the name Bill Peters. It was the first and last time McGivern used a pseudonym for crime fiction.

Eventually, McGivern's interest focused on the complex characterization of the police detective as fallible hero, the culpable human being on the front lines of civilization's perennial battle with a criminal element that threatens to undermine and destroy it. Specifically, McGivern centered his attention on the intrinsic nature of urban corruption, the two-sided, inherent duplicity of society. He concentrated on the darker, ambiguous side of human nature that is subsumed and obscured by the surface appearance of a functioning, law-abiding society.

In novels such as *The Big Heat, Rogue Cop* (1954), and *The Darkest Hour* (1955), McGivern places his protagonists in solitary—and lonely—confrontation with the seemingly overwhelming power of an underworld that thrives on duplicity. Although the detective/protagonist is clearly superior to his fellow officers in his ability to observe, investigate, and make deductions concerning a crime, that superiority is always taken for granted. For example, Mike Carmody, the protagonist of *Rogue Cop*, stops by a hotel room where a murder has been committed. His fellow detectives are in the middle of their investigation. It is not Carmody's case, but in a matter of minutes and in an offhand, matter-of-fact way, he solves the crime for his befuddled colleagues.

In his crime fiction, McGivern is never overly concerned with details of investigative deduction and solution; his emphasis is on character study. The reader's attention in *Rogue Cop* is focused on Carmody's inner struggle, the psychological/ethical/moral conflict that McGivern's protagonists invariably face. The depiction of their struggle frequently reflects the influence of McGivern's Catholic background and his abiding interest in man's need for a spiritual center. Essentially, McGivern illustrates a very basic conflict between good and evil. In these novels, evil in the modern world comes in a highly attractive and deceptive package, with money and power its primary attributes. It is simultaneously seductive and destructive, and its appeal is easily and readily rationalized.

In developing the character of Mike Carmody, McGivern has drawn, at least indirectly, on the New Testament story of the prodigal son. Seduced and corrupted, Carmody is a crooked cop, the scion of a loving Catholic family which he rejects. As the novel begins, he is a prodigal without a home to which he can return. His mother died when he was a child; his father, whose values and spiritual optimism Carmody cynically dismissed, lived long enough to know the pain of his son's corruption. In his attempt to justify his choices and the life he lives, Carmody has all but totally convinced himself that he is simply playing the percentages, living the good life that only a fool would reject. Yet the richly furnished apartment, the expensively tailored suits, and the other accoutrements of a life lived according to material wants all bear testimony to a moral, ethical, and spiritual poverty.

Carmody's redemption, along with the opportunity for retribution and subsequent atonement, comes after his younger brother, an incorruptible rookie cop, is murdered by racketeers because he has refused to follow his older brother's example. Bereft of family and career, Mike Carmody nevertheless regains in some semblance his lost integrity by turning State's evidence. The lost son returns, if not to the father, at least to the father's values. When Carmody becomes the star witness for the prosecution, however, his motivation is not only retribution and atonement; there is also an old-fashioned desire for revenge, another element of the darker side of human nature that plays a significant role in McGivern's fiction.

The motif of the good man in righteous pursuit of vengeance is the energizing force in several of McGivern's novels—including *The Big Heat, The Darkest Hour, Savage Streets* (1959), and *Reprisal* (1973). In *The Big Heat*, Dave Bannion, the protagonist, is a police detective who has rigorously maintained the straight and narrow path and is uncompromising in his opposition to racketeers and corrupt officials. Unlike Mike Carmody of *Rogue Cop*, Bannion has a spiritual center. (He reads, for example, the sixteenth century *Ascent of Mount Carmel* by Saint John of the Cross for guidance and perspective.) His meditations are put aside, however, when first a fellow police officer and later Kate, Bannion's wife, are killed by racketeers who enjoy respectable status in the community and the protection of corrupt police officials and politicians. Like a patriarch of the Old Testament, Bannion pursues his adversaries with the fury of an avenging angel. His winning struggle against seemingly overwhelming odds is a veritable Armageddon. When he and the forces of good have triumphed, he returns, at the conclusion of the novel, to his meditations on Saint John of the Cross.

In his exercise of the revenge motif, McGivern explores the gray areas of the issue as well. The law-abiding citizen, for example, vengeful because he is frustrated by the apparent inability of the police to exact justice in a legal system that seems to offer more protection to the criminal than to the victim, is effectively portrayed in *Reprisal* and *Savage Streets*. In both novels men whose lives, family, and property had always been insulated from crime suddenly become victims. That which had previously occurred only in the remote strata of society to which they were passive witnesses and bystanders has struck home, filling them with a sense of personal outrage and injustice.

*Savage Streets*, ostensibly a novel about juvenile delinquency and the lynch-mob mentality of vigilantism, reads like a sociological treatise. In this novel McGivern indicts middle-class, suburban America and the shallow values of a materialistic society. John Farrell and his neighbors live the comfortable commuter life of cocktail parties, backyard barbecues, and dinners at their restricted country club. When their children are threatened and intimidated by two teenage thugs, Farrell and the others become involved, attempting to intimidate the teenagers with their adult authority. The young hoodlums, however, are not intimidated, and a small war develops. When Farrell is driven to beat one of the young thugs senseless, mistakenly believing that this youth was responsible for the hit-and-run accident that sent Farrell's daughter to the hospital, he realizes what he has become. He attempts to reason with his vigilante neighbors to prevent further violence—but to no avail. Before Farrell can successfully enlist the police to halt the madness, one of his neighbors is dead, another boy is badly beaten, and a teenage girl is raped. In the course of the experience, Farrell comes to realize that there are actually two "gangs": one led by teens from the proverbial "wrong side of the tracks," the other by the exclusionary suburban set, whose property and career positions will be preserved at any cost, stopping, only by chance, just short of murder. The plot is a bit simplistic, but to his credit McGivern offers no easy answers to what he presents as a veiled class warfare. The focus in *Savage Streets* is on John Farrell, the typical American family man who comes to discover, after almost destroying his own life, that there is no satisfactory substitute for rule by law, regardless of how provocative the circumstances may be.

McGivern examined social issues in other crime novels, one of the best of which combines a social question with a well-plotted caper, a major robbery planned in extensive detail. In *Odds Against Tomorrow* (1957), Dave Burke, a former police officer who was fired from the force for taking bribes, and Novak, his accomplice, have planned a seemingly foolproof bank robbery. They require two additional men with special talents to make it work: John Ingram, a black man who needs money desperately to pay overdue gambling debts, and Earl Slater, a Southern redneck, a misfit who is painfully becoming aware that after distinguishing himself in wartime combat, he seems unable to do anything else. From the moment these two meet, it is clear that Slater's prejudice threatens the success of the robbery. Ironically, it is the failure of this desperate enterprise that brings Slater and Ingram together. Deserted by Novak after Burke is killed, they gradually become closer, even dependent on each other.

McGiven's political liberalism is clearly in evidence here, offering the failed robbery as a metaphor for a stalled society, impeded in its progress by bigotry. As is typical in McGivern's novels, the details of the well-planned robbery and its failure are of secondary interest. While his character study of Ingram is pedestrian and not particularly insightful, Slater proves a far more penetrating and interesting study. McGivern offers a vivid analysis of a frightened sociopath, a man desperate for love and security, whose only talent is for making enemies.

McGivern's novels of the 1970's and 1980's show a marked commercial bent and seem to have been written for the screen. This is hardly surprising since McGivern was a successful writer of screenplays and television scripts, and nine of his novels have been made into motion pictures. Novels such as *Night of the Juggler* (1975), about a Central Park serial killer, seem written more for film producers than for readers of crime fiction. *Caprifoil* (1972), however, is a first-rate espionage/secret agent thriller, worthy of comparison with the work of John le Carré.

McGivern's fiction is not without a lighter side, evidenced by the dual spoof of psychiatry and the caper plot in *Lie Down, I Want to Talk to You* (1967). Otis Pemberton, an overweight psychiatrist with a tendency to gamble (and lose), is a most unlikely and atypical McGivern protagonist. Pemberton is blackmailed into participating in a bank robbery by a patient. Since the patient has failed at previous robbery attempts, he needs Pemberton to "reprogram" him and his associates for success. Complicating the entire operation is a rival psychiatrist who has been treating the same patient and who ultimately becomes part of the scheme.

McGivern's books constitute crime fiction of a high order. In each, the actual crime and its concomitant details serve primarily as a point of departure for his highest interest: the texture of humanity that emerges with the creation and development of character. McGivern writes in the third person, combining spare prose and taut dialogue with an economical, highly selective use of descriptive detail. The situation in which the McGivern protagonist finds himself may be remote from the average reader's experience, but the reader readily empathizes; the angst McGivern depicts is universally felt and understood.

**Principal mystery and detective fiction**

NOVELS: *But Death Runs Faster*, 1948 (also as *The Whispering Corpse*); *Heaven Ran Last*, 1949; *Very Cold for May*, 1950; *Shield for Murder*, 1951; *Blondes Die Young*, 1952; *The Crooked Frame*, 1952; *The Big Heat*, 1952; *Margin of Terror*, 1953; *Rogue Cop*, 1954; *The Darkest Hour*, 1955 (also as *Waterfront Cop*); *The Seven File*, 1956 (also as *Chicago-7*); *Night Extra*, 1957; *Odds Against Tomorrow*, 1957; *Savage Streets*, 1959; *Seven Lies South*, 1960; *The Road to the Snail*, 1961; *A Pride of Place*, 1962; *A Choice of Assassins*, 1963; *The Caper of the Golden Bulls*, 1966; *Lie Down, I Want to Talk to You*, 1967; *Caprifoil*, 1972; *Reprisal*, 1973; *Night of the Juggler*, 1975; *Summitt*, 1982; *A Matter of Honor*, 1984.

SHORT FICTION: *Killer on the Turnpike*, 1961.

**Other major works**

NOVELS: *Soldiers of '44*, 1979; *War Games*, 1984.

SCREENPLAYS: *I Saw You What Did*, 1965; *The Wrecking Crew*, 1969; *Caprifoil*, 1973; *Brannigan*, 1975; *Night of the Juggler*, 1975.

TELEPLAYS: *San Francisco International Airport* series, 1970; *The Young Lawyers* series, 1970; *Banyon* series, 1972; *Kojak* series, 1973-1977.

NONFICTION: *Mention My Name in Mombasa: The Unscheduled Adventures of an American Family Abroad*, 1958 (with Maureen Daly McGivern); *The Seeing*, 1980 (with Maureen Daly McGivern).

**Bibliography**

Callendar, Newgate. Review of *Reprisal*, by William P. McGivern. *The New York Times Book Review* 78 (March 25, 1973): 49.

Hubin, Allen J. Review of *Night of the Juggler*, by William P. McGivern. *The Armchair Detective* 8 (May, 1975): 226.

Lewis, Steve. Review of *Reprisal*, by William P. McGivern. *The Mystery FANcier* 4 (March/April, 1980): 34.

Shibuk, Charles. Review of *Heaven Ran Last*, by William P. McGivern. *The Armchair Detective* 6 (May, 1973): 188.

*Richard Keenan*

# Helen MacInnes

**Born:** Glasgow, Scotland; October 7, 1907
**Died:** New York, New York; September 30, 1985

**Types of plot** • Amateur sleuth • espionage

**Contribution** • At the height of her popularity, Helen MacInnes was known as "Queen of International Espionage Fiction." Despite the fact that her novels contain much less sex and violence than others of the genre, they are highly suspenseful. In addition, they are based on an appreciation of justice, freedom, and individual dignity. Perhaps the most characteristic element of MacInnes's novels is their settings, which are invariably beautiful and of historic interest. The capital cities of Europe and its many forests, lakes, castles, and opera houses are described in such detail that the novels may be enjoyed as travel books. Brittany, Salzburg, Málaga, Venice, and Rome come alive for the reader. MacInnes's love for these and other spots of the world, as well as her appreciation of democratic values, illuminates and enhances her novels.

**Biography** • Helen Clark MacInnes was born on October 7, 1907, in Glasgow, Scotland, where she was also educated. She married Gilbert Highet, a Greek and Latin scholar, in 1932. To finance trips abroad they collaborated in translating books into English from German. The couple moved to the United States in 1937. After her son was born, MacInnes began writing her first novel. *Above Suspicion* (1941) not only was an immediate best-seller but also was made into a popular film, as were *Assignment in Brittany* (1942), *The Venetian Affair* (1963), and *The Salzburg Connection* (1968). The film *Assignment in Brittany* was used to help train intelligence operatives during World War II.

During the course of her life, MacInnes wrote twenty-one novels and a play. Her novels were highly successful, and more than 23 million copies of her books have been sold in the United States alone. They have been translated into twenty-two languages including Portuguese, Greek, Arabic, Tamil, Hindi, and Urdu. Her work is admired by both the general audience and professional intelligence agents. Allen Dulles, former head of the Central Intelligence Agency, called MacInnes a "natural master of the thriller" and included an excerpt from *Assignment in Brittany* in an anthology of espionage literature that he compiled. Not all of her novels, however, concerned espionage in foreign lands. *Friends and Lovers* (1947) was a semiautobiographical love story set at the University of Oxford in England, and *Rest and Be Thankful* (1949) satirized the New York literary and critical establishment, showing some of its members trying to survive at a dude ranch in Wyoming.

In 1985, MacInnes died in Manhattan following a stroke. Her death occurred shortly after her last novel, *Ride a Pale Horse* (1984), appeared on *The New York Times's* paperback best-seller list.

**Analysis** • Helen MacInnes began her first novel, *Above Suspicion,* after an apprenticeship which included translating German works with her husband and taking careful notes on the political situation in Germany. Like her succeeding novels, it is based on the necessity of resisting the advance of Nazism. During World War II, the enemy was the Gestapo, the German secret police. MacInnes writes that after the war, villainous Nazis were replaced by Communists and terrorists who were convinced of the superiority of their own ideologies and disdained Western democratic values, which they considered decadent. Because of their discipline, toughness, and efficiency, the enemies of freedom could achieve limited success in the short run but were ultimately doomed to be overwhelmed by the forces of good.

MacInnes disapproved heartily of dictatorships of both the Left and the Right. Indeed, she considered herself a Jeffersonian democrat, and her books promote the ideals of freedom and democracy. The earlier novels not only demonstrate the evils of Fascism but also insist on the danger of pacifism in the face of the Nazi threat. The later novels pitch the evils of Communism and the danger of appeasing the Soviet Union. MacInnes's work is not harmed by such overt political commentary. On the contrary, her novels lack the sense of languor and depression, even boredom, that certain contemporary espionage novels exhibit. MacInnes's professional intelligence agents, a few of whom appear in more than one novel, are skillful operatives who love their country. There is no doubt in their minds that the Western democracies are morally superior to the governments of their enemies. This conviction is in strong contrast to the posture of the operatives in the novels of John le Carré or Len Deighton, who seem to see little difference between the methodology and goals of the Soviet Union and those of the West.

In order to convince the reader that Western intelligence operatives and American State Department personnel are truly patriotic, MacInnes affords her audience glimpses into the mental processes of her characters. They are not professional agents, but they learn the craft of intelligence quickly after they are recruited by a professional agent for a mission. MacInnes's early heroes are often academics, while later heroes include a music critic, an art consultant, and a playwright. Their occupations allow MacInnes to comment on the current state of painting, music, and theater, which, for the most part, she finds inferior to the comparable arts of the past. These heroes are typically good-looking, gentle, and kind, as well as brave, intelligent, and resourceful, but they are also lonely. Not at all promiscuous, these young men are waiting for the right woman to come along, and by the conclusion of nearly all the novels, they are usually committed to a monogamous relationship. The contrast with Ian Fleming's James Bond is clear. Also unlike James Bond, MacInnes's heroes are not super-athletes and they do not possess technical devices with seemingly magical powers.

In *Above Suspicion*, Mrs. Frances Myles is the principal character, although her husband Richard proves to be braver, calmer, and more capable than she. In subsequent novels, MacInnes uses male heroes. Although she pays lip service to the idea of female equality, she seems to be afraid to compromise her heroines' "femininity" by making them too intelligent or too brave. Young, beautiful women exist either to be rescued by the hero or, if they are enemy agents, to tempt him. The plucky heroine is frequently pitted against a sexually predatory villainess; the latter may attract the hero initially but eventually disgusts him. This situation changes slightly in *The Snare of the Hunter* (1974), where the hero is aided by Jo Corelli, MacInnes's version of the liberated career woman who is able to take charge.

In this and other ways, MacInnes always tried to be current. For details concerning espionage techniques, she drew on evidence collected by the Federal Bureau of Investigation. Many of her plots were suggested by current events. The plot of *The Double Image* (1966), for example, was suggested by news reports that the grave of a Nazi war criminal was found to be bogus. This event reminded her of the possibility that several Communist spies had masqueraded as Nazis during World War II, as Richard Sorge, a real historical figure, had done. MacInnes has also been lauded for the accurate manner in which she described the Communist influence on the Algerian revolt against France, which took place in the early 1960's. Indeed, she considered herself obligated not to falsify the past. It is interesting, however, that in her earlier novels she was more accurate about the details of the craft of espionage than in her later books. In the later novels, she chose to ignore certain technological advances, particularly in communications, because she believed that dedicated personnel were more important than gadgets.

MacInnes is most accurate in her use of locale. In *Above Suspicion*, the reader is given a picture of prewar Oxford, Paris, and Austria. In *Assignment in Brittany*, the reader is shown Brittany as it must have been when the Nazis first came to power; *North from Rome* (1958) affords the reader a tour of Italy; in *Decision at Delphi* (1961), the reader is taken on an excursion through Greece, and *Message from Málaga* (1971) is set in Spain. *The Double Image* and *The Salzburg Connection* focus on postwar Austria, a mecca for tourists visiting concert halls, opera houses, and quaint mountain villages. In fact, MacInnes's most graphic writing is devoted to the historic delights of Europe and parts of Asia. In *Prelude to Terror* (1978), she describes the Neustrasse, a street in the Austrian town of Grinzing:

> It was lined with more vintners' cottages, their window boxes laden with bright petunias. Each had its walled courtyard, whose wide entrance doors stood partly open to show barrels and tables and more flowers. All of them had their own individual vineyards, long and narrow, stretching like a spread of stiff fingers up the sloping fields.

MacInnes's language is simple but evocative. The accurate descriptions of her settings, as well as her obvious love for them, lend a depth and a resonance to her novels, affording them an additional dimension few other espionage novels achieve. Since her plots are structured around a chase, they are exciting. Reader interest is further heightened by the love story, which is an intrinsic element of these novels. Unless the hero and heroine are already married to each other, two attractive young people will certainly meet and fall in love. To this mixture of travelogue and romance, MacInnes adds elements of action and suspense, as the hero and heroine must avoid capture, torture, and even death.

MacInnes's storytelling is tightly controlled. She keeps the reader's attention by providing only small bits of information at a time and by provoking concern at appropriate intervals. Will the garage mechanic unknowingly betray the heroine to her enemy? Will the villain reach the hidden door and escape? In all the novels, the protagonists are in danger, but only minor characters, or evil ones, die or get seriously hurt. Murder and mayhem either occur offstage or are not described vividly, which is clearly not standard practice in the contemporary espionage novel. Another unusual element in these novels is the emphasis on romance coupled with an absence of sexual description. The limited amount of sexual activity that does occur is glossed over as discreetly as it would have been in a Victorian novel.

Without relying on graphic descriptions of violence or sexual behavior, MacInnes has managed to entertain a generation of readers by keeping them in great suspense as she exposes her extraordinarily likable characters to familiar dangers. She has made it apparent that just as her characters barely manage to avoid disaster, so too are democracy and freedom constantly threatened by the forces of terror and chaos. In addition to the stratagems MacInnes employs to involve the reader, the chases, which often serve as the foundation of her plots, take place in some of the most picturesque settings in the world.

### Principal mystery and detective fiction

SERIES: Robert Renwick: *Hidden Target,* 1980; *Cloak of Darkness,* 1982.

OTHER NOVELS: *Above Suspicion,* 1941; *Assignment in Brittany,* 1942; *While Still We Live,* 1944; (also as *The Unconquerable*); *Horizon,* 1945; *Neither Five Nor Three,* 1951; *I and My True Love,* 1953; *Pray for a Brave Heart,* 1955; *North from Rome,* 1958; *Decision at Delphi,* 1961; *The Venetian Affair,* 1963; *The Double Image,* 1966; *The Salzburg Connection,* 1968; *Message from Málaga,* 1971; *The Snare of the Hunter,* 1974; *Agent in Place,* 1976; *Prelude to Terror,* 1978; *Ride a Pale Horse,* 1984.

### Other major works

NOVELS: *Friends and Lovers,* 1947; *Rest and Be Thankful,* 1949.

PLAY: *Home Is the Hunter,* 1964.

TRANSLATIONS: *Sexual Life in Ancient Rome,* 1934 (with Gilbert Highet; by Otto Kiefer); *Friedrich Engels: A Biography,* 1936 (with Gilbert Highet; by Gustav Mayer).

**Bibliography**
Boyd, Mark K. "The Enduring Appeal of the Spy Thrillers of Helen MacInnes." *Clues: A Journal of Detection* 4 (Fall/Winter, 1983): 66-75.
Breit, Harvey. *The Writer Observed.* Cleveland: World Publishing, 1956.
Seymour-Smith, M. *Novels and Novelists.* London: Windward, 1980.

*Barbara Horwitz*

# Ngaio Marsh

**Born:** Christchurch, New Zealand; April 23, 1895
**Died:** Christchurch, New Zealand; February 18, 1982

**Types of plot** • Police procedural • thriller

**Principal series** • Roderick Alleyn, 1934-1982.

**Principal series character** • RODERICK ALLEYN is a superintendent in the CID, married to Agatha Troy Alleyn, with one son, Ricky. At the outset, Alleyn is forty-two years old and single. He possesses an ironic wit which often runs to facetiousness. His preciosity is offset by his self-deprecating manner and his natural egalitarianism in a class-conscious society.

**Contribution** • Ngaio Marsh's novels embody many of the traditions of British Golden Age detective fiction. Most critics include her among the "Grand Dames": Dorothy L. Sayers, Agatha Christie, and Margery Allingham. She enjoyed a writing career second only to Christie's in longevity and productivity. She is separated from her colleagues by her New Zealand background and loyalties, which give her a different, "outsider's" view of the England about which she writes. She transcends many of the familiar limitations of detective fiction as she creates an aristocratic professional policeman who solves crimes committed in theaters, drawing rooms, and the New Zealand wilderness. Marsh writes with a uniquely well-honed ear for dialogue and how it reveals character. Her genius lies in her synthesis of three great traditions: detective fiction, character study, and the novel of manners.

**Biography** • Edith Ngaio Marsh's life begins, appropriately enough, with a mystery. Though she was born April 23, 1895, in Christchurch, New Zealand, her father listed her natal year as 1899. This act generated confusion about which the author herself remains vague in her autobiography. She describes her father as an absentminded eccentric descended from commercially successful English stock. Her mother, Rose Elizabeth Seager Marsh, was a second-generation New Zealand pioneer. Though never financially comfortable, her parents provided their only child with an excellent secondary education at St. Margaret's College, where one teacher instilled in her "an abiding passion for the plays and sonnets of Shakespeare." This passion interrupted her subsequent education in art at the University of Canterbury when she was invited to join the Allan Wilkie Company to act in Shakespearean and contemporary drama. She spent two years learning her chosen craft under Wilkie's tutelage and four more years as a writer, director, and producer of amateur theatricals in New Zealand.

In 1928, Marsh visited friends in England who persuaded her to open a small business in London. The business flourished, as did her writing. Inspired by either Dorothy L. Sayers or Agatha Christie (her memory contradicts itself), she began her first detective novel, which was published as *A Man Lay Dead* in 1934. Shortly thereafter, she returned to New Zealand and remained there through World War II, serving in the Ambulance Corps and writing twelve more mysteries by the end of the war. Perhaps her best among these books is *Vintage Murder* (1937), which incorporates many of her themes and settings.

After the war Marsh traveled extensively, maintained homes in both London and New Zealand, wrote more mysteries, and directed plays, primarily those of William Shakespeare, for the student-players of the University of Canterbury. Her contributions were honored by the university in 1962 when the Ngaio Marsh Theatre was opened on the campus. In 1966, the queen declared her a Dame of the British Empire. Other honors include the 1977 Grand Master Award from the Mystery Writers of America and induction into the Detection Club of Great Britain. On February 18, 1982, Dame Ngaio died in her home in Christchurch.

**Analysis** • In many ways, Ngaio Marsh's mysteries follow the rules of detective fiction as prescribed by S. S. Van Dine in 1928. These rules emphasize the genre's intellectual purity: the puzzle, the clues, the solution. They insist upon fairness for the reader: The author must not indulge himself with hidden clues, professional criminals, spies, or secret cults. No mere trickery should sully the game between the author and the reader. There is an implicit emphasis upon the classical dramatic unities of time, place, and action. In *A Man Lay Dead*, her first novel, Marsh adheres to these strictures with spare character and place description, well-planted but subtle clues to the murderer's motives and identity, and a quick solution. On the strength of this novel and the several that followed, one critic referred to her as "the finest writer in England of the pure, classical puzzle whodunnit." Yet to insist upon her books as "pure" is misleading. By the time she had written three novels, she was challenging some of Van Dine's most sacred tenets—not his doctrine of fairness and logical deduction but his demand for simplicity in all but plot. Her challenge succeeded in cementing her reputation as a novelist without sacrificing her commitment to detective fiction. She so successfully joined the elements of character and tone with the detective yarn that she provides a link between the older traditions of Charles Dickens and Wilkie Collins, and the newer writings of Agatha Christie.

In her first six novels, Marsh introduces characters and settings to which she will return with more sophistication later. Her murders nearly always occur in some sort of theater in front of witnesses. Among the witnesses and suspects are her artistic characters, a few mysterious foreigners, the occasional fanatic, and usually one or two pairs of lovers. Their observations are shaped into the solution by Marsh's detective, Roderick Alleyn, of Scotland Yard. It is

his character that unites these disparate people and places. Marsh introduces
Alleyn through the eyes of Angela North in *A Man Lay Dead*:

> Alleyn did not resemble a plain-clothes policemen, she felt sure, nor was he in the
> romantic manner–white-faced and gimlet-eyed. He looked like one of her Uncle
> Hubert's friends, the sort they knew would "do" for house-parties.

He is the younger son of a peer, educated at Oxford, courteous, but always
somewhat detached. Alleyn's fastidious nature, combined with his facetious
wit, confuses those who expect either a foppish amateur or the plodding copper. Marsh aimed at creating a normal man whose personality never cloyed or
bored his creator.

Alleyn also possesses a dry, almost peculiar sense of humor about his work.
In *Enter a Murderer* (1935), he leaves headquarters remarking "Am I tidy? . . . It
looks so bad not to be tidy for an arrest." Earlier, he had described himself as
feeling "self-conscious" about asking suspects for fingerprints. Despite Jessica
Mann's contention in *Deadlier than the Male: Why Are Respectable English Women
So Good at Murder?* (1981) that Alleyn does not change or develop in the thirty-
two novels, Marsh gradually introduces different aspects of his personality. In
*Artists in Crime* (1938), Alleyn falls in love and is refused, though not absolutely, but in *Death in a White Tie* (1938), he has won the hand of Agatha Troy,
a famous painter. By 1953, in *Spinsters in Jeopardy*, the couple has a son, Ricky.
Troy and Ricky occasionally embroil Alleyn in mysteries that arise in the
course of their careers or lives. Their presence assists Marsh in moving Alleyn
into the murder scene. Amateurs might happen upon crime with rather ap-
palling frequency, but a professional policeman must be summoned.

In *Death in a White Tie*, Alleyn's character and pedigree are assured. This
novel is pivotal in Marsh's development of character description and social
analysis. She quietly opens the drawing-room door onto the secrets, misery,
and shallowness of those involved in "the season" in London. Lady Alleyn,
the mother of the detective, and Agatha Troy attend the debutante parties, including a memorable one at which a popular older gentleman, Lord Robert,
who is known by the improbable nickname "Bunchy" and the Dickensian last
name Gospell, is murdered. Murder is not the worst of it; blackmail, bastardy,
adultery, bad debts, and many other ills beset these social darlings. As Bunchy
himself ruminates:

> he suddenly felt as if an intruder had thrust open all the windows of [his] neat little
> world and let in a flood of uncompromising light. In this cruel light he saw the people
> he liked best and they were changed and belittled. . . . This idea seemed abominable
> to Lord Robert and he felt old and lonely for the first time in his life.

Moments later, Bunchy is murdered. Alleyn, who was his friend, is called in to
investigate.

During the investigation Marsh introduces him to some of her favorite
types: the "simple soldier-man" who fought the war from the home front, the
gauche American lady (whose venality drives her to accept payment for spon-

soring an awkward debutante who is part Jewish), the quintessential cad who cheats at cards, and the callow youth rescued from his own obtuseness by his clever girl. These characters begin to emerge from the cardboard restrictions deemed appropriate for classical detective fiction. Marsh adds grace notes of humor, such as General Halcut-Hackett's outburst: "'Some filthy bolshevistic fascist,' shouted the General, having a good deal of difficulty with this strange collection of sibilants. He slightly dislodged his upper plate but impatiently champed it back into position." Marsh's ear for such verbal quirks as well as her eye for color and line truly set her apart from the conventions of detective fiction characterizations. In praising Agatha Christie for her books, Marsh commented that Christie was at her best in plotting: "Her characters are two-dimensional. . . . To call them silhouettes is not to dispraise them." Marsh described herself as trying "to write about characters in the round and [being] in danger of letting them take charge." Although some critics charge that in *Death of a Peer* (1940), the Lamprey family and their peculiarities do overwhelm the mystery, she never loses the struggle with these lively, complicated folk—rather, she enriches the yarn, encouraging her readers to care more fully about who is innocent or guilty.

In *Overture to Death* (1939), Marsh expands her repertoire of characters by developing a type that will reappear several times throughout her subsequent novels—the iron-willed, often sexually repressed spinster. Her two old maids, Eleanor Prentice and Idris Campanula, rival each other for domination of community good works and for the affections of the naïve rector. Eleanor, "thin, colorless . . . disseminated the odor of sanctity." Her best friend and yet most deadly competitor, Idris, is described as a "large and arrogant spinster with a firm bust, a high-colored complexion, coarse gray hair, and enormous bony hands." Throughout the novel, the tension between their artificial civility toward each another and their jaw-snapping, claw-sharpening ill will fuels the plot. Idris is the victim of a bizarre and deadly booby trap. She is shot, while playing the piano, by a pistol propped between the pegs where the piano wires were affixed. A loop of string tied around the trigger had been fastened to the soft-pedal batten, and pushing the pedal discharged the report into her face. As Alleyn discovers, Eleanor, driven to desperation by what she regarded as her rival's ultimate success with the rector, cleverly utilized what had begun as a harmless joke set with a child's water pistol for her own nefarious purpose. Such an involved means of murder is typical of Marsh's imagination. In this novel and others, she murders her victims by grisly methods: decapitation, meat skewers through the eye, boiling mud, and suffocation in a wool press. Though Marsh never ceased to insist that she was squeamish, her sense of the dramatic demanded a dramatic dispatch of the victim.

Running throughout all Marsh's novels is a wry sense of humor, often turned inward. Since she considered that her life's work was in theater rather than in detective fiction, Marsh often parodied the conventions of detective novels in her own works. In her first novel, Alleyn comments, "Your crime books will have told you that under these conditions the gardens of the great are as an open book to us sleuths." In *Death in a White Tie*, Marsh quotes part of the oath of the prestigious detection club when she has Lord Robert exclaim, "No jiggery-pokery." *Overture to Death* finds a police sergeant lamenting that "these thrillers are ruining our criminal classes," and in *Vintage Murder*, Alleyn remarks sarcastically, "so the detective books tell us, . . . and they ought to know." In none of the works of the other Grand Dames of detective fiction is this self-mockery so pronounced, though Allingham and Sayers both professed, like Marsh, to be more seriously occupied in other pursuits. Marsh echoes Rebecca West's statement: "There is this curious flight that so many intelligent women make into detective writing" in *Black Beech and Honeydew: An Autobiography* (1966, revised 1981). According to Marsh, "If I have any indigenous publicity value it is, I think for work in the theater rather than for detective fiction. . . . Intellectual New Zealand friends tactfully avoid all mention of my published work, and if they like me, do so, I cannot but feel, in spite of it." Toward the end of her life, however, Marsh, in a revised edition of her autobiography, did acknowledge the benefits of her writing, for without its profits she could never have directed student theater and have indulged her passion for Shakespearean production.

No discussion of Ngaio Marsh, her life, or her detective fiction can afford to ignore her loyalty to her native New Zealand and its influence upon her fiction. Four of her novels take place in New Zealand, with the faithful Alleyn still in command. In each of these novels, the setting plays an important part in the mystery; indeed, the country becomes a character—lovingly and lyrically examined in Marsh's prose. Certainly the most beautiful aspects of the country are discussed in *Vintage Murder*. This novel, an early one, contains many elements of what would become vintage Marsh: Alleyn, the theater, a bizarre murder, a cast of flamboyant actors, and the country. Though Marsh paints hauntingly stark portraits of rural England, nowhere does her painterly sense serve her so well as at home. New Zealand, Alleyn senses, is a new world, clean, light, immaculate; it purges the squalid and revitalizes the jaded. In the forest, he muses:

> There was something primal and earthy about this endless interlacing of greens. It was dark in the bush, and cool, and the only sound there was the sound of trickling water, finding its way downhill to the creek. There was the smell of wet moss, of cold wet earth. . . . Suddenly, close at hand, the bird called again—a solitary call, startlingly like a bell.

The forest renews him, stimulates his senses and his imagination. Marsh weaves the love of her land and of her people—Maori and Paheka alike—into her novels with elegant prose and a colorful palette.

These are "Marshmarks" as one observer has noted: sound deductive logic to please the conventions of the detective story, colorful but willful characters skillfully endowed with dialogue that is as lively as thought, and a sense of atmosphere and place that is palpable. Each of these qualities transforms her novels from a clever puzzle into an analysis of character and manners.

## Principal mystery and detective fiction

SERIES: Roderick Alleyn: *A Man Lay Dead,* 1934; *Enter a Murderer,* 1935; *The Nursing-Home Murder,* 1935 (with Henry Jellett); *Death in Ecstasy,* 1936; *Vintage Murder,* 1937; *Artists in Crime,* 1938; *Death in a White Tie,* 1938; *Overture to Death,* 1939; *Death at the Bar,* 1940; *Death of a Peer,* 1940 (also as *Surfeit of Lampreys*); *Death and the Dancing Footman,* 1941; *Colour Scheme,* 1943; *Died in the Wool,* 1945; *I Can Find My Way Out,* 1946; *Final Curtain,* 1947; *Swing, Brother, Swing,* 1949 (also as *A Wreath for Rivera*); *Opening Night,* 1951 (also as *Night at the Vulcan*); *Spinsters in Jeopardy,* 1953 (also as *The Bride of Death*); *Scales of Justice,* 1955; *Death of a Fool,* 1956 (also as *Off with His Head*); *Singing in the Shrouds,* 1958; *False Scent,* 1960; *Hand in Glove,* 1962; *Dead Water,* 1963; *Killer Dolphin,* 1966 (also as *Death at the Dolphin*); *Clutch of Constables,* 1968; *When in Rome,* 1970; *Tied Up in Tinsel,* 1972; *Black as He's Painted,* 1974; *Last Ditch,* 1977; *Grave Mistake,* 1978; *Photo-Finish,* 1980; *Light Thickens,* 1982.

## Other major works

PLAYS: *The Nursing-Home Murders,* 1935 (with Jellett); *False Scent,* 1961; *A Unicorn for Christmas,* 1965; *Murder Sails at Midnight,* 1972.

TELEPLAY: *Evil Liver,* 1975.

NONFICTION: *New Zealand,* 1942 (with Randall Matthew Burdon); *A Play Toward: A Note on Play Production,* 1946; *Perspectives: The New Zealander and the Visual Arts,* 1960; *Play Production,* 1960; *Black Beech and Honeydew: An Autobiography,* 1966, revised 1981.

CHILDREN'S LITERATURE: *A Three-Act Special,* 1960; *Another Three-Act Special,* 1962; *The Chrismas Tree,* 1962; *New Zealand,* 1964.

## Bibliography

Acheson, Carole. "Cultural Ambivalence: Ngaio Marsh's New Zealand Detective Fiction." *Journal of Popular Culture,* Fall, 1985, p. 159-174.

Bargainnier, Earl F. "Ngaio Marsh." In *Ten Women of Mystery,* edited by Earl F. Bargainnier. Bowling Green, Ohio: Bowling Green State University Popular Press, 1981.

_____. "Roderick Alleyn: Ngaio Marsh's Oxonian Superintendent." *The Armchair Detective* 11 (January, 1978): 63-71.

_____. "Ngaio Marsh's 'Theatrical' Murders." *The Armchair Detective* 10 (April, 1977): 175-181.

Boon, Kevin. *Ngaio Marsh.* Wellington, New Zealand: Kotuku Publications, 1996.

Haycraft, Howard. *Murder for Pleasure: The Life and Times of the Detective Story.* New York: Biblio & Tannen, 1968.

Klein, Kathleen Gregory, ed. *Great Women Mystery Writers: Classic to Contemporary.* Westport, Conn.: Greenwood Press, 1994.

Lewis, Margaret. *Ngaio Marsh: A Life.* Scottsdale, Ariz.: Poisoned Pen Press, 1998.

"Marsh, Ngaio." In *Mystery and Suspense Writers: The Literature of Crime, Detec-*

*tion, and Espionage*, edited by Robin W. Winks and Maureen Corrigan. New York: Charles Scribner's Sons, 1998.

McDorman, Kathryne Slate. *Ngaio Marsh*. Boston: Twayne, 1991.

Rahn, B. J., ed. *Ngaio Marsh: The Woman and Her Work*. Metuchen, N.J.: Scarecrow Press, 1995.

Symons, Julian. *Mortal Consequences: A History from the Detective Story to the Crime Novel*. London: Faber & Faber, 1972.

Weinkauf, Mary S. and Mary A. Burgess. *Murder Most Poetic: The Mystery Novels of Ngaio Marsh*. San Bernardino, Calif.: Brownstone Books, 1996.

*Kathryne S. McDorman*

# Margaret Millar

**Born:** Kitchener, Ontario, Canada; February 5, 1915
**Died:** Santa Barbara, California; March 26, 1994

**Also wrote as** • M. Sturm

**Types of plot** • Psychological • inverted

**Principal series** • Dr. Paul Prye, 1941-1942 • Inspector Sands, 1943-1945 • Tom Aragon, 1976-1982.

**Principal series characters** • DR. PAUL PRYE is a youngish, very tall and very bookish (his favorite author is William Blake) psychoanalyst who tends to get involved in murder mysteries. A bit clumsy but quick on the repartee, Prye attracts and is attracted to beautiful women.
• INSPECTOR SANDS is both less flamboyant and less visually conspicuous than Paul Prye. He is described as "a thin, tired-looking middle-aged man with features that fitted each other so perfectly that few people could remember what he looked like." Inspector Sands is with the Toronto Police Department and has almost as much trouble keeping his police cohorts in line as he has with the ingenious murderers prowling the streets of Toronto. He is, however, always successful, thanks to his intelligence and quiet insistence.
• TOM ARAGON, though a series character, has greater depth than Prye or Sands, and his books hold a darker tone more in keeping with the artistic psychological thrillers that Millar had developed by that time. A young Hispanic lawyer, Aragon is very junior in his firm, and his talents at detection are sometimes tried by uncertainty or moral doubts about the investigation. His chief emotional support is his wife, Laurie MacGregor, with whom he has a modern, long-distance relationship, as she lives and works in another city; their frequent phone conversations help him clarify aspects of his cases.

**Contribution** • Margaret Millar began her writing career with three successive novels about the amusing psychoanalyst-detective Dr. Paul Prye, but she became successful when she decided to make the psychological profiles of demented criminals and their victims her focus. With *The Iron Gates* (1945), her sixth book, Millar scored her first major success. The book centers on the effect which the monsters of fear can have on the mind of an outwardly happy, well-adjusted, well-to-do woman.

Since *The Iron Gates*, Millar has written more than a dozen books of suspense, most of which have been both critically acclaimed and commercially successful. She helped turn the psychological thriller into an art form, and she created books brimming with three-dimensional characterizations: real, breathing people, portrayed in crisp, vivid prose.

Millar's novels are concerned with the inner life of the individual, with the distortions of reality that psychopathology and stressful situations can forge in the mind. Although Millar did not focus as heavily upon social analysis as did her husband Ross Macdonald, her novels do present current social concerns whose treatment deepens over the span of her work. Her characters exist in Freudian microcosms, shaped and determined by their significant relationships: parent/child, husband/wife, brother/sister.

**Biography** • Margaret Ellis Sturm was born in Kitchener, Ontario, Canada, on February 5, 1915, to Henry William and Lavinia Ferrier Sturm. Young Margaret's first love was music. She studied the piano from an early age and became an accomplished player, giving recitals when she was still in high school. At the Kitchener-Waterloo Collegiate Institute, she was a member of the debating team, along with Kenneth Millar, who would later become her husband. Their first stories appeared together in their high school magazine, *The Grumbler*, in 1931. While attending the University of Toronto from 1933-1936, Margaret majored in classics and developed a lifelong interest in psychology that would figure strongly in her work. She and Kenneth were married on June 2, 1938, after his graduation from the same university.

After the birth of her only child, Linda Jane, in 1939, Millar was ordered to remain in bed due to a heart ailment. An invalid for some time, she began to write mysteries, achieving early success with *The Invisible Worm* (1941)—a success that allowed her husband to give up teaching high school and return to graduate school full time. Margaret's success also inspired Kenneth to begin his own attempts at writing; as her first reader and editor (though never her collaborator), he said that he learned to write from observing her work. To avoid confusion with his wife's growing fame, he adopted the pen name Ross Macdonald. Ironically, though both were successful crime novelists, and she the more widely read at the outset, his reputation would eventually eclipse hers.

While Kenneth served in the U.S. Navy, Margaret relocated the family to Santa Barbara, with which she had fallen in love during a trip to see him off. Santa Barbara would be a frequent setting in her novels, thinly disguised as "Santa Felicia" and "San Felice," and her books were often bathed in the brilliant sunlight of her adopted home. For a short period Millar worked as a screenwriter in Hollywood (1945-1946), but the bulk of her literary output was novels—mostly, but not exclusively, mysteries.

Millar and her husband shared a passion for environmental concerns that led them to found a chapter of the National Audubon Society in Santa Barbara, protest an oil spill and establish the Santa Barbara Citizens for Environmental Defense, and work together to protect the endangered California condor. They were ardent dog-lovers and bird-watchers, and nearly collaborated on *The Birds and the Beasts Were There* (1968), which Margaret would eventually write alone.

Millar and her husband also shared the tragedy of their troubled daughter. At the age of seventeen, Linda killed a child while driving under the influence of alcohol. Two years later she dropped out of college because of the continuing weight of guilt and psychological problems. Though she later returned to her family, she died at age thirty-one, in 1970. Millar published nothing for six years after her daughter's death.

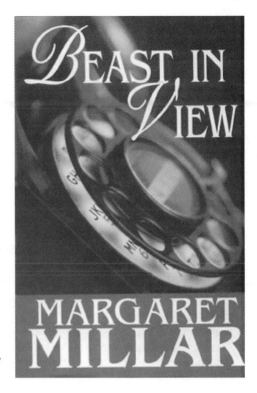

Millar attributed her interest in writing detective novels to having been an avid reader of suspense fiction from the age of eight. She became a world-class bestseller, and her books were translated into French and Swedish. She twice received the coveted Edgar Allan Poe Award from the Mystery Writers of America, for *Beast in View* (1955) and *Banshee* (1983). Two other novels, *How Like an Angel* (1962) and *The Fiend* (1964), were also runners-up for Edgar awards. The Mystery Writers of America honored her with the Grand Master Award for lifetime achievement in 1983 and made her the organization's president from 1957-1958. In 1965, she was named the *Los Angeles Times* Woman of the Year. Faced with increasing blindness and grieving over her husband's suffering and death from Alzheimer's disease in 1983, Millar completed only one more novel after that year. She died of a heart attack on March 26, 1994.

**Analysis** • Margaret Millar first began writing in the style of classic Golden Age detection, with series characters, plots that challenge readers to race to solve the crime before the end, final revelatory chapters, and even her version of the English country-house mystery. Each of her series characters appears in three books, though one, *The Devil Loves Me* (1942), includes both Prye and Sands. Her first books, *The Invisible Worm* (1941) and *The Weak-Eyed Bat* (1942), were good-natured, amusing mysteries with some clever psychological twists and insights. With her short series featuring the Toronto detective Inspector Sands, she settled into a more serious style and began to establish herself as a master of the psychological thriller.

The first of her books to win both critical and popular acclaim was *The Iron Gates*. This was her second and last book with Sands as the detective-hero. For decades, Millar abandoned the series format and wrote her novels as separate works of fiction which share only an emphasis on the psychological portrait. Each of her novels (until the Tom Aragon series in 1976) introduces the reader to a completely new cast of characters and set of circumstances. In her three or four best books, such as *The Fiend, How like an Angel,* and *Beast in View,* Millar has created highly original and self-contained works of literature that would not have been served by having to conform to a series format.

It can be argued that the second of Millar's series characters, Inspector Sands, simply faded into the background of her books. He is a thoroughly uninteresting character whose sole mark of distinction is that he has no distinction. Indistinguishable from millions of other graying, middle-aged men, he has "no strong sense of identity" and lives "in a vacuum." With Millar's interest in the psychologically and physically colorful, such a character was bound to be short-lived.

Millar's final venture into the realm of the series detective, with Tomas Aragon, belongs more to the psychological portrait novels of her later writing. Dark and often disturbing in tone, the three Aragon books are far from the amusement of Prye or the careful and successful detection of Sands. Aragon is thrust into situations that test his morals as well as his detecting skills, and he himself is nearly the victim of some of his mysteries, as in *Ask for Me Tomorrow* (1976), in which he is framed for a series of murders that follow his efforts at investigation–an investigation that he later learns has made him an unwitting accomplice of the murderer.

While Millar does not follow any set formula in writing her novels, there are several features they share. Complex webs of plotting provide a high level of suspense that is usually resolved in the end in a final revelatory scene. During the course of the novel, shifts in perception and ongoing reinterpretations create a whirling effect of constant surprise in which things are never as they seem. For the most part, Millar's talent at plotting and penetrating characterization makes these shifts wholly believable, as the reader constantly comes to new understandings along with the characters. Each of her books focuses on the inner life of one character. Usually this character is under some kind of stress, caused by either a set of outward circumstances that challenges the character's notions about reality or some kind of psychological disorder. In *Banshee,* the mysterious circumstances surrounding a young girl's death change all the people around her and their relationships in sad and shocking ways. In *The Fiend,* the protagonist is a young man whose mental problems cause his sense of reality and agency to slip.

*The Fiend* brings out another feature of Millar's books: The reader is invited to merge his consciousness with that of the protagonist, Charlie Gowen, a convicted child molester. Once inside Gowen's mind, the reader is treated to a ride on an experiential roller coaster. The world perceived by Charlie Gowen–or any other of Millar's mental cases–is distorted. Reality changes shape, and what was familiar becomes alien and threatening. In Charlie Gowen's world, children are not simply smaller and cuter than adults, they are dangerously alluring.

Most of Millar's books written after the Sands series are not whodunits per se. They are psychological thrillers, where the suspense lies in the acts of deception–either by cunning criminals, as in *An Air That Kills* (1957), or by a tormented mind, as in *Beast in View*–that implant distortions into the minds of the other characters and the reader. The books are chronicles of psychological afflictions and their slow and painful unraveling.

*Beast in View*, one of Millar's best, tells the story of a woman with a disorder known in psychology as multiple personality. Helen Clarvoe, a rich and lonely spinster, is being persecuted by Evelyn Merrick, a homicidal and demented young woman whom she once knew. The book chronicles the movements and thoughts of the two women as they dance a dance of death and destruction, only to merge them at the end as the two sides of one woman. Clearly influenced by the theories of both Sigmund Freud and R. D. Laing, the book is a record of the effects parental pressure can have when exerted on a fragile personality.

In *How like an Angel*, Millar focuses on another weak and defenseless person: a man caught between two women, one strong and domineering, the other offering him pleasure and a chance to assert himself. Millar also introduces in this book one of California's numerous religious sects, replete with a slightly deranged leader, a rich and senile old woman, and a coven of colorful and clearly drawn disciples in white robes and bare feet. The hero of the book, Quinn, a sometime Las Vegas detective and gambler down on his luck, embarks on a quest for truth like a prince in a fairy tale. In the end, he has obtained not only knowledge about the mysterious events surrounding the disappearance and presumed death of Patrick O'Gorman but also insights about himself and the world that allow him to claim the prize and marry the princess/widow.

In *How like an Angel*, as in all Millar's books, the emphasis is on characterization and on psychological revelations. Millar is a master of describing children, primarily little girls. She has created a series of portraits of nine-year-old girls starting with *The Cannibal Heart* (1949) and culminating with *The Fiend*. The portrait in *How like an Angel* of the pimpled teenage girl is wonderfully penetrating and compelling. Even in weaker books, such as *Banshee*, which is marred by overwriting and bad similes, there are two fascinating portrayals of young girls who invite the reader into their world of fantasy and confusion about the verbal and physical behavior of grown-ups.

Even when the central character is an adult, he or she is often remarkably childish and lost in a confusing world belonging to and defined by others. In *The Fiend*, the two protagonists, Charlie Gowen and his fiancée, Louise Lang, are outsiders who cannot fit into the adult world of marriage and adultery. In Charlie's case the result has been disastrous: He, with his nine-year-old emotions and adult body, has forced himself onto a little girl. He suffers the consequences, jail and lifelong apprehension (will he do it again?).

In the character of Charlie Gowen, Millar's writing is at its best. One sees her ability to depict a beleaguered mind. Yet in Charlie's character one also sees Millar's primary weakness: the creation of believable dialogue. Charlie Gowen is a college-educated man who holds down a job, but he speaks like a nine-year-old boy. It is hard to accept that he could have been graduated from even the fifth grade, much less college, and it is equally hard to believe that he has a job and manages to stay out of a mental institution.

That children are trapped inside adults is a central idea in Millar's books. Another character in *The Fiend*, the immature Kate Oakley, combines an inability to face the world without the mediating agency of a man with a childish distrust and hatred of men. She is a typical Millar character, unable to function as an adult in her private or public life. Almost all Millar's books feature characters who are locked in an infantile universe, with no escape other than crime and murder.

It is interesting that these books that chronicle the lives and worlds of people who cannot cope are written with almost clinical detachment. Millar seems to be more interested in dissecting sick minds than in expressing any sympathy for those who suffer or in trying to assess the social causes of individual disaster. The stories are absorbing because they are so convincingly told. Even Millar's weakest books are so suspenseful that neither bad similes nor her propensity for heavy-handed metaphor turns the reader away. Before everything else, Millar is a master of the plot, of the slow unfolding of a multifaceted story. Her psychological insight, great as it is, remains secondary to the genius of her architectonic plots.

### Principal mystery and detective fiction

SERIES: Tom Aragon: *Ask for Me Tomorrow*, 1976; *The Murder of Miranda*, 1979; *Mermaid*, 1982. Dr. Paul Prye: *The Invisible Worm*, 1941; *The Weak-Eyed Bat*, 1942; *The Devil Loves Me*, 1942. Inspector Sands: *Wall of Eyes*, 1943; *The Iron Gates*, 1945 (also as *Taste of Fears*).

OTHER NOVELS: *Fire Will Freeze*, 1944; *Do Evil in Return*, 1950; *Rose's Last Summer*, 1952 (also as *The Lively Corpse*); *Vanish in an Instant*, 1952; *Beast in View*, 1955; *An Air That Kills*, 1957 (also as *The Soft Talkers*); *The Listening Walls*, 1959; *A Stranger in My Grave*, 1960; *How like an Angel*, 1962; *The Fiend*, 1964; *Beyond This Point Are Monsters*, 1970; *Banshee*, 1983; *Spider Webs*, 1986.

### Other major works

NOVELS: *Experiment in Springtime*, 1947; *It's All in the Family*, 1948; *The Cannibal Heart*, 1949; *Wives and Lovers*, 1954.

SHORT FICTION: *Early Millar: The First Stories of Ross Macdonald and Margaret Millar*, 1982 (with Ross Macdonald).

NONFICTION: *The Birds and Beasts Were There*, 1968.

### Bibliography

Bruccoli, Matthew J. *Ross Macdonald/Kenneth Millar: A Descriptive Bibliography.* Pittsburgh, Penn.: University of Pittsburgh Press, 1983.

Cooper-Clark, Diana. *Designs of Darkness: Interviews with Detective Novelists.*

Bowling Green, Ohio: Bowling Green State University Popular Press, 1983.

Klein, Kathleen Gregory, ed. *Great Women Mystery Writers: Classic to Contemporary.* Westport, Conn.: Greenwood Press, 1994.

Lachman, Marvin. "Margaret Millar: The Checklist of an Unknown Mystery Writer." *The Armchair Detective* 3 (October, 1970): 85-88.

"Millar, Margaret." In *Mystery and Suspense Writers: The Literature of Crime, Detection, and Espionage*, edited by Robin W. Winks and Maureen Corrigan. New York: Charles Scribner's Sons, 1998.

Reilly, John M. "Margaret Millar." In *Ten Women of Mystery*, edited by Earl F. Bargainnier. Bowling Green, Ohio: Bowling Green State University Popular Press, 1981.

Sandoe, James. "Dagger of the Mind." *Poetry* 68 (1946): 146-163.

*Per Schelde*
*Updated by C. A. Gardner*

# E. Phillips Oppenheim

**Born:** London, England; October 22, 1866
**Died:** St. Peter Port, Guernsey; February 3, 1946

**Also wrote as** • Anthony Partridge

**Types of plot** • Espionage • thriller • police procedural

**Contribution** • E. Phillips Oppenheim contributed more than 150 novels to the mystery/detective genre. Because he served in the British Ministry of Information during World War I, Oppenheim was privy to at least some of the workings of the British Secret Service, and his protagonists are frequently Secret Service employees. There are no detective series in Oppenheim's work; each novel introduces a new set of characters. Oppenheim wrote about wealthy supermen and their way of life. His largely upper-class characters share a love of good wine and smoke exotic cigarettes. The women are beautiful and virtuous. While the men fall in love in almost every novel, the excitement of adventure takes precedence over that of romance. Oppenheim claimed to have begun each book with "a sense of the first chapter and an inkling of something to follow," and his plots are rarely dull.

That the plots of his immense oeuvre are not repetitive is a credit to Oppenheim's fertile imagination. Most of his books involve some kind of international intrigue, and many of them reveal a surprise hero. His single greatest literary influence was probably his neighbor in the French Riviera, Baroness Orczy, author of *The Scarlet Pimpernel* (1905). Louis, the maître d' of the Milan Hotel in *A Pulpit in the Grill Room* (1938) and *The Milan Grill Room: Further Adventures of Louis, the Manager, and Major Lyson, the Raconteur* (1940), is reminiscent of Orczy's armchair detective, The Old Man in the Corner.

**Biography** • Edward Phillips Oppenheim was born in London on October 22, 1866. He left the Wyggeston Grammar School in Leicester in 1882 before graduation because his father, a leather merchant, was having financial problems. During World War I, Oppenheim served in the British Intelligence Service, an experience that fed his imagination. He married New Englander Elsie Hopkins, and the couple had one daughter. Until World War II, they lived on the French Riviera; forced to leave, they moved to Guernsey, in the Channel Islands. Oppenheim, who occasionally wrote under the name Anthony Partridge, died in St. Peter Port, Guernsey, on February 3, 1946.

**Analysis** • E. Phillips Oppenheim, dubbed "The Prince of Storytellers," was a master of the spy novel. As a longtime resident of the French Riviera,

Oppenheim kept his finger on the European pulse; he located his intrigues in Poland, Russia, England, and Africa, as well as in a small, imaginary European country. He was a monarchist whose characters did not like Germany, Russia, Socialism, or Communism. Oppenheim boasted that he had foreseen the expansionist ambitions of Russia, Japan, and, particularly, Germany. His writing before World War I was so anti-German, in fact, that his name was on a list of British citizens to be eradicated if the Germans successfully invaded England. Ironically, when the Germans did obtain control of the Channel Islands, the Luftwaffe chose Oppenheim's house on Guernsey as their headquarters.

In *A Maker of History* (1905), a young Englishman obtains a copy of a secret treaty between the kaiser and the czar detailing an agreement to wage war against England. In *The Double Traitor* (1915), a diplomat obtains a list of the German spies in England and is able to identify them when war breaks out. In *The Kingdom of the Blind* (1916), an English aristocrat proves to be a German spy. Oppenheim had little faith in the ability of the League of Nations or the United Nations to obtain a permanent world peace, and he frequently emphasized the power and importance of secret societies engaged in world trade.

Among the novels that established Oppenheim's reputation as a spy novelist was *Mysterious Mr. Sabin* (1898), in which the protagonist steals British defense documents to sell to Germany. He plans to use the money to finance a twentieth century French revolution. Sabin's secret society, however, orders him to burn the documents obtained through blackmail, and Sabin must convince the other characters that he meant well all along.

Another successful novel, *The Great Impersonation* (1920), describes the impersonation of the German Major-General Baron Leopold von Ragastein in England by his former Etonian classmate Everard Dominey. Ragastein's intent is to influence enough British citizens to keep England from entering World War I against Germany. His attempt is frustrated by his double, Dominey, a British aristocrat who has become an alcoholic. (This novel was later adapted as a film, featuring Edmund Lowe.)

In the prophetic novel *The Dumb Gods Speak* (1937), Oppenheim describes the discovery of an all-powerful weapon in the year 1947. Yet an atomic bomb it is not: It is an electrical ray that can stop fleets of warships in the ocean without any casualties. In the novel, a single American warship defeats Japan by immobilizing its entire fleet. The people of the world deplore this action so much that they legislate against any future wars. In *The Wrath to Come* (1924), a German-Japanese plot for a joint attack on the United States is uncovered and prevented by the appearance of a *deus ex machina* in the form of a document.

In the novel *Miss Brown of X.Y.O.* (1927), the bored secretary Miss Brown is sitting on the steps of a London mansion with her typewriter when she is called in to take a deposition from a dying famous explorer. If the dictated information should fall into the hands of the Bolsheviks, a European war would result. The dying explorer proves to be a healthy secret agent, and after withstanding many enemy attempts to steal the important document, Miss Brown and the agent not only save Europe from war but also fall in love.

Oppenheim's sympathy with the wealthy and aristocratic is demonstrated in both *Up the Ladder of Gold* (1931) and *The Gallows of Chance* (1934). In the first novel, a fantasy about the power of money, the rich American Warren Rand corners the gold market and, using this power, tries to convince the nations of the world not to go to war for forty years. Rand commits crimes for a good cause, and clearly Oppenheim approved. In *The Gallows of Chance*, Lord Edward Keynsham, a member of an illegal bootlegging syndicate, is allowed to escape indictment for murder because he is beloved in his community. Indeed, he will marry his love, Katherine Brandt, an otherwise law-abiding leading actress who knows of his crimes. His best friend, Sir Humphrey Rossiter, resigns as Home Secretary to escape the duty of prosecuting Lord Edward. This occurs in spite of the fact that Lord Edward and his syndicate had kidnapped Sir Humphrey and threatened to hang him unless he met their demands to stay the execution of a convicted murderer.

In *Mr. Mirakel* (1943), the protagonist sets up a utopia to which he takes his followers; they escape with him, not only from war but also from an earthquake. The powerful leader is able to convince his followers that they will achieve a lasting peace.

One of Oppenheim's most unusual books, *The Seven Conundrums* (1923), has a Faustian theme. Maurice Little, Leonard Cotton, and Rose Mindel, three down-at-the-heel performers, sell their souls to Richard Thomson in return for professional and financial success. In seven different actions, the three go where they are told and carry out Thomson's typed and mysteriously delivered orders. After each order is carried out, they question Thomson. Instead of a reply, he counters with "That is the First [or Second . . .] Conundrum." Although the performers refer to Thomson as Mephistopheles privately, he promises to return their souls at the end of a year; at that time, he supplies answers to all seven conundrums and reveals his own identity as a member of the British Secret Service. The structure, the allusions, and the credible love story make *The Seven Conundrums* one of Oppenheim's finest works of fiction.

While many of Oppenheim's tales of intrigue involve spies acting alone, *The Ostrekoff Jewels* (1932) pits American diplomat Wilfred Haven against a beautiful Russian spy, Anna. The two escape from Russia together, the last leg of their journey to England taking place on a commandeered, antiquated, German plane. Not until the end of the novel does Wilfred trust Anna, although he has fallen in love with her at first sight. She proves to be the Princess Ostrekoff, the rightful owner of the crown jewels for which Wilfred has risked life and career.

Mr. Treyer in *The Strangers' Gate* (1939) is another of the Germans determined to topple the British government. In this story, Nigel Beverley, president of a British-owned company, represents the Crown. In a situation unusual for an Oppenheim protagonist, Nigel has to choose between three women: his fiancée, a wealthy socialite who is the daughter of his business partner, Lord Portington; Katrina, a beautiful opera singer who is the mistress of Prince Nicolas of Orlac and who makes advances toward Nigel; and Marya, an impoverished princess from Orlac who has been reared in a convent. Nigel chooses the innocent Marya, who will learn how to be the wife of a prominent businessman-socialite. The action centers on the conflicting attempts of Great Britain and Germany to control the bauxite mines of Orlac.

Whether detective story or straight espionage, E. Phillips Oppenheim's fiction is infused with his love of storytelling. So successful was his writing career that Oppenheim was able to enjoy the same luxurious life-style of many of his characters. Read by millions of thrill seekers, his works betray his interest in "world domination for good purpose, especially pacifism, his admiration for the superman of wealth, and his fascination with the game of world politics played as on a chess board."

## Principal mystery and detective fiction

NOVELS: *Expiation*, 1887; *The Peer and the Woman*, 1892; *A Monk of Cruta*, 1894 (also as *The Tragedy of Andrea*); *A Daughter of the Marionis*, 1895 (also as *To Win the Love He Sought*); *False Evidence*, 1896; *The Postmaster of Market Deignton*, 1896; *A Modern Prometheus*, 1896; *The Mystery of Mr. Bernard Brown*, 1896 (also as *The New Tenant* and *His Father's Crime*); *The Wooing of Fortune*, 1896; *The World's Great Snare*, 1896; *The Amazing Judgment*, 1897; *As a Man Lives*, 1898 (also as *The Yellow House*); *A Daughter of Astrea*, 1898; *Mysterious Mr. Sabin*, 1898; *The Man and His Kingdom*, 1899; *Mr. Marx's Secret*, 1899; *A Millionaire of Yesterday*, 1900; *Master of Men*, 1901 (also as *Enoch Strone*); *The Survivor*, 1901; *The Traitors*, 1902; *The Great Awakening*, 1902 (also as *A Sleeping Memory*); *A Prince of Sinners*, 1903; *The Yellow Crayon*, 1903; *The Master Mummer*, 1904; *The Betrayal*, 1904; *Anna the Adventuress*, 1904; *A Maker of History*, 1905; *Mr. Wingrave, Millionaire*, 1906 (also as *The Malefactor*); *A Lost Leader*, 1906; *The Vindicator*, 1907; *The Missioner*, 1907; *The Secret*, 1907 (also as *The Great Secret*); *Conspirators*, 1907 (also as *The Avenger*); *Berenice*, 1907; *The Ghosts of Society*, 1908 (also as *The Distributors*); *Jeanne of the Marshes*, 1908; *The Governors*, 1908; *The Kingdom of Earth*, 1909 (also as *The Black Watcher*); *The Moving Finger*, 1910 (also as *The Falling Star*); *The Illustrious Prince*, 1910; *The Missing Delora*, 1910 (also as *The Lost Ambassador*); *Passers-By*, 1910; *The Golden Web*, 1910 (also as *The Plunderers*); *Havoc*, 1911; *The Tempting of Tavernake*, 1911 (also as *The Temptation of Tavernake*); *The Court of St. Simon*, 1912 (also as *Seeing Life*); *The Lighted Way*, 1912; *The Mischief-Maker*, 1912; *The Double Life of Mr. Alfred Burton*, 1913; *The Way of These Women*, 1913; *A People's Man*, 1914; *The Vanished Messenger*, 1914; *The Black Box*, 1914; *The Double Traitor*, 1915; *Mr. Grex of Monte Carlo*, 1915; *The Kingdom of the Blind*, 1916; *The Hillman*, 1917; *The Cinema Murder*, 1917 (also as *The Other Romilly*); *The Zeppelin's Passenger*, 1918 (also as *Mr. Lessingham Goes Home*); *The Pawns Count*, 1918; *The Curious Quest*, 1918 (also as *The Amazing Quest of Mr. Ernest Bliss*); *The Strange Case of Mr. Jocelyn Thew*, 1919 (also as *The Box with Broken Seals*); *The Wicked Marquis*, 1919; *The Devil's Paw*, 1920; *The Great Impersonation*, 1920; *Jacob's Ladder*, 1921; *Nobody's Man*, 1921; *The Profiteers*, 1921; *The Evil Shepherd*, 1922; *The Great Prince Shan*, 1922; *The Mystery Road*, 1923; *The Inevitable Millionaires*,

1923; *The Passionate Quest,* 1924; *The Wrath to Come,* 1924; *Gabriel Samara,* 1925 (also as *Gabriel Samara, Peacemaker*); *Stolen Idols,* 1925; *The Interloper,* 1926 (also as *The Ex-Duke*); *The Golden Beast,* 1926; *Harvey Garrard's Crime,* 1926; *Prodigals of Monte Carlo,* 1926; *Miss Brown of X.Y.O.,* 1927; *The Fortunate Wayfarer,* 1928; *Matorni's Vineyard,* 1928; *The Light Beyond,* 1928; *Blackman's Wood,* 1929; *The Glenlitten Murder,* 1929; *The Treasure House of Martin Hews,* 1929; *The Lion and the Lamb,* 1930; *The Million Pound Deposit,* 1930; *Up the Ladder of Gold,* 1931; *Simple Peter Cradd,* 1931; *Moran Chambers Smiled,* 1932 (also as *The Man from Sing Sing*); *The Ostrekoff Jewels,* 1932; *Jeremiah and the Princess,* 1933; *Murder at Monte Carlo,* 1933; *The Strange Boarders of Palace Crescent,* 1934; *The Bank Manager,* 1934 (also as *The Man Without Nerves*); *The Gallows of Chance,* 1934; *The Battle of Basinghall Street,* 1935; *The Spy Paramount,* 1935; *The Bird of Paradise,* 1936 (also as *Floating Peril*); *Judy of Bunter's Buildings,* 1936 (also as *The Magnificent Hoax*); *The Dumb Gods Speak,* 1937; *Envoy Extraordinary,* 1937; *The Mayor on Horseback,* 1937; *The Colossus of Arcadia,* 1938; *The Spymaster,* 1938; *Exit a Dictator,* 1939; *Sir Adam Disappeared,* 1939; *The Strangers' Gate,* 1939; *The Grassleyes Mystery,* 1940; *Last Train Out,* 1941; *The Shy Plutocrat,* 1941; *The Man Who Changed His Plea,* 1942; *Mr. Mirakel,* 1943.

SHORT FICTION: *The Long Arm of Mannister,* 1908; *The Double Four,* 1911 (also as *Peter Ruff and the Double Four*); *Peter Ruff,* 1912; *Those Other Days,* 1912; *For the Queen,* 1912; *Mr. Laxworthy's Adventures,* 1913; *The Amazing Partnership,* 1914; *The Game of Liberty,* 1915 (also as *The Amiable Charlatan*); *Mysteries of the Riviera,* 1916; *Ambrose Lavendale, Diplomat,* 1920; *Aaron Rod, Diviner,* 1920; *The Honourable Algernon Knox, Detective,* 1920; *Michael's Evil Deeds,* 1923; *The Seven Conundrums,* 1923; *The Terrible Hobby of Sir Joseph Londe, Bt.,* 1924; *The Adventures of Mr. Joseph P. Cray,* 1925; *The Little Gentleman from Okehampstead,* 1926; *The Channay Syndicate,* 1927; *Madame,* 1927 (also as *Madame and Her Twelve Virgins*); *Mr. Billingham, The Marquis and Madelon,* 1927; *Nicholas Goade, Detective,* 1927; *Chronicles of Melhampton,* 1928; *The Exploits of Pudgy Pete and Co.,* 1928; *The Human Chase,* 1929; *Jennerton and Co.,* 1929; *What Happened to Forester,* 1929; *Slane's Long Shots,* 1930; *Sinners Beware,* 1931; *Inspector Dickins Retires,* 1931 (also as *Gangster's Glory*); *Crooks in the Sunshine,* 1932; *The Ex-Detective,* 1933; *General Besserley's Puzzle Box,* 1935; *Advice Limited,* 1935; *Ask Miss Mott,* 1936; *Curious Happenings to the Rooke Legatees,* 1937; *And Still I Cheat the Gallows: A Series of Stories,* 1938; *A Pulpit in the Grill Room,* 1938; *General Besserley's Second Puzzle Box,* 1939; *The Milan Grill Room: Further Adventures of Louis, the Manager, and Major Lyson, the Raconteur,* 1940; *The Great Bear,* 1943; *The Man Who Thought He Was a Pauper,* 1943; *The Hour of Reckoning, and The Mayor of Ballydaghan,* 1944.

## Other major works

PLAYS: *The Money-Spider,* 1908; *The King's Cup,* 1909 (with H. D. Bradley); *The Gilded Key,* 1910; *The Eclipse,* 1919 (with Fred Thompson).

NONFICTION: *My Books and Myself,* 1922; *The Quest for Winter Sunshine,* 1927; *The Pool of Memory: Memoirs,* 1941.

## Bibliography

Gadney, Reg. "Switch Off the Wireless—It's on Oppenheim." *London Magazine* 10 (June, 1970): 19-27.

Overton, Grant. "A Great Impersonation by E. Phillips Oppenheim." In *Cargoes for Crusoes*. Boston: Little, Brown, 1924.

Standish, Robert. *The Prince of Storytellers: The Life of E. Phillips Oppenheim.* London: Peter Davies, 1957.

Stokes, Sewell. "Mr. Oppenheim of Monte Carlo." *The Listener* 60 (1958): 344-345.

Wellman, Ellen, and Wray O. Brown. "Collecting E. Phillips Oppenheim (1866-1946)." *Private Library: Quarterly Journal of the Private Library Association* 6 (Summer, 1983): 83-89.

*Sue Laslie Kimball*

# Baroness Orczy

**Born:** Tarna-Örs, Hungary; September 23, 1865
**Died:** London, England; November 12, 1947

**Type of plot** • Amateur sleuth

**Principal series** • The Old Man in the Corner, 1905-1925 • Lady Molly of Scotland Yard, 1910 • Patrick Mulligan, 1928.

**Principal series characters** • THE OLD MAN IN THE CORNER (BILL OWEN), an extremely eccentric man who spends much of his time in a restaurant, the A.B.C. Shop, working untiringly at tying and untying knots in a piece of string. He is ageless and apparently unchanging. Not much concerned with justice or morality, he is interested in crime "only when it resembles a clever game of chess, with many intricate moves which all tend to one solution, the checkmating of the antagonist–the detective force of the country." Like all amateur sleuths, the old man has his Watson, a female journalist by the name of POLLY BURTON. An invariably baffled reader of stories of mysterious deaths in the newspapers, she comes to the A.B.C. Shop to hear the old man unravel the mystery.
  • LADY MOLLY OF SCOTLAND YARD is a strong-willed, direct, and clever woman who time after time manages to beat her male colleagues at the game of crime solving. She is somewhat of a feminist, if only in the sense that she claims that her feminine intuition–as opposed, presumably, to male intellect and logical thinking–equips her better for the job of detecting than any man. Lady Molly has a confidante and foil, MARY, a young policewoman who tells the story and represents the intrigued but skeptical reader.
  • PATRICK MULLIGAN, an Irish lawyer, is a hero of still another volume of detective stories written by the prolific baroness. Both the Lady Molly and the Patrick Mulligan stories are far inferior to the first two volumes of stories about the Old Man in the Corner, although they are very similar in both construction and execution.

**Contribution** • One student of crime literature calls Baroness Orczy's stories about the Old Man in the Corner "the first significant modern stories about an armchair detective." They are also rather unusual because of the purely cerebral interest the old man has in crime as a kind of mind game. The extent of his amorality is brought out in the story of "The Mysterious Death in Percy Street." In this story, Polly Burton realizes, after the old man has laid all the evidence and a damning piece of evidence–a length of rope with expert knots on it–before her, that the old man is the murderer, reveling in his own cleverness.

All the stories about the Old Man in the Corner and his journalist friend, Polly Burton, are set in the A.B.C. Shop, where he habitually sits, as the baroness describes him in her autobiography, "in his big checked ulster [and] his horn-rimmed spectacles," with "his cracked voice and dribbling nose and above all . . . his lean, bony fingers fidgeting, always fidgeting with a bit of string." Either he or Polly brings up some mysterious death or crime that is currently intriguing the public. The events are outlined by the old man, who, when he is not sitting in his corner, is an avid reader of newspapers and spectator in courtrooms. He is unfailingly–and jeeringly–contemptuous of the police and their feeble efforts at untying the knots clever criminals tie. With Polly as a respectful but not necessarily credulous listener, he proceeds–once the facts as he sees them are presented–to point to the logical and necessary solution to the mystery. He scoffs at offering his insights to the police because he is sure that they would not listen to him, who, after all, is merely an amateur, and because he admires the clever criminal who can outwit the entire Scotland Yard. Thus, the emphasis is on the ingeniously planned crime and the intelligent, rigidly logical unraveling of it, not on psychology, human relations, or morality.

**Biography** • Emma Magdalena Rosalia Maria Josefa Barbara Orczy was born in Hungary on September 23, 1865, the daughter of Baron Felix Orczy, an able composer and conductor, and Emma Orczy (née Wass). Problems, among which was a peasant uprising, convinced the Orczys to move first to Budapest, then to Brussels, followed by Paris and, finally, London. Young Emma, or Emmuska, as she preferred to be called, was educated first as a musician and later, when it was decided upon the advice of Franz Liszt–a family friend–that she did not have the gift of music, as an artist. Emmuska attended the West London and Heatherly schools of art. She showed promise and was for several years an exhibitor at the Royal Academy. While she was at the Heatherly School of Art, the young Hungarian met another student, Montagu Barstow, who was to become her husband.

It is intriguing that a woman who did not speak a word of English until she was fifteen years of age should have become one of the most prolific and popular writers of her time, writing more than thirty books in her adopted language. The baroness has explained how the idea of becoming a writer first came to her. She and her husband were staying with a family whose members wrote stories that they sold to popular magazines. Orczy, observing that people with little education who had never traveled were successful as authors, decided that she, with her international background and solid education, should be able to do at least as well. She wrote two stories and found to her joy not only that they were accepted immediately–by *Pearson's Magazine*–for the amount of ten guineas but also that the editor asked that she give him first refusal on any future stories she wrote. A literary career had begun.

It was suggested to the baroness that she write detective stories, somewhat in the style of the then very popular Sherlock Holmes stories. As a result, she

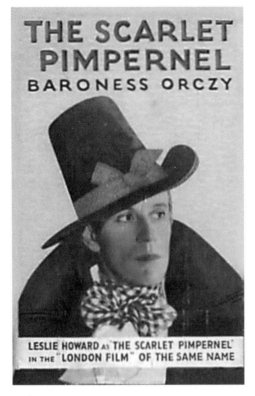

**THE SCARLET PIMPERNEL**

**BARONESS ORCZY**

LESLIE HOWARD ᴬˢ THE SCARLET PIMPERNEL' IN THE "LONDON FILM" OF THE SAME NAME

created the strange old man who sits in his unobtrusive corner, playing with his string and expounding in a haughty and self-assured manner to the lady reporter from *The Evening Observer* on crime and criminals. The stories caught on and ran as a series in *The Royal Magazine* before their publication in book form under the title *The Old Man in the Corner* in 1909.

The baroness produced four series of stories featuring Bill Owen, the peculiar old man, and Polly Burton. The first two series ran in *The Royal Magazine* from 1901 to 1904 and were later published as *The Old Man in the Corner*; the third series was first published in book form as *The Case of Miss Elliott* in 1905. The fourth and last series was published in 1925 as *Unravelled Knots*. Baroness Orczy is most famous, however, not for her detective stories but for being the author of that epic of trans-Channel derring-do and genteel romance, *The Scarlet Pimpernel* (1905).

At the outbreak of World War I, Barstow and Orczy moved to Monte Carlo, where they lived until his death in 1943; at that time, the baroness moved back to London. During her later years, Orczy's literary output slowed down considerably, although she kept writing until the end—her autobiography, *Links in the Chain of Life* (1947), being her last published work. Baroness Orczy died in London, at the age of eighty-two, in 1947.

**Analysis** • Although Baroness Orczy wrote more than thirty volumes of fiction, she is remembered principally as the author of the books about the Scarlet Pimpernel and to a lesser degree for her stories about the armchair detective in the corner of the A.B.C. Shop, Bill Owen. The first of these stories, "The Fenchurch Street Mystery," appeared in the May, 1901, issue of *The Royal Magazine* and is typical of all of them.

Polly Burton, a journalist at *The Evening Observer*, is sitting in the A.B.C. Shop reading her newspaper and minding her own business when a curious little man irritably pushes his glass away and exclaims, "Mysteries! . . . There is no such thing as a mystery in connection with any crime, provided intelligence is brought to bear upon its investigation." Burton is, not surprisingly, somewhat taken aback by being spoken to by a total–and very strange–stranger, but even more so because he seems to have read her thoughts: She is reading an article in the paper dealing with crimes that have frustrated the police.

Such is the opening of the first story about the Old Man in the Corner. Each of the stories is structured in the same way: First, the reader is drawn into the mystery to be investigated and solved via a conversation in the A.B.C. Shop between the two series protagonists; next, the data of the case in question are presented–usually by Bill Owen. Finally, Owen presents a neat, logical solution.

In the exposition phase the old man gives what almost amounts to an eye-witness account of the facts of the case. He often carries with him photographs he has taken or obtained of the protagonists of the case or, as is the case in "The Fenchurch Street Mystery," copies of pertinent letters or other documents. The old man also spends a considerable amount of his time in court-rooms listening to cases and taking notes. He is always early enough to get a seat in the first row, enabling him to see and hear everything. His account of the facts is lively and full of colorful adjectives and verbatim quotes from witnesses. He makes sure to call Burton's attention to those aspects of the case that seem to him pertinent to its solution.

Despite the old man's care to present the case so that all an intelligent person has to do is make logical deductions, Burton, like the police before her, invariably has to give up and leave the unraveling of the mystery to her interlocutor. The cases discussed at the A.B.C. Shop are to everyone but Owen true mysteries that seem to resist all attacks. To Owen there are no mysteries. He is so cocksure about this that he irritates Burton, who insists that crimes the police have despaired of solving are, for all intents and purposes, insoluble. The old man demurs: "I never for a moment ventured to suggest that there were no mysteries to the *police*; I merely remarked that there were none where intelligence was brought to bear upon the investigation of crime." He has deep contempt for the public, the journalists covering crimes, and, especially, the police. The last phase of each story is the protracted denouement: the Old Man in the Corner demonstrating how, with a minimum of insight into the human psyche and a keen intelligence, he can make any case that to the rest of the world is opaque become crystal clear.

This three-part structure is characteristic of every one of the stories about the Old Man in the Corner. Orczy makes the reader her confidant and interlocutor. The stories are told in the first person by Polly Burton as if she were telling them to a friend over a cup of tea. The relationship between the reader and the narrator is, in other words, somewhat like that between Polly Burton herself and the old man who tells his stories to her. This device of pulling the reader into the narrative by making him an intimate, common in nineteenth century literature, is used to great effect by Orczy.

The stories move back and forth in time and place, between the present in the A.B.C. Shop and the various events in the past that are presented as facts pertinent to the case. The old man creates in vivid narrative the situations in which the protagonists in the case have found themselves, or he re-creates the testimonies of witnesses at the trial in colloquial detail and color. Thus, the reader must follow the case on two levels: as Polly Burton's alter ego or confidant and as a witness to key events and the proceedings in court. The mixture is both entertaining and pleasing.

In the end, the reader, along with Polly Burton, must put up with the old man's annoying complacency and self-congratulation as he points out where the police and everybody else went wrong. The old man jeers at the police and brims over with conceit because he has presented all the evidence so that any intelligent person should be able to come to the one and only conclusion to the case, the conclusion that he has made and that makes sense of all the facts. When he has made the last knot on his string and thrown his pearls before the swine, he gets up, leaving Polly and the reader to wonder what exactly has happened. Have they just witnessed a brilliant amateur sleuth at work, or is the old man a hoax, fleet of fingers and mouth but actually merely testing the credulity of lady novelists and their readers?

Perhaps the most interesting aspect of the stories about the Old Man in the Corner is that they are totally devoid of morality and human compassion. The world conjured up by the author is one where greed and the will to outsmart society's laws and their representatives reign supreme. The emphasis is on how a smart criminal can get away with nearly anything. The criminal described and hailed as a hero by the old man—and by extension by his author and her alter ego, Polly Burton, who is only minimally interested in seeing justice served—is a virtual Nietzschean superman, a Raskolnikov who is not plagued by the monsters of conscience and who is never caught. If a criminal comes to a bad end in the stories, it is through the agency of fate, not the police or society. The successful culprit, as in "The Dublin Mystery," sometimes lives only a short time to enjoy the results of his mischief before being overtaken by fate and a natural death. It is almost as if the author wanted to suggest that even if the agents of socially defined justice are slow of wit, the most vicious of malefactors—the father murderer ("The Dublin Mystery") and the murderer of the rightful heir to the earldom ("The Tremarn Case"), to name two examples—will eventually be brought to justice and executed by some kind of higher agency.

This bare-knuckled social Darwinism, where the smart outwit, defraud, and kill the less smart with no immediate punishment, is both the strength and the weakness of Orczy's stories. The Old Man in the Corner and his cases are interesting because they introduce readers to an amoral universe that lies beyond the stories found in the newspapers. These stories are superior to the later series about Lady Molly of Scotland Yard and the Irish lawyer Patrick Mulligan because they are not sentimental. Their amoral tone is refreshing because it is so unexpected and so unusual. The weakness, however, is that it is hard for the reader to care about anything or anybody in the stories. The two protagonists, Polly Burton and Bill Owen, are too sketchy and, in Owen's case, too unsympathetic to like, and the people whose dramas are being retold are unreal and even unbelievable, mere shadows of real people, pawns to be moved about on the old man's chessboard.

The stories about the Old Man in the Corner are good early examples of the armchair-detective subgenre, with interesting and well-designed plots. Their weakness lies in the characterizations and in a certain moral and emotional callousness.

## Principal mystery and detective fiction

SERIES: Lady Molly of Scotland Yard: *Lady Molly of Scotland Yard*, 1910. Patrick Mulligan: *Skin o' My Tooth*, 1928. The Old Man in the Corner: *The Case of Miss Elliott*, 1905; *The Old Man in the Corner*, 1909 (also as *The Man in the Corner*); *The Old Man in the Corner Unravels the Mystery of the Khaki Tunic*, 1923; *The Old Man in the Corner Unravels the Mystery of the Pearl Necklace, and The Tragedy in Bishop's Road*, 1924; *The Old Man in the Corner Unravels the Mystery of the Russian Prince and of Dog's Tooth Cliff*, 1924; *The Old Man in the Corner Unravels the Mystery of the White Carnation, and The Montmartre Hat*, 1925; *The Old Man in the Corner Unravels the Mystery of the Fulton Gardens Mystery, and The Moorland Tragedy*, 1925; *Unravelled Knots*, 1925.

OTHER NOVELS: *Castles in the Air*, 1921; *The Miser of Maida Vale*, 1925; *The Celestial City*, 1926.

OTHER SHORT FICTION: *The Man in Grey, Being Episodes of the Chouan Conspiracies in Normandy During the First Empire*, 1918.

## Other major works

NOVELS: *The Emperor's Candlesticks*, 1899; *The Scarlet Pimpernel*, 1905; *By the Gods Beloved*, 1905 (also as *Beloved of the Gods* and *The Gates of Kamt*); *A Son of the People*, 1906; *I Will Repay*, 1906; *In Mary's Reign*, 1907; *The Tangled Skein*, 1907; *Beau Brocade*, 1907; *The Elusive Pimpernel*, 1908; *The Nest of the Sparrowhawk*, 1909; *Petticoat Government*, 1910 (also as *Petticoat Rule*); *A True Woman*, 1911 (also as *The Heart of a Woman*); *Meadowsweet*, 1912; *Fire in the Stubble*, 1912 (also as *The Noble Rogue*); *Eldorado: A Story of the Scarlet Pimpernel*, 1913; *Unto Caesar*, 1914; *The Laughing Cavalier*, 1914; *A Bride of the Plains*, 1915; *The Bronze Eagle*, 1915; *Leatherface: A Tale of Old Flanders*, 1916; *A Sheaf of Bluebells*, 1917; *Lord Tony's Wife: An Adventure of the Scarlet Pimpernel*, 1917; *Flower o' the Lily*, 1918; *The League of the Scarlet Pimpernel*, 1919; *His Majesty's Well-Beloved*, 1919; *The First Sir Percy: An Adventure of the Laughing Cavalier*, 1920; *Nicolette*, 1922; *The Triumph of the Scarlet Pimpernel*, 1922; *The Honourable Jim*, 1924; *Pimpernel and Rosemary*, 1924; *Sir Percy Hits Back: An Adventure of the Scarlet Pimpernel*, 1927; *Blue Eyes and Grey*, 1928; *Marivosa*, 1930; *A Child of the Revolution*, 1932; *A Joyous Adventure*, 1932; *The Way of the Scarlet Pimpernel*, 1933; *A Spy of Napoleon*, 1934; *The Uncrowned King*, 1935; *Sir Percy Leads the Band*, 1936; *The Divine Folly*, 1937; *No Greater Love*, 1938; *Mam'zelle Guillotine: An Adventure of the Scarlet Pimpernel*, 1940; *Pride of Race*, 1942; *Will-o'-the-Wisp*, 1947.

SHORT FICTION: *The Traitor*, 1912; *Two Good Patriots*, 1912; *The Old Scarecrow*, 1916; *A Question of Temptation*, 1925; *Adventures of the Scarlet Pimpernel*, 1929; *In the Rue Monge*, 1931.

PLAYS: *The Scarlet Pimpernel*, 1903 (with Montagu Barstow); *The Sin of William Jackson*, 1906 (with Barstow); *Beau Brocade*, 1908 (with Barstow); *The Duke's Wager*, 1911; *The Legion of Honour*, 1918; *Leatherface*, 1922 (with Caryl Fiennes).

NONFICTION: *Les Beaux et les dandys des grands siècles en Angleterre*, 1924; *The Scarlet Pimpernel Looks at the World*, 1933; *The Turbulent Duchess: H. R. H. Madame la Duchesse de Berri*, 1935; *Links in the Chain of Life*, 1947.

TRANSLATIONS: *Old Hungarian Fairy Tales*, 1895 (with Barstow); *The Enchanted Cat*, 1895; *Fairyland's Beauty (The Suitors of the Princess Fire-Fly)*, 1895; *Uletka and the White Lizard*, 1895.

## Bibliography

Bargainnier, Earl F. "Lady Molly of Scotland Yard." *The Mystery FANcier* 7 (July/August, 1983): 15-19.

_____. "The Old Man in the Corner." *The Mystery FANcier* 7 (November/December, 1983): 21-23.

Bleiler, E. F. Introduction to *The Old Man in the Corner: Twelve Mysteries*. New York: Dover, 1980.

Braybrooke, Patrick. *Some Goddesses of the Pen*. London: C. W. Daniel, 1927.

Dueren, Fred. "Was the Old Man in the Corner an Armchair Detective?" *The Armchair Detective* 14 (Summer, 1981): 232-235.

Klein, Kathleen Gregory, ed. *Great Women Mystery Writers: Classic to Contemporary*. Westport, Conn.: Greenwood Press, 1994.

Nachison, Beth. Introduction to *The Scarlet Pimpernel*. New York: Acclaim Books, 1997.

Rutland, Arthur. "Baroness Orczy." *The Bookman* April, 1913, p. 193-201.

*Per Schelde*

# Sara Paretsky

**Born:** Ames, Iowa; June 8, 1947

**Types of plot** • Hard-boiled • private investigator

**Principal series** • V. I. Warshawski, 1982-    .

**Principal series characters** • V. I. WARSHAWSKI, a female private investigator in her mid-thirties who practices in Chicago. She is a tough professional with a wry sense of humor, and she specializes in financial crime.
• DR. LOTTY HERSCHEL, Warshawski's closest friend, is a woman in her fifties who operates a clinic for women and children. She is a renowned perinatalogist at the fictional Beth Israel Hospital.
• MURRAY RYERSON, head of the crime desk at the fictitious Chicago *Herald-Star*, often feeds Warshawski information, but more often than not, he is eager for leads on her investigations. Ryerson and Warshawski were lovers early in the series and have since devolved into drinking buddies.
• BOBBY MALLORY, Warshawski's frequent nemesis, is a friendly lieutenant on the Chicago police force who provides the foil needed by most private investigators.
• MR. CONTRERAS, Warshawski's retired, nosey codger of a next-door neighbor.

**Contribution** • Sara Paretsky is notable in the mystery/detective genre for her ability to shift the conventions of the hard-boiled private investigator tradition to a female character. V. I. Warshawski is a tough-minded, able woman whose gender does not hamper her in the line of duty. Paretsky takes many opportunities to play against the expectations of the genre and to point out the competence of women in roles traditionally held by men. Paretsky imbues Warshawski with wit, cynicism, and a feminist perspective that allows her to deliver sardonic observations about her interactions and adventures. One of the most sharply drawn of the first wave of female private investigators, Paretsky's protagonist has also paved the way for subsequent, equally distinctive generations of the breed.

Warshawski is one of the most sharply drawn of the steadily growing tribe of female private investigators.

**Biography** • Reared in Kansas within a large family which was liberal and socially active—except where it concerned the roles of girls and women—Sara Paretsky began creating heroines and stories for herself early on. While her brothers were sent to college, she was sent to secretarial school, so she worked to put herself through college on her own. She later settled in Chicago, the city that provides the generous, colorful details of her novels' settings. She earned a doctorate in history at the University of Chicago but has no formal training in fiction writing. She was working as an executive at a large insurance company when she began writing detective fiction; this background is apparent in the insurance company-related plots and setting of her first three novels.

Paretsky credits the women's movement of the 1960's with helping her to see that she could "occupy public space," and she later used the visibility afforded by her success in the socially conscious tradition in which she was reared. A founding member of Sisters in Crime, she mentors high school students in downtown Chicago and has endowed scholarships for students in the sciences and arts.

Dorothy L. Sayers's attention to relationships and class issues has influenced Paretsky's work, but her novels replace Sayers's typically lettered style with a more colloquial, vigorously American and contemporary assessment of relationships and of women's social roles. One of her reasons for creating the V. I. Warshawski series was to portray a woman character freed from stereotypically passive feminine traits.

**Analysis** • Sara Paretsky's V. I. Warshawski series simultaneously works within and comments on the conventions of the hard-boiled genre by changing the gender of the central character. The tough, hard-boiled dick, who operates alone, outside traditional law-and-order systems, is a mythic figure of American folklore. He is typically envisioned as Humphrey Bogart, wearing a raincoat and a slouch hat, squinting over a perpetually smoking cigarette.

V. I. Warshawski is carved from the Sam Spade tradition—with a few humorous references to Nancy Drew—and yet her gender makes for a very different reading of the same character type. When the hard-boiled characteristics are assigned to a woman—traditionally women figure in this detective genre merely as the private eye's love interest or the femme fatale—the device can offer insights into the nature of gender roles and a refreshing new slant on the genre's conventions.

Warshawski's gender adds another dimension to the detective's traditional marginality with respect to dominant legal and social systems. While the myth of the male hero allows for the individual man to buck the system, or at least step outside it by riding off on his lone horse into the sunset, women are generally expected to remain protected by, if not subservient to, the dictates of law and order. Warshawski is a member in good standing of the Illinois bar but gave up her career in the district attorney's office to work alone.

Warshawski's choice to strike out on her own continually infuriates police lieutenant Bobby Mallory, a character who serves several functions in Paretsky's narratives. On one hand, the Mallory character is relatively predictable within the conventions of the genre. He is Warshawski's link with the system; he resents her intrusions on his cases, yet admires her ability to get the results from which his position keeps him.

In addition to being the aggravated law enforcement officer, Mallory serves now and then as a father figure for Warshawski. The usually predictable relationship is given a new dimension by the gender considerations. Mallory worked with Warshawski's father, who was an officer on the Chicago police force. Mallory glowers paternally at Warshawski when she gets involved in cases that seem inevitably to cross his desk, but his anger is a mixture of professional jealousy and fatherly concern.

The Warshawski character is crafted with the mix of cynicism and compassion that marks the best of the private investigators. Her specialty is financial crime, a venue that has allowed Paretsky to comment on corrupt bureaucracies and the machinations of those in the higher strata of the social order. *Indemnity Only* (1982) centers on an insurance hoax perpetrated by the officers of Ajax Insurance, a company later involved with illegal dealings and intrigue in the shipping industry in *Deadlock* (1984).

In 1992's *Guardian Angel* Warshawski unearths a complex bond-parking conspiracy, in *Tunnel Vision* (1994) there is a money laundering scheme involving Iraq, and *Hard Time* (1999) takes on the subject of the privatization of American prisons and the curruption and abuse—all for the sake of financial gain—it affords. Yet all of these novels deal with a great deal more than fianancial crime, for the financial crimes usually reside at the nexus of many other social ills—homicide, spouse and child abuse, exploitation of illegal aliens, homelessness, corrupt polititians, venal lawyers, and cruelty to animals.

Although Warshawski frequently deals with the chief executive officers of large corporations, her clients tend to be middle to lower class. Her own financial status is best described as "down at the heels"—her office location is in an old, dimly lit building near the financial district in downtown Chicago. The elevator to her fourth-floor suite rarely works, and the building lobby is often home to street people. Warshawski's setup is reminiscent of Toby Peters's office locale in Stuart M. Kaminsky's detective series.

Warshawski's lack of a generous income does not cramp her style. She can afford the Johnny Walker she regularly orders at the Golden Glow, a serious drinker's bar in the south Loop run by a dignified black woman named Sal. Paretsky's attention to detail helps to build a convincing portrait of Warshawski as a woman comfortable in her surroundings, one who knows exactly what she needs and who can navigate through the obstacles that come her way.

The Warshawski stories are written in the first person, which gives the narrator the observer's status, always slightly marginal to the events she describes. Warshawski is something of a loner. Rather than playing sports, she stays in shape by running in the early mornings along Lake Michigan. Her running, her scotch drinking, and her often insulting irreverence evince her comfort with her outsider status.

In contrast to the detached cynicism of most of the male characters in the genre, however, Warshawski tends to become personally involved in the events she describes and to evoke the larger picture into which they fit. Indeed, in *Hard Time* she gets so involved—against the advice and pleadings of her friends—that she ends up in prison for several chapters. Warshawski, in fact, is quick to joke about her well-developed sense of social justice and her ability to do automatic affirmative action tallies in large groups of people. Her feminism, too, is displayed through humor, often in the aphorisms by which she operates. Paretsky thus contributes to the subtly crusading spirit that pervades the genre but refrains from didacticism by continually commenting on her sarcastic observation of social mores.

Warshawski's closest friend, Dr. Lotty Herschel, often serves as a model of social consciousness which Paretsky contrasts with the corruption of top-heavy bureaucracies. A Viennese immigrant, Herschel fled Nazism by coming to the United States. She has dedicated her life to helping disadvantaged people as a response to the evils she has personally endured. Herschel is a woman of stature within the medical field. In addition to her regular duties as a perinatalogist at Beth Israel Hospital, she runs a clinic for low-income families in the run-down Chicago neighborhood where Warshawski rents an apartment.

Herschel is a woman with enormous personal dignity and compassion; her commitment to her work supersedes expectations of the more traditional female role. Although her suitors are distinguished gentlemen, she refuses to marry. Herschel offers companionship and support, and she is even something of a role model. Her advice provides a counterpoint to Mallory's blustery admonitions to be more of a conventional "girl."

Herschel figures largely in *Bitter Medicine* (1987), the fourth novel in the Warshawski series and Paretsky's first excursion outside the realm of financial crime. Warshawski is present at the scene of the untimely death of a pregnant teenage girl, who happens to be the sister of Herschel's nurse. Consuelo's death at a tidy suburban hospital whose staff is unaccustomed to treating low-income emergency patients raises the specter of malpractice suits against both the hospital and Lotty Herschel. When Herschel's partner, Malcolm Tregiere, is murdered and his dictation on Consuelo's case is missing, Warshawski begins to seek out the pattern that ties together Consuelo's death, Tregiere's murder, an antiabortion rally at Herschel's clinic, and the less-than-honest machinations of the suburban hospital's administration. *Guardian Angel* finds Warshawski pursuing a course of action that puts her and Lotty at odds and strains their friendship. Herschel also figures prominently in "Pietro Andromache," a story from the 1995 collection of Warshawski tales, *Windy City Blues*.

Bobby Mallory is somewhat displaced in *Bitter Medicine* by Detective Rawlings, a black man assigned to the case. Attention to racial issues is an integral part of the story's development, from Warshawski's maneuverings through the intricacies of implicit racism toward her Hispanic friend to a Hispanic gang's probable involvement in the murder of a black doctor. The gang theme allows Paretsky to place her female sleuth on turf usually addressed only by white male cops in violent displays of machismo.

*Bitter Medicine* allows Warshawski her first trip outside Chicago's city limits, and it gives Paretsky the opportunity for some playful commentary on the difference between affluent suburban and low-income city values. Warshawski's former husband, Richard Yarborough, appears for the first time as the high-priced lawyer representing a sleazy antiabortionist. Warshawski's dialogues with Yarborough are intentionally nasty. He has exchanged his marriage with her for one with a more traditionally feminine woman, and he is easily angered at Warshawski's frank jabbing at his bourgeois life-style. The Chicago suburbs appear as empty, sanitized havens from the gang violence and poverty of inner-city living—a milieu which Warshawski prefers.

Paretsky's novels often open with seductive descriptions of the Chicago locale in which Warshawski thrives, evoking the special relationship between the dick and the city for which Raymond Chandler, in his tributes to Los Angeles, is famous. Most of the Warshawski series takes place in the heat of the summer. The steamy atmosphere tends to intensify Warshawski's interactions with other characters and her own dogged pursuit of her cases.

Warshawski's method is relatively unscientific. She pokes around talking to people and begins to fit events and suspects into logical patterns. Paretsky's plots grow complex and then unravel by accretion—their climactic moments are ones of logical disclosure rather than fast chases or violent encounters. Yet they do not lack suspense or tension—Warshawski's methods are frequently illegitimate, if not illegal. For example, she is adept with lock-picking tools left in her possession by a burglar she once defended in the district attorney's office. She gathers information directly from her sources, which often involves nighttime visits to offices in which she does not belong.

Warshawski is not above relying on her feminine wiles to advance her cause, but Paretsky uses her heroine's moments of false identity and disguise to comment on the traditional expectations of the female role. If some men generally expect women to be less intelligent than Warshawski, she will impersonate a more foolish woman in order to get some piece of vital information. In her own guise, she is adamant that no one condescend to her, and her feminism is more pronounced.

In the tradition of the detached observer, Warshawski's relationships with men are casual and short-lived, rarely figuring prominently in the development of the plot. More traditional detective stories typically punish sexually active women under the auspices of the femme fatale stereotype. Warshawski's casual, healthy attitude toward her sexual encounters reflects the feminist premise that grounds Paretsky's writing.

Warshawski and journalist Murray Ryerson are occasional lovers, but their interactions are based more on mutual respect, affection, and the sharing of information than on building a long-term, secure commitment. In *Deadlock* and *Killing Orders* (1985), Warshawski takes up with an English reinsurance broker named Roger Ferrant, whose expertise gives Paretsky an outlet for information on securities and insurance transactions necessary for her plots. In *Bitter Medicine,* Warshawski has an affair with Peter Burgoyne, the head of obstetrics at Friendship V Hospital (he was the doctor in charge during Consuelo's treatment and subsequent death). Warshawski's involvement with Burgoyne eventually becomes suspect when she realizes that he and the hospital administrator have been involved in Tregiere's murder and the cover-up of various illicit operations and false advertising practices. She takes up with a new beau in *Guardian Angel,* only to have him decide to step back from the relationship because of her lone wolf style in *Tunnel Vision.*

Warshawski's lack of permanent romantic involvements is incidental to Paretsky's stories. Her character's professional veneer is fleshed out with humanizing notes from her family history. Like the city she loves, Warshawski is a melting pot of ethnicity—her mother was an Italian immigrant who married a Polish Jew. *Killing Orders* embroils Warshawski in a case that touches her personally when her Aunt Rosa is accused of placing counterfeit securities in a safe. There is little love lost between Warshawski and her reproving, hostile aunt, but family obligations require that Warshawski see the case through. In the process, emotional ghosts add a more complex layer to Warshawski's personality. Another aunt, this one good-natured but alcoholic and underhanded, gets Warshawski involved in arson, the homicide of a young hooker, and other difficulties in *Burn Marks.* The spirit of her innocent, revered mother is evoked in each of Paretsky's stories with mention of the red Venetian wine glasses that were her mother's legacy. In "Grace Notes," another story in *Windy City Blues,* a long-lost cousin turns up looking for sheet music that belonged to Warshawski's mysterious mother, and a bit more is revealed about her. In *Hard Time,* events and losses cause Vic to contemplate her mother's death on other levels.

The details of the Chicago setting help to particularize the Warshawski series and lend it veracity. Each story is a compelling travelogue into the intricacies of one of Chicago's many locales: finance networks (*Indemnity Only*), shipyards (*Deadlock*), Catholic dioceses in ethnic neighborhoods (*Killing Orders*), and suburban hospital settings (*Bitter Medicine*). The mix of fiction and fact in Warshawski's wry descriptions provides Paretsky with an outlet for the acute, sardonic social observations in which she specializes.

Not a polite, urbane lady sleuth in the Sayers tradition, Sara Paretsky's V. I.

Warshawski is a female private investigator based on the traditional male model. The female dick has gained a certain ascendency in the genre. Warshawski is kin to an ever-growing host of female detectives fashioned in the hard-boiled tradition.

The new women investigators are smart, physical, hard-living women, whose facility to move through the cracks and underbellies of big cities makes them well suited to their work. Although hard-boiled, such a character is not afraid to let her emotions and intuition influence the way she handles her cases. Paretsky and other women mystery/detective writers are reshaping a pervasive American myth by creating admirable female characters who get the job done as well as—or better than—their male predecessors.

## Principal mystery and detective fiction

SERIES: V. I. Warshawski: *Indemnity Only*, 1982; *Deadlock*, 1984; *Killing Orders*, 1985; *Bitter Medicine*, 1987; *Blood Shot*, 1988; *Burn Marks*, 1990; *Toxic Shock*, 1990; *Guardian Angel*, 1992; *V. I. Warshawski*, 1993; *Tunnel Vision*, 1994; *Ghost Country*, 1998; *Hard Time*, 1999.

SHORT FICTION: *A Taste of Life and Other Stories*, 1995; *Windy City Blues*, 1995; *V. I for Short*, 1995; *V. I. Warshawski Stories*, 1995.

## Other major works

*Raymond Chandler's Philip Marlowe*, 2000 (with others).

*Beastly Tales: The Mystery Writers of America Anthology*, 1989; *A Woman's Eye: New Stories by the Best Women Crime Writers*, 1991; *Women on the Case*, 1996.

## Bibliography

Klein, Kathleen Gregory, ed. *Great Women Mystery Writers: Classic to Contemporary*. Westport, Conn.: Greenwood Press, 1994.

Lukacks, John. Review of *Killing Orders*, by Sara Paretsky. *The New Yorker* 61 (September 2, 1985): 87-88.

"Paretsky, Sara." In *Mystery and Suspense Writers: The Literature of Crime, Detection, and Espionage*, edited by Robin W. Winks and Maureen Corrigan. New York: Charles Scribner's Sons, 1998.

Rozan, S. J. "Sara Paretsky: A Gun of One's Own." *Publisher's Weekly* 246, no. 43 (October 25, 1999): 44.

Smith, Joan. "Whose Eyes." *New Statesman* 111 (April 25, 1986): 27-28.

Stasio, Marilyn. "Lady Gumshoe: Boiled Less Hard." *The New York Times Book Review* 90 (April 28, 1985): 1.

Vicarel, Jo Ann. Review of *Bitter Medicine*, by Sara Paretsky. *Library Journal* 112 (May 1, 1987): 86.

*Jill Dolan*
*Updated by Fiona Kelleghan and Jessica Reisman*

# Robert B. Parker

**Born:** Springfield, Massachusetts; September 17, 1932

**Types of plot** • Private investigator • hard-boiled

**Principal series** • Spenser, 1973-      • Jesse Stone, 1997-      • Sunny Randall.

**Principal series characters** • SPENSER, an unmarried private investigator fired from the Boston police force, is around forty years old. Tough, intelligent, and irreverent, with interests ranging from sports and bodybuilding to literature and gourmet foods, he lives by a strict code of honor while operating on the fringes of the system which his work helps support.

• SUSAN SILVERMAN, Spenser's longtime girlfriend, is in her mid-thirties and divorced. A guidance counselor and later a psychologist, she is bright, articulate, and analytical. Although their personal philosophies are often in conflict, she provides a balance of tenderness and emotion in Spenser's life.

• HAWK is Spenser's friend and frequent ally, an enigmatic black man with ties to Boston's criminal underworld. Cold-blooded and amoral, yet fiercely loyal, he is a man of massive strength and biting wit who shares key points of Spenser's code of masculine ethics yet remains—unlike Spenser—unhampered by the dictates of conscience.

• JESSE STONE, a homicide detective hired as the police chief of Paradise, Massachusetts. Recently divorced, he has a love-hate relationship with his aspiring-actress ex-wife and a similar relation with an ever-ready bottle of Scotch. He has a complex emotional life that remains mostly internal, for he strives to be a "strong, silent" good cop.

• SUNNY RANDALL, a college graduate and former cop turned private eye. Smart and courageous, she is recently divorced, enjoys painting, and loves her miniature bull terrier, Rosie. Her best friend is Spike, a gay man. She has some resemblances to Spenser but is less ready for commitment, needing her space from her ex-husband, an Irish mobster named Richie Burke—with whom she still spends time—and her policeman father.

**Contribution** • Robert B. Parker fashioned his popular spenser series in the tradition of the detective novels of Dashiell Hammett and Raymond Chandler, creating a hero who is tough, principled, and tenacious. In fact, after Chandler's death it was Parker who was invited to complete a three-chapter manuscript begun by Chandler that was published as *Poodle Springs* (1989). In 1991, Parker wrote *Perchance to Dream*, a continuation of Chandler's 1939 *The Big Sleep*, featuring Carmen Sternwood from that novel.

Spenser's hard-boiled persona, however, is tempered with liberal doses of sarcastic, even playful, humor, and Parker has given his character a fully developed personal life which plays as great a part in the novels as do the cases on which Spenser works. As the series has evolved, Parker has increased his concentration on his character's philosophy and code of ethics, using Spenser's relationships with Susan Silverman and Hawk—and the differences in outlook among all three—as a springboard into conversations which examine the deeply held convictions by which Spenser lives. Spenser's long and complex affair with Susan has also served as a forum for an exploration of male-female relationships and the specific problems inherent in a relationship between a traditional hard-boiled hero and a liberated career woman.

The character of Spenser inspired the 1985-1988 television series *Spenser: For Hire*. The Spenser novels *Thin Air* (1995; aired 2000) and *Small Vices* (1997; aired 1999) were made into television films for the A&E network. *Thin Air* features appearances by Robert Parker (in a cameo), his wife, and their son Daniel, an actor.

**Biography** • Robert Brown Parker was born in Springfield, Massachusetts, on September 17, 1932. The son of Carroll Snow, a telephone company executive, and Mary Pauline (Murphy) Parker, a teacher, he attended Colby College in Waterville, Maine, and was graduated in 1954 with a degree in English. After a two-year stint in the U.S. Army, in which he served in the infantry in Korea, he married teacher Joan Hall, his college sweetheart. He attended graduate school at Boston University, where he received his M.A. in English in 1957. He then worked at various jobs before returning to Boston University in 1962 to obtain his Ph.D. His doctoral dissertation was titled "The Private Eye in Hammett and Chandler."

Parker was employed as a technical writer by the Raytheon Company in Andover and later as an advertising writer by Prudential Insurance in Boston. During the early 1960's, he was also a film consultant and the cochairman of the Parker-Farman advertising agency. In 1962 he returned to Boston University as a lecturer, continuing his teaching career throughout the 1960's as an English instructor first at Massachusetts State College in Bridgewater and later at Boston's Northeastern University, where he became an assistant professor in 1968 and an associate professor in 1974. In 1978, he retired. The Parkers have two sons, David and Daniel, and live in Cambridge, Massachusetts. Robert and Joan Parker founded Pearl Productions, a Boston-based independent film company named after their short-haired pointer, Pearl, who has been featured in Parker's fiction.

Parker's writing career began with contributions to the *Lock Haven Review* and the *Revue des langes vivantes* and as one of several editors of a book entitled *The Personal Response to Literature*, which was published in 1970. In 1973, he coedited *Order and Diversity: The Craft of Prose* with Peter L. Sandberg and cowrote *Sports Illustrated Training with Weights* with John R. Marsh—weight training plays a role in the Spenser novels. Also in 1973, the first of the

Spenser books, *The Godwulf Manuscript*, was published.

Since beginning the series, Parker has generally written one Spenser novel per year, and his characters are the basis for the 1980's television series *Spenser: For Hire.* In 1976, he received the Edgar Allan Poe Award for the year's best mystery and detective novel for his fourth Spenser book, *Promised Land* (1976).

**Analysis** • With the creation of Spenser, the tough, wisecracking Boston private investigator, Robert B. Parker has cast his series of detective novels firmly in the mold of such hard-boiled investigators as Dashiell Hammett's Sam Spade and Raymond Chandler's Philip Marlowe. Like those characters, Spenser (Parker has given his hero only one name) is a fundamentally decent man who nevertheless functions on the fringes of society and can handle himself with equal ease—and insouciance—in the face of underworld kingpins and figures of legitimate wealth and power. His hard-boiled credentials are impeccable: He is tough, courageous, and unshakably resolute in his determination to finish an investigation once it has begun, and he possesses the tongue-in-cheek wit with which hard-boiled heroes are wont to defy authority or defuse tension. A onetime cop who clashed with his superiors, Spenser is by nature a man who chafes at authority and functions best when the only rules governing his behavior are his own.

Spenser's code of ethics is perhaps the central thematic concern of the series, and Parker explores the subject in a variety of ways. The earlier books rely primarily on the character's actions to define his approach to life, while later entries in the series often contain dialogues between Spenser and Susan or Spenser and Hawk which outline the detective's personal code. It is an outlook which can most accurately be described as Hemingwayesque by way of Raymond Chandler's mean streets, drawing as it does on a tradition of masculine behavior that prizes strength, courage, honor, self-possession, and an unassailable belief in the essential correctness of one's convictions. Spenser is a man who could move easily among the heroes of any of Ernest Hemingway's novels, and the books are full of scenes of the detective sizing up other men he meets and finding them worthy of his respect—or his contempt—based on their adherence to similar standards.

This behavior is seen most clearly in Spenser's friendship with Hawk, who proves an invincible and unwaveringly loyal ally despite his own renegade status as what might be termed an independent contractor in Boston's underworld. Untroubled by a conscience, Hawk—unlike Spenser—is capable of murdering an unarmed man, yet their differences are insignificant next to the unstated bond they share as men who have taken each other's measure and found themselves equal in every respect. Despite this bond, however, their friendship remains stereotypically masculine, unencumbered by shared emotional revelations or time spent together outside the framework of a working relationship.

Spenser and Susan discuss the nature of his friendship with Hawk in *Cere-*

*mony* (1982), during their preparations for Thanksgiving dinner. Susan notes, "You trust Hawk with your life or mine. You expect him to risk his life for you—I know you'd risk yours for him—and you don't even know what he does on Thanksgiving." This comment causes Spenser to muse, "I tried to think of the right way to say it. Hawk and I both knew and we knew without having to say it or even think it." This sense of unspoken knowing is crucial to Spenser's code—and from it comes the degree of self-knowledge that makes him able to assess his abilities accurately and trust his judgment absolutely in situations of extreme danger.

The most overt explanation of Spenser's code occurs in *Early Autumn* (1981), in which the detective takes a troubled teenager named Paul Giacomin under his wing and provides the boy with a crash course in acceptable masculine behavior. Much of the book is set in the woods, where Spenser has taken Paul to help him build a cabin over the course of a summer. As the two work together, Spenser places the boy on a regimen of physical conditioning and talks with him openly and at length about the beliefs which govern his own behavior. By the story's close, Paul has become self-reliant and opted for a career as a dancer—but a dancer with the tongue-in-cheek manner of a hard-boiled detective.

Yet Parker has not allowed Spenser to rest comfortably within the traditional limits of the genre. Playing against type, he has given his detective qualities that set him apart from his hard-boiled brethren. Some of these characteristics grow directly out of the genre's conventions while others are unique to Spenser, but all of them serve to add depth and scope to a character who is operating within a style of fiction in which the central figure often remains enigmatic. The result is a well-defined hero whose personality—and personal life—are as important to the novels as the plots themselves.

Chief among Spenser's traits are his physical strength and his ability to best almost any opponent in a fight. Yet Parker does not ask the reader to take this as a given; he provides a rational basis for his character's physical prowess. Spenser was once a boxer, and he both jogs and works out regularly—activities which are frequently chronicled in the books. The inclusion of scenes involving Spenser at the gym or out for an early morning run lends a believability to the character as one sees the effort behind the end result. Other memorable elements in Spenser's personality are his love of literature, music, and good food and his skills as a health-conscious gourmet cook. The contrast which arises from Parker's juxtapositioning of these interests with the brutality and violence of Spenser's line of work is entirely deliberate, precluding as it does any attempt on the reader's part to pigeonhole Spenser based on his profession.

It is in the area of Spenser's emotional life, however, that Parker truly moves beyond the conventions of the hard-boiled genre, developing the detective's relationship with Susan Silverman from book to book as the series progresses. When the two first meet, in *God Save the Child* (1974), the second book in the series, Spenser is also seeing another woman, and his interest remains divided between them until the fourth book, *Promised Land*. Spenser is by nature a loner, and the decision to allow Susan to play a part in his life beyond that of occasional companionship is one which he does not reach easily. The effect this has on his life is summed up by Paul Giacomin, the young boy from *Early Autumn* and the only other close emotional tie in the detective's life. Commiserating with Spenser in *The Widening Gyre* (1983) during a troubled time in Spenser's and Susan's relationship, Paul notes, "What's happened to you is that you've let Susan inside, and you've let me inside. Before us you were invulnerable. You were compassionate but safe. . . ." For Spenser, love is dangerous because it leaves him at risk, with an aspect of his life that is no longer under his control.

When she enters the series, Susan is a high-school guidance counselor, and she soon begins to serve as an intelligent, compassionate sounding board for Spenser as he works through the sometimes complex moral and ethical issues of his work. A crucial turning point in their relationship occurs in *Mortal Stakes* (1975), in which a guilt-stricken Spenser turns to Susan for help after setting up the deaths of two men. His ability to open himself up to her emotionally (with the aid of a bottle of Wild Turkey) and her ability to understand the code by which he lives—although she does not share it herself—mark the beginning of a sense of commitment between the two which will deepen as the series progresses.

Spenser's relationship with Susan also allows Parker to explore the potential conflicts between a traditional hard-boiled hero and a modern, liberated woman. Beginning with *The Widening Gyre*, Susan enters a period of self-analysis which leads her to pull back from the intensity of her relationship with Spenser as she moves from Boston to Washington, D.C., to work on a doctorate in psychology. *Valediction* (1984) finds her accepting a job in San Francisco and informing Spenser that, although she still loves him, she is seeing another man, while *A Catskill Eagle* (1985) brings matters to a crux when Susan begins a dangerous affair with the son of a powerful businessman with underworld ties.

Throughout Susan's period of soul-searching, which she explains to Spenser as a need to define herself apart from her life with him, the detective is forced to abide by the rules which Susan sets for their relationship and to cope with the pain which arises from his prolonged state of emotional limbo. It is an unfamiliar situation for him and one which he endures out of a conviction that his love for Susan matters more to him than a sense of control. In a genre dominated by brief encounters and femmes fatales, Spenser's desire for commitment—despite a brief and tragic affair with a client in *A Savage Place* (1981)—is rare and the time spent by Parker examining the couple's relationship even rarer. Susan is a strong and independent figure within the series, an admirable choice on Parker's part which he temporarily—and surprisingly—abandons in *A Catskill Eagle*. In that novel, Susan's time apart from Spenser proves dangerous, as she becomes unable to break with her lover and must be rescued by Spenser and Hawk. This lapse aside, however, the pair share a loving and supportive relationship marked by bantering wit, strong physical attraction, and occasional professional collaboration. For example, in *Sudden Mischief* (1998), Susan's ex-husband gets into bad-money trouble that drags Susan down with him, and Susan and Spenser confront him and set wrongs to rights together.

The wit and wisecracks in the Spenser novels are not limited to Spenser and Susan's romance—they are a hallmark of Parker's style. The books are written in the first person from Spenser's point of view, and his sense of humor draws on the irreverent wit which has characterized many hard-boiled heroes. It is a quality which Parker utilizes to good effect as Spenser uses irreverent quips to show affection, skewer pomposity, and flaunt his lack of regard for authority. His wisecracks include quotes from song lyrics, literary references, and barbs which often go over the heads of their intended victims.

Parker's writing is also characterized by both crisp narrative scenes and occasionally heavy-handed philosophizing which is as reminiscent of Hemingway as is Spenser's personal code. One of his most effective stylistic devices, however, is his use of extremely detailed descriptions of each character's clothing and appearance and of the meals which Spenser consumes during the course of the books. *Ceremony* contains an entire chapter—though a brief one—devoted solely to a description of Spenser and Susan's Thanksgiving together, beginning with their glasses of freshly squeezed orange juice in the morning and ending with both characters dozing in front of the television following after-dinner coffee and Grand Marnier. The action of the plot stops for the course of the chapter, but the description adds immeasurably to the color and flavor of the novel. Glimpses such as these into Spenser's private life and personal code make Parker's detective hero memorable and help place Parker among the ranks of the best and most popular writers in the genre.

Parker struck out in new directions in the late 1990's with the publication of *Night Passage* (1997), featuring homicide detective Jesse Stone, and with *Family Honor* (1999), featuring a young female private eye, Sunny Randall. Stone has been a cop in Los Angeles married to an aspiring actress, but when he catches her in bed with a film producer, he turns to alcohol for solace. As *Night Passage* opens, Stone accepts a job as chief of police in a Boston suburb where, he learns, the mayor was hoping precisely for an alcoholic cop who would not be too observant.

Parker told an interviewer he decided to write a series in third-person point of view "and which would feature a character who was a bit younger than Spenser and who was not quite so Spenser-like." There are resemblances, however. Stone is strong, attractive to women, and capable of the well-timed wisecrack, but he is the silent type, his romantic entanglements are more complex, and his drinking problem hinders his desire to be a good cop doing the right thing. The wealthy coast-town setting provides a tasty new atmosphere for Parker's brand of satire.

Sunny Randall is also tough, like Spenser, but not averse to the occasional dig at the stereotypical private eye. When asked by the runaway teenager whom she was hired to find, "You're a girl like me, for crissake, what are you going to do?," Sunny replies, "It would be nice if I weighed two hundred pounds and used to be a boxer. But I'm not, so we find other ways." Parker created the character of Sunny for actress Helen Hunt to star in film adaptations of his novels. The Sunny Randall books were instantly popular, perhaps more so than the Stone books, which are more serious in tone.

Parker has earned his sobriquet "the dean of American crime fiction" and is deservedly ranked with the triumvirate of Dashiell Hammett, Raymond Chandler, and Ross MacDonald.

### Principal mystery and detective fiction

SERIES: Spenser: *Surrogate*, 1982; *The Godwulf Manuscript*, 1973; *God Save the Child*, 1974; *Mortal Stakes*, 1975; *Promised Land*, 1976; *The Judas Goat*, 1978; *Looking for Rachel Wallace*, 1980; *Early Autumn*, 1981; *A Savage Place*, 1981; *Ceremony*, 1982; *The Widening Gyre*, 1983; *Valediction*, 1984; *A Catskill Eagle*, 1985; *Taming a Sea-Horse*, 1986; *Pale Kings and Princes*, 1987; *Crimson Joy*, 1988; *Playmates*, 1989; *Stardust*, 1990; *Pastime*, 1991; *Double Deuce*, 1992; *Paper Doll*, 1993; *Walking Shadow*, 1994; *Thin Air*, 1995; *Chance*, 1996; *Small Vices*, 1997; *Sudden Mischief*, 1998; *Hush Money*, 1999; *Hugger Mugger*, 2000; Potshot, 2001. Jesse Stone: *Night Passage*, 1997; *Trouble in Paradise*, 1998. Sunny Randall: *Family Honor*, 1999; *Perish Twice*, 2000; *Gunman's Rhapsody*, 2001.

### Other major works

NOVELS: *Three Weeks in Spring*, 1978 (with Joan Parker); *Wilderness*, 1979; *Love and Glory*, 1983; *Poodle Springs*, 1989 (with Raymond Chandler); *Perchance to Dream*, 1991; *All Our Yesterdays*, 1994; *Three Weeks in Spring*, 1978 (with Joan Parker); *The Private Eye in Hammett and Chandler*, 1984; *Parker on Writing*, 1985; *A Year at the Races*, 1990 (with Joan H. Parker); *Spenser's Boston*, 1994 (with Kasho Kamugai); *Boston: History in the Making*, 1999.

NONFICTION: *Sports Illustrated Training with Weights*, 1973 (with John R. Marsh).

EDITED TEXTS: *The Personal Response to Literature*, 1970 (with others); *Order and Diversity: The Craft of Prose*, 1973 (with Peter L. Sandberg); *The Best American Mystery Stories*, 1997.

### Bibliography
Carter, Steven R. "Spenser Ethics: The Unconventional Morality of Robert B. Parker's Traditional American Hero." *Clues: A Journal of Detection* 1 (Fall/Winter, 1980): 109-118.

Donovan, M. "Robert Parker Brings a Soft Touch to the Hard-boiled School of Mystery Writing." *People Weekly* 21 (May 7, 1984): 58.

*Newsweek.* Review of *Taming a Sea-Horse*, by Robert B. Parker. 108 (July 7, 1986): 60.

Parker, Robert B. and Anne Ponder. "What I Know About Writing Spenser Novels." In *Colloquium on Crime: Eleven Renowned Mystery Writers Discuss Their Work*, edited by Robin W. Winks. New York: Scribner, 1986.

"Parker, Robert." In *Mystery and Suspense Writers: The Literature of Crime, Detection, and Espionage*, edited by Robin W. Winks and Maureen Corrigan. New York: Charles Scribner's Sons, 1998.

Tallett, Dennis. *The Spenser Companion*. Santa Barbara, Calif.: Companion Books, 1997.

Wright, S. "Robert Parker: We Weren't Blessed with an Ideal Close Relationship: We Earned It." *Vogue* 177 (December, 1987): 176.

*Janet E. Lorenz*
*Updated by Fiona Kelleghan*

# Elizabeth Peters

## Barbara Mertz

**Born:** Canton, Illinois; September 29, 1927

**Also wrote as** • Barbara Michaels

**Type of plot** • Amateur sleuth

**Principal series** • Jacqueline Kirby, 1972-    • Vicky Bliss, 1973-    • Amelia Peabody Emerson, 1975-    .

**Principal series characters** • JACQUELINE KIRBY, an attractive, middle-aged librarian with grown children. With her glasses sliding down her nose and her copper-colored tresses falling down in moments of excitement, she uses her sharp brain and lethal handbag in solving mysteries. She enters each story with some academic swain but leaves with another man, usually the cop.
• VICKY BLISS, a tall, blonde art historian with a keen sense of humor and a healthy interest in men. Drawn into mysteries by her work at a Munich museum, she solves them with intelligence, low cunning, and breaking and entering, rescuing herself and often the hero.
• SIR JOHN SMYTHE is the *nom de guerre* of Vicky's lover, an English art thief of good family. He claims to be a coward but comes through when needed. He disappears at the end of every mystery, only to embroil Vicky in another scam in the next.
• HERR PROFESSOR DOKTOR SCHMIDT is the rotund, romantic head of the Munich museum.
• AMELIA PEABODY EMERSON, an independent, independently wealthy, Victorian Englishwoman. When traveling to Egypt, she falls in love with the country, pyramids, and Egyptologist RADCLIFFE EMERSON. She marries Emerson. Armed with an irrepressible faith in her medical and detective abilities (as well as a steel-shanked parasol and a pistol), she manages everyone and everything. A feminist but passionately fond of her husband and sensible of her son's shortcomings, she comments acerbically on Victorian mores and solves mysteries by leaping to conclusions based on intuition, blithely changing her theories as they become untenable.

**Contribution** • Elizabeth Peters rescues the detective story heroine from the awful fate of being dowdy, a victim, or a twit. The heroines of her suspense-romances are beautiful, intelligent, independent women who easily attract men, but they solve their mysteries with their own intelligence. In a *Library Journal*

502

interview in 1992, Peters explained, "I like to write about ordinary women who are faced with a situation where they have to show gumption, courage, and wit."

In her series characters, Peters has created three different, autonomous heroines whose worth, and self-worth, do not depend on the possession of a male. At one end of the spectrum there is Jacqueline Kirby, who is totally autonomous and takes her love where she finds it, without apology. At the other end is Amelia Peabody Emerson, whose husband regards her as his equal, while the reader and Amelia know that she is his superior. The intermediate stage is occupied by Vicky Bliss, for whom Peters has invented Sir John Smythe, a delightful but unsuitable lover who disappears at the end of each book, thus relieving Vicky of the responsibilities of marriage and leaving her free to play the field.

**Biography** • Elizabeth Peters was born Barbara Gross on September 29, 1927, in Canton, Illinois, the daughter of Earl and Grace (Tregellas) Gross. She attended the Oriental Institute of the University of Chicago, where she studied Egyptology. Peters received a Ph.B. in 1947 and an M.A. in 1950, the same year she married Richard R. Mertz. She completed her Ph.D. in 1952 with a dissertation titled "Certain Titles of the Egyptian Queens and Their Bearing on the Hereditary Right to the Throne."

Following a pattern typical of her generation, Peters worked after marriage as a typist and secretary before having a baby. She followed her husband to various cities in the United States and abroad, cities which she would later use as settings in her fiction both as Elizabeth Peters and as Barbara Michaels, a pseudonym under which she has written gothic romances.

Under her own name, Peters published two popular books about Egypt, one in 1964 and another in 1966; her first Barbara Michaels book was published in 1966. When her editor suggested that she write more lighthearted books about modern heroines using exotic locales, she borrowed the names of her two children, Elizabeth and Peter, to form her new pseudonym, Elizabeth Peters. A true storyteller, she has produced at least two books per year and, in 1985, four. Peters was divorced in 1969. Her two-hundred-year-old stone house outside Frederick, Maryland, reportedly houses cats, dogs, antiques, and a ghost.

A former president of the American Crime Writers League, Peters was a member of the editorial board of *The Writer*, the editorial advisory board of *KMT, A Modern Journal of Ancient Egypt*, and the board of governors of the American Research Center in Egypt as of 2001. In 1989, Hood College named her an honorary Doctor of Human Letters. In 1990, she won the Agatha for best novel for *Naked Once More*, and in 1998 the Mystery Writers of America named her a Grand Master.

**Analysis** • By the time Barbara Mertz began writing as Elizabeth Peters, her talents as a spinner of romances were already well developed. Writing her dissertation had taught her to handle a long manuscript. In the late 1950's, she and her husband, Richard Mertz, collaborated on several thrillers; although these early works were never published, they served as an apprenticeship in form, plotting, and character development. Her first published novel was *The Master of Black Tower* (1966), a gothic romance.

Soon afterward her editor suggested that she write the contemporary romances she later published under the pseudonym Elizabeth Peters. In these books she has successfully managed the transition to a lighter style while retaining her mastery of the romance, manipulating and expanding the form but retaining its major elements and adapting them to modern settings.

Peters believes that the "softer" mysteries written from a female point of view are as valid as the more violent thrillers written from a male point of view. Among the universal fictional themes of money, power, and love, Peters, like most women, lists love first, but as a scholar she places truth before all else, so a major theme in her books is the conflict between faith/superstition and reason, with reason winning every time. Despite their comic elements, both Amelia Peabody and her husband Emerson (they first appear in *Crocodile on the Sandbank*, 1975) are true turn-of-the-century logical positivists in their rational, secular, scientific mind-set. Emerson is violently anticlerical and democratic, and Amelia, while firmly believing that if He exists, God is an Englishman, is nevertheless a feminist and an egalitarian, believing

squarely in the value of education as a means of producing a new and better society. Emerson's violent strictures on archaeological method show the scientific mind at work bringing order and method to this new field, and his slanderous comments on his colleagues reflect accurately relations between early (and present-day) Egyptologists.

Indeed, Peters did more than draw upon her archaeological knowledge to create this, her most popular series. Though wholly her own, with complex personalities, Peters's characters are loosely based on historical figures. Radcliffe Emerson is similar in many ways to the early Egyptologist William Flinders Petrie-both are handsome, dark-haired and bearded, with amazing energy, competitive spirits, quick tempers, and apt appellations bestowed by Egyptian workmen: "Father of Curses" for Emerson, "Father of Pots" for Petrie.

Amelia has a namesake in Amelia B. Edwards, a Victorian woman who wrote the travel diary *A Thousand Miles Up the Nile*. She lends Amelia Peabody her taste for adventure and her eccentricity, as well as the nickname of one of Edwards's friends, "Sitt Hakim," or "Lady Doctor." Another of Amelia's spiritual forebears is Lady Hilda Petrie, wife of Sir Flinders. Hilda was also a scholar who enjoyed the archaeological life and was, like Amelia, unstoppable in her investigations. Actual historical figures make brief appearances throughout the series, lending verisimilitude–a few of these are E. A. Wallis Budge, the keeper of the Egyptian collection at the British Museum and Emerson's professional rival, and James E. Quibell, who requests medicine for Petrie's party during a documented historical occurrence. The excavation sites and travel routes are so well detailed that Amelia's adventures may be followed on a map or excavation guide. Finally, Amelia's voice and writing style are a perfect match for the journals, diaries, and letters of Victorian women travelers, with the original historical spellings of Arab and Egyptian names intact.

Between 1972 and 1975, Peters established three series characters through which she could explore a second theme, that of the autonomous female character, a woman whose happiness is not dependent on capturing a man. With the characters of Jacqueline Kirby, Vicky Bliss, and Amelia Peabody Emerson, Peters has developed three variants of the independent woman, at the same time ringing changes on the romance form by creating heroines for whom marriage and monogamy are not life's most important issues. At the same time, she avoids the rape solution common to romances, in which the strong-minded heroine is overcome by superior force.

All Peters's heroines are committed to some abstract value, whether it be truth, scholarly integrity, or Jacqueline Kirby's simple belief that murder is wrong. That is why her heroines, even the least experienced, must solve the problem which the book presents, no matter what the danger.

University librarian Jacqueline Kirby, who first appears in *The Seventh Sinner* (1972), is decidedly independent. A mature woman with two children in their early twenties, she makes no mention of the children's father. During the course of the series she exhibits several personas. As the stereotypical librarian, with her long copper hair snatched back in a tight bun and a pair of glasses perched precariously on her nose, she is the complete professional; with her hair flowing down her back and her voluptuous body clad in an emerald silk pants suit, flirting with some suave man old enough to be a suitable target, she is a satirical version of the Total Woman.

Kirby's sharp mind is furnished with a mixed bag of information which she uses to unravel the mystery, elucidating it in the library at the end of the book. Her trademark is a large handbag containing a faintly satirical variety of useful objects. The purse itself often comes in handy as a weapon. Another constant is that she enters the action with an academic swain but leaves the party

with a debonair cop, proving herself to be not only autonomous but also as attractive to men of action as she is to men of intellect.

Kirby is not only independent, indeed she is cynical and hard-nosed, willingly placing herself and others in jeopardy to solve the mystery. In her, Peters has developed a woman with a tough mind and high standards who is,
nevertheless, extremely sexy. Peters uses the series to criticize the classical
mystery form; more specifically, in *The Murders of Richard III* (1974), she draws
on her knowledge of Ricardian scholarship to provide a corrective to Josephine Tey's uncritical *The Daughter of Time* (1951).

Peters's second autonomous heroine, Vicky Bliss, is an art historian with
long blonde hair and a magnificent figure; she is sexually active but not interested in marriage. In fact, like most attractive professional women, she finds
men drawn to her for all the wrong reasons. Intelligent and active, she is not
above breaking and entering in pursuit of the solution to the mystery, which
she explains in classic fashion in the last chapters.

What is unique to the Bliss series is the slim, blond, English jewel thief and
confidence man Sir John Smythe, who first appears in *Street of the Five Moons*
(1978). Smythe commonly avoids violence by withdrawing from the action,
but when Vicky is involved, he cannot choose that option but must stand and
fight. In an inversion of the typical romance plot, Bliss usually rescues Sir
John as they solve the mystery. After several romantic interludes—Smythe is
an accomplished lover—he disappears, leaving Vicky holding the bag, only to
appear in the next book, to her mingled delight and disgust. The love-hate relationship between the two adds tension and spice to the plots.

In Smythe, Peters has developed the perfect foil and demon lover for an autonomous woman. His disappearance relieves Bliss of the necessity of facing
the two-career problem, and since his occupation violates everything for
which she stands, the reader knows that if the two are ever to marry, it will be
Sir John who must give up his life and adjust to Vicky, and not the reverse.

Peters develops her final variation of the autonomous female character in
Amelia Peabody in *Crocodile on the Sandbank.* This series, unlike the others, is
written in the august and convoluted prose common to Victorian novels and
is at once a crashingly good high romance and a satire so delicious that large
portions of it beg to be read aloud.

In *Crocodile on the Sandbank*, Peters uses stock characters such as the Plain
Jane, the Innocent Heiress, the Irascible Grandfather, the Wicked Cousin, the
Faithless Lover, the Poor-But-Honest Hero, and the Bad-Tempered-But-Lov-
able Older Man and stock situations such as the midnight elopement and the
missing will, but she infuses new vitality and a large dose of humor into a plot
that is as old as the Egyptian tombs in which it is set. With wicked wit, Peters
brings her fast-paced novel crashing to a highly satisfying conclusion: the unmasking of the wicked and married bliss for both pairs of lovers.

The arrival of a son in *The Curse of the Pharaohs* (1981) completes the Emerson family. Walter Peabody Emerson, called "Ramses" because of the resemblance of his profile to that pharaoh's, is the perfect academic offspring—"cata-

strophically precocious," long-winded, and nearly always right. Amelia sees Ramses through the unsentimental eye with which she views the universe, recognizing his strengths (he is very bright and always obedient) and weaknesses (he would get dirty in a vacuum and has a fine Jesuitical mind which allows him to escape parental prohibitions). She addresses him as if he were an adult. Ramses allows Peters to comment acerbically on children and domesticity.

Amelia is not only the central character; indeed, she is, like most wives, the engine that makes everything work. While she loves her husband and son passionately, she sees them with a clear eye and manages them firmly, Emerson with sex and Ramses with direct orders. She also manages everything else. Her excursions into detecting lead the couple into deadly peril, from which Ramses has lately taken to rescuing them, once from being immured in a flooded tomb (*The Mummy Case*, 1985) and once from a cellar in the decaying castle of a depraved aristocrat (*The Deeds of the Disturber*, 1988).

Using the style and plot devices of the gothic romance in this series, Peters combines the theme of marriage between a man and a woman who are equals in every way with an investigation into the conflict between faith and reason in which the ghosts and walking mummies are explained rationally as the concoctions of the villains.

Although Peters bowed to her publisher's requests for more "sensational" titles for several of the earlier Amelia Peabody Emerson books (*The Curse of the Pharaohs* and *The Mummy Case*), the series later followed her original artistic intent of using lines from Egyptian literature that have symbolic significance for the story at hand. The titles thus add a further element to the mystery, as readers seek the source of the quote and consider its relevance.

Peters's heroines can be divided into two types. The first is an inexperienced young woman, often a student, who makes errors of judgment which lead her into danger. Using her intelligence and rising above her fear, she solves the puzzle and wins love, but she is often helped by the hero and sometimes gives up her work to join in his. With a bit more experience, she will grow into the second type, that of the mature, independent women, such as Jacqueline Kirby, Vicky Bliss, and Amelia Peabody, who go willingly into danger in pursuit of a solution to the puzzle.

The other females in Peters's books are more typical romance characters. More alluring or more sophisticated, although less intelligent, than the heroines, they use their appeal to captivate the male characters. Their suggestive walks and tight clothing show them to be no ladies, and they may develop into villains.

Her male characters are less fully characterized than the women and also fall into romance categories. There are always at least two men competing for the heroine's attention, and the man who seems to be the hero, often a slim but strong blond, usually turns out to be the villain, while the almost ugly man, who behaves suspiciously for two hundred pages, turns into both hero and true love during the action that ends the story. While the men are not exactly stick characters, they are less fully realized than either the good or the bad women.

Because Peters's main themes have to do with the individual struggle for self-definition and love, she focuses her plots on matters of private rather than public morality. She uses her historical training to create realistic plots that involve genuine historical problems or artifacts. For added romance, she locates the stories in glamorous foreign cities or at archaeological sites and exploits her special knowledge to provide verisimilitude in the story line. In *The Jackal's Head* (1968), model Althea Tomlinson discovers the secret of her father's death as well as the lost tomb of Nefertiti in Egypt. Undergraduate Carol Farley journeys to Mexico and falls in love with pyramids while searching for her runaway father and helping to break a drug ring in *The Night of Four Hundred Rabbits* (1971). D. J. Abbott, a graduate student in anthropology, discovers human remains along with mammoth bones in Arizona in *Summer of the Dragon* (1979). Vicky Bliss pursues the Schliemann treasure in Bavaria in *Trojan Gold* (1987), a pre-Viking chalice in Sweden in *Silhouette in Scarlet* (1983), and an art forgery ring in Rome in *Street of the Five Moons*.

While the Jacqueline Kirby books are more classically plotted mysteries, their plots still revolve around private vices and satirize petty human pretensions. *The Murders of Richard III* makes fun of the antiquarian defenders of Richard, *Die for Love* (1984) mocks a convention of romance writers in New York, and in *The Seventh Sinner* plagiarism motivates murder in a Roman art institute.

Peters sees the exotic locales and sophisticated people in her stories through mildly Puritan and very American eyes. The foreign city is a place of excitement, danger, and decadence, where the heroine must fight to protect her values and virtue. People of wealth or good family who do not also work for a living are soft and corrupt. The villain is often a suave and superficially attractive aristocrat, while the hero is a hard-working American who is knowledgeable but uncorrupted by foreign ways.

Peters's heroines, however, are not Puritans. They regard sex as a normal human instinct and enjoy it, or expect to enjoy it. Love is distinguished from sex and is an irrational but pleasant state achieved only with the right man. Its arrival is sudden, unbidden, and final. Jacqueline Kirby's rejection of love's final solution to her problems and Vicky Bliss's half love for her disappearing jewel thief do not invalidate this generalization but point up the independence of the two women and keep the reader turning the pages to find out whether this time it will be different. If it is, it will be the men who change, and the characters will be promoted to the bliss of an equal relationship like that enjoyed by the Emersons.

Peters has frequently commented in articles and interviews about her series characters. While some mystery authors have found series characters limiting, Peters sees the special requirements of a series character as both challenging and, in some ways, freeing. The challenge comes from the need to reintroduce the characters each time without boring continuing readers, as well as having to discard otherwise worthwhile plots that are not right for a particular character. Peters has solved the latter problem by alternating work among three different series and her non-series fiction as Barbara Michaels. The rewards for Peters are worth the effort: Within a series, characters can truly grow and develop, providing greater interest for readers and an opportunity for ongoing craftsmanship for the author.

Peters's style is light and breezy. Her heroines, even the youngest, have a humorous attitude toward the world and have, or gain, a wry self-knowledge. Her more mature heroines have a sharp eye for hypocrisy and a cynical wit that makes the exposition and the dialogue crackle. With all of its violence and corruption, Peters's world is an essentially rational and happy one in which the evildoer has produced an imbalance. Her heroines use their intelligence and courage to correct that imbalance and live happily ever after.

## Principal mystery and detective fiction

SERIES: Vicky Bliss: *Borrower of the Night*, 1973; *Street of the Five Moons*, 1978; *Silhouette in Scarlet*, 1983; *Trojan Gold*, 1987; *Night Train to Memphis*, 1994. Amelia Peabody Emerson: *Crocodile on the Sandbank*, 1975; *The Curse of the Pharaohs*, 1981; *The Mummy Case*, 1985; *Lion in the Valley*, 1986; *The Deeds of the Disturber*, 1988 *The Last Camel Died at Noon*, 1991; *The Snake, the Crocodile, and the Dog*, 1992; *The Hippopotamus Pool*, 1996; *Seeing a Large Cat*, 1997; *The Ape Who Guards the Balance*, 1998; *The Falcon at the Portal*, 1999; *He Shall Thunder in the Sky*, 2000; *Lord of the Silent*, 2001. Jacqueline Kirby: *The Seventh Sinner*, 1972; *The Murders of Richard III*, 1974; *Die for Love*, 1984; *Naked Once More*, 1989.

OTHER NOVELS: *The Jackal's Head*, 1968; *The Camelot Caper*, 1969; *The Dead Sea Cipher*, 1970; *The Night of Four Hundred Rabbits*, 1971 (also as *Shadows in the Moonlight*); *Legend in Green Velvet*, 1976 (also as *Ghost in Green Velvet*); *Devil-May-Care*, 1977; *Summer of the Dragon*, 1979; *The Love Talker*, 1980; *The Copenhagen Connection*, 1982.

## Other major works

NOVELS: *The Master of Black Tower*, 1966; *Sons of the Wolf*, 1967 (also as *Mystery on the Moors*); *Ammie, Come Home*, 1968; *Prince of Darkness*, 1969; *The Dark on the Other Side*, 1970; *The Crying Child*, 1971; *Greygallows*, 1972; *Witch*, 1973; *House of Many Shadows*, 1974; *The Sea King's Daughter*, 1975; *Patriot's Dream*, 1976; *Wings of the Falcon*, 1977; *Wait for What Will Come*, 1978; *The Walker in Shadows*, 1979; *The Wizard's Daughter*, 1980; *Someone in the House*, 1981; *Black Rainbow*, 1982; *Here I Stay*, 1983; *The Grey Beginning*, 1984; *Be Buried in the Rain*, 1985; *Shattered Silk*, 1986; *Search the Shadows*, 1987; *Smoke and Mirrors*, 1989; *Into the Darkness*, 1990; *Vanish with the Rose*, 1992; *Houses of Stone*, 1993; *Stitches in Time*, 1995; *Other Worlds*, 1999.

NONFICTION: *Temples, Tombs, and Hieroglyphs: The Story of Egyptology*, 1964, revised 1978 and 1990 (as *Temples, Tombs, and Hieroglyphs: A Popular History of Ancient Egypt*); *Red Land, Black Land: The World of the Ancient Egyptians*, 1966, revised 1978; *Two Thousand Years in Rome*, 1968 (with Richard Mertz).

EDITED TEXT: *Elizabeth Peters Presents Malice Domestic: An Anthology of Original Traditional Mystery Stories*, 1992 (with Martin H. Greenberg).

## Bibliography

Grape, Jan, and Dean James. *Deadly Women*. New York: Carroll & Graf, 1998.

*Library Journal*. Review of *The Deeds of the Disturber*, by Elizabeth Peters. 108 (May 1, 1988): 94.

_____. Review of *Trojan Gold*, by Elizabeth Peters. 112 (April 1, 1987): 166.

Peters, Elizabeth. Interview. *The Writer* 98 (September, 1985): 9.

Peters, Elizabeth. "Series Characters: Love 'em or Leave 'em." *The Writer* 107, no. 4 (April, 1994): 9-13.

*Publishers Weekly*. Review of *The Mummy Case*, by Elizabeth Peters. 227 (January 18, 1985): 64.

Smith, Linell. "Don't Call Her 'Prolific,'" *Baltimore Sun*, April 29, 1998, p. 1E.

*Marilynn M. Larew*
*Updated by C. A. Gardner*

# Ellis Peters

## Edith Mary Pargeter

**Born:** Horsehay, Shropshire, England; September 28, 1913
**Died:** Shropshire, England; October 14, 1995

**Types of plot** • Amateur sleuth • historical • police procedural • thriller

**Principal series** • Felse family, 1951-1978 • Brother Cadfael, 1977-1995.

**Principal series characters** • GEORGE FELSE, Detective Sergeant and later Detective Chief Inspector of the Criminal Investigation Department (C.I.D.) in Comerford, a provincial town in central England. Felse is a highly professional and honest police officer. A middle-aged family man, Felse is deeply in love with his wife and devoted to their son. He is dependable, mature, understanding, and reasonable.
• BERNARDA (BUNTY) ELLIOT FELSE, the wife of George Felse. A concert contralto before she married George, Bunty is a loyal and devoted wife and mother. Intelligent, sensitive, and thoughtful, she proves to be shrewd and fearless when she accidentally becomes involved in detection.
• DOMINIC FELSE, the son of George and Bunty Felse. Dominic matures in the course of the series from a thirteen-year-old boy who discovers the corpse in his father's first murder case to a young University of Oxford graduate. Engaging, adventurous, and aware, Dominic figures directly as an amateur detective in several of the novels, and peripherally in the others.
• BROTHER CADFAEL, a twelfth century Benedictine monk. A Welshman in his early sixties, Cadfael fought in the Crusades and had several amatory adventures as a young man before retiring to Shrewsbury Abbey. His youthful experiences gave him an understanding of human nature, and his present work as gardener and medicinal herbalist figures in his detection of criminals.
• PRIOR ROBERT, a monk of Shrewsbury Abbey. Around fifty years of age, he is handsome, aristocratic, authoritative, and ambitious. His scheming for power in the abbey sets him at odds with Brother Cadfael and makes him that character's principal foil.
• HUGH BERINGAR, Sheriff of Shrewsbury. A bold and keenly intelligent man in his early twenties, he is the friend and principal secular ally of Brother Cadfael and aids him in solving several of his cases.

**Contribution** • Ellis Peters's Felse family series and her chronicles of Brother Cadfael are in the British tradition of detective fiction writers such as P. D. James and Ruth Rendell. These writers' works, while displaying the careful and suspenseful plotting characteristic of the detective genre, frequently transcend the effect of pure entertainment and share with the traditional "literary" novel the aims of engaging in complex examinations of human character and psychology and achieving thematic depth and moral vision.

Peters herself expressed her dislike for the distinction between detective fiction and serious novels and succeeded in interweaving traditional novelistic materials—love interests, the study of human growth and maturation, the depiction of communities and their politics—with the activity of crime solving. The Brother Cadfael chronicles are her most popular as well as her most impressive achievement, locating universal human situations in the meticulously particularized context of twelfth century England. These novels are masterpieces of historical reconstruction; they present a memorable and likable hero, Brother Cadfael, and a vivid picture of medieval life, in and out of the monastery, in its religious, familial, social, political, and cultural dimensions.

**Biography** • Ellis Peters was born Edith Mary Pargeter on September 28, 1913, in Horsehay, Shropshire, England, the daughter of Edmund Valentine Pargeter and Edith Hordley Pargeter. ("Ellis Peters" is a pen name which she adopted in 1959 after having published numerous books; she used it exclusively as a writer of detective fiction.) She attended Dawley Church of England Elementary School in Shropshire and Coalbrookdale High School for Girls, and earned an Oxford School Certificate. She worked as a pharmacist's assistant and dispenser in Dawley from 1933 to 1940. During this time, she also began writing novels on a wide range of historical and contemporary subjects; the first was *Hortensius, Friend of Nero* (1936). From 1940 to 1945, she served as a petty officer in the Women's Royal Naval Service, receiving the British Empire Medal in 1944. During World War II she developed an interest in Czechoslovakia because she was haunted by the Western powers' betrayal of that country at Munich. After the war, she translated many volumes of prose and poetry from the Czech and Slovak and continued writing her own fiction.

Her first detective novel, which she published as Edith Pargeter in 1951, was *Fallen into the Pit*. It initiated a series of thirteen novels featuring the Felse family, a series which continued until 1978. Peters wrote five other detective novels and numerous detective short stories during this period as well. Her interests in music, theater, and art are reflected in several of these works. In 1977, she began publishing the Brother Cadfael novels.

As both Edith Pargeter and Ellis Peters, this writer received much recognition for her work, including the Mystery Writers of America Edgar Allan Poe Award in 1962 for *Death and the Joyful Woman* (1961), which was cited as the best mystery novel of the year; the Czechoslovak Society for International Relations Gold Medal in 1968; and the Crime Writers' Association Silver Dagger in 1981 for *Monk's-Hood* (1980). Edith Mary Pargeter died on October 14, 1995.

**Analysis** • Ellis Peters came to detective fiction after many years of novel writing. Disliking the frequently made distinction between detective novels, or "thrillers," as she calls them, and serious novels, she stresses that "the thriller *is a novel.* . . . The pure puzzle, with a cast of characters kept deliberately two-dimensional and all equally expendable at the end, has no attraction for me." Her detective novels bear witness both to her life experiences and to her statements about her art.

Peters is essentially a social novelist. Murder serves as her occasion to dramatize a wide variety of human interactions and motivations in settings that are vividly realized. One might think of an Ellis Peters mystery in terms of a set of concentric circles. At the center is the detective character, usually preoccupied at the beginning of the novel with something other than crime. Frequently, he or she is an amateur who assumes the role of detective only circumstantially. The amateur status of several of her detectives allows Peters to move the narrative comfortably beyond crime into other areas such as love relationships, family interactions, and the struggles of adolescents maturing toward self-discovery. Except for *Death Mask* (1959), Peters's detective novels are always narrated from a third-person point of view through an anonymous persona. Peters is able to narrow or broaden her perspective with ease, and therefore to present the inner workings of her central characters' minds and to focus on external matters—landscapes, social or historical background, local customs—with equal skill.

The central character is generally carefully placed within the circle of a close family or community that is described in depth. The earlier mysteries often focus on C.I.D. Detective Sergeant George Felse of Comerford, his wife, Bunty, and their son Dominic. Although George and Dominic are the most actively involved in detection, Bunty too becomes accidentally involved in solving a murder in *The Grass-Widow's Tale* (1968). Peters's later series places its central character, Brother Cadfael, within the twelfth century Benedictine community of monks at the Abbey of St. Peter and St. Paul in Shrewsbury, England. Although the Felse family series ranges in locale from central England to such places as the Cornish coast, Scotland, Czechoslovakia, Austria, and India, the Brother Cadfael novels usually stay within the vicinity of Shrewsbury, allowing Peters to develop her picture of medieval life in great depth.

Beyond these family and community circles, there are larger milieus. For the Felse family, these include a variety of worlds—for example, those of concert musicians, of diplomats, and of professional thieves. Brother Cadfael and his fellow monks live in the Shropshire of the late 1130's and earlier 1140's and frequently find themselves caught in the political strife between Empress Maud and her cousin King Stephen, who contend for the British crown. At other times, the political feuds are more local if not less complex and bitter.

Typically, Peters's detective novels begin at a fairly leisurely pace. In *The Grass-Widow's Tale,* for example, Bunty Felse at the outset is frustrated by the fact that her husband and son are going to be absent on her forty-first birthday, doubtful about her identity and accomplishments, and gloomily pondering "age, infirmity, and death." The plot of this novel takes many surprising twists and turns before focusing upon the solution of a murder and robbery case, a

case which becomes the occasion for Bunty to find renewed meaning in her life and to discover some precious truths about the nature of human love. In *A Morbid Taste for Bones: A Mediaeval Whodunnit* (1977), the first chronicle of Brother Cadfael, Peters begins with the background for the Shrewsbury monks' mission to Wales to obtain the bones of Saint Winifred and proceeds to dramatize the initial results of that mission and to establish the novel's major characters and subplots. It is only on page ninety-one of this 256-page novel that a murder case surfaces.

Once the scenes have been set and the characters established, Peters's detective novels become absorbingly suspenseful and often contain exciting action scenes. *The Grass-Widow's Tale* includes a terrifying episode in which Bunty and her companion, Luke, must fight their way out of a cottage in which they are being held by a gang of ruthless professional criminals who are planning to murder them. *Saint Peter's Fair* (1981), one of the most suspenseful of the Brother Cadfael chronicles, features a remarkable chase-and-rescue sequence.

A highly skillful creator of suspense, Peters proves to be at least as gifted as a student of human character. She has explained her interest in crime novels thus:

> The paradoxical puzzle, the impossible struggle to create a cast of genuine, rounded, knowable characters caught in conditions of stress, to let readers know everything about them, feel with them, like or dislike them, and still to try to preserve to the end the secret of which of these is a murderer—this is the attraction for me.

The most successfully realized of Peters's characters is Brother Cadfael, who combines worldly wisdom and experience with moral and spiritual insight. He is a middle-aged man who entered monastic life after fighting for many years in the Crusades. His experiences and travels to such places as Venice, Cyprus, and the Holy Land afforded him a knowledge of human nature unusual in a monk and developed in him courage and a liking for adventure. He came to know not only the ways of men but also those of women; he has been a lover as well as a warrior, and he readily acknowledges that he committed a fair share of "mischief" as a younger man.

This "mischief" is to be distinguished, however, from evil. Brother Cadfael is essentially a good man. It was the desire to develop his spiritual side that led him to retire to the Benedictine abbey at Shrewsbury, where he has been living as a monk for fifteen years when the chronicles begin.

Cadfael's experiences of a life of action set him apart from most of the other monks; his experiences as a monk, in turn, set him apart from people living a worldly life. Even his birthplace sets him apart: He is a Welshman in an English monastery. Like many other famous detective heroes, Cadfael is unique in his milieu, a more complete person than his contemporaries. As a man of action, moreover, he shares the abilities, though never the ruthlessness, of hard-boiled detectives, while as a participant in the contemplative life, he bears some resemblance to armchair detectives.

At the abbey, Brother Cadfael is in charge of a flourishing garden. He specializes in herbs used for seasoning and medicine. Some of these herbs can be dangerous, and, to Cadfael's horror, malefactors sometimes steal them from the garden to use them as poisons. Cadfael becomes involved in several of his cases through such circumstances. In *Monk's-Hood*, for example, he commits himself to solve the murder of Master Bonel, who died after being served a dinner sent from the monastery. The dish proved to be laced with liniment prepared by Cadfael himself and containing monkshood (wolfsbane), a deadly poison.

Cadfael's garden is a living symbol of the hero himself as well as of the human world around him. Growth takes place there, as it does in human life, growth of things either healthful and nourishing or harmful. Just as Brother Cadfael cultivates, nurtures, and controls his plants, so too does he foster the proper kinds of growth in his community. In a number of the chronicles, Cadfael has a young assistant, a novice monk whom he lovingly guides toward psychological and spiritual maturity. Sometimes this guidance takes the form of transplanting. In *A Morbid Taste for Bones*, Cadfael recognizes that Brother John lacks a vocation for the monastery and eventually helps him to begin a new life with the woman with whom he falls in love in Wales. In *The Devil's Novice* (1983), Cadfael obtains justice for Brother Meriet, a "green boy" who has been banished to the monastery for a crime he did not commit. Cadfael's detective activities extend the gardening metaphor further—he weeds out undesirable elements in his community and distinguishes the poisonous from the harmless. Cadfael's herbs are most beneficial as medicinal aids, and he himself is, ultimately, not merely an amateur detective but also a healer of physical, moral, and spiritual maladies.

In his role as healer, Brother Cadfael exemplifies Peters's principal concerns as a novelist. She has commented, "It is probably true that I am not very good at villains. The good interest me so much more." Her villains are typically motivated by ambition or greed, dehumanizing vices that lead them to murder and treachery. The element of treachery makes Cadfael's cases something more than simply puzzles to be solved; it invests them with an enhanced moral dimension. Peters declares that she has "one sacred rule" about her detective fiction, apart from treating her characters "with the same respect as in any other form of novel":

> It is, it ought to be, it must be, a morality. If it strays from the side of the angels, provokes total despair, wilfully destroys—without pressing need in the plot—the innocent and the good, takes pleasure in evil, that is unforgivable sin. I use the word deliberately and gravely.

The villains in the Brother Cadfael series characteristically attempt to destroy "the innocent and the good." Brother Cadfael repeatedly becomes involved in his cases when a young person is unjustly accused of murder. In *A Morbid Taste for Bones*, for example, Engelard, an exiled Englishman in love with the Welsh squire Rhisiart's daughter, is wrongly thought to have killed Rhisiart, who had opposed Engelard's suit. The murderer proves instead to be a fanatically ambitious young monk. Brother Cadfael works to prove the innocence of Master Bonel's stepson Edwin when Bonel dies of poisoning in *Monk's-Hood*. A complicating motivational force in this novel is the fact that Edwin is the son of Richildis, Cadfael's sweetheart of long ago, whom he has not seen in forty-two years. In *The Leper of Saint Giles* (1981), the lovely Iveta is about to be married by her ambitous and greedy guardians to a man she does not love. When that man's mangled body is found in a forest, the man she loves is accused of the murder, and Brother Cadfael steps in to prove that he is innocent. Cadfael saves Liliwin, a traveling performer who seeks sanctuary at the abbey, and proves his innocence of robbery and murder in *The Sanctuary Sparrow* (1983).

While threats to innocent young men in the Brother Cadfael chronicles usually take the form of false accusations of crime, threats to innocent young women tend to involve actual or potential entrapments requiring their rescue, as in *One Corpse Too Many* (1979) and *Saint Peter's Fair*. Peters's young female characters are not passive victims, however, but intelligent, persistent, and courageous, and they frequently work with Brother Cadfael in solving his cases. In doing so, these young women are motivated not only by the desire for justice but also by love. Young love, at first thwarted and then fulfilled, is omnipresent in these novels, and Brother Cadfael is its chief facilitator. As surely and steadily as he brings murderers to the bar of justice, he brings lovers to the altar of marriage. The chronicles of Brother Cadfael follow the literary tradition of social comedy, affirming love, thwarting whatever blocks it, reestablishing the social order that has been upset by ambition, greed, and murder, and promoting the continuity of that order in future generations.

While Edith Pargeter will ever be better known as her alter ego, Ellis Peters, the success of the Brother Cadfael series brought recognition to all of her writings. In 1991 Mysterious Press began reissuing the Felse novels, and these were followed in 1993 by *The Heaven Tree* (1960), *The Green Branch* (1962), and *The Scarlet Seed* (1963) bound as a set and rechristened the *Heaven Tree* trilogy. Though these historical novels did not enjoy the acclaim of the Cadfael series, they were created with the same eye for detail and filled with the lively atmosphere of medieval Britain.

The last Brother Cadfael novel, *Brother Cadfael's Penance* (1994) was published a year before the author's death. The series attained even greater fame when the BBC produced several television installments starring Derek Jacobi as Brother Cadfael. The books have also been recorded and a line of Brother Cadfael paraphernalia, including maps, handbooks, needlework, glassware, and trinkets is available in the United Kingdom and the United States.

To Pargeter/Peters this was all icing on the cake; her goals were purely literary when she was writing her historical characters, "to demonstrate," as Rosemary Herbert wrote in *Publishers Weekly* in 1991, "that people from distant ages can be portrayed with vitality and intimacy." In this, Pargeter more than succeeded—millions mourned her death at age eighty-two and the loss of her extraordinary creations.

### Principal mystery and detective fiction

SERIES: Brother Cadfael: *A Morbid Taste for Bones: A Mediaeval Whodunnit,* 1977; *One Corpse Too Many,* 1979; *Monk's-Hood,* 1980; *Saint Peter's Fair,* 1981; *The Leper of Saint Giles,* 1981; *The Virgin in the Ice,* 1982; *The Sanctuary Sparrow,* 1983; *The Devil's Novice,* 1983; *Dead Man's Ransom,* 1984; *The Pilgrim of Hate,* 1984; *An Excellent Mystery,* 1985; *The Raven in the Foregate,* 1986; *The Rose Rent,* 1987; *The Hermit of Eyton Forest,* 1988; *The Confession of Brother Haluin,* 1988; *The Heretic's Apprentice,* 1990; *The Potter's Field: The Seventeenth Chronicle of Brother Cadfael, of the Benedictine Abbey of Saint Peter and Saint Paul, at Shrewsbury,* 1990; *The Summer of the Danes,* 1991; *The Holy Thief,* 1992; *Brother Cadfael's Penance,* 1994. The Felse Family: *Fallen into the Pit,* 1951; *Death and the Joyful Woman,* 1961; *Flight of a Witch,* 1964; *A Nice Derangement of Epitaphs,* 1965 (also as *Who Lies Here?*); *The Piper on the Mountain,* 1966; *Black Is the Colour of My True-Love's Heart,* 1967; *The Grass-Widow's Tale,* 1968; *The House of Green Turf,* 1969; *Mourning Raga,* 1969; *The Knocker on Death's Door,* 1970; *Death to the Landlords!,* 1972; *City of Gold and Shadows,* 1973; *Rainbow's End,* 1978.

OTHER NOVELS: *Death Mask,* 1959; *The Will and the Deed,* 1960 (also as *Where There's a Will*); *Funeral of Figaro,* 1962; *The Horn of Roland,* 1974; *Never Pick Up Hitch-Hikers!,* 1976.

OTHER SHORT FICTION: *The Assize of the Dying,* 1958.

### Other major works

NOVELS: *Hortensius, Friend of Nero,* 1936; *Iron-Bound,* 1936; *The City Lies Foursquare,* 1939; *Ordinary People,* 1941 (also as *People of My Own*); *She Goes to War,* 1942; *The Eighth Champion of Christendom,* 1945; *Reluctant Odyssey,* 1946; *Warfare Accomplished,* 1947; *The Fair Young Phoenix,* 1948; *By Firelight,* 1948 (also as *By This Strange Fire*); *Lost Children,* 1951; *Holiday with Violence,* 1952; *This Rough Magic,* 1953; *Most Loving Mere Folly,* 1953; *The Soldier at the Door,* 1954; *A Means of Grace,* 1956; *The Heaven Tree,* 1960; *The Green Branch,* 1962; *The Scarlet Seed,* 1963; *A Bloody Field by Shrewsbury,* 1972; *Sunrise in the West,* 1974; *The Dragon at Noonday,* 1975; *The Hounds of Sunset,* 1976; *Afterglow and Nightfall,* 1977; *The Marriage of Meggotta,* 1979.

SHORT FICTION: *The Lily Hand and Other Stories,* 1965; *A Rare Benedictine,* 1988; *Feline Felonies,* 1993 (with others).
RADIO PLAY: *The Heaven Tree,* 1975.
NONFICTION: *The Coast of Bohemia,* 1950; *Shropshire,* 1992 (with Roy Morgan; also as *Ellis Peters's Shropshire*); *Strongholds and Sanctuaries: The Borderland of England and Wales,* 1993 (with Roy Morgan).
TRANSLATIONS: *Tales of the Little Quarter,* 1957 (by Jan Neruda); *The Sorrowful and Heroic Life of John Amos Comenius,* 1958 (by Frantisek Kosík); *A Handful of Linden Leaves: An Anthology of Czech Poetry,* 1958; *Don Juan,* 1958; (by Josef Toman); *The Abortionists,* 1961 (by Valja Stýblová); *Granny,* 1962 (by Bozena Nemcová); *The Linden Tree,* 1962 (with others); *The Terezin Requiem,* 1963 (by Josef Bor); *Legends of Old Bohemia,* 1963 (by Alois Jirásek); *May,* 1965 (by Karel Hynek Mácha); *The End of the Old Times,* 1965 (by Vladislav Vancura); *A Close Watch on the Trains,* 1968 (by Bohumil Hrabal; also as *Closely Watched Trains*); *Report on My Husband,* 1969 (by Josefa Slánská); *A Ship Named Hope,* 1970 (by Ivan Klíma); *Mozart in Prague,* 1970 (by Jaroslav Seifert).

## Bibliography

Greeley, Andrew M. "Ellis Peters: Another Umberto Eco?" *The Armchair Detective* 18 (Summer, 1985): 238-245.
Herbert, Rosemary. "Ellis Peters: The Novelist Cum Historian Has Written a New Mystery About Her Ever-Popular Sleuth, a Twelfth-Century Monk," *Publishers Weekly* 238, no. 36 (August 9, 1991): 40.
Kaler, Anne K., ed. *Cordially Yours, Brother Cadfael.* Bowling Green, Ohio: Bowling Green State University Press, 1998.
Klein, Kathleen Gregory, ed. *Great Women Mystery Writers: Classic to Contemporary.* Westport, Conn.: Greenwood Press, 1994.
Hubin, Allen J. Review of *One Corpse Too Many,* by Ellis Peters. *The Armchair Detective* 14 (Winter, 1981): 19.
Lewis, Steve. Review of *A Morbid Taste for Bones,* by Ellis Peters. *The Mystery FANcier* 4 (July/August, 1980): 37.
Lewis, Margaret. *Edith Pargeter–Ellis Peters.* Chester Springs, Penn.: Dufour Editions, 1994.
Whiteman, Robin. *The Cadfael Companion: The World of Brother Cadfael.* Rev. ed. London: London: Little, Brown, 1995.

*Eileen Tess Tyler*
*Updated by Fiona Kelleghan*

# Edgar Allan Poe

**Born:** Boston, Massachusetts; January 19, 1809
**Died:** Baltimore, Maryland; October 7, 1849

**Types of plot** • Amateur sleuth • psychological

**Principal series** • C. Auguste Dupin, 1841-1844.

**Principal series character** • C. AUGUSTE DUPIN is a young French gentleman of an illustrious family who has been reduced to living on a modest inheritance in Paris. Extremely well-read, highly imaginative, and master of a keen analytical ability, Dupin is the original armchair detective, the progenitor of every amateur sleuth in detective fiction from Sherlock Holmes to the present.

**Contribution** • Although Edgar Allan Poe's career was relatively short, he was the leading figure in the mid-nineteenth century transformation of the legendary tale into the sophisticated form now known as the short story. Experimenting with many different styles and genres—the gothic tale, science fiction, occult fantasies, satire—Poe gained great recognition in the early 1840's for his creation of a genre that has grown in popularity ever since—the tale of ratiocination, or detective story, which features an amateur sleuth who by his superior deductive abilities outsmarts criminals and outclasses the police.

"The Murders in the Rue Morgue" and "The Mystery of Marie Roget," the first two works in the Dupin series, created a small sensation in the United States when they were first published. Following fast upon these works was "The Gold Bug," which, although not featuring Dupin, focused on analytical detection; it was so popular that it was immediately reprinted three times. "The Purloined Letter," the third and final story in the Dupin series, has been the subject of much critical analysis.

**Biography** • Edgar Allan Poe was born in Boston, Massachusetts, on January 19, 1809. When his parents, David Poe, Jr., and Elizabeth Arnold Poe, indigent actors, died when he was two years old, Poe was taken in by a wealthy tobacco exporter, John Allan. In 1826, Poe entered the University of Virginia but withdrew after less than a year because of debts Allan would not pay. After a brief term in the army, Poe entered West Point Academy, argued further with Allan about financial support, and then purposely got himself discharged. In 1831, he moved to Baltimore, where he lived with his aunt, Maria Clemm, and her daughter Virginia.

After winning a short-story contest sponsored by a Philadelphia newspaper, Poe was given his first job as an editor on the *Southern Literary Messenger* in

*Edgar Allan Poe.* (Library of Congress)

Richmond, Virginia. During his two-year tenure, he gained considerable public attention with his stories. With the end of that job, Poe, who had by this time both a new wife (his cousin Virginia) and his aunt to support, took his small family to Philadelphia, where he published some of his best-known works—*The Narrative of Arthur Gordon Pym of Nantucket* (1838), "Ligeia," "The Fall of the House of Usher," and "William Wilson."

At this point, Poe discovered a new way to capitalize on his popularity as a critic, writer, and generally respected man of letters. He joined the lecture circuit, delivering talks on poetry and criticism in various American cities. Poe continued to present lectures on literature for the last five years of his life, with varying degrees of acclaim and success, but never with enough financial reward to make his life comfortable. Even the immediate sensation created by his poem "The Raven," which was reprinted throughout the country and which made Poe an instant celebrity, still could not satisfy the need for enough funds to support his family.

On a trip from Richmond to New York, Poe, a man who could not tolerate alcohol, stopped in Baltimore and began drinking. After he was missing for several days, he was found on the street, drunk and disheveled. Three days later, he died of what was diagnosed as delirium tremens.

**Analysis** • Although Edgar Allan Poe is credited as the creator of the detective story and the character type known as the amateur sleuth, Auguste Dupin and his ratiocinative ability were clearly influenced by other sources. Two probable sources are Voltaire's *Zadig* (1748) and François-Eugène Vidocq's *Mémoires de Vidocq, chef de la police de sûreté jusqu'en* (1827; *Memoirs of Vidocq, Principal Agent of the French Police*, 1828). Poe mentions Zadig in "Hop-Frog" and thus most likely knew the story of Zadig's ability to deduce the description of the king's horse and the queen's dog by examining tracks on the ground and hair left on bushes. He also mentions Vidocq, the first real-life detective, in "The

Murders of the Rue Morgue" as a "good guesser," but one who could not see clearly because he held the object of investigation too close.

Poe's creation of the ratiocinative story also derives from broader and more basic interests and sources. First, there was his interest in the aesthetic theory of Samuel Taylor Coleridge, heavily indebted to nineteenth century German Romanticism. In several of Poe's most famous critical essays, such as his 1842 review of Nathaniel Hawthorne's *Twice-Told Tales* (1837) and his theoretical articles, "Philosophy of Composition" in 1846 and "The Poetic Principle" in 1848, Poe develops his own version of the theory of the art work as a form in which every detail contributes to the overall effect. This organic aesthetic theory clearly influenced Poe's creation of the detective genre, in which every detail, even the most minor, may be a clue to the solution of the story's central mystery.

The development of the mystery/detective genre also reflected the influence of gothic fiction. The gothic novel, based on the concept of hidden sin and filled with mysterious and unexplained events, had, like the detective story, to move inexorably toward a denouement that would explain all the previous puzzles. The first gothic novel, Horace Walpole's *The Castle of Otranto* (1764), with its secret guilt and cryptic clues, was thus an early source of the detective story.

A third source was Poe's fascination with cryptograms, riddles, codes, and other conundrums and puzzles. In an article in a weekly magazine in 1839, he offered to solve any and all cryptograms submitted; in a follow-up article in 1841, he said that he had indeed solved most of them. Although Poe demonstrated his skill as a solver of puzzles in many magazine articles, the most famous fictional depiction of his skill as a cryptographer is his story "The Gold Bug."

William Legrand, the central character in "The Gold Bug," shares some characteristics with Poe's famous amateur sleuth, Dupin. Legrand is of an illustrious family, but because of financial misfortunes, he has been reduced to near poverty. Although he is of French ancestry from New Orleans, he lives alone on an island near Charleston, South Carolina. In addition, like Dupin, he alternates between melancholia and enthusiasm, which leads the narrator (also like the narrator in the Dupin stories) to suspect that he is the victim of a species of madness.

The basic premise of the story is that Legrand is figuratively bitten by the gold bug after discovering a piece of parchment on which he finds a cryptogram with directions to the buried treasure of the pirate Captain Kidd. As with the more influential Dupin stories, "The Gold Bug" focuses less on action than on the explanation of the steps toward the solution of its mystery. In order to solve the puzzle of the cryptogram, Legrand demonstrates the essential qualities of the amateur detective: close attention to minute detail, extensive information about language and mathematics, far-reaching knowledge about his opponent (in this case Captain Kidd), and, most important, a perceptive intuition as well as a methodical reasoning ability.

Poe's famous gothic stories of psychological obsession, such as "The Black Cat," "The Tell-Tale Heart," "The Fall of the House of Usher," and "Ligeia," seem at first glance quite different from his ratiocinative stories of detection. In many ways, however, they are very similar: Both types depend on some secret guilt that must be exposed; in both, the central character is an eccentric whose mind seems distant from the minds of ordinary men; and both types are elaborate puzzles filled with clues that must be tied together before the reader can understand their overall effect.

"The Oblong Box" and "Thou Art the Man," both written in 1844, are often cited as combining the gothic and the ratiocinative thrusts of Poe's genius. The narrator of "The Oblong Box," while on a packet-ship journey from Charleston, South Carolina, to New York City, becomes unusually curious about an oblong pine box which is kept in the state room of an old school acquaintance, Cornelius Wyatt. In the course of the story, the narrator uses deductive processes to arrive at the conclusion that Wyatt, an artist, is smuggling to New York a copy of Leonardo da Vinci's "The Last Supper" done by a famous Florentine painter.

When a storm threatens to sink the ship, Wyatt ties himself to the mysterious box and, to the horror of the survivors, sinks into the sea with it. Not until a month after the event does the narrator learn that the box contained Wyatt's wife embalmed in salt. Although earlier in the story the narrator prided himself on his superior acumen in guessing that the box contained a painting, at the conclusion he admits that his mistakes were the result of both his carelessness and his impulsiveness. The persistent deductive efforts of the narrator to explain the mystery of the oblong box, combined with the sense of horror that arises from the image of the artist's plunging to his death with the corpse of his beautiful young wife, qualifies this story, although a minor tale in the Poe canon, as a unique combination of the gothic and the ratiocinative.

"Thou Art the Man," although often characterized as a satire of small-town life and manners, is also an interesting but minor contribution to the genre. The story is told in an ironic tone by a narrator who proposes to account for the disappearance of Mr. Barnabus Shuttleworthy, one of the town's wealthiest and most respected citizens. When Shuttleworthy's nephew is accused of murdering his uncle, Charley Goodfellow, a close friend of Shuttleworthy, makes every effort to defend the young man. Every word he utters to exalt and support the suspected nephew, however, serves only to deepen the townspeople's suspicion of him.

Throughout the story, Goodfellow is referred to as "Old Charley" and is praised as a man who is generous, open, frank, and honest. At the story's conclusion, he receives a huge box supposedly containing wine promised him by the murdered man before his death. When the box is opened, however, the partially decomposed corpse of Shuttleworthy sits up in the box, points his finger at Goodfellow, and says, "Thou art the man!" Goodfellow, not surprisingly, confesses to the murder.

Although the basic ironies of Charley's not being such a "good fellow" after all and of his efforts to have the nephew convicted even as he pretended to have him exonerated are central to the story's plot, the final irony focuses on the means by which Goodfellow is made to confess. It is Goodfellow's frankness and honesty which causes the narrator to distrust him from the beginning and thus find the corpse, stick a piece of whale bone down its throat to cause it to sit up in the box, and use ventriloquism to make it seem as if the corpse utters the words of the title. The tale introduces such typical detective-story conventions as the creation of false clues by the criminal and the discovery of the criminal as the least likely suspect.

It is in the C. Auguste Dupin stories, however, that Poe develops most of the conventions of the detective story, devices that have been used by other writers ever since. The first of the three stories, "The Murders in the Rue Morgue," is the most popular because it combines horrifying, seemingly inexplicable events with astonishing feats of deductive reasoning. The narrator, the forerunner of Dr. Watson of the Sherlock Holmes stories, meets Dupin in this story and very early recognizes that he has a double personality, for he is both wildly imaginative and coldly analytical. The reader's first encounter with Dupin's deductive ability takes place even before the murders occur, when he seems to read his companion's mind by responding to something that the narrator had only been thinking. When Dupin explains the elaborate method by which he followed the narrator's thought processes by noticing small details and associating them, the reader has the beginning of a long history of fictional detectives taking great pleasure in recounting the means by which they solved a mystery.

Dupin's knowledge of the brutal murder of a mother and daughter on the Rue Morgue is acquired by the same means that any ordinary citizen might learn of a murder—the newspapers. As was to become common in the amateur-sleuth genre, Dupin scorns the methods of the professional investigators as being insufficient. He argues that the police find the mystery insoluble for the very reason that it should be regarded as easy to solve, that is, its bizarre nature; thus, the facility with which Dupin solves the case is in direct proportion to its apparent insolubility by the police.

The heart of the story focuses on Dupin's extended explanation of how he solved the crime rather than on the action of the crime itself. The points about the murder that stump the police—the contradiction of several neighbors who describe hearing a voice in several foreign languages, and the fact that there seems to be no possible means of entering or exiting the room where the murders took place—actually enable Dupin to master the case. He accounts for the foreign-sounding voice by deducing that the criminal must have been an animal; he explains the second point by following a mode of reasoning based on a process of elimination to determine that apparent impossibilities are in fact possible. When Dupin reveals that an escaped orangutan did the killing, the Paris prefect of police complains that Dupin should mind his own business. Dupin is nevertheless content to have beaten the prefect in his own realm; descendants of Dupin have been beating police inspectors ever since.

"The Mystery of Marie Roget," although it also focuses on Dupin's solving of a crime primarily from newspaper reports, is actually based on the murder of a young girl, Mary Cecilia Rogers, near New York City. Because the crime had not been solved when Poe wrote the story, he made use of the facts of the case to tell a story of the murder of a young Parisian girl, Marie Roget, as a means of demonstrating his superior deductive ability.

The story ostensibly begins two years after the events of "The Murders in the Rue Morgue," when the prefect of police, having failed to solve the Marie Roget case himself, worries about his reputation and asks Dupin for help. Dupin's method is that of the classic armchair detective; he gathers all the copies of the newspapers which have accounts of the crime and sets about methodically examining each one. He declares the case more intricate than that of the Rue Morgue because, ironically, it seems so simple.

One of the elements of the story that makes it less popular than the other two Dupin tales is the extensive analysis of the newspaper articles in which Dupin engages—an analysis which makes the story read more like an article critical of newspaper techniques than a narrative story. In fact, what makes Poe able to propose a solution to the crime is not so much his knowledge of crime as his knowledge of the conventions of newspaper writing. In a similar manner, it was his knowledge of the conventions of novel-writing that made it possible for him to deduce the correct conclusion of Charles Dickens's novel *Barnaby Rudge: A Tale of the Riots of '80* (1841) the previous year when he had read only one or two of the first installments.

Another aspect of "The Mystery of Marie Roget" which reflects Dupin's deductive genius and which has been used by subsequent detective writers is his conviction that the usual error of the police is to pay too much attention to the immediate events while ignoring the peripheral evidence. Both experience and true philosophy, says Dupin, show that truth arises more often from the seemingly irrelevant than from the so-called strictly relevant. By this means, Dupin eliminates the various hypotheses for the crime proposed by the newspapers and proposes his own hypothesis, which is confirmed by the confession of the murderer.

Although "The Mystery of Marie Roget" contains some of the primary conventions that find their way into later detective stories, it is the least popular of the Dupin narratives not only because it contains much reasoning and exposition and very little narrative, but also because it is so long and convoluted. Of the many experts of detective fiction who have commented on Poe's contribution to the genre, only Dorothy L. Sayers has praised "The Mystery of Marie Roget," calling it a story especially for connoisseurs, a serious intellectual exercise rather than a sensational thriller such as "The Murders in the Rue Morgue."

Professional literary critics, however, if not professional detective writers, have singled out "The Purloined Letter" as the most brilliant of Poe's ratiocinative works. This time, the crime is much more subtle than murder, for it focuses on political intrigue and manipulation. Although the crime is quite simple—the theft of a letter from an exalted and noble personage—its effects are quite complex. The story depends on several ironies: First, the identity of the criminal is known, for he stole the letter in plain sight of the noble lady; second, the letter is a threat to the lady from whom he stole it only as long as he does nothing with it; and third, the Paris Police cannot find the letter, even though they use the most sophisticated and exhaustive methods, precisely because, as Dupin deduces, it is in plain sight.

Also distinguishing the story from the other two is Dupin's extended discussion of the important relationship between the seemingly disparate talents of the mathematician and the poet. The Minister who has stolen the letter is successful, says Dupin, for he is both a poet and a mathematician. In turn, Dupin's method of discovering the location of the letter is to take on the identity of a poet and mathematician, thus allowing him to identify with the mind of the criminal. The method follows the same principle used by a young boy Dupin knows of who is an expert at the game of "even and odd," a variation of the old game of holding an object behind one's back and asking someone to guess which hand holds the prize. The boy always wins, not because he is a good guesser, but because he fashions the expression on his face to match the face of the one holding the object and then tries to see which thoughts correspond with that expression.

The various techniques of deduction developed by Poe in the Dupin stories are so familiar to readers of detective fiction that to read his stories is to be reminded that very few essential conventions of the genre have been invented since Poe. Indeed, with the publication of the Dupin stories, Poe truly can be said to have single-handedly brought the detective story into being.

### Principal mystery and detective fiction

SHORT FICTION: *Tales of the Grotesque and Arabesque*, 1840; *The Prose Romances of Edgar Allan Poe*, 1843; *Tales*, 1845; *The Works of the Late Edgar Allan Poe*, 1850.

### Other major works

NOVEL: *The Narrative of Arthur Gordon Pym of Nantucket*, 1838.

PLAY: *Politian*, 1835.

POETRY: *Tamerlane and Other Poems*, 1827; *Al Aaraaf, Tamerlane, and Minor Poems*, 1829; *Poems*, 1831; *The Raven and Other Poems*, 1845; *Eureka: A Prose Poem*, 1848; *Poe: Complete Poems*, 1959.

NONFICTION: *The Letters of Edgar Allan Poe*, 1948; *Literary Criticism of Edgar Allan Poe*, 1965.

MISCELLANEOUS: *The Collected Works of Edgar Allan Poe*, 1969, 1978.

### Bibliography

Allen, Michael. *Poe and the British Magazine Tradition*. New York: Oxford University Press, 1969.

Bloom, Clive, ed. *Nineteenth-Century Suspense: From Poe to Conan Doyle*. New York: St. Martin's Press, 1988.

Buranelli, Vincent. *Edgar Allan Poe.* New York: Twayne, 1961.

Carlson, Eric W., ed. *A Companion to Poe Studies.* Westport, Conn.: Greenwood Press, 1996.

_____. ed. *The Recognition of Edgar Allan Poe.* Ann Arbor: University of Michigan Press, 1966.

Davidson, Edward H. *Poe: A Critical Study.* Cambridge, Mass.: Belknap Press of Harvard University Press, 1957.

Dayan, Joan. *Fables of Mind: An Inquiry into Poe's Fiction.* New York: Oxford University Press, 1987.

Irwin, John T. *The Mystery to a Solution: Poe, Borges, and the Analytic Detective Story.* Baltimore, Md.: Johns Hopkins University Press, 1994.

Lee, A. Robert, ed. *Edgar Allan Poe: The Design of Order.* Totowa, N.J.: Barnes & Noble, 1987.

Lehman, David. *The Perfect Murder: A Study in Detection.* New York: Free Press, 1989.

Magistrale, Tony. *Student Companion to Edgar Allan Poe.* Westport, Conn.: Greenwood Press, 2001.

Magistrale, Tony and Sidney Poger. *Poe's Children: Connections between Tales of Terror and Detection.* New York: Peter Lang, 1999.

Meyers, Jeffrey. *Edgar Allan Poe: His Life and Legacy.* New York: Charles Scribner's Sons, 1992.

Quinn, Arthur H. *Edgar Allan Poe: A Critical Biography.* New York: D. Appleton-Century, 1941.

Quinn, Patrick F. *The French Face of Edgar Poe.* Carbondale: Southern Illinois University Press, 1957.

Regan, Robert, ed. *Poe: A Collection of Critical Essays.* Englewood Cliffs, N.J.: Prentice-Hall, 1967.

Silverman, Kenneth, ed. *New Essays on Poe's Major Tales.* New York: Cambridge University Press, 1993.

Thomas, Dwight, and David K. Jackson. *The Poe Log: A Documentary Life of Edgar Allan Poe, 1809-1849.* Boston: G. K. Hall, 1987.

*Charles E. May*

# Bill Pronzini

**Born:** Petaluma, California; April 13, 1943

**Also wrote as** • Russell Dancer • Robert Hart Davis (with Jeffrey M. Wallman) • Jack Foxx • Romer Zane Grey (with Wallman) • William Jeffrey (with Wallman) • Rick Renault (with Wallman) • Alex Saxon

**Type of plot** • Private investigator

**Principal series** • The Nameless Detective, 1969-    • Carmody, 1970-1992 • Quincannon and Carpenter, 1985-1998.

**Principal series characters** • THE NAMELESS DETECTIVE, a private eye, formerly a fifteen-year veteran of the San Francisco Police Department. About forty-seven years old at the start of the series, Nameless has aged through the years, and, by 1988, is actively considering retirement. He is sloppy, moderately overweight, unmarried, and concerned both with his health and with being loved. His two real obsessions, however, are collecting pulp magazines and trying to make the world a better place.

    • LIEUTENANT "EB" EBERHARDT, a detective for the San Francisco Police Department at the outset of the series, is Nameless's closest friend and has appeared in all the series' novels and most of the stories. The two met as trainees at the police academy. Nameless turns to Eb for help, whether working on a case or working through a personal problem. Eb eventually joins Nameless as a partner in his agency after retiring from the police department.

    • CARMODY, an international dealer in "legal and extralegal services and material" who occasionally does detective work. An American, he lives in isolation on the Spanish island of Majorca. He is the flinty, silent type, with a good tan and green eyes; he smokes thin black cigars and drives a 911-T Porsche Targa.

    • JOHN FREDERICK QUINCANNON, a former Secret Service agent and reformed alcoholic, would like to form a sexual relationship with his partner, Sabina Carpenter, but she dodges his advances. He works as a detective in San Francisco of the 1890's.

    • SABINA CARPENTER is a widow and a former Pinkerton Agency detective. Quincannon's equal at witty banter, she teams up with him to solve a variety of "impossible" crimes.

**Contribution** • Bill Pronzini's Nameless novels move the hard-boiled detective genre toward a new kind of authenticity. To the unsentimental realism of Dashiell Hammett, the descriptive power of Raymond Chandler, and the psychological depth of Ross Macdonald, all meant to transcend the artificial atmosphere of the "English" detective story, Pronzini adds attention to everyday human problems—emotional as well as physical. Nameless struggles with health concerns of varying seriousness and also spends a modest but significant portion of his narrative seeking stable female companionship. He ages and on occasion gets depressed. In short, Nameless is revealed in a way that would be utterly foreign to a character such as Hammett's Sam Spade or Chandler's Philip Marlowe.

Pronzini also seeks heightened authenticity, largely shedding the toughguy image associated with the hard-boiled genre. To be sure, Nameless is tough. He doggedly seeks the truth and unhesitatingly puts himself into risky situations. Nameless eschews violence and sarcasm, however, and he is willing, at least occasionally, to wear his heart on his sleeve. Indeed, Nameless does nothing to hide the fact that he cares about people and is generally sympathetic. He cultivates a good working relationship with the police and with few exceptions stays on the right side of the law. Pronzini also occasionally works in some of the banality and drudgery involved with real-life private investigation.

All this is mixed in with some of the more classic hard-boiled elements: twisting plots, sparsely furnished offices, feverish pace, compelling descriptions of California settings (though Nameless does occasionally leave the state, pursuing one case in Europe), and a hero so dedicated to his vocation that he will often go without sleep and will sometimes work without fee. In addition, the very namelessness of Pronzini's detective harks back to Hammett's Continental Op. It is, in fact, the blend of old with new that makes Pronzini's series unique.

Yet Pronzini does not merely build on the work of the three authors mentioned above. Through Nameless's love of the pulps, the reader is reminded that many fine writers have helped to shape and promote the hard-boiled genre—a significant bibliographic contribution on Pronzini's part.

**Biography** • Bill Pronzini was born on April 13, 1943, in Petaluma, a small town north of San Francisco in California, to Joseph and Helen Gruder Pronzini. Joseph Pronzini was a farm worker. The younger of two children, Bill was reared in Petaluma, where he attended the local schools. He wrote his first novel at the age of twelve. In high school, he began collecting pulp magazines. It was at this point that Pronzini did his first professional writing, working as a reporter for the Petaluma *Argus Courier* from 1957 to 1960. After attending Santa Rosa Junior College for two years, Bill refused a journalism scholarship to Stanford University, choosing instead to become a free-lance fiction writer. During the early years of his writing career, Bill supplemented his income by working at various times as a newsstand clerk, warehouseman, typist, salesman, and civilian guard with the marshal's office.

Pronzini married Laura Patricia Adolphson in May, 1965. The following year, he sold his first story, "You Don't Know What It's Like," to the *Shell Scott*

*Mystery Magazine.* Pronzini was divorced in 1967. His writing career flourished, however, and he had short stories published in a variety of pulp magazines. One product of this period was his unnamed detective: *The Snatch,* published in 1971, was Pronzini's first novel featuring Nameless. Pronzini moved to Majorca in 1971. There he met Brunhilde Schier, whom he married in 1972. They lived in West Germany before moving back to San Francisco in 1974.

Pronzini has gone on to become one of the most prolific authors of his time, producing more than thirty novels and hundreds of stories in a variety of genres: detective, Western, and science fiction. In addition to those works published under his own name, Pronzini has written novels and short stories using the pseudonyms Jack Foxx, Alex Saxon, and Russell Dancer. He has also been a prolific collaborator, working with such authors as Barry N. Malzberg, Jeffrey M. Wallman, Michael Kurland, Collin Wilcox, and Marcia Muller. In addition to his writing, Pronzini has edited a number of books in the mystery, Western, and science-fiction fields.

Pronzini's quantitative achievements have been augmented by qualitative ones. While he has yet to achieve the high literary acclaim accorded Hammett, Chandler, and Macdonald, he is greatly respected by his fellow writers of mysteries and has won a number of awards, including the Mystery Writers Association Scroll Award for the best first novel (1971) and the Private Eye Writers of America Shamus Award for the Best Private Eye Novel of 1981 (*Hoodwink,* 1981, *Boobytrap,* 1998). *Snowbound* (1974) earned the Grand Prix de la Literature Policière as the best crime novel published in France in 1988, and *A Wasteland of Strangers* was nominated for the best crime novel of 1997 by both the Mystery Writers of America and the International Crime Writers Association. He received "The Eye," the Lifetime Achievement Award (presented in 1987) from the Private Eye Writers of America.

**Analysis** • While Bill Pronzini has produced stories and novels at a truly enviable pace, both he and his critics have accorded the Nameless series a special status. First, it is clear that Pronzini himself identifies strongly with the Nameless detective. Indeed, this is one reason his hero has remained without a name. In addition, the Nameless series has been recognized as marking the literary high point of Pronzini's career. It is this body of work for which Pronzini will probably be remembered, for the Nameless series has staying power derived both from its faithfulness to the well-hallowed tradition of the hardboiled detective story and from its innovations and freshness within that tradition.

The hard-boiled detective story goes back to the 1920's, when Hammett, taking advantage of the flourishing trade in pulp magazines and the stylistic trends of the times, almost single-handedly established a new subgenre of popular fiction. Drawing on his experience as a Pinkerton's detective, Hammett brought a new realism and depth to crime fiction while holding to the constraints of the pulp market. These constraints dictated plenty of action and consummate directness of expression. The result was a hybrid literary form with elements of both high and low art—something roughly akin, both conceptually and chronologically, to the Marx brothers' *A Night at the Opera* (1935). The hard-boiled genre expanded quickly and profusely. As Pronzini and others have remarked, numerous authors, some well-known, others relatively obscure, though often talented, went on to produce notable works within it. In addition, the genre was a natural for films and later for television. The action-oriented, economic prose and crisp dialogue of hard-boiled stories translated readily to both the large and the small screen, resulting in classic films such as *The Maltese Falcon* (1941) and popular television programs such as *Peter Gunn, The Rockford Files,* and *Spenser: For Hire.* In short, the hard-boiled detective became a significant mythic figure in American culture, one that, for all its very considerable international appeal, remains as distinctly American as jazz.

Why has the hard-boiled detective had so broad and lasting an appeal? He or she (the female of the species having emerged during the 1970's and 1980's) has been likened to a modern-day knight, defending the weak, seeking truth, and striving for justice in ways that legal authorities cannot or will not duplicate. Put another way, the hard-boiled detective is an independent agent who acts as he does because it is right, not for material gain or out of blind allegiance to a cause, and who is willing to face stiff opposition in the name of principle. In contrast to stereotypical bureaucratic torpor, the hard-boiled detective is also a person of action, a doer, living up to the dictates of a demanding personal code. Thus, the hard-boiled detective must not only pass up wealth and other modern measures of "success" but also risk grave personal danger. It is this precarious existence which dictates that the detective be a loner; privation and danger are his or her crosses to bear and are not readily transferable to loved ones and other intimates.

Pronzini's Nameless series consciously carries on this tradition both stylistically and substantively. Using the genre's classic, first-person narrative, lean prose, and crisp dialogue, Pronzini portrays Nameless as being nearly everything the detective as modern-day knight is supposed to be. Nameless helps the weak, at times working without pay to do so. For example, in the early stories "It's a Lousy World" and "Death of a Nobody," Nameless takes up the causes of an ex-con and a derelict, both of whom have been killed. There are no wealthy relatives footing the bill, thus no hope for a paycheck. Yet Nameless follows through, simply because he cares about the sanctity of every human life, not merely those for whom a fee can be collected. He also cares about the quality of each life, a characteristic which leads his friend Eb to call him a "social worker." Beyond this universal compassion lies a hunger for truth in all of its complexity (as opposed to mere appearances) and for thoroughgoing justice (rather than the rough equivalent provided by law). In order to pursue these goals, Nameless must devote himself single-mindedly to his investigations, wading through a sea of lies, warding off threats, and ignoring weariness to the point of exhaustion. Nameless does all this and more in the name of a higher code, a modern form of chivalry aimed at making the world a better place in which to live.

Nevertheless, the Nameless series does more than simply pay homage to the hard-boiled genre; it adds a new twist or two to the tradition. Drawing on the model of Thomas B. Dewey's detective, "Mac," Pronzini has aimed for a new kind of "authenticity," eschewing the more superficial and fantastic elements of the genre. Nameless starts off his literary existence middle aged and paunchy, anything but the romanticized figure often presented, particularly in screen variations of the hard-boiled tradition. Nor is Nameless always wildly successful in his endeavors: He is sometimes mistaken about things and sometimes used.

In a more conspicuous break with the hard-boiled tradition, Nameless is far less private about the details of his life and his needs than are most of the classic hard-boiled characters. Nameless has a long-running, close friendship with a San Francisco cop named Eberhardt (Eb). He also has had two enduring relationships with women—first with Erica Coates, who turns down Nameless's proposal because of his line of work, and later with Kerry Wade, although a bad first marriage keeps Kerry from marrying Nameless. In addition, the reader is given details of Nameless's state of physical well-being that the Continental Op or Sam Spade would never have dreamed of sharing. These run the gamut from Nameless's bouts with heart-burn to a tumor and the possibility of lung cancer. (It is the later which induces Nameless to quit smoking.)

In addition to these very human insights, Pronzini's hero is much less prone to play the tough guy. Nameless rarely breaks the law or engages in violence. Indeed, he almost always refuses to carry a gun, especially later in the series, and he throws the only gun he owns into the ocean in *Dragonfire* (1982).

Pronzini's quest for heightened authenticity (or what one pair of critics has called "unromanticized realism") has been additionally enhanced in three specific ways that deserve to be noted. First, by making Nameless a collector of pulp magazines and an expert on the hard-boiled genre in particular, Pronzini has not merely been autobiographical. He has also moved his hero one step away from the fictional world toward the world of the reader. The pulps are real. Though the stories in the pulps are fictional, these fictions are read and collected by real people. Nameless reads and collects these works. Therefore, Nameless is (or, at least, seems) more real.

Second, Pronzini has preserved continuity between the stories and novels of the series, leaving situations hanging and having Nameless and Eb age somewhat realistically from work to work. Both characters have changing relationships with the opposite sex and both experience career shifts. Like everyone, Nameless and his friend must deal with the trials, tribulations, and occasional comforts of the human life cycle.

Finally, Pronzini twice has collaborated with other authors of detective fiction to produce works which provide mutual validation for the main characters involved. Nameless does not merely exist in the minds of Pronzini and his readers. He also cohabits San Francisco with Collin Wilcox's Lieutenant Frank Hastings and Marcia Muller's Sharon McCone. In something akin to the way governments extend or deny one another diplomatic recognition, these authors have brought their fictional characters closer to life through these collaborations, making them more authentic in the process. The result has been the creation of a unique character and series in the hard-boiled tradition as well as the emergence of a significant audience for Pronzini's Nameless stories and novels.

A final comment or two should be added regarding the anonymity of Pronzini's best-known character, particularly since it may seem difficult to find a connection between this aspect of Pronzini's series and his quest for authenticity. It could be argued that the reality of Pronzini's character is best preserved by not tying him down to a name which can easily be proved fictional. Yet Nameless apparently owes his condition to two factors largely separate from the quest for authenticity: serendipity and the close indentification of Pronzini with his character. Pronzini claims no profound goal in leaving his hero nameless—merely that no name suited the man: "Big, sort of sloppy Italian guy who guzzles beer, smokes too much and collects pulp magazines. What name fits a character like that? Sam Spadini, Philip Marlozzi?" Additionally, Pronzini admits that his character is autobiographical, reflecting his own perceptions and reactions:

> Nameless and I are the same person; or, rather, he is an extrapolation of me. His view of life, his hang-ups and weaknesses, his pulp collecting hobby—all are essentially mine. . . . So, even though I can't use it, his name is Bill Pronzini.

Indeed, when Pronzini's hero is referred to in one of the sections of *Twospot* (1978), a collaborative effort with Collin Wilcox, he is called "Bill." Thus, while the situation does not handicap the series—some readers are even intrigued by it—the precise meaning of the hero's anonymity is unclear and possibly not very important. Indeed, it seems ironic to be told the details of Nameless's life, where he lives (the upstairs apartment of a Victorian house in Pacific Heights), whom he sees, how he amuses himself, and yet never learn his name. Whether this irony is intended is left unclear.

In the mid-1980's, Pronzini allowed his love of the Western genre—he has edited dozens of Western anthologies and collections—to spill over into his mystery writing with the invention of two new series characters. John Quincannon and his partner (and unrequited love interest), Sarah Carpenter, are detectives working in San Francisco of the 1890's. Chiefly they solve locked-room mysteries and other "impossible" crimes, although they do encounter the occasional six-gun or thrown punch.

Though the team appears in only two novels and one short-story collection as of 2001, they have achieved critical acclaim. One critic wrote that the historical setting contains "some of the most elaborate landscapes since those of Arthur Morrison in the 1890's," adding of the Delta region of the Sacramento River east of San Francisco that "this watery region is marked as being peculiarly Pronzini's own."

J. G. Ballard has suggested that delta regions represent the Unconscious, a sort of living map of the interior landscape of part of the human mind." The story "Burgade's Crossing," for example, involves a search of the landscape for the possible site of a premeditated murder, so that the setting itself almost acts as a character.

Whether they will be developed to the extent of the Nameless Detective remains to be seen. With or without a name, Pronzini's detective does achieve a significant level of authenticity and freshness. Joining the ranks of today's liberated man, Nameless is unafraid to cry or communicate his emotional needs, fears, and concerns. He is willing to confess his desire to be loved and to have at least a few close friends. Nameless provides an alternative to the tough-guy private eyes of old.

## Principal mystery and detective fiction

SERIES: The Nameless Detective: *The Snatch*, 1971; *The Vanished*, 1973; *Undercurrent*, 1973; *Blowback*, 1977; *Twospot*, 1978 (with Collin Wilcox); *Labyrinth*, 1979; *Hoodwink*, 1982; *Scattershot*, 1982; *Dragonfire*, 1982; *Bindlestiff*, 1983; *Casefile*, 1983; *Quicksilver*, 1984; *Nightshades*, 1984; *Double*, 1984 (with Marcia Muller); *Bones*, 1985; *Deadfall*, 1986; *Shackles*, 1988; *Jackpot*, 1990; *Breakdown*, 1991; *Quarry*, 1992; *Epitaphs*, 1992; *Demons*, 1993; *Criminal Intent 1: All New Stories*, 1993 (with Muller and Ed Gorman); *Hardcase*, 1995; *Sentinels*, 1996; *Spadework: A Collection of "Nameless Detective" Stories*, 1996; *Illusions*, 1997; *Boobytrap*, 1998; *Crazybone*, 2000. Quincannon and Carpenter: *Quincannon*, 1985; *Beyond the Grave*, 1986 (with Muller); *Carpenter and Quincannon, Professional Detective Services*, 1998. Carmody: *A Run in Diamonds*, 1973; *Carmody's Run*, 1992.

OTHER NOVELS: *The Stalker*, 1971; *Panic!*, 1972; *The Jade Figurine*, 1972; *A Run in Diamonds*, 1973; *Snowbound*, 1974; *Dead Run*, 1975; *Games*, 1976; *The Running of Beasts*, 1976 (with Barry N. Malzberg); *Freebooty*, 1976; *Acts of Mercy*, 1977 (with Malzberg); *Wildfire*, 1978; *Night Screams*, 1979 (with Malzberg); *Masques*, 1981; *Day of the Moon*, 1983; *The Eye*, 1984 (with John Lutz); *The Lighthouse*, 1987 (with Muller); *The Hangings*, 1989; *Firewind*, 1989; *Stacked Deck*, 1991; *With an Extreme Burning*, 1994; *The Tormentor*, 1994; *Blue Lonesome*, 1995; *A Wasteland of Strangers*, 1997; *Nothing But the Night*, 1999; *In an Evil Time*, 2001.

## Other major works

NOVELS: *Prose Bowl*, 1980 (with Malzberg); *The Cambodia File*, 1980 (with Jack Anderson); *The Gallows Land*, 1983; *Starvation Camp*, 1984; *The Horse Soldiers*, 1987 (with Greenberg); *The Last Days of Horse-Shy Halloran*, 1987; *The Gunfighters*, 1988 (with Greenberg).

SHORT FICTION: *A Killing in Xanadu*, 1980; *Graveyard Plots: The Best Short Stories of Bill Pronzini*, 1985; *Small Felonies: Fifty Mystery Short Shorts*, 1988; *The Best Western Stories of Bill Pronzini*, 1990; *Duo*, 1998 (with Muller); *Sleuths*, 1999; *Night Freight*, 2000; *Oddments: A Short Story Collection*, 2000; *All the Long Years: Western Stories*, 2001.

NONFICTION: *Gun in Cheek: A Study of "Alternative" Crime Fiction*, 1982; *San Francisco*, 1985 (with Larry Lee, Mark Stephenson and West Light); *1001 Midnights: The Aficionado's Guide to Mystery and Detective Fiction*, 1986 (with Muller); *Son of Gun in Cheek*, 1987; *Six-Gun in Cheek: An Affectionate Guide to the "Worst" in Western Fiction*, 1997.

EDITED TEXTS: *Tricks and Treats*, 1976 (with Joe Gores; also as *Mystery Writers Choice*); *Midnight Specials*, 1977; *Dark Sins, Dark Dreams*, 1977 (with Malzberg); *Werewolf*, 1979; *Shared Tomorrows: Collaboration in SF*, 1979 (with Malzberg); *Bug-Eyed Monsters*, 1980 (with Malzberg); *The Edgar Winners: 33rd Annual Anthology of the Mystery Writers of America*, 1980; *Voodoo!*, 1980; *Mummy!*, 1980; *Creature!*, 1981; *The Arbor House Treasury of Mystery and Suspense*, 1981 (with John D. MacDonald, Malzberg, and Greenberg; also abridged as *Great Tales of Mystery and Suspense*, 1985); *The Arbor House Necropolis: Voodoo!, Mummy!, Ghoul!*, 1981 (also as *Tales of the Dead*); *The Arbor House Treasury of Horror and the Supernatural*, 1981 (with Malzberg and Greenberg; also abridged as *Classic Tales of Horror and the Supernatural*); *Specter!*, 1982; *The Arbor House Treasury of Great Western Stories*, 1982 (with Greenberg; also abridged as *Great Tales of the West*); *Great Tales of the West*, 1982 (with Greenberg); *The Arbor House Treasury of Detective and Mystery Stories from the Great Pulps*, 1983 (also as *Tales of Mystery*); *The Web She Weaves: An Anthology of Mystery and Suspense Stories by Women*, 1983 (with Muller); *The Mystery Hall of Fame*, 1984 (with Charles G. Waugh and Greenberg); *Baker's Dozen: 13 Short Mystery Novels*, 1984 (with Greenberg; also as *The Mammoth Book of Short Crime Novels*); *Baker's Dozen: Thirteen Short Spy Novels*, 1984 (with Greenberg; also as *The Mammoth Book of Short Spy Novels*); *The Western Hall of Fame*, 1984 (with Greenberg); *The Reel West*, 1984 (with Greenberg); *Child's Ploy: An Anthology of Mystery and Suspense Stories*, 1984 (with Muller); *Witches' Brew: Horror and Supernatural Stories by Women*, 1984 (with Muller); *The Best Western Stories of Steve Frazee*, 1984 (with Greenberg); *The Western Hall of Fame: An Anthology of Classic Western Stories Selected by the Western Writers of America*, 1984 (with Greenberg); *The Best Western Stories of Wayne D. Overholser*, 1984 (with Greenberg); *The Lawmen*, 1984 (with Greenberg); *The Mystery Hall of Fame: An Anthology of Classic Mystery and Suspense Stories Selected by the Mystery Writers of America*, 1984 (with Greenberg and Charles G. Waugh); *The Outlaws*, 1984 (with Greenberg); *She Won the West: An Anthology of Western and Frontier Stories by Women*, 1985 (with Muller); *Baker's Dozen: 13 Short Espionage Novels*, 1985 (with Greenberg); *Chapter and Hearse: Suspense Stories about the World of Books*, 1985 (with Muller); *The Cowboys*, 1985 (with Greenberg); *Dark Lessons: Crime and Detection on Campus*, 1985 (with Muller); *The Deadly Arts*, 1985 (with Muller); *The Ethnic Detectives: Masterpieces of Mystery Fiction*, 1985 (with Greenberg); *Kill or Cure: Suspense Stories about the World of Medicine*, 1985 (with Muller); *Murder in the First Reel*, 1985 (with Charles G. Waugh and Greenberg); Police Procedurals, 1985 (with Greenberg); *The Second Reel West*, 1985 (with Greenberg); *A Treasury of Civil War Stories*, 1985 (with Greenberg); *A Treasury of World War II Stories*, 1985 (with Greenberg); *The Warriors*, 1985 (with Greenberg); *The Wickedest Show on Earth: A Carnival of Circus Suspense*, 1985 (with Muller); *Women Sleuths*, 1985 (with Greenberg); *Best of* the West: Stories That Inspired Classic Western Films, 1986-1988, 3 vols. (with Greenberg); *Great Modern Police Stories,* 1986 (with Greenberg); *Locked Room Puzzles,* 1986 (with Greenberg); *Mystery in the Mainstream: An Anthology of Literary Crimes,* 1986 (with Greenberg and Malzberg; also as *Crime and Crime Again: Mystery Stories by the World's Great Writers*); *The Railroaders,* 1986 (with Greenberg); *The Steamboaters,* 1986 (with Greenberg); *The Third Reel West,* 1986 (with Greenberg); *Wild Westerns: Stories from the Grand Old Pulps,* 1986; *101 Mystery Stories,* 1986 (with Greenberg); *Baker's Dozen: 13 Short Detective Novels,* 1987 (with Greenberg); *The Best Western Stories of Lewis B. Patten,* 1987 (with Greenberg); *The Cattlemen,* 1987 (with Greenberg); *The Gunfighters,* 1987 (with Greenberg); *The Horse Soldiers,* 1987 (with Greenberg); *Manhattan Mysteries,* 1987 (with Carol-Lynn Rössel Waugh and Greenberg); *Prime Suspects,* 1987 (with Greenberg); *Suspicious Characters,* 1987 (with Greenberg); *Uncollected Crimes,* 1987 (with Greenberg); *Cloak and Dagger: A Treasury of 35 Great Espionage Stories,* 1988 (with Greenberg); *Criminal Elements,* 1988 (with Greenberg); *Homicidal Acts,* 1988 (with Greenberg); *Lady on the Case,* 1988 (with Muller and Greenberg); *The Mammoth Book of Private Eye Stories,* 1988 (with Greenberg; also as *The Giant Book of Private Eye Stories*); *Cloak and Dagger,* 1988 (with Greenberg); *The Texans,* 1998 (with Greenberg); *Homicidal Acts,* 1988 (with Greenberg); *The Arizonans,* 1989 (with Greenberg); *The Best Western Stories of Frank Bonham,* 1989 (with Greenberg); *The Best Western Stories of Loren D. Estleman,* 1989 (with Greenberg); *The Californians,* 1989 (with Greenberg); *Felonious Assaults,* 1989 (with Greenberg); *The Mammoth Book of World War II Stories,* 1989; *More Wild Westerns,* 1989; *The Best Western Stories of Ryerson Johnson,* 1990 (with Greenberg); *The Californians: The Best of the West,* 1990 (with Greenberg); *Christmas Out West,* 1990 (with Greenberg); *New Frontiers,* 1990 (with Greenberg); *The Northerners,* 1990 (with Greenberg); *The Best Western Stories of Les Savage, Jr.,* 1991; *The Montanans,* 1991 (with Greenberg); *The Best Western Stories of Ed Gorman,* 1992 (with Greenberg); *Combat!: Great Tales of World War II,* 1992 (with Greenberg); *In the Big Country: The Best Western Stories of John Jakes,* 1993 (with Greenberg); *The Mammoth Book of Short Crime Novels,* 1996 (with Greenberg; also as *The Giant Book of Short Crime Stories*); *American Pulp,* 1997 (with Gorman and Greenberg); *Hard-Boiled: An Anthology of American Crime Stories,* 1997 (with Jack Adrian); *Detective Duos,* 1997 (with Muller); *Under the Burning Sun: Western Stories by H. A. DeRosso,* 1997; *The Best of the American West: Outstanding Frontier Fiction,* 1998 (with Greenberg); *Renegade River: Western Stories by Giff Cheshire,* 1998; *Heading West: Western Stories by Noel M. Loomis,* 1999); *Pure Pulp,* 1999 (with Gorman and Greenberg); *Riders of the Shadowlands: Western Stories by H. A. de Rosso,* 1999; *War Stories,* 1999 (with Greenberg); *Tracks in the Sand: Western Stories by H. A. DeRosso,* 2001.

## Bibliography
Baker, Robert A., and Michael T. Nietzel. *Private Eyes: One Hundred and One Knights, A Survey of American Detective Fiction, 1922-1984.* Bowling Green, Ohio: Bowling Green State University Popular Press, 1985.

Isaac, Frederick. "Nameless and Friend: An Afternoon with Bill Pronzini." *Clues* 4, no. 1 (Spring-Summer, 1983): 35-52.

Lee, Wendi. "Partners in Crime, Part II: Marcia Muller and Bill Pronzini." *Mystery Scene* 42 (1994): 18.

Nevins, Francis M., Jr., and Bill Pronzini. "Bill Pronzini: A Checklist." *The Armchair Detective* 13 (Fall, 1980): 345-350.

Perry, Anne. "What's Your Motive." *Publisher's Weekly* 247, no. 43 (October 23, 2000): 43.

Randisi, Robert J. "An Interview with Bill Pronzini." *The Armchair Detective* January, 1978, p. 46-48.

*Ira Smolensky*
*Marjorie Smolensky*
*Updated by Fiona Kelleghan*

# Ellery Queen

**Authors** • Frederic Dannay (1905-1982) and Manfred B. Lee (1905-1971) • Avram Davidson (1924-    ) • Richard Deming (1915-    ) • Edward D. Hoch (1930-    ) • Stephen Marlowe (1928-    ) • Talmadge Powell (1920-    ) • Theodore Sturgeon (1918-    ) • John Holbrook Vance (1917-    ).

**Type of plot** • Amateur sleuth

**Principal series** • Ellery Queen, 1929-1971 • Drury Lane, 1932-1933 • Tim Corrigan, 1966-1968 • Mike McCall, 1969-1972.

**Principal series characters** • ELLERY QUEEN, a mystery writer and an amateur sleuth. Single, he lives with his father in New York City. In his mid-twenties when the series begins, he is middle-aged by its close and has lost much of the effete brittleness of character that marked his earliest appearances. Brilliant and well-read, he has a restless energy and a sharp grasp of nuance and detail that he brings to bear on the crimes he investigates—and later records in murder mystery form. He is sometimes deeply affected by the cases on which he works and often blames himself for failing to arrive at a quicker solution.

• INSPECTOR RICHARD QUEEN, Ellery's father, a respected member of the New York Police Department. A longtime widower, fond of snuff, he lives with his adored son, whom he often consults on particularly difficult cases. A kindly man who is nevertheless tough and persistent in his pursuit of the truth, he enjoys an affectionate, bantering relationship with Ellery.

• DJUNA, the Queens' young houseboy and cook, appears regularly throughout the earlier books in the series. A street waif when he is first taken in by Inspector Queen, he takes charge of the two men's Upper West Side apartment while still a teenager. Bright, slight of build, and possibly a Gypsy by birth, he is tutored and trained by Ellery and his father and greatly admires them both.

**Contribution** • The novels and short stories of Ellery Queen span four decades and have sold more than 150 million copies worldwide, making Queen one of the mystery genre's most popular authors. (For the sake of clarity and simplicity, "Ellery Queen" will be referred to throughout this article as an individual, although the name is actually the pseudonym of two writers, Frederic Dannay and Manfred B. Lee, and several other writers who worked with them.) Queen is also the leading character in his own novels.

Queen's early novels are elaborate puzzles, carefully plotted and solved with almost mathematical logic and precision. They represent a style of detective fiction which flourished in the 1920's, and Queen's contributions have become classics of the form. As the series progressed and Queen developed as a

*Frederic Dannay.* (Library of Congress)

character, the books improved in depth and content, sometimes incorporating sociological, political, or philosophical themes. Their settings range from New York to Hollywood to small-town America, and each is examined with perceptive intelligence. In several of the series' later books, Queen abandons outward reality for the sake of what Frederic Dannay termed "fun and games," letting a mystery unfold in a setting that is deliberately farfetched or farcical.

Queen's novels and stories are also famed for several key plot devices which have become trademarks of his style. Among them are the dying message (a clue left by the victim to the killer's identity), the negative clue (a piece of information which should be present and is notable by its absence), the challenge to the reader (a point in the story at which Queen addresses the reader directly and challenges him to provide the solution), and the double solution (in which one, entirely plausible solution is presented and is then followed by a second, which offers a surprising twist on the first).

Queen's contributions to the field of mystery and detection are not limited to his novels and short stories. *Ellery Queen's Mystery Magazine,* begun in 1941, remains one of the world's leading mystery publications, printing stories by a wide range of authors, while Queen the detective has also been the hero of a long-running radio series, *The Adventures of Ellery Queen* (1939-1948), and several television series, the first of which aired in 1950. In addition, Queen founded the Mystery Writers of America and edited dozens of mystery anthologies and short-story collections.

**Biography** • The two men who together invented the Ellery Queen persona were Brooklyn-born cousins, Frederic Dannay and Manfred Bennington Lee. In reality, their famous alter ego is a pseudonym for two pseudonyms: Dannay was born Daniel Nathan, while Lee's real name was Manford Lepofsky. Both were born in 1905, and both attended Boys' High School in Brooklyn. Lee went on to receive a degree from New York University in 1925, where he pursued what was to be a lifelong interest in music. In 1942, Lee married actress Kaye

Brinker, his second wife, with whom he had eight children—four daughters and four sons. Dannay was married three times: in 1926 to Mary Beck (who later died), with whom he had two sons; in 1947 to Hilda Wisenthal (who died in 1972), with whom he had one son; and in 1975 to Rose Koppel.

During the 1920's, Dannay worked as a writer and art director for a New York advertising agency, while Lee was employed, also in New York, as a publicity writer for several film studios. In 1928, the two cousins began collaborating on a murder mystery, spurred on by a generous prize offered in a magazine detective-fiction contest. The two won the contest, but the magazine was bought by a competitor before the results were announced. The following year, however, Frederick A. Stokes Company, the publishing house cosponsoring the contest, published the cousins' novel, *The Roman Hat Mystery* (1929), and Ellery Queen was born.

By 1931, Dannay and Lee were able to quit their jobs and devote themselves completely to their writing, producing one or two books a year throughout the 1930's. During this period, the pair also wrote briefly under the name Barnaby Ross, publishing the four books which make up the Drury Lane series, *The Tragedy of X* (1932), *The Tragedy of Y* (1932), *The Tragedy of Z* (1933), and *Drury Lane's Last Case* (1933). The bulk of their energy, however, was directed toward Ellery Queen, and the series flourished. Queen's stories were a regular feature in many magazines of the period, and their popularity brought Dannay and Lee to Hollywood, which would later serve as the setting for several of their books.

It was also during the 1930's that Ellery Queen began making appearances on the lecture circuit, and Dannay and Lee's background in advertising and publicity came into play. It was virtually unknown in the early stages of their career that Queen was actually two men, and the cousins perpetuated their readers' ignorance by sending only Dannay, clad in a black mask, to give the lectures. Later, Lee would also appear, as Barnaby Ross, and the pair would treat audiences to a carefully planned "literary argument" between their two fictional creations. It was not until the cousins first went to Hollywood that the world learned that Ellery Queen was actually Dannay and Lee.

During the 1940's, Dannay and Lee produced fewer books and stories, choosing instead to devote themselves to the weekly radio show, *The Adventures of Ellery Queen*, which ran until 1948. In 1941, the pair also created *Ellery Queen's Mystery Magazine*, with Dannay serving as the principal editor. Their collaboration continued throughout the 1950's and 1960's as they produced more Queen novels and stories, edited numerous anthologies and short-story collections, and cofounded the Mystery Writers of America. Dannay also wrote an autobiographical novel, *The Golden Summer* (1953), under the name Daniel Nathan. In 1958, they published *The Finishing Stroke*, a book intended as the last Queen mystery, but they returned to their detective five years later and eventually produced seven more Queen novels, the last of which, *A Fine and Private Place*, appeared in 1971, the year of Lee's death. Dannay continued his work with the magazine until his own death eleven years later.

Among the critical acclaim and wide array of awards Dannay and Lee received were numerous Edgar Allan Poe awards and a Grand Masters Award from the Mystery Writers of America and a place on a 1951 international list of the ten best active mystery writers. Throughout their long partnership, the pair, who bore a remarkable resemblance to each other and often finished each other's sentences in conversations, steadfastly refused to discuss the details of their collaboration. The division of labor between them, in terms of plotting, characterization, and editing, remains unknown.

It is known, however, that during their lifetimes Lee and Dannay's pseudonym became a house name, and numerous mystery novels by Ellery Queen were published by other writers under Lee's or Dannay's supervision. This type of collaboration began in the early 1940's with novelizations of filmscripts. Eventually, two new series characters were introduced under Queen's name: Tim Corrigan and Mike McCall. Some of the authors who wrote as Ellery Queen have been identified: Avram Davidson, Richard Deming, Edward D. Hoch, Stephen Marlowe, Talmadge Powell, Theodore Sturgeon, and John Holbrook Vance.

**Analysis** • Like Agatha Christie, Queen was a master of intricate plotting. From the very first of the Ellery Queen novels, *The Roman Hat Mystery*, his cases are cunningly devised puzzles which the reader must work to assemble along with Queen. Unlike some practitioners of the art, Queen is a believer in fair play; all the pieces to his puzzles are present, if the reader is observant enough to spot them. One of the features of many of the books is Queen's famous "challenge to the reader," in which the narrator notes that all the clues have now been presented and diligent mystery lovers are invited to offer their own solutions before reading on to learn Ellery's. The mysteries abound with misdirections and red herrings, but no vital clue is ever omitted or withheld—although arcane bits of knowledge are sometimes required to reach the proper solution.

In Queen's earliest books, all of which sport "nationality" titles such as *The Egyptian Cross Mystery* (1932) or *The Chinese Orange Mystery* (1934), the clever plotting is often at the expense of character development (as is also true of Christie). The Ellery Queen featured in these novels is a rather cool, bloodless character—an assessment shared by at least one half of the writing partnership which created him. According to Francis M. Nevins, Jr., in his later years Lee was fond of referring to the early Ellery as "the biggest prig that ever came down the pike." It is an accurate description, and one which Queen sought to change later in his career.

Ellery appears in the early books as a brilliant, self-absorbed gentleman sleuth, complete with pince-nez and a passion for rare books. As the series progressed, he slowly grew into a character of some depth and feeling, although he never reached the level of three-dimensional humanity achieved by Dorothy L. Sayers in her development of Lord Peter Wimsey. Indeed, Wimsey is an apt comparison for Queen; both are gentleman sleuths with scholarly interests who begin their fictional careers more as caricatures than characters. Yet Sayers fleshed out her detective so successfully in the following decade and a half that Wimsey's emotional life becomes a central feature in several of her later novels. Queen, on the other hand, is humanized and sketched in without ever becoming a truly compelling figure apart from his dazzling crime-solving talents.

Character development aside, however, Queen's mysteries employ several ingenious recurring plot devices which have become trademarks of the series. Chief among these is the "dying message," in which the victim somehow provides a vital clue to his killer's identity, a ploy which would play an important part in many of the series' later books. It first appeared in *The Tragedy of X*, a Drury Lane novel originally written under the name Barnaby Ross and later reissued with Ellery Queen listed as the author. *The Scarlet Letters* (1953) features one of the most gripping examples of the device, as a dying man leaves a clue for Ellery by writing on the wall in his own blood. *The Roman Hat Mystery* contains another important trademark, the "negative clue," in this case a top hat which should have been found with the victim's body but is missing. The negative clue exemplifies Queen's skills as a detective: He is able to spot not only important evidence at the scene but also details which should have been present and are not.

Another familiar motif in Queen's stories is a carefully designed pattern of clues, sometimes left deliberately by the murderer, which point the way to the crime's solution. *The Finishing Stroke* contains a superb example of the technique in its description of a series of odd gifts left on the twelve days of Christmas for the murderer's intended victim (although the fact that a knowledge of the Phoenician alphabet is necessary to arrive at the solution may strike some readers as unfair). Several of the plots, including those of four back-to-back novels, *Ten Days' Wonder* (1948), *Cat of Many Tails* (1949), *Double, Double* (1950), and *The Origin of Evil* (1951), hinge on a series of seemingly unrelated events, with the murderer's identity hidden within the secret pattern which connects them.

Several of Queen's books also contain "double solutions," with Ellery providing an initial, plausible solution and then delving deeper and arriving at a second, correct conclusion. This device brings added suspense to the stories, as well as opening the door to the realm of psychological detection into which Queen sometimes ventures. In *Cat of Many Tails*, Ellery's initial conclusion, plausible except for one small detail, is forced upon him by a guilt-stricken suspect who is attempting to shield the true murderer. A similar situation arises in *And on the Eighth Day* (1964), when Ellery is deliberately misled—this time by a suspect with noble motives—into providing an incorrect solution that leads to a man's death.

The psychological motivations of his characters play an increasingly important part in Queen's books as the series progresses. One of the author's favorite ploys is the criminal who uses other characters to carry out his plans, a situation which occurs in *Ten Days' Wonder, The Origin of Evil,* and *The Scarlet Letters*. In these cases, Ellery is forced to look beyond the physical details of the crime and search for insight into the mind of the murderer. Often the quarry he seeks is toying with him, taking advantage of the knowledge that Queen is his adversary to tease him with clues or lead him astray. At the close of both *Ten Days' Wonder* and *Cat of Many Tails*, Ellery is overcome with guilt, blaming himself for not solving the cases more quickly and possibly preventing further deaths. Indeed, *Cat of Many Tails* opens with Ellery so shattered by his confrontation with Diedrich Van Horn, the villain of *Ten Days' Wonder*, that he has given up sleuthing altogether—until his father's pleas draw him into a suspenseful serial killer case.

The filial relationship between Ellery and Inspector Richard Queen plays a far greater part in the series' earlier books than it does in later ones. Queen and his father share a Manhattan apartment located on West Eighty-seventh Street (the site of New York's famous Murder Ink bookstore), and Inspector Queen's long career with the police force provides an entrée for Ellery to many of his cases. The two are devoted to each other, and the inspector's admiration for his son's brilliant detective powers knows no bounds. Eventually, however, Queen the author may have believed that he had exhausted the possibilities of the father-son crime-solving team, for Ellery's later cases tend to occur away from home.

A wider variety of settings for his books also gave Queen the opportunity to work a thread of sociological observations throughout his later stories. *Calamity Town* (1942) is set in the small community of Wrightsville (also the setting for *Double, Double*), and Queen colors his story with details of small-town life. Queen knew that there is a particular horror inherent in crimes which shatter an apparently tranquil and unspoiled community. Yet urban crimes have their own form of terror, one which Queen examines in *Cat of Many Tails* as the serial killer strikes seemingly random victims and brings New York City to the brink of panic and chaos. The action shifts from Greenwich Village and Times Square to Harlem and the Upper East Side as Ellery searches for the thread that links the victims' lives. In other Queen novels, Hollywood comes under close scrutiny, sometimes with bemused humor and amazement (*The Four of Hearts*, 1938) or contempt for its greed and power-seeking (*The Origin of Evil*).

*The Origin of Evil* is also representative of the forays into philosophy and religion which Queen undertakes on occasion. This story, whose title is a play on Charles Darwin's *On the Origin of Species* (1859), explores mankind's innate capacity for evil. Religious philosophy is given an interesting twist in *And on the Eighth Day*, in which Ellery stumbles upon a lost desert community and is taken by them to be a prophet whose coming had been foretold to them. Although he believes that their reaction to him is based on a series of misunderstandings and coincidences, he finds that his presence among them has indeed come at a crucial time, and the fulfillment of their ancient prophecy unfolds before his eyes. One chapter, in a clear biblical reference, consists simply of the sentence "And Ellery wept."

Ellery Queen's novels and stories are mysteries with classic components: a murder, a set of clues, a group of suspects, and a gifted detective capable of assembling a revealing picture out of seemingly unrelated facts. Queen's long career as a writer gave him the opportunity to play with the mystery genre, exploring a wide range of settings and themes as he took his character from a "priggish" youth to a more satisfyingly three-dimensional middle age. Yet Queen's enduring popularity remains grounded in those classic elements, and his work stands as proof that there are few things that will delight a reader like a baffling, carefully plotted mystery.

## Principal mystery and detective fiction

SERIES: Tim Corrigan: *Where Is Bianca?*, 1966; *Who Spies, Who Kills?*, 1966; *Why So Dead?*, 1966; *How Goes the Murder?*, 1967; *Which Way to Die?*, 1967; *What's in the Dark?*, 1968 (also as *When Fell the Night*). Drury Lane: *The Tragedy of X*, 1932; *The Tragedy of Y*, 1932; *The Tragedy of Z*, 1933; *Drury Lane's Last Case*, 1933. Mike McCall: *The Campus Murders*, 1969; *The Black Hearts Murder*, 1970; *The Blue Movie Murders*, 1972. Ellery Queen: *The Roman Hat Mystery*, 1929; *The French Powder Mystery*, 1930; *The Dutch Shoe Mystery*, 1931; *The Greek Coffin Mystery*, 1932; *The Egyptian Cross Mystery*, 1932; *The American Gun Mystery*, 1933 (also as *Death at the Rodeo*); *The Siamese Twin Mystery*, 1933; *The Adventures of Ellery Queen*, 1934; *The Chinese Orange Mystery*, 1934; *The Spanish Cape Mystery*, 1935; *Halfway House*, 1936; *The Door Between*, 1937; *The Devil to Pay*, 1938; *The Four of Hearts*, 1938; *The Dragon's Teeth*, 1939 (also as *The Virgin Heiresses*); *The New Adventures of Ellery Queen*, 1940; *Ellery Queen, Master Detective*, 1941 (also as *The Vanishing Corpse*); *The Penthouse Mystery*, 1941; *Calamity Town*, 1942; *The Perfect Crime*, 1942; *The Murdered Millionaire*, 1942; *There Was an Old Woman*, 1943 (also as *The Quick and the Dead*); *The Murderer Is a Fox*, 1945; *Ten Days' Wonder*, 1948; *Cat of Many Tails*, 1949; *Double, Double*, 1950 (also as *The Case of the Seven Murders*); *The Origin of Evil*, 1951; *Calendar of Crime*, 1952; *The King Is Dead*, 1952; *The Scarlet Letters*, 1953; *QBI: Queen's Bureau of Investigation*, 1954; *Inspector Queen's Own Case*, 1956; *The Finishing Stroke*, 1958; *The Player on the Other Side*, 1963; *And on the Eighth Day*, 1964; *Beware the Young Stranger*, 1965; *Queens Full*, 1965; *The Fourth Side of the Triangle*, 1965; *A Study in Terror*, 1966 (also as *Sherlock Holmes vs. Jack the Ripper*); *Face to Face*, 1967; *QED: Queen's Experiments in Detection*, 1968; *The House of Brass*, 1968; *The Last Woman in His Life*, 1970; *A Fine and Private Place*, 1971.

OTHER NOVELS: *The Last Man Club*, 1940; *The Glass Village*, 1954; *Dead Man's Tale*, 1961; *Death Spins the Platter*, 1962; *Kill As Directed*, 1963; *Murder with a Past*, 1963; *Wife or Death*, 1963; *The Last Score*, 1964; *The Golden Goose*, 1964; *Blow Hot, Blow Cold*, 1964; *The Four Johns*, 1964 (also as *Four Men Called John*); *The Killer Touch*, 1965; *The Copper Frame*, 1965; *A Room to Die In*, 1965; *The Devil's Cook*, 1966; *Losers, Weepers*, 1966; *The Madman Theory*, 1966; *Shoot the Scene*, 1966; *Guess Who's Coming to Kill You?*, 1968; *Cop Out*, 1969; *Kiss and Kill*, 1969.

CHILDREN'S LITERATURE (as Ellery Queen, Jr.): *The Black Dog Mystery*, 1941; *The Green Turtle Mystery*, 1941; *The Golden Eagle Mystery*, 1942; *The Red Chipmunk Mystery*, 1946; *The Brown Fox Mystery*, 1948; *The White Elephant Mystery*, 1950; *The Yellow Cat Mystery*, 1952; *The Blue Herring Mystery*, 1954; *The Mystery of the Merry Magician*, 1961; *The Mystery of the Vanished Victim*, 1962; *The Purple Bird Mystery*, 1965; *The Silver Llama Mystery*, 1966.

**Other major works**

PLAYS: *Danger, Men Working*, c. 1936 (with Lowell Brentano); *Ellery Queen, Master Detective*, 1940 (with Eric Taylor).

RADIO PLAYS: *The Adventures of Ellery Queen*, 1939-1948.

NONFICTION: *The Detective Short Story: A Bibliography*, 1942; *Queen's Quorum: A History of the Detective-Crime Short Story As Revealed by the 106 Most Important Books Published in This Field Since 1845*, 1951, revised 1969; *In the Queen's Parlor and Other Leaves from the Editors' Notebook*, 1957; *Ellery Queen's International Case Book*, 1964; *The Woman in the Case*, 1966 (also as *Deadlier Than the Male*); *Queen's Quorum: A History of the Detective-Crime Short Story as Revealed by the 125 Most Important Books Published in This Field, 1845-1967*, 1986.

EDITED TEXTS: *Challenge to the Reader*, 1938; *101 Years' Entertainment: The Great Detective Stories, 1841-1941*, 1941, revised 1946; *Sporting Blood: The Great Sports Detective Stories*, 1942 (also as *Sporting Detective Stories*); *The Female of the Species: The Great Women Detectives and Criminals*, 1943 (also as *Ladies in Crime: A Collection of Detective Stories by English and American Writers*); *The Misadventures of Sherlock Holmes*, 1944; *Best Stories from "Ellery Queen's Mystery Magazine,"* 1944; *The Adventures of Sam Spade and Other Stories*, by Dashiell Hammett, 1944 (also as *They Can Only Hang You Once*); *Rogues' Gallery: The Great Criminals of Modern Fiction*, 1945; *The Continental Op*, by Hammett, 1945; *The Return of the Continental Op*, by Hammett, 1945; *To the Queen's Taste: The First Supplement to "101 Years' Entertainment," Consisting of the Best Stories Published in the First Five Years of "Ellery Queen's Mystery Magazine,"* 1946; *Hammett Homicides*, by Hammett, 1946; *The Queen's Awards*, 1946-1959; *Dead Yellow Women*, by Hammett, 1947; *Murder by Experts*, 1947; *The Riddles of Hildegarde Withers*, by Stuart Palmer, 1947; *Dr. Fell, Detective*, by John Dickson Carr, 1947; *The Department of Dead Ends*, by Roy Vickers, 1947; *The Case Book of Mr. Campion*, by Margery Allingham, 1947; *Twentieth Century Detective Stories*, 1948, revised 1964; *Nightmare Town*, by Hammett, 1948; *Cops and Robbers*, by O. Henry, 1948; *The Literature of Crime: Stories by World-Famous Authors*, 1950 (also as *Ellery Queen's Book of Mystery Stories*); *The Creeping Siamese*, by Hammett, 1950; *The Monkey Murder and Other Hildegarde Withers Stories*, by Palmer, 1950; *Woman in the Dark*, by Hammett, 1952; *Mystery Annals*, 1958-1962; *Ellery Queen's Anthology*, 1959-1973; *To Be Read Before Midnight*, 1962; *A Man Named Thin and Other Stories*, by Hammett, 1962; *Mystery Mix*, 1963; *Double Dozen*, 1964; *Twelve*, 1964; *Twentieth Anniversary Annual*, 1965; *Lethal Black Book*, 1965; *Crime Carousel*, 1966; *All-Star Lineup*, 1966; *Poetic Justice: Twenty-three Stories of Crime, Mystery, and Detection by World-Famous Poets from Geoffrey Chaucer to Dylan Thomas*, 1967; *Mystery Parade*, 1968; *Murder Menu*, 1969; *The Case of the Murderer's Bride and Other Stories*, by Erle Stanley Gardner, 1969; *Minimysteries: Seventy Short-Short Stories of Crime, Mystery, and Detection*, 1969; *Murder—In Spades!*, 1969; *Shoot the Works!*, 1969; *Grand Slam*, 1970; *Mystery Jackpot*, 1970; *P As in Police*, by Lawrence Treat, 1970; *Headliners*, 1971; *The Golden Thirteen: Thirteen First Prize Winners from "Ellery Queen's Mystery Magazine,"* 1971; *The Spy and the Thief*, by Edward D. Hoch, 1971; *Mystery Bag*, 1972; *Ellery Queen's Best Bets*, 1972; *Amateur in Violence*, by Michael Gilbert, 1973; *Crookbook*, 1974; *Christmas Hamper*, 1974; *Kindly Dig Your Grave and Other Stories*, by Stanley Ellin, 1975; *Aces of Mystery*, 1975; *Murdercade*, 1975; *Masters of Mystery*, 1975; *Giants of Mystery*, 1976; *Crime Wave*, 1976; *Magicians of Mystery*, 1976; *How to Trap a Crook and Twelve Other Mysteries*, by Julian Symons, 1977; *Searches and Seizures*, 1977; *Champions of Mystery*, 1977; *Faces of Mystery*, 1977; *Who's Who of Whodunits*, 1977; *Masks of Mystery*, 1977; *Japanese Golden Dozen: The Detective Story World in Japan*, 1978; *A Multitude of Sins*, 1978; *Napoleons of Mystery*, 1978; *The Supersleuths*, 1978; *Secrets of Mystery*, 1979; *Wings of Mystery*, 1979; *Scenes of the Crime*, 1979; *Circumstantial Evidence*, 1980; *Veils of Mystery*, 1980; *Windows of Mystery*, 1980; *Crime Cruise Round the World*, 1981; *Doors to Mystery*, 1981; *Eyes of Mystery*, 1981; *Eyewitnesses*, 1981; *Maze of Mysteries*, 1982; *Book of First Appearances*, 1982 (with Eleanor Sullivan); *Lost Ladies*, 1983 (with Sullivan); *The Best of Ellery Queen*, 1983; *Lost Men*, 1983 (with Sullivan); *Prime Crimes*, 1984 (with Sullivan); *The Best of Ellery Queen: Four Decades of Stories from the Mystery Masters*, 1985 (with Martin H. Greenberg); *Ellery Queen's Blighted Dwellings: Stories Collected from Issues of Ellery Queen's Mystery Magazine*, 1986 (with Eleanor Sullivan); *Six of the Best: Short Novels by Masters of Mystery*, 1989; *The Tragedy of Errors and Others: With Essays and Tributes to Recognize Ellery Queen's Seventieth Anniversary*, 1999.

**Bibliography**

Baker, Robert A., and Michael T. Nietzel. *Private Eyes: One Hundred and One Knights—A Survey of American Detective Fiction, 1922-1984*. Bowling Green, Ohio: Bowling Green State University Popular Press, 1985.

Boucher, Anthony. *Ellery Queen: A Double Profile*. Boston: Little, Brown, 1951.

Geherin, David. *The American Private Eye: The Image in Fiction*. New York: Frederick Ungar, 1985.

Karnick, S. T. "Mystery Men." *National Review* 52, no. 4 (March 6, 2000): 59-61.

Nevins, Francis M., Jr. *Royal Bloodline: Ellery Queen, Author and Detective*. Bowling Green, Ohio: Bowling Green State University Popular Press, 1974.

Nevins, Francis M., Jr., and Ray Stanich. *The Sound of Detection: Ellery Queen's Adventures in Radio*. Madison, Ind.: Brownstone, 1983.

"Queen, Ellery." In *Mystery and Suspense Writers: The Literature of Crime, Detection, and Espionage*, edited by Robin W. Winks and Maureen Corrigan. New York: Charles Scribner's Sons, 1998.

Sullivan, Eleanor. *Whodunit: A Biblio-Bio-Anecdotal Memoir of Frederic Dannay, "Ellery Queen."* New York: Targ Editions, 1984.

*Janet E. Lorenz*

# Ruth Rendell

## Ruth Grasemann

**Born:** London, England; February 17, 1930

**Also wrote as** • Barbara Vine

**Types of plot** • Amateur sleuth • police procedural • psychological • thriller

**Principal series** • Inspector Reginald Wexford, 1964-   .

**Principal series characters** • CHIEF DETECTIVE INSPECTOR REGINALD WEXFORD of Scotland Yard is a lifelong resident of Kingsmarkham, Sussex. He knows his fellow residents as well as the literary works to which he frequently alludes. Fifty-two at his first appearance, he is happily married to Dora Wexford and devoted to their two adult daughters. His sensitivity to human motivations enables him to solve the most complex mysteries.
• DETECTIVE INSPECTOR MIKE BURDEN, Wexford's subordinate and friend, is twenty years younger than Wexford, a police officer who is intelligent but whose understanding of people is hampered by his prudishness. After he loses his young wife, he despairs, but eventually he learns to love again, remarries, and becomes a better father and a more tolerant man.

**Contribution** • Ruth Rendell was one of the most significant new writers to emerge during the late 1960's, when psychological realism replaced the earlier tradition of mannered and elegant mysteries. Whether a Rendell book approaches psychological analysis obliquely–through the detective work of Inspector Wexford–or penetrates the mind of the killer himself, it always presents crime as arising out of the criminal's character. Rendell's work is clearly contemporary, her style crisp and detached, her settings suburban. Among her dull, unimaginative middle-class or lower-middle-class characters, murder would seem to be unlikely; nevertheless, her novels prove that in this environment monotony can become deadly, pettiness can lead to viciousness, and any number of characters, frustrated and imprisoned, might well strike out. It is Rendell's profoundly ironic vision of life and the thorough, complexly intelligent way in which she unfolds it that make her novels extraordinary.

**Biography** • Ruth Rendell was born Ruth Grasemann on February 17, 1930, in London, England. Her parents were Arthur and Ebba Elise Grasemann. After going to school in Essex, she left in 1948 to become a reporter and subeditor at the *Essex Express and Independent,* where she worked for four years. Meanwhile, she married Donald Rendell; they later had a son.

After years of receiving rejection slips for her short stories, Rendell at last aroused a publisher's interest with a light comedy. Instead of rewriting it, as the publisher had suggested, she submitted a mystery novel, did some revising, and had it accepted for publication. This was her first novel, *From Doon with Death* (1964), which introduced Chief Inspector Reginald Wexford to the British reading public; the book was an immediate success. In the following year, with its publication in the United States, Rendell's reputation was established on both sides of the Atlantic.

By the 1970's, P. D. James and Rendell were considered the two major English successors to Agatha Christie. Rendell's short-story collection *The Fallen Curtain and Other Stories* (1976) brought to her an Edgar Allan Poe Award from the Mystery Writers of America; she received the Silver Cup from Current Crime for a Wexford novel, *Shake Hands Forever* (1975); she won the Gold Dagger from the Crime Writers' Association for the psychological thriller *A Demon in My View* (1976). *The Lake of Darkness* (1980) claimed the National Arts Council Book Award for genre fiction. Nor did the awards depend on the magic name Rendell. In 1986, when *A Dark-Adapted Eye* appeared under the pseudonym Barbara Vine, it too won an Edgar. In 1990 she was given the *Sunday Times* Literary award and the Crime Writers' Association Cartier Diamond Dagger for outstanding contribution to the genre. In 1996, the Commander of the British Empire Award was added to the list. She has also received the highest Edgar honor, the Grand Master Award.

**Analysis** • Although Ruth Rendell, her publishers, her critics, and her reading public carefully divide her works into the Wexford series and novels of suspense, the difference is more a matter of approach than of tone. The Wexford books begin with a murder and work in typical police-procedural fashion to the solution of that murder, while the novels of suspense, which have appeared in alternation with the others, trace the psychological development of a murderer or a victim, sometimes one and the same, "ordinary" people who include mothers, housekeepers, interior designers, bridesmaids, painters and artisans, nursing home patients, dogwalkers, activists, and others.

The two kinds of novels, however, are more alike than different. Earlier English house-party novels were in many ways akin to comedies of manners; the writer did not attack the norms of the society itself but simply the foolish or vicious who deviate from those norms. In these earlier mysteries, the murder was not merely an interruption of the delightful pattern of talk, games, and visits; it was a breach of decorum as well. Once the murderer was unmasked and removed, the innocent could proceed with trivial but pleasant lives, lives dominated not by dull routine but by rational or even providential order. Rendell's books are very different. Although her middle-class or lower-middle-class characters work, shop, eat, and watch television in patterns which vary little from day to day, most of them find neither happiness nor security in their routines. They simply pass the time, avoiding a confrontation with the real misery and meaninglessness of their lives. When the murderer is removed from society, there is no real reestablishment of order; too many other unhappy characters remain in their perilous balance between quiet desperation and violence.

Perhaps because he has lived for so long with a wife and two daughters, Rendell's Inspector Wexford is especially sensitive to domestic arrangements. In *From Doon with Death*, for example, he senses foul play when a wife disappears, leaving the spotless house which she obviously values. In *A Guilty Thing Surprised* (1970), it is the difference between a filthy house and a clean shed which enables him to understand Sean Lovell, the would-be rock star, who has made the shed his sanctuary and his stage.

The success of Wexford's investigations depends not upon mere skill at observation in the Sherlock Holmes tradition, but more profoundly upon his ability to fit the details of setting to the preoccupations of the people whom he meets. In *The Veiled One* (1988), for example, he finds it significant that one householder chooses to live in an almost empty house, while her attic is stuffed with comfortable furniture; in *An Unkindness of Ravens* (1985), he notices that Joy Williams's daughter is stuffed into a tiny bedroom, while her son has the larger room, which most parents would give to their daughter. From such details, Wexford deduces the resentments from which may spring murder.

Although Wexford and Burden possess clear standards of good and evil to guide their own behavior and although both of them are fortunate enough to attract love, their lives are not easier than those of others. Burden's first wife dies, and he suffers from grief; after he remarries, his new wife nearly has a nervous breakdown during her pregnancy. Wexford himself worries about his daughters, who marry, get divorced, and sometimes quarrel with each other. By interweaving the details of her detectives' lives with their pursuit of killers, Rendell suggests an alternative to the petty cruelty, deceit, infidelity, and brutality which is so typical of the other characters: the understanding patience and forbearing love which enable Burden to wait out his wife's bad temper, which enable Wexford to understand his daughter's idealistic defiance of authority and to forgive her disregard of his own professional embarrassment.

The same ironic use of everyday detail, the same interplay between characters and their domestic surroundings, the same demarcation between characters who make the best of their lives and those who, obsessed by hatred or desire, make the worst of them is also seen in Rendell's suspense novels. In *To Fear a Painted Devil* (1965), the crucial object, pointed out in the prologue, is a gory painting of Salome holding John the Baptist's head. When the story moves to the present, the nine-year-old boy who had once been terrified by the painting is a grown man who is consistently nasty to his wife. When he dies, there seem to be no grounds for regret. Nevertheless, a doctor, who in this book takes the place of Wexford, is discontented with the verdict of accidental or natural death. His need to investigate further leads him behind the façade of neat gardens, tennis matches, and invitations for drinks to the discovery of a middle-aged man's obsession and a young woman's use of it to dispose of her husband. The seemingly respectable, prosperous, middle-class characters in this novel are revealed as liars, adulterers, and even murderers. Having observed the extent to which people can use others, it is not surprising that in the final moments of the novel the doctor seeks his home and his own loving wife as an antidote to his vision of evil.

Although *A Fatal Inversion* (1987) also involves a murder, in this case, there is no detective, amateur or professional. Instead, the novelist follows a group of successful men who have repressed the memory of those deaths for which they had been responsible a decade before. The focus is on an estate which the killer inherited, and in particular the house, filled with family treasures, where a group of young people attempted an irresponsible, hippielike existence. From contempt for the treasures of the past, which they destroyed or sold, they had proceeded to contempt for human life, kidnapping a baby, who subsequently died, and then killing one of their group who insisted on going to the police. When the body is accidentally discovered in a pet cemetery on the estate, the members of the group, now prominent in various fields, must face their guilt. Although at the end of the novel the police are no closer to solving the crime than they had been when the body was found and only the reader knows what really happened, clearly the wrongdoers have been sentenced to live with their actions.

Rendell's suspense novels explore, with an incomparable and compassionate acuity, the darkest spots in the human mind and spirit. In *The Bridesmaid* (1989), for example, she traces the path of an amiable young man from the unremarkable routine of his mundane, mildly unsatisfying days into troubled spheres he never imagined—and makes it, through her observance of detail and psychological realities, entirely credible. In *Keys to the Street* (1996), a young woman housesitting learns to what extremes of both tenderness and cruelty human nature is capable of going. *A Sight for Sore Eyes* (1998) slowly twines together the courses of three individuals damaged to very different effect by life and their own complex psychological reactions to pain and loss. In all her works, Rendell focuses unwaveringly on closeted acts of insanity and on the interdependent and tangled fragility of relationships among people, both familiars and strangers.

*The Veiled One* is typical of Rendell's ironic approach. The contemporary setting is a suburban shopping center; the corpse is that of a middle-aged woman, strangely garroted and left in a underground parking garage. The murder is first noticed by a woman, who then stands screaming at the locked gates of the center. She is observed by a man who spends much of his time at his window, watching people come and go from the center; the center is the most interesting place any of them ever go, except imaginatively in magazines or on television. Thus Rendell sums up the lives of her characters, whose movements in and out of the shopping center, the supermarket, the knitting shop, and the health-food store will provide the key to the murder which Inspector Wexford must solve.

The details which Wexford notices on his visit to the woman who found the body emphasize the relationship between surroundings and character, which is always stressed in a Rendell mystery. Dorothy Sanders lives in a house without charm or real comfort:

> Inside, the place was bleak and cavernous; carpets and central heating were not luxuries that Mrs. Sanders went in for. The hall floor was quarry-tiled, in the living room they walked on wood-grain linoleum and a couple of sparse rugs.

The coldness of the house reflects the coldness of Sanders's character. When her grown son, Clifford, is described as meekly sitting in his stocking feet so as not to dirty the floor, his mother's control over him is made clear. With such detailed descriptions of domestic surroundings, Rendell reveals a considerable amount about her characters and their relationships and thus prepares for the drama which is to ensue.

As Inspector Wexford knocks on the doors of the other neat suburban homes, he finds evidence of pretense, deceit, anger, and hatred. Lesley Arbel's attendance on her bereaved uncle, for example, turns out to be an attempt to retrieve some letters. Roy Carroll does not even pretend kindliness toward the world. His missing wife was obviously treated no more compassionately than his cowed dog. As for the murdered woman herself, she was willing to do anything for money, from persuading old people to change their wills to her final ingenious system of blackmail.

Because they are human, Wexford and Burden are not exempt from the evil which pervades the world. Throughout the novel, Wexford must struggle with his desire to force his daughter out of the antinuclear activism which he thinks caused the bombing of her car. He manages to keep his conscience clear, but Burden becomes obsessed with breaking the spirit of Clifford Sanders, at first because he is sure that Clifford is the killer but increasingly because it has become an exercise in power. When Clifford transfers his allegiance to his inquisitor, Burden rejects him; later, when Clifford, who is found innocent of the car-park murder, kills his mother, Burden is left with the question of his own responsibility in the matter. The quality shared by well-meaning characters such as Wexford, Burden, and the psychologist Serge Olson—who has been treating Clifford—is their values: They are impelled by a sense of duty as well as by an honest compassion for others. Therefore, they can provide the standard against which to measure the many characters who exhibit the worst in human behavior.

Like all Rendell novels, *The Veiled One* is dominated by a particular object—in this case, the circular knitting needle which Wexford concludes was the murder weapon. As Wexford visits women, watches them knit, notices flaws in lovingly knitted sweaters, stops in at the knitting shop in the mall, and finally times the murder by tracing a parcel of gray wool, he is moving toward the killer, Clifford's mother. Evidently, she has done away with a total of four people over a period of many years.

Nevertheless, order is not restored when she is eliminated by her son, as it would have been in one of the older house-guest mysteries. What is communicated and explored in Rendell's Wexford novels, the Barbara Vine works, and her collections of short fiction is that beneath the surface of everyday life evil is always lurking, that order itself is at best an ideal to which individuals can aspire, at worst a myth. It is this constant reminder of human malevolence which makes Rendell's works, beyond their realism of detail and character, so suspenseful, ironic, and unforgettable.

## Principal mystery and detective fiction

SERIES: Inspector Wexford: *From Doon with Death,* 1964; *A New Lease of Death,* 1967 (also as *Sins of the Fathers*); *Wolf to the Slaughter,* 1967; *The Best Man to Die,* 1969; *A Guilty Thing Surprised,* 1970; *No More Dying Then,* 1971; *Murder Being Once Done,* 1972; *Some Lie and Some Die,* 1973; *Shake Hands Forever,* 1975; *A Sleeping Life,* 1978; *Means of Evil and Other Stories,* 1979; *Death Notes,* 1981 (also as *Put On by Cunning*); *The Speaker of Mandarin,* 1983; *An Unkindness of Ravens,* 1985; *The Veiled One,* 1988; *The Second Wexford Omnibus,* 1988; *The Third Wexford Omnibus,* 1989; *Kissing the Gunner's Daughter,* 1992; *Simisola,* 1995; *Road Rage,* 1997; *Harm Done,* 1999.

OTHER NOVELS: *To Fear a Painted Devil,* 1965; *Vanity Dies Hard,* 1966 (also as *In Sickness and in Health*); *The Secret House of Death,* 1968; *One Across, Two Down,* 1971; *The Face of Trespass,* 1974; *A Demon in My View,* 1976; *A Judgment in Stone,* 1977; *Make Death Love Me,* 1979; *The Lake of Darkness,* 1980; *Master of the Moor,* 1982; *The Killing Doll,* 1984; *The Tree of Hands,* 1984; *Live Flesh,* 1986; *The New Girlfriend,* 1986; *A Dark-Adapted Eye,* 1986; *A Fatal Inversion,* 1987; *Talking to Strange Men,* 1987; *Heartstones,* 1987; *The House of Stairs,* 1988; *The Bridesmaid,* 1989; *Undermining the Central Line,* 1989; *Gallowglass,* 1990; *Going Wrong,* 1990; *King Solomon's Carpet,* 1991; *Asta's Book,* 1993 (also as Anna's Book); *The Crocodile Bird,* 1993; *No Night Is Too Long,* 1994; *The Brimstone Wedding,* 1996; *The Keys to the Street,* 1996; *The Chimney Sweeper's Boy,* 1998; *A Sight for Sore Eyes,* 1999; *Grasshopper,* 2001.

OTHER SHORT FICTION: *The Fallen Curtain and Other Stories,* 1976; *The Fever Tree and Other Stories of Suspense,* 1984; *The New Girl Friend and Other Stories of Suspense,* 1986; *Collected Stories,* 1988; *The Copper Peacock Short Stories,* 1991; *The Fever Tree and Other Stories,* 1992; *Blood Lines: Long and Short Stories,* 1996; *Pirhana to Scurfy and Other Stories,* 2001.

## Other major works

NONFICTION: *Ruth Rendell's Suffolk,* 1992 (with Paul Bowden).

EDITED WORKS: *Dr. Thorne,* 1991 (by Anthony Trollope); *The Reason Why: An Anthology of the Murderous Mind,* 1995.

## Bibliography
Bakerman, Jane S. "Rendell Territory." *The Mystery Nook* 10 (May, 1977): A1.
_____. "Ruth Rendell." In *Ten Women of Mystery,* edited by Earl F.

Bargainnier. Bowling Green, Ohio: Bowling Green State University Popular Press, 1981.

Klein, Kathleen Gregory, ed. *Great Women Mystery Writers: Classic to Contemporary.* Westport, Conn.: Greenwood Press, 1994.

Miller, Don. "A Look at the Novels of Ruth Rendell." *The Mystery Nook* 10 (May, 1977): A7-A17.

"Rendell, Ruth." In *Mystery and Suspense Writers: The Literature of Crime, Detection, and Espionage,* edited by Robin W. Winks and Maureen Corrigan. New York: Charles Scribner's Sons, 1998.

Rowland, Susan. *From Agatha Christie to Ruth Rendell.* New York: St. Martin's Press, 2000.

Symons, Julian. *Bloody Murder: From the Detective Story to the Crime Novel: A History.* Rev. ed. New York: Viking, 1985.

Tallett, Dennis. *The Ruth Rendell Companion.* Santa Barbara, Calif.: Companion Books, 1995.

Wyndham, Francis. "Deadly Details." *The Times Literary Supplement,* June 5, 1981, p. 626.

*Rosemary M. Canfield-Reisman*
*Updated by Fiona Kelleghan and Jessica Reisman*

# Mary Roberts Rinehart

**Born:** Pittsburgh, Pennsylvania; August 12, 1876
**Died:** New York, New York; September 22, 1958

**Type of plot**   Amateur sleuth

**Principal series** • Miss Pinkerton, 1914-1942.

**Principal series character** • HILDA ADAMS, a trained nurse, is called "Miss Pinkerton" by DETECTIVE INSPECTOR PATTON, who makes sure that she attends the bedside of prominent citizens who suffer illness or nervous collapse after a robbery, murder, or family crisis. Single, sensible, intelligent, and strong-willed, she is twenty-nine in her first appearance and thirty-eight by the last.

**Contribution** • In a 1952 radio interview, Mary Roberts Rinehart said that she had helped the mystery story grow up by adding flesh and muscle to the skeleton of plot. Beginning at the height of the Sherlock Holmes craze, Rinehart introduced humor and romance and created protagonists with whom readers identified. Thus, the emotions of fear, laughter, love, and suspense were added to the intellectual pleasure of puzzle tales. *The Circular Staircase* (1908) was immediately hailed as something new, an American detective story that owed little to European influences and concerned characteristically American social conditions.

Rinehart's typical novel had two lines of inquiry, often at cross purposes, by a woman amateur and by a police detective. The woman, lacking the resources and scientific laboratories to gather and interpret physical evidence, observes human nature, watches for unexpected reactions, and delves for motive. The necessary enrichment of background and characterization forced the short tale (which was typical at the turn of the century) to grow into the detective novel. Critics sometimes patronize Rinehart as inventor of the "Had-I-But-Known" school of female narrators who withhold clues and stupidly prowl around dark attics. Her techniques, however, were admirably suited to magazine serialization. In addition to its influence on detective fiction, Rinehart's work led to the genre of romantic suspense.

**Biography** • Mary Roberts was reared in Pittsburgh, Pennsylvania. Her father was an unsuccessful salesman, and her mother took in roomers. At fifteen, Mary was editing her high school newspaper and writing stories for *Pittsburgh Press* contests. In 1893 she entered nurse's training at a hospital whose public wards teemed with immigrants, industrial workers, and local prostitutes. In

1895 her father committed suicide. Mary Roberts completed her training and, in April, 1896, married a young physician, Stanley Rinehart.

In the next six years she had three sons, helped with her husband's medical practice, and looked for a means of self-expression. By 1904 she was selling short stories to *Munsey's Magazine, Argosy,* and other magazines. *The Circular Staircase* was published, and *The Man in Lower Ten* (1909) became the first detective story ever to make the annual best-seller list.

In 1910-1911, the Rineharts traveled to Vienna so that Stanley Rinehart could study a medical specialty. During the next few years, Rinehart concentrated on books with medical and political themes. When war broke out, she urged *The Saturday Evening Post* to make her a correspondent. In 1915 reporters were not allowed to visit the Allied lines, but Rinehart used her nurse's training to earn Red Cross credentials. She examined hospitals, toured "No Man's Land," and interviewed both the King of Belgium and the Queen of England.

Her war articles made Rinehart a public figure as well as a best-selling novelist. She covered the political conventions of 1916 (taking time out to march in a women's suffrage parade) and turned down an offer to edit *Ladies' Home Journal.* In 1920 two plays written with Avery Hopwood were on Broadway. *The Bat* had an initial run of 878 performances and eventually brought in more than nine million dollars. Rinehart lived in Washington, D.C., during the early 1920's. In 1929 two of her sons set up a publishing firm in partnership with John Farrar. Annual books by Mary Roberts Rinehart provided dependable titles for the Farrar and Rinehart list.

Rinehart moved to New York in 1935, following her husband's death in 1932, and continued an active life. Eleven of her books made best-seller lists between 1909 and 1936. The comic adventures of her dauntless spinster heroine Tish had been appearing in *The Saturday Evening Post* since 1910. During the 1930's, she also produced an autobiography, wrote the somber short fiction collected in *Married People* (1937), and underwent a mastectomy. In 1946 Rinehart went public with the story of her breast cancer and urged women to have examinations. Her last novel was published in 1952, although a story in *Ellery Queen's Mystery Magazine* in 1954 neatly rounded out the half century of detective writing since her poem "The Detective Story"–a spoof of the Sherlock Holmes craze–appeared in *Munsey's Magazine* in 1904. She died in 1958.

**Analysis** • Mary Roberts Rinehart significantly changed the form of the mystery story in the early years of the twentieth century by adding humor, romance, and the spine-chilling terror experienced by readers who identify with the amateur detective narrator. Borrowing devices from gothic novels of the late eighteenth and early nineteenth centuries and from sensation fiction of the 1860's, Rinehart infused emotion into the intellectual puzzles of ratiocination which dominated late nineteenth and early twentieth century magazines. By securing identification with the central character, she made readers share the perplexity, anxiety, suspense, and terror of crime and detection. Since she did not deal in static cases brought to a master detective for solution but rather with stories of ongoing crime, in which the need for concealment escalates as exposure approaches, the narrator almost inevitably becomes a target and potential victim.

Rinehart's typical mystery has two investigators. One is a professional detective and the other a woman amateur who narrates the story. All the important characters must be sufficiently developed so that the amateur can make deductions by watching their emotional responses and penetrating their motives. Rinehart's books also include both romance (sometimes between the two detectives) and humor. *The Man in Lower Ten,* her first full-length mystery, was intended as a spoof of the pompous self-importance with which Great Detectives analyzed clues.

Like many readers, Rinehart used mysteries for escape; the "logical crime story," she wrote, "provided sufficient interest in the troubles of others to distract the mind from its own." On the wards of a busy urban hospital she had seen "human relations at their most naked." In writing, however, she "wanted escape from remembering" and therefore chose "romance, adventure, crime, . . . where the criminal is always punished and virtue triumphant."

She saw the mystery as "a battle of wits between reader and writer," which consists of two stories. One is known only to the criminal and to the author; the other is enacted by the detective. These two stories run concurrently. The reader follows one, while "the other story, submerged in the author's mind [rises] to the surface here and there to form those baffling clews." In "The Repute of the Crime Story" (*Publishers Weekly,* February 1, 1930), Rinehart outlined the "ethics" of crime writing. The criminal

> should figure in the story as fully as possible; he must not be dragged in at the end. There must be no false clues. . . . Plausibility is important, or the story may become merely a "shocker." The various clues which have emerged throughout the tale should be true indices to the buried story, forming when assembled at the conclusion a picture of that story itself.

In most of Rinehart's mysteries the "buried story" is not simply the concealment of a single crime. Also hidden—and explaining the criminal's motives—are family secrets such as illegitimacy, unsuitable marriages, or public disgrace. This material reflects the sexual repression and social hypocrisy embodied in Victorian culture's effort to present an outward appearance of perfect respectability and moral rectitude. Rinehart forms a bridge between the sensational novels of the 1860's, which had used similar secrets, and the twentieth century psychological tale. Clues locked in character's minds appear in fragments of dream, slips of the tongue, or inexplicable aversions and compulsions. In a late novel, *The Swimming Pool* (1952), the amateur detective enlists a psychiatrist to help retrieve the repressed knowledge. Even in her earliest books Rinehart used Freudian terminology to describe the unconscious.

Rinehart's stories typically take place in a large house or isolated wealthy community. In British mysteries of the interwar years a similar setting provided social stability; in Rinehart, however, the house is often crumbling and the family, by the end of the tale, disintegrated. The secret rooms, unused attics, and hidden passageways not only promote suspense but also symbolize the futile attempt of wealthy people to protect their status by concealing secrets even from one another. These settings also allow for people to hide important information from motives of privacy, loyalty to friends, and distaste for the police. In the Miss Pinkerton series (two stories published in *The Saturday Evening Post* in 1914, a collection of short fiction published in 1925, novels dated 1932 and 1942, and an omnibus volume published under the title *Miss Pinkerton* in 1959), Inspector Patton uses nurse Hilda Adams as an agent because when any prominent family is upset by crime, "somebody goes to bed, with a trained nurse in attendance."

Relations between the professional detective and the woman amateur—who is generally an intelligent and spirited single woman in her late twenties or early thirties—are marked by mutual respect and friendly sparring. Rinehart was not ignorant of scientific methods; her medical training made her perfectly comfortable with physiological evidence and the terminology of coroners' reports. The official detective discovers physical clues and uses police resources to interview witnesses and tail suspects. Yet, as the narrator of *The Circular Staircase* says, "both footprints and thumb-marks are more useful in fiction than in fact." The unofficial detective accumulates a separate—and often contradictory—fund of evidence by observing people's reactions, analyzing unexpected moments of reticence, understanding changes in household routine, and exploring emotional states. The official detective enlists her aid, but she may conceal some information because she senses that he will laugh at it or because she is afraid that it implicates someone about whom she cares. She ventures into danger to conduct investigations on her own partly because she wants to prove the detective wrong and partly because of her own joy in the chase.

Although she wrote several essays on the importance to women of home and family life, Rinehart was an active suffragist and proud of having been a "pioneer" who went into a hospital for professional training at a time "when young women of my class were leading their helpless protected lives." In her work, Rinehart used women's "helplessness" and repression as a convincing psychological explanation for failure to act, for deviousness, and even for crime. In *The Circular Staircase*, a young woman complains of the humiliation of being surrounded by "every indulgence" but never having any money of her own to use without having to answer questions. The sexual repression and social propriety of women forced to depend on relatives for support because class mores prohibit their employment breed bitterness and hatred. Rinehart's explicit yet empathetic exploration of motives for crime among women of the middle and upper classes is a marked contrast to the misogyny of the hard-boiled school.

The innovations of Rinehart's formula were almost fully developed in her first published book, *The Circular Staircase*. The wry tone, the narrator's per-

sonality, the setting, and the foreshadowing are established in the opening
sentence:

> This is the story of how a middle-aged spinster lost her mind, deserted her domes-
> tic gods in the city, took a furnished house for the summer out of town, and found
> herself involved in one of those mysterious crimes that keep our newspapers and de-
> tective agencies happy and prosperous.

Rachel Innes shares certain traits with Anna Katharine Green's Amelia
Butterworth—both are inquisitive spinsters of good social standing—but Rinehart's humor, her economical and spirited narration, and her ability to manage multiple threads of a complex plot made an instant impact on reviewers.

The house that Rachel Innes rents is a typical Rinehart setting with its
twenty-two rooms, five baths, multiple doors, French windows, unused attics,
and a circular staircase off the billiard room which was installed apparently so
licentious young men could get up to bed without waking anyone. In addition,
the electric company which serves the remote locale regularly shuts down at
midnight. Before many days have passed, Rachel Innes is awakened by a gun-
shot at three o'clock in the morning and discovers, lying at the bottom of the
circular staircase, the body of a well-dressed gentleman whom she has never
seen before.

The romantic complications which shortly ensue confound the mystery.
Rachel Innes's nephew and niece (Halsey and Gertrude) are both secretly engaged, and each has some possible provocation for having murdered the in-
truder. Fear that her nephew or niece might be involved gives Rachel Innes a
reason to conceal information from the detective, Jamieson. At the same time,
some of the evidence that seems to point toward Halsey or Gertrude arises
from their attempts to preserve the secrecy of their romantic attachments.

There are actually two "buried stories" in *The Circular Staircase*, although
both Jamieson and Innes believe that they are on the track of a single criminal.
The "outcroppings" that provide clues toward the solution of one mystery
therefore lay false trails for the other. One involves a secret marriage (or
pseudomarriage), an abandoned child, and a vengeful woman; the other is a
banker's scheme to stage a fake death so that he can escape with the proceeds
of an embezzlement. The ongoing efforts to conceal the second crime lead to
further murders and then to Halsey's disappearance. That is a significant emotional shift; the tale now concerns not only the process of detection but also
the threat of danger to characters about whom the reader cares. Rinehart
orchestrates the suspense with additional gothic elements, a midnight dis-
interment, and a hair-raising climax in which Innes is trapped in the dark with
an unknown villain in a secret chamber that no one knows how to enter. The
identification of reader with detective and the sure-handed manipulation of
suspense and terror are hallmarks of the Rinehart style (and of a great many
subsequent thrillers).

The competition between the woman amateur and the male professional is
to some degree a conflict between intuitive and rational thinking. While

Jamieson accumulates physical evidence and investigates public records, Innes listens to the tones that indicate concealment, understands when people are acting against their will, and believes her senses even when they seem to perceive the impossible. At one point her nephew says, "Trust a woman to add two and two together, and make six." She responds,

> If two and two plus X make six, then to discover the unknown quantity is the simplest thing in the world. That a household of detectives missed it entirely was because they were busy trying to prove that two and two make four.

Both the suspense and the humor are heightened by Rinehart's facility with language. Her use of a middle-aged spinster's genteel vocabulary to describe crime, murder, and terror is amusing, and her ease with other dialects and with the small linguistic slips that mar a banker's disguise in the role of a gardener show the range of her verbal resources.

In a later generation, when some of Rinehart's innovations had been incorporated in most crime fiction and others had given rise to the separate genre of romantic suspense, critics of the detective story frequently wrote condescendingly of her as the progenitor of the Had-I-But-Known school of narration. The device grew from the demands of magazine writing; only two of Rinehart's mysteries had their initial publication in book form. When writing serials, she pointed out, each installment "must end so as to send the reader to the news stand a week before the next installment is out." The narrator's veiled reference to coming events arouses suspense and maintains the reader's anxious mood.

Mary Roberts Rinehart began writing mysteries two years after *The Hound of the Baskervilles* (1902) was published; she was already well established by the heyday of British classical detection, published throughout the hard-boiled era, and was still writing when Ian Fleming started work on the James Bond books. By the time Rinehart died, her books had sold more than eleven million copies in hardcover and another nine million in paperback. The bibliographical record presents some problems. Rinehart identified seventeen books as crime novels; in these, the central action is an attempt to discover the causes of a murder. Almost all of her fiction, however, combines romance, humor, violence, and buried secrets, and paperback reprints often use the "mystery" label for books which Rinehart would not have put into that category. There are also variant British titles for some books and a number of omnibus volumes that collect novels and short stories in various overlapping configurations.

## Principal mystery and detective fiction

SERIES: Miss Pinkerton: *Mary Roberts Rinehart's Crime Book*, 1925; *Miss Pinkerton*, 1932 (also as *Double Alibi*); *Haunted Lady*, 1942; *Miss Pinkerton*, 1959.

OTHER NOVELS: *The Circular Staircase*, 1908; *The Man in Lower Ten*, 1909; *The Window at the White Cat*, 1910; *Where There's a Will*, 1912; *The Case of Jennie Brice*,

1913; *The After House*, 1914; *Sight Unseen, and The Confession*, 1921; *The Red Lamp*, 1925 (also as *The Mystery Lamp*); *The Bat*, 1926 (with Avery Hopwood); *Two Flights Up*, 1928; *The Door*, 1930; *The Album*, 1933; *The Wall*, 1938; *The Great Mistake*, 1940; *The Yellow Room*, 1945; *The Swimming Pool*, 1952 (also as *The Pool*).

OTHER SHORT FICTION: *Alibi for Isabel and Other Stories*, 1944; *Episode of the Wandering Knife: Three Mystery Tales*, 1950 (also as *The Wandering Knife*); *The Frightened Wife and Other Murder Stories*, 1953.

PLAY: *The Bat*, 1920 (with Hopwood).

## Other major works

NOVELS: *When a Man Marries*, 1909; *The Street of Seven Stars*, 1914; *K*, 1915; *Long Live the King!*, 1917; *The Amazing Interlude*, 1918; *Twenty-three and a Half Hours' Leave*, 1918; *Dangerous Days*, 1919; *The Truce of God*, 1920; *A Poor Wise Man*, 1920; *The Breaking Point*, 1921; *The Trumpet Sounds*, 1927; *Lost Ecstasy*, 1927 (also as *I Take This Woman*); *This Strange Adventure*, 1929; *Mr. Cohen Takes a Walk*, 1933; *The State Versus Elinor Norton*, 1933 (also as *The Case of Elinor Norton*); *The Doctor*, 1936; *The Curve of the Catenary*, 1945; *A Light in the Window*, 1948.

SHORT FICTION: *The Amazing Adventures of Letitia Carberry*, 1911; *Tish*, 1916; *Bab: A Sub-Deb*, 1917; *Love Stories*, 1919; *Affinities and Other Stories*, 1920; *More Tish*, 1921; *Temperamental People*, 1924; *Tish Plays the Game*, 1926; *The Romantics*, 1929; *Married People*, 1937; *Tish Marches On*, 1937; *Familiar Faces: Stories of People You Know*, 1941; *The Best of Tish*, 1955.

PLAYS: *A Double Life*, 1906; *Seven Days*, 1907 (with Hopwood); *Cheer Up*, 1912; *Spanish Love*, 1920 (with Hopwood); *The Breaking Point*, 1923.

SCREENPLAY: *Aflame in the Sky*, 1927 (with Ewart Anderson).

NONFICTION: *Kings, Queens, and Pawns: An American Woman at the Front*, 1915; *Through Glacier Park: Seeing America First with Howard Eaton*, 1916; *The Altar of Freedom*, 1917; *Tenting Tonight: A Chronicle of Sport and Adventure in Glacier Park and the Cascade Mountains*, 1918; *Isn't That Just like a Man!*, 1920; *The Out Trail*, 1923; *Nomad's Land*, 1926; *My Story*, 1931; (revised as *My Story: A New Edition and Seventeen New Years*, 1948); *Writing Is Work*, 1939.

## Bibliography

Bachelder, Frances H. *Mary Roberts Rinehart: Mistress of Mystery*. San Bernardino, Calif.: Brownstone Books, 1993.

Bargainnier, Earl F., ed. *Ten Women of Mystery*. Bowling Green, Ohio: Bowling Green State University Popular Press, 1981.

Cohn, Jan. *Improbable Fiction: The Life of Mary Roberts Rinehart*. Pittsburgh, Penn: University of Pittsburgh Press, 1980.

Doran, George H. *Chronicles of Barrabas, 1884-1934*. New York: Harcourt, Brace, 1935.

Downing, Sybil, and Jane Valentine Barker. *Crown of Life: The Story of Mary Roberts Rinehart*. Niwot, Colo.: Roberts Rinehart Publishers, 1992.

Fleenor, Julian E., ed. *The Female Gothic*. Montreal: Eden Press, 1983.

Klein, Kathleen Gregory, ed. *Great Women Mystery Writers: Classic to Contempo-

*rary*. Westport, Conn.: Greenwood Press, 1994.
MacLeod, Charlotte. *Had She But Known: A Biography of Mary Roberts Rinehart*. New York: Mysterious Press, 1994.
Nye, Russel B., ed. *New Dimensions in Popular Culture*. Bowling Green, Ohio: Bowling Green State University Popular Press, 1972.

*Sally Mitchell*

# Lawrence Sanders

**Born:** Brooklyn, New York; 1920
**Died:** Pompano Beach, Florida, February 7, 1998

**Also wrote as** • Lesley Andress

**Types of plot** • Police procedural • private investigator • espionage • amateur sleuth • hard-boiled

**Principal series** • Edward X. Delaney, 1970-1985 • Peter Tangent, 1976-1978 • Commandment, 1978-1991 • Archy McNally, 1992-1997.

**Principal series characters** • EDWARD X. DELANEY, a retired Chief of Detectives of the New York City Police Department. Known as "Iron Balls" among longtime departmental members, he is in his mid-fifties. A man of uncompromising integrity who revels in the smallest investigative details, Delaney is well-read, enjoys food enormously, possesses a sardonic sense of humor, and can laugh at himself. He insists that reason must prevail and maintains that his work as a police detective helps to restore a moral order quickly falling into ruins.

• PETER TANGENT is a quasi investigator in West Africa for an American oil company. He is nonheroic but capable of recognizing and admiring heroism in others. Initially he comes to West Africa as an exploiter of the political chaos there, but, by coming to know a genuine native hero, he loses some of his cynicism.

• ARCHIBALD MCNALLY, debonair playboy and amateur sleuth, directs a small department (personnel: one) dedicated to Discreet Inquiries at the law firm of McNally & Son, which is led by his father, Prescott McNally. Expelled from Yale Law School because of public streaking, Archy failed to secure a law degree and instead investigates potentially embarrassing matters for the elite of Palm Beach. Often seen wearing his favorite puce beret, this loquacious dandy enjoys driving his red Miata, eating fine foods, and drinking a marc accompanied by an English Oval before retiring each evening. Each Discrete Inquiry evolves into a full-fledged mystery.

**Contribution** • The range of Lawrence Sanders's novels covers the classic police procedural, the private investigator, the amateur sleuth, the hard-boiled, and the espionage genres. He has made some distinctive contributions to detective fiction by crossing and combining the conventions of the police procedural with those associated with the private investigator and/or the amateur sleuth. By synthesizing these genres, he has been able to expand his areas of interest and inquiry, blending the seasoned perceptions of the professional with the original perceptions of the amateur. While working within the tradition of both Raymond Chandler and Dashiell Hammett, Sanders has added technical innovations of his own, notably in *The Anderson Tapes* (1970), an entire novel created out of a Joycean montage gleaned from police reports, wiretaps, and listening devices.

Sanders became a best-selling novelist with this first book and remained so with each subsequent novel. Most important, however, is the complexity of the characters he has added to detective fiction. They are mature, multifaceted, and perplexing. His heroes probe their criminals with a Dostoevskian level of insight rare in popular crime fiction. Unlike any other practitioner of the genre, Sanders unashamedly takes as the principal content in his two major series the most basic ethical and moral precepts of a Judeo-Christian society: the deadly sins and the commandments. He also explores in great depth the qualities which the pursued and the pursuer secretly share. In his final series, the Archibald McNally books, Sanders continued to deliver a high quality mystery novel utilizing the talents of an amateur sleuth. These are by far his most lighthearted novels, yet the antics of his engaging characters in no way diminish the impact of his stories or their ability to question the darker side of human behavior.

**Biography** • Lawrence Sanders was born in Brooklyn, New York, in 1920, and was reared and educated in the Midwest, specifically Michigan, Minnesota, and Indiana. He was graduated from Wabash College in Crawfordsville, Indiana, earning a B.A. degree in literature in 1940. The literary allusions in Sanders's works attest his formal education. It was the encouragement of a ninth-grade English teacher, however, that caused him to entertain seriously the notion of becoming a professional writer. The English teacher published in the school paper a book review written by the young Sanders; once he saw his byline in print, he knew that he wanted to be a writer.

After four years in the United States Marine Corps, from 1943 to 1946, Sanders returned to New York City and began working in the field of publishing. He worked for several magazines as an editor and as a writer of war stories, men's adventure stories, and detective fiction. He eventually became feature editor of *Mechanix Illustrated* and editor of *Science and Mechanics*. Utilizing information that he had gained in the course of editing articles on surveillance devices, Sanders wrote *The Anderson Tapes*, an audaciously innovative first novel for a fifty-year-old man—and one that foreshadowed the Watergate break-in.

After 1970, the year in which *The Anderson Tapes* was published, Sanders produced at least one novel per year. His first novel made him wealthy enough to devote himself full-time to his own writing. Most of his crime novels became bestsellers, and several were made into successful films. Lawrence Sanders died on February 7, 1998 in Pompano Beach, Florida.

**Analysis** • Some of Lawrence Sanders's early works have been collected in a book titled *Tales of the Wolf* (1986). These stories were originally published in detective and men's magazines in 1968 and 1969 and concern the adventures of Wolf Lannihan, an investigator for International Insurance Investigators, or Triple-I. Wolf Lannihan is a hard-boiled detective who describes women in terms of their sexual lure ("She was a big bosomy Swede with hips that bulged her white uniform") and criminals by their odor ("He was a greasy little crumb who wore elevator shoes and smelled of sardines"). Like Chandler's Philip Marlowe, he keeps a pint of Jim Beam in the bottom drawer of his desk for emergencies. These stories follow the pattern of the classic hard-boiled, hard-drinking, irreverent loner who punches his way out of tight spots. While weak on originality, they do have their witty moments and can be read today as parodies of the hard-boiled style of writing popular in the 1930's.

It was, however, the first novel that Sanders wrote, *The Anderson Tapes*, that brought him success as a writer of detective fiction. He had blue-penciled other writers for twenty-odd years as an editor for pulp and science magazines and churned out adventure stories at night during that time. In despair over the abominable writing he was editing, he determined to write an innovative detective novel. *The Anderson Tapes* became an immediate best-seller and was made into a film starring Sean Connery.

Sanders has talked about his method of composition in several articles, and the outstanding characteristic of his comments and advice is utter simplicity. Having started out in the 1960's writing gag lines for cheesecake magazines and fast-paced formula fiction for men's adventure magazines, war magazines, and mystery pulps, he had become adept at writing tight, well-plotted stories to hold the reader's attention:

> When you're freelancing at seventy-five dollars a story, you have to turn the stuff out fast, and you can't afford to rewrite. You aren't getting paid to rewrite. You can't afford to be clever, either. Forget about how clever you are. Tell the damn story and get on with it. I know a guy who kept rewriting and took eighteen years to finish a novel. What a shame! It was probably better in the first version.

Sanders's views about the writer's vocation are refreshingly democratic and pragmatic. He insists that anyone who can write a postcard can write a novel:

> Don't laugh. That's true. If you wrote a postcard every day for a year, you'd have 365 postcards. If you wrote a page every day, you'd have a novel. Is that so difficult? If you have something to say and a vocabulary, all you need is a strict routine.

Sanders's next novel was *The First Deadly Sin* (1973), and it was an even bigger success than *The Anderson Tapes*. Some critics believe it to be his masterpiece because it possesses in rich and varied abundance all the literary devices, techniques, and characters that his readers have come to expect. Although Captain Edward X. Delaney was first seen in the second half of *The Anderson Tapes*, as he took absolute charge of an invading police force, in *The First Deadly Sin*, the reader sees him as a complete character in his home territory. A commanding presence, he is a mature, complex man who understands clearly the viper's tangle of administrative and political infighting. He has operated within the labyrinthine organization of the police force for many years and become a captain, though not without making some uncomfortable compromises.

The key to understanding Edward X. Delaney is the quotation from Fyodor Dostoevski's *Besy* (1871-1872; *The Possessed,* 1913) that Sanders plants in *The First Deadly Sin*: "If there was no God, how could I be a captain?" Delaney is tortured by the possibility of a world without meaning, and he yearns for an earlier, innocent world that has deteriorated into a miasma of demolished orders and become an existential nightmare in which no authority exists except the law itself. He views himself as a principal agent of this last remaining order, the law. The fallen world he inhabits is very much a wasteland, fragmented by corruption, chaos, and evil. For Delaney, evil exists and is embodied in criminals who break the law. He lives next door to his own precinct on the Upper East Side of Manhattan. He cannot separate his integrity from his life as an officer of the law: They are one. Without a god or an order outside himself, Delaney cannot be a captain because the order necessary to create and enforce such hierarchical categories no longer exists. In an earlier time, he might have become a priest, but he realizes that the Church too has fallen victim to bureaucratic chaos and corruption.

Delaney must attend to the smallest details because they may become the keys to solving the mystery, to revealing its order. Delaney possesses an essentially eighteenth century mind; he believes that when one accumulates enough details and facts, they will compose themselves into a total meaningful pattern: Everything must cohere. His work provides the facts and, therefore, controls and determines the outcome. It is that control that gives his life and work meaning. Without it, his world remains an existential void.

Edward X. Delaney is not, however, a dreary thinking machine; he possesses an incisive sense of humor about others and himself. He can be refreshingly sardonic, especially when his wife, Monica, points out his little quirks. A firm believer in women's intuition, Delaney asks her advice when he finds himself hopelessly mired in the complications of a particularly elaborate series of crimes, such as the serial murders of both *The First Deadly Sin* and *The Third Deadly Sin* (1981). It is both the human and the professional Chief Delaney that Gregory Mcdonald parodies in several of his crime novels. In these parodies, he takes the form of Inspector Francis Xavier Flynn of the Boston Police Department, a resourceful, civilized, and impudent supercop.

First Deputy Commissioner Ivar Thorsen, known as the Admiral, appears in all the Deadly Sin novels, serving to call Delaney to adventure. Perpetually beleaguered, he furnishes, as he sips Delaney's Glenfiddich, three key ingredients to assure Delaney's success: a description of the complexities of the crime, an analysis of the political pressures deriving from the inability of the New York City Police Department to solve the crime, and protection for Delaney so that he may bring his peculiar and sometimes questionable procedures into play (thus circumventing the bureaucratic barriers that consistently hamper the investigation). Abner Boone, Delaney's psychologically wounded protégé, appears in most of the Deadly Sin novels. He is described as horse-faced, with a gentle and overly sensitive temperament. He can sympathize with Delaney because they are both disillusioned romantics (Delaney lost his innocence when he saw a German concentration camp in 1945). Delaney trusts Boone because he is without cynicism, and there is nothing he detests more than cynicism and its source, self-pity.

Many of the women in Sanders's novels are either castrating bitch god-desses or nourishing mother types. Celia Montfort, in *The First Deadly Sin*, pro-vides the narcissistic Daniel Gideon Blank with what he perceives as a conduit to the primal, amoral energies of primitive man; through Celia, Daniel, who has become a Nietzschean superman, is relieved of any guilt for his actions. Bella Sarazen, whose name embodies her pragmatic and warlike sexuality, performs any act if the price is right in *The Second Deadly Sin* (1977). The pro-miscuously alcoholic but loving Millie Goodfellow in *The Sixth Commandment* (1978) helps the equally alcoholic but clever field investigator Samuel Todd to uncover the rotten secrets of Coburn, New York, a dying upstate hamlet steeped in paranoia and guilt.

Of the four major villains in these novels, two are women. Zoe Kohler's first name, which is derived from the Greek word meaning "life," ironically defines her function throughout *The Third Deadly Sin*. Although a victim of Ad-dison's disease, she moves throughout the novel as the castrating goddess par excellence, luring her victims to hotel rooms, exciting them with the promise of sexual ecstasy, and then slashing their sexual organs to pieces with a knife. She, like Daniel Blank, is one of Sanders's Midwest monsters, victims of the kind of sexual and emotional repression that only the Puritan Midwest can produce. Zoe Kohler's psychological and physical illnesses have produced in her a maniacal lust turned upside down, a classic form of sexual repression whose cause is rejection and whose manifestation is vengeful behavior of the most violent kind. The other female villain, the psychologist of *The Fourth Deadly Sin* (1985), suffers no physical illness which exacerbates her emotional condition. Rather, her anger, which is the fourth deadly sin, is a response to her husband's extramarital affair. She is a privileged, wealthy, highly edu-cated woman who knows exactly what she is doing; her crime is all the more heinous because it is premeditated.

The most frightening villain in all Sanders's crime novels, however, is Daniel Gideon Blank; he is also the author's most complex, believable, and magnifi-cently malignant character. He is taken directly from the Old Testament and Dante's *Inferno*. His first name, Daniel, comes from the Hebrew word meaning "God is my judge," certainly an ironic choice of name since Daniel Blank com-mits numerous murders throughout the novel. Blank's middle name, Gideon, refers to a famous Hebrew judge and literally means "a warrior who hews or cuts down his enemies." The last name of Sanders's antihero suggests the empty, impotent, and gratuitous nature of the murders he commits.

Blank is an Antichrist figure, Christ become Narcissus—not the Man for Others who sacrifices himself for the salvation of mankind, but the man who sacrifices others for his own salvation, to fill in the Blank, as it were. He identifies himself as "God's will" and calls himself "God on earth," particularly at the orgasmic moment of the actual sinking of his weapon into a hapless victim's skull. He identifies himself with the computer he brings with him to his new job and states, "I am AMROK II." A true narcissist, Daniel Blank, by identifying himself as AMROK II, sets himself up as both the founder of a church, Jesus Christ, and Peter, whose name means "rock" and who was designated by Christ to be the Church's first leader.

The key to Delaney's genius as an investigator can be found in examining his relationship with the criminals themselves. It is a complex relationship that entails serious psychological risks for him because the pursued and the pursuer secretly share some key characteristics. Toward the end of *The First Deadly Sin*, Delaney writes an article on this Dostoevskian theme:

> It was an abstruse examination of the sensual . . . affinity between hunter and hunted, of how, in certain cases, it was necessary for the detective to penetrate and assume the physical body, spirit and soul of the criminal in order to bring him to justice.

Needless to say, Delaney's wife gently persuades him not to publish it, because he, like Daniel Blank, has been tempted into the destructive element and risks losing himself in it.

Archibald McNally, a bon vivant amateur detective, leads the division of Discreet Inquiries for his father at the law firm McNally & Son. Set among the elite of Palm Beach, Florida, each tale in the series resonates with a cast of eccentric characters. Debonair and possessing a vocabulary the like of which most people only dream, Archy lives the life of a playboy as well as he can from his small apartment on the top floor of his parent's house. His keen fashion sense (peony patterned jackets, vermilion loafers, and gamboling rabbit boxers) complements the high esteem in which he holds culinary masterpieces, and the reader can look forward to extensively detailed descriptions of his best gastronomical finds.

Binky Watrous, Archy's sometimes sidekick, is notable for his constant lack of money and uncanny ability to imitate birdcalls. Connie Garcia is Archy's love interest, described by him as a Latin femme fatale who is, "soft, loving, blithe, spirited, jealous, distrustful, and vengeful." She invariably discovers the gross infidelities Archy effortlessly commits throughout the course of each story and makes him pay before taking him back once again. When Archy needs assistance from the local police, he turns to Al Rogoff, a man built like a steamroller who uses a "good ol' boy" act to hide his sharp intelligence:

> "You know a guy named Peter Gottschalk?" "Yes, I know Peter. He's a member of the Pelican Club." "Is he off-the-wall?" "I really couldn't say. From what I've heard,

he's been known to act occasionally in an outré manner." "Outré," Rogoff repeated. "Love the way you talk." "Why are you asking about Peter Gottschalk?" "Because early this morning, about two or three, he outred his father's car into an abutment on an overpass out west."

The Pettibones run the Pelican Club, a members-only establishment featuring a crest of "a pelican rampant on a field of dead mullet". The grounds-keeper and cook of the McNally household, Jamie and Ursi Olson, occasionally offer insights into the world of the hired help of Palm Beach County.

Each story begins with Prescott McNally, Archy's father, assigning Archy a Discreet Inquiry related in some way to one of his clients. Archy's ability to forge relationships with those involved in the investigation is instrumental, and almost all of his detecting is achieved through conversations or interactions. Written entirely from his perspective, the style is conversational in tone and quite engaging. Archy uses a journal in which to record his observations, and the keen intellect often masked by his whimsical nature becomes evident as the solution to each case unfolds.

Sanders did not confuse lightheartedness with shallowness, however. Archy confronts several situations that do not blithely roll off of his playboy veneer. A true departure from Sanders's earlier works, the McNally books expose the depth of his talent. An ability to move from the realm of hard-boiled detective fiction to that of a rollicking amateur detective successfully takes extraordinary skill, and Lawrence Sanders had it.

### Principal mystery and detective fiction

Lawrence Sanders was one of the finest writers of detective fiction in the United States. His style resonates not only with the snappy dialogue of Raymond Chandler and Dashiell Hammett but also with the long, balanced sentences of the most accomplished American and British classic writers, such as Henry James, Nathaniel Hawthorne, F. Scott Fitzgerald, and William Faulkner.

The moral enigmas present in his earlier works evoke the persistently tormenting conflicts of a Charles Dickens or a Fyodor Dostoevski. Like all serious writers, Sanders is disturbed by important questions. He can evoke and sustain, as few modern writers can, a deeply disturbing sense of sin and courageously plunges into an exploration of the lines between guilt and innocence, responsibility and victimization, heredity and environment. He resists easy answers to complex situations, entering fully into each case, struggling alongside his characters. Even in his later works this struggle is evident, although the presentation alters dramatically. Taking the keen dialogue and well developed plots into a fresh setting, Sanders displays an almost frivolous side while still delivering excellent detective fiction. Sanders was one of the most important and innovative writers of crime fiction of the twentieth century.

SERIES:

Commandment: *The Sixth Commandment*, 1978; *The Tenth Commandment*, 1980; *The Eighth Commandment*, 1986; *The Seventh Commandment*, 1991.

Timothy Cone: *The Timothy Files,* 1987; *Timothy's Game,* 1988.

Edward X. Delaney: *The Anderson Tapes,* 1970; *The First Deadly Sin,* 1973; *The Second Deadly Sin,* 1977; *The Third Deadly Sin,* 1981; *The Fourth Deadly Sin,* 1985.

Peter Tangent: *The Tangent Objective,* 1976; *The Tangent Factor,* 1978.

Archy McNally: *McNally's Secret,* 1992; *McNally's Luck,* 1992; *McNally's Risk,* 1993; *McNally's Caper,* 1994; *McNally's Trial,* 1995; *McNally's Puzzle,* 1996; *McNally's Gamble,* 1997; *McNally's Dilemma,* 1999 (with Vincent Lardo); *McNally's Folly,* 2000 (with Lardo); *McNally's Chance,* 2001 (with Lardo).

OTHER SHORT FICTION: *Tales of the Wolf,* 1986.

### Other major works

NOVELS: *The Pleasures of Helen,* 1971; *Love Songs,* 1972; *The Tomorrow File,* 1975; *The Marlow Chronicles,* 1977; *Caper,* 1980; *The Case of Lucy Bending,* 1982; *The Seduction of Peter S.,* 1983; *The Passion of Molly T.,* 1984; *The Loves of Harry Dancer,* 1986; *Capital Crimes,* 1989; *Dark Summer,* 1989; *Stolen Blessings,* 1989; *Sullivan's Sting,* 1990; *Private Pleasures,* 1994; *The Adventures of Chauncey Alcock,* 1997 (with others); *Guilty Pleasures,* 1998; *Guilty Secrets,* 1998.

NONFICTION: *Handbook of Creative Crafts,* 1968 (with Richard Carol).

EDITED TEXT: *Thus Be Loved,* 1966.

### Bibliography

Hubin, Allen J. Review of *The Second Deadly Sin,* by Lawrence Sanders. *The Armchair Detective* 11 (January, 1978): 18.

Nelson, William. "Expiatory Symbolism in Lawrence Sanders' *The First Deadly Sin.*" *Clues: A Journal of Detection* 1 (Fall/Winter, 1980): 71-76.

Nelson, William, and Nancy Avery. "Art Where You Least Expect It: Myth and Ritual in the Detective Series." *Modern Fiction Studies* 19 (Autumn, 1983): 463-474.

Stasio, Marilyn. "Lawrence Sanders, 78, Author of Crime and Suspense Novels." *New York Times,* February 12, 1998, p. B11.

Washer, Robert E. Review of *The Anderson Tapes,* by Lawrence Sanders. *The Queen Canon Bibliophile* 2 (February, 1970): 17.

*Patrick Meanor*
*Updated by C. A. Gardner*

# Dorothy L. Sayers

**Born:** Oxford, England; June 13, 1893
**Died:** Witham, Essex, England; December 17, 1957

**Type of plot** • Master sleuth

**Principal series** • Lord Peter Wimsey, 1923-1937.

**Principal series characters** • LORD PETER WIMSEY, a wealthy aristocrat, Oxford graduate, book collector, wine connoisseur, and lover of fast cars, cricket, and crime. Though he gives the appearance, particularly in the early novels, of being a foppish playboy, his flippancy masks intelligence, conscience, and sensitivity.
• BUNTER, an imperturbable, supremely competent manservant. He served under Wimsey in World War I, then became his valet, bringing his master through a war-induced breakdown. His skills range from photographing corpses and cooking superb meals to extracting crucial evidence from cooks and housemaids over tea in the servants' quarters.
• CHIEF-INSPECTOR CHARLES PARKER, a Scotland Yard detective, is Lord Peter's friend and later his brother-in-law. He provides a calm, rational balance to Wimsey's flamboyant personality.
• HARRIET VANE, the detective novelist with whom Lord Peter falls in love as he saves her from the gallows in *Strong Poison* (1930). Independent, capable, and proud, she refuses to marry him until she is convinced that their marriage can be an equal partnership.

**Contribution** • Dorothy L. Sayers never considered her detective novels and short stories to be truly serious literature, and once Lord Peter Wimsey had provided a substantial income for her, she turned her attention to religious drama, theology, and a translation of Dante's *La divina commedia* (c. 1320; *The Divine Comedy*). Yet she wrote these popular works with the same thoroughness, commitment to quality, and attention to detail that infuse her more scholarly writings. Her mystery novels set a high standard for writers who followed her—and there have been many. Her plots are carefully constructed, and she was willing to spend months, even years, in researching background details. What gives her works their lasting appeal, however, is not the nature of the crimes or the cleverness of their solutions. Readers return to the novels for the pleasure of savoring Sayers's wit, her literary allusions, the rich settings, the deftly developed characters, and, above all, her multitalented aristocratic sleuth, Lord Peter Wimsey. Blending the conventions of detective fiction with social satire and unobtrusively interweaving serious themes, she fulfilled her

Dorothy L. Sayers. (Library of Congress)

goal of making the detective story "once more a novel of manners instead of a pure crossword puzzle."

**Biography** • Dorothy Leigh Sayers was born in Oxford, England, on June 13, 1893, the only child of the Reverend Henry Sayers, headmaster of the Christ Church Choir School, and his talented wife, Helen Leigh Sayers. When Dorothy was four, the family moved to the fen country immortalized in *The Nine Tailors* (1934), and there she was educated by her parents and governesses. By the time she entered the Godolphin School in Salisbury in 1909, she was fluent in French and German and an avid reader and writer. Her life as a pampered only child did not, however, prepare her well to fit in with her contemporaries, and she found real friends only when she entered Somerville College, Oxford, in 1912. There she participated enthusiastically in musical, dramatic, and social activities and won first-class honors in French. She was among the first group of women granted degrees in 1920.

After leaving Oxford in 1915, she held a variety of jobs, finally settling at Benson's Advertising Agency in London as a copywriter. Shortly after she joined Benson's, she began work on her first detective novel, *Whose Body?* (1923). Following its publication, she took a leave of absence from her work, ostensibly to work on a second book but in reality to give birth to a son out of wedlock. One of her biographers, James Brabazon, has identified her child's father as a working-class man to whom she may have turned in reaction to a painful affair with the writer John Cournos.

She placed her son in the care of a cousin, returned to work, and two years later married Captain Oswald Arthur "Mac" Fleming, another man who shared almost none of her intellectual interests. Fleming, a divorced journalist, suffered throughout most of their married life from physical and psychological damage resulting from his service in World War I. She and Fleming informally adopted her son in 1934, but the boy continued to live with her cousin, and she never told him that he was her own child.

In this decade of personal stress, Sayers's career as a detective novelist was taking shape. By 1937 she had published more than a dozen books and was recognized as one of England's best mystery writers. In the last twenty years of her life, she devoted her energies to becoming an articulate spokeswoman for the Church of England and a respected Dante scholar. She did not quite abandon her earlier pursuits, maintaining a strong interest in the Detection Club, which she had helped found in 1930. She died in 1957.

**Analysis** • In her introduction to *The Omnibus of Crime* (1928-1934), Dorothy L. Sayers writes that the detective story "does not, and by hypothesis never can, attain the loftiest level of literary achievement.... It rarely touches the heights and depths of human passion." It is, she adds,

> part of the literature of escape, and not of expression. We read tales of domestic un-happiness because that is the kind of thing which happens to us; but when these things gall too close to the sore, we fly to mystery and adventure because they do not, as a rule, happen to us.

Clearly, she cherished no ambition of finding literary immortality in the adventures of Lord Peter Wimsey. Nevertheless, she brought to the craft of writing detective fiction a scholar's mind and a conviction that any work undertaken is worth doing well, qualities that have won acclaim for her as one of the best mystery writers of the twentieth century.

Her biographers have suggested that the impetus for her writing of mystery stories was economic. Still financially dependent on her parents in her late twenties, she began work on *Whose Body?* in 1921 as one last effort to support herself as a writer. In a letter to her parents, she promised that if this effort were unsuccessful, she would give up her ambitions and take a teaching position—not a career she coveted. Her choice of this genre was a sensible one for her purposes. Mysteries were enormously popular in England and America in the 1920's and 1930's, and by 1937, when Lord Peter Wimsey made his last major appearance, her twelve detective novels and numerous short stories had guaranteed her a substantial income for the rest of her life.

Having chosen her form, Sayers entered upon her task with diligence, studying the work of the best of her predecessors, particularly Edgar Allan Poe, Sir Arthur Conan Doyle, and Wilkie Collins. She applied her academic training to the genre, its history, its structures, and its compacts with its readers. Her efforts were so successful that only a few years after the publication of her first novel she was asked to edit a major anthology of detective stories and to write an introduction that is both a short history of the genre and an analysis of its major characteristics.

Sayers's work is not, on the surface, especially innovative. Particularly in her early work, she used the popular conventions of the form—mysterious methods of murder, amoral villains, and the clever amateur detective in the tradition of C. Auguste Dupin, Sherlock Holmes, and E. C. Bentley's Philip Trent. From the beginning, however, she lifted the quality of the mystery novel. First, as critic and detective novelist Carolyn Heilbrun notes, "Miss Sayers wrote superbly well." A reader can open her books to almost any page and find lines that reflect her pleasure in a well-turned phrase. She enjoyed experimenting with different types of styles, even imitating Wilkie Collins's *The Moonstone* (1868) by using letters to tell the story in *The Documents in the Case* (1930; with Robert Eustace).

Sayers was a skillful creator of plots, adhering firmly to the "fair play" she describes in her introduction to *The Omnibus of Crime*: "The reader must be given every clue—but he must not be told, surely, all the detective's deductions, lest he should see the solution too far ahead." Her adherence to this principle is especially clear in her short stories, both those featuring Wimsey and those involving her second amateur detective hero, Montague Egg. Egg, a traveling salesman of wine and spirits, is a master interpreter of the hidden clue and another delightful character, though the stories about him tend to be more formulaic than the Wimsey tales.

Sayer's full-length novels are unusual in the variety of crimes and solutions they depict. She never fell into a single pattern of plot development, and in fact she argued that a successful mystery writer cannot do that, for each work arises out of a different idea, and each idea demands its own plot: "To get the central idea is one thing: to surround it with a suitable framework of interlocking parts is quite another. . . . idea and plot are two quite different things." The challenge is to flesh out the idea in a suitable sequence of events and to develop characters in ways that make these events plausible.

The character most crucial to the effectiveness of the mystery novel is, naturally, that of the detective. Sayers developed Lord Peter Wimsey gradually over the fifteen years in which she wrote about him. In his first appearances he is a rather stereotypical figure, comprising elements of Trent, Holmes, and P. G. Wodehouse's Bertie Wooster, the quintessential "silly-ass-about-town." In his first case, he greets the discovery of a body in a bathtub, clad only in a pair of gold-rimmed eyeglasses, with gleeful enthusiasm. Sayers herself might later have considered him too gleeful; as she wrote in her introduction to *The Omnibus of Crime*, "The sprightly amateur must not be sprightly all the time, lest at some point we should be reminded that this is, after all, a question of somebody's being foully murdered, and that flippancy is indecent."

At the beginning of his career, Wimsey is distinguished chiefly by superficial attributes—wealth; an aristocratic upbringing; interest in rare books, wine, and music; skill in languages; arcane knowledge in a variety of fields; and the services of the unflappable Bunter. While the early Wimsey is, in Margaret Hannay's words, something of a "cardboard detective," nevertheless there are in him elements that allowed Sayers to "humanize him" in her later works. He is shown in *Whose Body?* and *Unnatural Death* (1927) to have moments of self-doubt as he contemplates his responsibility for actions that follow upon his intervention into the crimes. His moral sensitivity is also revealed in his sympathetic response to the irritating but understandable war victim George Fentiman in *The Unpleasantness at the Bellona Club* (1928), who so bitterly resents his dependence on his wife. The later Lord Peter retains the ability to "talk piffle" as a mask to cover his intelligence, but his detecting is now seen not as an amateur's game but as work in service of truth. His stature is also increased by his work for the Foreign Office, which sends him out to exercise his conversational skills as a diplomat.

As Sayers acknowledges in her essay "Gaudy Night," in which she discusses the composition of the novel of the same name, Peter's growth came largely in response to the creation of Harriet Vane in *Strong Poison*. Sayers invented Harriet, she confessed, with the idea of marrying him off before he consumed her whole existence. When she came to the end of the novel, however, her plan would not work. "When I looked at the situation I saw that it was in every respect false and degrading; and the puppets had somehow got just so much flesh and blood in them that I could not force them to accept it without shocking myself." The only solution, she decided, was to make Peter "a complete human being, with a past and a future, with a consistent family and social history, with a complicated psychology and even the rudiments of a religious outlook." In the novels written after 1930, Wimsey becomes wiser, more conscious of the complexities of human feelings, less certain of the boundaries of good and evil. As he becomes a more complex figure, the novels in which he appears begin to cross the border between the whodunit and the novel of manners.

Another major factor in Sayers's success as a mystery writer was her ability to create authentic, richly detailed settings for her work. "Readers," she says in "Gaudy Night,"

> seem to like books which tell them how other people live—any people, advertisers, bell-ringers, women dons, butchers, bakers or candlestick-makers—so long as the detail is full and accurate and the object of the work is not overt propaganda.

She alludes here to the three novels many readers consider her best—*Murder Must Advertise* (1933), *The Nine Tailors*, and *Gaudy Night* (1935). In each she drew on places and people she knew well to create worlds that her readers would find appealing.

From her nine years as copywriter with Benson's, Sayers created Pym's Publicity in *Murder Must Advertise*. There is an aura of verisimilitude in every detail, from the office politics to the absurd advertisements for "Nutrax for Nerves" to the Pym's-Brotherhood annual cricket match. Sayers even borrowed Benson's spiral iron staircase as the scene of Victor Dean's murder, and she drew on her own successful "Mustard Club" campaign for Wimsey's brilliant cigarette-advertising scheme, "Whiffle your way around Britain."

Sayers set *The Nine Tailors* in a village in the fen country much like the parish in which her father served for most of her childhood and adolescence. The plot depends heavily on the practice of bell-ringing, which Sayers studied for two years before she completed her novel. Her account of the mechanics of draining the fen country and the attendant dangers of flooding shows equally careful research. Many of the greatest delights of the book, however, lie in the evocation of village life, epitomized in the final scene, in which the inhabitants of Fenchurch St. Paul have taken refuge from the floodwaters in the huge church:

A curious kind of desert-island life was carried on in and about the church, which, in course of time, assumed a rhythm of its own. Each morning was ushered in by a short and cheerful flourish of bells, which rang the milkers out to the cowsheds in the graveyard. Hot water for washing was brought in wheeled waterbutts from the Rectory copper. Bedding was shaken and rolled under the pews for the day. . . . Daily school was carried on in the south aisle; games and drill were organized in the Rectory garden by Lord Peter Wimsey; farmers attended to their cattle; owners of poultry brought the eggs to a communal basket; Mrs. Venables presided over sewing-parties in the Rectory.

The mystery plot is here grounded in a world of rich and poor, old and young, that seems to go on beyond the confines of the novel.

For some readers the most interesting community of all those that Sayers depicted is Shrewsbury College, the setting for *Gaudy Night*—one of the first works of a still-popular type of detective fiction, the university mystery. Shrewsbury is closely modeled on Somerville, where the author spent three of the most personally rewarding years of her life. Although her picture of life in the Senior Common Room did not win universal approval from her Somerville acquaintances, she captured brilliantly the camaraderie and rivalries of the educational institution, the dedication of committed teachers to their students and their scholarly disciplines, and the undergraduates' struggle to deal with academic and social pressures.

Sayers's settings come to life chiefly through their inhabitants, many of whom have little do with the solution to the mystery but much to do with the lasting appeal of the works. Every reader has favorite characters: old Hezekiah Lavender, who tolls the passing of human life on the venerable bell Tailor Paul; Tom Puffett, the loquacious chimney sweep in *Busman's Honeymoon* (1937); Ginger Joe, the young fan of fictional detective Sexton Blake who provides Wimsey with an important clue in *Murder Must Advertise*; Miss Lydgate, the kindly scholar in *Gaudy Night*. These characters are often seen most vividly through their own words. Lord Peter's delightful mother, the Dowager Duchess of Denver, is instantly recognizable for her stream-of-consciousness conversation, dotted with malapropisms that cover underlying good sense. Wimsey's indefatigable spinster investigator, Miss Climpson, is best known through her self-revelatory letters, which are as full of italics as Queen Victoria's diaries:

> My train got in quite late on Monday night, after a *most dreary* journey, with a *lugubrious* wait at *Preston*, though thanks to your kindness in insisting that I should travel *First-class*, I was not really at all tired! Nobody can realise what a *great* difference these extra comforts make, especially when one is *getting on* in years, and after the *uncomfortable* travelling which I had to endure in my days of poverty, I feel that I am living in almost *sinful* luxury!

Of Wimsey himself, Carolyn Heilbrun wrote, "Lord Peter's audience, if they engage in any fantasy at all about that sprig of the peerage, dream of having him to tea. They don't want to *be* Lord Peter, only to know him, for the sake of hearing him talk." It might even be said that good conversation finally brings Peter and Harriet Vane together, for it is talk that establishes their mutual respect, allowing them to reveal their shared commitment to intellectual honesty and their mutual conviction that husband and wife should be equal partners.

Taken as a whole, the conversations of Sayers's characters dazzle readers with the skill and erudition of their author, who reproduces the voices from many levels of English society while keeping up a steady stream of allusion to works as diverse as Dante's *The Divine Comedy*, Robert Burton's *The Anatomy of Melancholy* (1621), the operettas of Gilbert and Sullivan, and the adventures of fictional character Sexton Blake.

While Sayers's brilliant handling of plot, character, setting, and dialogue would probably have made her novels classics in the genre without additional elements, these works are also enriched by serious themes that preoccupied her throughout her career: the place of women in society, the importance of work, and the nature of guilt and innocence.

The works show a recurrent concern with the problems of the professional woman searching for dignity and independence in a man's world. Sayers embodies these concerns in such characters as Ann Dorland in *The Unpleasantness at the Bellona Club*, Marjorie Phelps, Sylvia Marriott, and Eiluned Price in *Strong Poison*, Miss Meteyard in *Murder Must Advertise*, and especially Harriet Vane, the character who most resembles her author. Wimsey is attractive to all these women not so much for his undeniable sex appeal as for his taking them seriously as human beings. If Sayers can be said to have fallen in love with her detective, as many have suggested, it is surely this quality that she found most appealing. She argues passionately in her lecture *Are Women Human?* (1971) that women should be treated as individuals, not as members of an inferior species:

> "What," men have asked distractedly from the beginning of time, "what on earth do women want?" I do not know that women, *as* women, want anything in particular, but as human beings they want, my good men, exactly what you want yourselves: interesting occupation, reasonable freedom for their pleasures, and a sufficient emotional outlet. What form the occupation, the pleasures and the emotion may take, depends entirely upon the individual.

As this quotation suggests, Sayers's concern with the place of woman in society is closely related to her belief that each person needs to find his or her own proper work and do it well. This idea, later to be the major theme of her religious drama *The Zeal of Thy House* (1937) and her theological volume *The Mind of the Maker* (1941), is central to the action of *Gaudy Night* and to the development of Peter and Harriet's relationship. The plot of his novel arises out of a young scholar's suppression of evidence that would invalidate the argument of his master's thesis, an action whose discovery led to his professional disgrace and eventually to his suicide. His wife sets out to avenge his death on the woman scholar who discovered his fraud. While Sayers does not deny the moral ambiguities in the situation, she makes it clear that fraudulent scholarship is no minor matter. One must do one's work with integrity, regardless of personal considerations.

Acting on this conviction, Lord Peter urges Harriet to "abandon the jig-saw kind of story and write a book about human beings for a change," even if it means confronting painful episodes from her past. When she responds, "It would hurt like hell," he replies, "What would that matter, if it made a good book?" She interprets his respect for her work as respect for her integrity as a human being and moves a step closer to accepting his proposal of marriage.

The issue of guilt and innocence—more fundamentally, of good and evil—is handled more obliquely. As R. D. Stock and Barbara Stock note in their essay "The Agents of Evil and Justice in the Novels of Dorothy L. Sayers," the nature of the criminals changes during the course of the author's career. In most of the early novels the criminal is a cold, heartless villain, quite willing to sacrifice others for his or her own goals. In the later works, however, the author shows her readers a world in which guilt and innocence are less clear-cut. The victims, such as Campbell in *The Five Red Herrings* (1931) and Deacon in *The Nine Tailors*, are thoroughly unsympathetic figures. Their killers are seen not as monsters but as human beings caught in circumstances they are not strong enough to surmount. In *The Nine Tailors* the murderers are the bells, inanimate objects controlled by individuals who share in the guilt of all humanity. This novel reflects Sayers's conviction, stated in *The Mind of the Maker*, that "human situations are subject to the law of human nature, whose evil is at all times rooted in its good, and whose good can only redeem, but not abolish, its evil."

By moving away from "the jig-saw kind of story" to deal with issues of moral and intellectual complexity, Sayers was enlarging the scope of her genre but also testing its limits. One of the great appeals of detective stories, she once wrote, is that they provide readers who live in a world full of insoluble problems with problems that unfailingly have solutions. Her last works still provide answers to the questions around which her plots revolve: Who killed the man whose body was found in Lady Thorpe's grave? Who was disrupting Shrewsbury College? Who murdered Mr. Noakes? These solutions do not, however, answer all the questions raised: What are one's obligations to other human beings, even if they are wrongdoers? When does one become a contributor to the development of another's guilt? What are the moral consequences of solving crimes? It is not surprising that she felt the need to move on to literary forms that would allow her to deal more directly with these issues, though there are many readers who wish she had continued to let Lord Peter and Harriet explore them.

By the time Dorothy Sayers ended Wimsey's career with several short stories written in the late 1930's and early 1940's, she had left an indelible mark on the twentieth century detective story. Her world of aristocrats and man-servants, country vicars, and villages in which everyone had a place and stayed in it, was vanishing even as she wrote about it; Wimsey tells Harriet at one point, "Our kind of show is dead and done for." Yet her works continue to appeal to large numbers of readers. Why? Some readers simply desire to escape the problems of the present–but the secret of Sayers's popularity surely goes beyond that. Her reputation rests partly on her superb handling of language, her attention to details of plot and setting, her humor, and her memorable characters. Yet it is ultimately those elements that push at the boundaries of the detective stories that have kept her works alive when those of many of her popular contemporaries have vanished. She left her successors a challenge to view the mystery novel not simply as entertainment (though it must always be that) but also as a vehicle for both literary excellence and reflection on serious, far-reaching questions.

## Principal mystery and detective fiction

SERIES: Lord Peter Wimsey: *Whose Body?*, 1923; *Clouds of Witness*, 1926; *Unnatural Death*, 1927 (also as *The Dawson Pedigree*); *The Unpleasantness at the Bellona Club*, 1928; *Lord Peter Views the Body*, 1928; *Strong Poison*, 1930; *The Five Red Herrings*, 1931 (also as *Suspicious Characters*); *Have His Carcase*, 1932; *Murder Must Advertise*, 1933; *Hangman's Holiday*, 1933; *The Nine Tailors*, 1934; *Gaudy Night*, 1935; *Busman's Honeymoon*, 1937; *In the Teeth of the Evidence and Other Stories*, 1939; *Striding Folly*, 1972.

OTHER NOVELS: *The Documents in the Case*, 1930 (with Robert Eustace); *The Floating Admiral*, 1931 (with others); *Ask a Policeman*, 1933 (with others); *Six Against the Yard*, 1936 (with others; also as *Six Against Scotland Yard*); *Double Death: A Murder Story*, 1939 (with others); *The Scoop, and Behind the Scenes*, 1983 (with others); *Crime on the Coast, and No Flowers by Request*, 1984 (with others).

## Other major works

PLAYS: *Busman's Holiday*, 1936 (with Muriel St. Clare Byrne); *The Zeal of Thy House*, 1937; *He That Should Come*, 1939; *The Devil to Pay, Being the Famous Play of John Faustus*, 1939; *Love All*, 1940; *The Man Born to Be King: A Play-Cycle on the Life of Our Lord and Saviour Jesus Christ*, 1941-1942; *The Just Vengeance*, 1946; *The Emperor Constantine*, 1951 (revised as *Christ's Emperor*, 1952).

POETRY: *Op. 1*, 1916; *Catholic Tales and Christian Songs*, 1918; *Lord, I Thank Thee–*, 1943; *The Story of Adam and Christ*, 1955.

NONFICTION: *Papers Relating to the Family of Wimsey*, 1936; *An Account of Lord Mortimer Wimsey, the Hermit of the Wash*, 1937; *The Greatest Drama Ever Staged*, 1938; *Strong Meat*, 1939; *Begin Here: A War-Time Essay*, 1940; *Creed or Chaos?*, 1940; *The Mysterious English*, 1941; *The Mind of the Maker*, 1941; *Why Work?*, 1942; *The Other Six Deadly Sins*, 1943; *Unpopular Opinions*, 1946; *Making Sense of the Universe*, 1946; *Creed or Chaos? and Other Essays in Popular Theology*, 1947; *The Lost Tools of Learning*, 1948; *The Days of Christ's Coming*, 1953, revised 1960; *Introductory Papers on Dante*, 1954; *The Story of Easter*, 1955; *The Story of Noah's Ark*, 1955; *Further Papers on Dante*, 1957; *The Poetry of Search and the Poetry of Statement, and Other Posthumous Essays on Literature, Religion, and Language*, 1963; *Christian Letters to a Post-Christian World*, 1969; *Are Women Human?*, 1971; *A Matter of Eternity*, 1973; *Wilkie Collins: A Critical and Biographical Study*, 1977 (edited by E. R. Gregory); *The Letters of Dorothy L. Sayers, 1937-1943*, 1998.

CHILDREN'S LITERATURE: *Even the Parrot: Exemplary Conversations for Enlightened Children*, 1944.

TRANSLATIONS: *Tristan in Brittany*, 1929 (by Thomas the Troubadour); *The Heart of Stone, Being the Four Canzoni of the "Pietra" Group*, 1946 (by Dante); *The Comedy of Dante Alighieri the Florentine*, 1949-1962 (cantica III with Barbara Reynolds); *The Song of Roland*, 1957.

EDITED TEXTS: *Oxford Poetry 1917*, 1918 (with Wilfred R. Childe and Thomas W. Earp); *Oxford Poetry 1918*, 1918 (with Earp and E. F. A. Geach); *Oxford Poetry 1919*, 1919 (with Earp and Siegfried Sassoon); *Great Short Stories of Detection, Mystery, and Horror*, 1928-1934 (also as *The Omnibus of Crime*); *Tales of Detection*, 1936.

## Bibliography

Brabazon, James. *Dorothy L. Sayers: A Biography*. London: Gollancz, 1981.

Brown, Janice. *The Seven Deadly Sins in the Work of Dorothy L. Sayers*. Kent, Ohio: Kent State University Press, 1998.

Brunsdale, Mitzi. *Dorothy L. Sayers: Solving the Mystery of Wickedness*. New York: Berg, 1990.

Coomes, David. *Dorothy L. Sayers: A Careless Rage for Life*. Oxford: Lion, 1992.

Dale, Alzina Stone. *Maker and Craftsman: The Story of Dorothy L. Sayers*. Wheaton, Ill.: H. Shaw Publishers, 1992.

Dale, Alzina Stone, ed. *Dorothy L. Sayers: The Centenary Celebration*. New York: Walker, 1993.

Freeling, Nicolas. *Criminal Convictions: Errant Essays on Perpetrators of Literary License*. Boston: D. R. Godine, 1994.

Hannay, Margaret P., ed. *As Her Whimsey Took Her: Critical Essays on the Work of Dorothy L. Sayers*. Kent, Ohio: Kent State University Press, 1979.

Hitchman, Janet. *Such a Strange Lady: An Introduction to Dorothy L. Sayers*. New York: Harper & Row, 1975.

Hone, Ralph. *Dorothy L. Sayers, a Literary Biography*. Kent, Ohio: Kent State University Press, 1979.

Kenney, Catherine McGehee. *The Remarkable Case of Dorothy L. Sayers*. Kent, Ohio: Kent State University Press, 1990.

Lewis, Terrance L. *Dorothy L. Sayers' Wimsey and Interwar British Society*. Lewiston, N.Y.: E. Mellen Press, 1994.

McGregor, Robert Kuhn, and Ethan Lewis. *Conundrums for the Long Week-End: England, Dorothy L. Sayers, and Lord Peter Wimsey*. Kent, Ohio: Kent State University Press, 2000.

Pitt, Valerie. "Dorothy Sayers: The Masks of Lord Peter." In *Twentieth-Century Suspense: The Thriller Comes of Age*, edited by Clive Bloom. New York: St. Martin's Press, 1990.

Reynolds, Barbara. *Dorothy L Sayers: Her Life and Her Soul*. Rev. ed. London: Hodder & Stoughton, 1998.

*Elizabeth Johnston Lipscomb*

# Georges Simenon

**Born:** Liège, Belgium; February 13, 1903
**Died:** Lausanne, Switzerland; September 4, 1989

**Also wrote as** • Bobette • Christian Brulls • Germain d'Ântibes • Jacques Dersonne • Georges d'Isly • Jean Dorsage • Luc Dorsan • Jean du Perry • Georges-Martin Georges • Gom Gut • Kim • Victor Kosta • Plick et Plock • Poum et Zette • Georges Sim • Georges Simm • Gaston Vialis • Gaston Viallis • G. Violio • G. Violis • X

**Types of plot** • Police procedural • psychological

**Principal series** • Inspector Maigret, 1930-1972.

**Principal series character** • JULES MAIGRET, Chief Inspector of the Police Judiciaire (the French equivalent of Scotland Yard). He is about forty-five in most of the stories, although there are a few which look forward to his retirement or backward to his first cases. He and his self-effacing, intuitively understanding wife have no children, their one daughter having died in infancy. His approach is to penetrate the particular world of each event, getting to know the causative factors and interrelationships among those involved; he often feels a strong bond with the criminals, so that when he brings them to justice he is left with ambivalent feelings.

**Contribution** • Georges Simenon's extremely prolific writing career provided fans of the *roman policier* with a number of unrelated crime novels marked by extreme fidelity to detail, and with the series featuring Inspector Maigret. The novels featuring Maigret represent a fusion of the American detective story tradition with French realism. The stories are somewhat reminiscent of the American hard-boiled school, particularly the works of Ross Macdonald, in the lack of sentimental justice and in the often-fatalistic plots in which "old sins cast long shadows" and bring about current tragedies. The psychological realism of the more tightly drawn Maigret characters, however, is more reminiscent of François Mauriac or Julien Green. Moreover, the conclusions are usually less devastating than those of the hard-boiled mysteries, and there is often an element of muted optimism in the Maigret novel.

*Le cas de Simenon*, or Simenon's case, has long been argued in critical circles: Are not his detective stories more than genre pieces, and do they not approach literature? His many other novels use the same devices and express the same themes as his Maigret stories: the desire for home and the impossibility of finding it; the destructive potency of the past; the futility of flight; the fatal seductiveness of illusion. His major contribution consists of the vividly drawn, almost symbiotic relationship between criminal and inspector–and the portrait of Maigret himself as he enters into the scene of each event pertaining to the crime, his vision informed by the French maxim *tout comprendre, c'est tout pardonner* (to understand all is to forgive all).

**Biography** • Georges Joseph Christian Simenon was born on February 13, 1903, in Liège, Belgium. His father, Désiré Simenon, was an accountant from a solid petit bourgeois background; his mother, Henriette Brull, came from a family known for financial instability and social snobbery. The contrast between his paternal and maternal families preoccupied Simenon and often figures in his stories, which tend to idealize the petit bourgeois life and cruelly satirize the pretentious social climbers of the upper-middle class.

Simenon's family was never well-off, and his education was interrupted by the need to earn money when he learned (at age sixteen) that his father was seriously ill. After failing at two menial jobs, he became a cub reporter, at which he was an immediate success. While working at a newspaper and frequenting a group of young artists and poets, he wrote his first novel, *Au pont des arches* (1921), at age seventeen. In 1920 he became engaged to Regine Renchon and enlisted in the army; in 1922 he went to Paris, and he was married the following year. At this time he was writing short stories for Paris journals with amazing rapidity; he wrote more than one thousand stories over the next few years. For two years he was secretary to two young aristocrats, and through them, especially the second, the Marquess de Tracy, he made literary connections. In 1924 he began writing popular novels at an incredible rate. The first, a romance titled *Le Roman d'une dactylo* (1924; the novel of a secretary), was written in a single morning. Simenon ordinarily spent three to five days writing a novel; he was once hired to write a novel in three days before the public in a glass cage, but the publisher who set up the stunt went bankrupt before the event. In 1929 he wrote his first Maigret, *Pietr-le-Letton* (1931; *Maigret and the Enigmatic Lett,* 1963); Maigret was an instant success.

In 1939 Simenon's son Marc was born, but his marriage was already in trouble, partly because of his rapacious womanizing (in later life, in a typical Simenon embellishment, he claimed to have had sexual relations with ten thousand women). In the 1940's he traveled to the United States, where he lived for ten years in relative contentment, adding to his repertoire of atmospheres. In 1949 he was divorced from Regine; the day after the divorce was finalized he married Denyse Ouimet, with whom the couple had been traveling. That year his second son, Johnny, was born to Denyse. He and Denyse had two more children, Marie-Georges (born in 1953) and Pierre (born in 1959, after their return to Europe).

Denyse's alcoholism led to their separation and a bitter literary attack on Simenon in her memoirs, *Un Oiseau pour le chat* (1978). Vilifying the father adored by Marie-Georges, the book contributed to their daughter's depression and suicide in 1978. After her death, Simenon was wracked by guilt and memorialized his daughter in *Mémoires intimes* (1981; *Intimate Memoirs*, 1984), "including Marie-Jo's book," drawing in part on notes, diaries, letters, and voice recordings that Marie-Georges left behind. Though scandal resulted from the revelation that her suppressed incestuous love for her father may have led to her death, a potentially greater scandal was itself suppressed by Denyse's lawyers, who recalled the books to censor the story of Marie-Jo's sexual abuse by her mother at the age of eleven. Unable to reconcile with Denyse, Simenon would live out the rest of his days with his Italian companion Teresa Sburelin.

For most of Simenon's writing life he produced from one to seven novels a year, writing both Maigrets and serious novels. In 1973 he decided to stop producing novels, and after that time he wrote only autobiographical works, including the controversial *Intimate Memoirs*.

**Analysis** • Georges Simenon began his writing career with romances, envisioning an audience of secretaries and shopgirls, but he soon began to imagine another kind of mass audience and another genre. He began writing short thrillers in his early twenties, and one of these, *Train de nuit* (1930), featured a policeman named Maigret, although this Maigret was only a shadow character. The full embodiment of Maigret came to Simenon all at once after three glasses of gin on a summer afternoon:

> As Simenon walked, a picture of his principal character came to him: a big man, powerful, a massive presence rather than an individual. He smoked his pipe, wore a bowler hat and a thick winter coat with a velvet collar (both later abandoned as fashions in police clothing changed). But he did not see his face. *Simenon has never seen the face of Jules Maigret.* "I still do not know what his face looks like," he says. "I only see the man and his presence."

The first Maigret, *Maigret and the Enigmatic Lett*, was begun the next day, finished within a few more days, and promptly sent to Fayard, Simenon's publisher. Yet it was not the first Maigret to appear; Simenon rapidly wrote four more, so that five Maigret novels appeared almost simultaneously and established this popular new detective firmly in the French mind.

Inspector Maigret of the Police Judiciaire is the idealized father figure whose life in many ways reflects that of Désiré Simenon. Born into a petit bourgeois household, he has the close tie to the land and the contentment in small pleasures of the senses associated with petit bourgeois life. He enjoys his pipe and the air on a clear Paris day and the meals prepared for him by his wife, a self-effacing woman whose almost wordless sympathy is equaled in detective fiction only by that of Jenny Maitland. Saddened by his intuitive understanding of the underside of life (and also by the death of his only child—which puts him in the class of the wounded detective), he desires to bring about healing more than to bring criminals to justice. Since his personal desires do not always merge with his professional duties, he is sometimes unhappy about the results of his investigations.

Maigret's method is intuitive rather than ratiocinative, which places him outside the locked-room armchair-detective school. Indeed, Maigret often says, "I never think." He means that he feels and senses instead of figuring, and he arrives at his intuitions by immersing himself completely in the milieu of the crime. As he becomes more and more involved with the figures of the incident, he learns to think as they do, and the truth emerges. It is ironic that although the Maigret books followed one another with such astonishing rapidity, there is no classical Maigret plot. Although usually the criminal is caught and brought to justice, occasionally he escapes; now and then he is punished despite Maigret's deep regrets; at least once the wrong man is executed. The stories do not provide the archetypal pleasure of the Agatha Christie type of plot, in which the villain is caught and the society thus purged. Rather, there is often a sense of the relativity of innocence and guilt, and the inescapability of evil. Moreover, it is somewhat misleading to think of the novels as police novels, for Maigret is often fighting the system as well as the criminals. Hampered by bureaucratic shackles and a superior (Judge Comeliau) who represents reason over intuition and head over heart, Maigret is pressed from both sides in his effort to provide some healing for the fractured human beings he encounters.

What makes the Maigrets a momentous departure from the traditional realm of the detective story, though, is not the characterization of Maigret, however intriguing he may be. It is their realism, built on intensely observed detail and grounded in a rich variety of settings, from the locks along the Seine to the countryside of the Loire valley. The stories enter into particular trades and professions, always describing by feel as well as by sight, so that the reader has a sense of having been given an intimate glimpse into a closed world. Even in *Maigret* (1934; *Maigret Returns*, 1941), the novel that was intended to conclude the series, the details of the retirement cottage are so subtly and lovingly sketched that readers automatically make the comparison between the country life and the Paris to which Maigret is driven to return by the pressure of events. Simenon was a newspaperman par excellence, and his powers of observation and description are his genius. In the context of the novels, the details of weather, dress, and furniture acquire symbolic significance. It is

this evocative use of the concrete that raises the Maigrets from the genre and makes them, like Graham Greene's thrillers, literature.

The first batch of Maigrets consisted of nineteen novels written over four years, from 1930 to 1934, and ending with *Maigret Returns*, which is atypically set in Maigret's retirement years. It would seem that Simenon had decided to leave Maigret to cultivate his garden. Simenon then wrote a number of other novels, some of which received critical acclaim, and *le cas de Simenon* was very much in the national press. André Gide was one of the writer's greatest fans, especially appreciating the nondetective novels; what he found to be Simenon's most compelling quality applies to the Maigrets as well as the other novels. Gide credited Simenon with "a striking, haunting vision of the lives of others in creating living, gasping, panting beings." Other fans bemoaned the lack of new Maigrets; one even sent a cable to the Police Judiciaire reporting that Maigret was missing. Indeed, Simenon was publicly so involved with Maigret that he could not leave him long in his garden; in 1939, the writer began the second series of novels concerning the popular detective. He continued writing Maigrets along with his other stories until he finally stopped writing novels altogether in the early 1970's.

The non-Maigret novels with which he interspersed the Maigrets had many of the characteristics of the detective story, except that usually there was little (if any) focus on detection. These are psychological crime novels somewhat similar to the non-Inspector Wexford novels of Ruth Rendell: The character of the criminal is dissected, his effect on others is analyzed, and an ironic discrepancy develops between his self-image and the way he is perceived. The atmosphere tends to be colder and more clinical because of the absence of the father figure, Maigret. Ironically, the theme in these stories is often the need for warmth, identification, family.

Perhaps typical of the non-Maigret is *Le Locataire* (1934; *The Lodger*, 1943), a story of a homeless Jew who impulsively commits a casual and brutal murder and then finds a home in a boardinghouse. The atmosphere of the boardinghouse—its standard decor, its trivial and yet telling conversations—is so perfectly portrayed that it is easy to connect this pension with Simenon's mother's experience taking in roomers. The focus of the story is the myth of home with which the exiled Elie comforts himself, a myth that has a dimension of truth. Even when caught (the police are in the background, and readers barely encounter them but do see the results of their investigations), Elie is followed by the dream of home he has invented, as the owner of the boardinghouse goes to see Elie off on the convict ship.

Criminals notwithstanding, these novels are not fully realized detective stories, because the discovering or unraveling aspect is missing (as well as the complementary balance between investigator and culprit, who in the Maigrets are often something like father and errant son). These other novels are more like case studies that underscore the unpredictability of the human animal in the most extreme circumstances. The Maigret addict who is also a general detective-story fan may be unable to make the transition.

The second Maigrets did not begin appearing until 1942, when four of them appeared in rapid succession to launch the new series. Many of these new Maigrets do not contain the detective's name in the title, causing some confusion among Maigret fans and those who would choose only Simenon's non-Maigret novels. Much critical discussion has focused on the differences between the new and the old series, but in fact the later Maigrets are not substantially different from the early ones, although it might be argued that they show more careful attention to plot and that they have a higher proportion of main characters who are *ratés*–failures–of one sort or another. One unarguable difference, too, is that they reflect Simenon's American experience, even going so far as to introduce an American policeman who serves as foil and apprentice to Maigret.

Considering *le cas de Simenon* and the mixture of detective novels and other novels, as well as the characteristic Simenon plots and themes in both, it is worth comparing the French novelist with Graham Greene, who also wrote a mixture of thrillers and literary novels and dealt with the same materials in both. The French failures in the Maigrets correspond with Greene's seedy British types. The themes of flight, of the need to escape self, of intuitive penetration of the darknesses of human existence are parallel. Both authors use precise, concrete details to communicate a moral ambience. An important difference is that Greene's Catholic underpinnings are not present in Simenon's novels, or at least are not immediately evident. Some critics have claimed to see them, and Simenon, who claimed agnosticism, has conceded that there may be something to the religious claims made for his work.

The reliable character of Maigret carries Simenon's detective novels even when their plots fail. Fatherly, reflective, Maigret makes the reader believe that justice will be done if it is humanly possible–a qualification that sets these novels apart from the Golden Age detective stories by such writers as Agatha Christie and Dorothy L. Sayers, in which justice is always done. In the typical Maigret, the detective is filling his pipe at the beginning of the story and looking out his office window at some unpleasant manifestation of Paris weather when the case begins. He consults his officers, the same characters briefly but effectively sketched in novel after novel: the young Lapointe, whom Maigret fathers (and calls by the familiar *tu*); the Inspector's old friend Janvier; the miserable Lognon who is like Eeyore in *Winnie-the-Pooh* (1926), always feeling abused and neglected; and others. (Sometimes the inspector is at home, asleep, when the call comes–and his wife has everything ready for his departure before he hangs up.) Throughout the investigation, he orders some characteristic drink (different drinks for different cases) at various cafés, while Mme Maigret's cassoulets or tripes go cold at home. (Some of Maigret's favorite dishes make the American reader's hair stand on end.) When the criminal is finally apprehended and his confession recorded, Maigret often goes home to eat and to restore himself in the comfort of his wife's silent sympathy. The reader is always prepared for Maigret's little idiosyncrasies and for those of the other recurrent characters; thus, the ritual is enacted successfully even if there is some standard deviation from the typical plot, such as the escape of the criminal or a final sense that justice was not quite done.

Despite the pleasant familiarity of the characters and the archetypal paternalism of the inspector, style and theme give the Maigret novels depth. The smallest observations—how a prostitute's face looks when dawn comes in the course of questioning, what is in an aggressively house-proud bourgeoise's kitchen, what the nightclub owner's wife does each night to prepare for the club's opening—these things are so convincingly portrayed that the reader feels that he too is penetrating into the mystery. The mystery is the secret of the human heart, as it is in Graham Greene's novels. Simenon's style is not hard-boiled, nor is it overly descriptive. It is evocative and direct—a few words, a detail, a snatch of dialogue carry multiple suggestions. A half sentence may intimate an entire complex relationship between a husband and wife. The recurrent weather details make the reader gain a sense of the atmosphere. Simenon's details not only are visual but also appeal to the other senses, particularly the tactile. The reader feels on his own skin the fog that is blurring Maigret's vision; he too glories in the occasional clear day. Simenon's use of the concrete is not unlike Colette's; indeed, this famous celebrant of the sensual was Simenon's adviser and friend.

As has been suggested, the flaw in the Maigret story is most often the plot; Simenon claimed to give little attention to plotting, and even not to know how a story would end until he had finished it. Nevertheless, his best plots are psychological tours de force. The unveiling of character is steady throughout the series of events; readers sense the intuitive rightness of Maigret's insights, and, at the end, they find that the motive meshes with the deed.

Not all of his stories, however, afford this sense of closure. *Maigret au Picratt's* (1951; *Maigret in Montmartre*, 1963) is a case in point. In this story the focus is on the victim, a twenty-year-old nightclub stripper who becomes after her death a fully realized character, through the course of the investigation. She is given a subtle case-study history and a network of believable motivations, and through analysis of her life Maigret is able to identify her killer. Yet this killer remains a shadow character himself, and therefore the final scenes in which the police track him down are somewhat anticlimactic. One expects some final revelation, some unveiling of the killer's nature, but none is forthcoming.

Other stories, such as *Maigret et M. Charles* (1972; *Maigret and Monsieur Charles*, 1973), focus on both criminal and victim, so that the conclusion has no (or at least fewer) loose ends. It is indeed rare that the plot of any Maigret is itself particularly compelling. Plot is a function of character in Simenon's works, and the success or failure of plot hinges on the adequate development and believable motivation of the people involved. The early Maigrets, such as *Le Charretier de la Providence* (1931; *Maigret Meets a Milord*, 1963), are particularly susceptible to weakness in plot. This story gives an intriguing, provocative picture of a criminal in whom the reader somehow cannot quite believe.

No one, however, reads Maigrets for the plot. They are read for character, for atmosphere, for the ritual of detection, for the more subtle benefits of this genre of literature, including no doubt the values Aristotle found in tragedy: the purging of pity and fear. Simenon's true genius lay in his merging of French realism with the traditional detective story, with the effect that the detective-story understanding of justice is modified to an ideal that is appropriate for life in the real world. Justice in the Maigret stories is not a negative, fatalistic force, as it usually is in the stories of the hard-boiled school (some of which have no winners in the end except the investigator, and all he has gained is the sad truth). Nor is justice the inexorable working out of divine retribution as it is in the Golden Age stories, in which evil is purged and the innocent are left ready to begin new lives. Rather, Simenon's world is a complex and ambiguous place where evil and good are closely related and cannot always be separated. There is still, however, a chance for purgation and rededication, usually supplied by the intuitive researches of that archetypal father figure, Inspector Maigret.

The last Maigret, *Maigret and Monsieur Charles*, appeared in 1972; after that, Simenon announced that he would write no more novels. *Maigret and Monsieur Charles* is a subtle psychological study of an unhealthy relationship. This story, satisfying on levels of plot, character, and theme, makes an appropriate farewell to Maigret. The hundreds of Maigret novels and short stories Simenon wrote over a period of forty years will continue to appeal not only to detective-story fans but also to those readers attracted to evocative description and intrigued by the darker side of human experience.

## Principal mystery and detective fiction

SERIES: Inspector Maigret: *Pietr-le-Letton,* 1931 (*Maigret and the Enigmatic Lett,* 1963; also as *The Strange Case of Peter the Lett*); *M. Gallet, décédé,* 1931 (*Maigret Stonewalled,* 1963; also as *The Death of M. Gallet*); *Le Pendu de Saint-Pholien,* 1931 (*Maigret and the Hundred Gibbets,* 1963; also as *The Crime of Inspector Maigret*); *Le Charretier de la Providence,* 1931 (*Maigret Meets a Milord,* 1963; also as *The Crime at Lock 14*); *La Tête d'un homme,* 1931 (*A Battle of Nerves,* 1940); *Le Chien jaune,* 1931 (*A Face for a Clue,* 1940); *La Nuit du Carrefour,* 1931 (*Maigret at the Crossroads,* 1964; also as *The Crossroads Murders*); *Un Crime en Hollande,* 1931 (*A Crime in Holland,* 1940); *Au rendez-vous des terre-neuvas,* 1931 (*The Sailors' Rendez-vous,* 1970); *La Danseuse du Gai-Moulin,* 1931 (*At the Gai-Moulin,* 1940); *La Guinguette à deux sous,* 1932 (*The Guinguette by the Seine,* 1940); *Le Port des brumes,* 1932 (*Death of a Harbour Master,* 1942); *L'Ombre chinoise,* 1932 (*Maigret Mystified,* 1964; also as *The Shadow in the Courtyard*); *L'Affaire Saint-Fiacre,* 1932 (*Maigret Goes Home,* 1967; also as *The Saint-Fiacre Affair*); *Chez les Flamands,* 1932 (*The Flemish Shop,* 1940); *Le Fou de Bergerac,* 1932 (*The Madman of Bergerac,* 1940); *Liberty-Bar,* 1932 (English translation, 1940); *L'Écluse numéro un,* 1933 (*The Lock at Charenton,* 1941); *Maigret,* 1934 (*Maigret Returns,* 1941); *Maigret revient,* containing *Cécile est morte, Les Caves du Majestic,* and *La Maison du juge,* 1942 (*Maigret and the Spinster,* 1977; *Maigret and the Hotel Majestic,* 1977; and *Maigret in Exile,* 1978) *Signé Picpus,* 1944 (*To Any Lengths,* 1958); *L'Inspecteur cadavre*, 1944; *Les Nouvelles Enquêtes de Maigret*, 1944 (*The Short Cases of Inspector Maigret*, 1959); *Félicie est là*, 1944; *La Pipe de Maigret*, 1947 (*Maigret's Pipe*, 1977); *Maigret se fâche*, 1947 (*Maigret in Retirement*, 1976); *Maigret à New York*, 1947 (*Inspector Maigret in New York's Underworld*, 1956); *Maigret et l'inspecteur malchanceux*, 1947 (also as *Maigret et l'inspecteur malgraceux*, translated in *Maigret's Christmas*, 1951); *Les Vacances de Maigret*, 1948 (*No Vacation for Maigret*, 1959; also as *Maigret on Holiday*); *Maigret et son mort*, 1948 (*Maigret's Special Murder*, 1964; also as *Maigret's Dead Man*); *La Première Enquête de Maigret (1913)*, 1949 (*Maigret's First Case*, 1970); *Mon Ami Maigret*, 1949 (*My Friend Maigret*, 1969; also as *The Methods of Maigret*); *Maigret chez le coroner*, 1949 (*Maigret and the Coroner*, 1980); *Maigret et la vieille dame*, 1950 (*Maigret and the Old Lady*, 1965); *L'Amie de Mme Maigret*, 1950 (*Madame Maigret's Friend*, 1960; also as *Madame Maigret's Own Case*); *Maigret et les petits cochons sans queue*, 1950; *Un Noël de Maigret*, 1951 (*Maigret's Christmas*, 1951); *Les Mémoires de Maigret*, 1951 (*Maigret's Memoirs*, 1963); *Maigret au Picratt's*, 1951 (*Maigret in Montmartre*, 1963; also as *Inspector Maigret and the Strangled Stripper*); *Maigret en meublé*, 1951 (*Maigret Takes a Room*, 1965; also as *Maigret Rents a Room*); *Maigret et la grande perche*, 1951 (*Maigret and the Burglar's Wife*, 1969; also as *Inspector Maigret and the Burglar's Wife*); *Maigret, Lognon, et les gangsters*, 1952 (*Maigret and the Gangsters*, 1974; also as *Inspector Maigret and the Killers*); *Le Révolver de Maigret*, 1952 (*Maigret's Revolver*, 1969); *Maigret et l'homme du banc*, 1953 (*Maigret and the Man on the Bench*, 1975); *Maigret a peur*, 1953 (*Maigret Afraid*, 1961); *Maigret se trompe*, 1953 (*Maigret's Mistake*, 1964); *Maigret à l'école*, 1954 (*Maigret Goes to School*, 1964); *Maigret et la jeune morte*, 1954 (*Maigret and the Young Girl*, 1965; also as *Inspector Maigret and the Dead Girl*); *Maigret chez le ministre*, 1955 (*Maigret and the Calame Report*, 1969; also as *Maigret and the Minister*); *Maigret et le corps sans tête*, 1955 (*Maigret and the Headless Corpse*, 1967); *Maigret tend un piège*, 1955 (*Maigret Sets a Trap*, 1965); *Un Échec de Maigret*, 1956 (*Maigret's Failure*, 1962); *Maigret s'amuse*, 1957 (*Maigret's Little Joke*, 1965; also as *None of Maigret's Business*); *Les Scrupules de Maigret*, 1958 (*Maigret Has Scruples*, 1959); *Maigret voyage*, 1958 (*Maigret and the Millionaires*, 1974); *Maigret et les témoins récalcitrants*, 1959 (*Maigret and the Reluctant Witnesses*, 1964); *Une Confidence de Maigret*, 1959 (*Maigret Has Doubts*, 1968); *Maigret aux assises*, 1960 (*Maigret in Court*, 1961); *Maigret et les vieillards*, 1960 (*Maigret in Society*, 1962); *Maigret et le voleur paresseux*, 1961 (*Maigret and the Lazy Burglar*, 1963); *Maigret et les braves gens*, 1962 (*Maigret and the Black Sheep*, 1976); *Maigret et le client du samedi*, 1962 (*Maigret and the Saturday Caller*, 1964); *Maigret et le clochard*, 1963 (*Maigret and the Bum*, 1973; also as *Maigret and the Dossier*); *La Colère de Maigret*, 1963 (*Maigret Loses His Temper*, 1967); *Maigret et le fantôme*, 1964 (*Maigret and the Apparition*, 1975; also as *Maigret and the Ghost*); *Maigret se défend*, 1964 (*Maigret on the Defensive*, 1968); *La Patience de Maigret*, 1965 (*The Patience of Maigret*, 1966); *Maigret et l'affaire Nahour*, 1966 (*Maigret and the Nahour Case*, 1967); *Le Voleur de Maigret*, 1967 (*Maigret's Pickpocket*, 1968); *Maigret à Vichy*, 1968 (*Maigret in Vichy*, 1969; also as *Maigret Takes the Waters*); *Maigret hésite*, 1968 (*Maigret Hesitates*, 1970); *L'Ami d'enfance de Maigret*, 1968 (*Maigret's Boyhood Friend*, 1970); *Maigret et le tueur,* 1969 (also as *Le Meurtre d'un étudiant; Maigret and the Killer,* 1971); *Maigret et le marchand de vin,* 1970 (*Maigret and the Wine Merchant,* 1971); *La Folle de Maigret,* 1970 (*Maigret and the Madwoman,* 1972); *Maigret et l'homme tout seul,* 1971 (*Maigret and the Loner,* 1975); *Maigret et l'indicateur,* 1971 (*Maigret and the Informer,* 1973; also as *Maigret and the Flea*); *Maigret et M. Charles,* 1972 (*Maigret and Monsieur Charles,* 1973).

OTHER NOVELS: *L'Orgueil qui meurt,* 1925; *Nox l'insaisissable,* 1926; *Aimer, mourir,* 1928; *Une Femme à tuer,* 1929; *Pour venger son père,* 1931; *Marie-Mystère,* 1931; *Le Rêve qui meurt,* 1931; *Baisers mortels,* 1931; *Le Relais d'Alsace,* 1931 (*The Man from Everywhere,* 1942); *Victime de son fils,* 1931; *Âme de jeune fille,* 1931; *Les Chercheurs de bonheur,* 1931; *L'Épave,* 1932; *La Maison de l'inquiétude,* 1932; *Matricule 12,* 1932; *Le Passager du Polarlys,* 1932 (*Danger at Sea,* 1954; also as *The Mystery of the Polarlys*); *La Figurante,* 1932; *Fièvre,* 1932; *Les Forçats de Paris,* 1932; *La Fiancée du diable,* 1933; *La Femme rousse,* 1933; *Le Château des Sables Rouges,* 1933; *Deuxième Bureau,* 1933; *Les Gens d'en face,* 1933 (*The Window over the Way,* 1966; also as *Danger Ashore*); *L'Âne Rouge,* 1933 (*The Night-Club,* 1979); *La Maison du canal,* 1933 (*The House by the Canal,* 1948); *Les Fiançailles de M. Hire,* 1933 (*Mr. Hire's Engagement,* 1956); *Le Coup de lune,* 1933 (*Tropic Moon,* 1942); *Le Haut Mal,* 1933 (*The Woman in the Gray House,* 1944); *L'Homme de Londres,* 1933 (*Newhaven-Dieppe,* 1944); *Le Locataire,* 1934 (*The Lodger,* 1943); *L'Évasion,* 1934; *Les Suicidés,* 1934 (*One Way Out,* 1943; also as *Escape in Vain*); *Les Pitard,* 1935 (*A Wife at Sea,* 1949); *Les Clients d'Avrenos,* 1935; *Quartier nègre,* 1935; *Les Demoiselles de Concarneau,* 1936 (*The Breton Sisters,* 1943); *45° à l'ombre,* 1936; *Long Cours,* 1936 (*The Long Exile,* 1982); *L'Évadé,* 1936 (*The Disintegration of J. P. G.,* 1937); *L'Île empoisonnée,* 1937; *Seul parmi les gorilles,* 1937; *Faubourg,* 1937 (*Home Town,* 1944); *L'Assassin,* 1937 (*The Murderer,* 1963); *Le Blanc à lunettes,* 1937 (*Tatala,* 1943); *Le Testament Donadieu,* 1937 (*The Shadow Falls,* 1945); *Ceux de la soif,* 1938; *Les Trois Crimes de mes amis,* 1938; *Chemin sans issue,* 1938 (*Blind Alley,* 1946; also as *Blind Path*); *L'Homme qui regardait passer les trains,* 1938 (*The Man Who Watched the Trains Go By,* 1958); *Les Rescapés du Télémaque,* 1938 (*The Survivors,* 1965); *Monsieur la Souris,* 1938 (English translation, 1950; also as *The Mouse*); *Touriste de bananes: Ou, Les Dimanches de Tahiti,* 1938 (*Banana Tourist,* 1946); *La Marie du port,* 1938 (*A Chit of a Girl,* 1949; also as *The Girl in Waiting*); *Le Suspect,* 1938 (*The Green Thermos,* 1944); *Les Sœurs Lacroix,* 1938 (*Poisoned Relations,* 1950); *Le Cheval Blanc,* 1938 (*The White Horse Inn,* 1980); *Chez Krull,* 1939 (English translation, 1966); *Le Bourgemestre de Furnes,* 1939 (*Burgomaster of Furnes,* 1952); *Le Coup de vague,* 1939; *Les Inconnus dans la maison,* 1940 (*Strangers in the House,* 1954); *Malempin,* 1940 (*The Family Life,* 1978); *Cour d'assises,* 1941 (*Justice,* 1949); *La Maison des sept jeunes filles,* 1941; *L'Outlaw,* 1941 (*The Outlaw,* 1986); *Bergelon,* 1941 (*The Delivery,* 1981); *Il pleut, bergère . . . ,* 1941 (*Black Rain,* 1965); *Le Voyageur de la Toussaint,* 1941 (*Strange Inheritance,* 1958); *Oncle Charles s'est enfermé,* 1942 (*Uncle Charles Has Locked Himself In,* 1987); *Le Veuve Couderc,* 1942 (*The Widow,* 1955; also as *Ticket of Leave*); *La Vérité sur Bébé Donge,* 1942 (*I Take This Woman,* 1953; also as *The Trial of Bébé Donge*); *Le Fils Cardinaud,* 1942 (*Young Cardinaud,* 1956); *Le Rapport du gendarme,* 1944 (*The Gendarme's Report,* 1951); *Le Fenêtre des Rouet,* 1945 (*Across the Street,* 1954); *La Fuite de Monsieur Monde,* 1945 (*M. Monde Vanishes,* 1967); *L'Aîné des Ferchaux,* 1945 (*Magnet of Doom,* 1948; also as *The First Born*); *Les Noces de Poitiers,* 1946; *Le Cercle des Mahe,* 1946; *Trois Chambres à Manhattan,* 1946 (*Three Beds in Manhattan,* 1964); *Au bout du rouleau,* 1947; *Le Clan des Ostendais,* 1947 (*The Ostenders,* 1952); *Lettre à mon juge,* 1947 (*Act of Passion,* 1952); *Le Destin des Malou,* 1947 (*The Fate of the Malous,* 1962); *Le Passager clandestin,* 1947 (*The Stowaway,* 1957); *Pedigree,* 1948 (English translation, 1962); *Le Bilan Malétras,* 1948 (*The Reckoning,* 1984); *La Jument perdue,* 1948; *La Neige était sale,* 1948 (*The Stain in the Snow,* 1964; also as *The Snow Was Black*); *Le Fond de la bouteille,* 1949 (*The Bottom of the Bottle,* 1954); *Les Fantômes du chapelier,* 1949 (*The Hatter's Ghosts,* 1956); *Les Quatre Jours du pauvre homme,* 1949 (*Four Days in a Lifetime,* 1953); *Un Nouveau dans la ville,* 1950; *Les volets verts,* 1950 (*The Heart of a Man,* 1951); *L'Enterrement de Monsieur Bouvet,* 1950 (*The Burial of Monsieur Bouvet,* 1955; also as *Inquest on Bouvet*); *Tante Jeanne,* 1951 (*Aunt Jeanne,* 1953); *Le Temps d'Anaïs,* 1951 (*The Girl in His Past,* 1952); *Une Vie comme neuve,* 1951 (*A New Lease on Life,* 1963); *Marie qui loche,* 1951 (*The Girl with a Squint,* 1978); *La Mort de Belle,* 1952 (*Belle,* 1967); *Les Frères Rico,* 1952 (*The Brothers Rico,* 1967); *Antoine et Julie,* 1953 (*Magician,* 1955; also as *Antoine and Julie*); *L'Escalier de fer,* 1953 (*The Iron Staircase,* 1963); *Feux rouges,* 1953 (*The Hitchhiker,* 1967; also as *Red Lights*); *Crime impuni,* 1954 (*The Fugitive,* 1955; also as *Account Unsettled*); *L'Horloger d'Everton,* 1954 (*The Watchmaker of Everton,* 1967); *Le Grand Bob,* 1954 (*Big Bob,* 1972); *Les Témoins,* 1955 (*The Witnesses,* 1956); *La Boule noire,* 1955; *Les Complices,* 1956 (*The Accomplices,* 1963); *En cas de malheur,* 1956 (*In Case of Emergency,* 1958); *Le Petit Homme d'Arkhangelsk,* 1956 (*The Man from Arkangel,* 1966); *Le Fils,* 1957 (*The Son,* 1958); *Le Nègre,* 1957 (*The Negro,* 1959); *Strip-tease,* 1958 (English translation, 1959); *Le Président,* 1958 (*The Premier,* 1966); *Le Passage de la ligne,* 1958; *Dimanche,* 1959 (*Sunday,* 1966); *La Vieille,* 1959 (*The Grandmother,* 1980); *Le Veuf,* 1959 (*The Widower,* 1961); *L'Ours en peluche,* 1960 (*Teddy Bear,* 1972); *Betty,* 1961 (English translation, 1975); *Le Train,* 1961 (*The Train,* 1966); *La Porte,* 1962 (*The Door,* 1964); *Les Autres,* 1962 (*The House on the Quai Notre-Dame,* 1975); *Les Anneaux de Bicêtre,* 1963 (*The Bells of Bicêtre,* 1964; also as *The Patient*); *La Chambre bleue,* 1964 (*The Blue Room,* 1964); *L'Homme au petit chien,* 1964 (*The Man with the Little Dog,* 1965); *Le Petit Saint,* 1965 (*The Little Saint,* 1965); *Le Train de Venise,* 1965 (*The Venice Train,* 1974); *Le Confessionnal,* 1966 (*The Confessional,* 1968); *La Mort d'Auguste,* 1966 (*The Old Man Dies,* 1967); *Le Chat,* 1967 (*The Cat,* 1967); *Le Déménagement,* 1967 (*The Move,* 1968; also as *The Neighbors*); *La Prison,* 1968 (*The Prison,* 1969); *La Main,* 1968 (*The Man on the Bench in the Barn,* 1970); *Il y a encore des noisetiers,* 1969; *Novembre,* 1969 (*November,* 1970); *Le Riche Homme,* 1970 (*The Rich Man,* 1971); *La Disparition d'Odile,* 1971 (*The Disappearance of Odile,* 1972); *La Cage de verre,* 1971 (*The Glass Cage,* 1973); *Les Innocents,* 1972 (*The Innocents,* 1973).

OTHER SHORT FICTION: *Les Treize Mystères,* 1932; *Les Treize Énigmes,* 1932; *Les Treize Coupables,* 1932; *Les Sept Minutes,* 1938; *Le Petit Docteur,* 1943; *Les*

*Dossiers de l'Agence O,* 1943; *Nouvelles exotiques,* 1944; *On ne tue pas les pauvres types,* 1947; *Le Bateau d'Émile,* 1954; *La Rue aux trois poussins,* 1963; *La Piste du Hollandais,* 1973.

## Other major works

NOVELS: *Au pont des arches,* 1921; *Le Roman d'une dactylo,* 1924; *Amour d'exilée,* 1924; *Les Larmes avant le bonheur . . . ,* 1924; *L'Heureuse Fin,* 1925; *Pour le sauver,* 1925; *Pour qu'il soit heureux!,* 1925; *L'Oiseau blessé,* 1925; *La Fiancée fugitive,* 1925; *Entre deux haines,* 1925; *Ceux qu'on avait oubliés,* 1925; *À l'assaut d'un cœur,* 1925; *Étoile de cinéma,* 1925; *La Prêtresse des Vaudoux,* 1925; *Au Grand 13,* 1925; *Un Viol aux q'uat'z arts,* 1925; *Perversités frivoles,* 1925; *Plaisirs charnels,* 1925; *La Noce à Montmartre,* 1925; *Aux vingt-huit négresses,* 1925; *Voluptueuses étreintes,* 1925; *Amour d'Afrique,* 1926; *L'Orgueil d'aimer,* 1926; *Celle qui est aimée,* 1926; *Les Yeux qui ordonnent,* 1926; *De la rue au bonheur,* 1926; *Que ma mère l'ignore!,* 1926; *Un Peche de jeunesse,* 1926; *Se Ma Tsien, le sacrificateur,* 1926; *Liquettes au vent,* 1926; *Une Petite très sensuelle,* 1926; *Orgies bourgeoises,* 1926; *L'Homme aux douze étreintes,* 1926; *Nini voilée,* 1926; *Histoire d'un pantalon,* 1926; *Mémoires d'un vieux suiveur,* 1926; *Nichonnette,* 1926; *Défense d'aimer,* 1927; *Le Cercle de la soif,* 1927 (also as *Le Cercle de la mort*); *Le Feu s'éteint,* 1927; *Les Voleurs de navires,* 1927; *Un Monsieur libidineux,* 1927; *Lili-Tristresse,* 1927; *Un Tout Petit Cœur,* 1927; *La Pucelle de Bénouville,* 1927; *Étreintes passionnées,* 1927; *Une Môme dessalée,* 1927; *L'Envers d'une passion,* 1927; *Le Semeur de larmes,* 1928; *Songes d'été,* 1928; *Le Sang des Gitanes,* 1928; *Aimer d'amour,* 1928; *Le Monstre blanc de la Terre de Feu,* 1928 (also as *L'Île de la Désolation*); *Le Lac d'angoisse,* 1928 (also as *Le Lac des esclaves*); *La Maison sans soleil,* 1928; *Miss Baby,* 1928; *Chair de beauté,* 1928; *Le Secret des Lamas,* 1928; *Les Maudits du Pacifique,* 1928; *Le Roi des glaces,* 1928; *Le Sous-marin dans la forêt,* 1928; *Les Nains des cataractes,* 1928; *Les Cœurs perdus,* 1928; *Annie, danseuse,* 1928; *Dolorosa,* 1928; *Les Adolescents passionnés,* 1928; *Mademoiselle X . . . ,* 1928; *Le Désert du froid qui tue,* 1928 (also as *Le Yacht Fantôme*); *Cœur exalté,* 1928; *Trois Cœurs dans la tempête,* 1928; *Le Fou d'amour,* 1928; *Les Amants de la mansarde,* 1928; *Un Jour de soleil,* 1928; *Un Soir de vertige . . . ,* 1928; *Brin d'amour,* 1928; *Les Cœurs vides,* 1928; *Cabotine,* 1928; *Un Petit Corps blessé,* 1928; *Haïr à force d'aimer,* 1928; *L'Étreinte tragique,* 1928; *Un Seul Baiser . . . ,* 1928; *L'Amour méconnu,* 1928; *L'Amant fantôme,* 1928; *Madame veut un amant,* 1928; *Les Distractions d'Hélène,* 1928; *L'Amour à Montparnasse,* 1928; *Des gens qui exagerent,* 1928; *Un Petit Poison,* 1928; *Bobette et ses satyres,* 1928; *Une Petite dessalée,* 1928; *Rien que pour toi,* 1929; *Le Roi du Pacific,* 1929 (also as *Le Bateaud'Or*); *L'Île des maudits,* 1929 (also as *Le Naufrage du Pélican*); *La Fiancée aux mains de glace,* 1929; *Destinées,* 1929; *La Femme qui tue,* 1929; *Les Bandits de Chicago,* 1929; *Les Contrebandiers de l'alcool,* 1929; *La Panthère borgne,* 1929; *La Police scientifique,* 1929; *Les Deux Maîtresses,* 1929; *L'Île des hommes roux,* 1929; *Le Gorille-Roi,* 1929; *En Robe de mariée,* 1929; *La Femme en deuil,* 1929; *Les Mémoires d'un prostitué par lui-même ,* 1929; *La Fille de l'autre,* 1929; *Cœur de poupée,* 1929; *Deux Cœurs de femmes,* 1929; *Le Mirage de Paris,* 1929; *L'Épave d'amour,* 1929; *L'Amour et l'argent,* 1929; *Un Drôle de coco,* 1929; *Une*

*Ombre dans la nuit,* 1929; *La Victime,* 1929; *Voleuse d'amour,* 1929; *Nuit de Paris,* 1929; *Celle qui revient,* 1929; *Trop beau pour elle!,* 1929; *Le Parfum du passé,* 1929; *Hélas! je t'aime* . . . , 1929; *La Merveilleuse Aventure,* 1929; *Les Pirates du Texas,* 1929 (revised as *La Chasse au whisky,* 1934); *L'Amant sans nom,* 1929; *Un Drame au Pôle sud,* 1929; *Captain S.O.S.,* 1929; *Lily-Palace,* 1929; *Nez d'argent,* 1930 (revised as *Le Paria des bois sauvages,* 1933); *Mademoiselle Million,* 1930; *La Femme 47,* 1930; *L'Homme qui tremble,* 1930; *L'Oeil de l'Utah,* 1930; *Le Pêcheur de Bouées,* 1930; *Le Chinois de San Francisco,* 1930; *Jacques d'Antifer, roi des Îles du Vent,* 1930 (revised as *L'Heritier du corsaire,* 1934); *Train de nuit,* 1930; *L'Inconnue,* 1930; *Les Amants du malheur,* 1930; *Celle qui passé,* 1930; *La Femme ardente,* 1930; *Petite Exilée,* 1930; *La Porte close,* 1930; *La Poupée brisée,* 1930; *Les Étapes du mensonge,* 1930; *Le Bonheur de Lili,* 1930; *Un Nid d'amour,* 1930; *Bobette, mannequin,* 1930; *La Puissance du souvenir,* 1930; *Cœur de jeune fille,* 1930; *Sœurette,* 1930; *Lil-Sourire,* 1930; *Folie d'un soir,* 1930; *L'Homme de proie,* 1931; *Les Errants,* 1931; *Katia, acrobate,* 1931; *L'Homme à la cigarette,* 1931; *La Maison de la haine,* 1931; *La Double Vie,* 1931; *Pauvre amante!,* 1931; *Jehan Pinaguet: Histoire d'un homme simple,* 1991.

SHORT FICTION: *Nuit de Noces,* 1926; *Double noces* and *Les Noces ardentes,* 1926; *Paris-Leste,* 1927; *La Folle d'Itteville,* 1931.

PLAY: *La Neige était sale,* 1951 (adapted with Fréderic Dard)

NONFICTION: *La Mauvaise Étoile,* 1938; *Je me souviens,* 1945; *L'Aventure,* 1945; *Long Cours sur les rivières et canaux,* 1952; *Le Roman de l'homme,* 1959 (*The Novel of Man,* 1964); *La Femme en France,* 1959; *Entretien avec Roger Stephanie,* 1963; *Ma Conviction profonde,* 1963; *La Paris de Simenon,* 1969 (*Simenon's Paris,* 1970); *Quand j'étais vieux,* 1970 (*When I Was Old,* 1971); *Lettre à ma mère,* 1974 (*Letter to My Mother,* 1976); *Des Traces de pas,* 1975; *Un Homme comme un autre,* 1975; *Les Petits Hommes,* 1976; *Vent du nord, vent du sud,* 1976; *À la découverte de la France,* 1976 (with Francis Lacassin and Gilbert Sigaux); *À la recherche de l'homme nu,* 1976 (with Lacassin and Sigaux); *Un Banc au soleil,* 1977; *De la cave au grenier,* 1977; *À l'abri de notre arbre,* 1977; *Tant que je suis vivant,* 1978; *Vacances obligatoires,* 1978; *La Main dans la main,* 1978; *Au-delà de ma porte-fenêtre,* 1978; *Je suis resté un enfant de chœur,* 1979; *À quoi bon jurer?,* 1979; *Point-virgule,* 1979; *Le Prix d'un homme,* 1980; *On dit que j'ai soixante-quinze ans,* 1980; *Quand vient le froid,* 1980; *Les Libertés qu'il nous reste,* 1980; *La Femme endormie,* 1981; *Jour et nuit,* 1981; *Destinées,* 1981; *Mémoires intimes,* 1981 (*Intimate Memoirs,* 1984).

## Bibliography

Assouline, Pierre. *Simenon: A Biography.* New York: Knopf, 1997.

Becker, Lucille Frackman. *Georges Simenon Revisited.* New York: Twayne, 1999.

Bresler, Fenton. *The Mystery of Georges Simenon: A Biography.* New York: Beaufort, 1983.

Cowley, Malcolm, ed. *Writers at Work: The "Paris Review" Interviews, First Series.* New York: Penguin, 1977.

Eskin, Stanley G. *Simenon.* Jefferson, N.C.: McFarland, 1987.

Freeling, Nicolas. *Criminal Convictions: Errant Essays on Perpetrators of Literary License.* Boston: D. R. Godine, 1994.

Marnham, Patrick. *The Man Who Wasn't Maigret: A Portrait of Georges Simenon.* New York: Farrar, Straus, Giroux, 1993.

Narcejac, Thomas. *The Art of Simenon.* London: Routledge & Kegan Paul, 1952.

Raymond, John. *Simenon in Court.* London: H. Hamilton, 1968.

"Simenon, Georges." In *Mystery and Suspense Writers: The Literature of Crime, Detection, and Espionage,* edited by Robin W. Winks and Maureen Corrigan. New York: Charles Scribner's Sons, 1998.

Young, Trudee. *Georges Simenon: A Checklist of His Maigret and Other Mystery Novels and Short Stories in French and English Translations.* Metuchen, N.J.: Scarecrow, 1976.

*Janet McCann*
*Updated by C. A. Gardner*

# Maj Sjöwall and Per Wahlöö

## Maj Sjöwall

**Born:** Stockholm, Sweden; September 25, 1935

## Per Wahlöö

**Born:** Göteborg, Sweden; August 5, 1926
**Died:** Malmö, Sweden; June 22, 1975

**Also wrote as** • Peter Wahlöö

**Type of plot** • Police procedural

**Principal series** • Martin Beck, 1965-1975.

**Principal series characters** • MARTIN BECK, a member and eventually the head of the Stockholm homicide squad, is tall, reserved, and sometimes melancholy. Fortyish and unhappily married when the series begins, Beck is intelligent, painstaking, patient, and conscientious. He is a skilled police detective who is often troubled by the role which the police play in Swedish society.
 • LENNART KOLLBERG, Beck's colleague and closest friend, is good natured, stocky, and a devoted family man. A pacifist by nature, his growing disillusionment with changes in the police system after its nationalization in 1965 eventually leads him to resign.
 • GUNVALD LARSSON, a member of the Stockholm homicide squad, is tall, brawny, taciturn, cynical, and often short-tempered. Unmarried and a loner, he is fastidious in his dress and efficient in the performance of his job. He is a hardworking professional with little time for interpersonal relationships.
 • FREDRIK MELANDER, originally a homicide-squad detective, later transferred to the burglary and violent crimes division. Married and a father, he is valued by his colleagues for his astonishing, computer-like memory and is notorious for his frequent trips to the men's room.
 • EINER RÖNN, a member of the homicide squad, is an efficient but unremarkable detective. Rarely promoted, he is one of Gunvald Larsson's few friends.

**Contribution** • The ten novels in the Martin Beck series, written by husband-and-wife team Per Wahlöö and Maj Sjöwall, chronicle the activities of the Stockholm homicide squad from 1965–the year in which the Swedish police force was nationalized–to 1975. Conceived as one epic novel, Beck's story was written and published at the rate of one installment per year—documenting the exact happenings of the years in which they were composed, down to flight numbers and departure times, political events, and the weather.

The books trace the changes in the police force and its relationship to Swedish society as well as the personal lives of the homicide detectives themselves. Marked by dry humor and painstaking attention to detail, they capture both the interplay among the principal characters and the exhaustive amounts of routine research that go into solving a crime. Writing in a detached, clinical style, Sjöwall and Wahlöö paint a portrait of Sweden in the late 1960's and early 1970's as a bourgeois welfare state in which crime is steadily on the rise and the police are seen increasingly by the public as tools of the government rather than as allies of the people. Using the crime novel as a mirror of the ills of the socialist state, Sjöwall and Wahlöö transformed the genre into a vehicle for addressing wrongs, rather than diffusing social anxiety. Until their work, the police procedural had been little appreciated in Sweden; the Beck series influenced Swedish successors such as K. Arne Blom, Olov Svedelid, Kennet Ahl, and Leif G. W. Persson to adopt a similar approach of social awareness.

**Biography** • Peter Fredrik Wahlöö was born on August 5, 1926, in Göteborg, Sweden, the son of Waldemar Wahlöö and Karin Helena Svensson Wahlöö. He attended the University of Lund, from which he was graduated in 1946, and began a career as a journalist. Throughout the 1950's, Wahlöö wrote about criminal and social issues for several Swedish magazines and newspapers before publishing his first novel, *Himmelsgetan*, in 1959. Also deeply involved in left-wing politics, Wahlöö was deported from Francisco Franco's Spain in 1957 for his political activities.

Prior to his success as coauthor of the Martin Beck books, Wahlöö's published novels were translated into English under the name Peter Wahlöö. Like the Beck books, Wahlöö's other novels are chiefly concerned with philosophical and sociological themes, examining through fiction the relationship of people to the society in which they live. Wahlöö is the author of two detective novels—*Mord på 31: A våningen* (1964; *Murder on the Thirty-first Floor*, 1966; filmed as *Kamikaze 1989* in 1984) and *Stålspånget* (1968; *The Steel Spring*, 1970)—featuring Chief Inspector Jensen, a police detective in an unnamed, apathetic northern country clearly intended as a bleak projection of Sweden's future. Wahlöö also wrote scripts for radio, television, and film, and translated some of Ed McBain's 87th Precinct novels into Swedish.

Maj Sjöwall (sometimes transliterated as Sjoewall) was born in Stockholm, Sweden, on September 25, 1935, the daughter of Will Sjöwall and Margit Trobaeck Sjöwall. After studying journalism and graphics in Stockholm, she became both a magazine art director and a publishing-house editor. She was working as a journalist when she first met Wahlöö, to whom she was married in 1962. After studying journalism and graphics at Stockholm, she became both a magazine art director and a publishing house editor.

While working for magazines published by the same company, Sjöwall and

Wahlöö met and found their social views closely matched. Married in 1962, they composed a monumental outline for the Beck series, conceived as a single epic 300 chapters long, divided into ten books for the sake of convenience. Sitting across the dining room table from each other, they simultaneously wrote alternate chapters while their children (Lena, Terz, and Jens) slept.

Perhaps because of journalistic backgrounds that fostered spare, disciplined writing with precise details, their styles meshed seamlessly. The couple shared a desire to use the format of the detective novel to examine deeper issues within Swedish society; Wahlöö said they intended to "use the crime novel as a scalpel cutting open the belly of the ideologically pauperized and morally debatable so-called welfare state of the bourgeois type." The first Martin Beck novel, *Roseanna*, appeared in 1965. Sjöwall and Wahlöö collaborated on other projects as well, including a comparison of police methods in the United States and Europe and the editing of the literary magazine *Peripeo*. Maj Sjöwall is also a poet.

The Martin Beck series was published and acclaimed in over twenty countries, garnering such awards as the Sherlock Award from the Swedish newspaper *Expressen* in 1968, the Edgar from the Mystery Writers of America in 1971, and the Italian Gran Giallo Città di Cattolica Prize in 1973, all for *Den skrattande polisen* (1968; *The Laughing Policeman*, 1970). The novel was filmed in 1973, with its setting transposed to San Francisco. *Den vedervärdige mannen från Säffle* (1971; *The Abominable Man*, 1972) was filmed as *The Man on the Roof* in 1977. Six books were adapted for television in Sweden.

Per Wahlöö died of pancreatic disease on June 22, 1975. Afterward, Sjöwall wrote one other novel, *Kvinnan som liknade Garbo* (1990), coauthored with with Tomas Ross.

**Analysis** • The ten novels which constitute the Martin Beck series represent a remarkable achievement in the realm of mystery and detective fiction. Begun in 1965 and completed in 1975, the year of Per Wahlöö's death, the books chronicle a decade in the lives of the members of the Stockholm Police homicide squad, focusing primarily on detective Martin Beck, who becomes the head of the squad by the end of the series. The nationalization of the Swedish police force in the early 1960's—an event to which Sjöwall and Wahlöö refer in *Polismördaren: roman om ett brott* (1974; *Cop Killer*, 1975) as the creation of a state within the state—led the couple to plan a series of ten books which would reflect the changes taking place in Swedish society. Using crime as the basis for their examination, they planned the books as one continuous story told in ten segments, each of which constitutes a separate novel, with characters who recur throughout the series and whose lives change as it progresses.

In choosing the crime novel as the setting for their study, Sjöwall and Wahlöö selected a medium which would allow their characters to interact with all strata of Swedish society, and the cases in the Martin Beck books involve criminals and victims who are drug addicts, sex murderers, industrialists, tourists, welfare recipients, members of the bourgeoisie, and—in a plot which eerily foreshadowed subsequent events–the Swedish prime minister. The police force in most countries, perhaps more than any other group, deals directly with the end result of social problems, both as they affect the social mainstream and as they relate to those who fall through society's cracks, and the crimes which form the plots of the Beck novels are often a direct outgrowth of existing sociological conditions.

The arc which the series follows moves from fairly straightforward, although horrifying, murders and sex crimes to cases that increasingly reflect the growing violence in most Western societies throughout the 1960's and early 1970's. The first book in the series, *Roseanna*, details the squad's efforts to track down the lone, disturbed murderer of a young American tourist, while the final entry, *Terroristema* (1975; *The Terrorists*, 1976), finds the detectives attempting to thwart the plans of an international assassin during the visit of a right-wing American senator. (The fact that both characters are Americans is almost certainly intentional, as the books often make mention of the level of crime and the availability of guns in the United States, which is seen as a cautionary model of an excessively violent society.)

The decaying relationship between the police and Swedish society is depicted in the series as an outgrowth of the role the nationalized police force came to play in Sweden's bureaucratic welfare society. This position is outlined in the final pages of *The Terrorists* by Martin Beck's closest friend, Lennart Kollberg, who has left the force: "They made a terrible mistake back then. Putting the police in the vanguard of violence is like putting the cart before the horse." Kollberg's comment puts into words the implied criticism throughout the series of the use of police violence to combat rising social violence.

The source of that violence is seen by Sjöwall and Wahlöö as a by-product of Western economic systems. In the same book, another character remarks, "For as long as I can remember, large and powerful nations within the capitalist bloc have been ruled by people who according to accepted legal norms are simply criminals." In the series' sixth book, *Polis, polis, potatismos!* (1970; *Murder at the Savoy*, 1971), the murder of a wealthy business executive and arms trafficker is traced to a former employee who lost his job, his home, and his family as a result of the executive's ruthless policies. As the story unfolds, it becomes clear that the crime has removed a despicable man from the world, although his "work" will be carried on by his equally unsavory associates. The book ends with Martin Beck unhappy in the knowledge that the man he has caught will spend years in prison for murdering a corrupt man whose callousness Beck despises. As Kollberg notes near the end of *The Terrorists*, "Violence has rushed like an avalanche throughout the whole of the Western world over the last ten years." The book ends with the former police detective playing the letter *X* in a game of Scrabble and declaring, "Then I say X–X as in Marx."

The climate of the 1960's, with its antiwar protests and generation-based schisms, also fuels the negative view of the police. In *The Laughing Policeman*, Beck's teenage daughter, Ingrid, tells him that she had once boasted to her friends that her father was a policeman, but she now rarely admits it. The general mood of the 1960's, combined with the easy availability of drugs and the growing number of citizens living on social welfare rolls, places the police more and more often at odds with ordinary men and women. Sometimes driven by desperation, these citizens commit crimes which were once the province of hardened criminals: A young mother robs a bank in *Det slutna rummet* (1972; *The Locked Room*, 1973); a middle-class teenage boy in *Cop Killer* becomes the object of a manhunt after a crime spree leads to a policeman's death; and a naïve young girl living on the fringes of society shoots the prime minister in *The Terrorists*.

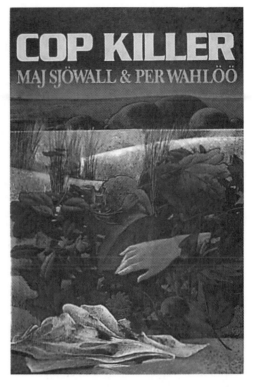

Yet the corruption filtering down through Swedish society from its upper echelons also leaves its peculiar mark on those crimes which have always been associated with the general populace, infecting their modus operandi with a shocking disregard for justice and human life. In *The Laughing Policeman*, a successful businessman who murdered his lover twenty-five years earlier shoots all the passengers on a city bus because two of them have knowledge which might expose him. *Cop Killer* offers a variation on this theme, with its story of a wealthy man who murders his mistress in the manner of a sex crime in order to throw suspicion on a man once convicted of a similar offense. In both cases, the perpetrators' only thoughts are to protect themselves—and the comfortable lives they have built within their communities—and they do so at a terrible cost to all notions of justice and the sanctity of human life.

Sjöwall and Wahlöö use not only their plots but their characters as well in their dramatization of the changes in Swedish society during the period covered by the series. Beck, a tall, reserved, often-melancholy man whose years of police work have not impaired his ability to judge each victim and each criminal individually, is the central figure. The moral complexities of his work often trouble Beck—a fact reflected in his sour stomach and slight stoop—yet he carries on in his profession, seeking a philosophical middle road which will allow him to reconcile those aspects of the job which he abhors with those which he believes fulfill a useful social function. Over the course of the series' ten years, his marriage worsens, he separates from his wife, his relationship with his daughter strengthens, and he falls in love with Rhea Nielsen, a good-humored earth mother of a woman whose cooking and companionship go a long way toward improving Beck's personal life—and digestion.

Beck's friend and colleague, Lennart Kollberg, also serves as a barometer for the times. Unlike Beck, Kollberg is happily married—he fathers two children during the series—and possessed of a far more effusive personality. The course which Kollberg's professional life will follow is set in motion during *Roseanna*, the series' first book, when he shoots and kills a man. The event has a profound effect on him, and he becomes the most outspoken opponent of the increasing use of police violence throughout the books. In defiance of police regulations, Kollberg afterward refuses to carry a loaded gun, and his growing dissatisfaction with the role of the police in society finally culminates in his resignation at the end of the ninth book, *Cop Killer*. He appears in *The Terrorists* as a fat, contented househusband, minding his children while his wife happily pursues a career.

The remaining recurring characters in the series appear primarily in their professional capacities and are used by Sjöwall and Wahlöö to round out the homicide squad and reflect the interplay of personalities which exists in any working situation. Individuals come and go within the structure of the squad: Fredrik Melander is transferred to another division; an ambitious young detective named Benny Skacke opts for a transfer to Malmö after a mistake that nearly costs Kollberg his life; detective Åke Strenström is among those murdered on the bus in *The Laughing Policeman*; and his girlfriend, Åsa Torell, joins the force as a reflection of the changing role of women during the 1960's and 1970's. (The ebb and flow within the force is also carried over into the outside world, with characters who figured in earlier cases reappearing later in the series.) Beck has an amiable, ongoing association with Per Månsson, his counterpart in Malmö. All these characters serve to illustrate the wide range of personality types who choose police work as a career—a theme which takes a dark turn in *The Abominable Man*, when a former policeman turns murderer and sniper after his wife dies in the custody of a corrupt and sadistic officer.

The tragic motive that lies at the heart of *The Abominable Man* has its roots in the psychological makeup of both the killer and his first victim, a crucial point throughout the Martin Beck series. For Sjöwall and Wahlöö, psychological traits are often inextricably bound to sociological forces. In the case of *The Abominable Man*, police corruption perpetuated the career of the sadistic officer whose actions drove his future murderer to the brink of madness. The books delve deeply into the social and psychological factors that set the stage for each crime.

The Martin Beck books fall under the heading of police procedurals, and Sjöwall and Wahlöö's writing style has the clinical, matter-of-fact tone of tough journalistic reporting. The series is characterized by an exceptionally thorough attention to detail that reflects the painstaking process of sifting through vast amounts of information and leaving no lead uninvestigated.

Cases often hinge on a remembered shred of evidence or an incorrectly recalled detail, and the role which luck and happenstance sometimes play is
never ignored. Sjöwall and Wahlöö frequently present interviews and confes-
sions in the form of typed transcripts, and the books' descriptions are both
vivid and utterly unsensationalized.

Given the serious nature of the series' themes, then, and the somber tone of
its individual plots, the books' considerable wit and humor come as a pleasant
surprise. Droll asides and dryly ironic exchanges of dialogue alleviate the atmosphere of Scandinavian gloom that permeates the novels, with flashes of
humor becoming more frequent as the writers progress further into the series
and develop a surer grasp of their themes and characters. *The Locked Room*
contains a comically executed SWAT-style raid that could easily have been
lifted from a Keystone Kops film, and there are sly references throughout the
series to the characters' reading preferences, which run to Raymond Chandler and Ed McBain. (In one of the final books, Beck is referred to in a newspaper article as "Sweden's Maigret.") The dour, dismally unphotogenic Gunvald Larsson is also a recurring source of amusement as his picture finds its
way into the newspaper several times—with his name always misspelled.

Best among the series' running jokes, however, are two radio patrolmen
named Kristiansson and Kvant, memorable solely for their inexhaustible capacity for bungling. They are the bane of Larsson's existence as they mishan-
dle evidence, lose suspects, and even catch a murderer while answering nature's call in the bushes of a city park. Nothing in the lighthearted manner in
which they are portrayed prepares the reader for the shock of Kvant's death
by sniper fire in *The Abominable Man.* He is replaced in the next book by the
equally inept Kvastmo, but the effect of his shooting brings home the degree
to which Sjöwall and Wahlöö have successfully created a world which mirrors
real life—a world in which crime and violence can alter the course of a human
life in an instant. The role which the police should play in such a world is a
complex issue, and it constitutes the heart of Sjöwall and Wahlöö's work.

### Principal mystery and detective fiction

SERIES: Martin Beck: *Roseanna,* 1965 (English translation, 1967); *Mannen
som gick upp in rök,* 1966 (*The Man Who Went Up in Smoke,* 1969); *Mannen pa
balkongen,* 1967 (*The Man on the Balcony: The Story of a Crime,* 1967); *Den
skrattande polisen,* 1968 (*The Laughing Policeman,* 1968); *Brandbilen som försvann,*
1969 (*The Fire Engine That Disappeared,* 1970); *Polis, polis, potatismos!,* 1970
(*Murder at the Savoy,* 1971); *Den vedervärdige mannen från Säffle,* 1971 (*The Abominable Man,* 1972); *Det slutna rummet,* 1972 (*The Locked Room,* 1973);
*Polismördaren: roman om ett brott,* 1974 (*Cop Killer: The Story of a Crime,* 1975);
*Terroristema,* 1975 (*The Terrorists,* 1976). Chief Inspector Jensen (by Per
Wahlöö): *Mord på 31: A våningen,* 1964 (*Murder on the Thirty-first Floor,* 1966;
also as *The Thirty-First Floor*); *Stålsprånget,* 1968 (*The Steel Spring,* 1970).

## Other major works

NOVELS: (by Per Wahlöö): *Himmelsgetan,* 1959 (revised as *Hövdingen,* 1967); *Vinden och regnet,* 1961; *Lastbilen,* 1962 (*The Lorry,* 1968; also as *A Necessary Action*); *Uppdraget,* 1963 (*The Assignment,* 1965); *Generalerna,* 1965 (*The Generals,* 1974). (by Maj Sjöwall): *Kvinnan som liknade Garbo* (with Tomas Ross), 1990.
SHORT FICTION: *Det växer inga rosor på Odenplan,* 1964.

## Bibliography

Bailey, O. L. "Mysteries in Review." *Saturday Review* 55 (August 5, 1972): 61-62.

Benstock, Bernard. "The Education of Martin Beck." In *Art in Crime Writing: Essays on Detective Fiction,* edited by Bernard Benstock. New York: St. Martin's Press, 1983.

Duffy, Martha. "Martin Beck Passes." *Time* 106 (August 11, 1975): 58.

Maxfield, James F. "The Collective Detective Hero: The Police Novels of Maj Sjöwall and Per Wahlöö." *Clues: A Journal of Detection* 3 (Spring/Summer, 1982): 70-79.

Occhiogrosso, Frank. "The Police in Society: The Novels of Maj Sjöwall and Per Wahlöö." *The Armchair Detective* 12 (Spring, 1979): 174-177.

Palmer, Jerry. "After the Thriller." *Thrillers: Genesis and Structure of a Popular Genre.* New York: St. Martin's Press, 1979.

Symons, Julian. *Mortal Consequences: A History, from the Detective Story to the Crime Novel.* London: Faber & Faber, 1972.

Van Dover, J. Kenneth. *Polemical Pulps: The Martin Beck Novels of Maj Sjöwall and Per Wahlöö.* San Bernardino, Calif.: Brownstone Books, 1993.

White, Jean M. "Wahlöö/Sjöwall and James McClure: Murder and Politics." *The New Republic* 175 (July 31, 1976): 27-29.

*Janet E. Lorenz*
*Updated by C. A. Gardner*

# Martin Cruz Smith

**Born:** Reading, Pennsylvania; November 3, 1942

**Also wrote as** • Nick Carter • Jake Logan • Martin Quinn • Simon Quinn

**Types of plot** • Amateur sleuth • espionage • police procedural

**Principal series** • Roman Grey, 1971-1972 • Nick Carter, 1972-1973 • The Inquisitor, 1974-1975 • Arkady Renko, 1981-     .

**Principal series characters** • ROMAN GREY, a Gypsy antique dealer in his early thirties, living in New York City. Grey (or Romano Gry–his Gypsy name) walks the line between Gypsy and *gaja* (non-Gypsy). Dating a *gaja* woman and trusted by a *gaja* police officer, he works on criminal cases for Gypsy honor.
    • FRANCIS XAVIER KILLY, a lay brother of the Vatican's Militia Christi and a former CIA agent, known as the Inquisitor. A shrewd investigator, he combines physical skill with intellect to maneuver his way through church politics and international crises.
    • ARKADY RENKO, a dedicated Russian detective, who wore his Soviet identity as a badge of honor until the rise of *glasnost* threw the country into turmoil. Despite personal tragedies and political disorder, Renko is a dogged investigator willing to put his life on the line for duty and honor.

**Contribution** • Martin Cruz Smith's novel *Gorky Park* (1981), his most important work, showcases his power to create believable characters within the mystery genre. The hero in *Gorky Park*, Arkady Renko, is the prototypical investigator–intelligent, cynical, beleaguered by a cheating wife and cheating superiors–who is also proud to be Russian. The villain, American John Osborne, is slippery and homicidal. Smith's ability to make the murderous KGB officer Pribluda more sympathetic than the privileged Osborne proves his skill with plot and characterization. For the most part, Smith's language is compact, page-turner prose. He generally describes the grotesque–such as the dwarf, Andreev, in *Gorky Park* and the bat caves in *Nightwing* (1977)–without relying on metaphor. Smith is notable as well for his ability to paint a convincing portrait of societies and institutions, such as the bureaucracy in *Gorky Park*, and of the dynamic between a couple, such as the relationship between Anna Weiss and Joe Pena in *Stallion Gate* (1986). He has contributed to an understanding of humans' relationship to other animals with the mythic interaction between man and animal depicted in *Nightwing, Gorky Park*, and *Gypsy in Amber* (1971).

**Biography** • Martin Cruz Smith, born Martin William Smith on November 3, 1942, in Reading, Pennsylvania, is the son of John Calhoun, a musician, and Louise Lopez Smith, an Indian rights activist. Smith was graduated from the University of Pennsylvania in 1964 with a bachelor of arts degree and then worked as a reporter for the *Philadelphia Daily News* in 1965. He was employed by Magazine Management from 1966 to 1969. On June 15, 1968, he married Emily Arnold, a chef.

In 1970, he published his first novel, *The Indians Won*, which was reviewed in science fiction journals. From 1970 through 1976, he wrote and published many mystery and adventure novels under various pseudonyms. Written under the name Martin Smith, *Gypsy in Amber* and *Canto for a Gypsy* (1972) indicate his fascination with mismatched partners, a motif that resurfaces in *Gorky Park*. *Gypsy in Amber* earned a nomination by the Mystery Writers of America as the best first mystery novel of 1971.

In 1973, Smith spent two weeks in the Soviet Union researching a book that was to include a Soviet detective working with an American detective to solve a murder. Refused permission to return to the Soviet Union, he did further research by interviewing Soviet émigrés about life in their homeland.

His Inquisitor series, published in 1974-1975 under the name of Simon Quinn, was received with considerable interest. His first substantial success as a writer, however, occurred in 1977 with the publication of *Nightwing*. This book was nominated by the Mystery Writers of America for the 1978 Edgar Allan Poe Award. In 1977, Smith also had his middle name legally changed from William to Cruz, his maternal grandmother's first name.

The success of *Nightwing* allowed Smith to focus on completing his Russian mystery, *Gorky Park*, which was published in 1981. The popularity of *Gorky Park* enabled Smith to spend the next five years researching and writing his novel about the Manhattan Project test site in New Mexico, *Stallion Gate*, published in 1986. Smith has lived with his wife and children in New York, California, and New Mexico.

**Analysis** • Martin Cruz Smith works best within the police procedural formula. Smith often uses mismatched partners to investigate a crime. The partners in the Gypsy series are Roman Grey and Harry Isadore. Isadore, the New York Police Department's expert on Gypsies, "may still be a sergeant at forty-nine" but can deliver "a lovely lecture on Gypsies at City College." The almost trusting relationship between Grey and Isadore, hindered only by Isadore's occasional unfulfilled threat to arrest Grey, leads the reader to respect the partners in the Gypsy series and see their work as complementary. In *Nightwing*, however, the partners are a bat killer, Hayden Paine, and an Indian deputy, Youngblood Duran, whose relationship is stormy, marked by death threats backed up by loaded guns. Paine has been hired by leaders of a Navajo reservation to locate the source of an outbreak of the plague. Duran is investigating the death of an Indian medicine man who was apparently killed by a wild animal. Both investigations lead to one source: vampire bats that carry bubonic plague. The partners meet for the last time in the middle of the Painted Desert and then seek the bat cave together. The partners' antagonism gives way in the end to Duran's memorializing Paine as a hero for his extermination of the bats.

In *Gorky Park*, Smith was able to create detective partners who are combative and cooperative in a much more satisfying fashion. These investigators, the Russian Arkady Renko and the American James Kirwill, initially threaten each other. Whereas in *Nightwing* the threat begins with tense but quiet accusation, Renko and Kirwill first meet at the scene of the murder in Gorky Park, where Kirwill comes close to killing Renko. Their fistfight, which Renko loses, is followed by Kirwill's shooting at Renko:

> When Arkady stepped forward, the hand lowered. He saw a barrel. The man aimed with both hands the way detectives were trained to fire a gun, and Arkady dove. He heard no shot and saw no flash, but something smacked off the ice behind him and, an instant later, rang off stones.

As Renko continues his investigation, he in turn nearly kills the American:

> Arkady wasn't aware of raising the makeshift gun. He found himself aiming the barrel at a point between Kirwill's eyes and pulling the trigger so that the doubled rubber band and plunger started to move smoothly. At the last moment he aimed away. The closet jumped and a hole two centimeters across appeared in the closet door beside Kirwill's ear. Arkady was astonished. He'd never come close to murdering anyone in his life, and when the accuracy of the weapon was considered he could as easily have killed as missed. A white mask of surprise showed where the blood had drained around Kirwill's eyes.

Now the partners are even: Each has nearly shot the other. The symmetry in physical risk between the two culminates in Kirwill's death at John Osborne's hand; just as Renko was stabbed in Moscow, so is Kirwill stabbed in New York. In New York, the partners have been able to overcome their differences and work together to net Osborne.

Mismatched lovers, too, are sources of conflict in the Roman Grey series, in *Nightwing*, in *Gorky Park*, and in *Stallion Gate*. Roman Grey's love for a non-Gypsy, Dany Murray, offends other Gypsies, who often accuse him of being Anglicized by her. His cooperation with Sergeant Isadore further provokes the Gypsies' ire. As a Gypsy colleague says to Grey in *Canto for a Gypsy*, "Each day I see you are more with them than us. First the girl and then the police. Maybe you want to be the first Gypsy in their heaven?" Suspicion and mistrust between ethnic groups is also evident in *Nightwing*, only this time the protagonist's group is the Hopi Indians. Youngblood Duran must endure racist comments directed toward his white lover, Anne Dillon; other Indians tell him she is only interested in him for sex. The racist preoccupation with "sex with the savage" also figures in *Stallion Gate*, in which the mismatched couple, like the couple in *Nightwing*, begin with sex and then fall in love. In both instances, Smith portrays the man as the more romantic and vulnerable of the lovers.

Vulnerability and romance are shared by the mismatched lovers in *Gorky*

*Park,* Irina Asanova and Arkady Renko. The crucial difference between them is that Renko is Russian but Irina, though born in the Soviet Union, refuses to be Russian. Renko's involvement with Irina is highly dangerous because she is a dissident whose principal goal is to emigrate. Their attraction, like that of Smith's other couples, is intensely physical and develops from sex to love.

These mismatched lovers all undergo trials by fire in their relationships. In *Canto for a Gypsy,* Grey envisions his love leaving him because she will not be able to fit in with his Gypsy life, particularly during a trip through Europe:

> She wouldn't break during the first month . . . because she had determination. But determination would only take her so far. Her fascination of Rom would turn to disgust. Their car would carry the stench of sweat and anger. She wouldn't fight, she would just go home. Roman knew it as certainly as he knew at this moment she couldn't believe it would ever happen.

Here Grey's dilemma with a non-Gypsy lover is apparent: Either he gives up his travels as a Gypsy (which is tantamount to giving up life as a Gypsy) or he loses the woman he loves.

Leaving on a trip is also central to the plot of *Nightwing,* and as in the earlier book, is a test of love. Early in the novel, Anne Dillon tells Youngblood Duran, the deputy investigating the death of the medicine man, that she will soon be leaving the reservation and that she wants him to come with her; he refuses to leave. After he finds her nearly dead in the desert, however, the only survivor of the group of desert campers, he declares, "My reservation days are over and I'm going to join the living. I finally figured it out. You're my ticket from here because I love you enough to be where you are, wherever that is." The relationship that began as a strong sexual attraction endures and grows, culminating with the pair riding off together at the end of the book, like the lovers in *Canto for a Gypsy.*

In *Gorky Park,* however, though the lovers pass their test, they are not given a happily-ever-after ending. After Renko and Asanova have endured KGB questioning regarding the months during which Renko was recovering from his stab wound, the couple is together in New York City. Asanova has acted as Osborne's lover so that Osborne would bring Renko to New York. The mark of her love for Renko is not, however, prostituting herself for him; she had already prostituted herself to get out of the Soviet Union. The test of her love, instead, is her willingness to go back with him, as she first asserts in New York and reaffirms in their finals words to each other:

> She took a dozen steps. "Will I ever hear from you?" She looked back, her eyes haggard and wet.
> "No doubt. Messages get through, right? Times change."
> At the gate she stopped again. "How can I leave you?"
> "*I* am leaving *you.*"

The words "Times change" suggest that there may be for this couple some hope for the future. Most of Smith's mysteries end with some expression of hope of a future together for the mismatched couple.

The universes Smith creates place man in a mythic relationship with animals. In *Gypsy in Amber,* the confrontation between good and evil (Roman Grey and Howard Hale) is mediated by a sacrificed goat. Indeed, the goat strikes the final blow:

> Howie still looked like a broken bust put back, subtly, completely ruined. Roman pulled the goat out of his arms. Its absence left two spongy holes in Howie's chest where its horns had cradled. The animal's gold, gun-slit eyes caught the first light of day as it broke over the pines.
> "Howie sacrificed himself," Hillary said.

The goat, which has been tied on Grey's back, for much of the final battle between Howie and Grey, has shielded Grey from death many times and in the end is a sacrificial animal, archetypal figure of early Western mythology.

The sacrificial relationship between animal and man is further explored in *Nightwing,* only here the man sacrifices himself to the animal. Hayden Paine describes a symbiosis between the vampire bat and Central American Indian civilizations:

> "The vampire lives off large mammals that sleep in herds. It lives off cattle and horses. There weren't any cattle and horses in the New World until the Spanish brought them. What do you think the vampires lived on before then? Name me the one large American mammal that slept together in herds, or villages."
> A light-headed sensation came over Anne.
> "You mean, people?"
> "Yes, that's exactly what I mean. People. Which is why all the old vampire roosts were found next to villages. Of course, we can only speculate on the details of this relationship. Whether one vampire colony would establish territoriality over a particular village and defend its feeding ground against other colonies."

Paine points out that what man gained from this relationship was a god. He speculates on the meaning of religious sacrifice for the Central American Indian tribes. Paine's obsession with the vampire bat reflects the intricacy of man's relationship with animals; in Paine's case, killing the animals meant killing himself.

The relationship between man and animal is further explored in *Gorky Park,* in which the caged sables being smuggled to America become a metaphor for an ironic and perverse sort of freedom. The three murder victims in Gorky Park were caring for and helping to smuggle sables; the victims were living in a shack, their own cage, feeding the other caged victims. Renko considers the pathos in their circumstances as he investigates the crime. In the end, Renko cannot shoot the sables that have been smuggled to America. Just as he frees Irina Asanova, he ends by freeing the sables, once again meting out justice.

Martin Cruz Smith's novels keep the reader turning the pages quickly. His sentences are most often short and emphatic, with repetition and parallelism as important devices. For example, Arkady considers the nature of Osborne:

Arkady felt cold, as if the windows had opened. Osborne was not sane, or not a man. If money could grow bones and flesh it would be Osborne. It would wear the same cashmere suit; it would part its silver hair the same way; it would have the same lean mask with its expression of superior amusement.

Smith achieves success as a writer not through flamboyant style but by placing his protagonists in situations that require them to confront their own codes of ethics. A natural storyteller, he explores man's relationship with his culture. The couples in his books, lovers as well as detective partners, are most real when they are downcast and threatened by the powers that be. Smith's strengths lie in his ability to portray people's responses to crisis—including their frustration, weakness, and cynicism.

Arkady Renko returned for two more adventures in *Polar Star* (1989) and *Red Square* (1992), the former with Renko at sea, literally, on the Russian fishing vessel of the title; and the latter exploring the seamy underbelly of postcommunist Moscow. However, the Renko in *Havana Bay* (1999) is a shadow of his former self and intent only on dying. While trying to kill himself, he is attacked and instinctively fights back, only to regret his natural response to self-preservation. When asked to locate an old friend, the reluctant hero travels to Cuba and is immersed in intrigue—enough to keep his suicidal thoughts at bay.

Whether writing about a Russian investigator or a Gypsy antique dealer, the CIA or the KGB, Los Alamos or Moscow, Smith, dubbed the "mastercraftsman of the good read" by Tony Hillerman, continues to deliver in the new millennium.

## Principal mystery and detective fiction

SERIES: Nick Carter: *The Inca Death Squad,* 1972; *Code Name: Werewolf,* 1973; *The Devil's Dozen,* 1973. Roman Grey: *Gypsy in Amber,* 1971; *Canto for a Gypsy,* 1972. The Inquisitor: *His Eminence, Death,* 1974; *Nuplex Red,* 1974; *The Devil in Kansas,* 1974; *The Last Time I Saw Hell,* 1974; *The Midas Coffin,* 1975; *Last Rites for the Vulture,* 1975. Arkady Renko: *Nightwing,* 1977; *Gorky Park,* 1981; *Polar Star,* 1989; *Red Square,* 1992; *Havana Bay,* 1999.

OTHER NOVELS: *The Analog Bullet,* 1972; *The Human Factor,* 1975; *Stallion Gate,* 1986.

## Other major works

NOVELS: *The Indians Won,* 1970; *The Adventures of the Wilderness Family,* 1976; *North to Dakota,* 1976; *Ride for Revenge,* 1977; *Pikes Peak Shoot-Out,* 1994; *Ghost Town,* 1994; *Blood Trail,* 1994; *Rose,* 1996.

## Bibliography

Dove, George N. "Case in Point: *Gorky Park.*" *The Mystery FANcier* 6 (July/August, 1982): 9-11, 18.

Junker, Howard, ed. *The Writer's Notebook.* San Francisco: HarperCollins West, 1995.

Prescott, Peter S. "The Making of a Bestseller." *Newsweek,* May 25, 1981, 77, 79-80.

Smith, Martin Cruz. Interview. *The New York Times Book Review* 86 (May 3, 1981): 46.

Vespa, Mary. "A Literary Capitalist Named Martin Cruz Smith Mines Moscow in *Gorky Park.*" *People,* May 25, 1981.

*Janet T. Palmer*
*Updated by Fiona Kelleghan*

# Mickey Spillane

## Frank Morrison Spillane

**Born:** Brooklyn, New York; March 9, 1918

**Types of plot** • Hard-boiled • private investigator • thriller

**Principal series** • Mike Hammer, 1947-1984 • Tiger Mann, 1964-1966.

**Principal series characters** • MIKE HAMMER, a New York City private investigator, is in his mid-twenties and is a just-returned World War II veteran as the series opens. Thereafter, he ages gradually to about forty. Irresistible to sexually aggressive women, he remains unmarried. Tough, crusading, and violent, with a simplistic personal sense of justice, he pursues murderers, and the organizations shielding them, on their own ground and with their own tactics.
 • VELDA, Hammer's sexy secretary, is also a private investigator. She serves as his surrogate mother and mistress and is one of the few people whom he loves and trusts.
 • CAPTAIN PATRICK CHAMBERS, a New York City homicide detective, is a foil for Hammer as well as a friend who, though bound to rules and regulations, understands and generally assists him.

**Contribution** • Mickey Spillane is more a phenomenon of popular culture than an arresting literary figure. His twenty-two books, particularly the Mike Hammer series, have had international sales of more than 67 million copies. Of the top ten best-selling fictional works published between 1920 and 1980, seven were Spillane's, and in the detective-fiction genre few have exceeded his sales. Spillane can attribute part of his popularity to having created in Mike Hammer the quintessentially simplistic avenger-crusader. Crimes in which Hammer becomes involved are personal. Usually the slaying of an old buddy or of a small-timer whom he has encountered and liked prompts him to saddle up, lock, and load. His vengeance is violent, direct, and—compared to that dispensed by the courts—swift. Without any crimes really being solved, a raw, hangman's justice is realized—illegally, but not without some assistance from the law. Readers are also treated to whole squads of sexually aggressive women who find Hammer, or his counterparts in other books, Tiger Mann or Gillian Burke, irresistible.

Spillane's entertainment appeal lies in his simplistic characterization, his heroes' direct assault upon their enemies—and thereby upon one aspect of an increasingly organized, violent, and impersonal society—and sexual encounters without the preliminary bouts, encounters that sanction at least a double standard, and perhaps no standard at all. Yet Spillane's loose plotting, scant characterizations, and violent resolutions have a comic book's color and directness, an honesty of sorts, allowing readers' vicarious (and basically harmless) indulgence in a succession of common fantasies and prejudices. He popularized pulp fiction in a way it had not quite been popularized previously, gaining an audience which included those who did not read books and those who read lots of books—they all read Mickey Spillane.

**Biography** • Frank Morrison Spillane was born on March 9, 1918, in Brooklyn, New York, the son of an Irish bartender. He grew up, by his own report, in one of the tougher neighborhoods of Elizabeth, New Jersey. Little is known about his early schooling. In the mid-1930's he attended Kansas State College, hoping eventually to study law. During the summers, he was captain of the lifeguards at Breezy Point, Long Island.

In 1935, when he was seventeen, he began selling stories to the pulps. He was able to pay his college tuition by writing for radio and by writing comic books. (He claims to have been one of the originators of the Captain Marvel and Captain America comics, which enjoyed enormous popularity in the 1930's and 1940's.) During World War II, he served in the United States Army Air Force, training cadets and in time flying fighter missions. After the war, he briefly worked as a trampoline artist for Barnum and Bailey's circus.

Spillane's success as a writer really begain in 1947, with the publication of what remains his most popular book, *I, the Jury*. In 1952, after half a dozen additions to the series, he was converted to the Jehovah's Witnesses, whose Fundamentalist views are sometimes apparent in his work. Over the next twenty-fives years, a score of the Hammer tales, or minor variants of them, appeared.

Divorced once, Spillane married a woman much his junior, Sherri—a model whom he had met when she posed for the cover of one of his books—in 1965. Along with producer Robert Fellows, Spillane formed an independent film company in Nashville, Tennessee, in 1969 for the filming of features and television productions, while continuing his other writing. Mike Hammer's adventures were depicted in several films of the 1950's, as well as in a television series. Spillane cowrote the screenplay for—and even starred as Mike Hammer in—*The Girl Hunters*, a 1963 film. Later incarnations of Mike Hammer have included a syndicated television series.

Spillane received the lifetime achievment award from the Private Eye Writers of America in 1983 and the Edgar Allan Poe Grand Master award from the Mystery Writers of America in 1995, although he has always frankly disdained such recognition, insisting that he writes simply to make money. In that he has succeeded amply. In his later years, he lived in South Carolina, enjoying the outdoors, his beach house, his pets, and his wealth.

**Analysis** • Using an idiom familiar to Mickey Spillane, his work may qualify simply as "trash." He states frankly that none of his books has required more than a few days to write and that they have been written according to formula, and for money. Those critics who have not dismissed him out of hand have generally reacted to him caustically. It has been pointed out that he debases women, reducing them to sex objects, and frequently evil ones at that. His handling of sex, stripped of any tenderness, intimacy, or romance, is perceived by many to be pornographic. The violence and gore he hurls at the reader have been condemned as gratuitous and revolting. His plots have been deemed shaky, his characterizations thin, his dialogue wooden. In sum, by any criteria, comparisons with the classic writers in his field—Dashiell Hammett, Raymond Chandler, or Ross Macdonald—simply fail.

Yet the larger question of why millions have read Spillane's books remains. The fact is that, in spite of a lack of craftsmanship, Spillane entertains. He does so swiftly, requiring neither intellection nor furrowed brows from his readers. Moreover, in a complex, pluralistic, multiracial, and often-menacing urban world, he simplifies life, playing upon basic cultural instincts and prejudices. He provides cheap escape.

Mike Hammer (or his surrogates—it is all the same) is a tough private eye, a loner who before the bottom of page 2 in any volume of the series is confronted with a killing that has personal meaning to him. In *I, the Jury*, Hammer's wartime buddy and best friend, Jack Williams, has been shot by a .45 and left to die slowly, crawling before his executioner. In *Vengeance Is Mine!* (1950), Chester Wheeler, Hammer's casual drinking companion, is murdered while he and Hammer, dead drunk, share the same bed. In *Survival . . . Zero!* (1970), a petty pickpocket whom Hammer knew, Lippy Sullivan, calls him while dying with a knife in his back. Such murders invariably launch Hammer's personal crusade to locate the slayer and avenge the death.

The ubiquitous Captain Patrick Chambers, Hammer's detective friend and sometime backup, always warns Hammer to stay off the case, taking the role of society's spokesman calling for orderly investigation within the law. The rules are stated, however, only to alert the reader to the fact that they are about to be broken. Soon Pat and Hammer, in leapfrog fashion, are finding and sharing clues. Pat's actions are implicit acknowledgment that corruption, bureaucratic mismanagement, and public apathy make true justice impossible to attain except outside the law.

As the pursuit progresses, Hammer touches upon an attitude that is widespread among Americans: a mistrust of huge organizations. In *One Lonely Night* (1951), Hammer seeks a killer who is linked to the Communist Party of America; in *Kiss Me, Deadly* (1952), the Mafia lurks, pulling the strings. In *The Girl Hunters* (1962), the killer's shield is an international terrorist organization, as it is also in *Survival . . . Zero!* In *The Big Kill* (1951), Hammer stands against an extensive blackmail ring.

An antiorganizational, antiauthoritarian bias is only one of many common prejudices that are expressed by Hammer (or Johnny McBride, Tiger Mann, or Gill Burke). Hammer detests New York City, "queers" or "faggots," "Commies," district attorneys, the Federal Bureau of Investigation (FBI), counterespionage agencies, punks, hoods, successful criminals (particularly drug dealers), modern robber barons, most police officials, and skinny women.

In pursuit of his enemies, Hammer (and Spillane's other heroes) becomes a one-man war wagon, armed with Old Testament injunctions—particularly "an eye for an eye, a tooth for a tooth." In *One Lonely Night* his urge to kill is so powerful that a terrified woman whom he has rescued from a rapist leaps off a bridge to her death after she sees the lust for killing in his face. Later, in the same book, he butchers a number of political radicals with an FBI machine gun. With his "rod," he lays open the jaw of another enemy, breaks his teeth, and kicks them down his throat. In *My Gun Is Quick* (1950), he takes Feeney Last's head "like a sodden rag and smashed and smashed and smashed and there was no satisfying, solid thump, but a sickening squashing sound that splashed all over me." The greatest cruelties are reserved for prime objects of Hammer's revenge. Unlike the hero avengers in the detective fiction of Chandler and Hammett, who generally leave final vengeance to the cops or to the intervention of fate, Spillane's avengers attend personally to their usually grisly executions. Thus, William Dorn and Renee Talmadge, the principal villains of *Survival . . . Zero!*, their backs against the wall, are persuaded by Hammer that he is going to blow them away with his trademark .45. The prospect terrifies them into swallowing cyanide capsules—only to be shown by a jeering Hammer that his gun is empty. Oscar, the villainous Communist in *One Lonely Night*, finally trapped beneath a burning beam and painfully being consumed by the fire, is told that as soon as a fireman comes through the window to rescue him—if he is not already dead by then—Hammer will blow his head off. No treatment is too inhuman for "the greatest Commie louse of them all." Hammer's dispatching in *I, the Jury* of Carol Manning, the gorgeous psychiatrist turned dope-ring leader and the slayer of his best friend, is classic. Cornered at last, she strips naked to distract him from the murder weapon nearby. Resisting chastely, he shoots her in the stomach.

> Pain and unbelief.
> "How c-could you?" she gasped.
> I had only a moment before talking to a corpse, but I got it in.
> "It was easy," I said.

The myriad women encountered by Hammer in the course of his crusades are invariably busty, leggy, gorgeous, and sexually aggressive, fantasy creatures descended from the pin-up girls of the 1940's and 1950's. Though he is described as homely, Hammer's wild brown-green Irish eyes and his air of violence and power prove overwhelmingly attractive to a parade of sex kittens. The sexual encounters in Spillane's books are described without clinical details, so that to modern readers they may seem old-fashioned and humorous rather than pornographic. Hammer beds his women shamelessly, and the double standard prevails, but his sexual acts are implied rather than described. Instead, Spillane depicts for his readers a continuous strip tease, a procession of sex-starved women putting on and taking off clothes, lounging in provocative poses, and making themselves utterly available to Hammer.

Yet the stereotyping of female sexual displays and the movement of voluptuous women in and out of Hammer's range are less important than Spillane's
reliance—as humanist critic John Cawelti suggests—on violence for his chief
stimulus. It is the imminent capacity of Spillane's heroes for violence, after all,
not their looks or lines, that attracts women in the first place: the same deadli-
ness that terrifies the villains.

Spillane's crusaders, in any event, are ambivalent about women. His female characters are either sex objects notable for their capacity to tempt or,
like Velda, alternately jealous and tolerant aides-de-camp, who mother the
protagonist, comfort him, and readily accept him in bed. There is no way of
knowing whether Spillane purposefully pandered to certain audiences with
what many critics (male and female alike) consider his chauvinism and degradation of women. There is no doubt, however, that the "manly" behavior
("macho" postdates Spillane) of both his villains and his protagonists reflected—and still reflects—one widespread view of men's relations with women.
Instinctively, Spillane grasped and exploited these common desires and fantasies.

In comparison to many late twentieth century bestsellers and films, with
their anatomization of sex and liberal use of crude, graphic language, Spillane
seems almost quaint, even puritanical. Four-letter words, or their equivalents,
are fairly rare in his works; sex is not comparably explicit. Drugs do not constitute an amusing recreation; indeed, they are treated as debilitating, ultimately deadly (although there is cultural acceptance of drinking and smoking). Hammer is fiercely loyal to his friends and, despite his sexual escapades,
always goes back to the waiting Velda. Spillane's heroes are champions of the
underdog; they protect women and children against multiple menaces. They
display a puritanical sense of mission, righteousness, and an evangelical zeal.

After a seven-year hiatus, Spillane and Hammer returned in *Black Alley*
(1996), with a few marked differences. Though the story is essentially the
same, and Hammer still gets involved only to find out who gunned down an
old army buddy, the hard-boiled hero has mellowed just a bit: He admits to
liking Richard Wagner's music and admits to Velda that she's the one and actually proposes to her. In addition, his usual methods are hampered by the
fact that he has been seriously wounded. No longer able to beat things out of
people, he must actually follow clues. Moreover, on doctor's orders, he cannot consummate his relationship with Velda. It makes for an interesting
change.

Written for the adult postwar generation, Spillane's novels are dated and,
like much popular music and many films, are rapidly becoming period pieces.
Mike Hammer, for example, is often short of "dough," "jack," or "long
green." He "packs" a "rod" and drives a "jalopey." For him and other of
Spillane's avengers, the "monikers" assigned to women are "girlie," "sugar
pie," "broad," "babe," "kitten," "pet," and "kid." Hard-boiled as they are, they
saw "wow," "swell," "yup," "bub," "boy oh boy," "okeydoke," "jeez," and
"pal." "Punks" get "plugged" or "bumped off" with "slugs" before they are

"dumped." Enemies put "the bee" on Hammer; "wolves" or "drips" stalk Velda; both are sometimes "scared out of their pants" by "tough eggs" and manage to "scram" or simply "blow"—unless Pat and "the harness bulls" rescue them before Mike says "something dirty."

In an era before "hairball" and "scumbag" would sound mild, Spillane entertained readers with his novel raciness. As a part of the popular culture and an archetype of pulp fiction, Spillane's heroes may fade into the past, but elements that he popularized, basic and one-dimensional as they are, will remain.

## Principal mystery and detective fiction

SERIES: Mike Hammer: *I, the Jury*, 1947; *Vengeance Is Mine!*, 1950; *My Gun Is Quick*, 1950; *The Big Kill*, 1951; *One Lonely Night*, 1951; *Kiss Me, Deadly*, 1952; *The Girl Hunters*, 1962; *The Snake*, 1964; *The Twisted Thing*, 1966; *The Body Lovers*, 1967; *Survival... Zero!*, 1970; *Mike Hammer: The Comic Strip*, 1982-1984. Tiger Mann: *Day of the Guns*, 1964; *Bloody Sunrise*, 1965; *The Death Dealers*, 1965; *The By-Pass Control*, 1967; *Black Alley*, 1996; *The Mike Hammer Collection*, 2001.

OTHER NOVELS: *The Long Wait*, 1951; *The Deep*, 1961; *The Delta Factor*, 1967; *The Erection Set*, 1972; *The Last Cop Out*, 1973.

OTHER SHORT FICTION: *Me, Hood!*, 1963; *The Flier*, 1964; *Return of the Hood*, 1964; *Killer Mine*, 1965; *Me, Hood!*, 1969; *The Tough Guys*, 1969; *Tomorrow I Die*, 1984.

## Other major works

SCREENPLAY: *The Girl Hunters*, 1963 (with Roy Rowland and Robert Fellows).

EDITED TEXTS: *Murder Is My Business*, 1994 (with Max Allen Collins)

CHILDREN'S LITERATURE: *The Day the Sea Rolled Back*, 1979; *The Ship That Never Was*, 1982.

## Bibliography

Banks, R. Jeff. "Spillane's Anti-Establishmentarian Heroes." In *Dimensions in Detective Fiction*, edited by Larry N. Landrum, Pat Browne, and Ray B. Browne. Bowling Green, Ohio: Bowling Green State University Popular Press, 1976.

Cawelti, John G. "The Spillane Phenomenon." In *Adventure, Mystery, and Romance: Formula Stories as Art and Popular Culture*. Chicago: University of Chicago Press, 1976.

LaFarge, Christopher. "Mickey Spillane and His Bloody Hammer." In *Mass Culture*, edited by Bernard Rosenberg and David Manning White. Glencoe, Ill.: Free Press, 1957.

Penzler, Otto. *Mickey Spillane*. New York: Mysterious Bookshop, 1999.

"Spillane, Mickey." In *Mystery and Suspense Writers: The Literature of Crime, Detection, and Espionage*, edited by Robin W. Winks and Maureen Corrigan. New York: Charles Scribner's Sons, 1998.

Symons, Julian. *Mortal Consequences: A History, from the Detective Story to the Crime Novel.* London: Faber & Faber, 1972.

Weibel, Kay. "Mickey Spillane as a Fifties Phenomenon." In *Dimensions of Detective Fiction,* edited by Larry N. Landrum, Pat Browne, and Ray B. Browne. Bowling Green, Ohio: Bowling Green State University Popular Press, 1976.

Winks, Robin. *Modus Operandi: An Excursion into Detective Fiction.* Boston: D. R. Godine, 1982.

*Clifton K. Yearley*
*Updated by Fiona Kelleghan and Jessica Reisman*

# Robert Louis Stevenson

**Born:** Edinburgh, Scotland; November 13, 1850
**Died:** Apia, Samoa; December 3, 1894

**Types of plot** • Historical • horror • psychological • thriller

**Contribution** • Robert Louis Stevenson must be seen as an unknowing progenitor of the mystery/detective genre. He was essentially a romantic writer attempting to be taken seriously in a mainstream literary world caught up in the values of realism and naturalism. As a romantic writer, he strongly affirmed the preeminent right of incident to capture the reader's attention. He countered Jane Austen's polite cup of tea with Dr. Jekyll's fantastic potion; he left the discreet parsonage to others, while he explored the mysteries of Treasure Island; he eschewed the chronicling of petty domestic strife and struck out instead to write about, not the uneventful daily life of ordinary men, but rather their extraordinary daydreams, hopes, and fears.

Stevenson also insisted on the importance of setting to a narrative. As he writes in "A Gossip on Romance," "Certain dank gardens cry aloud for a murder." The creation of atmosphere has been an important element in mystery fiction since Edgar Allan Poe first had his amateur French sleuth, Monsieur Dupin, investigate the murders in the Rue Morgue. The rugged Spanish Sierras of Stevenson's "Olalla" are, in their own way, as unforgettable as the Baker Street lodgings of Sherlock Holmes and Dr. Watson.

Stevenson also had a profound interest in psychology. His emphasis on the criminal's motivation, rather than on his identity, clearly presages the method of much contemporary, post-Freudian, mystery-suspense fiction. In Stevenson's "Markheim," the reader witnesses a murder early in the story and has no doubt about the identity of the murderer; the interest lies in the murderer's motivation, in his emotional and intellectual response to his crime. In terms of plotting, setting, and characterization, Stevenson is a master of all the elements which became so important to the development of the mystery/detective genre.

**Biography** • Stevenson is one of those intriguing writers, like Oscar Wilde, whose life often competes with his works for the critics' attention. He was born Robert Louis Balfour Stevenson on November 13, 1850, in Edinburgh. He was the only child of Thomas and Margaret Isabella (Balfour) Stevenson. His father, grandfather, and two uncles were harbor and lighthouse engineers who had hopes that Stevenson would follow in their profession. Stevenson, however, was a sickly child whose interest in lighthouses was of the romantic, rather than the structural, sort. Although he studied engineering, and then law,

Robert Louis Stevenson. (Library of Congress)

to please his family, it was apparent early that he was destined to become a writer.

Stevenson chose his companions from among the writers and artists of his day, such as William Ernest Henley, Sidney Colvin, and Charles Baxter. One friend, Leslie Stephen, editor of *Cornhill* magazine, published some of his early essays. His first book, *An Inland Voyage* (1878), was not published until he was twenty-eight years old.

While studying art in France, Stevenson fell in love with Fanny Van de Grift Osborne, who returned reluctantly to her San Franciscan husband, Samuel C. Osborne, in 1878. Stevenson pursued her to the United States, and after her divorce in 1880, they were married. Unfortunately, Stevenson's tubercular condition was a constant difficulty for him; thus, the couple spent the first ten years of their marriage trying to find a congenial climate within easy reach of Edinburgh. That took the Stevensons to the great spa towns of Hyères, Davos, and Bournemouth—places of refuge where he wrote his first novel, *Treasure Island* (1883), as well as *A Child's Garden of Verses* (1885), *Kidnapped* (1886), and his first world-renowned work, *The Strange Case of Dr. Jekyll and Mr. Hyde* (1886).

In 1887, Stevenson's father died, setting him free to search the globe for a safe harbor. First, he went to Lake Saranac in New York for a cure which appeared to arrest his disease, then on to San Francisco, from which he began his South Seas cruise on the *Casco*. His eighteen months on the high seas took him to Tahiti, Australia, Hawaii, and finally his beloved Samoa. In 1889, Stevenson bought property which he named Vailima on a little island called Upolu and settled down to the most creative days of his life. It was there that he composed the compelling fragment *Weir of Hermiston* (1896), which most critics consider to be his most masterful piece of prose. He also fought hard for the political rights of the Samoans, who grieved after his death of a cerebral hemorrhage, on December 3, 1894, as fully as those who understood that the Western world had lost one of its finest writers.

**Analysis** • Probably the best known of Robert Louis Stevenson's mature works is *The Strange Case of Dr. Jekyll and Mr. Hyde.* It has, in Western culture, somewhat the stature of a number of other supernatural tales with archetypal plots, such as Mary Wollstonecraft Shelley's *Frankenstein* (1818) and Bram Stoker's *Dracula* (1897). Readers unfamiliar with the novel, or even Stevenson's authorship of it, can still recount in fairly accurate detail the lineaments of the plot. The work's tremendous popularity undoubtedly has much to do with the aspects of action, character, and setting which now characterize so many mystery and detective novels.

Mr. Hyde's notorious crimes include trampling an innocent little girl in the street and leaving her to suffer unaided, bludgeoning to death an old man of considerable reputation, supposedly blackmailing the kindly benefactor Dr. Jekyll, and committing a variety of unnameable sins against propriety and morality, the likes of which were best left to the Victorian imagination. Stevenson's Hyde is as dark a character as any who ever stalked the streets of London, and his outward appearance creates disgust wherever he goes. No one could fault *The Strange Case of Dr. Jekyll and Mr. Hyde* for a lack of incident. In describing action, Stevenson is evocative, not explicit. His writing is reminiscent of the somewhat abstract style of Henry James in his psychological thriller *The Turn of the Screw* (1898). That is not really surprising, since the two men had a deep respect for each other's work.

While there is no detective per se in *The Strange Case of Dr. Jekyll and Mr. Hyde*, there is the lawyer Mr. Utterson, whose curiosity, aroused by the strange stipulations of Dr. Jekyll's will, prompts him to attempt to solve the mystery of Mr. Hyde. Stevenson believed that the reader is most contented when he thoroughly identifies with the characters in a story. It is impossible not to empathize with the rational, but rather pedestrian, Mr. Utterson as he wrestles with a reality too bizarre for him to comprehend. Mr. Utterson serves the essential function, so ably executed by Dr. Watson throughout the Sherlock Homes series, of providing a defective intelligence who moves the story forward, while always keeping the suspense at a nearly unbearable pitch. This thrusting of ordinary people into extraordinary circumstances has also become a mainstay of the modern mystery/detective genre.

Stevenson's skill in explicating psychological motivation is so strong that the reader even finds himself forcibly identifying with Dr. Jekyll and his evil alter ego, or *Doppelgänger*, Mr. Hyde. It is a well-known hallmark of later mystery fiction to find something noble, or at least exceptional, in the criminal mind, but it was still a novelty in 1886. Writers of the late twentieth century have asked, quite frequently, as Peter Shaffer does in his psychological mystery play *Equus* (1973), which is more to be admired—a banal normalcy or an exhilarating and unique madness. (Victorians were more likely to see the answer to this question as obvious.)

While Stevenson was a tremendous romantic in terms of plot and character, he had a rare gift for the realistic rendering of setting. Just as later mystery writers are scrupulous about forensic detail, Stevenson was a passionate observer and recorder of nature and cityscapes. He even put forth the paradoxical idea, in an essay entitled "The Enjoyment of Unpleasant Place," that given enough time, all settings, even the most inhospitable, could yield a measure of understanding and contentment. A good example of Stevenson's style and attention to salient detail is this short description of the back entrance to Dr. Jekyll's laboratory:

> The door, which was equipped with neither bell nor knocker, was blistered and distained. Tramps slouched into the recess and struck matches on the panels; children kept shop upon the steps; the schoolboy had tried his knife on the mouldings; and for close on a generation, no one had appeared to drive away these random visitors or to repair their ravages.

Any number of Stevenson's other works can also be studied as precursors to the mystery/detective genre, because even while he might be working within the rubric of the boys' adventure story or the gothic tale, his fundamental interest in vigorous action, strong character delineation, and detailed settings creates the kind of suspense one associates with mystery and detective fiction.

For example, *Treasure Island* is full of adventure, which in another setting might be called crime. There are shootings, stabbings, and treachery enough for even the most lurid-minded reader. With the shipwrecks, the malaria, and the harshness of the elements, a tale full of incident emerges. There is also no dearth of mystery: What is the meaning of the black spot? Who is the mysterious blind man? Where is Treasure Island? How do the men aboard the *Hispaniola* find the liquor to get drunk? Who is the "man of the island"? What eventually becomes of Long John Silver?

Long John Silver, the opportunistic but charming pirate, is one of Stevenson's most captivating rogues. Perfectly motivated by enlightened self-interest, his shifts of loyalty almost inevitably move the plot. One identifies with him as surely as one identifies with the spry, touchingly adolescent protagonist. As for setting, one does not even need the supplied treasure map to amble competently, though mentally, around the island. Yet attention must be paid, because without a strong sense of place the mysteries of the island would remain inexplicable.

In *Treasure Island*, as in most of his other works, Stevenson is unusually modern in giving away the ending of the story at the outset, so that the focus of the reader's suspense is not specifically on the denouement but on the nature of the events leading up to it. The reader knows, for example, from the first page, that Jim Hawkins will survive and attain the hidden treasure, because Hawkins is clearly retelling the tale of Treasure Island from the vantage of his secure future. The reader also knows in the short story "Markheim" that Markheim is the man who murdered the antique dealer, although the reader is encouraged to be curious about why he committed the murder. In both cases Stevenson maintains suspense, not around the questions of whether the treasure will be found or whether Markheim is the killer but around the questions of how the treasure will be found and at what human cost and why Markheim kills the antique dealer and at what spiritual price. This preoccupation with process and psychology, rather than brute facts, is a characteristic of much contemporary mystery and detective writing, as can be seen quite clearly in many of Alfred Hitchcock's films.

Stevenson's works, like those of Edgar Allan Poe, were often dismissed and undervalued in the 1920's and 1930's. Certainly *Treasure Island* suffers if compared with Herman Melville's *Moby Dick* (151), "Markheim" may well seem a poor thing next to Fyodor Dostoevski's *Crime and Punishment* (1866), and "Olalla" pales beside Joseph Sheridan Le Fanu's story "Carmilla." Yet to have written works which bear comparison with all these classics is by no means a small accomplishment. Such has been the plight of many writers in the mystery and detective genre, to have been the beloved of the common reader during their lives and to have their work criticized by academics after their deaths.

Any reader who wants to assure himself of Stevenson's excellent style has only to read a passage of his description, such as this view of Notre Dame on a winter's night in Paris from Stevenson's first published story, "A Lodging for the Night":

> High up overhead the snow settled among the tracery of the cathedral towers. Many a niche was drifted full; many a statue wore a long white bonnet on its grotesque or sainted head. The gargoyles had been transformed into great false noses, drooping towards the point. The crockets were like upright pillows swollen on one side. In the intervals of the wind, there was a dull sound of dripping about the precincts of the church.

There is no question that this is a setting that cries out for a mystery, not for a garden party.

Stevenson's "shilling shockers" and boys' adventures clearly boast intricate and eventful plots, psychologically authentic characterizations, and powerfully observed and conveyed settings. Clearly, Stevenson's fiction was an important precedent to work carried on in the twentieth century by other popular and talented writers in the mystery/detective genre.

## Principal mystery and detective fiction

NOVELS: *Treasure Island*, 1883; *The Dynamiter*, 1885; *The Strange Case of Dr. Jekyll and Mr. Hyde*, 1886; *The Master of Ballantrae*, 1888; *The Wrong Box*, 1889 (with Lloyd Osbourne); *The Wrecker*, 1892; *The Body Snatcher*, 1895; *The Suicide Club*, 1895.

SHORT FICTION: *The New Arabian Nights*, 1882; *More New Arabian Nights*, 1885; *The Merry Men and Other Tales and Fables*, 1887.

## Other major works

NOVELS: *Prince Otto*, 1885; *Kidnapped*, 1886; *Catriona*, 1893; *The Ebb-Tide*, 1894 (with Osbourne); *Weir of Hermiston*, 1896; *St. Ives*, 1897.

SHORT FICTION: *Island Nights' Entertainments*, 1893; *Tales and Fantasies*, 1905.

PLAYS: *Deacon Brodie,* 1880; *Macaire,* 1885 (with William Ernest Henley); *The Hanging Judge,* 1914 (with Fanny Van de Grift Stevenson).

POETRY: *Moral Emblems,* 1882; *A Child's Garden of Verses,* 1885; *Underwoods,* 1887; *Ballads,* 1890; *Songs of Travel,* 1895.

NONFICTION: *An Inland Voyage,* 1878; *Picturesque Notes on Edinburgh,* 1878; *Travels with a Donkey in the Cevennes,* 1879; *Virginibus Puerisque,* 1881; *Familiar Studies of Men and Books,* 1882; *The Silverado Squatters: Sketches,* 1883; *Memories and Portraits,* 1887; *The South Seas: A Record of Three Cruises,* 1890; *Father Damien,* 1890; *Across the Plains,* 1892; *A Footnote to History,* 1892; *Amateur Emigrant,* 1895; *Vailima Letters,* 1895; *The Letters of Stevenson to His Family and Friends,* 1899, 1911.

## Bibliography

Bell, Ian. *Robert Louis Stevenson: Dreams of Exile, A Biography.* Edinburgh: Mainstream, 1992.

Bevan, Bryan. *Robert Louis Stevenson: Poet and Teller of Tales.* London: Rubicon Press, 1993.

Calder, Jenni. *Robert Louis Stevenson: A Life Study.* New York: Oxford University Press, 1980.

_____, ed. *Robert Louis Stevenson: A Critical Celebration.* Totowa, N.J.: Barnes & Noble, 1980.

Daiches, David. *Robert Louis Stevenson and His World.* London: Thames & Hudson, 1973.

Eigner, Edwin. *Robert Louis Stevenson and Romantic Tradition.* Princeton, N.J.: Princeton University Press, 1966.

Elwin, Malcolm. *The Strange Case of Robert Louis Stevenson.* London: Macdonald, 1950.

McLynn, Frank. *Robert Louis Stevenson: A Biography.* New York: Random House, 1993.

Veeder, William, and Gordon Hirsch. *Dr. Jekyll and Mr. Hyde After One Hundred Years.* Chicago: University of Chicago Press, 1988.

*Cynthia Lee Katona*

# Mary Stewart

**Born:** Sunderland, Durham, England; September 17, 1916

**Type of plot** • Thriller

**Contribution** • Mary Stewart is the preeminent writer of the romantic thriller. She raised the standard of the genre partly by innovations in character, moving beyond the convention of the helpless heroine which dominated romantic fiction in the mid-1950's; she created charming, intelligent, capable young women with whom the reader could identify. She also discarded the convention of the hero's casual and uncaring attitude toward violence. Her heroines and heroes are ordinary people, not especially endowed with courage or heroism, who are thrust into dangerous and challenging situations in which they must make choices. Other qualities of her work which have made her one of the best-selling novelists in the world include an elegant and graceful style and the use of attractive, authentic settings, usually in Europe.

**Biography** • Mary Florence Elinor Stewart was born on September 17, 1916, in Sunderland, County Durham, England. Her father, Frederick A. Rainbow, was a clergyman, and her mother, Mary Edith Rainbow, came from a family of New Zealand missionaries. Stewart was one of three children. When she was seven, the family moved to the mining village of Shotton Colliery in County Durham, and Stewart attended a number of different schools before going to Durham University in 1935. At university, she became president of the Women's Union and of the Literary Society; she was graduated in 1938 with a first class honors degree in English.

In 1939, she received a diploma in the theory and practice of teaching. She then taught at a school in Middlesborough, in northern England, before becoming head of English and classics at Worcester School, in the Midlands. In 1941, she received an M.A. from Durham University and was appointed assistant lecturer in English; during the last years of World War II, she served part-time in the Royal Observer Corps.

In 1945, Stewart married Frederick Henry Stewart, who at the time was a lecturer in geology at Durham University. From 1948 until 1956, Mary Stewart continued her work as lecturer at the university, but on a part-time basis, and she also taught at St. Hild's Teacher Training College in Durham. In 1956, she gave up teaching to concentrate on her writing. She had been writing stories and poems since she was a child, and during her teaching career her poems had been published in the *Durham University Journal*. She started her first novel with no thought of publication, but her husband persuaded her to submit the manuscript to a publisher. *Madam, Will You Talk?* was published in

1955, and Stewart's literary career had begun. The Stewarts then moved from Durham to Edinburgh, where Frederick Stewart had been appointed professor of geology at the university. Between 1955 and 1984, Stewart published nineteen novels, including three for children. In 1960 she won the British Crime Writers' Association Award.

**Analysis** • Mary Stewart's comments on her own work in an article published in *The Writer* in 1970 provide an illuminating account of her development and her principal concerns as a novelist. Her first five novels she describes as "exploratory," for she was experimenting with a variety of different forms. *Madam, Will You Talk?* is a chase story with all the traditional elements of the thriller. The plot, which hinged on a series of improbable coincidences, was woven around the theme of a "fatedriven love, self-contained, all-else-excluding." *Wildfire at Midnight* (1956) is a classic detective story, the writing of which, she says, honed certain technical skills. Nevertheless, she was impatient and dissatisfied with the necessary emphasis on plot rather than character and disliked the conventional detective story, in which "pain and murder are taken for granted and used as a parlor game." In *Thunder on the Right* (1957) she experimented for the first and only time with a third-person narrator. In spite of the limitations a first-person narrator imposes in some areas (detailed description can be given only, for example, of events in which the narrator is a direct participant), Stewart came to prefer it because of the "vividness, personal involvement and identification" which it makes possible. Stewart's skillful handling of this form of narration so as to evoke these responses in her readers contributes in no small measure to her popularity.

Perhaps the hallmark of Stewart's fiction can be found in her description of what she was attempting in her first five novels. They were:

> a deliberate attempt . . . to discard certain conventions which seemed . . . to remove the novel of action so far from real life that it became a charade or a puzzle in which no reader could involve himself sufficiently really to care. I tried to take conventionally bizarre situations (the car chase, the closed-room murder, the wicked uncle tale) and send real people into them, normal everyday people with normal everyday reactions to violence and fear; people not "heroic" in the conventional sense, but averagely intelligent men and women who could be shocked or outraged into defending, if necessary with great physical bravery, what they held to be right.

These concerns are readily apparent in her fourth and fifth novels, *Nine Coaches Waiting* (1958) and *My Brother Michael* (1960). *Nine Coaches Waiting* is a gothic tale, designed as a variation on the Cinderella story. Young Linda Martin accepts a post as English governess to the nine-year-old Comte Philippe de Valmy, at a remote chateau in High Savoy. She falls in love with the boy's cousin, Raoul de Valmy, but comes to suspect that he is part of a plot against the boy's life. Faced with the choice between love and duty—which Stewart has identified as the main theme of the novel—she puts the boy's welfare first, while hoping against hope that her lover is innocent. Her virtue wins its inevitable reward; in the denouement, the wicked uncle, who is behind the plot, shoots himself, and Cinderella gets her Prince Charming. Although the plot is fragile, Stewart cleverly maintains the suspense with a mix of familiar elements: surprise revelations, sudden and unexpected confrontations, a search–during which the hardly-daring-to-breathe heroine comes within a whisker of being discovered–and a chase. Some ingenious variations include a sleepwalking villainess unconsciously revealing her guilt à la Lady Macbeth and a romantic red herring in the form of a tall, attractive Englishman who befriends the heroine early in the novel–but who never comes as prominently into the story as the reader, cunningly tricked by Stewart, expects. Linda herself is a typical Stewart heroine. She is modest, tactful, and considerate, possesses integrity but is not a prig (she is capable of some white lies), is vulnerable and understandably frightened at what she has got herself into, but is also resourceful and capable, fully prepared to do what the situation demands of her.

A similar description could be applied to Camilla Haven, the heroine of *My Brother Michael.* Her charmingly self-deprecating sense of humor, revealed early in the novel by her alarming incompetence behind the wheel of an unfamiliar car in an unfamiliar country, quickly endears her to the reader. Caught up in a series of dangerous events in Delphi, she rises to the occasion not without self-doubt but also with considerable bravery.

Her companion, Simon Lester, is a typical Stewart hero. He first meets Camilla when he takes over the wheel of her car and gets her out of a difficult driving situation (difficult for her, that is–Stewart's men are always superb drivers). Simon possesses an easy, relaxed self-confidence, a quiet strength, competence, and great determination. He stays cool under pressure and rarely betrays much excitement or emotion.

In her article for *The Writer,* Stewart remarks that she had become tired of the convention under which the romantic hero was "unthinkingly at home with violence," and such a description could certainly not be applied to Simon. The violence in which he becomes involved is forced on him; he is a schoolmaster who teaches classics, so that violence is hardly his natural mode of operation. Stewart also comments that she rejected the concept of the hero as a social misfit, a type which was becoming fashionable at the time (she was referring to the literary movement embodied in the so-called Angry Young Men of the 1950's in Great Britain). On the contrary, Simon Lester, like all of her heroes, is unfailingly polite, courteous, and chivalrous, amply possessed, as Stewart put it, of "the civilized good manners that are armour for the naked nerve." He also embodies the common sense and "liberal ideas" which Stewart admires. The latter can be seen, for example, in his reflective comment on the odd ways of the Greek peasantry: "I think that most things can be forgiven to the poor." It is one of the most memorable lines in any of Stewart's novels.

*My Brother Michael* was inspired by Stewart's first visit to Greece, and a large part of the novel's appeal lies in the richly evoked setting of Delphi. In this passage, for example, Stewart re-creates the landscape around Parnassus in elegant, meandering rhythms and poetic images:

All along the Pleistus–at this season a dry white serpent of shingle beds that glittered in the sun–all along its course, filling the valley bottom with the tumbling, whispering green-silver of water, flowed the olive woods; themselves a river, a green-and-silver flood of plumy branches as soft as sea spray, over which the ever-present breezes slid, not as they do over corn, in flying shadows, but in whitening breaths, little gasps that lift and toss the olive crests for all the world like breaking spray. Long pale ripples followed one another down the valley.

The setting is not merely background adornment; Stewart uses it to create an atmosphere of a land still populated by the ancient gods, whose presence can be felt by those of subtle sense and pulse. Here is Apollo's temple:

From where we were the pillars seemed hardly real; not stone that had ever felt hand or chisel, but insubstantial, the music-built columns of legend: Olympian building, left floating–warm from the god's hand–between sky and earth. Above, the indescribable sky of Hellas; below, the silver tide of the olives everlastingly rippling down to the sea. No house, no man, no beast. As it was in the beginning.

Classical allusions abound throughout the narrative; Stewart expects her reader to recognize them, and they are an integral part of plot and theme. Indeed, the climax of the plot comes when Camilla discovers a statue of Apollo, untouched and unseen for two thousand years. The theme of the novel has similarities with Aeschylus's *Oresteia* (458 B.C.); the name of Orestes, the avenger of a murdered relative, is invoked on more than one occasion as Simon Lester is forced into avenging the murder of his brother, an event that had taken place fifteen years previously. Violent events in the past cast long shadows over the present, but the Furies are eventually satisfied.

The formula which worked so well in *My Brother Michael* was repeated, with different ingredients, in *This Rough Magic* (1964), which has proved to be one of Stewart's most popular novels. Four million copies were sold over the decade following its publication. Instead of Delphi, the setting is the island of Corfu, and the literary allusions are not to the classics but to William Shakespeare. The opening gambit is familiar: the heroine on holiday in an exotic clime. True to type, Lucy Waring is young and middle-class, modest enough to blush but spirited enough to tackle a villain. Stewart, as always, knows how to lead her reader astray: Once more there is a romantic red herring, a tall English photographer, who this time turns out to be the villain, whereas the likeliest candidate for villain eventually wins the lady's hand.

The strength of the novel lies in the characters, who are well drawn, if not in great depth, a strong plot with plenty of twists and surprises, a careful building of suspense, and the usual exciting (and violent) climax. The novel's charm lies in its setting, its wealth of incidental detail–ranging from the habits of dolphins to local folklore about Corfu's patron saint–and the ingenious way in which Stewart weaves Shakespeare's play *The Tempest* (1611) into the fabric of the story. The theory of one of the characters, a retired actor famous for his role as Prospero, is that Corfu is the magic island depicted in *The Tempest*, and allusions to the play crop up on every other page. Stewart may be writing popular fiction, but her reader is certainly at an advantage if he or she is literate; the allusions are not limited to *The Tempest* but include *King Lear* (c. 1605-1606), *Much Ado About Nothing* (c. 1598-1599), and William Congreve's Restoration drama *The Way of the World* (1700). (An amusing example occurs in the 1965 book *Airs Above The Ground*, in which an ignorant mother prattles about a passage in the Bible, which she cannot quite remember, about a thankless child being sharper than a serpent's tooth—actually an image from *King Lear*.)

Literary allusions also enrich *Touch Not the Cat* (1976), one of Stewart's best novels, a sophisticated, cleverly plotted gothic mystery which holds its interest until the end and never slackens pace. The action takes place in an old moated grange in the Midlands which belongs to the Ashleys, a venerable English family with a historical pedigree going back to Tudor times and beyond. The plot is set in motion by a cryptic message from a dying man (Stewart employed a similar device in *My Brother Michael*), which leads the heroine, Bryony Ashley, on a trail of clues leading to valuable old books, Roman villas, surprise inheritances, and the unmasking of treacherous cousins. Juxtaposed to the main narrative are a series of brief flashbacks to a tragic love affair involving one of the Ashley ancestors, which eventually turns out to have a vital bearing on the present. The story also includes the novel device of telepathic lovers, a device which Stewart handles convincingly, with subtlety and insight. As usual, she erects a smokescreen to throw the reader off the romantic trail. It is all told with Stewart's customary grace and economy of style. Her light, fluent prose is always a pleasure to read, and it is with some justice that her novels have been hailed as "genuine triumphs of a minor art."

Stewart's later novels, *Thornyhold* (1988), *The Stormy Petrel* (1991), and *Rose Cottage* (1997), are less gripping fare than her fiction of the 1950's and 1960's. Stewart returns to England for her settings, and continues her formula of a young woman encountering a strange new home and stranger family or neighbors, but these are drawn in pastels rather than the vivid colors of the Continent, true cozies and rarely thrilling.

## Principal mystery and detective fiction

NOVELS: *Madam, Will You Talk?*, 1955; *Wildfire at Midnight*, 1956; *Thunder on the Right*, 1957; *Nine Coaches Waiting*, 1958; *My Brother Michael*, 1960; *The Ivy Tree*, 1961; *The Moon-Spinners*, 1962; *This Rough Magic*, 1964; *Airs Above the Ground*, 1965; *The Gabriel Hounds*, 1967; *The Wind off the Small Isles*, 1968; *Touch Not the Cat*, 1976; *Thornyhold*, 1988; *The Stormy Petrel*, 1991; *Rose Cottage*, 1997.

## Other major works

NOVELS: *The Crystal Cave*, 1970; *The Hollow Hills*, 1973; *The Last Enchantment*, 1979; *The Wicked Day*, 1983; *The Prince and the Pilgrim*, 1995.

POETRY: *Frost on the Window and Other Poems*, 1990.

RADIO PLAYS: *Lift from a Stranger*, 1957-1958; *Call Me at Ten-Thirty*, 1957-1958; *The Crime of Mr. Merry*, 1957-1958; *The Lord of Langdale*, 1957-1958.

CHILDREN'S LITERATURE: _The Little Broomstick,_ 1971; _Ludo and the Star Horse,_ 1974; _A Walk in Wolf Wood,_ 1980.

## Bibliography

Duffy, Martha. "On the Road to Manderley." _Time_ 97 (April 12, 1971): 95-96.

Hemmings, F. W. J. "Mary Queen of Hearts." _New Statesman_ 70 (November 5, 1965): 698-699.

Friedman, Lenemaja. _Mary Stewart._ Boston: Twayne, 1990.

Newquist, Roy. _Counterpoint._ Chicago: Rand McNally, 1964.

Robertson, N. "Behind the Best Sellers." _The New York Times Book Review_ 84 (September 2, 1979): 18.

Wiggins, Kayla McKinney. "'I'll Never Laugh at a Thriller Again': Fate, Faith, and Folklore in the Mystery Novels of Mary Stewart." _Clues_ 21, no. 1 (Spring-Summer, 2000): 49-60.

_Bryan Aubrey_
_Updated by Fiona Kelleghan_

# Rex Stout

**Born:** Noblesville, Indiana; December 1, 1886
**Died:** Danbury, Connecticut; October 27, 1975

**Types of plot** • Master sleuth • private investigator

**Principal series** • Nero Wolfe, 1934-1985 • Tecumseh Fox, 1939-1941.

**Principal series characters** • NERO WOLFE, a private detective and recluse, is often goaded into taking on cases by desperate clients—or by his chief assistant, ARCHIE GOODWIN, who in many ways is Wolfe's alter ego. Wolfe is fat (nearly three hundred pounds), intellectual, and something of a romantic. Goodwin, the narrator of all the Wolfe novels, is lean, well built, and practical. Between them, they make an unbeatable—if often irritable—team. Goodwin is a shrewd observer and researcher; he finds the facts. Wolfe is the theoretician and tactician; he knows how to manipulate circumstances and make the most of the evidence Goodwin hands him.
  • TECUMSEH FOX, more physically active than Nero Wolfe, operates out of his large farm in Westchester County which his neighbors call "The Zoo." He is a daring private detective and breaks the law if he believes that a client's case is at stake.

**Contribution** • Next to Arthur Conan Doyle's Sherlock Holmes and Dr. Watson, Rex Stout's Nero Wolfe and Archie Goodwin may be the most memorable detective team in the history of the murder mystery genre. For more than forty years Stout was able to sustain his series of Nero Wolfe novels and short stories with amazing verve and consistency. Goodwin is the hard-boiled detective, ferreting out facts and collecting information from unusual sources. He brings the world to the contemplative, isolated Wolfe, who rarely leaves his home on business. He is the great mind secluded in his large, three-story brownstone on West Thirty-fifth Street in New York City. Without Goodwin, Wolfe would have to deal with the world much more directly; his mind would be cluttered with minutiae. With Goodwin as his detail man, Wolfe manages to hew his cases into a pleasing, aesthetic shape. When he solves a crime, he has simultaneously unraveled a mystery and tied up many loose ends that have bothered Goodwin and the other characters. As Wolfe suggests in several of the novels, he is an artist. He lives quietly and in virtual solitude, for that is his way of imposing his vision on the world. On those rare occasions when he is forced to leave his house, he as much as admits that sometimes the order he would like to bring to things is threatened by a chaotic and corrupt society he only momentarily manages to subdue.

**Biography** • Rex Stout was born on December 1, 1886, in Noblesville, Indiana, to John Wallace and Lucetta Todhunter Stout. The next year his family moved to Kansas, where he grew up in Wakarusa and Bellview as the sixth of nine children. He lived on a farm, which he remembered fondly in later years, while his father became superintendent of schools in Shawnee County. John Wallace Stout seems to have been a fair-minded parent as well as a great disciplinarian and fearful authority figure. Lucetta Todhunter Stout was a highly intelligent but rather reserved person who did little to encourage her children. As a result, her son Rex learned to rely on his own resources at a very early age.

John Wallace Stout owned more than one thousand books, all of which his son had read by the age of eleven. Rex Stout was a precocious student, a spelling champion, and an avid reader of poetry with a prodigious memory. His father was involved in politics, which became one of the future novelist's lifelong interests. The Stout family's theatricals, composed and performed at home, made Rex Stout a self-assured speaker and debater. It is not hard to see this background reflected in the duels of wit between the characters in his detective novels.

In his youth, Stout was a great traveler, a sailor, a self-made businessman, and a free-lance writer before publishing his first Nero Wolfe novel in 1934. He turned to mystery writing after a respectable but undistinguished effort to write fiction that would compete in seriousness with the work of F. Scott Fitzgerald, William Faulkner, and the other great twentieth century modernist writers. Before the Wolfe series, his modestly successful novels explored complex psychological themes and human characters. Yet through the evolution of the Nero Wolfe series, with its repeating characters and themes, he was able to approach a complex interpretation of human nature.

Very active in World War II as a propagandist for the American government, a controversial supporter of the Vietnam War, and a staunch opponent of J. Edgar Hoover's Federal Bureau of Investigation (FBI), Stout was himself a complex man. His fierce interests in politics and society are apparent in the Nero Wolfe series—although his main character is far more aloof from current affairs than Stout ever was. Rex Stout died in October, 1975.

**Analysis** • In Edgar Allan Poe's short story "The Purloined Letter," the model for much of modern detective fiction, M. Auguste Dupin solves a mystery by cerebration; that is, he persistently thinks through the circumstances of the case, questioning the motives of the culprit and putting himself in the criminal's place so that he can reenact the conditions of the crime. Dupin rarely leaves his room, for he works by ratiocination—Poe's term for the detective's cognitive ability to catch and to outwit the guilty party. Dupin is a man of thought, not a man of action. He is also something of a mystery himself, a remote figure whom his assistant and interlocutor (also the narrator of the story) has trouble fathoming. Dupin, in short, is the cultivated, urban intellectual who prevails in an environment that values strength of mind and mental resourcefulness. "The Purloined Letter," then, is as much about the narrator's fascination with the detective's mind as it is about catching the villain.

Nero Wolfe is a direct descendant of Dupin. He hates to leave his house on West Thirty-fifth Street in New York City. Except in extremely rare instances, all appointments with clients are in Wolfe's brownstone. The detective has traveled widely—he even owns a house in Egypt—but it is a principle with him not to leave home on business. Archie Goodwin—Wolfe's sidekick, detail man, inquisitor, and protector—is the legman, the detective's link with the outside world. Goodwin prefers to believe that Wolfe is lazy; that is the reason the detective refuses to budge from his lair. Wolfe is sedentary, but his lack of physical exercise is more than a quirk. As his name Nero suggests, he has tyrannically created his own empire out of his towering ego. A man so bent on enjoying his own pleasures (chiefly a greenhouse with three hundred orchids and gourmet meals served by his live-in cook), to the exclusion of all others, has the perfect personality to pit against the egos of criminals, confidence men, and murderers. Wolfe knows what human greed means. He himself works for high fees that support his sybaritic existence.

Wolfe is wedded to his daily routines: breakfast at eight in his bedroom, two hours with his orchids from nine to eleven, office hours from eleven to quarter past one, then lunch and more office hours until four, after which he devotes two more hours to his orchids. Dinner is at half past seven. Goodwin knows better than to disturb the detective when he is working with his flowers, and only emergencies interrupt the other parts of the fixed schedule. This profound sense of order, of instituting a household staff that caters to his habits, is what motivates Wolfe to apprehend murderers—those disrupters of a peaceful and harmonious society. As his last name suggests, he is also a predator. Killers must be caught in Nero Wolfe novels, because they ultimately threaten his own safety; they sometimes intrude into his Manhattan brownstone or violate the lives of others in ways that offend Wolfe's belief (never stated in so many words) that urban man has a right to organize his life in a highly individual, even eccentric, manner. Caring so passionately about his own security, Wolfe is moved to take on cases where another's well-being is menaced.

Although there are significant women characters in the Nero Wolfe series, their values, characters, and concerns are never central. Wolfe himself is leery of women, especially younger ones. At the conclusion of *In the Best Families* (1950), it is a joke to Goodwin that a woman has finally got close enough to Wolfe to make him smell of perfume. Goodwin is a chauvinist. He can be rather condescending with women. Occasionally, as in *And Be a Villain* (1948), a female character becomes the focal point of the story. In general, however, the power and fascination of Stout's fictional world is male.

Almost every Wolfe novel has this continuing cast of characters: Goodwin (who often has to spur Wolfe into action), Fritz (Wolfe's brilliant, conscientious cook in charge of pleasing his palate every day), Theodore (the orchid nurse), and Saul Panzer, Fred Durkin, and Orrie Cather (Wolfe's operatives, called in to help research and waylay suspects). Inspector Cramer of the New York Police Department is Wolfe's competitor, sometimes his ally, depending on the nature of the case and on whether Wolfe has information that will help the police and encourage them to tolerate his investigations. Wolfe has contact with a newspaperman, Lon Cohen, who passes along tips to Goodwin or plants items in the press at Wolfe's behest. Wolfe's organization of his household and his talent for manipulating the press and the police also speak to his consummate talents as a modern, urban detective.

It is indicative of the strengths of the Nero Wolfe series that the first novel, *Fer-de-Lance* (1934), and the last published before his death, *A Family Affair* (1975), are considered to be among Stout's best work. Every novel is characterized by Goodwin's exasperated familiarity with Wolfe's idiosyncrasies. Somehow Stout is able to create, almost immediately, the illusion of an ongoing world outside the particular novel's plot. Instead of explaining Wolfe's routine with his flowers, for example, Goodwin simply alludes to it as a habit. Gradually, in the course of the novel, brief and recurrent references to the routine are so embedded in the narrative that the presumption of a real world is easily assimilated. Indeed, the solving of a crime becomes inherently fascinating because it is contrasted implicitly with Wolfe's thoroughly regularized agenda. In other words, the detective must settle the case in order to preserve his deeply domestic order.

*And Be a Villain,* for example, begins with Goodwin filling out Wolfe's income tax forms: "For the third time I went over the final additions and subtractions on the first page of Form 1040, to make good and sure." It is typical of Stout to start a book in the middle of some action. In this case, the way Goodwin does Wolfe's income tax not only suggests his meticulous technique but also introduces the importance of money in the detective's world. He usually works only when he is forced to replenish the income he spends so extravagantly. "To make good and sure" is also characteristic of Goodwin's clipped speech. He never says more than really needs to be said. He works for Wolfe because he is efficient and accurate. He is by nature a man who wants to get things right—whether it is adding up figures or finding the real murderer.

*And Be a Villain* is the first novel of the Zeck trilogy—arguably the finest work in the Nero Wolfe series. Certainly the trilogy is representative of the series, and in its depiction of society, human character, and politics it demonstrates some of the most ambitious work ever attempted by a detective story writer. In the Zeck trilogy, Stout exploits and expands the strengths of the murder mystery genre to a point beyond which the genre cannot go without forsaking the conventions of the plot and of the detective's own personality.

In *And Be a Villain,* Wolfe is hired to investigate the murder of Cyril Orchard, the publisher of a horse-racing tip sheet, who is murdered in sensational fashion. He is the victim of a poison that is put into a soft drink that is sponsored on a popular radio show. Nearly all concerned with the show are suspects. Wolfe has to work hard to get them to tell the truth, since they conceal evidence embarrassing to the show's star, Madeleine Fraser. At first, this cover-up obscures the true nature of the case, for what Wolfe learns is that Fraser gets indigestion from her sponsor's beverage. On the live program she has always had a taped bottle filled with cold coffee to simulate the soft drink. Someone switched bottles, however, and Orchard drank what turned out to be the poisoned potion. The suspicion, then, is that Fraser was the true target of the poisoner. Not until Wolfe happens to read a newspaper account of the death of Beulah Poole, publisher of an economic forecasting tip sheet, does he realize that some larger conspiracy is at work and that Orchard was indeed the intended murder victim.

Behind the scenes of the Zeck trilogy is the mastermind, Arnold Zeck, who calls Wolfe to persuade him to drop the case. It seems Wolfe has stumbled upon a scam involving blackmail of prominent professionals and business-men who are forced to take out expensive subscriptions to the tip sheets. Zeck is a very powerful, ruthless, and corrupt figure who buys politicians and poses as a philanthropist. In the event, Wolfe solves the crime and apprehends the murderer without having to confront Zeck. The implication, however, is that Wolfe dreads the day when he will have to battle Zeck. It will mean a revolu-tion in his own life, including his departure from his beloved brownstone in order to bring his adversary down. Worse than that, Wolfe implies, he may not be successful.

Each novel in the Zeck trilogy brings Wolfe closer to the confrontation with absolute evil. Striking in all three novels is Wolfe's admission that his tri-umphs are momentary and local. The very model of the self-sufficient, im-pregnable detective, Wolfe suddenly seems incredibly vulnerable—really a very insignificant figure when matched against Zeck's crime empire. When one of Zeck's minions, Louis Rony, is murdered and Wolfe refuses to stop his investigation in *The Second Confession* (1949), Zeck has his men machine-gun Wolfe's rooftop orchid greenhouse. That is a shocking invasion of Wolfe's do-main. Although it is not the first time that Wolfe has suffered intrusions, Zeck has a societal organization—virtually a government unto itself—that could very well obliterate the detective. For much of the novel Rony has been suspected of being a secret Communist Party member; originally Wolfe was engaged to expose Rony's true political affiliations. Yet, as in *And Be a Villain*, the plot be-comes much more complex, more disturbing. Rony, it is learned, was a Party member and a Zeck operative, a kind of double agent. Wolfe again escapes a showdown with Zeck once this fact is known, since Zeck apparently believes that Rony betrayed him.

Finally, in *In the Best Families*, Wolfe is driven underground, for he has come too close to the center of Zeck's operations. In the previous two novels, Zeck has warned Wolfe to be careful, while expressing the highest admiration for Wolfe's techniques. After all, Wolfe has also built up an intricate if much smaller organization. Like Zeck, he is one of a kind. Like Zeck, he is rarely seen outside his headquarters. The difference between the two men is that Zeck wants to penetrate society from within. He wants to control the most im-portant political and financial institutions; he wants to make them perfect ex-tensions of his will. Wolfe, on the other hand, exploits society only to the ex-tent necessary to foster his deeply personal desires. He is as selfish and egotistical as Zeck, but he recognizes the rights and responsibilities of other individuals and organizations. For Zeck there can be only one organization, his own. Wolfe, on the other hand, happily pays his income tax and cooperates with the police when they can help him or lies to them when it is necessary to solve a case. Yet he has a sense of limits. His logic of organization turns inward, toward his own appetites, his own home. Zeck, on the other hand, would make the world his oyster if he had a chance.

Wolfe knows all these things about Zeck, so in the final volume of the trilogy he challenges Zeck on his own territory. Wolfe flees his brownstone, surfaces in California, loses more than one hundred pounds, slicks back his hair, grows a beard, talks through his nose, and is unrecognizable as himself. He works up a scam that fits him solidly into Zeck's organization. Like Poe's detective, Wolfe puts himself in the villain's place. Wolfe must make himself over and actually commit crimes to catch a criminal.

The Zeck trilogy is a powerful political and ethical statement, and yet it never loses its focus as detective fiction. Zeck is still the personal symbol of corruption as he would be in a Dashiell Hammett novel—to name another important model for detective fiction. Wolfe immediately gains ten pounds after successfully penetrating Zeck's organization and bringing down its master. He has gone through an agony of self-denial in order to get Zeck and rejects Goodwin's notion that he should stay in shape. Wolfe must return to fatness, for he has come perilously close to destroying his own identity. In earlier novels it has been enough for Wolfe to outwit his opponents, to absorb their psychology and turn it against them. Here he does that, but also much more. In the Zeck trilogy he must follow a policy. He must be political if he is to destroy not only the man but also his empire. David R. Anderson is right. At heart, Wolfe is a romantic who shies away from a society that cannot fulfill his aesthetic and moral craving for perfection. Knowing how decadent life is "out there," he must create a world of his own that is as flawless as he can make it.

The Zeck trilogy represents the middle period of the Nero Wolfe series. As Anderson also notes, the trilogy represents a "rite of passage" for Goodwin and Wolfe. Zeck has been their greatest challenge, and through him they have learned just how dependent they are on each other. When Wolfe flees his home in *In the Best Families* without a word to his partner, Goodwin feels abandoned but easily supports himself as a detective. Yet he continues to wonder whether Wolfe will reappear and is gratified when the detective surfaces and clues Goodwin into his plan to topple Zeck. The fact is that without Wolfe, Goodwin's work would be lucrative but unimaginative. Without Goodwin, Wolfe has been able to plan his plot against Zeck, but he cannot execute it. The loner—and he is incredibly alone during the months he works at penetrating Zeck's organization—cannot ultimately exist alone. The shock of separation, Anderson observes, is what eventually reunites this quarrelsome partnership. Inspector Cramer predicts in *In the Best Families* that Zeck is out of reach. That would be true if Goodwin and Wolfe did not know how to trust each other. In the reconciliation of opposites evil cannot triumph. Zeck has failed to divide and conquer Wolfe's world–although one of the many amusing ironies in this novel occurs when Wolfe (pretending to be Roeder, a Zeck operative) hires Goodwin to do a job for Zeck.

For all the routine of Wolfe's life, there is considerable variety in the series. While he constantly affirms that he does not leave home on business, for example, there are several instances in the series when he does. In spite of their close, daily association Wolfe still does things that surprise Goodwin. That is perhaps the freshest aspect of the Wolfe novels when they are considered in terms of the murder mystery genre. Each novel repeats the central facts about Wolfe and his entourage without becoming tiresome. In the Nero Wolfe series, invention and convention are complementary qualities. They are what makes the series cohere. A man of the most studied habits, Nero Wolfe knows when it is crucial that he break the pattern.

## Principal mystery and detective fiction

SERIES: Tecumseh Fox: *Double for Death,* 1939; *Bad for Business,* 1940; *The Broken Vase,* 1941. Nero Wolfe: *Fer-de-Lance,* 1934 (also as *Meet Nero Wolfe*); *The League of Frightened Men,* 1935; *The Rubber Band,* 1936 (also as *To Kill Again*); *The Red Box,* 1937 (also as *The Case of the Red Box*); *Too Many Cooks,* 1938; *Some Buried Caesar,* 1938 (also as *The Red Bull*); *Over My Dead Body,* 1940; *Where There's a Will,* 1940; *Black Orchids,* 1942 (also as *The Case of the Black Orchids*); *Not Quite Dead Enough,* 1944; *The Silent Speaker,* 1946; *Too Many Women,* 1947; *And Be a Villain,* 1948 (also as *More Deaths Than One*); *The Second Confession,* 1949; *Trouble in Triplicate,* 1949; *In the Best Families,* 1950 (also as *Even in the Best Families*); *Three Doors to Death,* 1950; *Murder by the Book,* 1951; *Curtains for Three,* 1951; *Triple Jeopardy,* 1951; *Prisoner's Base,* 1952 (also as *Out Goes She*); *The Golden Spiders,* 1953; *The Black Mountain,* 1954; *Three Men Out,* 1954; *Before Midnight,* 1955; *Might As Well Be Dead,* 1956; *Three Witnesses,* 1956; *If Death Ever Slept,* 1957; *Three for the Chair,* 1957; *Champagne for One,* 1958; *And Four to Go,* 1958 (also as *Crime and Again*); *Plot It Yourself,* 1959 (also as *Murder in Style*); *Too Many Clients,* 1960; *Three at Wolfe's Door,* 1960; *The Final Deduction,* 1961; *Gambit,* 1962; *Homicide Trinity,* 1962; *The Mother Hunt,* 1963; *Trio for Blunt Instruments,* 1964; *A Right to Die,* 1964; *The Doorbell Rang,* 1965; *Death of a Doxy,* 1966; *The Father Hunt,* 1968; *Death of a Dude,* 1969; *Please Pass the Guilt,* 1973; *A Family Affair,* 1975; *Death Times Three,* 1985.

OTHER NOVELS: *The Hand in the Glove,* 1937 (also as *Crime on Her Hands*); *Mountain Cat,* 1939; *Red Threads,* 1939; *Alphabet Hicks,* 1941 (also as *The Sound of Murder*).

OTHER SHORT FICTION: *Justice Ends at Home and Other Stories,* 1977.

## Other major works

NOVELS: *Her Forbidden Knight,* 1913; *Under the Andes,* 1914; *A Prize for Princes,* 1914; *The Great Legend,* 1916; *How like a God,* 1929; *Seed on the Wind,* 1930; *Golden Remedy,* 1931; *Forest Fire,* 1933; *O Careless Love!,* 1935; *Mr. Cinderella,* 1938.

NONFICTION: *The Nero Wolfe Cook Book*, 1973 (with others).

EDITED TEXTS: *The Illustrious Dunderheads*, 1942; *Rue Morgue No. 1*, 1946 (with Louis Greenfield); *Eat, Drink, and Be Buried*, 1956 (also as *For Tomorrow We Die*).

MISCELLANEOUS: *Corsage*, 1977.

## Bibliography

Anderson, David R. *Rex Stout*. New York: Frederick Ungar, 1984.

Baring-Gould, William S. *Nero Wolfe of West Thirty-fifth Street: The Life and Times of America's Largest Private Detective*. New York: Viking Press, 1969.

Darby, Ken. *The Brownstone House of Nero Wolfe, as Told by Archie Goodwin*. Boston: Little, Brown, 1983.

McAleer, John J. *Queen's Counsel: Conversations with Ruth Stout on Her Brother Rex Stout*. Ashton, Md.: Pontes Press, 1987.

_____. *Rex Stout: A Biography*. 1977. Reprint. Boston: Little, Brown, 1994.

"Stout, Rex." In *Mystery and Suspense Writers: The Literature of Crime, Detection, and Espionage*, edited by Robin W. Winks and Maureen Corrigan. New York: Charles Scribner's Sons, 1998.

Townsend, Guy M., John J. McAleer, and Boden Clarke, eds. *The Works of Rex Stout: An Annotated Bibliography and Guide*. 2d ed. San Bernardino, Calif.: Borgo Press, 1995.

Van Dover, J. Kenneth. *At Wolfe's Door: The Nero Wolfe Novels of Rex Stout*. San Bernardino, Calif.: Borgo Press, 1991.

*Carl Rollyson*

# Julian Symons

**Born:** London, England; May 30, 1912
**Died:** Walmer, Kent, England; November 19, 1994

**Types of plot** • Inverted • psychological

**Principal series** • Chief Inspector Bland, 1945-1949 • Francis Quarles, 1961-1965 • Detective Chief Superintendent Hilary Catchpole, 1994-1996.

**Principal series characters** • CHIEF INSPECTOR BLAND, a police investigator. Appropriately named, the plodding Bland is not impressive or even confidence-inspiring at his first appearance. Subsequent appearances, however, prove him to be capable and efficient, even if unimaginative.
• FRANCIS QUARLES, a private investigator who sets up his practice shortly after World War II. Large of build and flamboyantly dandyish of costume, Quarles masks his efficiency and astuteness behind deceptively languorous behavior.
• DETECTIVE CHIEF SUPERINTENDENT HILARY CATCHPOLE, a police investigator. Virtuous and compassionate, solidly middle-class, happily married to a jovial wife, Catchpole represents the stalwart hero of the people, the prototypical "good man."

**Contribution** • Julian Symons has produced a body of crime fiction that has moved beyond genre formulas with its emphasis on the artistic representation of a particular worldview and its exploration of the human psyche under stress, with its ironic commentary on a world in which the distinctions between the lawbreaker and the forces of law frequently blur into uselessness. Symons views the crime novel as a vehicle for analysis of the effects of societal pressures and repressions on the individual. Symons has mainly concentrated on psychological crime novels that delineate what he calls "the violence that lives behind the bland faces most of us present to the world." Typically, his characters are ordinary people driven to extreme behavior, average citizens caught in Hitchcockian nightmares; the focus is on the desperate actions prompted by the stresses of everyday life. Symons has expanded the limits of the crime novel, proving through his work that a popular genre, like orthodox fiction, can serve as a vehicle for a personal vision of Western society gone awry, of human lives in extremis.

Any assessment of Symons's contribution to crime literature must include mention of his two important histories of the genre: *The Detective Story in Britain* (1962) and *Bloody Murder: From the Detective Story to the Crime Novel* (1972,

1985, 1993; published in the United States as *Mortal Consequences: A History, from the Detective Story to the Crime Novel*). In both of these works, Symons details what he perceives to be a shift in both popularity and emphasis in the genre from the elegantly plot-driven classic detective story of the Golden Age of the 1920's and 1930's to the more psychologically oriented crime novel with its emphasis on character and motivation.

**Biography** • Julian Gustave Symons (the name rhymes with "women's") was born on May 30, 1912, in London, England, the last child in a family of seven. His parents were Minnie Louise Bull Symons and Morris Albert Symons, but Julian never learned his father's original name or nationality. A seller of secondhand goods until World War I brought him profits as an auctioneer, the elder Symons was a strict Victorian-era father.

As a child, Julian suffered from a stammer that placed him in remedial education despite his intelligence; overcoming his speech problems and excelling as a student, Symons nevertheless ended his formal education at fourteen and began an intense program of self-education that encompassed all that was best in literature. Julian Symons worked variously as a shorthand typist, a secretary in an engineering firm, and an advertising copywriter and executive, all in London, before he became established as an important and prolific writer of crime fiction.

At first glance, Symons's literary career appears to fall rather neatly into two distinct and contradictory phases: radical poet in the 1930's, and Tory writer of crime fiction. A founder of the important little magazine *Twentieth Century Verse* and its editor from 1937 to 1939, Symons was one of a group of young poets who in the 1930's were the heirs apparent to Stephen Spender and W. H. Auden. Before the outbreak of World War II, Symons was already the author of two volumes of poetry and was acquiring a reputation as an insightful and astute literary critic.

In 1941, Symons married Kathleen Clark; they had two children, Sarah and Maurice. From 1942 to 1944, Symons saw military service in the Royal Armoured Corps of the British army. A major turning point in Symons's career was the publication of his first crime novel, *The Immaterial Murder Case* (1945). Originally written as a spoof of art movements and their followers, this manuscript had languished in a desk drawer for six years until Kathleen encouraged him to sell it to supplement his wages as a copywriter.

The success of this and the novel that followed, *A Man Called Jones* (1947), provided Symons with the financial security he needed to become a full-time writer and spend time on books that required extensive research. With his fourth novel, *The Thirty-first of February* (1950), Symons began to move away from the classic detective forms to more experimental approaches. He supplemented his freelance income with a weekly book review column, inherited from George Orwell, in the *Manchester Evening News* from 1947-1956. Through the years, he also wrote reviews for the *London Sunday Times* (1958-68), served as a member of the council of Westfield College, University of London (1972-

75), and lectured as a visiting professor at Amherst College, Massachusetts (1975-76).

A cofounder of the Crime Writers Association, Symons served as its chair from 1958 to 1959. That organization honored him with the Crossed Red Herrings Award for best crime novel in 1957 for *The Colour of Murder*, a special award for *Crime and Detection* in 1966, and the Cartier Diamond Dagger Award for lifetime achievement in 1990. Symons also served on the board of the Society of Authors from 1970-1971, succeeded Agatha Christie as president of the Detection Club from 1976-1985, and presided over the Conan Doyle Society from 1989-1993. The Mystery Writers of America honored him with the Edgar Allan Poe Award for *The Progress of a Crime* in 1961, a special award for *Bloody Murder* in 1973, and the Grand Master award in 1982. The Swedish Academy of Detection also made him a grand master, in 1977; he won the Danish Poe-Kluhben in 1979 and was named a fellow of the Royal Society of Literature in 1975. His final novel, *A Sort of Virtue: A Political Crime Novel*, appeared in 1996—two years after his death.

**Analysis** • While Julian Symons's intricately crafted crime novels have their roots in the classic detective tradition, they also represent his lifelong fascination with genre experimentation, with moving beyond the confines of the tightly structured detective story which provides, through a sequence of cleverly revealed clues, an intellectually satisfying solution to a convoluted crime puzzle. In *Mortal Consequences*, Symons has made clear the distinctions he draws between the detective story and the crime novel. To Symons, the detective story centers on a Great Detective in pursuit of a solution to a crime, generally murder. Major emphasis is placed on clues to the identity of the criminal; in fact, much of the power of the detective story derives from the author's clever manipulation of clues and red herrings. Typically, the British detective story is socially conservative, set in a rural England that still reflects the genteel lifestyle of a bygone age. The crime novel, by contrast, generally has no master detective, but rather probes the psychology of individuals who have been driven by their environment—usually urban or suburban—to commit crimes or to become victims. Quite often the crime novel is critical of the social order, especially of the ways in which societal pressures and institutions gradually and inexorably destroy the individual.

Although Symons began his career with three formula detective novels featuring Chief Inspector Bland of the slow but adequate methodology, he soon abandoned both the form and the icon for the more ambitious project of using crime literature as social criticism. Nevertheless, these three early novels manifest in embryonic form the themes that dominate Symons's later fiction: the social personas that mask the true identity and motivations of an individual, the games people play in order to keep their masks in place, and the social pressures that force those masks to fall away, leaving the individual vulnerable and uncontrollable. In fact, masks and game-playing are the dominant motifs in Symons's fiction, functioning at times as metaphors for escape from the more unpleasant realities of existence. About his decision to move beyond the series detective, Symons said, "if you want to write a story showing people involved in emotional conflict that leads to crime, a detective of this kind is grit in the machinery."

In Symons's crime novels, the central focus is frequently on individuals who are driven to violent behavior by external forces over which—or so they believe—they have no control. "The private face of violence fascinates me," Symons acknowledged in an interview. More specifically, Symons is intrigued by the violence inherent in suburban dwellers, in respectable middle-class people who commute daily to numbingly dull jobs and return home to stiflingly placid homes and families in cozy English neighborhoods. Not for Symons the placid world of the English village will its hollyhocks and quaint cottages and population of genial eccentrics. His is the world of the ordinary and the average, at home and in the workplace; he delineates the sameness of workaday routine and the anonymity of the business world that neatly crush the individuality out of all but the most hardy souls, that goad the outwardly sane into irrational and destructive actions. Symons has commented that in his work he consciously uses acts of violence to symbolize the effects of the pressures and frustrations of contemporary urban living. How these pressures result in bizarre and uncontrollable behavior is sharply described in *The Tigers of Subtopia and Other Stories* (1982), a collection of stories about the latent tiger buried in the most innocuous of suburban denizens, about submerged cruelty and violence released by seemingly inconsequential everyday occurrences.

Nearly all Symons's characters disguise their true selves with masks, socially acceptable personas that hide the tigers inside themselves, that deny the essential human being. The early work *A Man Called Jones* unravels the mystery surrounding a masked man who calls himself Mr. Jones. Bernard Ross, prominent Member of Parliament in *The Detling Secret* (1982), once was Bernie Rosenheim. May Wilkins in *The Colour of Murder*, anxious to hide the existence of a thieving father and an alcoholic mother, takes refuge behind a forged identity as a nice young married woman who gives bridge parties and associates with the right sort of people. Adelaide Bartlett (*Sweet Adelaide*, 1980) plays the part of an adoring and dutiful wife even after she has murdered her husband. In *The Pipe Dream* (1958), the mask is literal and very public. Disguised as "Mr. X—Personal Investigator," Bill Hunter, a popular television personality, conceals the fact that he is really O'Brien, a onetime prison inmate. When his charade is exposed and he loses his job, he becomes Mr. Smith, with disastrous consequences. False identities are important to *Bogue's Fortune* (1956), *The Belting Inheritance* (1965), and *The Man Whose Dreams Came True* (1968). Many of Symons's protagonists masquerade behind aliases: Anthony Jones as Anthony Bain-Truscott or Anthony Scott-Williams, Arthur Brownjohn alias Major Easonby Mellon, Paul Vane as Dracula. Each of these characters is forced at some point to come to terms with one of the truths of Julian Symons's world: The person behind the mask cannot—must not—be denied, and role-playing cannot be continued indefinitely. Person and persona must be integrated or face destruction.

In order to maintain the fictions of their public personas, Symon's characters often play elaborate games with themselves and with others. Lenore Fetherby, in an effort to acquire irrefutable proof that she is her sister Annabel Lee, sets up a complicated trans-Atlantic charade in which she (as Annabel) has an intense affair with a bookish American professor who can be relied upon to remember his only romance. May Wilkins pretends to outsiders that her marriage is the perfect union of two ambitious young people. Determined to make his way in a class-dominated society, Bernard Ross disguises his Jewish ancestry by concocting an appealingly down-to-earth background as the son of immigrant farmers in America. For others, games are safety mechanisms that allow people to cope with the tensions and insecurities of urban existence. Mrs. Vane, bored and disillusioned by the failure of her marriage, takes refuge in endless bridge games. Bob Lawson works out his frustrations through visits to a prostitute who pretends to be a physician and subjects him to the various indignities of physical examinations.

Frequently, the game-playing takes on the more dangerous aspect of fantasy in which a character convinces himself of the truth of some impossible scenario and proceeds to live his life as though the fantasy were reality. Such is John Wilkins's problem in *The Colour of Murder.* Convincing himself, despite all the evidence to the contrary, that Sheila Morton nurses a secret passion for him, Wilkins forces his way into her company, even intruding on her vacation at a seaside resort. Consequently, he is convicted of her murder by a jury that, in an ironic parallel of his refusal to see the obvious vis-à-vis Sheila's feelings about him, chooses to misapprehend the clues and to believe Sheila's murder to be the result of Wilkins's thwarted passion.

For many characters, fantasy has more than one function. Not only does it enable the dreamer to exist comfortably within the mask, but also it becomes an avenue of escape from everyday monotony or an intolerable situation. Immersed from childhood in a fantasy about her aristocratic forebears and her true position in society, Adelaide Bartlett imagines herself too refined and too delicate for the grocer she is forced to marry. Her dreams of a pure love that permits only celibate relationships between the sexes lead her first to fantasize a chaste affair with a young minister, then to escape to monastic weekends alone at a seaside resort, and finally to murder the man whom she regards as a importunate, oversexed clod of a husband. Paul Vane of *The Players and the Game* (1972) has a fully realized fantasy life. As Vane, he is the efficient and respectable director of personnel of Timbals Plastics; as Dracula, he keeps a diary in which he records his alternative life. Ultimately, Dracula intrudes upon Vane's life; fantasy and reality collide. The results are tragic for both identities.

Symons would play upon the theme of identity from a different angle in some of his final works. In *Death's Darkest Face* (1990), a fictional version of Symons himself is asked to evaluate the progress of an unsuccessful investigation, and the intersection of the author's life with fiction lends belief to fictional characters who are in reality just so much paper-another series of masks.

In his final two novels, *Playing Happy Families* (1994) and *A Sort of Virtue* (1996), Symons once again takes up the series detective, this time with an amused affection that makes Detective Chief Superintendent Hilary Catchpole much more sympathetic to the reader than Symons's earlier investigators. Though Catchpole is a model of the virtuous policeman, his aspirations, foibles, and failings are all too human—he is a hero, but not the elevated supersleuth of Golden Age detective fiction. *A Sort of Virtue: A Political Crime Novel* provided Symons a last chance to comment on larger social issues. Catchpole's proffered epitaph, "He had a sort of virtue," stands in for Symons's final comment on human nature—an ever-surprising mixture of virtue and vice, in which the most realistic aspiration for heroes is simply to do more good than harm.

Throughout many of Symons's novels, his characters live within a stifling, inhibited society in which conformity and bland respectability are prized, and individuality has no place. Progress has created a mechanical world of routine, populated by automatons engaged in the single-minded pursuit of material and social success. Spontaneity, creativity, and play are discouraged by a moralistic society that has room only for those whose behavior is "suitable." The result is the tightly controlled public personas that mask all individual preferences and needs, personas that ultimately become operative not only in the professional life but also at home.

For many of Symons's characters, role-playing or an active fantasy life often begin as harmless activities which serve to relieve the stresses induced by society's demands and restrictions. In a number of instances, however, the games and the fantasies gradually begin to take precedence over real life, and the individual begins to function as though the imaginary life were real. Tragedy often ensues. Symons has pointed out that all human beings can be broken under too much pressure; his characters—especially those whose energies are devoted to maintaining two separate identities, and who crack under the strain of the effort—prove the truth of that observation. The quiet average neighborhood in a Symons novel seethes with malevolence barely concealed by civilized behavior.

In the Symons crime novel violence is not an irregularity as it so often is in the classic detective story. Violence—physical, psychological, moral, spiritual—is inherent in the society that suppresses and represses natural actions and desires. Behind the stolid façades of suburban houses, beneath the calm faces of workaday clones, hides the potential for irrationality and violence, denied but not obliterated. "The thing that absorbs me most," says Symons, "is the violence behind respectable faces." In his novels, it is the assistant managers and personnel directors and housewives—good, solid, dependable people—whose carefully designed masks crumple and tear under the pressures of life. Violence erupts from those of whom it is least expected.

In short, the concerns of crime writer Julian Symons are the same concerns addressed by mainstream fiction. Symons portrays microcosms of Western civilization in decay; he describes a world in which the individual has no place, communication is impossible, and acceptable behavior is defined by a society determined to eliminate all rebellion against the common standard. He examines the fate of those who will not or cannot conform, and he lays the blame for their tragedies on an environment that shapes and distorts the human psyche into an unrecognizable caricature of humanity.

Like those writers who have earned their reputations in the literary mainstream, Symons has created a body of work that embodies a distinctive view of life, a concern with the effects of society on the fragile human psyche, and a realistic portrayal of the alienation and frustration of individuals in late twentieth century England, still struggling to regain a sense of equilibrium decades after World War II. His characters, like so many in twentieth century fiction, are fragmented selves who acknowledge some facets of their identities only in fantasy or role-playing and who otherwise devote all of their energies to repressing their less socially acceptable personas. As a writer of crime fiction, Julian Symons has opened up innumerable possibilities for innovation and experimentation in the genre; as a serious writer and critic, he has brought to a popular form the serious concerns and issues of the twentieth century novel at its best.

## Principal mystery and detective fiction

SERIES: Chief Inspector Bland: *The Immaterial Murder Case*, 1945; *A Man Called Jones*, 1947; *Bland Beginning*, 1949 (also as *Bland Beginning: A Detective Story*). Francis Quarles: *Murder! Murder!*, 1961; *Francis Quarles Investigates*, 1965. Detective Chief Superintendent Hilary Catchpole: *Playing Happy Families*, 1994; *A Sort of Virtue: A Political Crime Novel*, 1996.

OTHER NOVELS: *The Thirty-first of February*, 1950 (also as *The 31st of February*); *The Broken Penny*, 1953; *The Narrowing Circle*, 1954; *The Paper Chase*, 1956 (also as *Bogue's Fortune*); *The Colour of Murder*, 1957 (also as *The Color of Murder*); *The Gigantic Shadow*, 1958 (also as *The Pipe Dream*); *The Progress of a Crime*, 1960; *The Killing of Francie Lake*, 1962 (also as *The Plain Man*); *The End of Solomon Grundy*, 1964; *The Belting Inheritance*, 1965; *The Man Who Killed Himself*, 1967; *The Man Whose Dreams Came True*, 1968; *The Man Who Lost His Wife*, 1970; *The Players and the Game*, 1972; *The Plot Against Roger Rider*, 1973; *A Three-Pipe Problem*, 1975 (also as *A Three Pipe Problem*); *The Blackheath Poisonings: A Victorian Murder Mystery*, 1978 (also as *The Blackheath Poisonings*); *Sweet Adelaide: A Victorian Puzzle Solved*, 1980 (also as *Sweet Adelaide*); *The Detling Murders*, 1982 (also as *The Detling Secret*); *The Name of Annabel Lee*, 1983; *The Criminal Comedy of the Contented Couple*, 1985 (also as *A Criminal Comedy*); *Criminal Acts*, 1987; *Did Sherlock Holmes Meet Hercule . . .* , 1988; *The Kentish Manor Murders*, 1988; *Death's Darkest Face*, 1990; *Portraits of the Missing: Imaginary Biographies*, 1992; *Something Like a Love Affair*, 1992; *The Advertising Murders*, 1992.

OTHER SHORT FICTION: *The Julian Symons Omnibus*, 1967; *Ellery Queen Presents Julian Symons' How to Trap a Crook, and Twelve Other Mysteries*, 1977; *The Great Detectives: Seven Original Investigations*, 1981; *The Tigers of Subtopia and Other Stories*, 1982 (also as *Somebody Else and Other Stories*); *The Man Who Hated Television and Other Stories*, 1995.

## Other major works

SCREENPLAY: *The Narrowing Circle*, 1955

TELEPLAYS: *I Can't Bear Violence*, 1963; *Miranda and a Salesman*, 1963; *The Witnesses*, 1964; *The Finishing Touch*, 1965; *Curtains for Sheila*, 1965; *Tigers of Subtopia*, 1968; *The Pretenders*, 1970; *Whatever's Peter Playing At?*, 1974.

RADIO PLAYS: *Affection Unlimited*, 1968; *Night Ride to Dover*, 1969; *The Accident*, 1976.

POETRY: *Confusions About X*, 1939; *The Second Man*, 1943; *A Reflection on Auden*, 1973; *The Object of an Affair and Other Poems*, 1974; *Seven Poems for Sarah*, 1979.

NONFICTION: *A. J. A. Symons: His Life and Speculations*, 1950, revised 1986; *Charles Dickens*, 1951; *Thomas Carlyle: The Life and Ideas of a Prophet*, 1952; *Horatio Bottomley: A Biography*, 1955; *The General Strike: A Historical Portrait*, 1957; *The Hundred Best Crime Stories Published by the Sunday Times*, 1959 (also as *The One Hundred Best Crime Stories*); *The Thirties: A Dream Resolved*, 1960, revised 1975 (also as *The Thirties and the Nineties*); *A Reasonable Doubt: Some Criminal Cases Re-examined*, 1960; *The Detective Story in Britain*, 1962; *Buller's Campaign*, 1963; *England's Pride: The Story of the Gordon Relief Expedition*, 1965; *Crime and Detection: An Illustrated History from 1840*, 1966 (also as *A Pictorial History of Crime*); *Critical Occasions*, 1966; *Bloody Murder: From the Detective Story to the Crime Novel*, 1972, revised 1985, 1993 (also as *Mortal Consequences: A History, from the Detective Story to the Crime Novel*); *Between the Wars: Britain in Photographs*, 1972; *Notes from Another Country*, 1972; *The Tell-Tale Heart: The Life and Works of Edgar Allan Poe*, 1978; *Conan Doyle: Portrait of an Artist*, 1979; *The Modern Crime Story*, 1980; *Critical Observations*, 1981; *The Mystique of the Detective Story*, 1981; *Tom Adams' Agatha Christie Cover Story*, 1981 (with Tom Adams; also as *Agatha Christie: The Art of Her Crimes*); *A. J. A. Symons to Wyndham Lewis: Twenty-Four Letters*, 1982; *Crime and Detection Quiz*, 1983; *1948 and 1984: The Second Orwell Memorial Lecture*, 1984; *Two Brothers: Fragments of a Correspondence*, 1985; *Dashiell Hammett*, 1985; *Makers of the New: The Revolution in Literature, 1912-1939*, 1987; *Oscar Wilde: A Problem in Biography*, 1988; *The Thirties and the Nineties*, 1990; *Criminal Practices: Symons on Crime Writing 60's to 90's*, 1994.

EDITED TEXTS: *An Anthology of War Poetry*, 1942; *Selected Writings of Samuel Johnson*, 1949; *Carlyle: Selected Works, Reminiscences, and Letters*, 1955; *Essays and Biographies*, by A. J. A. Symons, 1969; *The Woman in White*, by Wilkie Collins, 1974; *The Angry Thirties*, 1976; *Selected Tales*, by Edgar Allan Poe, 1976; *The Angry Thirties*, 1976 (also as *The Angry 30's*); *Selected Tales*, by Edgar Allan Poe, 1976 (also as *The World's Classics: Edgar Allan Poe, Selected Tales*); *Verdict of*

*Thirteen: A Detection Club Anthology*, 1979; *The Complete Sherlock Holmes*, by Arthur Conan Doyle, 1981; *New Poetry 9*, 1983; *The Penguin Classic Crime Omnibus*, 1984; *The Essential Wyndham Lewis, An Introduction to His Work*, 1989.

## Bibliography
Cantwell, Mary. "Homicides, Victorian and Modern." *The New York Times Book Review* 88 (March 20, 1983): 12, 42.
Carter, Steven R. "Julian Symons and Civilization's Discontents." *The Armchair Detective* 12 (January, 1979): 57-62.
Cooper-Clark, Diana. *Designs of Darkness: Interviews with Detective Novelists.* Bowling Green, Ohio: Bowling Green State University Popular Press, 1983.
Craig, Patricia, ed. *Julian Symons at Eighty: A Tribute.* Helsinki, Finland: Eurographica, 1992.
Gray, Paul. "Crime and Craftsmanship." *Time* 121 (February 14, 1983): 82.
Grimes, Larry E. "Julian Symons." In *Twelve English Men of Mystery*, edited by Earl F. Bargainnier. Bowling Green, Ohio: Bowling Green State University Popular Press, 1984.
"Symons, Julian." In *Mystery and Suspense Writers: The Literature of Crime, Detection, and Espionage*, edited by Robin W. Winks and Maureen Corrigan. New York: Charles Scribner's Sons, 1998.
Walsdorf, Jack, and Kathleen Symons, eds. *Julian Symons Remembered: Tributes From Friends.* Council Bluffs, Iowa: Yellow Barn Press, 1996.
Walsdorf, John J., and Bonnie J. Allen. *Julian Symons: A Bibliography with Commentaries and a Personal Memoir.* New Castle, Del.: Oak Knoll Press, 1996.

*E. D. Huntley*
*Updated by Fiona Kelleghan and C. A. Gardner*

# Josephine Tey

## Elizabeth Mackintosh

**Born:** Inverness, Scotland; 1896 or 1897
**Died:** London, England; February 13, 1952

**Also wrote as** • Gordon Daviot

**Type of plot** • Police procedural

**Principal series** • Alan Grant, 1929-1952.

**Principal series characters** • ALAN GRANT, a Scotland Yard police detective. He is a shrewd reader of human faces who relies on his "flair," an ingenious, intuitive knack for solving cases. Although he makes mistakes, his intelligence sets him apart from most fictional police detectives, who lack his imagination, initiative, and cosmopolitan outlook.
• SERGEANT WILLIAMS, Grant's sidekick, who furnishes Grant with detailed information gleaned from his meticulous investigations.

**Contribution** • Although Alan Grant is a recurring character in Josephine Tey's detective novels, he is not always the main character. As in *To Love and Be Wise* (1950), he may be introduced at the beginning of a novel but not figure prominently until a crime has been committed. In *The Franchise Affair* (1948), he plays only a minor role. Tey is exceptional in not following the conventional plots of mystery and detective stories. She is more interested in human character. Grant is important insofar as he comes into contact with murder victims and suspects, but usually the human scene is fully described before Grant appears, or the other characters are fleshed out as he encounters them. Consequently, Tey's novels never seem written to formula or driven by a mere "whodunit" psychology. She is interested, rather, in human psychology as it is revealed in the commission of a crime, a disappearance, or a case of imposture. Often readers who do not like the conventions of detective stories like Tey because her novels seem organic; that is, they grow out of what is revealed about the characters. If Tey writes mysteries, it is because human character is a mystery.

**Biography** • Josephine Tey was born in Inverness, Scotland, where she attended the Royal Academy and studied the humanities. After she was graduated, she continued course work in physical culture at the Anstey Physical College and taught the subject for several years in English schools. She gave up teaching in 1926 to look after her invalid father at their family home. As Gordon Daviot, she wrote novels, short stories, and plays. Her greatest success in the theater came with the production of *Richard of Bordeaux* (1932), based on the life of Richard III and starring John Gielgud.

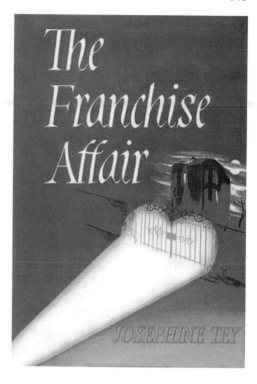

In private life, Tey was Elizabeth Mackintosh. She seemed to have few interests besides horse racing and fishing, both of which figure in her fiction. In a letter to a fellow mystery writer she confessed that she did not read many mysteries. She was a very shy woman with few close friends. She granted no press interviews. It was characteristic of her to have lived with her fatal illness for a year before her death without telling anyone about it. She never married. The strongest women in her fiction are single, and her detective, Alan Grant, is a bachelor who shares many of his creator's interests, including a devotion to the theater.

**Analysis** • Josephine Tey's first detective novel, *The Man in the Queue* (1929), introduced Alan Grant of Scotland Yard. Grant is a man with considerable style. As later novels indicate, he is regarded as somewhat suspect at the Yard because of his "flair." He might be just a bit too intelligent. His superiors fear that his wit may cause him to be too ingenious, to make too much of certain evidence with his fancy interpretations. Indeed, in *The Man in the Queue*, Grant's brilliance almost does lead him to the wrong conclusion. Some reviewers thought that Tey spent too much time conveying the mental processes of her detective. A greater fault of her first detective novel, however, is the stabbing of the man in the queue—which is done in public in a crowded line of people. Reviewers wondered why the man did not cry out. None of Tey's subsequent detective novels depends on gimmickry, however, and with the exception of *The Daughter of Time* (1951), Grant's thoughts are not the focus of the narrative.

*The Man in the Queue* also introduced Grant's sidekick, Sergeant Williams. As in the classic detective story, Williams plays a kind of Dr. Watson to Grant's Sherlock Holmes. Grant, however, is much more appreciative of Williams, his detail man, than Holmes is of Watson. Grant relies on Williams for meticulous investigations and often goes over the details to be sure that he

(Grant) has not missed anything. In other words, Williams is no mere sounding board, even if he worships Grant as his hero.

Except for *A Shilling for Candles* (1936), Tey wrote no Alan Grant novels in the 1930's, as though to prevent him from dominating her fiction. *Brat Farrar* (1949) is about an impostor who claims to be the heir to a huge family fortune. The heir is presumed to have committed suicide as a young boy, although the boy's body was never found. In a riveting narrative, Tey achieves the astonishing feat of getting readers to identify with the impostor, Brat Farrar, while deepening the mystery of how the heir actually met his death. As in several other novels, she raises intriguing questions about human identity, about how human beings take on roles that can both obscure and reveal reality.

Similarly, in *To Love and Be Wise*, an Alan Grant novel, the question at first seems to be what happened to Leslie Searle, an American photographer who has befriended an English family. He disappears on an outing with Walter Whitmore, an English radio personality who is suspected of doing away with Searle because of Searle's involvement with Whitmore's fiancée. By the time Grant becomes deeply involved in the case, the novel is half over and the reader's interest is increasingly focused on exactly who Leslie Searle was. How is it that he insinuated himself into the lives of an English family? What was there about him that made him so appealing? Grant has to pursue these questions before finally realizing that Leslie Searle is not the victim but the perpetrator of a crime.

The most celebrated Alan Grant novel is *The Daughter of Time*. Grant is laid up with an injury in the hospital. He asks his close friend, the actress Martha Hallard (another regular character in the Grant series), to bring him a set of prints. Among other things, Hallard supplies him with a print of the portrait of Richard III, which is on display at the National Gallery in London. Grant is stunned that Richard's keenly intelligent and compassionate face is nothing like the villain portrayed by Shakespeare and Sir Thomas More. With the assistance of an American student, Grant engages in a full-scale research project to exonerate Richard III from the charge of murdering the princes in the Tower and of being the most villainous king in English history.

*The Daughter of Time* has been extravagantly praised as a tour de force, a unique combination of the detective story and a work of history. It has also been disdained as a prejudiced book that libels historians for supposedly blackening Richard's name based on insufficient or biased evidence. It is true that Tey does not offer all the evidence that has been used to confirm Richard's guilt. Worse, the novel has internal flaws. For a novelist who was usually so perceptive about human character, Tey saw only the bright side of Richard's public character and did not make allowances for the brutal age in which he lived, an age in which struggles for the throne often led to bloodshed. In Tey's favor, however, the conventions of the mystery/detective genre may also be held accountable: The form mandates that a criminal be caught. If Richard III is not the villain, then Henry VII must be. Tey's detective amasses a case against Richard's successor. Historians have other options and have conducted much closer studies of Richard III's England than can be permitted in a detective novel. Most readers have found *The Daughter of Time* to be an invigorating work of fiction, particularly appealing for the unusual interpretation of historical events, whatever credence one gives to that interpretation.

The real strength of *The Daughter of Time* lies in Tey's emphasis on Grant as an interpreter of the evidence. Although he attacks historians, his methods are not out of line with what R. G. Collingwood has recommended in *The Idea of History* (1946). In fact, Collingwood invents a detective story in order to explain how a historian interprets evidence. Even if Grant makes the wrong judgments of history, the important thing is that he is not content to look at secondary sources—that is, other histories of Richard III. Instead, he consults the records and documents produced during Richard's brief reign. Grant tries to use his experience as a detective, his ability to read human faces, to interpret Richard's life and work. Grant asks hard questions. He actively investigates the historical evidence and does not rely on authorities. Tey shrewdly gets readers to identify with Grant by having him slowly discover the evidence and then put it to the test of his formidable skepticism.

*The Daughter of Time* is different from the other Grant novels in that Grant displays more confidence than he does elsewhere. In the other novels he has definite mental and physical weaknesses. Something in the English climate makes him sniffle. In *The Singing Sands* (1952), he retreats to the Scottish highlands to steady himself; in pursuit of a murderer, he is also on the verge of a nervous breakdown. Yet is it his very vulnerability that helps him to identify with others and to see his way through to the solution of his cases.

Much of the beauty of Tey's writing derives from her love of the English and Scottish countryside. When things go awry in this charming, family-oriented world, it is absolutely imperative that the detective restore equilibrium. The scenes in *The Singing Sands* of Grant fishing in Highland streams remain vivid long after the plot of the novel is forgotten. In *Brat Farrar*, which is not part of the Grant series, Tey makes an impostor her main character and makes his identification with an English family and its home such a powerful theme that it becomes imperative that the criminal somehow be able to redeem himself—which he does by discovering the real murderer of the twin whom he has impersonated.

One of the common pitfalls of serial detective fiction is that it can become routinized and thus predictable, the detective employing the same set of gestures and methods that have proved effective and popular in previous novels. This is never so with Tey. Each case confronting Grant is unique, and he must fumble to discover the appropriate technique. Circumstances always influence the way Grant handles a case. In spite of his prodigious mental gifts, he is not presented as a Great Detective who is the equal of every mystery. He profits from lucky accidents, from the suggestions of others, and from the mistakes of criminals. As a result, the reader's interest is drawn to Grant's character as well as the mysteries he is trying to solve.

It is striking what a clean, highly individualized world Tey presents in her detective fiction. There are relatively few murders and gruesome incidents. The police and the other institutions of society are never seen as corrupt. Rather, it is human character that is crooked or degenerate. In other words, Tey's crimes become moral but never sociological problems. She is a keen observer of society but shies away from generalizations about class and economic structure.

Given a sufficient interest in crime, an amateur can become a detective. Such is the case in *Miss Pym Disposes* (1946). Set in a physical education college, this novel draws upon Tey's own experience. Miss Lucy Pym is a best-selling author. She has also been a schoolmistress and now finds herself teaching temporarily at a girls' school. When she prevents a girl from cheating on an exam, she is compulsively drawn into a murder and devises an extralegal punishment for the criminal that leads to disaster. The novel is a brilliant attack on the high-and-mighty detectives who dispense their own brand of justice and are contemptuous of the police. Given the destructive way Miss Pym disposes of her case, it is no wonder that Tey did not follow this very popular novel with a sequel. Tey rejected the notion that a detective can solve case after case neatly and efficiently. As a result, she only wrote eight mystery/detective novels; each one had to be unique, and each successive novel was as carefully devised as the previous one.

During Tey's lifetime two of her works (*A Shilling for Candles, The Franchise Affair*) were turned into films, most notably the former which served as the basis for Alfred Hitchcock's *Young and Innocent* (1937). Brat Farrar, however, was the subject of two adaptations, first as television movie for the BBC, and then as part of the network's perennially popular *Mystery!* series.

Though Tey died in the mid-twentieth century, her works were still in print at the turn of the century. Her crowning achievement, *The Daughter of Time*, which had been recorded for posterity by Derek Jacobi, had been digitally remastered and released in late 2000. Few mystery writers, past or present, have written with such diversity or originality; Tey's small body of work has more than withstood the test of time.

### Principal mystery and detective fiction

SERIES: Alan Grant: *The Man in the Queue*, 1929 (also as *Killer in the Crowd*); *A Shilling for Candles*, 1936; *The Franchise Affair*, 1948; *To Love and Be Wise*, 1950; *The Daughter of Time*, 1951; *The Singing Sands*, 1952.

OTHER NOVELS: *Miss Pym Disposes*, 1946; *Brat Farrar*, 1949 (also as *Come and Kill Me*).

### Other major works

NOVELS: *Kif: An Unvarnished History*, 1929; *The Expensive Halo*, 1931; *The Privateer*, 1952.

PLAYS: *Richard of Bordeaux*, 1932; *The Laughing Woman*, 1934; *Queen of Scots*, 1934; *The Stars Bow Down*, 1939; *Leith Sands and Other Short Plays*, 1946; *The Little Dry Thorn*, 1947; *Valerius*, 1948; *Dickon*, 1953; *Sweet Coz*, 1954; *Plays*, 1953-1954.

RADIO PLAYS: *Leith Sands*, 1941; *The Three Mrs. Madderleys*, 1944; *Mrs. Fry Has a Visitor*, 1944; *Remember Caesar*, 1946; *The Pen of My Aunt*, 1950; *The Pomp of Mr. Pomfret*, 1954; *Cornelia*, 1955.
NONFICTION: *Claverhouse*, 1937.

## Bibliography

Charney, Hanna. *The Detective Novel of Manners: Hedonism, Morality, and the Life of Reason*. Rutherford: Fairleigh Dickinson University Press, 1981.

Davis, Dorothy Salisbury. "On Josephine Tey." *The New Republic* 131 (September 20, 1954): 17-18.

Klein, Kathleen Gregory. "Josephine Tey." In *St. James Guide to Crime and Mystery Writers*, edited by Jay P. Pederson and Taryn Benbow-Pfalzgraf. Detroit: St. James Press, 1996.

Mann, Jessica. *Deadlier than the Male: Why Are Respectable English Women So Good at Murder?* New York: Macmillan, 1981.

Rollyson, Carl. "The Detective as Historian: Josephine Tey's *The Daughter of Time*." *Iowa State Journal of Research* 53 (August, 1978): 21-30.

Roy, Sandra. *Josephine Tey*. Boston: Twayne, 1980.

Smith, M. J. "Controversy: Townsend, Tey, and Richard III, a Rebuttal." *The Armchair Detective* 10 (October, 1977): 317-319.

Symons, Julian. *Mortal Consequences: A History, from the Detective Story to the Crime Novel*. London: Faber & Faber, 1972.

Talburt, Nancy Ellen. *Ten Women of Mystery*, edited by Earl F. Bargainner. Bowling Green, Ohio: Bowling Green State University Popular Press, 1981.

"Tey, Josephine." In *Mystery and Suspense Writers: The Literature of Crime, Detection, and Espionage*, edited by Robin W. Winks and Maureen Corrigan. New York: Charles Scribner's Sons, 1998.

Townsend, Guy M. "Richard III and Josephine Tey: Partners in Crime." *The Armchair Detective* 10 (July, 1977): 211-224.

*Carl Rollyson*
*Updated by Fiona Kelleghan and Taryn Benbow-Pfalzgraf*

# Ross Thomas

**Born:** Oklahoma City, Oklahoma; February 19, 1926
**Died:** Santa Monica, California; December 18, 1995

**Also wrote as** • Oliver Bleeck

**Types of plot** • Espionage • amateur sleuth • thriller

**Principal series** • McCorkle and Padillo, 1966-1990 • Philip St. Ives, 1969-1976 • Artie Wu and Quincy Durant, 1978-1992.

**Principal series characters** • "MAC" MCCORKLE, the undescribed viewpoint character, is probably in his late thirties as the McCorkle and Padillo series begins. With Mike Padillo, he runs a saloon first in Bonn and then in Washington, D.C. Mac's Place features high prices, low lights, and honest drinks. A typical understated American, Mac was behind the lines in Burma during World War II and can handle himself in a fight when necessary. His bonding to his partner and his commitment to finishing the dirty work so that he can return to drinking motivate his actions.

• MIKE PADILLO, half-Estonian and half-Spanish, with a facility for languages and violence, is blackmailed into military intelligence during World War II and into working for an unnamed Central Intelligence Agency (CIA) competitor after the war. All he wants is to run a good saloon, but Mac's Place provides his cover as well. Cynical and suspicious, he wants to come in out of the cold but is not allowed to do so. His relationship with Mac is a tribute to male bonding.

• PHILIP ST. IVES is a former newspaper columnist who has a wide acquaintanceship among shady characters. He uses that knowledge to act as a go-between in ransoming stolen objects, in the process finding himself obliged to solve the crimes involved, although he is loyal to the criminals until they deceive him in some way.

• MYRON GREENE is St. Ives's attorney and accountant. A corporate lawyer with a taste for flashy clothes and cars, he would not be caught dead trying a case in court but revels in his connection to the seamy life through St. Ives. Cases usually come in through Greene.

• ARTIE WU is more than six feet tall and weighs nearly 250 pounds. The illegitimate son of the illegitimate daughter of the last Manchu emperor and semiserious claimant to the throne, he met Quincy Durant in an orphanage, and they have been partners in crime ever since. An expert in classic con games, he is the planner of the pair. He is married, with two sets of twins.

• QUINCY DURANT, tall, thin, and nervous as a coiled spring, is the action man, although his talent as a planner of con games is not to be despised either. His love life usually complicates things.

• OTHERGUY OVERBY is so called because when the gaff is blown, it is always "the other guy" who is left holding the bag. An experienced con man, Otherguy gives the impression he might sell out the partnership, but he never quite does.

**Contribution** • Ross Thomas has made the rotten worlds of politics, finance, and espionage as familiar to readers as the headlines in their daily newspapers. Crossing the mean, dark streets lined with executive suites and using the eye of a reporter and the tongue of an adder with a malicious sense of humor, he makes the reader feel like an eavesdropper in the halls of power, often using the inside political manipulator as hero. As Oliver Bleeck, he has invented a new occupation for amateur sleuth Philip St. Ives. As a professional go-between, he dabbles in crimes ranging from art theft to Cold War double-crosses.

**Biography** • Ross Elmore Thomas was born on February 19, 1926, in Oklahoma City, Oklahoma, to J. Edwin and Laura (Dean) Thomas. He began his education as a thriller writer while a reporter on the *Daily Oklahoman* in his hometown before serving as a U.S. Army infantryman in the Philippines during World War II. After he graduated from the University of Oklahoma in 1949, he directed public relations for the National Farmers Union and later for the Volunteers in Service to America (VISTA). Thomas managed election campaigns in the United States—for two union presidents, for a Republican Senate nominee, and for a Democratic governor of Colorado. Interestingly, he also advised an African leader who was running for the post of prime minister in Nigeria, though without success.

Thomas covered Bonn, Germany, for the Armed Forces Network in the late 1950's and served as a consultant/political mastermind to the United States government from 1964 to 1966 before publishing his first thriller, *The Cold War Swap*, a book that won the Mystery Writers of America Edgar Allan Poe Award in 1967. In 1974, he married Rosalie Appleton. He always cast a cynical eye on institutions and society at home and abroad, dissecting both with the wit of a morgue attendant and a wiretapper's ear for dialogue. *Briarpatch* (1984) won Thomas another Edgar, and *Chinaman's Chance* (1978) was selected by the Independent Mystery Bookseller's Association as one of the 100 Favorite Mysteries of the Century. Thomas served a term as president of the Mystery Writers of America. All of his novels remain in print, a feat of which few writers can boast.

**Analysis** • If Ross Thomas needed any apprenticeship in writing fiction, he served it during his year as reporter, public relations man, and political manager. His first novel, *The Cold War Swap*, was published three years after John le Carré's pathbreaking *The Spy Who Came in from the Cold* (1963) captured the attention of readers by inverting the morality of the espionage novel. In his first offering, Thomas showed that he was already a master of the Hobbesian world of espionage double-cross where every man is against every other, the only rule is survival, and the agents from both sides are more sympathetic characters than their masters. His hero, Mike Padillo, is a fully "amortized agent"–the agency's investment in him has long since paid off handsomely. He is to be traded to the Soviets for a pair of gay National Security Agency (NSA) defectors. His triumph, if it can be called that, is in carrying out his mission without falling into the hands of either side.

Thomas's universe is not the weary world of fallen empire inhabited by le Carré's neurasthenic heroes but the permanently rotten one invented by the creators of the hard-boiled American detective. In it, few men (and fewer women) are loyal, everything is for sale, and everything is connected–in the worst possible way. His men are professionals whose only pride is in their professionalism and their survival. They survive because a few people have followed E. M. Forster's advice to remain loyal to their friends rather than to their nation, or because they can buy aid from those who have no loyalties. Heroes cannot reform Thomas's world, but the quick or the unprincipled can manipulate it, briefly, in pursuit of the ancient triad of money, power, and sex.

Thomas's area of specialization is the world of the double-cross–espionage, politics, and the con game–and his viewpoint characters are men of a certain age and experience who can handle themselves in the board room, battle, or boudoir. Journalists, former spies, and political insiders, his heroes come in two kinds, those who, like the cowboy, do not go looking for trouble, and those who, like the private eye, do–for money. Those who do not go willingly into trouble have to be blackmailed into doing the job, and their only recompense is money, lots of it, and peace and quiet until the next time. In *Cast a Yellow Shadow* (1967), Mike Padillo agrees to assassinate the prime minister of a white-ruled African nation after Mac's wife is kidnapped. In *The Singapore Wink* (1969), Edward Cauthorne, former Hollywood stunt man and current dealer in vintage cars, agrees to go to Singapore to locate a man for the mob after several of his cars are vandalized. Hoods have also crushed the hands of Sidney Durant, his twenty-year-old body man, by slamming a car door on them repeatedly.

Those who do go willingly into trouble include con men Artie Wu and Quincy Durant, go-between Philip St. Ives, and a miscellaneous crew of journalists and political consultants whose job descriptions cannot be easily distinguished from those of the con men. The professionals cannot be distinguished in their expertise from the amateurs either, and the survival of all depends on quick reflexes fueled by low cunning, inside knowledge, and lashings of untraceable money. Thomas invents women characters who are as capable of violence, lust, greed, and chicanery as the men; they may be physically weaker, but they make up for it. Although they are usually subsidiary characters in the typical women's roles of secretary or assistant, there are exceptions. Georgia Blue (*Out on the Rim,* 1987) is a former Secret Service agent who has a role equal to the men's in persuading the Filipino revolutionary to retire to Hong Kong, and Wanda Gothar (*The Backup Men,* 1971) is an experienced member of a family that has been involved in espionage since the Napoleonic era. If the women are older, they are capable of the exercise of power, such as Gladys Citron (*Missionary Stew,* 1983), West Coast editor of a *National Enquirer*-type newspaper and former Office of Strategic Services (OSS) officer decorated personally by Charles de Gaulle for killing three dozen Germans. Realistically, most of the older women exercise power as wives or widows, and they do it by manipulation, at which they are as adept as the men around them. All Thomas's characters like sex the way they like food or drink.

Perhaps because Southerners have traditionally had verbal skills that take them into politics, or because Thomas is from the edge of the South, many of his political characters are convincing Southern gothics whose careers would enliven the dullest work of academic sociology. The seersucker-suited Clinton Shartelle, hired to manage the political campaign of the African chief Sunday Akomolo in *The Seersucker Whipsaw* (1967), describes his life in Denver to his associate, Peter Upshaw:

> I lived here in a house with my daddy and a lady friend from 1938 to 1939. Not too far from that ball park which is—you might have noticed—a somewhat blighted area. It was a plumb miserable neighborhood even then. I was sixteen-seventeen years old. My daddy and I had come out here from Oklahoma City in the fall driving a big, black 1929 LaSalle convertible sedan. We checked in at the Brown Palace and my daddy got himself a lease on a section of land near Walsenburg, found himself a rig and crew, and drilled three of the deepest dry holes you ever saw.

Shartelle's story goes on for several pages, and before he has finished, Thomas has involved the reader in a three-dimensional character whose childhood has produced a man of flexible morals with a gift of gab that could charm a sheriff bent on eviction or an outraged creditor. He is a man drawn to political manipulation just as naturally as steel filings are drawn to a magnet.

The minor characters Thomas creates are as fully drawn as the major ones. The reader comes to understand them as clearly as he understands his own quirky relatives. The reader can never tell, however, whether the cab driver whose long life story Thomas relates will take his tip and disappear from the pages of the book, or whether he will play a larger part of the story. The characters are so engaging in their frankly seamy humanity that the reader is simply happy to meet them, even if only briefly. Certain minor character types, such as the Village Wise Man or Fixer, reappear in successive books. One of these of the Fixer type is David "Slippery" Slipper, white-haired and seventy-five, who

> had been, at various times, a New Deal White House aide, or to hear him tell it, "Harry Hopkins's office boy"; a spy of sorts for the wartime Office of Strategic Services; a syndicated columnist (121 daily newspapers); a biographer of the iron-willed Speaker of the House of Representatives, Thomas Brackett (Czar) Reed; an

Assistant Secretary of Agriculture (six months); a deputy Undersecretary of the Interior (ninety days); ambassador to Chad (one year, "the longest year of my life," he later said); and for the past fifteen years a political fixer and consultant who charged outrageous fees for his sensible, hardheaded advice.

After several more detailed paragraphs about Slippery, Thomas has him tell the hero to drop his investigation, and he disappears forever from *Missionary Stew*. These categories are not exclusively male. Señora Madelena de Romanones plays both the Village Wise Woman and Fixer characters in *Cast a Yellow Shadow*.

Thomas's spies and spymasters are painted as ridiculous and two-faced. The reader can never tell who is on which side, as even the hero is not always committed to conventional morality. The double-crosses come fast and furious, and the reader will always be wise to expect one more, unless he has just read the last line of the book. Thomas's male characters like fast, expensive cars, exotic weapons, and fast, exotic women. When he is setting up the story, Thomas can "tell the tale" better than any con man alive. His political manipulators are heroes as often as they are villains, and his union officials are simply normal men with a normal lust for power and money, not Working Class Heroes or Red Revolutionaries. In fact, his revolutionaries are normal men with normal lusts. The Libyans in *The Mordida Man* (1981) finally accept revenge when they cannot obtain the return of a kidnapped terrorist, and, in *Out on the Rim*, the aging Filipino rebel Alejandro Espiritu becomes so power-mad that he executes his own nephew without remorse, allowing Wu and Durant to carry out their mission to remove him (and keep a large portion of the money they were supposed to have used to bribe him).

Thomas has a crime-reporter's eye for concrete details such as the exact age of a building (and often its history), the number of steps in a flight of stairs, and the number of an airline flight and the precise number of minutes it takes off late. This use of detail creates a sense of reality so palpable that the reader can almost taste the dirt on the cement. Thomas's style, directly descended from the colorful speech of the oral tradition, is so wry and amusing that he makes the reader regret the homogenization of American English by television announcers and bureaucratic memorandum writers. His dialogue is realistic, and conversation between male friends, such as McCorkle and Padillo or Wu and Durant, is as elliptical as the exchange of a couple who have been married for fifty years.

Thomas takes his plots from the front pages of the daily papers, using his experience to invent an inside story that is more treacherous than reality. In *Yellow-Dog Contract* (1976), political campaign manager Harvey Longmore comes out of retirement to investigate the disappearance of a nationally known union leader. *The Porkchoppers* (1972) investigates a crooked, no-holds-barred union election. In *The Mordida Man*, the president's brother, a slick political manager, has been kidnapped by the Libyans. In *Out on the Rim*, Wu and Durant become entangled in the guerrilla war in the Philippines; with an immediacy unmatched by the experts who write for the op-ed pages, Thomas depicts the violence and corruption which plague that former American colony.

When Thomas writes as Oliver Bleeck, his voice is more serious, and the Philip St. Ives stories are closer to classical mysteries, but the characters are as closely observed and as colorful as they are in the Ross Thomas books. The crime situations allow him to include overweight, overworked, and underpaid cops, whose lives are as disorderly as they are human, and St. Ives is more nearly a hard-boiled, if amateur, detective, whose own life in a seedy New York residence hotel is not any more orderly than anybody else's. He is as competent and as tricky as Thomas's other heroes, but his soul is darker than the souls of the enthralling manipulators who find real joy–and profit–in the tawdry world around them.

In his books, Ross Thomas has invented a complex world of greed, lust, and chicanery where inside knowledge and money are the only security, a world of betrayal where the quick and flexible may, for a while, stay alive, find a good woman, and come out a bit ahead. And maybe even get in a few licks for the good guys in the process.

## Principal mystery and detective fiction

SERIES: McCorkle and Padillo: *The Cold War Swap*, 1966 (also as *Spy in the Vodka*); *Cast a Yellow Shadow*, 1967; *The Backup Men*, 1971; *Twilight at Mac's Place*, 1990. Philip St. Ives: *The Brass Go-Between*, 1969; *Protocol for a Kidnapping*, 1971; *The Procane Chronicle*, 1971 (also as *The Thief Who Painted Sunlight* and *St. Ives*); *The Highbinders*, 1974; *No Questions Asked*, 1976. Artie Wu and Quincy Durant: *Chinaman's Chance*, 1978; *Out on the Rim*, 1987; *Voodoo, Ltd.*, 1992.

OTHER NOVELS: *The Seersucker Whipsaw*, 1967; *The Singapore Wink*, 1969; *The Fools in Town Are on Our Side*, 1970; *The Porkchoppers*, 1972; *If You Can't Be Good*, 1973; *The Money Harvest*, 1975; *Yellow-Dog Contract*, 1976; *The Eighth Dwarf*, 1979; *The Mordida Man*, 1981; *Missionary Stew*, 1983; *Briarpatch*, 1984; *The Fourth Durango*, 1989; *Spies, Thumbsuckers, Etc.*, 1989; *Ah, Treachery*, 1994.

## Other major works

SCREENPLAY: *Hammett*, 1983 (with Dennis O'Flaherty and Thomas Pope).
NONFICTION: *Warriors for the Poor: The Story of VISTA*, 1969 (with William H. Crook); *Cop World: Inside an American Police Force*, 1985.

## Bibliography

Donovan, Mark. "With Twenty-first Thriller, Writer Ross Thomas Just Might Hit It Big–Not That He Hasn't Been Trying." *People Weekly* 28 (November 30, 1987): 109.

Grimes, William. "Ross Thomas, 69, An Author of Stylish Political Thrillers." *The New York Times*, December 19, 1995, p. B14.

Hiss, Tony. "Remembering Ross Thomas." *The Atlantic Monthly* 278, no. 5 (November, 1996): 117.

Leggett, John. *Ross and Tom: Two American Tragedies.* Rev. ed. New York, Simon and Schuster, 2000.
Lehman, David. "Thrillers." *Newsweek* 105 (April 22, 1985): 58.
*The New York Times.* Review of *Briarpatch,* by Ross Thomas. March 3, 1985, p. 35.
*Time.* Review of *Out on the Rim,* by Ross Thomas. 130 (September 28, 1987): 67.

*Marilynn M. Larew*
*Updated by Fiona Kelleghan*

# Jim Thompson

**Born:** Anadarko, Oklahoma Territory; 1906
**Died:** Hollywood, California; April 7, 1977

**Types of plot** • Inverted • hard-boiled • psychological

**Contribution** • Jim Thompson brought a level of psychological realism to crime novels seldom achieved by writers in that or any other genre. He explored the criminal mind in chilling and powerful first-person narrations, presenting the ordinary world through the eyes of brutal and brutalized killers to whom commonplace morality and rules of behavior do not apply. Thompson's killers tell their stories and describe their savage behavior without entirely losing the reader's sympathy and understanding, yet Thompson did not justify or excuse his criminals because of their warped environments, nor did he maintain the reader's sympathy by providing his killers with unusually despicable victims. He achieved something much more difficult: He convincingly presents a world that causes readers to suspend their ordinary moral judgments as too simplistic and abstract to apply to the margins of society inhabited by his characters.

**Biography** • Jim Thompson's childhood was quite unconventional, according to his wife, Alberta. He grew up in Oklahoma, Texas, and Nebraska, where his brilliant and charismatic but erratic father first triumphed and then hit the bottom in one career after another, finally going bankrupt in oil after having made millions. Jim Thompson shared his father's brilliance and his inability to establish order in his life. While still in high school, he began his long struggle with alcohol, despairing at the meaninglessness of life and generating a self-destructive rage at the stupidity and parochialism of society around him.

He attended the University of Nebraska for a few years and married Alberta there in 1931. To feed his wife and three children during the Great Depression, he worked in hotels, oil fields, collection agencies, and vegetable fields. He had had his first story published at age fifteen and then earned extra money by writing true crime stories, character sketches, and vignettes of his experiences with the down-and-out people around him. His appointment in the late 1930's as director of the Oklahoma Writers Project inspired him to break into the larger publishing world. He wrote two excellent novels, *Now and on Earth* (1942) and *Heed the Thunder* (1946), but despite praise from critics neither book sold. Thompson worked on several major newspapers and briefly served as editor-in-chief of *Saga* magazine.

In 1949 he wrote his first mystery, *Nothing More than Murder*. It was followed by a string of mysteries, written rapidly and in streaks: Twelve books appeared between 1952 and 1954.

Hindered by alcoholism and never financially secure, Thompson always tapped the writing markets available to him. In the 1950's he collaborated on two screenplays for films directed by Stanley Kubrick, *The Killing* (1956) and *Paths of Glory* (1957), and wrote for several television series. He lived for his writing, Alberta said, and after strokes ended that part of his life, he deliberately starved himself to death, by her account. At the time of his death—April 7, 1977—none of his books was in print in the United States.

Yet Thompson was not forgotten. Several films were made from his books: *The Killer Inside Me* (1952) in 1976, *The Getaway* (1959) in 1972, *Série Noire* in 1979 (based on the novel *A Hell of a Woman*, 1954), and *Coup de Torchon* in 1981 (based on the novel *Pop. 1280*, 1964). In the 1980's, publishers began reprinting Thompson's works. They found a market among those who remembered his paperback originals and among members of a new generation who responded to his nihilistic vision of life. Ten years after Thompson's death, most of his novels were back in print.

**Analysis** • Diversity of themes and settings characterizes Jim Thompson's paperback originals. He wrote fictionalized autobiography, explored the unstable, high-pressure world of confidence rackets, and used the hard-boiled crime style to write black comedy, including a comic masterpiece, *Pop. 1280*.

Thompson's crime novels also take up diverse social themes. As John Steinbeck described the plight of Okies forced off their land and surviving through hard work and strength of character, the Oklahoma-born Thompson portrayed another class of Southwestern people, often long detached from the land, living by wits and luck on the margins of society. In terse paragraphs he describes the social and economic impact of soil erosion, the betrayal of the people by railroad corruption, the shenanigans of corrupt politicians, and the human costs of the communist witch-hunt of the 1950's. He explores the constricted lives of sharecroppers and the plight of Indians (*Cropper's Cabin*, 1952), the disease of alcoholism (*The Alcoholics*, 1953), and the source and nature of black rage (*Nothing but a Man*, 1970; *Child of Rage*, 1972).

Thompson's reputation and rediscovery rests above all on his unparalleled ability to portray a killer's mind, often in powerful first-person narrations by a disintegrating criminal personality. Deputy Sheriff Lou Ford, who narrates *The Killer Inside Me*, stands out from the people around him only because he is friendlier and nicer. His quiet, smiling exterior masks inner rage. "I've loafed around the streets sometimes, leaned against a store front with my hat pushed back and one boot hooked back around the other," he says.

> Hell, you've probably seen me if you've ever been out this way—I've stood like that, looking nice and friendly and stupid, like I wouldn't piss if my pants were on fire. And all the time I'm laughing myself sick inside. Just watching the people.

Ford, a brilliant young man hiding behind a mask of bland, cliché-spouting stupidity, knows that he is sick. He gently explains to a young delinquent whom he has befriended and is preparing to kill that straight society, while tolerating terrible social injustices, has no place for people like the young man, who commit minor transgressions:

> They don't like you guys, and they crack down on you. And the way it looks to me they're going to be cracking down harder and harder as time goes on. You ask me why I stick around, knowing the score, and it's hard to explain. I guess I kind of got a foot on both fences, Johnnie. I planted 'em there early and now they've taken root, and I can't move either way and I can't jump. All I can do is wait until I split. Right down the middle. That's all I can do. . . .

Ford describes the widening split within him. Deputy Sheriff Ford does not carry a gun: "People are people, even when they're a little misguided," he says. "You don't hurt them, they won't hurt you. They'll listen to reason." Reason vanishes, however, when he goes to the home of Joyce Lakeland, a pretty young woman engaged in minor prostitution. He tells her to keep her hustling low-key or leave town; she hits him; he beats her unconscious but, once awake, she responds to him sexually, pulling him into a sadomasochistic relationship. As Ford is drawn to her again and again, he feels "the sickness" returning. He had been sexually abused as a child and had himself molested young girls, for which his brother had been blamed and imprisoned. Now as the sickness returns he struggles to hold himself together. "I knew she was making me worse; I knew that if I didn't stop soon I'd never to able to. I'd wind up in a cage or the electric chair." He finally (apparently) beats Joyce to death, a crime that sets off a chain of events forcing him to kill person after person, including his longtime sweetheart. The sickness gains increasing control. A drifter threatens to expose him: "I grinned, feeling a little sorry for him. It was funny the way these people kept asking for it. . . . Why'd they all have to come to me to get killed? Why couldn't they kill themselves?" In the end, he deliberately walks into a trap and brings his story to a powerful, fiery climax:

> Yeah, I reckon that's all unless our kind gets another chance in the Next Place. Our kind. Us people.
> All of us that started the game with a crooked cue, that wanted so much and got so little, that meant so good and did so bad.

Thompson explored the criminal mind in other books. In *Pop. 1280*, Nick Corey, high sheriff of a county in a Southern state, tells his story. The sheriff's job allows him to pursue his favorite activities: eating, sleeping, and bedding women. The voters ask little from him except that he entertain them with his bland ignorance. They enjoy making fun of him, thinking that he is too stupid to understand. As an election approaches, however, some voters want action. Nick begins to clean things up in his own way, first offhandedly shooting a couple of pimps who were making a nuisance of themselves, then engaging in a string of murders to hide his crime. In the end, Nick decides that he is probably Christ, sent by God to "promote" sinners to Glory by killing them.

The disturbing element in Thompson's work comes partly because it rings

true; it explains the newspaper stories of bland, quiet people who turn into serial killers. Thompson's world is frightening also because he has a peculiar
ability to describe the mind of brutal killers while retaining the reader's sympathy for them. They are victims themselves, sometimes brutalized as children, sometimes racked by alcoholism and poverty, sometimes, as in the case
of Lou Ford, losing a desperate struggle to hold onto mental stability. All live
in a world that has given little but suffering to them or to their victims.

There is no moral center in the world Thompson presents. Concepts of
right and wrong are not applicable; platitudes about crime not paying are
meaningless. The moral structure that adequately guides most people through
life seems shallow and remote in Thompson's world; simple problems of surface morality are not what his characters confront. Psychiatrists cannot understand people such as him, Lou Ford says:

> We might have the disease, the condition; or we might just be cold-blooded and
> smart as hell; or we might be innocent of what we're supposed to have done. We
> might be any one of those three things, because the symptoms we show would fit
> any one of the three.

Insanity, guilt, and innocence dissolve into the same behavior.

Thompson does not relieve the reader's fear by bringing in detectives to
tidy matters up and reestablish moral norms. Nor does he use love or friendship to lighten the world his characters inhabit. The love that William "Kid"
Collins feels for Fay Anderson in *After Dark, My Sweet* (1955) requires him, a
mentally unstable former boxer, deliberately to provoke Fay into killing him;
only in that way can he save her. In *The Getaway*, Carter "Doc" McCoy and
Carol McCoy, who love each other and are married, commit robbery and
murder and make a run across the United States for the Mexican border.
Their love is eroded by the knowledge that if extreme conditions have pushed
them into killing once, they can kill again, even each other. At the end, figuratively, perhaps literally, in Hell, each is trying to kill the other in order to
avoid being killed.

The world sketched by Thompson is bleak, marked by random violence
and undeserved suffering. Life reminds Kid Collins of a concrete pasture:
"You keep going and going, and it's always the same everywhere. Wherever
you've been, wherever you go, everywhere you look. Just grayness and hard-
ness, as far as you can see." Perhaps, Lou Ford hopes, there will be something
better in the Next Place, but there seems little promise of that. God is not
dead, says the young black man, Allen Smith, in *Child of Rage*:

> Madmen never die. . . . He is still in business on the same old corner. I have seen
> him there myself, showering riches on rascals, and tendering dung and piss to wid-
> ows and orphans and stealing pennies from blind men. . . . The Lord . . . is patently as
> nutty as a goddamned bedbug.

The power of Thompson's writing, whether he is portraying the bleak
world of a disintegrating personality or the black comedy of a con man pursu-

ing his swindle, comes from his simple, direct narration. Even in his third-person stories, he keeps the focus so tightly bound to the central character's viewpoint that the external world is warped into a personal vision. Thompson experimented with shifting viewpoints in some novels. In *The Criminal* (1953) and *The Kill-Off* (1957), he uses multiple first-person narrators. In *A Hell of a Woman*, multiple narrative comes from different parts of Frank "Dolly" Dillon's disintegrating personality, with two endings of the novel interchanging line by line, describing Dolly's castration in one and his death by suicide in another.

Thompson wrote rapidly, polishing page by page as he wrote, and, recalls his publisher Arnold Hano, he found it difficult to rewrite. Sometimes he was so drained by the end of a book that he tacked on a hasty conclusion simply to get it over with. If some endings are weak, others are extraordinarily strong: Mafia hit man Charles "Little" Bigger longing for death as his lover hacks him to pieces (*Savage Night*, 1953); the disintegration of Dolly Dillon's life in drugs, alcohol, and insanity; the violent and sad end of Lou Ford, who seeks death to end his sickness; the hell in which Doc and Carol McCoy find themselves; the melancholy of a brooding Nick Corey, who, having come to view himself as Jesus Christ carrying out God's will by killing sinners, confesses, in the last line, "I don't no more know what to do than if I was just another lousy human being!"

## Principal mystery and detective fiction

NOVELS: *Nothing More than Murder*, 1949; *The Killer Inside Me*, 1952; *Cropper's Cabin*, 1952; *The Alcoholics*, 1953; *Bad Boy*, 1953; *The Criminal*, 1953; *Recoil*, 1953; *Savage Night*, 1953; *A Swell-Looking Babe*, 1954; *The Golden Gizmo*, 1954; *A Hell of a Woman*, 1954; *The Nothing Man*, 1954; *Roughneck*, 1954; *After Dark, My Sweet*, 1955; *The Kill-Off*, 1957; *Wild Town*, 1957; *The Getaway*, 1959; *The Transgressors*, 1961; *The Grifters*, 1963; *Pop. 1280*, 1964; *Texas by the Tail*, 1965; *Ironside*, 1967; *South of Heaven*, 1967; *The Undefeated*, 1969; *Nothing but a Man*, 1970; *Child of Rage*, 1972; *King Blood*, 1973; *The Ripoff*, 1985; *Fireworks: The Lost Writings of Jim Thompson*, 1988.

## Other major works

NOVELS: *Now and on Earth*, 1942; *Heed the Thunder*, 1946.

SCREENPLAYS: *The Killing*, 1956 (with Stanley Kubrick); *Paths of Glory*, 1957 (with Kubrick and Calder Willingham).

## Bibliography

Brewer, Gay. *Laughing Like Hell: The Harrowing Satires of Jim Thompson*. San Bernardino, Calif.: Borgo Press, 1996.

Cassill, R. V. "*The Killer Inside Me*: Fear, Purgation, and the Sophoclean Light." In *Tough Guy Writers of the Thirties*, edited by David Madden. Carbondale: Southern Illinois University Press, 1968.

Collins, Max Allan. *Jim Thompson: The Killers Inside Him*. Cedar Rapids, Iowa: Fedora Press, 1983.

McCauley, Michael J. *Jim Thompson: Sleep with the Devil.* New York: Mysterious Press, 1991.

Madigan, Mark J. "'As True and Direct as a Birth or Death Certificate': Richard Wright on Jim Thompson's *Now and On Earth.*" *Studies in American Fiction* 22, no.1 (Spring, 1994): 105.

O'Brien, Geoffrey. "Jim Thompson, Dimestore Dostoevsky." In *Cropper's Cabin.* Berkeley, Calif.: Great Arts Books, 1952.

Polito, Robert. *Savage Art: A Biography of Jim Thompson.* New York: Alfred A. Knopf, 1995.

_____, and Michael McCauley. "Jim Thompson: Lost Writer." In *Fireworks: The Lost Writings of Jim Thompson.* New York: Donald I. Fine, 1988.

Sallis, James. *Difficult Lives: Jim Thompson, David Goodis, Chester Himes.* Brooklyn, N.Y.: Gryphon Books, 1993.

Stansberry, Domenic. *Manifesto for the Dead.* Sag Harbor, N.Y.: Permanent Press, 2000.

Thomson, David. "The Whole Hell Catalog: Reconsideration, Jim Thompson." *The New Republic* 192 (April 15, 1985): 37-41.

*William E. Pemberton*

# Lawrence Treat

**Born:** New York, New York; December 21, 1903
**Died:** Oak Bluffs, Massachusetts; January 7, 1998

**Also wrote as** • Lawrence A. Goldstone

**Types of plot** • Private investigator • police procedural

**Principal series** • Carl Wayward, 1940-1943 • Mitch Taylor/Jub Freeman/ Bill Decker, 1945-1960.

**Principal series characters** • CARL WAYWARD, a psychology professor specializing in criminology, becomes involved in murder cases as a consultant but quickly takes charge. He is in his thirties, and he is married during the course of the series. An intellectual, he is motivated by the challenge of matching wits with criminals and utilizing his expertise.

• MITCH TAYLOR is a typical big-city cop, mainly interested in avoiding trouble, bucking for promotion, and living simply with his wife and children. He is proud of his uniform and has a sense of duty but is not above minor graft and avoiding work whenever possible.

• JUB FREEMAN, who sometimes teams up with Taylor, is a "new type" cop whose passion is scientific detection. He is married during the course of the series. In his forays into the field to gather evidence, he displays a certain gaucheness in dealing with the public.

• LIEUTENANT BILL DECKER, in charge of the Homicide Division, knows how to handle cops–with a pat on the back and a kick in the pants. He lets his men break rules and cut corners when necessary. Decker was the prototype of hundreds of tough-talking, hard-driving fictional successors.

**Contribution** • Lawrence Treat is generally regarded as the father of the police procedural, that subgenre of detective fiction that emphasizes the realistic solution of mysteries through routine police methods, including dogged interrogations, stakeouts, tailings, and heavy utilization of the technology of the police laboratory. Treat established some of the conventions of the police procedural that have appeared almost unfailingly in novels in this category ever since. Among them is the convention of the cop who is unable to maintain a normal family life because his work requires irregular hours and alienates him from everyone except other cops. Another convention is the theme of rivalry and tension within the law enforcement agency, caused by many different personalities trying to win glory and avoid blame. Finally, there is the convention of the policeman being a hated outsider, lied to, ridiculed, maligned, and occasionally made the target of attempted seduction. These conventions have become familiar not only in police procedural novels but also in motion pictures about policemen and in such popular television series as *Dragnet* and *Hill Street Blues.*

**Biography** • Lawrence Treat was born Lawrence Arthur Goldstone on December 21, 1903, in New York City (he changed his name legally in 1940). He had an excellent education, obtaining a B.A. from Dartmouth College in 1924 and a law degree from Columbia University in 1927.

Treat practiced law for only a short time. For many years he had wanted to write, and he was writing poetry while still in law school. He had practiced law for only three months when his firm broke up in 1928, and the partners gave him ten weeks' salary (three hundred dollars). He determined to devote his time to writing. He went to Paris, wrote poetry and worked at odd jobs, and roomed with an old camp counselor and his wife in Brittany. Treat soon came to realize that even if he were a much better poet, he would still be unable to make a living at that craft. A mystery magazine he picked up in a Paris bookstore changed his career. Treat's earliest contributions to mystery fiction were picture puzzles, some of which were collected in *Bringing Sherlock Home* (1930).

After returning in the United States, he married Margery Dallet in June, 1930. During the 1930's, a period of frustration and indecision, he began writing for pulp mystery magazines (he wrote about three hundred short stories and twenty novels during his lifetime). His marriage to Margery ended in divorce in 1939. During a period of frustration and indecision, he discovered the world of detective magazines and reasoned that his legal background and literary interests made him well qualified to succeed in that field. He learned his trade by writing one story per day for a solid month.

Treat's early detective novels featuring the highly intellectual and academically oriented Carl Wayward were well-written and received favorable reviews. Yet they were stuck in the conventional mold of the British or classic mystery and did not represent a significant contribution to the genre. During the latter years of World War II, he met two laboratory research people who stimulated him to take a fresh approach. He also took a seminar in police supervisory work and became acquainted with many working policemen. This experience led to his publication in 1945 of *V as in Victim*, the first police procedural ever written.

Treat has published hundreds of short stories in such magazines as *Mike Shayne Mystery Magazine, Ellery Queen's Mystery Magazine,* and *Alfred Hitchcock's Mystery Magazine.* While living in Yorktown Heights, New York, he taught mystery writing at Columbia University, New York University, and elsewhere. He married Rose Ehrenfreund in 1943; they moved to Martha's Vineyard in 1972.

He received two Edgar Allan Poe Awards (for "H as in Homicide," 1964, and *The Mystery Writer's Handbook,* 1976) from the Mystery Writers of America, of which he was both a founder and a president.

**Analysis** • Lawrence Treat received a much better education than the typical mystery writer, and the positive and negative effects of it are evident in his writings. His first mystery novels feature Carl Wayward, a college professor with marked tendencies toward social and intellectual snobbishness. Wayward is not exactly an amateur sleuth, the favored protagonist of the classic school of mystery fiction; he specializes in criminology, which gets him involved in cases as a consultant, not unlike the great Sherlock Holmes. Yet Wayward seems to be perpetually on sabbatical, and his supposed knowledge of criminology rarely surfaces during his investigations. He is indistinguishable from the typical amateur sleuth, who takes up investigations out of idle curiosity or sympathy for someone involved and whose immensely superior intellect enables him to make fools of the bumbling police.

*H as in Hangman* (1942) is probably the best and most characteristic of the four Carl Wayward novels. It is set in Chautauqua, the famous resort founded in the nineteenth century to bring enlightenment to the masses. Wayward is there to lecture on criminal psychology; his professional contempt for this system of popular adult education is such, however, that it is difficult for the reader to understand why he has chosen to participate at all. Most of the principal characters are American equivalents of the upper- and upper-middle-class types found in typical British mysteries of the classic school, such as those of Agatha Christie. They lounge on porches sipping tea and lemonade, discussing highbrow subjects or gossiping rather viciously about absent acquaintances. The few who are not being supported by relatives or inherited property are vaguely involved in "stocks and bonds" or some other occupation which pays well without demanding much of their attention. Wayward himself is able to spend most of his time leaning against something with his left hand in the side pocket of his tweed jacket. It is a closed environment, the *sine qua non* of the classic school, which conveniently limits the number of suspects to a manageable handful of known and socially acceptable individuals when the first murder is committed.

The victim, an elderly music professor who has been a leader in the Chautauqua movement for decades, is found hanged in the bell tower shortly after he or his murderer has alerted the whole community that something dastardly was afoot by playing the bells at an ungodly hour. The carillon performer did not choose anything vulgar such as "Pop Goes the Weasel" but played a portion of "Ase's Death" from Edvard Grieg's *Peer Gynt Suite* (1867). Instead of a rope, the dead man was hanged with a cello string. Such "smart aleck kills," which Raymond Chandler reviled, are characteristic of the classic school of detective fiction. The leisure-class characters, the circumscribed setting in which the soon-to-be suspects are almost formally introduced, the tidbits of culture and arcane information, the gothic overtones of the modus operandi, and the incompetent sheriff who begs Wayward for help are some of the features that mark the Wayward novels as derivative ventures.

Treat's Wayward novels show intelligence and literary talent. He had started with aspirations to write poetry and quality mainstream novels and,

like Ross Macdonald in later years, had had to step down in class for pragmatic reasons. Critics recognized the quality of his writing and praised his
Wayward novels. Nevertheless, he dropped his intellectual hero unceremoni-
ously in 1943; two years later, he produced a mystery novel which not only
represented a quantum leap forward in his writing career but also became a
landmark in the genre.

*V as in Victim*, published in 1945, is regarded as the first police procedural.
It is such a dramatic departure from the Wayward novels that it seems not to
have been written by the same person. Set in the heart of Manhattan, it con-
veys a feeling not unlike that of the *noir* literature and films which had been
flourishing during the war years. As in many of the novels by Cornell
Woolrich, the people in *V as in Victim* seem dwarfed and intimidated by their
towering, dehumanized environment. Treat's language, too, departed radi-
cally from the gracefully turned phrases in the Wayward books: His police
procedurals sound American rather than Anglophilic. A few elitist characters
remain, but now they seem to be living on borrowed time. They have discovered adultery and dry martinis.

It is interesting to speculate on what factors could have caused such a remarkable change in the whole approach of a writer. Treat has not discussed
this subject in print, but clues can be garnered from his books, facts of his personal life, and the period during which he matured as a writer. He went
through a divorce. Then there was the war. He was not personally involved,
but there are many indications in his books, notably in *H as in Hunted* (1946),
that as a sensitive, artistic person he was strongly affected by reports of the
atrocities that were perpetrated in Europe and Asia during those fateful years.
Treat was undoubtedly influenced by the *Black Mask* school of writers, including Dashiell Hammett. Motion pictures must have been another influence:
They became more proletarian and less elitist during the war years and have
remained so ever since. There was the beginning of the white flight from the
big cities which would undermine the tax base and result in physical and
moral deterioration. There was the influx of minorities, all suspicious, hostile,
and alienated. Big cities in the United States were becoming sinister places.
All these undercurrents of change can be felt in *V as in Victim*, published in
that historic year of 1945, when Germany surrendered and the atom bombs
were dropped on Japan.

One of the positive effects of Treat's extensive formal education was his intellectual discipline. When he decided to write a realistic novel about working
policemen, he went about it with a thoroughness worthy of another lawyer-
mystery writer, Erle Stanley Gardner. Treat's exposure to real hard-nosed
cops in the precinct station, in the laboratories, in the field, and after hours in
the taprooms undoubtedly had a strong influence on his writing. He also did
much academic-type research. In his preface to *The Mystery Writer's Handbook*
(1976), he reveals his wide knowledge of the literature covering various aspects of the crime field, including law, forensic medicine, ballistics, and fin-
gerprinting. Carl Wayward may have been a criminologist in name, but his

creator actually became one. Since *V as in Victim* was to have such an important influence, it was fortunate for the development of this subgenre that Treat was a learned and conscientious craftsman.

There was an inherent contradiction within the police procedural from its very beginnings. Treat wanted to create realistic cops going about their work in a realistic manner, but at the same time he wanted to retain the traditional element of mystery—that is, the process of discovering who among a limited cast of clearly established characters committed a particular crime. In reality, many crimes are never solved or even investigated but merely documented; the records are then held in open files until someone informs or confesses. Policemen do not have the luxury of working on only one case at a time, like the private eye or amateur sleuth. They are often yanked off one case and assigned to another because there are too many murderers and not enough detectives. In the process of tailing a suspect or questioning informants, a policeman may come upon a different crime which will lead him off on a tangent. Furthermore, there is no such thing as a limited cast of interrelated suspects in a city of millions of strangers. Any attempt to impose artificial boundaries around an urban crime would only lead to absurdity.

Treat recognized these problems and tried various means to get around them without giving up the traditional mystery. In *H as in Hunted*, for example, his focal character is a man who was imprisoned and tortured by the Nazis and has come back to New York to confront the coward who betrayed him. Jub Freeman becomes involved because he is a boyhood friend of the protagonist, but by focusing on a civilian, Treat is able to limit his story to a single mystery and a single cast of suspects. Unfortunately, this approach weakens the book as a police procedural and makes it more like a Cornell Woolrich-type novel of private vengeance. In *Lady, Drop Dead* (1960), the feckless Mitch Taylor is involved in the story, but the protagonist is a private detective, which makes this police procedural veer dangerously close to being a private-eye novel reminiscent of Raymond Chandler.

Eventually, Treat moved his three sustaining characters, Taylor, Freeman, and Decker, out of New York entirely, evidently hoping that the traditional mystery element in his plots would seem less incongruous in a smaller city. Yet though you can take a writer out of New York, you cannot always take New York out of a writer. Treat's unidentified city seems like an older and less hectic New York but is still too big and impersonal to provide a comfortable home for the apparatus of the traditional British mystery yarn. *Lady, Drop Dead*, the last of the Taylor/Freeman/Decker series, still reads like a set piece. Its limited cast of suspects is assembled in a classic finale so that the real murderer—who is the one the reader most suspected simply because he is the one who seemed least likely—can break down and unburden his conscience with a detailed confession.

The police procedural has evolved and proliferated since *Lady, Drop Dead* was published in 1960, but Treat did not participate in its development. His formal education may have saddled him with too much esteem for tradition and thus been an inhibiting factor. His police procedurals, like his Carl Wayward novels, seem to belong to an older, safer, much slower-moving world, but he deserves great credit for having originated this fascinating form of mystery fiction.

### Principal mystery and detective fiction

SERIES: Mitch Taylor/Jub Freeman/Bill Decker: *V as in Victim*, 1945; *H as in Hunted*, 1946; *Q as in Quicksand*, 1947 (also as *Step into Quicksand*); *T as in Trapped*, 1947; *F as in Flight*, 1948; *Over the Edge*, 1948; *Big Shot*, 1951; *Weep for a Wanton*, 1956; Lady, *Drop Dead*, 1960. Carl Wayward: *B as in Banshee*, 1940 (also as *Wail for the Corpses*); *D as in Dead*, 1941; *H as in Hangman*, 1942; *O as in Omen*, 1943.

OTHER NOVELS: *Run Far, Run Fast*, 1937; *The Leather Man*, 1944; *Trial and Terror*, 1949; *Venus Unarmed*, 1961.

OTHER SHORT FICTION: *P as in Police*, 1970.

### Other major works

NONFICTION: *Bringing Sherlock Home*, 1930; *Crime and Puzzlement: 24 Solve-Them-Yourself Picture Mysteries*, 1981 (with Leslie Cabarga, 1981); *Crime and Puzzlement 2: More Solve-Them-Yourself Picture Mysteries*, 1982 (with Kathleen Borowik); *The Clue Armchair Detective: Can You Solve the Mysteries of Tudor Close?*, 1983 (with George Hardie; also as *The Cluedo Armchair Detective*); *Crime and Puzzlement 3: 24 Solve-Them-Yourself Picture Mysteries*, 1988 (with Paul Karasik); *Crimes to Unravel*, 1988; *Crime and Puzzlement, My Cousin Phoebe: 24 Solve-Them-Yourself Picture Mysteries*, 1991 (with Dean Bornstein); *Crime and Puzzlement 5, On Martha's Vineyard, Mostly: 24 Solve-Them-Yourself Picture Mysteries*, 1993 (with Paul Karasik).

CHILDREN'S LITERATURE: *You're the Detective!*, 1983.

EDITED TEXTS: *Murder in Mind: An Anthology of Mystery Stories by the Mystery Writers of America*, 1967; *The Mystery Writer's Handbook*, 1976 (with Herbert Brean); *A Special Kind of Crime*, 1982.

### Bibliography

Breen, Jon L. "The Police Procedural." In *Mystery and Suspense Writers: The Literature of Crime, Detection, and Espionage*, edited by Robin W. Winks and Maureen Corrigan. New York: Charles Scribner's Sons, 1998.

Dove, George N. *The Police Procedural.* Bowling Green, Ohio: Bowling Green State University Popular Press, 1982.

"Lawrence Treat, 94, Prolific Mystery Writer." *The New York Times,* January 16, 1998, p. B11

*The New Yorker.* Review of *Trial and Terror*, by Lawrence Treat. 25 (August 20, 1949): 120.

"Treat, Lawrence." In *St. James Guide to Crime and Mystery Writers*, edited by Jay P. Pederson and Taryn Benbow-Pfalzgraf. 4th ed. Detroit: St. James Press, 1996.

Washer, Robert. Review of *P as in Police* in *The Queen Canon Bibliophile*, by Lawrence Treat. 3 (April, 1971): 18.

*Bill Delaney*
*Updated by Fiona Kelleghan*

# S. S. Van Dine

## Willard Huntington Wright

**Born:** Charlottesville, Virginia; October 15, 1888
**Died:** New York, New York; April 11, 1939

**Type of plot** • Master sleuth

**Principal series** • Philo Vance, 1926-1939.

**Principal series characters** • PHILO VANCE, a debonair, aristocratic, brilliant amateur sleuth. A dilettante whose one passion is art, he is also well versed in psychology, skilled at sports and games, and the author of studies on polo, hieroglyphics, physics, criminology, Florentine and Chinese art, Greek drama, and Norwegian fishing. A handsome bachelor, he is thirty-two years old at the beginning of the series. In personality he is reserved, cynical, and whimsical.

• S. S. VAN DINE, a Harvard classmate, attorney, manager of financial and personal affairs, and friend and constant companion of Philo Vance. Like Sherlock Holmes's friend Dr. Watson, Van Dine, self-described as "a commonplace fellow, possessed of a conservative and rather conventional mind," serves as a foil to the brilliant and fascinating Vance, and as narrator of his murder cases.

• JOHN F. X. MARKHAM, District Attorney of New York, is a longtime friend of Vance, upon whom he depends for help in solving difficult cases. His personality is in contrast to Vance's; he is "sternly aggressive, brusque, forthright, and almost ponderously serious." An "indefatigable worker" and "utterly incorruptible," he holds Vance's respect.

• ERNEST HEATH, sergeant of the Homicide Bureau, is the man officially in charge of Vance's cases. At first he resents Vance's participation, and often he is irritated by his mannerisms, but he comes to respect and admire his abilities. Heath is unimaginative but diligent.

**Contribution** • S. S. Van Dine is a significant figure in the history of detective fiction, both as a theorist and as a practitioner of the genre. As a theorist, he articulated a strict code of "fairness" in the plotting of the detective novel and enunciated important ideas about the nature of the genre's appeal. *The Benson Murder Case* (1926) and *The Canary Murder Case* (1927) attracted a new audience for detective fiction in the United States, bringing it to the attention and serious consideration of intellectual and sophisticated readers and initiating what has come to be known as the Golden Age of American detective fiction. In the 1920's and 1930's, Van Dine's Philo Vance novels were the most widely read detective stories in the United States. They inspired thirty-one motion pictures, filmed between 1929 and 1947, and a popular weekly radio series, *Philo Vance*, during the 1940's.

**Biography** • S. S. Van Dine was born Willard Huntington Wright on October 15, 1888, in Charlottesville, Virginia, the son of Archibald Davenport Wright and Annie Van Vranken Wright. (Wright adopted his pen name, based on Van Dyne—an old family name—and the abbreviation of "steamship," when he turned to writing detective fiction.) Van Dine attended St. Vincent College, Pomona College, and Harvard University and also studied art in Munich and Paris. In 1907, he became a literary and art critic for the *Los Angeles Times*. During his distinguished career in this field, Van Dine published books on art, literature, philosophy, and culture. Also in 1907, he married Katharine Belle Boynton; they had one daughter and were divorced in 1930. He later married Eleanor Pulapaugh.

From 1912 to 1914, Van Dine edited *The Smart Set*, a sophisticated New York literary magazine, to which he attracted important new authors. He continued his career as critic and journalist until 1923, when a demanding work schedule caused his health to deteriorate. Confined to bed with a heart ailment for more than two years and forbidden by his physician to do any serious work, he spent his convalescence assembling and analyzing a two-thousand-volume collection of detective fiction and criminology. These activities inspired him to write a detective novel of his own. As S. S. Van Dine, he submitted to a publisher thirty thousand words of synopsized plans for three novels. The expanded draft of the first plan appeared in 1926 as *The Benson Murder Case*.

This novel introduces Philo Vance, the hero of the most popular American detective series in its day. Van Dine also wrote several short detective films for Warner Bros. from 1931 to 1932 (their titles and exact dates are not known).

The twelve Philo Vance novels brought wealth to their heretofore debt-ridden author, enabling him to cultivate a luxurious life-style comparable to that of his fictional hero. Van Dine lived in a penthouse, delighted in witty and erudite conversation, fine cuisine, costly wines, and elegant clothes, and spent his very large income rapidly; he left an estate of only thirteen thousand dollars when he died on April 11, 1939.

**Analysis** • The development of S. S. Van Dine's theory and the composition of his early detective novels occurred at the same time—during his two-year convalescence beginning in 1923. Writing under his real name, Van Dine articulated his theory of detective fiction in a detailed historical introduction to his anthology *The Great Detective Stories: A Chronological Anthology* (1927). Van Dine's theory underlies "Twenty Rules for Writing Detective Stories" (1928), his acerbically witty credo, which, as he affirmed, was "based partly on the practice of all the great writers of detective stories, and partly on the promptings of the honest author's inner conscience." Van Dine's theory is important in its own right as well as in the context of detective writers' concerns about the integrity of the genre during this period. His theory is also borne out to a large degree in the Philo Vance novels, although significant departures from it may be observed.

In his 1927 introduction, Van Dine begins by distinguishing detective fiction from all other categories of fiction. "Popular" rather than "literary," it is unlike other kinds of popular fiction—romance, adventure, and mystery (that is, novels of international intrigue and suspense)—in that it provides not a passive emotional thrill but an engaging intellectual challenge. Rather than merely awaiting "the author's unraveling of the tangled skein of events," the reader of a detective novel experiences "the swift and exhilarating participation in the succeeding steps that lead to the solution." Van Dine sees the detective novel as unlike "fiction in the ordinary sense." It is an "intellectual game, . . . a complicated and extended puzzle cast in fictional form," and puzzles, he avers, have been mankind's "chief toy throughout the ages." Van Dine likens the detective novel to the crossword puzzle:

> In each there is a problem to be solved; and the solution depends wholly on mental processes—on analysis, on the fitting together of apparently unrelated parts, on a knowledge of the ingredients, and, in some measure, on guessing. Each is supplied with a series of overlapping clues to guide the solver; and these clues, when fitted into place, blaze the path for future progress. In each, when the final solution is achieved, all the details are found to be woven into a complete, interrelated, and closely knitted fabric.

All the Philo Vance novels are intricately plotted; several underscore the puzzle element. In *The Bishop Murder Case* (1929), for example, clues to a series of murders include allusions to Mother Goose rhymes, mathematical theories, and chess moves. Vance himself approaches his cases as if they were puzzles or mathematical problems; he is an adherent of "cold, logical exactness in his mental processes."

The solution to be sought in a detective novel, according to Van Dine, is ideally that of a murder: "Crime has always exerted a profound fascination over humanity, and the more serious the crime the greater has been that appeal." He said that he considered "murder" the strongest word in the English language, and he used it in the title of each of his Philo Vance novels.

For a puzzle to be enjoyable—and solvable—it must be logical and fair. Many of Van Dine's twenty rules address the issue of fairness. For example, "The reader must have equal opportunity with the detective for solving the mystery. All clues must be plainly stated and described" (rule 1); "No willful tricks or deceptions may be placed on the reader other than those played legitimately by the criminal on the detective himself" (rule 2); "The detective himself, or one of the official investigators, should never turn out to be the culprit . . ." (rule 4); "The culprit must be determined by logical deductions—not by accident or coincidence or unmotivated confession . . ." (rule 5).

Van Dine stresses that the detective writer must be ingenious but never implausible: "A sense of reality is essential to the detective novel." The ideal material for the plot is commonplace, not exotic; the detective writer's task is "the working of familiar materials into a difficult riddle" which, if the reader should go back over the book after reading it the first time "he would find that the solution had been there all the time if he had had sufficient shrewdness to grasp it." The Philo Vance novels meet this criterion, for the most part. Vance typically solves his cases by a process of elimination and through his knowledge, both academic and intuitive, of human psychology.

Although, unlike romances or adventure novels, the detective novel, according to Van Dine, must have only enough atmosphere to establish the "pseudo-actuality" of its plot, setting, as opposed to atmosphere, is crucial:

> The plot must appear to be an actual record of events springing from the terrain of its operations; and the plans and diagrams so often encountered in detective stories aid considerably in the achievement of this effect. A familiarity with the terrain and a belief in its existence are what give the reader his feeling of ease and freedom in manipulating the factors of the plot to his own (which are also the author's) ends.

Accordingly, the Philo Vance novels usually feature maps and room diagrams. They also present a fascinatingly detailed picture of upper-class life in New York City in the 1920's and 1930's.

The style of a detective story, according to Van Dine, must aid in creating the sense of reality and verisimilitude; it "must be direct, simple, smooth, and unencumbered." It must be unemotional as well, and thus contribute to what is for Van Dine "perhaps the outstanding characteristic of the detective novel"–unity of mood, a mood conducive to "mental analysis and the overcoming of difficulties." In the Philo Vance novels, accordingly, the author presents himself through the narratorial persona of S. S. Van Dine, the protagonist's lawyer and companion. The narrator's status as an attorney serves to underscore the importance of logical analysis and objectivity, but his style, especially in the later novels, is frequently mannered and elaborate, and he digresses frequently into lengthy disquisitions, complete with footnotes, about such matters as art, archaeology, music, mathematics, criminology, and religion–typically in their most esoteric manifestations.

Van Dine's recommendations about characterization suggests that he thinks of characters–excluding the detective hero himself–primarily as pieces in a puzzle. Although they must not be "too neutral and colorless" (which would spoil the effect of verisimilitude), the detective writer should avoid delineating them "too fully and intimately." Characters should "merely fulfill the requirements of plausibility, so that their actions will not appear to spring entirely from the author's preconceived scheme." They are not to fall in love, since "the business at hand is to bring a criminal to the bar of justice, not to bring a lovelorn couple to the hymeneal altar" (rule 3); nor are they to belong to "secret societies, camorras, mafias" (rule 13), or, it appears, to be professional criminals, who are the concern of police departments, "not of authors and brilliant amateur detectives" (rule 17).

Story materials, plot, atmosphere, setting, style, narration, mood, characterization–according to Van Dine's theory all of these are strictly functional parts of a puzzle to be solved, counters in an exciting mental game. The primary player in this game is the detective hero and, vicariously, the reader. Van Dine's ideal detective hero stands in contrast to his world. He is singular. In fact, Van Dine rules that "There must be but one detective–that is, but one protagonist of deduction–one *deus ex machina.*" To have more than one detective would be to confuse the reader: "It's like making the reader run a race with a relay team" (rule 9). The detective is singular, not only in number, but, more important, in kind. His brilliance sets him above others, especially the police. Preferably, he is an amateur, and this status divorces him from mundane considerations such as earning a living or gaining a promotion. In Van Dine's view he is at once godlike, heroic (like Oedipus), wise ("the Greek chorus of the drama"), and fascinating:

> All good detective novels have had for their protagonist a character of attractiveness and interest, of high and fascinating attainments–a man at once human and unusual, colorful and gifted.

Philo Vance meets these criteria. The opening chapter of the first volume of the series, *The Benson Murder Case,* provides a detailed character portrait of Vance. He is described as "a man of unusual culture and brilliance." He is learned in psychology and criminology, enjoys music, and has a passion for art; he is an authority on it as well as "one of those rare human beings, a collector with a definite philosophic point of view." "Unusually good-looking" and in dress "always fashionable–scrupulously correct to the smallest detail–yet unobtrusive," Vance is skilled in various sports and games: He is an expert fencer, his golf handicap is only three, he is a champion at polo, and he is an "unerring" poker player. An "aristocrat by birth and instinct, he held himself severely aloof from the common world of men." Vance is a snob both intellectually and socially: "He detested stupidity even more, I believe, than he did vulgarity or bad taste."

Reactions to Vance over the years have differed widely and range from fascination and adulation to the bemused annoyance of Ogden Nash's famous lines, "Philo Vance/ Needs a kick in the pance." In the later novels his mannerisms sometimes seem self-parodic. Although he did not always avoid them, it is evident in the following passage from *The Benson Murder Case* that Van Dine knew the risks he was taking with his characterizations of Vance:

> Perhaps he may best be described as a bored and supercilious, but highly conscious and penetrating, spectator of life. He was keenly interested in all human reactions; but it was the interest of the scientist, not the humanitarian. Withal he was a man of rare personal charm. Even people who found it difficult to admire him found it equally difficult not to like him. His somewhat quixotic mannerisms and his slightly English accent and inflection–a heritage of his postgraduate days at Oxford–impressed those who did not know him well as affectations. But the truth is, there was very little of the *poseur* about him.

Van Dine was very interested in the philosophy of Friedrich Nietzsche; in 1915, in fact, he published a book titled *What Nietzsche Taught*. His ideal detective hero bears significant resemblance to the Nietzschean *Übermensch* (literally, "overman"), who, unlike common human beings, has managed to overcome his passions, has genuine style, is creative, and is above ordinary morality. Van Dine's Philo Vance is a self-professed disciple of Nietzschean philosophy, and in *The Bishop Murder Case* he plays the part of an *Übermensch* when he avoids being murdered by switching poisoned drinks with Professor Bertrand Dillard, the killer he has been investigating. Reproached by the district attorney for taking the law into his own hands, Vance says,

> ". . . I felt no more compunction in aiding a monster like Dillard into the Beyond than I would have in crushing out a poisonous reptile in the act of striking."
> "But it was murder!" exclaimed Markham in horrified indignation.
> "Oh, doubtless," said Vance cheerfully. "Yes—of course. Most reprehensible. . . . I say, am I by any chance under arrest?"

Here Vance does what the author or reader would, perhaps, like to do—deliver justice, not merely to facilitate it through his detection.

Van Dine's theory posits the detective as an alter ego for both author and reader. The detective is

> at one and the same time, the outstanding personality of the story, . . . the projection of the author, the embodiment of the reader, . . . the propounder of the problem, the supplier of the clues, and the eventual solver of the mystery.

For Van Dine, then, the detective hero serves the function not only of entertainment but also of wish fulfillment: He satisfies a fantasy about intellectual and moral power. Ultimately and paradoxically, therefore, fictional realism and strict logic serve in Van Dine's theory of detective fiction a compelling fantasy that cannot be satisfied in the real world of human society.

### Principal mystery and detective fiction

SERIES: Philo Vance: *The Benson Murder Case*, 1926; *The Canary Murder Case*, 1927; *The Greene Murder Case*, 1928; *The Bishop Murder Case*, 1929; *The Scarab Murder Case*, 1930; *The Kennel Murder Case*, 1933; *The Dragon Murder Case*, 1934; *The Casino Murder Case*, 1934; *The Garden Murder Case*, 1935; *The Kidnap Murder Case*, 1936; *Philo Vance Murder Cases*, 1936; *The Gracie Allen Murder Case*, 1938 (also as *The Smell of Murder*); *The Winter Murder Case*, 1939.

OTHER NOVEL: *The President's Mystery Story*, 1935 (with others).

### Other major works

NOVEL: *The Man of Promise*, 1916.

SCREENPLAY: *The Canary Murder Case*, 1929 (with others).

NONFICTION: *Europe After 8:15*, 1914 (with H. L. Mencken and George Jean Nathan); *Modern Painting: Its Tendency and Meaning*, 1915; *What Nietzsche Taught*, 1915; *The Creative Will: Studies in the Philosophy and Syntax of Aesthetics*, 1916;

*The Forum Exhibition of Modern American Painters, March Thirteenth to March Twenty-fifth, 1916,* 1916; *Informing a Nation,* 1917; *Misinforming a Nation,* 1917; *The Future of Painting,* 1923; *I Used to Be a Highbrow But Look at Me Now,* 1929.

EDITED TEXTS: *The Great Modern French Stories,* 1917; *The Great Detective Stories: A Chronological Anthology,* 1927.

## Bibliography

Braithwaite, William Stanley. "S. S. Van Dine-Willard Huntington Wright." In *Philo Vance Murder Cases.* New York: Charles Scribner's Sons, 1936.

Crawford, Walter B. "The Writings of Willard Huntington Wright." *Bulletin of Bibliography* 24 (May-August, 1963): 11-16.

Garden, Y. B. "Philo Vance: An Impressionistic Biography." In *Philo Vance Murder Cases.* New York: Charles Scribner's Sons, 1936.

Hageman, E. R. "Philo Vance's Sunday Nights at the Old Stuyvesant Club." *Clues: A Journal of Detection* 1 (Fall/Winter, 1980): 35-41.

Loughery, John. *Alias S. S. Van Dine.* New York: Scribner, 1992.

_____. "The Rise and Fall of Philo Vance: Time and Hollywood Eroded the Essence of This Erudite Sleuth." *The Armchair Detective* 20 (1987): 64-71.

Penzler, Otto. *S. S. Van Dine.* New York: Mysterious Bookshop, 1999.

Tuska, Jon. *Philo Vance: The Life and Times of S. S. Van Dine.* Bowling Green, Ohio: Bowling Green State University Popular Press, 1971.

"Van Dine, S. S." In *Mystery and Suspense Writers: The Literature of Crime, Detection, and Espionage,* edited by Robin W. Winks and Maureen Corrigan. New York: Charles Scribner's Sons, 1998.

*Eileen Tess Tyler*

# Robert H. Van Gulik

**Born:** Zutphen, Netherlands; August 9, 1910
**Died:** The Hague, Netherlands; September 24, 1967

**Type of plot** • Historical

**Principal series** • Judge Dee, 1949-1968.

**Principal series characters** • JUDGE DEE, a district magistrate, married, with three wives who live together harmoniously, providing the perfect team for his favorite game, dominoes. A fervent Confucian, he administers his many official responsibilities justly, seeking to maintain social order and respect for justice.
• MA JOONG, the son of a junk cargo owner, trained in boxing and intended for a career in the army. Having accidentally killed a cruel magistrate, he is forced to live as a bandit. Fond of women and drink, he is physically fearless but somewhat superstitious.
• HOONG LIANG, a servant in the household of Judge Dee's father. He insists on following the judge to the provinces. Completely loyal, he in turn has the complete trust of the judge.
• CHIAO TAI, from a good family, also forced to become a highwayman because of a corrupt official. He offers his services to the judge, stipulating only that he be allowed to resign if he finds the man responsible for the death of his comrades. Intelligent, thoughtful, and shy, he is unlucky in love.
• TAO GAN, seeking revenge on the world for the base behavior of his beloved wife, becomes an itinerant swindler. His familiarity with the criminal underworld and his skill with disguises make him an effective fourth assistant. Parsimonious to the extreme, he will scheme for free meals whenever possible.

**Contribution** • Robert H. van Gulik's stories of Judge Dee are fine examples of the historical mystery novel, which recaptures a bygone era even as it tells a good story. Though his stories are fictions, his training as a scholar and a diplomat enabled him to draw upon a vast store of historical material to enrich his mystery novels.
Noting, during his diplomatic service in Asian countries, that even poor translations of Western detective stories were enthusiastically received by Japanese and Chinese readers, van Gulik decided to demonstrate the strong tradition of Chinese detective stories that already existed. Starting with a translation of an anonymous eighteenth century novel about Judge Dee, he went on

to write several more of his own. He originally wrote them in English, then translated some for serial publication in Japanese journals. Western audiences found them so interesting that he decided to continue writing in English, and he translated his own work. He was thus responsible for introducing the classical Chinese detective story to the West, while the minutiae of the novels and his scholarly notes appended to the novels provide glimpses of the ancient Chinese way of life.

**Biography** • Born in Zutphen, the Netherlands, on August 9, 1910, to Willem Jacabus van Gulik, a physician, and his wife, Bertha de Ruiter, Robert Hans van Gulik displayed an interest in Oriental language and culture as a boy. The Chinese inscriptions on his father's collection of porcelain intrigued him, and he started studying Chinese in the Chinatown section of Batavia, Java, where his father was serving in the Dutch army. Back in the Netherlands for his college education, van Gulik took up law and languages at the University of Leiden, adding Japanese, Tibetan, Sanskrit, and Russian to his list of languages. His thesis, *Hayagriva: The Mantrayanic Aspect of Horse-Cult in China and Japan*, won for him a Ph.D. with honors from the University of Utrecht in 1935. His entry into the Netherlands Foreign Service led to postings in China, India, and Japan. In Chung-king, China, in 1943 he met and married Shui Shih-Fang, with whom he had three sons and a daughter.

Van Gulik's career as a diplomat flourished, bringing him many awards and honors. Despite the constant moves—which took him to Washington, D.C., the Middle East, Malaysia, Japan, and Korea—van Gulik continued his scholarly activities, researching, translating, editing, and writing. He was a skilled calligrapher—a rare talent for a Westerner—and had some of the other preoccupations of a traditional Chinese gentleman, collecting rare books, scroll paintings, musical instruments, and art objects. Of the breed of scholars who found meaning in small, esoteric subjects, he wrote, for example, two monographs on the ancient Chinese lute, which he himself played, and translated a famous text on ink stones. A talented linguist, historian, and connoisseur, van Gulik published scholarly articles on a variety of topics about traditional Chinese life, ranging from Chinese classical antiquity (c. 1200 B.C.-A.D. 200) to the end of the Ch'ing Dynasty (A.D. 1644-1911). It was through his mysteries about Judge Dee that van Gulik popularized the specialized knowledge of Chinese life he had gained. Having finally obtained the post of ambassador from the Netherlands to Japan in 1965, he died two years later of cancer in his homeland, on September 24, 1967.

**Analysis** • In his brief notes explaining the origins of his collection of short stories, *Judge Dee at Work* (1967), Robert H. van Gulik mused on the importance of each of his three careers: As a diplomat, he dealt with matters of temporary significance; as a scholar, he confined himself to facts of permanent significance; as a mystery writer, he could be completely in control of the facts and give free play to his imagination. It is the interplay of these separate experiences which give van Gulik's Judge Dee novels a distinct position in the genre of historical mystery novels.

A real historical figure who was politically important during the Tang Dynasty (618-907), Judge Dee was more popularly remembered as a folk figure, not unlike the Robin Hood of English folk history. The first appearance in English of the famed detective-magistrate Di Ren-jie (630-700) was in van Gulik's translation of an anonymous novel of the eighteenth century, *Wu-ze-tian-si-da-qi-an*, published as *Dee goong an* (1949). The success of his translation led van Gulik to write his own stories. Though he drew upon his scholarly background and interest in China to find stories, create accurate details, and provide illustrations, the Judge Dee stories are fictional, based on the Chinese form but adapted to Western audiences.

In his translator's preface, van Gulik points out five distinct features of Chinese detective stories. Rather than the cumulative suspense that characterizes Western whodunits, Chinese stories introduce the criminal at the beginning, explaining the history of and the motive for the crime. The pleasure for the reader lies in the intellectual excitement of following the chase. Nor are the stories bound to the realistic: Supernatural elements abound, animals and household items give evidence in court, and the detective might pop into the Nether World for information. Other characteristics have to do with the Chinese love and patience for voluminous detail: long poems, philosophical lectures, and official documents pad the purely narrative, resulting in novels of several hundred chapters; then too, each novel may be populated with two hundred or more characters. Finally, the Chinese sense of justice demands that the punishment meted out to the criminal be described in gruesome detail, sometimes including a description of the punishment the executed criminal receives in the afterlife.

These elements are toned down considerably or eliminated entirely in the stories that van Gulik wrote. In *The Chinese Lake Murders* (1960), for example, the first, short chapter is a diary entry by an official who has fallen in love with the woman who is to be a murder victim. It appears to be a confession of sorts, but one that is so intensely brooding, vague, and mystical that its purport becomes clear only toward the end of the story. Van Gulik thus neatly manages to include a convention while adapting it. Similarly, Judge Dee is often confronted with tales of haunted monasteries, temples invaded by phantoms, mysterious shadowy figures flitting in deserted houses, and other supernatural elements. A sensitive person, the judge is also often overcome by an inexplicable sense of evil in certain locations, which prove to be the sites of brutal torture or murder or burial—information revealed only after the judge has determined the mysteries' solutions. While his assistants are sometimes spooked by tales of ghosts and spirits, van Gulik portrays his judge primarily as a rational man suspicious of tales of the supernatural, and indeed most of these otherworldly elements prove to be concoctions fashioned by the criminals for their own convenience.

The van Gulik narrative flow is interrupted only by his own maps and illustrations, which are based on but not exact reproductions of Chinese woodblock prints; though a short poem or an official account may occasionally appear, they are strictly related to the story. Van Gulik retains the characteristic of the anonymous eighteenth century Judge Dee novel in telling three separate stories which prove to be related. Though he borrowed freely from his historical research, combining stories from disparate sources, van Gulik's considerable inventiveness and storytelling ability are evident in the way he can maintain the reader's interest in three separate stories. The list of dramatic *personae*, grouping the characters by story, is provided as a guide and numbers only a dozen or so.

While the traditional form is skillfully adapted to modern audiences, what remains completely faithful to the original Chinese detective story is the position of the detective figure, who was always a judge. In the pre-Communist social structure, the district magistrate had so many responsibilities over the affairs of the citizens in his jurisdiction that his title meant "the father-and-mother official." The term "judge" may therefore sound slightly misleading, for not only was a crime reported to the district magistrate but also he was in charge of investigating it, questioning suspects, making a decision, and sentencing. The wide powers that he wielded are fully delineated in van Gulik's novels. Judge Dee is regularly portrayed presiding over the daily sessions, resplendent in his official dark green robe with a black winged hat, his constabulary with whips and truncheons ready at his command. The habit, startling to twentieth century readers, was to treat anyone who came to the tribunal, defendant and complainant, the same way. Both had to kneel, hands behind them, in front of the judge, who could command his constables to whip or otherwise torture any recalcitrant suppliant. Particularly stubborn or arrogant people, such as the artist in *The Chinese Maze Murders* (1956), could be beaten into unconsciousness. The Chinese system of justice also required that criminals confess their crimes, even if they had to be tortured into confession, and the forms of death were gruesome. Judge Dee's way of cutting a deal with a criminal sometimes is to offer a more merciful form of death in return for cooperation. People who bore false witness could also be severely punished.

Though he will resort to such powers of his authority when necessary, Judge Dee solves cases because of his careful sifting of evidence, his powers of observation, and his experience and understanding of human nature. A firm upholder of the traditional Chinese values, Judge Dee exercises his power wisely. It is the higher purpose of justice which rules his decisions: The main purpose of the law, he realizes, is to restore the pattern disrupted by the crime, to repair the damage as much as possible. So it is that Judge Dee will sometimes start his tenure in a remote district which is in disarray, ruling over a populace made cynical by previous weak or corrupt officials or in the grip of evil men. The process of solving the murder mysteries is intrinsically linked to the process of restoring order and respect for the law and the imperial court.

Also typical of the Chinese detective story are the four assistants to the judge, often recruited from the "brothers of the green woods"–that is, bandits. Though his first and most trusted assistant, Sergeant Hoong Liang, is a faithful family retainer who follows the judge to the various outlying provinces in which the judge wants to work, the other three are reformed men. Ma Joong and Chiao Tai are typical of their ilk in that they are honest men who have been forced by circumstances into a life of crime. They meet Judge Dee when they attempt to rob him on the highway (*The Chinese Gold Murders*, 1959). Delighted by this rare opportunity to practice his swordsmanship, Judge Dee pulls out a family heirloom, the legendary sword Rain Dance, and is so annoyed when a group of officers comes to his rescue that he claims the highwaymen as his assistants. The two bandits are so impressed that they ask to be taken into his service. The fourth assistant, Tao Gan, similarly volunteers to join the judge. In contrast to the corrupt officials who caused honest men to become criminals, Judge Dee is thus neatly shown as a just and admirable man. The assistants are very useful in gathering evidence among the populace for the cases, and Judge Dee himself will take to the streets incognito. These reconnoitering missions provide little touches of ribald humor in the novels but also give readers a sense of the very hard life of common people, scrambling for their daily bowl of rice, subject to invasions from the northern borders. After the first five novels, van Gulik decided to simplify the pattern, for a "new" Judge Dee series; he dropped all but one assistant and focused more on character development. In response to popular demand, he brought back Sergeant Hoong, who had been killed in a previous novel.

Other historically accurate characteristics tend to simplify the narrative in predictable ways. Van Gulik toned down the vehement xenophobia of the truly devout Confucianist judge; even so, Judge Dee is openly contemptuous of foreign influences such as Buddhism or Taoism; even when Tatars, Indians, or Koreans are not actually criminals, they are suspect and considered dangerous. He prefers didactic poetry to love songs and while he may say, in a tolerant spirit, that what people do in the privacy of their own homes is their business, any character who deviates from the norm in his sexual preference or social behavior is suspect.

The author's scholarly training and interest are evident in other ways. His interest in art is manifest in the number of illustrations which enliven the novels; one, *The Phantom of the Temple* (1966), is based on the Judge Dee strips he created for Dutch and Scandinavian newspapers. One incident reveals the connection between van Gulik's scholarship and mystery writing. The Japanese publisher of *The Chinese Maze Murders* insisted on an image of a female nude for the cover. Seeking to verify his view that the prudish Confucianist tradition precluded the art of drawing nude human bodies, van Gulik discovered instead that an antique dealer had a set of printing blocks of an erotic album from the Ming period, which in turn led him to publish two scholarly books on the subject of erotic art and sexual life in ancient China. Beyond the care for historical accuracy, however, van Gulik's interest in art is integrally important in the mystery novels. Paintings are important as clues; two contrasting pictures of a pet cat and Judge

Dee's careful observation of the position of the sun in each lead him to a solution in *The Haunted Monastery* (1962), for example.

In the context of the Western mystery novel tradition, such features as maps, lists, and illustrations are typical of puzzle-plots. Some of the motifs in the Judge Dee novels may be more familiar to the devotee of the tougher kind of hard-boiled novels, however, such as the distinct misogyny which permeates the novels. The custom of poor families selling daughters to brothel houses and the reverence for sons over daughters are undoubted if sad historical facts. Still, the number of beautiful young women who are kidnapped, locked up, beaten, and otherwise tortured and killed in the course of the novels is cumulatively oppressive. By extension, incestuous and sadomasochist characters appear often.

As a detective figure, even with the vast powers he has, Judge Dee is not portrayed solely as the Great Detective, the brilliantly intuitive crime solver who never falters. In *The Chinese Nail Murders* (1961), he comes perilously close to losing both his job and his head when he orders that a grave be dug up and then cannot find any evidence of murder. In deep despair, he prepares himself for disgrace, saved only by the help of a beautiful woman he has come to admire very much, wistfully recalling his father's words that it is very lonely at the top. Such touches of psychological individuality are lightly done. The emphasis on the social role rather than the individual characterizes van Gulik's style: Phrases such as "the judge barked" and a liberal use of exclamation marks in dialogue suggest the peremptory nature of the detective's task.

Ever the scholar, van Gulik included a postscript, detailing the origins of his stories, with remarks on relevant Chinese customs. Even without these aids, his Judge Dee stories provide a generalized picture of ancient Chinese life and have repopularized the Chinese equivalent of Sherlock Holmes.

## Principal mystery and detective fiction

SERIES: Judge Dee: *Dee goong an,* 1949 (translation of portions of an anonymous eighteenth century Chinese novel; *Celebrated Cases of Judge Dee,* 1976); *The Chinese Maze Murders,* 1956; *New Year's Eve in Lan-Fang,* 1958; *The Chinese Bell Murders,* 1958; *The Chinese Gold Murders,* 1959; *The Chinese Lake Murders,* 1960; *The Chinese Nail Murders,* 1961; *The Red Pavilion,* 1961; *The Haunted Monastery,* 1962; *The Lacquer Screen,* 1963; *The Emperor's Pearl,* 1963; *The Willow Pattern,* 1965; *The Monkey and the Tiger,* 1965; *The Phantom of the Temple,* 1966; *Murder in Canton,* 1966; *Judge Dee at Work,* 1967; *Necklace and Calabash,* 1967; *Poets and Murder,* 1968 (also as *The Fox-Magic Murders*).

OTHER NOVEL: *Een gegeven dag,* 1963 (*The Given Day,* 1964).

## Other major works

NOVELS: *De nacht van de tijger: Een rechter tie verhaal,* 1963; *Vier vingers: Een rechter tie verhaal,* 1964.

NONFICTION: *Hayagriva: The Mantrayanic Aspect of Horse-Cult in China and Japan,* 1935; *The Lore of the Chinese Lute,* 1940; *Hsi K'ang and His Poetical Essay on the Lute,*

1941; *Pi-Hsi-T'u-K'ao, Erotic Colour Prints of the Ming Period,* 1951; *De Boek Illustratie in Het Ming Tijdperk,* 1955; *Chinese Pictorical Art as Viewed by the Connoisseur,* 1958; *Sexual Life in Ancient China,* 1961; *The Gibbon in China,* 1967.

TRANSLATIONS: *Urvaci,* 1932; *Mi Fu on Inkstones,* 1938; *T'ang-Yin-Pi-Shih (Parallel Cases from Under the Peartree),* 1956.

EDITED TEXT: *Ming-Mo I-Seng Tung-Kao-Chan-Shih Chi-K'an,* 1944.

MISCELLANEOUS: *The English-Blackfoot Vocabulary,* 1930 (with C. C. Uhlenbeck); *The Blackfoot-English Vocabulary,* 1934 (with Uhlenbeck); *Ch'un-Meng-So-Yen, Trifling Tale of a Spring Dream,* 1950.

## Bibliography

Bishop, John L. "Some Limitations of Chinese Fiction." *Harvard-Yenching Institute Studies,* no. 21 (1966): 237-245.

Lach, Donald F. Introduction to *The Chinese Gold Murders.* Chicago: University of Chicago Press, 1977.

Mugar Memorial Library. *Bibliography of Dr. R. H. van Gulik (D.Litt.).* Boston: Boston University, 1968.

Sarjeant, William Antony S. "A Detective in Seventh-Century China: Robert van Gulik and the Cases of Judge Dee." *The Armchair Detective* 15, no. 4 (1982): 292-303.

Starrett, Vincent. "Some Chinese Detective Stories." In *Bookman's Holiday.* New York: Random House, 1942.

Van de Wetering, Janwillem. *Robert van Gulik: His Life, His Work.* 1987. Reprint. New York: Soho Press, 1998.

"Van Gulik, Robert." In *Mystery and Suspense Writers: The Literature of Crime, Detection, and Espionage,* edited by Robin W. Winks and Maureen Corrigan. New York: Charles Scribner's Sons, 1998.

*Shakuntala Jayaswal*

# Edgar Wallace

**Born:** Greenwich, England; April 1, 1875
**Died:** Beverly Hills, California; February 10, 1932

**Types of plot** • Private investigator • police procedural • thriller

**Principal series** • The Four Just Men, 1905-1928 • J. G. Reeder, 1925-1932.

**Principal series characters** • LEON GONZALEZ, RAYMOND POICCART, GEORGE MANFRED, and MIQUEL THERY constitute the group in the original work *The Four Just Men* (1905), and three of them reappear in later Four Just Men books. These characters are determined, like The Three Musketeers, to take justice into their own hands.
• MR. J. G. REEDER is a more traditional English detective. With his square derby, mutton-chop whiskers, tightly furled umbrella, spectacles, large old-fashioned cravat, and square-toed shoes, this elderly gentleman carries a Browning automatic and fears no one, despite a feigned apologetic habit. Claiming that he has a criminal mind and using his power of recollection (and a great collection of newspaper clippings), Reeder has the goods on everyone involved in his specialty—financial-related murder.

**Contribution** • Edgar Wallace's publication of more than 170 books, an impressive list of short stories, comedies, plays, and screenplays—as well as his lifetime career as journalist, correspondent, and editor—marks him as the best-selling English author of his generation and one of the most prolific. Howard Haycraft declared that Wallace's "vast audience gave him an influence, in popularizing the genre, out of all proportion to the actual merit of his writing." He made the thriller popular in book form, and on stage and screen, throughout the English-speaking world. Only John Creasey, with his more than five hundred novels, wrote more than Wallace, and perhaps Agatha Christie was the only mystery/detective writer whose novels attracted more readers.

The best of Wallace's detective fiction recounts the cases of Mr. J. G. Reeder, a very British sleuth of valiant courage whose triumphs are won by both chance and deduction. The critics Stefan Benvenuti and Gianni Rizzoni observe that Wallace "concentrated on the extravagant, the exotic, and the freely fantastic, all interpreted in a style derived from the Gothic novel." He steered clear of sex or controversy, but he often challenged the system of justice of his era and pointed to errors in police practices.

**Biography** • Richard Horatio Edgar Wallace was born on April 1, 1875, in Greenwich, England, the son of Polly Richards and Richard Edgar, unwed members of an acting company. As an illegitimate child, Wallace was placed in the home of George and Millie Freeman in Norway Court, London, where he spent his boyhood as Dick Freeman until he ran away to join the army at the age of eighteen. Like his mother and grandmother, he loved the theater and, without much formal education, learned to read primarily from public library books. He soon was writing verses of his own.

Wallace joined the Royal West Kent Regiment as an enlisted private; in July, 1896, he sailed on a troopship to South Africa. After six years of military service as a hospital orderly, he bought his own discharge and became a celebrated war correspondent in the Boer Wars. Wallace was named to the staff of the London *Daily Mail* and covered the end of the war in South Africa. He married a minister's daughter, Ivy Caldecott, in April, 1901, in Cape Town and at the end of the war returned to make his home in England. The couple had three children before they were divorced in 1919. Soon after, Wallace married his secretary of five years, Violet "Jim" King; in 1923, they had a daughter, Penelope.

Plagued by debts left unpaid in South Africa and new bills accumulating in London, he began writing plays and short stories while serving as correspondent or editor for various newspapers. His lifelong love of gambling at horse racing led him into writing and editing several racing sheets, but his losses at the tracks continually added to his debts. Blessed with an indomitable sense of optimism and self-confidence, he drove himself as a writer and established his name as an author. In 1905, Wallace wrote and published his first great novel, *The Four Just Men*. After a series of lawsuits forced the *Daily Mail* to drop him as a reporter, he was able to draw upon his experience in the Boer Wars and his assignments in the Belgian Congo, Canada, Morocco, Spain, and London slums, which provided rich material for short stories and novels.

On the advice of Isabel Thorne, fiction editor for Shurey's Publications, Wallace began a series for the *Weekly Tale-Teller* called "Sanders of the River," based upon his experiences in the Congo. He was editor of *Town Topics*, a sports weekly, when World War I broke out in 1914. From the second day of the war until the Armistice, for twelve guineas a week, he wrote six daily articles for the *Birmingham Post*, summarizing the war news, which were published in nine volumes under the title *The War of the Nations: A History of the Great European Conflict* (1914-1919). Using dictation, he increased his writing speed, producing a series of paperback war novels. He also wrote his first motion-picture script, on the life of Edith Cavell, the English nurse who, in 1915, was executed in German-occupied Belgium for aiding the escape of Allied soldiers.

The last ten years of Wallace's life were the most rewarding. Success as a playwright came with the 1926 production of *The Ringer* in London. Numerous plays were produced, many more novels were published, and he continued to edit a Sunday newspaper and write a daily racing column. In 1931, he sailed to the United States to write for film studios in California; there, he collaborated with other writers on a horror film that later became *King Kong* (1933). Suddenly taken ill, he died on February 10, 1932, at the age of fifty-six.

**Analysis** • Edgar Wallace carved a permanent niche in the early twentieth century development of the mystery/detective novel. His books featured heroes and villains that were accessible to the reading public of his generation. Wallace patriotically upheld the British flag in his own life and in the fictional lives of his detectives. In his novels and stories, those who commit murder die for their crimes. The protagonists of *The Four Just Men* (and others in that series) go above the law when justice is not properly meted out by the courts or when the criminal escapes unpunished. These just men are heroes who redress wrongs and often succeed after the authorities have failed. When Wallace capitalized upon this theme, his characters were do-gooders of a romantic cut: Right and wrong were clearly distinguished in these works, the heroes of which persevered until good triumphed over evil.

Within the English-speaking world of the 1920's, Edgar Wallace became a widely read author; even in postwar Germany, he was hailed for his enormous popularity. Most scholars of detective fiction agree that he was instrumental in popularizing the detective story and the thriller. Libraries had to stock dozens of copies of each of his best works for decades. Somehow, Wallace was closely in tune with his times and his readers, as Margaret Lane makes clear in her biography of the writer:

> "Edgar Wallace," wrote Arnold Bennett in 1928, "has a very grave defect, and I will not hide it. He is content with society as it is. He parades no subversive opinions. He is 'correct.'" This was a shrewd observation and was never more plainly demonstrated than by Edgar's newspaper work during the war. It was not that he feared to cross swords with public opinion; he always, most fully and sincerely, shared it.

Wallace shifted from newspaper writing to writing short stories, novels, and plays after his war experiences in South Africa. His natural ability to describe graphically events for readers of daily papers led to longer feature articles that reflected popular opinion. Driven by debt, and born with a sense of ambition and self-confidence, Wallace struggled to find his literary identity. Anxious to cash in on his first great mystery thriller, *The Four Just Men*, he published and advertised it himself, offering a reward for the proper solution (which consumed all the income from the novel's successful sales). By the time *The Four Just Men* appeared, Wallace had developed the technique that would become the hallmark of much of his mystery/detective fiction. His editor had honed his short stories into very salable copy, and his characters had become real people in the minds of British readers. His biographer Margaret Lane summarizes his maturity in style:

> He realised, too, that these stories were the best work he had ever done, and that at last he was mastering the difficult technique of the short story. He evolved a favourite pattern and fitted the adventures of his characters to the neat design. He would outline a chain of incidents to a certain point, break off, and begin an apparently independent story; then another, and another; at the crucial point the several threads would meet and become one, and the tale would end swiftly, tied in a neat knot of either comedy or drama.

In 1910, while Wallace wrote and edited racing sheets, he observed legal and illegal activities by the best and the worst characters of the race-track crowd, activities that eventually emerged in his mystery fiction. *Grey Timothy* (1913), a crime novel about racing, paralleled two of his mystery books, *The Fourth Plague* (1913) and *The River of Stars* (1913). His more famous *Captain Tatham of Tatham Island* (1909; revised as *The Island of Galloping Gold*, 1916) also had a racing theme.

Wallace scoffed at critics who declared that his characters were paper-thin; others from more literary and academic circles denounced him for not writing more carefully, with greater depth to his plots and characters. In spite of these criticisms, before World War I Wallace had found his place as a mystery writer: "That is where I feel at home; I like actions, murderings, abductions, dark passages and secret trapdoors and the dull, slimy waters of the moat, pallid in the moonlight."

Many editors and readers believed that Wallace had close ties with the criminal world and that his characters were taken from real life, but according to his daughter-in-law that was not so. Perhaps Al Capone of Chicago (whose home Wallace visited in 1929) came the closest to his vision of the super-criminal. He promptly wrote one of his best plays, *On the Spot* (1930), about the American gangster. Yet in *People: A Short Autobiography* (1926), Wallace devotes a chapter to his knowledge of criminals and the reasons for their law-breaking. He declared:

> To understand the criminal you must know him and have or affect a sympathy with him in his delinquencies. You have to reach a stage of confidence when he is not showing off or lying to impress you. In fact, it is necessary that he should believe you to be criminally minded.

Whether it was Detective Surefoot Smith, Educated Evans, Carl Rennett, Timothy Jordan, Superintendent Bliss, Inspector Bradley, or Mr. Reeder, Wallace spun his yarns with equal knowledge about the skills, habits, and frailties of both murderers and their detectors.

Various efforts to classify Wallace's works of mystery/detective fiction have failed, but certain series and types of plot do emerge. The Four Just Men series was published between 1905 and 1928. There are the police novels—including his famous *The Ringer* (1926), *The Terror* (1929), and *The Clue of the Silver Key* (1930)—and the thrillers, such as *The Green Archer* (1923), *The India-Rubber Men* (1929), and the classic *The Man from Morocco* (1926). The J. G. Reeder series, begun in 1925 with *The Mind of Mr. J. G. Reeder*, was brought to its height with the popular *Red Aces* (1929). Yet many of Wallace's detective stories were short stories that overlapped such categories or were not collected until after his death.

Many of Wallace's works reflect his generation's reluctance to accept the authority of "science." While other authors after 1910 were incorporating scientific equipment such as lie detectors into their detective works, his London crime fighters used old-fashioned wits instead of newfangled widgets. While many authors turned to more modern, psychological solutions for murder mysteries, Wallace believed that his readers would be lost in such heavy character analysis; he did not let such new devices spoil the fun. Mr. Reeder relies upon his own phenomenal memory (buttressed by musty scrapbooks of murder cases), his incriminating evidence often coming from unsuspecting sources. When he astonishes his superiors of Scotland Yard, his conclusions are based on information found outside the criminal labs. Wallace's haste to write his stories led him to depend upon his own fertile mind; seldom did he leave his study to search for more documentary detail.

His readers loved his fantastic and scary secret passages, hiding places, trapdoors, and mechanical death-dealing devices. (He let his imagination roam like that of a science-fiction writer.) The setting for many of his novels was London, which provided a wide variety of suburbs, railroads, and steamship docks through which the underworld characters prowled and detectives searched. Although his work is sometimes marred by sloppy writing, the fast pace of Wallace's stories thrilled his readers to their sudden conclusions—the culprit revealed, arrested, or killed all within the last few pages.

### Principal mystery and detective fiction

SERIES: Four Just Men: *The Four Just Men*, 1905, revised 1906, 1908; *The Law Council of Justice*, 1908; *The Just Men of Cordova*, 1917; *Jack o'Judgement*, 1920; *The Law of the Four Just Men*, 1921; *The Three Just Men*, 1925; *Again the Three Just Men*, 1928 (also as *The Law of the Three Just Men* and *Again the Three*). J. G. Reeder: *The Mind of Mr. J. G. Reeder*, 1925 (also as *The Murder Book of J. G. Reeder*); *Terror Keep*, 1927; *Red Aces*, 1929; *Mr. Reeder Returns*, 1932 (also as *The Guv'nor and Other Stories*).

OTHER NOVELS: *Angel Esquire*, 1908; *Captain Tatham of Tatham Island*, 1909 (revised as *The Island of Galloping Gold*, 1916; also as *Eve's Island*); *The Nine Bears*, 1910 (also as *The Other Man, Silinski, Master Criminal*, and *The Cheaters*); *The Fourth Plague*, 1913; *Grey Timothy*, 1913 (also as *Pallard the Punter*); *The River of Stars*, 1913; *The Man Who Bought London*, 1915; *The Melody of Death*, 1915; *The Clue of the Twisted Candle*, 1916; *The Debt Discharged*, 1916; *The Tomb of Ts' in*, 1916; *Kate Plus Ten*, 1917; *The Secret House*, 1917; *Down Under Donovan*, 1918; *The Man Who Knew*, 1918; *The Green Rust*, 1919; *The Daffodil Mystery*, 1920; *The Book of All Power*, 1921; *The Angel of Terror*, 1922 (also as *The Destroying Angel*); *Captains of Souls*, 1922; *The Crimson Circle*, 1922; *The Flying Fifty-five*, 1922; *Mr. Justice Maxwell*, 1922; *The Valley of Ghosts*, 1922; *The Clue of the New Pin*, 1923; *The Green Archer*, 1923; *The Missing Million*, 1923; *The Dark Eyes of London*, 1924; *Double Dan*, 1924 (also as *Diana of Kara-Kara*); *The Face in the Night*, 1924; *Room 13*, 1924; *Flat 2*, 1924, revised 1927; *The Sinister Man*, 1924; *The Three Oaks Mystery*, 1924; *Blue Hand*, 1925; *The Daughters of the Night*, 1925; *The Fellowship of the Frog*, 1925; *The Gaunt Stranger*, 1925 (also as *The Ringer*); *The Hairy Arm*, 1925 (also as *The Avenger*); *A King by Night*, 1925; *The Strange Countess*, 1925; *Barbara on Her Own*, 1926; *The Black Abbot*, 1926; *The Day of Uniting*, 1926; *The Door with Seven Locks*, 1926; *The Joker*, 1926 (also as *The Colossus*); *The Man from Morocco*,

1926 (also as *The Black*); *The Million Dollar Story*, 1926; *The Northing Tramp*, 1926 (also as *The Tramp*); *Penelope of the Polyantha*, 1926; *The Square Emerald*, 1926 (also as *The Girl from Scotland Yard*); *The Terrible People*, 1926; *We Shall See!*, 1926 (also as *The Gaol Breaker*); *The Yellow Snake*, 1926; *The Ringer*, 1926; *Big Foot*, 1927; *The Feathered Serpent*, 1927; *The Forger*, 1927 (also as *The Clever One*); *The Hand of Power*, 1927; *The Man Who Was Nobody*, 1927; *The Squeaker*, 1927 (also as *The Squealer*); *The Traitor's Gate*, 1927; *Number Six*, 1927; *The Double*, 1928; *The Thief in the Night*, 1928; *The Flying Squad*, 1928; *The Gunner*, 1928 (also as *Gunman's Bluff*); *The Twister*, 1928; *The Golden Hades*, 1929; *The Green Ribbon*, 1929; *The India-Rubber Men*, 1929; *The Terror*, 1929; *The Calendar*, 1930; *The Clue of the Silver Key*, 1930; *The Lady of Ascot*, 1930; *White Face*, 1930; *On the Spot*, 1931; *The Coat of Arms*, 1931 (also as *The Arranways Mystery*); *The Devil Man*, 1931 (also as *The Life and Death of Charles Peace*); *The Man at the Carlton*, 1931; *The Frightened Lady*, 1932; *When the Gangs Came to London*, 1932.

OTHER SHORT FICTION: *Sanders of the River*, 1911; *The People of the River*, 1912; *The Admirable Carfew*, 1914; *Bosambo of the River*, 1914; *Bones, Being Further Adventures in Mr. Commissioner Sanders' Country*, 1915; *The Keepers of the King's Peace*, 1917; *Lieutenant Bones*, 1918; *The Adventures of Heine*, 1919; *Bones in London*, 1921; *Sandi, The King-Maker*, 1922; *Bones of the River*, 1923; *Chick*, 1923; *Educated Evans*, 1924; *More Educated Evans*, 1926; *Sanders*, 1926 (also as *Mr. Commissioner Sanders*); *The Brigand*, 1927; *Good Evans!*, 1927 (also as *The Educated Man–Good Evans!*); *The Mixer*, 1927; *Again Sanders*, 1928; *Elegant Edward*, 1928; *The Orator*, 1928; *Again the Ringer*, 1929 (also as *The Ringer Returns*); *Four Square Jane*, 1929; *The Big Four*, 1929; *The Black*, 1929, revised 1962; *The Ghost of Down Hill*, 1929; *The Cat Burglar*, 1929; *Circumstantial Evidence*, 1929; *Fighting Snub Reilly*, 1929; *The Governor of Chi-Foo*, 1929; *The Little Green Men*, 1929; *Planetoid 127*, 1929; *The Prison-Breakers*, 1929; *Forty-eight Short Stories*, 1929; *For Information Received*, 1929; *The Lady of Little Hell*, 1929; *The Lone House Mystery*, 1929; *The Reporter*, 1929; *The Iron Grip*, 1929; *Mrs. William Jones and Bill*, 1930; *Killer Kay*, 1930; *The Lady Called Nita*, 1930; *Sergeant Sir Peter*, 1932; *The Steward*, 1932; *The Last Adventure*, 1934; *The Undisclosed Client*, 1962; *The Man Who Married His Cook and Other Stories*, 1976; *Two Stories, and the Seventh Man*, 1981; *The Sooper and Others*, 1984.

## Other major works

NOVELS: *The Duke in the Suburbs*, 1909; *Private Selby*, 1912; *1925: The Story of a Fatal Peace*, 1915; *Those Folks of Bulboro*, 1918; *The Books of Bart*, 1923; *The Black Avons*, 1925 (also as *How They Fared in the Times of the Tudors, Roundhead and Cavalier, From Waterloo to the Mutiny*, and *Europe in the Melting Pot*).

SHORT FICTION: *Smithy*, 1905 (revised as *Smithy, Not to Mention Nobby Clark and Spud Murphy*, 1914); *Smithy Abroad: Barrack Room Sketches*, 1909; *Smithy's Friend Nobby*, 1914 (also as *Nobby*); *Smithy and the Hun*, 1915; *Tam o' the Scouts*, 1918; *The Fighting Scouts*, 1919.

PLAYS: *An African Millionaire*, 1904; *The Forest of Happy Dreams*, 1910; *Dolly Cutting Herself*, 1911; *Hello, Exchange!*, 1913 (also as *The Switchboard*); *The Manager's Dream*,

1913; *Whirligig,* 1919 (with Wal Pink and Albert de Courville; also as *Pins and Needles*); *M'Lady,* 1921; *The Whirl of the World,* 1924 (with Courville and William K. Wells); *The Looking Glass,* 1924 (with Courville); *The Ringer,* 1926; *The Mystery of Room 45,* 1926; *Double Dan,* 1926; *The Terror,* 1927; *A Perfect Gentleman,* 1927; *The Yellow Mask,* 1927; *The Flying Squad,* 1928; *The Man Who Changed His Name,* 1928; *The Squeaker,* 1928 (also as *Sign of the Leopard*); *The Lad,* 1928; *Persons Unknown,* 1929; *The Calendar,* 1929; *On the Spot,* 1930; *The Mouthpiece,* 1930; *Smoky Cell,* 1930; *Charles III,* 1931; *The Old Man,* 1931; *The Case of the Frightened Lady,* 1931 (also as *Criminal at Large*); *The Green Pack,* 1932.

SCREENPLAYS: *Nurse and Martyr,* 1915; *The Ringer,* 1928; *Valley of the Ghosts,* 1928; *The Forger,* 1928; *Red Aces,* 1929; *The Squeaker,* 1930; *Should a Doctor Tell?,* 1930; *The Hound of the Baskervilles,* 1931 (with V. Gareth Gundrey); *The Old Man,* 1931; *King Kong,* 1933 (with others).

POETRY: *The Mission That Failed! A Tale of the Raid and Other Poems,* 1898; *Nicholson's Nek,* 1900; *War! and Other Poems,* 1900; *Writ in Barracks,* 1900.

NONFICTION: *Unofficial Dispatches,* 1901; *Famous Scottish Regiments,* 1914; *Field-Marshall Sir John French and His Campaigns,* 1914; *Heroes All: Gallant Deeds of War,* 1914; *The Standard History of the War,* 1914-1916; *The War of the Nations: A History of the Great European Conflict,* 1914-1919; *Kitchener's Army and the Territorial Forces: The Full Story of a Great Achievement,* 1915; *People: A Short Autobiography,* 1926; *This England,* 1927; *My Hollywood Diary,* 1932; *A Fragment of Medieval Life,* 1977?

## Bibliography

Croydon, John. "A Gaggle of Wallaces: On the Set with Edgar Wallace." *The Armchair Detective* 18, no. 1 (Winter, 1985): 64-68.

Dixon, Wheeler Winston. "The Colonial Vision of Edgar Wallace." *Journal of Popular Culture* 32, no. 1 (Summer, 1998): 121-139.

Godden, Ian H. "Nothing More Than a Little Innocent Murdering: Edgar Wallace's Policemen, A Brief Survey." *CADS: Crime and Detective Stories* 18-19 (February-October, 1992).

Hogan, John A. "Real Life Crime Stories of Edgar Wallace." *Antiquarian Book Monthly Review* 12, no. 11 (November, 1985).

_____. "The 'Unknown' Edgar Wallace." *CADS: Crime and Detective Stories* 2 (November, 1985): 14-16.

Lane, Margaret. *Edgar Wallace: The Biography of a Phenomenon.* New York: Doubleday, Doran, 1939.

Lofts, William Oliver Guillemont. "The Hidden Gems of Edgar Wallace." *Book and Magazine Collector* 95 (February, 1992): 30-39.

Morland, Nigel. The Edgar Wallace I Knew." *The Armchair Detective* 1, no. 3 (April, 1968): 68-81.

_____. "Edgar Wallace: The Man and the Legend." *Creasey Mystery Magazine* 8, no. 1 (March, 1964): 14-21.

_____. "Unforgettable Edgar Wallace." *Reader's Digest* 106, no. 636 (April, 1975): 110-115.

"Wallace, Edgar." In *Mystery and Suspense Writers: The Literature of Crime, Detection, and Espionage,* edited by Robin W. Winks and Maureen Corrigan. New York: Charles Scribner's Sons, 1998.

Wallace, Ethel, and Haydon Talbot. *Edgar Wallace by His Wife.* London: Hutchinson, 1932.

Watson, Colin. "King Edgar, and How He Got His Crown." In *Snobbery with Violence: Crime Stories and Their Audience.* New York: Mysterious, 1990.

*Paul F. Erwin*

# Joseph Wambaugh

**Born:** East Pittsburgh, Pennsylvania; January 22, 1937

**Types of plot** • Police procedural • historical

**Contribution** • Joseph Wambaugh, the Los Angeles policeman who became a best-selling novelist, began writing out of a need to describe the Watts riots of the 1960's from the perspective of those police officers assigned to restore order there. He wanted to describe "what it was like for young men, young policemen, to grow up, on the streets, in that dreadful and fascinating era." The body of his work concerns American police procedure and the lives of those who belong to what has been called the "maligned profession." It is a world of frustrating, counterproductive rules and regulations drawn up by police administrators who have not been on the streets for years, a world where brutality mixes with courage, corruption with dedication, and evil with honor.

Although occasionally criticized for lengthy philosophical discourses and an undeveloped style, Wambaugh is more often praised for thoughtful and realistic storytelling, and he has been regarded as one of the "few really knowledgeable men who try to tell the public what a cop's life is like." Beginning with his first novel, *The New Centurions* (1970), positive popular response has led to the reproduction of Wambaugh's stories in other media such as film, television, and audio cassettes. His police officers were violent, afraid, foulmouthed, and fallible. "Do you like cops? Read *The New Centurions*," a *New York Times* reviewer wrote. "Do you hate cops? Read *The New Centurions*."

Critical acclaim for his writing began in 1974, when he received the Herbert Brean Memorial Award for *The Onion Field* (1973), which, according to *The New York Times* reviewer James Conaway, is equal to Truman Capote's *In Cold Blood* (1966) and placed Wambaugh in the tradition of Theodore Dreiser and James T. Farrell.

Wambaugh's books, gritty, hyperrealistic, and nonlinear, typically interweave several story lines at once. His characters are composites of real-life cops and criminals; his dialogue is praised and reviled as "outrageously colorful." What Wambaugh brought to detective fiction was actual life on the beat from a cop's perspective: the gallows humor, the ugliness, the drugs and booze, the boredom and the raw fear. "I didn't realize what I was doing, but I was turning the procedural around," Wambaugh told an interviewer. "The procedural is a genre that describes how a cop acts on the job; I was showing how the job might act on the cop . . . how it worked on his head."

Wambaugh shows that investigations can be mishandled and that police officers, who can be bigots, alcoholics, and hard cases, make bad errors of judgment. However, he believes that most Americans are unwilling to grasp the reality, the human cost, of police work. Wambaugh's books are enormously popular among cops as well as civilian readers because of their accuracy. "Police work is still, in my opinion, the most emotionally hazardous job on earth," he said in 2000. "Not the most physically dangerous, but the most emotionally dangerous."

**Biography** • The only child of Anne Malloy and Joseph Aloysius Wambaugh, Joseph Aloysius Wambaugh, Jr., was born on January 22, 1937, in East Pittsburgh, Pennsylvania. The German surname accounts for one-quarter of his ethnic heritage; the other three-quarters is Roman Catholic Irish. His was a family of hard workers, many of whom labored in the Pittsburgh steel mills.

Wambaugh's California settings originate in his personal experience. His father had been police chief in East Pittsburgh before the family moved to California in 1951. Three years later, Wambaugh left high school to enlist in the United States Marine Corps. During his service time, in 1956, he and Dee Allsup, a high school friend, his high school sweetheart, were married. They had three children; their son Mark would later die at the age of twenty-one. Upon Wambaugh's discharge from the Marines in 1957, the couple returned to California, where Wambaugh worked at different jobs while earning an associate degree in English from Chaffey College in 1958.

In 1960, Wambaugh graduated from California State College, Los Angeles, with a B.A. and joined the Los Angeles Police Department (LAPD) as a burglary detective. However casually he came to police work (he once told an interviewer that he joined the police department because he had "nothing better to do" and because the money was more than he had ever earned), he soon found himself deeply involved. He was a solid, common-sense investigator who cracked more than his share of tough cases. He has said that police work relaxed him and soothed his soul.

Wambaugh began writing after he became involved in helping to control the Watts riot. On August 11, 1965, six days of rioting began in the Watts section of South Central Los Angeles following a routine traffic stop. African Americans were tired of abusive treatment from white police officers in the cities, which included the use of water cannons, clubs, and

*Joseph Wambaugh.* (Library of Congress)

cattle prods. In the ensuring violence, thirty-four people were killed and 856 injured. Nearly four thousand people were arrested, and 209 buildings were destroyed. It was a difficult time for citizens and police alike.

Wambaugh intended to maintain both careers, as writer and policeman, but his status as a "celebrity cop" would not permit that option. In 1973, for example, he was presented with California State University's first outstanding-alumnus award. Interrupting police calls and visits at the Hollenbeck Station were one problem, but great tension developed from the changed relationships inside the department: "The other cops were starting to treat me differently–sort of like a star–and I couldn't bear being different." On March 1, 1974, he left the force.

As production consultant for the television series adapted from his novel *The Blue Knight* (1972), Wambaugh fought to maintain authenticity in the scripts. Indeed, his insistence has become legendary. He filed and won a lawsuit over violations committed against the text when *The Choirboys* (1975) was made into a film. Indeed, his literary career has been plagued with litigation. "I've been under continuous litigation for my writing since 1974," Wambaugh once told an interviewer. "There's a million ambulance chasers who say, 'Let's sue him!'"

The most famous case concerned the murders forming the basis of Wambaugh's *Echoes in the Darkness* (1987). On September 14, 1994, Philadelphia's Upper Merion High School principal Jay C. Smith, convicted of the murders of a school teacher and her two children, filed suit against Wambaugh, claiming that he had conspired with police investigators to conceal exculpatory evidence and to fabricate evidence linking Smith to the murders, in order to make money from the book and a television miniseries. Smith lost the case, although his conviction was overturned.

After being sued over *The Onion Field, Lines and Shadows,* and *Echoes in the Darkness,* Wambaugh swore off writing nonfiction. *The Blooding* (1989) was the only true-crime book he wrote that was not the subject of a defamation lawsuit. Wambaugh attributed this to the fact that it dealt not with Americans but with an English murder case.

Joseph and Dee Wambaugh eventually left Los Angeles for a house in Palm Springs and an estate overlooking the San Diego harbor and Coronado Island when he made his fortune with bestseller after bestseller.

**Analysis** • It is not the subject matter (crime and police work) or the types of characters (police officers, criminals, and victims) that distinguish Joseph Wambaugh's books: It is the intimacy he develops between the reader and the policemen. Like a trusted partner, the reader is privy to others' baser qualities–including vulgarity, bigotry, and cruelty. Yet the reader also comes to know human beings, and that knowledge allows for affection, sometimes admiration, and always a shared fatalism about police work: It is an after-the-fact effort–after the robbery, after the rape, after the child abuse, after the murder.

This fatalistic outlook does not develop from book to book; it is present in full measure from Wambaugh's first novel:

> It is the natural tendency of things toward chaos. . . . It's a very basic natural law Kilvinsky always said, and only the order makers could temporarily halt its march, but eventually there will be darkness and chaos. . . .

The point is convincingly dramatized through the police confrontations during the 1965 Armageddon known as the Watts riots.

Even the survivors–those policemen who finish enough shifts to reach retirement and the prized pension–pay with a piece of their souls. The wise Kilvinsky in *The New Centurions* learns all the natural laws and then shoots himself. Bumper Morgan, the blue knight in the book of that title, is the kind of police officer that radicals had in mind when shouting "pig." He is a fat, freeloading womanizer (teenage belly dancers preferred), and the reader would probably turn away in disgust if, beneath the crudity, loneliness and depression were not detectable.

Victimization of police officers is one of Wambaugh's recurring themes. They are victimized by the dislike of those they swear to protect and by the justice system they swear to uphold. Two of his books make this premise particularly convincing. Writing for the first time in the genre of the nonfiction, or documentary, novel, Wambaugh in *The Onion Field* painstakingly reconstructed the 1963 kidnapping of two fellow officers, the murder of one, and the trial that followed. During that trial, the surviving officer became as much a defendant as the two killers.

To the author's credit, however, he stays out of the story. Here, for example, are none of the awkward intrusions found in *The New Centurions*. Nowhere does one on-duty policeman turn to another and inquire about psychological-sociological implications, such as "Gus, do you think policemen are in a better position to understand criminality than, say, penologists or parole officers or other behavioral scientists?" The questions and answers have not disappeared, however. They are simply left either for the reader to ask and answer in the course of reading the book or for one of the force to understand as an integral part of the story. "I don't fudge or try to make it [a true-crime story] better by editorializing or dramatizing," Wambaugh said, "I try to be a real investigative reporter and write it as it happened as best I can."

The realization of Dick Snider in *Lines and Shadows* (1983) is a case in point. After watching San Diego cops chase illegal aliens through the city's San Ysidro section, Snider knows that the crime of illegal entry and the various authorities' efforts to stop it are simply shadows hiding the truth. Illegal entry is, in fact, only about money: "*There is not a significant line between two countries. It's between two economies.*"

In studying so closely the ruined careers, marriages, and lives of the Border Alien Robbery Force, the BARF Squad, as it became known, Wambaugh also provides an explicit answer to a puzzle within all of his books–indeed, to a puzzle about police inside or outside the covers of a book. Why would they want such a job? Wambaugh's answer is that they are caught up as the players in a national myth:

They gave their nightly performance and almost everyone applauded. They did it the only way they knew–not ingeniously, merely instinctively–by trying to resurrect in the late twentieth century a mythic hero who never was, not even in the nineteenth century. A myth nevertheless cherished by Americans beyond the memory of philosophers, statesmen, artists and scientists who really lived: the quintessentially American myth and legend of the Gunslinger, who with only a six-shooter and star dares venture beyond the badlands.

Those who recognize the myth and how they have been used by it clearly have great difficulty continuing to play their parts. Yet these are the most likable and most interesting policemen in Wambaugh's fiction–Martin Welborn, for example (*The Glitter Dome*, 1981). He is a ploddingly thorough detective, with a penchant for orderliness in his police work and in his personal life. Glasses in his kitchen cupboard rest "in a specifically assigned position." Drawers display dinner and cocktail napkins "stacked and arranged by size and color." Neither can he leave "out of place" an unsolved case or the memory of a mutilated child. He depends upon two universals: People always lie and, with less certainty, the devil exists (because "life would be unbearable if we didn't have the devil, now wouldn't it?"). What happens, then, when one of the universals is taken away? Yes, people always lie, but there is no evil and, consequently, no good. All that happens happens accidentally. With that realization, detecting who committed a crime and bringing the criminal to justice loses significance. So, too, does life, and Marty Welborn ends his by driving over a mountain cliff as he recalls the one perfect moment in his life. At the time, he had been a young, uniformed policeman, and he had just heard an old cardinal deliver a solemn high mass. As he kneeled to kiss the cardinal's ring, Welborn saw, in one perfect moment, the old priest's "*lovely crimson slippers.*"

While Martin Welborn is the totally professional police officer, a winner who nevertheless takes his life, Andrei Milhailovich Valnikov (*The Black Marble*, 1978) is a loser, a "black marble" who endures. Like Welborn, he has his reveries, usually drunken ones, of past perfect moments. Yet they come from a czarist Russia Valnikov never personally experienced. Such an absence of reality works perfectly with the constant losses in the detective's work. He cannot, for example, find his handcuffs, he gets lost on the streets of Los Angeles, and he is all the more touchingly comical for both the reveries and the misadventures. In Valnikov, Wambaugh demonstrates his ability to develop a memorable character.

As good as Wambaugh is at occasional character development, he is even better at telling amusing stories, as in *The Blue Knight* and *The Black Marble. The Glitter Dome, The Delta Star* (1983)–which was described by one reviewer as "Donald Westlake meets Ed McBain"–and *The Secrets of Harry Bright* (1985) are also amusing. None of these novels, however, measures up to the humor in *The Choirboys*. All that has been said about Wambaugh's humor in this book is true: It is "sarcastic and filled with scrofulous expletives"; it is "scabrous"; and it is often "intentionally ugly." Indeed, the reader may believe that laughing at *The Choirboys* is giving in to an adolescence long outgrown.

Wambaugh would be offended by none of this. He lists among his literary influences both Joseph Heller and Truman Capote on the one hand and humorists P. J. O'Rourke and Dave Barry, the Pulitzer-winning humor columnist, on the other. "I wanted to use the tools of gallows humor, satire, hyperbole, all of that, to make people laugh in an embarrassed way," Wambaugh told an interviewer. "I reread [Heller's] *Catch-22* and [Kurt Vonnegut's] *Slaughterhouse Five* to see how it was done in war novels. . . . I couldn't find anybody who'd done it in a police novel."

Typical of Wambaugh's humor is Officer Francis Tanaguchi's impression of Bela Lugosi in *The Choirboys*:

> For three weeks, which was about as long as one of Francis's whims lasted, he was called the Nisei Nipper by the policemen at Wilshire Station. He sulked around the station with two blood dripping fangs slipped over his incisors, attacking the throat of everyone below the rank of sergeant.

The jokes in *The Choirboys* are sandwiched between a prologue, three concluding chapters, and an epilogue filled with terror and insanity. Wambaugh's novel illustrates well an idea popularized by Sigmund Freud: Beneath a joke lies the most horrific of human fears.

However, Wambaugh's works became more light-hearted following *The Secrets of Harry Bright* (1985). "As I mellowed with age, or got farther from day-to-day police work, I wrote books that were more consciously entertaining," he said. "*Harry Bright* was the exception. I happen to like that book better than any of the other novels, but that one was so dark, I think I had to lighten up, it was all about fathers and sons and death."

His novels of the 1990's were broadly comical—*The Golden Orange* (1990), a tale of an alcoholic cop among the millionaires of the Gold Coast of Orange County; *Fugitive Nights* (1992), in which another alcoholic cop teams up with a female private eye to handle a drug-smuggling case, depending, as one reviewer said, mostly on vulgar police humor for its laughs;" *Finnegan's Week* (1993), a funny and witty thriller about toxic waste comparable to the works of Carl Hiaasen; and *Floaters* (1996), a romp concerning racing spies, saboteurs, scam artists, and hookers swarming around San Diego Bay, the site of the America's Cup international sailing regatta, into which two Mission Bay patrol-boat cops of the "Club Harbor Unit" get dragged out of their depth.

Several of Wambaugh's novels were adapted to film. *The New Centurions* (1972) starred George C. Scott; more successful was *The Black Marble*, directed by Harold Becker as a romantic comedy and produced by Frank Capra, Jr., and starring James Woods and Harry Dean Stanton. *The Choirboys* (1977) was disappointingly directed by Robert Aldrich; it is understandable why Wambaugh filed suit when he saw the results. *The Blue Knight* was filmed as a television miniseries of four one-hour installments in 1973; lead actor William Holden and director Robert Butler both received Emmy Awards for their work.

A second *Blue Knight* TV movie, filmed in 1975 and starring George Kennedy as seasoned cop Bumper Morgan, served as the pilot for a short-lived

TV series (1975-1976). *The Glitter Dome* (1985) was filmed for cable television and starred James Garner, John Lithgow, and Margot Kidder. *Fugitive Nights: Danger in the Desert* aired on television in 1993, with Teri Garr as leading lady. The nonfiction novels *The Onion Field* (motion picture) and *Echoes in the Darkness* (made-for-television miniseries re-released as video) were also filmed in 1979 and 1987, respectively. Wambaugh's fast-paced, violent, and funny writing continues to attract the attention of Hollywood.

Wambaugh, however, was dissatisfied with these adaptation projects— except for ones he contributed to. Television's regular series *Police Story* (1973-1980) was "based on his memoirs" and focused on the LAPD. A particularly interesting project was The Learning Channel's series *Case Reopened*, in which Lawrence Block, Ed McBain, and Wambaugh were asked to host hour-long segments about notorious unsolved crimes. Wambaugh's turn came with "The Black Dahlia," which aired October 10, 1999. The murder of Elizabeth Short had occurred when Wambaugh was ten, and during his rookie years on the beat he heard many anecdotes about the sensational manhunt. Despite his vow not to return to true-crime writing, Wambaugh reviewed the evidence and offered his own solution.

Of the crime committed as documented in *Echoes in the Darkness*, Wambaugh wrote, "Perhaps it had nothing to do with sin and everything to do with sociopathy, that most incurable of human disorders because all so afflicted consider themselves *blessed* rather than cursed." The fate of a policeman who becomes a best-selling author as a representative of the police to the rest of the human species might be considered both a blessing and a curse. Certainly Wambaugh's insights into the follies and struggles of humanity have proved a blessing for crime fiction.

## Principal mystery and detective fiction

NOVELS: *The New Centurions*, 1970; *The Blue Knight*, 1972; *The Choirboys*, 1975; *The Black Marble*, 1978; *The Glitter Dome*, 1981; *The Delta Star*, 1983; *The Secrets of Harry Bright*, 1985; *The Golden Orange*, 1990; *Fugitive Nights*, 1992; *Finnegan's Week*, 1993; *Floaters*, 1996.

## Other major works

SCREENPLAYS: *The Onion Field*, 1979; *The Black Marble*, 1980; *Echoes in the Darkness*, 1987.

NONFICTION: *The Onion Field*, 1973; *Lines and Shadows*, 1983; *Echoes in the Darkness*, 1987; *The Blooding*, 1989.

## Bibliography

Reed, J. D. "Those Blues in the Knights." *Time* 117 (June 8, 1981): 76-79.
Roberts, Steven V. "Cop of the Year." *Esquire* 80 (December, 1973): 15-53, 310, 314.
Wambaugh, Joseph. "Wambaugh Cops from Experience." Interview by J. Brady. *Writer's Digest* 53 (December, 1973): 9-16.

Van Dover, J. Kenneth. *Centurions, Knights, and Other Cops: The Police Novels of Joseph Wambaugh.* San Bernardino, Calif.: Brownstone Books, 1995.

Ziegler, Robert E. "Freedom and Confinement: The Policeman's Experience of Public and Private in Joseph Wambaugh." *Clues: A Journal of Detection* 3 (Spring/Summer, 1982): 9-16.

*Alice MacDonald*
*Updated by Fiona Kelleghan*

# Hillary Waugh

**Born:** New Haven, Connecticut; June 22, 1920

**Also wrote as** • Elissa Grandower • H. Baldwin Taylor • Harry Walker

**Types of plot** • Hard-boiled • police procedural • private investigator • thriller

**Principal series** • Sheridan Wesley, 1947-1949 • Fred Fellows, 1959-1968 • David Halliday, 1964-1966 • Frank Sessions, 1968-1970 • Simon Kaye, 1981-     .

**Principal series characters** • FRED FELLOWS, the chief of police in Stockford, Connecticut, is married, with four children. At first glance, Fellows is the stereotypical small-town policeman–the slightly overweight, tobacco-chewing storyteller. As criminals who choose to commit a crime in Stockford quickly learn, however, the truth of the matter is that Fellows is an extraordinarily good detective, solving his cases with a combination of solid police work and imaginative thinking. Fellows is fifty-three years old in his first novel (1959), and he ages slightly over the course of the eleven novels in which he appears.

• FRANK SESSIONS, a detective second grade in the homicide squad, Manhattan North, is divorced. A tough and capable detective, Sessions originally became a detective because his father was a policeman. Quick to dispel any idealistic notions about his job, Sessions is a veteran of more than sixteen years on the force who nevertheless remains passionate about justice. This passion is often tested in his brutal cases.

• SIMON KAYE, a private investigator, is single. An ex-cop, Kaye is a resourceful private eye who works in the same unnamed city in which he grew up. Around thirty years old, Kaye is a very physical investigator who is capable of inflicting as well as absorbing much physical damage. Often cynical and sarcastic, Kaye works as a detective to help people as individuals, not out of some overblown Don Quixote/Sir Galahad complex.

**Contribution** • One of the true pioneers of the police procedural, Hillary Waugh was not the first writer to use policemen as detectives, but he was one of the first to present a realistic portrait of policemen and police work, emphasizing all the details of the case from start to finish, including the dull legwork that is often ignored. This emphasis was picked up later by other writers such as Ed McBain and Dell Shannon. According to Julian Symons and others, Waugh's first police procedural, *Last Seen Wearing . . .* (1952), is one of he classics of detective fiction. Waugh's later police novels involving Fred Fellows and Frank Sessions are praised for their realism and polish. In his less-known works as well as in these police procedurals, Waugh is a master craftsman who knows how to tell a good story and construct a tight and suspenseful plot. His prolific and enduring career is a testament to his ability and innovation.

**Biography** • Hillary Baldwin Waugh was born on June 22, 1920, in New Haven, Connecticut. He remained in that city until he received his B.A. from Yale University in 1942. Straight from graduation, he entered the navy and became a pilot in the Naval Air Corps in May, 1943. He remained in the navy until January, 1946, achieving the rank of lieutenant. It was in the navy that he began to write his first mystery, which was published in 1947 as *Madam Will Not Dine Tonight.*

After his discharge from the navy, Waugh returned to New England. With the exception of some time in New York and Europe, Waugh has lived in Connecticut since that time. In 1951, he married Diana Taylor, with whom he had two daughters and one son. After a divorce in 1981, he married Shannon O'Cork. He has worked as a teacher (1956-1957), has edited a weekly newspaper (1961-1962), and has been involved in local politics, serving as First Selectman of Guilford, Connecticut (1971-1973). These vocations have always been secondary, though, to his writing.

A prolific writer, Waugh published more than forty novels in the forty-year span between 1947 and 1987. Waugh is also active in the Mystery Writers of America, being a past president of that organization.

**Analysis** • One of the most interesting aspects of the detective story is the vast variety of forms it has taken in its history. The police procedural, one major variation of the detective novel, got its start in the 1940's and 1950's with the work of writers such as Lawrence Treat and Hillary Waugh and has since become one of the most popular forms of the genre. This particular type of story follows the efforts of a policeman or a police force (not a gifted amateur or a private eye) working toward solving a case. Waugh himself explains this emphasis in an essay, "The Police Procedural," in John Ball's *The Mystery Story* (1976):

> The police procedural thrusts the detective into the middle of a working police force, full of rules and regulations. Instead of bypassing the police, as did its predecessors, the procedural takes the reader inside the department and shows how it operates.
>
> These are stories, not just about policemen, but about the world of the policeman. Police Inspector Charlie Chan doesn't belong. (There're no police.) Nor does Inspector Maigret. (There are police, but Maigret, like Chan, remains his own man.)

Thus, the police procedural presents a realistic milieu to the reader; the emphasis is upon the ordinary policemen who solve cases through a combination of diligence, intelligence, and luck. Waugh helped pioneer this particular form and remains one of its masters.

Waugh began to write while he was a pilot in the navy, and he began his career with three fairly standard private eye novels: *Madam Will Not Dine To-*

*night, Hope to Die* (1948), and *The Odds Run Out* (1949). He returned to the private eye form in the early 1980's with his Simon Kaye novels, a series of entertaining mysteries. It was in 1950, however, that Waugh began a work that would become an influential classic, a work that would help define the emerging type of detective novel known as the police procedural. In writing that novel, Waugh found himself influenced by an unlikely source. In 1949, he had read a book by Charles M. Boswell titled *They All Died Young: A Case Book of True and Unusual Murders* (1949). The book, a true-crime collection of ten stories about murders of young girls, had a tremendous impact on Waugh. "I went through those stories, one by one, and was never the same thereafter." Waugh resolved to write a detective story in the same matter-of-fact style as that of Boswell, a detective story that would show how the police of a small town would solve the case of the disappearance and murder of a college girl. That novel, which appeared in 1952 as *Last Seen Wearing...* , is still considered by many to be one of the best detective stories ever written.

The detectives in the story are Frank Ford and his sergeant, Burton Cameron, two ordinary policemen who are well-drawn and realistic characters. In fact, they were so realistic that the rough, grouchy Ford seemed to take over the work as the novel progressed. Waugh had originally intended the two to be modeled on the rather nondescript detectives of the true-crime stories—solid professionals with no outstanding features. Instead, the realistic, complex portrayal of the detectives became an important part of the story and was to become an important part of later successful police procedurals. Like the classic puzzle story or the private eye story, the successful police procedural depends upon and revolves around the detectives. Ford and Cameron lack the genius of Sherlock Holmes or the guile of Sam Spade, but they make up for that by being admirably professional policemen and believable, engaging characters.

Waugh had clearly hit upon a successful formula. In 1959, he returned to the idea of a small-town police force in *Sleep Long, My Love.* That novel featured a slightly overweight, folksy gentleman named Fred Fellows, the chief of police of Stockford, Connecticut. Over the next nine years, Fellows appeared in eleven novels, and it is these novels that show Waugh in full mastery of the form.

In the creation of Fellows, Waugh transformed a stereotype into a complex, three-dimensional character. Policemen in small towns have often been portrayed as inept and bumbling, if not incompetent and corrupt. Stockford is definitely a typical small town (except for its extraordinarily high crime rate), and Fellows is, on the surface, the typical small-town police chief. He is fifty-three at the beginning of the series, and he is married, father to four children—a devoted family man. He is slightly overweight, a source of anxiety for him. He chews tobacco and has nude pinups on the wall of his office. Deliberate and methodical, he has a penchant for telling stories in the manner of parables, using them to illustrate his thought processes. in his second adventure, *Road Block* (1960), one of the crooks planning a payroll holdup in Stockford dismisses Fellows and his force as "a bunch of hick cops." As that criminal and many others discover, the truth of the matter is that Fellows and his coworkers are a group of very talented policemen. In *Road Block*, Fellows tracks down the criminals by using the mileage on the odometer of a car and catches them by feeding them false reports over the police radio. Behind Fellows's genial, folksy manner, the reader discovers a complex individual—a policeman who is not bound by his office, but instead brings to it shrewdness and imaginative thinking.

In addition to introducing a realistic detective, Waugh set a precedent in the Fellows series by giving attention to the actual nuts and bolts of a police investigation. Rather than dismissing the details—the endless interviewing of suspects and witnesses, the tracking down of leads that prove to be false as well as those that are valuable, the combing of neighborhoods, the searching through all types of records—Waugh relishes them, utilizing them to create suspense. For an organized police force, bound by the legal system, cases are built piece by piece. Information comes in as bits and pieces—some useful, some worthless. Detection for Fellows and his men is pure work—work that sometimes leads nowhere, yet work that ultimately pays off. In Waugh's deft hands, the step-by-step, often-repetitive legwork of a case is never dull. By allowing the reader to focus on the detectives as they sort out the details of the case, Waugh builds suspense the same way his detectives build their cases, moving step by step. As he says, "The tension should build to an explosion, not a let-down."

All the novels in the Fellows series exhibit another strength of Waugh's writing—his tight, believable plots. Waugh does not use the multiple-case approach of later writers; each novel focuses on a single case, following it from beginning to end. *Road Block*, for example, begins with the crooks planning the holdup, and their plans are revealed in great detail. As the robbery unfolds and the plans go awry, the story moves swiftly. Time is of the essence for Fellows, and the novel reflects that. There is no time for subplots, and there are none. Every detail of the novel builds the suspense of the case, propelling it toward the climax.

Another example is *The Missing Man* (1964), which begins with the discovery of the body of a young woman on the beach of a lake near Stockford. The case is a frustrating one for Fellows and his men as they struggle to identify both the victim and her murderer; although it takes them weeks to solve the case, there are no extraneous subplots. This deliberate focus is a skillful way of building tension in the work, forcing the reader to continue turning pages. There are simply no lulls in the action.

After leaving Fred Fellows, Waugh turned his attention to another policeman, Detective Second Grade Frank Sessions of the homicide Squad, Manhattan North. Sessions first appeared in *30 Manhattan East* (1968), which appeared the same year as the last Fellows novel, *The Con Game*; he also appeared in *The Young Prey* (1969) and *Finish Me Off* (1970). With this trio of brutal and gritty novels, Waugh left the small-town locale of Fellows and Ford for the big city, but he did not abandon the strengths and innovations of his earlier works. As a central character, Sessions is complex enough to sustain the reader's interest. A sixteen-year veteran of the force, Sessions, like Fellows and Ford, is a true professional. On one hand, he sees police work for the demanding job that it is; on the other, he remains dedicated to that difficult job.

In the three Sessions novels, Waugh pays even more attention to the detailed legwork of the cases. The everyday workings of a police department are once again the primary focus, and the manner in which the homicide squad of Manhattan North goes about solving a case is examined very closely. The urban setting amplifies the importance of the tedious, repetitive legwork, for here it is even more difficult to reach a solution to a case. The late 1960's were an uneasy time in the history of America, and Waugh captures the uneasiness and unrest perfectly. It was an especially difficult time to be an urban policeman, and the Sessions novels reflect that. Like his other works, these novels demonstrate Waugh's mastery of the procedural; the three Sessions novels are textbook examples of tight, controlled plotting and masterful storytelling.

The police procedural form owes much to Hillary Waugh; that is apparent. Yet, for all of his pioneering and innovation, Waugh's greatest claim to fame is the simple fact that he is an excellent storyteller. All of his works—be they police procedurals, private eye novels, or other types of works—show this ability. His long career attests the fact that, above all, Hillary Waugh tells a story that people take great pleasure in reading.

## Principal mystery and detective fiction

SERIES: Fred Fellows: *Sleep Long, My Love,* 1959 (also as *Jigsaw*); *Road Block,* 1960; *That Night It Rained,* 1961; *The Late Mrs. D,* 1962; *Born Victim,* 1962; *Death and Circumstances,* 1963; *Prisoner's Plea,* 1963; *The Missing Man,* 1964; *End of a Party,* 1965; *Pure Poison,* 1966; *The Con Game,* 1968. David Halliday: *The Duplicate,* 1964; *The Triumvirate,* 1966. Simon Kaye: *The Glenna Powers Case,* 1980; *The Doria Rafe Case,* 1980; *The Billy Cantrell Case,* 1981; *The Nerissa Claire Case,* 1983; *The Veronica Dean Case,* 1984; *The Priscilla Copperwaite Case,* 1986. Frank Sessions: *30 Manhattan East,* 1968; *The Young Prey,* 1969; *Finish Me Off,* 1970. Sheridan Wesley: *Madam Will Not Dine Tonight,* 1947 (also as *If I Live to Dine*); *Hope to Die,* 1948; *The Odds Run Out,* 1949.

OTHER NOVELS: *Last Seen Wearing . . . ,* 1952; *A Rag and a Bone,* 1954; *The Case of the Missing Gardener,* 1954; *Rich Man, Dead Man,* 1956 (also as *Rich Man, Murder* and *The Case of the Brunette Bombshell*); *The Eighth Mrs. Bluebeard,* 1958; *The Girl Who Cried Wolf,* 1958; *Murder on the Terrace,* 1961; *Girl on the Run,* 1965; *The Trouble with Tycoons,* 1967; *Run When I Say Go,* 1969; *The Shadow Guest,* 1971; *Parrish for the Defense,* 1974 (also as *Doctor on Trial*); *A Bride for Hampton House,* 1975; *Seaview Manor,* 1976; *The Summer at Raven's Roost,* 1976; *The Secret Room of Morgate House,* 1977; *Madman at My Door,* 1978; *Blackbourne Hall,* 1979; *Rivergate House,* 1980; *Murder on Safari,* 1987.

**Other major works**

NONFICTION: *Hillary Waugh's Guide to Mysteries and Mystery Writing,* 1991.
EDITED TEXT: *Merchants of Menace,* 1969.

**Bibliography**

Ball, John, ed. *The Mystery Story.* San Diego: University Extension, University of California, 1976.
Barzun, Jacques, and Wendell Hertig Taylor. Introduction to *The Missing Man.* New York: Doubleday, 1964.
Dove, George N. "Hillary Waugh." In *The Police Procedural.* Bowling Green, Ohio: Bowling Green State University Popular Press, 1982.
_____. Introduction to *Last Seen Wearing . . .* New York: Carroll & Graf, 1990.
Penzler, Otto, ed. *The Great Detectives.* London: Little, Brown, 1978.

*Stephen Wood*

# Patricia Wentworth

## Dora Amy Elles Dillon Turnbull

**Born:** Mussoorie, India; 1878
**Died:** Camberley, Surrey, England; January 28, 1961

**Type of plot** • Private investigator

**Principal series** • Maud Silver, 1928-1961.

**Principal series characters** • MAUD SILVER, a professional private investigator, unmarried, operating her detective agency from her drawing room after her retirement from a position as governess. Her clients are usually young females who are friends or have been referred by friends. Seemingly acquainted with people throughout England, including the police, she works carefully and efficiently, not only proving the innocence of her clients but also reinstating their inevitable social respectability.
 • ERNEST LAMB, the woolly and not entirely skillful chief investigator who often works with Miss Silver. His three daughters are all named after flowers.
 • ETHEL BURKETT, Miss Silver's favorite niece, whose four young children receive most of the bounty from Miss Silver's perpetual knitting.
 • GLADYS ROBINSON, Miss Silver's other niece. Her complaints about her husband make her less than pleasant both to Miss Silver and to the reader.
 • RANDAL MARCH, the chief constable in the county where many of Miss Silver's cases occur. When she worked as a governess, Randal was her favorite child, and their devotion to each other remains.

**Contribution** • The more than seventy novels of Patricia Wentworth, more than half of which feature Miss Silver and/or Inspector Lamb, have been variously judged anodyne, dependable, and engaging—solid praise for such an extensive canon. Often compared to Jane Marple, Wentworth's heroine, Miss Silver, is enriched with much detail, making her one of the most successfully and clearly drawn private detectives in the genre. She inevitably brings a happy solution to varied maidens-in-distress who have been wrongly accused of crime and stripped of their good names and reputations. Wentworth's style, though in no way poetic or memorable, is sufficient to tell the story, and is, at times, mildly witty. Her plots play fair with the reader, even though they are at times highly unrealistic. They are successful, however, because they create considerable suspense by placing ordinary, decent people from comfortable English settings into extreme danger, a plot device which Wentworth helped to initiate. Like other prolific mystery writers, notably Agatha Christie, Wentworth wrote novels which are uneven in quality, with the least successful written at the end of her career. Yet her charming, rational heroine, Miss Silver, and her skill in creating suspense ensure Wentworth's lasting popularity as a writer of detective fiction.

**Biography** • Patricia Wentworth was born Dora Amy Elles in Mussoorie, India, in 1878. She was the daughter of a British army officer. She received a high school education at the Blackheath High School in London, where she and her two brothers had been sent to live with their grandmother. When she completed her education, she returned to India, where she married Colonel George Dillon in 1906. He died soon after, leaving her with three stepsons and a young daughter. She returned to England with the four children and established a successful writing career, publishing six well-received novels of historical fiction between 1910 and 1915.

In 1920, she married another British army officer, Lieutenant George Oliver Turnbull, and moved to Surrey. He encouraged and assisted her in her writing and served as a scribe while she dictated her stories, the two of them working only during the winter months between 5:00 and 7:00 P.M. In 1923, she began writing mystery novels with *The Astonishing Adventure of Jane Smith*; in 1928, she introduced Miss Silver in *Grey Mask*. Then, after an interim of nine years and fifteen mystery novels, she revived the Maud Silver character in 1937 and used her exclusively in her books written between 1945 and 1961. She died on January 28, 1961.

**Analysis** • Like many other prolific mystery novelists, Patricia Wentworth began her professional career writing in another genre, historical fiction. Unlike her peers, however, she earned a solid reputation as such a writer, with her first novel, *A Marriage Under the Terror* (1910), appearing in ten editions and winning a literary prize. She wrote five more historical novels, which were published annually through 1915. While technically unremarkable, these early volumes helped her develop style, plotting technique, and the extensive use of detail in characterization.

When she began writing mysteries in 1923, she was a polished writer already showing the traits which would become the hallmarks of her entire body of work. In her first novel of detection, *The Astonishing Adventure of Jane Smith*, while using generic mystery plot elements, she conjured up considerable suspense and intrigue. In many of her books, the typical English settings of pastoral country village or urban London gain deadly and suspenseful qualities with the emphasis upon secret passageways and gangs of disguised criminals who have mysterious though entirely mortal power. Such plot elements are saved from becoming silly and absurd throughout her work because of the suspense they consistently generate.

Wentworth's settings offer the orderly, romanticized views of England which the reader of English mystery novels has come to expect. The small English village, made most famous by Christie, contains within itself all the plot and character requirements. The village green is surrounded by a few small cottages with their requisite gardens; fewer still larger homes built in the Georgian style and filled with unpretentious furniture which, though worn, is very good indeed; a group of small shops containing collections of innocuous items for sale; and the necessary official places, a vicarage and a solicitor's office. Such exaggerated peace in the setting is stressed in order to create a strong contrast to the strange and nearly diabolical evil which enters and temporarily cankers the village. It is also the peace to which the village returns after Miss Silver has excised the evil. Thus, Wentworth uses setting in a traditional mystery fashion.

On the surface, too, her characters resemble those of Christie. First among them is Maud Silver herself, an elderly female whose powers of knitting and detection seem unbounded. Often compared to Jane Marple, she is only superficially similar. Interestingly, Miss Silver's appearance in *Grey Mask* predates that of Miss Marple in *Murder in the Vicarage* (1930) by two years. Wentworth's creation of Miss Silver is highly detailed, perhaps more than that of any other detective hero. These details function to make her comfortably familiar to the reader and often stunningly unpredictable to her foes. Nearly everything about her is misleadingly soft, pastel, and chintz, from her light blue dressing gown and pale smooth skin to her little fur tie and ribbon-and-flower-bedecked hat. She is not a fussy elderly lady, however, and, importantly, not an amateur. With her detective agency she has established a professional reputation, and her skills are acknowledged both financially and socially.

Other characters in the books, particularly the dozens of damsels in distress, may be fit into categories. This placement must be done with caution, however, in order to avoid the mistaken conclusion that they are similar, interchangeable, or two-dimensional. The damsels' behavior is a result of more than beauty and virtue; each has her own consistent weaknesses and idiosyncrasies which are not extraneous but primary sources for the movement of the plot. The characters who reappear from book to book are also endowed with their own traits, but they gain their entertainment value from the pleasant familiarity the reader soon establishes with them. A newly introduced character may suddenly realize that he or she knows one of Miss Silver's longtime favorites, a niece or a student perhaps, and the requisite order of social class, inherent in the world of the English detective story, is underscored.

Such order is clearly seen in Wentworth's plots. While plot conflicts range from the unlikely to the downright silly, they succeed because the characters who are placed in outlandish predicaments are themselves down to earth. Hence, manmade monsters threateningly lying in wait for realistic victims are not entirely foolish. Even when the threat seems to be an ordinary person using no mechanical monsters, he is horrible within; his evil becomes diabolical, almost unmotivated. It is comforting to purge such characters from the ordered society. Considered a pioneer in the use of artful suspense, Wentworth has been compared to Charlotte Armstrong, the most successful writer of suspenseful detective fiction. It is Wentworth's own method, however, to juxtapose the everyday and the horrible in order to sustain supense and bring consistently satisfying conclusions.

The style of Wentworth's novels, while often pedestrian, serves the plots well, particularly as a result of its nonintrusiveness. The reader pauses neither to admire its brilliance and wit nor to shake his head over the jarring clichés. In a chatty, second-person style, the nearly omniscient narrator briefs the reader on the personalities and motivations of the various characters and also allows the reader to hear their ongoing thoughts. Short lines of light wit also color the descriptions so that Wentworth's books become something other than reportage.

In *Miss Silver Comes to Stay* (1949), Wentworth presents a story typical of many of her successful novels. The closed setting of the small village of Melling provides the predictable scenes of a manor house library with doors leading to the garden, cottage parlors, a solicitor's office, and a general store. The proximity and the small number of these scenes enable the reader to imagine easily their location; further, it allows characters to socialize and to be aware of one another's business. The setting also functions as a presentation of the order to which this little village of Melling will return after Miss Silver removes the chaotic element.

The cast of characters, too, is pleasant and predictable. Miss Silver has come to Melling to visit her friend, appropriately named Cecilia Voycey. Acting as a foil to Miss Silver, she is an old school chum who chatters and gossips, while Miss Silver, on the other hand, quietly and methodically solves the murders. The heroine, Rietta Cray, is the damsel in distress, the leading suspect; for variation, however, she is forty-three years old, has big feet, and is often compared to Pallas Athene. In this volume, she becomes the wife of Chief Constable Randal March, the recurring character who is Miss Silver's favorite student from her governess days. He is attractive both in his admiration and affection for Miss Silver and in his common sense and wisdom. His subordinate, Inspector Drake, impetuous and imprecise, acts as his foil. The victim, James Lessiter, a wealthy lord of the manor, is amoral and unscrupulous, thereby arousing sufficient numbers of enemies who become suspects to puzzle the police. Both he and the second victim, Catherine Welby, are unlikable, which ensures that their deaths raise no grief in the other characters or in the reader. A final important suspect is Carr Robertson, Rietta Cray's twenty-eight-year-old nephew, whom she reared. He and his aunt are the chief victims of misplaced accusations; they are also both involved in their own starcrossed love affairs and are unable to marry their lovers. Thus Miss Silver not only purges the village of evil but also opens the path to love for four deserving people. She herself is drawn with no new strokes. A first-time reader is easily introduced to her knitting, good sense, and prim appearance, while the longtime reader of Miss Silver is seduced with the pleasure of familiarity.

The plot is not outlandish and depends upon only one scene of outrageous coincidence, the fact that Marjory Robertson, Carr's first wife, happens to have run away with Lessiter. Otherwise, the plot contains no twists which are not acceptable in the detective-story genre. A weakness of this particular story, however, is the lack of a sufficient number of suspects, and a few more lively red herrings are needed. The murder of Lessiter in his library is accomplished by bashing in his head with a fireplace poker. Ordinarily, men and not women commit murder using such means; still, only four men are possible suspects, one of whom is the loving and loyal Carr. The others are two minor characters, who are not involved enough to have committed the crime, and the real murderer himself. His means, motive, and opportunity for murdering Lessiter are logical but not overwhelming, and the solution is not one which completes a splendid puzzle. The pacing of the plot is classic, with the cast of characters being introduced as future suspects in the first few chapters and the murder scene being described in detail with the curtain drawn on the reader at the necessary moment. It is during this scene that Wentworth creates her standard suspense scene when the evil Lessiter acts as both the aggressor with Rietta and as the victim with the unknown murderer. Following this scene comes the questioning of suspects, the second murder, the discovery of secrets in everyone's closet, and the final revelation. The latter, however, is somewhat carelessly revealed too soon. The finger of blame seems not to point falsely at successive suspects; it simply appears and aims at the real killer. Clearly this work follows a formula plot and utilizes formula characters. Nevertheless, it is ordinarily with the expectation of such formula writing that the reader takes up such a book in the first place.

While language and style are appropriate, the dialogue is stilted and mannered. Descriptions of the physical are clear but often repetitious. The bloodied sleeve of Carr's raincoat, for example, the most gruesome image in the story, is noted an extraordinary number of times, considering that it is unimportant in the solution to the crime. In a similarly repetitive manner, lovers kiss, embrace, and kneel beside the beloved so many times that a pervasive tone of romance is cast over the entire story. Murder—romanticized, unregretted, and evil—suspensefully committed and covered up, with several pairs of happy lovers united in the end, thanks to Maud Silver: Such is the formula for the entire canon of Patricia Wentworth.

### Principal mystery and detective fiction

SERIES: Ernest Lamb: *The Blind Side*, 1939; *Who Pays the Piper?*, 1940 (also as *Account Rendered*); *Pursuit of a Parcel*, 1942. Maud Silver: *Grey Mask*, 1928; *The Case Is Closed*, 1937; *Lonesome Road*, 1939; *In The Balance*, 1941 (also as *Danger Point*); *The Chinese Shawl*, 1943; *Miss Silver Deals with Death*, 1943 (also as *Miss Silver Intervenes*); *The Clock Strikes Twelve*, 1944; *The Key*, 1944; *She Came Back*, 1945 (also as *The Traveller Returns*); *Pilgrim's Rest*, 1946 (also as *Dark Threat*); *Latter End*, 1947; *Wicked Uncle*, 1947 (also as *Spotlight*); *The Case of William Smith*, 1948; *Eternity Ring*, 1948; *Miss Silver Comes to Stay*, 1949; *The Catherine Wheel*, 1949; *The Brading Collection*, 1950; *Through the Wall*, 1950; *Anna, Where Are You?*, 1951 (also as *Death at Deep End*); *The Ivory Dagger*, 1951; *The Watersplash*, 1951; *Ladies' Bane*, 1952; *Vanishing Point*, 1953; *Out of the Past*, 1953; *The*

*Silent Pool*, 1954; *The Benevent Treasure*, 1954; *The Listening Eye*, 1955; *Poison in the Pen*, 1955; *The Gazebo*, 1956 (also as *The Summerhouse*); *The Fingerprint*, 1956; *The Alington Inheritance*, 1958; *The Girl in the Cellar*, 1961.

OTHER NOVELS: *The Astonishing Adventure of Jane Smith*, 1923; *The Red Lacquer Case*, 1924; *The Annam Jewel*, 1924; *The Black Cabinet*, 1925; *The Dower House Mystery*, 1925; *The Amazing Chance*, 1926; *Hue and Cry*, 1927; *Anne Belinda*, 1927; *Will-o'-the-Wisp*, 1928; *Fool Errant*, 1929; *The Coldstone*, 1930; *Beggar's Choice*, 1930; *Kingdom Lost*, 1930; *Danger Calling*, 1931; *Nothing Venture*, 1932; *Red Danger*, 1932 (also as *Red Shadow*); *Seven Green Stones*, 1933 (also as *Outrageous Fortune*); *Walk with Care*, 1933; *Devil-in-the-Dark*, 1934 (also as *Touch and Go*); *Fear by Night*, 1934; *Red Stefan*, 1935; *Blindfold*, 1935; *Hole and Corner*, 1936; *Dead or Alive*, 1936; *Down Under*, 1937; *Run!*, 1938; *Mr. Zero*, 1938; *Rolling Stone*, 1940; *Unlawful Occasions*, 1941 (also as *Weekend with Death*); *Silence in Court*, 1945.

## Other major works

NOVELS: *A Marriage Under the Terror*, 1910; *A Little More Than Kin*, 1911 (also as *More Than Kin*); *The Devil's Wind*, 1912; *The Fire Within*, 1913; *Simon Heriot*, 1914; *Queen Anne Is Dead*, 1915.

POETRY: *A Child's Rhyme Book*, 1910; *Beneath the Hunter's Moon: Poems*, 1945; *The Pool of Dreams: Poems*, 1953.

NONFICTION: *Earl or Chieftain? The Romance of Hugh O'Neill*, 1919.

## Bibliography

Amelin, Michael. "Patricia Wentworth." *Enigmatika* 25 (November, 1983): 3-9.

Cuff, Sergeant. Review of *The Alington Inheritance*, by Patricia Wentworth. *Saturday Review* 41 (June 14, 1958): 40.

_____. Review of *The Gazebo*, by Patricia Wentworth. *Saturday Review* 39 (June 9, 1956): 38.

Klein, Kathleen Gregory. *Great Women Mystery Writers*. Westport, Conn.: Greenwood Press, 1994.

Wynne, Nancy Blue. "Patricia Wentworth Revisited." *The Armchair Detective* 14 (1981): 90-92.

*Vicki K. Robinson*

# Donald E. Westlake

**Born:** Brooklyn, New York; July 12, 1933

**Also wrote as** • John B. Allen, Curt Clark, Tucker Coe, Timothy J. Culver, Morgan J. Cunningham, Samuel Holt, Sheldon Lord, Allan Marshall, Richard Stark, Edwin West, Edwina West, Edwin Wood

**Types of plot** • Inverted • hard-boiled • comedy caper • private investigator • thriller

**Principal series** • Parker, 1962-1974, 1997-    • Alan Grofield, 1964-1974 • Mitch Tobin, 1966-1972 • John Dortmunder, 1970-    .

**Principal series characters** • PARKER, a ruthless, brilliant master thief with no first name. Through an elaborate underground criminal network, Parker sometimes is recruited, sometimes recruits others, for daring thefts: an army payroll, an entire North Dakota town. Meticulous and coldly efficient, he will kill without compunction, but he abhors needless violence.

• ALAN GROFIELD, an aspiring actor, thief, and sometimes associate of Parker. Grofield is more charming, human, and humorous than Parker but equally conscienceless in perpetrating the thefts and scams by which he subsidizes his acting career.

• MITCH TOBIN, an embittered former cop, guilt-ridden because his partner was killed while Tobin was sleeping with a burglar's wife. Though he tries to hibernate in his Queens home, Tobin grows progressively more involved with other people by reluctantly solving several baffling murders. Eventually, he becomes a licensed private detective.

• JOHN DORTMUNDER, a likable two-time loser who lives a quiet domestic life with May, a grocery checker and shoplifter, when not pursuing his chosen career as a thief. Often lured into crimes against his will by Andy Kelp, Dortmunder designs brilliant capers that always go wrong somehow.

• ANDY KELP, an incurable optimist, is a car thief who steals only doctors' cars, a sucker for gadgets, and Dortmunder's longtime associate and jinx.

• STAN MURCH is a gifted getaway driver who monomaniacally discusses roads, routes, detours, and traffic jams, often with his mother, a cabdriver usually called "Murch's Mom."

• TINY BULCHER, a cretinous human mountain, leg-breaker, and threat to the peace, is often called "the beast from forty fathoms."

**Contribution** • By combining the intricate plotting characteristic of mystery writing with the deconstructive energies of comedy and satire, Donald E.

Westlake invented his own form of crime fiction, the comic caper. Comedy was a significant element in the fiction Westlake published under his own name during the late 1960's, beginning with *The Fugitive Pigeon* (1965). In those novels, harried protagonists bumblingly encounter the frustrations of everyday life while sidestepping dangerous enemies. Somehow, all the negative forces are rendered harmless in the end, as is usual in comedy. In the same period, Westlake's Richard Stark novels featuring Parker, the master thief, developed increasingly more complex capers, or "scores." With *The Hot Rock* (1970), Westlake united these two creative forces in a single work and found his perfect hero/foil, John Archibald Dortmunder.

In the series of novels that followed, Dortmunder designs capers as brilliant as Parker's. His compulsive associates follow through meticulously. Yet these capers never quite succeed. The reader, hypnotized by the intricacy and daring of Dortmunder's planning, watches in shocked disbelief as the brilliant caper inexorably unravels. The laughter that inevitably follows testifies to Westlake's mastery of this unique subgenre.

Some of his novels have been made into American, English, and French films starring actors as varied as Lee Marvin (*Point Blank*, 1967), Sid Caesar (*The Busy Body*, 1967), Jim Brown (*The Split*, 1968), Robert Redford (*The Hot Rock*, 1972), Robert Duvall (*The Outfit*, 1973), George C. Scott (*Bank Shot*, 1974), Dom DeLuise (*Hot Stuff*, 1979), Gary Coleman (*Jimmy the Kid*, 1983), Christopher Lambert (*Why Me?*, 1990), Antonio Banderas and Melanie Griffith (*Two Much*, 1996), and Mel Gibson (*Payback*, 1999). Westlake has also scripted several films, most famously his Academy Award-winning screenplay for *The Grifters* (1990, based on Jim Thompson's novel, directed by Stephen Frears and starring John Cusack, Angelica Huston, and Annette Bening). The Mystery Writers of America named Westlake a Grand Master in 1993.

**Biography** • Donald Edwin Westlake was born on July 12, 1933, in Brooklyn, New York, the son of Albert Joseph and Lillian Bounds Westlake. He was educated at Champlain College and the State University of New York at Binghamton and served in the United States Air Force, from 1954 to 1956. Westlake married Nedra Henderson in 1957, and they were divorced in 1966. He married Sandra Foley in 1967; they were divorced in 1975. These marriages brought Westlake four sons: Sean Alan, Steven Albert, Tod David, and Paul Edwin. In 1979, he married writer Abigail Adams, with whom he collaborated on two novels, *Transylvania Station* (1986) and *High Jinx* (1987).

After a series of jobs, including six months during 1958-1959 at the Scott Meredith literary agency, Westlake committed himself to becoming a full-time writer in 1959. He quickly became one of the most versatile and prolific figures in American popular literature. His first novel, *The Mercenaries*, published in 1960, was followed by more than sixty other titles, some published under Westlake's own name, some under the pen names Richard Stark, Tucker Coe, Curt Clark, and Timothy J. Culver. During 1967, for example, as

Richard Stark he published *The Rare Coin Score* and *The Green Eagle Score*, both featuring the ruthless thief Parker, and *The Damsel*, starring the more charming Alan Grofield. In the same year, *Anarchaos*, a work of science fiction, appeared under the pseudonym Curt Clark; Westlake's name was on the cover of *Philip*, a story for children, and the comic crime novel *God Save the Mark*. Since the latter received the Edgar Allan Poe Award from the Mystery Writers of America, it is evident that Westlake's writing was distinguished as well as prolific.

In an interview with *Publishers Weekly* in 1970, Westlake credited his experience in a literary agency for his understanding of the practical aspects of the literary life. His books have enjoyed good sales not only in the United States but also abroad, especially in England. Some of his novels have been made into American, English, and French films starring actors as varied as Jim Brown, Sid Caesar, Gary Coleman, Lee Marvin, Robert Redford, and George C. Scott.

**Analysis** • Donald E. Westlake's earliest novels were praised by the influential Anthony Boucher of *The New York Times* as highly polished examples of hard-boiled crime fiction. Although Westlake wrote only five novels exclusively in this idiom, concluding with the extremely violent *Pity Him Afterwards* in 1964, he did not entirely abandon the mode. The novels he wrote under the pen names Richard Stark (1962-1974) and Tucker Coe (1966-1972) all display elements of hard-boiled detective fiction. In fact, much of this work invites comparisons to that of Dashiell Hammett and Raymond Chandler. The resemblances, however, are much more a matter of tone than of character or structure. Although Tucker Coe's hero, Mitch Tobin, solves murder mysteries, he does so as a discredited policeman rather than as a private detective. The two Richard Stark series are even less traditional, since their protagonists are thieves and murderers. Illustrating the inverted mode of crime fiction, these novels draw the reader into sympathy with, or at least suspended judgment toward, Parker and Alan Grofield. Whether attributed to Stark or Coe, all these novels present a professionally controlled hard edge. When Westlake removed his own name from their covers, however, and turned to writing comic novels about crime and criminals, he discovered the form for which he was most constitutionally and artistically suited, and he launched a remarkably successful writing career.

Parker, the master thief, is a remarkable creation in himself: calculating, meticulous, highly inventive, totally lacking in normal human feelings. In some respects he resembles characters in the earlier novels published under Westlake's own name, but Parker elevates these qualities through exaggeration. For example, murder is easy for Parker, but small talk is difficult. So are most human relations, because Parker sees no practical advantage to such transactions. When involved in a caper, Parker is all business, so much so that he feels no sexual desire until the current heist is completed. Then he makes up for lost time. The purely instrumental nature of this character is further evident in the fact that he has only a surname. According to Francis M. Nevins, Jr., the first novel in the series, *The Hunter* (1962), came so easily to Westlake that he had written more than half the book before he noticed that Parker had no first name. By then, it was too late to add one unobtrusively. Since Parker normally operates under an alias in the sixteen novels in the series, this lack causes few problems. Parker was scheduled to wind up in the hands of the police at the end of *The Hunter*, and it was Westlake's editor at Pocket Books who recognized the potential for a series. Westlake easily arranged for Parker to escape and to pursue a successful criminal career, concluding in the bloody *Butcher's Moon* (1974).

The basic plot in the Parker novels, and in the Grofield series as well, is an elaborate robbery, heist, caper, or score. In *The Seventh* (1966), for example, the booty is the cash receipts of a college football game; in *The Green Eagle Score*, the payroll of an army base; in *The Score* (1964), all the negotiable assets in the town of Copper Canyon, North Dakota. Daring robberies on this scale require sophisticated planning, criminal associates with highly varied skills, weapons, transportation, electronic equipment, explosives, and perhaps uniforms, false identification, or other forms of disguise. Engaged by the detailed planning and execution of the caper, a reader temporarily suspends the disapproval that such an immoral enterprise would normally elicit. Thus, the reader experiences the release of vicarious participation in antisocial behavior.

Westlake cleverly facilitates this participation through elements of characterization. For example, Parker would unemotionally kill in pursuit of a score, and he can spend half a book exacting bloody revenge for a double cross, but he will not tolerate needless cruelty on the part of his colleagues. Furthermore, he maintains a rigid sense of fair play toward those criminals who behave honestly toward him. His conscientiousness is another winning attribute. In the same way, Grofield appeals to the reader because he is fundamentally an actor, not a thief. He steals only to support his unprofitable commitment to serious drama. In addition, although Grofield often collaborates with Parker on a caper, his wit and theatrical charm give him more in common with the comic protagonists of Westlake's *The Spy in the Ointment* (1966) and *High Adventure* (1985) than with the emotionless Parker. Thus, despite being far from rounded characters, both Parker and Grofield offer readers the opportunity to relish guilty behavior without guilt.

Westlake stopped writing these books because, he told interviewers, "Parker just wasn't alive for me." He had wearied of the noir voice. So Parker fans were delighted when, after twenty-three years, he returned in *Comeback* (1997) to steal nearly half a million dollars from a smarmy evangelist, only to find that a co-conspirator meant to kill Parker and keep the loot for himself. A *New York Times* Notable Book of the Year, the novel found a reception so hot that Richard Stark quickly followed them with *Backflash* (1998), *Payback* (1999), and *Flashfire* (2000).

Mitchell Tobin comes much closer to filling the prescription for a rounded fictional character, largely because of his human vulnerabilities and his burden of guilt. After eighteen years as a New York City policeman, Mitch was expelled from the force because his partner, Jock Sheehan, was killed in the line of duty while the married Tobin was in bed with Linda Campbell, the wife of an imprisoned burglar. Afterward, consumed by guilt but supported by his understanding wife Kate, Tobin tries to shut out the world by devoting all of his time and energy to building a high brick wall around his house in Queens. The world keeps encroaching, however, in the persons of desperate individuals needing help—usually to investigate a murder—but unable to turn to the police. A crime kingpin, a distant relative's daughter, the operator of a psychiatric halfway house, the homosexual owner of a chic boutique—all seek Tobin's aid. Partly in response to Kate's urging, partly because of his own residual sense of decency, Tobin takes the cases, suffers the resentment and hostility of the police, and solves the murders.

Although he returns to his wall after every foray into the outside world, with each case Tobin clearly takes another step toward reassuming his life, thereby jeopardizing his utility as a series character. In fact, Westlake wrote in the introduction to *Levine* (1984) that Tobin's character development inevitably led to the expiration of the series. In the final novel, *Don't Lie to Me* (1972), Tobin has a private investigator's license and is regularly working outside his home as night watchman at a graphics museum. Linda Campbell reappears, several murders take place, and a hostile cop threatens and beats Tobin, but Mitch copes with it all effectively and without excessive guilt—that is to say, he comes dangerously close to becoming the conventional protagonist of crime fiction. At this point, Westlake wisely abandoned the pen name Tucker Coe and turned to more promising subjects.

By 1972, the year of Mitch Tobin's disappearance, Westlake had already published, under his own name, seven comic novels about crime, including *The Hot Rock*, the first of the Dortmunder series. Thus, Westlake was already well on his way toward establishing his unique reputation in the field. Appearing at the rate of about one per year, beginning with *The Fugitive Pigeon* in 1965, these novels usually featured a down-to-earth, young, unheroic male hero, suddenly and involuntarily caught in a very tangled web of dangerous, often mob-related, circumstances. Charlie Poole, Aloysius Engle, J. Eugene Raxford, and Chester Conway are representative of the group. Though beset by mobsters, police, and occasionally foreign agents, these protagonists emerge, according to comic convention, largely unscathed, usually better off than when the action commenced, especially in their relations with women. In this respect they resemble Alan Grofield, as they do also in their personal charm and their sometimes witty comments on contemporary society. Westlake's achievement in these novels was demonstrated by their continuing favorable reception by reviewers such as Boucher and by the recognition conveyed by the Edgar Allan Poe Award for *God Save the Mark*.

The novels in the Dortmunder series depart from these patterns in various ways. For one thing, John A. Dortmunder is not young or particularly witty. Nor is he an innocent bystander: He is a professional thief. Furthermore, he is seldom much better off at the end of the novel than he was at the beginning, and his only romantic attachment is a long-standing arrangement with May, a food market checker, who fell in love with Dortmunder when she caught him shoplifting. Finally, Dortmunder is not a lone wolf, despite his frequently expressed wish to be one, but only one member of what is probably the least successful criminal gang of all time.

In the course of the novels making up the series, the membership of this gang varies somewhat, depending on the caper at hand. Dortmunder is always around to do the planning, even though the original idea for the crime is usually brought to him by someone else, often his old pal and nemesis, Andy Kelp. Kelp steals cars for a living, usually doctors' cars because they come with outstanding optional equipment and can be parked anywhere. Another regular gang member is Stan Murch, a getaway driver who talks obsessively about the shortest automotive distance between two points. He is often accompanied by his mother, a cynical New York cabbie who is usually referred to as "Murch's Mom." She and May sometimes act as a sort of ladies' auxiliary, making curtains in *Bank Shot* (1972), taking care of the kidnap victim in *Jimmy the Kid* (1974). The mammoth and very dangerous Tiny Bulcher is also frequently on hand. Sullen, ignorant, and violent, he often frightens his fellow crooks, but he is strong enough to lift or carry anything.

Among the early members of Dortmunder's gang are Roger Chefwick, expert on locks and safes and an obsessive model trains hobbyist; Wilbur Howey, who served forty-eight years in prison on a ten-year sentence because he could not resist the temptation to escape; and Herman X, whose criminal activities support both black activist political causes and a sybaritic life-style. As the series developed, extra hired hands became less frequent, although the regular planning sessions of Dortmunder, Kelp, Stan, and Tiny in the back room of Rollo's beloved and atmospheric bar remained de rigueur. Fictional criminals who can be categorized in this way according to their obsessions and character defects seem to belong more to the world of conventional Jonsonian comedy than to the frightening world of contemporary urban America. This disparity permits Westlake to approach disturbing subject matter in these novels without upsetting his readers.

The basic plot in the Dortmunder series, the comic caper, has a similar effect. In *Adventure, Mystery, and Romance: Formula Stories as Art and Popular Culture* (1976), John G. Cawelti argues that detective fiction generally functions as a comic genre because it subdues the threatening elements of life through the powers of mind and structure. Overly elaborate plotting, that is, inevitably triggers some sort of comic reader response. Even before discovering Dortmunder in 1970, Westlake showed evidence of a similar conviction in the incredibly complex kidnap caper he created for *Who Stole Sassi Manoon?* (1969). Later, *Help I Am Being Held Prisoner* (1974) developed another non-Dortmunder caper of Byzantine complexity, a double bank robbery conducted by prison inmates who have a secret passage to the outside world. In these novels, as in the Dortmunder and Parker series, the intricacy of the caper both enthralls readers and distracts them from the negative judgments they would make in real life.

The fundamental difference between the comic and the chilling capers lies in the degree to which Westlake permits realistic circumstances to undermine the design. Paradoxically, the comic variety entails a greater degree of realism. Though Parker must sometimes settle for a fraction of his anticipated haul, Dortmunder gets even less. Moreover, the antagonistic forces subverting Dortmunder's plans are rarely the sorts of dangerous assassins whom Parker encounters, but more mundane elements such as weather, illness, time, and coincidence—in other words, real life. The distinction of Westlake's comic caper novels, therefore, arises from his combining the coherence available only in elaborately constructed fiction with the comic incoherence familar to readers in their everyday lives. Such comedy, though often howlingly hilarious, is ultimately a serious, highly moral form of literature.

Westlake's *Humans* (1992) showed just how seriously he takes his comedy. In the 1990's he undertook a number of novels that are neither comedy capers (though they are occasionally highly comedic) nor hard-boiled. In *Smoke* (1995), Freddie Noon, a burglar, breaks into a secret tobacco research laboratory, swallows some experimental solutions, and finds himself invisible. *Humans*, however, is narrated by an angel, Ananayel, who has been sent by God to arrange the end of the world. "He" encounters obstacles not only from the resident devils, who will do anything to thwart God's will, but also from his growing love for a human woman.

*The Ax* (1997) addressed the phenomenon of the increasing, one might say hasty, layoffs and "down-sizing" in the name of the corporate bottom line that ruined hundreds of thousands of American lives during the period of greatest prosperity that America had ever known. The protagonist, Burke Devore, gets fired from his middle-management position at a paper mill, and his rage drives him to commit murder—in fact to commit mass murder.

The 1995 republication of 1982's *Kahawa* by Mysterious Press includes an introduction by Westlake that signalled how strongly he indicts the kind of crime about which he writes so (apparently) casually. It also showed that by comparison, even in the Parker novels there were lengths to which he would not go, a barrier beyond which lies soul-blanching horror. *Kahawa* is based on a true story: In Idi Amin's Uganda, a group of white mercenaries stole a coffee-payload railroad train a mile long and made it disappear. Of Uganda after Amin fled, Westlake writes in his introduction, "Five hundred thousand dead; bodies hacked and mutilated and tortured and debased and destroyed; corridors running with blood. . ." His research, he reported, "changed the character of the story I would tell. As I told my wife at the time, 'I can't dance on all those graves.'" One is reminded of Joseph Conrad's Marlow, in *Heart of Darkness* (1899), who murmurs as he looks upon civilized England, "And this also has been one of the dark places of the earth."

After spending considerable time in those dark places, many a writer turns to absurdism. Westlake's blessing is that, though his outrage seems to grow by the year, he has never lost his sense of humor. Although he documents the atrocities of Uganda, he also creates lovable characters over whom a reader might weep. Although he plans the end of the world, he dramatizes how precious and valuable are human follies and foible-filled lives. Westlake, after the 1990's, is no longer the madcap he pretends to be, who remarks, "It probably says something discreditable about me that I put the serious work under a pseudonym and the comic under my own name." Westlake's ever-evolving career has proven that he is not merely a "genius of comedy" or a "heist-meister." He has become one of the truly significant writers of the twentieth century.

## Principal mystery and detective fiction

SERIES:
John Dortmunder: *The Hot Rock*, 1970; *Bank Shot*, 1972; *Jimmy the Kid*, 1974; *Nobody's Perfect*, 1977; *Why Me?*, 1983; *Good Behavior*, 1985; *Drowned Hopes*, 1990; *Don't Ask*, 1993; *What's the Worst That Could Happen?*, 1996; *Bad News*, 2001. Alan Grofield: *The Score*, 1964; *The Damsel*, 1967; *The Blackbird*, 1969; *The Dame*, 1969; *Lemons Never Lie*, 1971.

Parker: *The Hunter*, 1962 (also as *Point Blank*); *The Man with the Getaway Face*, 1963 (also as *The Steel Hit*); *The Outfit*, 1963; *The Mourner*, 1963; *The Score*, 1964 (also as *Killtown*); *The Jugger*, 1965; *The Seventh*, 1966 (also as *The Split*); *The Rare Coin Score*, 1967; *The Green Eagle Score*, 1967; *The Black Ice Score*, 1968; *The Sour Lemon Score*, 1969; *Deadly Edge*, 1971; *Slayground*, 1971; *Plunder Squad*, 1972; *Butcher's Moon*, 1974; ; *Child Heist*, 1974; *Comeback*, 1998; *Backflash*, 1998; *Payback*, 1999. Mitch Tobin: *Kinds of Love, Kinds of Death*, 1966; *Murder Among Children*, 1968; *Wax Apple*, 1970; *A Jade in Aries*, 1971; *Don't Lie to Me*, 1972.

OTHER NOVELS: *The Mercenaries*, 1960 (also as *The Smashers*); *Killing Time*, 1961 (also as *The Operator*); *361*, 1962; *Killy*, 1963; *Pity Him Afterwards*, 1964; *The Fugitive Pigeon*, 1965; *The Handle*, 1966 (also as *Run Lethal*); *The Busy Body*, 1966; *The Spy in the Ointment*, 1966; *God Save the Mark*, 1967; *Who Stole Sassi Manoon?*, 1969; *Somebody Owes Me Money*, 1969; *Ex Officio*, 1970 (also as *Power Play*); *I Gave at the Office*, 1971; *Cops and Robbers*, 1972; *Gangway*, 1973 (with Brian Garfield); *Help I Am Being Held Prisoner*, 1974; *Two Much!*, 1975; *Brothers Keepers*, 1975; *Dancing Aztecs*, 1976 (also as *A New York Dance*); *Enough*, 1977; *Castle in the Air*, 1980; *Kahawa*, 1982; *High Adventure*, 1985; *Trust Me on This*, 1988; *The Fourth Dimension Is Death*, 1989; *The Perfect Murder*, 1991 (with others); *Smoke*, 1995; *Pity Him Afterwards*, 1996; *The Ax*, 1997; *The Hook*, 2000; *Corkscrew*, 2000.

OTHER SHORT FICTION: *The Curious Facts Preceding My Execution and Other Fictions*, 1968; *Levine*, 1984; *Tomorrow's Crimes*, 1989; *Horse Laugh and Other Stories*, 1991; *A Good Story and Other Stories*, 1999.

## Other major works

NOVELS: *Anarchaos*, 1967; *Up Your Banners*, 1969; *Adios, Scheherezade*, 1970; *A Likely Story*, 1984; *High Jinx*, 1987 (with Abby Westlake); *Transylvania Station*, 1987 (with Abby Westlake); *Sacred Monster: A Comedy of Madness*, 1989; *Humans*, 1992; *Baby, Would I Lie?: A Romance of the Ozarks*, 1994.

SCREENPLAYS: *Cops and Robbers*, 1972; *Hot Stuff*, 1975 (with Michael Kane); *The Stepfather*, 1987; *The Grifters*, 1990; *Why Me?*, 1990 (with Leonard Mass, Jr.).

TELEPLAYS: *Supertrain*, 1979; *Fatal Confession: A Father Dowling Mystery*, 1987; *Flypaper*, 1993.

NONFICTION: *Elizabeth Taylor: A Fascinating Story of America's Most Talented Actress and the World's Most Beautiful Woman*, 1961; *Under an English Heaven*, 1972.

CHILDREN'S LITERATURE: *Philip*, 1967.

EDITED TEXT: *Once Against the Law*, 1968 (with William Tenn); *Murderous Schemes: An Anthology of Classic Detective Stories*, 1996; *The Best American Mystery Stories*, 2000.

## Bibliography

Cawelti, John G. *Adventure, Mystery, and Romance: Formula Stories as Art and Popular Culture*. Chicago: University of Chicago Press, 1976.

DeAndrea, William L. "The Many Faces of Donald E. Westlake." *The Armchair Detective* 21, no. 4 (Fall, 1988): 940-960.

Dunne, Michael. "The Comic Capers of Donald Westlake." In *Comic Crime*, edited by Earl Bargainnier. Bowling Green, Ohio: Bowling Green State University Popular Press, 1987.

Long, Marion. "Looking on the Dark Side." *Mary Higgins Clark Mystery Magazine* 24, no. 7 (Fall, 1998)

Mantell, Suzanne. "Donald Westlake: Adept at Juggling." *Publishers Weekly* 247, no. 43 (October 23, 2000): 44.

Nevins, Francis M., Jr. "Donald Edwin Westlake." In *Twentieth-Century Crime and Mystery Writers*, edited by John M. Reilly. London: Macmillan, 1980.

West, J. Alec. "An Interview with Donald Westlake." *Murderous Intent Mystery Magazine* (Fall, 1997)

Westlake, Donald E. Introduction to *Levine*. New York: Mysterious, 1984.

"Westlake, Donald E." In *Mystery and Suspense Writers: The Literature of Crime, Detection, and Espionage*, edited by Robin W. Winks and Maureen Corrigan. New York: Charles Scribner's Sons, 1998.

*Michael Dunne*
*Updated by Fiona Kelleghan*

# Cornell Woolrich

## Cornell George Hopley-Woolrich

**Born:** New York, New York; December 4, 1903
**Died:** New York, New York; September 25, 1968

**Also wrote as** • George Hopley • William Irish

**Types of plot** • Psychological • thriller • police procedural • inverted • historical

**Principal series** • The "Black," 1940-1948.

**Contribution** • Cornell Woolrich's highly suspenseful plots are often recounted from the standpoint of leading characters who, however ordinary they may seem at the outset, become embroiled in strange and terrifying situations. Woolrich was particularly adept at handling questions of betrayal and suspicion, arousing doubts about characters' backgrounds and intentions. Works dealing with amnesia or other unknowing states of mind produce genuine tension, though in other hands such themes might seem forced and overused.

Woolrich rarely made use of master detectives or other agents committed to bringing criminals to justice. His policemen attempt as best they can to grapple with apparently inexplicable occurrences; some of them are willful and corrupt. When they reach solutions, often it is with the help of individuals who themselves have been suspected of or charged with criminal acts. One of Woolrich's strengths is the vivid depiction of stark emotional reactions; the thoughts and feelings of leading characters are communicated directly, often in sharply individual tones. Some of his plots revolve about methods of crime or detection which might seem ingenious in some instances and implausible in others. Taken as a whole, his work may appear uneven; his best tales, however, produce somber and deeply felt varieties of apprehension, plunging the reader into the grim, enigmatic struggles of his protagonists.

**Biography** • The dark forebodings which affected the author's works may have originated in his early life. Cornell George Hopley-Woolrich was born in New York City on December 4, 1903. His father was a civil engineer and his mother was a socialite; as a boy, Woolrich was often in Latin America. At about the age of eight, after seeing a production of Giacomo Puccini's *Madame Butterfly* (1904), he was overwhelmed with a profound sense of fatalism. When revolutions broke out in Mexico, he was fascinated by the fighting and collected spent cartridges that could be found on the street. It would appear that he was badly shaken by the eventual breakdown of his parents' marriage, which left him unusually dependent upon his mother.

In 1921, he entered Columbia University in New York, where courses in English may have spurred his interest in creative writing. One of his classmates, Jacques Barzun, later recalled that Woolrich was an amiable if somewhat distant individual. On one occasion, he was immobilized by a foot infection, an experience that may be reflected in the theme of enforced immobility which would appear in some of his later writings. During that time, however, under the name Cornell Woolrich he composed his first novel, *Cover Charge* (1926); this romantic work was favorably received. His *Children of the Ritz* (1927) won a prize offered jointly by *College Humor* magazine and a motion-picture company; Woolrich went to Hollywood in order to adapt a filmscript from that book. In 1930, he married Gloria Blackton, a film producer's daughter, but she left him after a few weeks. Woolrich may have had homosexual inclinations. After he returned to New York, he wrote other sentimental novels, the last of which was *Manhattan Love Song* (1932), before devoting his efforts entirely to mystery writing.

In 1934, his first crime and suspense stories were published in detective magazines. Even with the success of *The Bride Wore Black* (1940) and other full-length works, Woolrich remained a reclusive figure; frequently he would remain in his room at a residential hotel for long periods, venturing outside only when necessary. Success and public esteem apparently meant little to him, even when his works were widely distributed and had become known through films and other adaptations. In 1948, he won the Edgar Allan Poe Award of the Mystery Writers of America. His mother, to whom he remained devoted, died in 1957, and he dedicated the stories in *Hotel Room* (1958) to her. His ensuing despondency seemed to diminish his creative output. In addition to bouts of alcoholism, he developed diabetes; yet he ignored the progressive deterioration of his health. Gangrene affected one leg, but he left this condition unattended until it became necessary for doctors to amputate the limb. He finally suffered a stroke and died in his native city on September 25, 1968. Very few people attended his funeral. His will established a trust fund, dedicated to his mother's memory, in support of scholarships for the study of creative writing at Columbia.

**Analysis** • The stories which marked Cornell Woolrich's debut as a mystery writer display a fatalism which lends added weight to surprise endings and ironic twists. Almost invariably, seemingly innocuous situations become fraught with dangerous possibilities. Outwardly ordinary people prove to harbor devious and malign intentions; the innocent, by the odd machinations of fate, often find themselves enmeshed in the schemes of the guilty. Frequently, the outcome of these dark, troubled struggles remains in doubt, and Woolrich was not averse to letting characters perish or be undone by their own devices. Many of his works are set in New York or other large urban areas during the

Depression and depict people who, already impoverished and often desperate, are drawn relentlessly into yet more serious and threatening circumstances.

In Woolrich's first suspense work, "Death Sits in the Dentist's Chair," the mysterious demise of a man who has recently had his teeth filled leads to some frantic searching for the murderer. An unusual murder method is uncovered, and the protagonist is nearly poisoned during his efforts to show the culprit's mode of operation. In "Preview of Death," when an actress costumed in an old-fashioned hoop skirt is burned to death, a police detective shows how the fire could have been produced by one of her cohorts. "Murder at the Automat" leads to some anxious investigations when a man dies after eating a poisoned sandwich obtained from a machine; actually, the trick seems remarkably simple once the murderer's likely whereabouts have been reviewed. Other deadly devices, some outwardly improbable, appear in various stories.

In "Kiss of the Cobra," death from snake poison cannot easily be explained until it is learned how a strange Indian woman could have transferred venom to common articles used by her victims. Suggestions of supernatural agencies are developed more fully in "Dark Melody of Madness" (also known as "Papa Benjamin" and "Music from the Dark"), in which a musician all too insistently attempts to learn the secrets of voodoo from some practitioners of that dark religion. Although he can compel them to divulge the incantations that seemingly will summon malevolent spirits, such forces are not content to be used in the man's stage performances. Eventually, whether from the intervention of unearthly powers or from sheer fright, he collapses and dies. "Speak to Me of Death," which eventually was incorporated into another work, concerns a seemingly prophetic warning: When a wealthy old man is told that he will die at midnight, other interested parties take note of the means specified and gather to prevent harm from coming to him. In the end he falls victim not to any human agency or to anxiety and apprehension; rather, the original design is carried through in a wholly unexpected way. In Woolrich's stories, the distinction between known operations of the physical world and his characters' subjective beliefs is often left shadowy and uncertain; when improbable events take place, it is not always clear whether individual susceptibilities or the actual workings of malignant powers are responsible. Similarly, when protagonists are introduced in an intoxicated state, sometimes it cannot easily be determined whether they are actually responsible for deeds that were perpetrated when they were inebriated. In other stories, certain individuals are under the sway of narcotics, such as marijuana or cocaine.

At times, Woolrich's protagonists find themselves implicated in grim plots which begin with apparently incriminating situations and end with unusual resolutions. In "And So to Death" (better known as "Nightmare"), a man who has been found at the scene of a murder has some difficulty in persuading even himself that he is innocent, and only with the intervention of others can the facts in the case be established. Police procedures are often portrayed as arbitrary and brutal. A marathon dance contest furnishes the background for

"Dead on Her Feet," a macabre study of a killing in an unusual pose. When a girl is found rigid, not exhausted but actually murdered, a ruthless policeman forces a young man, weary and frightened, to dance with his dead partner; though soon afterward he is absolved, he breaks down under the strain and falls prey to uncontrollable mad laughter. In "The Body Upstairs," police torment a man with lighted cigarettes in an attempt to make him confess; all the while, another man on the force has tracked down the real killer.

If the innocent generally suffer in Woolrich's stories, it is also true that crime often fails to achieve its ends. Well-laid plans tend to go awry in strange or unanticipated ways. In "The Death of Me," a man determines to stage his own death in order to defraud his insurance company. He exchanges personal effects with someone who was killed at a railroad crossing, but this other man proves to have been a criminal who had stolen a large sum of money; thus, the protagonist is pursued both by the man's cohorts and by an insurance investigator. When he turns on his company's agent and kills him, he realizes that he will be subject to criminal charges under whichever name he uses. In "Three O'Clock," a man decides to eliminate his wife and her lover. He builds a time bomb which he installs in the basement of his house; once the mechanism is in place, however, he is accosted by burglars, who tie him up and leave him behind as the fateful countdown begins. After the man has abandoned all hope of rescue, it is discovered that the device had inadvertently been deactivated beforehand, but by then he has been driven hopelessly mad by his ordeal.

In other cases, those who in one way or another are confronted with crime are able to confound lawbreakers. In "Murder in Wax," a woman uses a concealed phonograph machine to record the testimony that is required to save her husband from murder charges. "After-Dinner Story" has the host at a social gathering using the threat of poison to elicit a vital admission from one of the guests. The notable story "It Had to Be Murder" (also known as "Rear Window") begins with a man with a cast on his leg casually observing others in his vicinity; some mysterious movements by a man at the window across from him attract his attention, and he arrives at the inference that his neighbor's wife has been murdered. Although at first the police are inclined to dismiss this theory, these suppositions prove to be correct, and an encounter at close quarters with the killer takes place before the matter is settled.

Woolrich's crime novels, notably those which came to be grouped together because of their common "color scheme"–the word "black" figures in the titles of six Woolrich novels–deal with more complex issues of anxiety and violence. Multiple killings, for example, raise questions about how apparently unrelated persons and occurrences may have become part of a larger web of havoc and destruction; the pattern is eventually explained by reference to previous events which have left the perpetrators permanently embittered and changed. In some cases, the murderer's actions and the efforts at detection are shown in alternating sequences, so that the overarching question becomes which side will prevail in the end. Although clues and testimony figure prominently in some works, the reader rarely is challenged directly by such means;

assessments of character and intentions often are equally significant. Problems of love frustrated or gone wrong frequently account for the single-minded intensity and twisted, circuitous logic underlying murderous deeds; some characters are driven by an anguished loneliness which has turned ordinary emotional impulses inside out.

The pursuit of revenge is a common motivation for crime in Woolrich's novels. In *The Bride Wore Black*, various murders seem to implicate a mysterious woman; it is learned that years earlier her husband was killed on the church steps immediately after their wedding ceremony, and she has vowed to eliminate those responsible. In some respects *Rendezvous in Black* (1948) is a haunting, bittersweet study in love denied. After the death of his fiancée, a man sets forth to inflict similar anguish on others who may have been involved; killing those whom each of them loved most, he leaves a trail of bodies which can be explained only when his original design is uncovered. All the while tangled, turbulent feelings have welled up within the killer; when a woman is hired by the police to lure him into the open, she creates the illusion that his beloved has returned to him.

Woolrich was adept at portraying the lonely desperation of those who must struggle against the most unfavorable odds to prove their innocence or to save loved ones. Sometimes it appears that sheer willpower and determination can triumph over the most imposing obstacles; even the most unlikely forms of evidence can be instrumental in efforts to find the real culprits. *The Black Curtain* (1941) concerns a man who has suffered a blow to the head which has effaced the memories of three years; uneasily, he sorts out the bits of information which may cast some light on the missing period of his life. It emerges that under another identity he was falsely implicated in a murder, and the actual perpetrators have been trying to do away with him for once and all. The protagonist's groping, agonizing attempts to learn about his own past, despite his fear that some terrible secret lies at the end of his quest, makes this work a highly compelling one. *The Black Angel* (1943) begins with a man's sentence to death for the murder of his presumed mistress; his wife believes in him implicitly, however, and as the date for the execution draws near she sets off on her own to clear him. Beginning only with a monogrammed matchbook and some entries in the victim's notebook, she succeeds finally in confronting the real killer. Along the way there are a number of unsettling encounters in the murky night world of call girls and criminal operators. A man who fled to Havana with a gangster's wife is implicated in her murder, in *The Black Path of Fear* (1944); dodging threats from several sides, he receives aid from some unexpected quarters, and eventually some bizarre and vicious criminals are brought to justice.

In many of Woolrich's works, time itself becomes an enemy. This motif is utilized most powerfully in *Phantom Lady* (1942), which begins 150 days before a man's scheduled execution. The time remaining, down to the final hour, is announced at the beginning of each chapter. The protagonist has been found guilty of murdering his wife, after no one would believe that he had actually been with another woman on the night in question. Even he has begun to doubt that she ever existed. Finally, after much fruitless searching, the mystery woman is located. The evidence used to bring her into the open is no more substantial than an old theater program. In the end, the real culprit turns out to be an individual who had been close to the condemned man. In *Deadline at Dawn* (1944), a man and a woman who happened to be at the scene of a killing must find the actual murderer within a matter of hours; chapter headings consist simply of clock faces showing how much closer the protagonists have come to freedom, or to disaster, at each turn.

Suspicion and conflict at close quarters also appears in Woolrich's works; while husbands and wives, and for that matter lovers of various sorts, often act on behalf of each other, when differences arise the results can be frightful and unsettling. In *Waltz into Darkness* (1947), set in New Orleans in 1880, a man seeks a mail-order bride, but he discovers that the woman he has married is not quite the one he had expected. His new wife appropriates his money, and he discovers that she probably had a hand in the death of his original betrothed. Yet she exercises a fatal sway over him, and though she mocks him for his apparent weakness, he believes that the signs of her deep underlying love for him are unmistakable. This curious polarity seems to enervate him and leave him without a will of his own; he commits murder for her sake, and even when he learns that she is slowly poisoning him, his devotion to her is so strong that he cannot save himself.

Woolrich frequently employed first-person narratives. Those works in which accounts of crime and detection follow each other on parallel courses utilize an omniscient narrator, who appears, however, never to be far from the thoughts, hopes, and fears of the leading characters. In some of his stories he adopts a lilting, sentimental tone for the recounting of romantic aspirations; the shock of disillusionment and distrust is conveyed in a jarring, somber fashion. In some of his later offerings such tendencies took on maudlin qualities, but at his best Woolrich could create an acute and well-drawn contrast between lofty ideals and close encounters with danger. Reactions to impending threats are expressed in a crisp, staccato tempo; blunt, numbing statements, either in direct discourse or in narration, generally bring matters to a head. Often situations are not so much described as depicted through the uneasy perspective of characters who must regard people and objects from the standpoint of their own struggles with imminent danger. Odd metaphors for frenzied and violent action sometimes lend ironic touches. In much of Woolrich's writing, action and atmosphere cannot readily be separated. Indeed, quite apart from the original conceptions that are realized in his leading works, the dark and penetrating power of his studies in mystery and fear entitle his efforts to be considered among the most important psychological thrillers to appear during the twentieth century.

### Principal mystery and detective fiction

SERIES: The "Black" series: *The Bride Wore Black,* 1940 (also as *Beware the Lady*); *The Black Curtain,* 1941; *Black Alibi,* 1942; *The Black Angel,* 1943; *The Black Path of Fear,* 1944; *Rendezvous in Black,* 1948.

OTHER NOVELS: *Phantom Lady,* 1942; *Deadline at Dawn,* 1944; *Night Has a Thousand Eyes,* 1945; *Waltz into Darkness,* 1947; *I Married a Dead Man,* 1948; *Fright,* 1950; *Savage Bride,* 1950; *You'll Never See Me Again,* 1951; *Strangler's Serenade,* 1951; *Death Is My Dancing Partner,* 1959; *The Doom Stone,* 1960; *Into the Night,* 1987.

OTHER SHORT FICTION: *I Wouldn't Be in Your Shoes,* 1943 (also as *And So to Death* and *Nightmare*); *After-Dinner Story,* 1944 (also as *Six Times Death*); *If I Should Die Before I Wake,* 1945; *The Dancing Detective,* 1946; *Borrowed Crimes,* 1946; *Dead Man Blues,* 1947; *The Blue Ribbon,* 1949 (also as *Dilemma of the Dead Lady*); *Somebody on the Phone,* 1950 (also as *The Night I Died* and *Deadly Night Call*); *Six Nights of Mystery,* 1950; *Eyes That Watch You,* 1952; *Bluebeard's Seventh Wife,* 1952; *Nightmare,* 1956; *Violence,* 1958; *Beyond the Night,* 1959; *The Ten Faces of Cornell Woolrich,* 1965; *The Dark Side of Love,* 1965; *Nightwebs,* 1971; *Angels of Darkness,* 1978; *The Fantastic Stories of Cornell Woolrich,* 1981; *Darkness at Dawn,* 1985; *Vampire's Honeymoon,* 1985; *Blind Date with Death,* 1986.

## Other major works

NOVELS: *Cover Charge,* 1926; *Children of the Ritz,* 1927; *Times Square,* 1929; *A Young Man's Heart,* 1930; *The Time of Her Life,* 1931; *Manhattan Love Song,* 1932.

SHORT FICTION: *Hotel Room,* 1958.

SCREENPLAY: *The Return of the Whistler,* 1948 (with Edward Bock and Maurice Tombragel).

## Bibliography

Boucher, Anthony. Introduction to *The Bride Wore Black.* New York: Simon & Schuster, 1940.

Ellison, Harlan. Introduction to *Angels of Darkness.* New York: Mysterious, 1978.

Kunitz, Stanley J., ed. *Twentieth Century Authors: First Supplement.* New York: Wilson, 1955.

Lee, A. Robert. "The View from the Rear Window: The Fiction of Cornell Woolrich." In *Twentieth-Century Suspense: The Thriller Comes of Age,* edited by Clive Bloom. New York: St. Martin's Press, 1990.

Nevins, Francis M., Jr. "Cornell Woolrich." *The Armchair Detective* 2 (October-April, 1968-1969): 25-28, 99-102, 180-182.

_____. *Cornell Woolrich: First You Dream, Then You Die.* New York: Mysterious, 1988.

_____. "Cornell Woolrich: The Years Before Suspense." *The Armchair Detective* 12 (Spring, 1979): 106-110.

Woolrich, Cornell. *Blues of a Lifetime: The Autobiography of Cornell Woolrich.* Bowling Green, Ohio: Bowling Green State University Popular Press, 1991.

"Woolrich, Cornell." In *Mystery and Suspense Writers: The Literature of Crime, Detection, and Espionage,* edited by Robin W. Winks and Maureen Corrigan. New York: Charles Scribner's Sons, 1998.

*J. R. Broadus*

# Israel Zangwill

**Born:** Whitechapel, London, England; January 21, 1864
**Died:** Midhurst, Sussex, England; August 1, 1926

**Type of plot** • Police procedural

**Contribution** • Israel Zangwill, hailed in his time as "the Dickens of the ghetto" and praised as a peer of classic writers such as Thomas Hardy, Henry James, Rudyard Kipling, and George Bernard Shaw, made his single outstanding contribution to the realm of mystery fiction when he was twenty-seven years old. Serialized in 1891 and subsequently published in book form, *The Big Bow Mystery*, Zangwill's unique crime novel, has been termed the first full-length treatment of the locked-room motif in detective literature. Israel Zangwill has thus come to be proclaimed the father of this challenging mystery genre, and properly so. On the fictional trail to the solution of the Big Bow murder, the author's professional sleuths, along with a number of amateur newspaper theorists and assorted curbstone philosophers, offer a number of ingenious alternate explanations of the puzzle, possible hypotheses which through the years have inspired other literary craftsmen involved in constructing and disentangling locked-room mysteries. In addition, *The Big Bow Mystery* offers a graphic picture of late Victorian life in a seething London working-class neighborhood. Zangwill effectively combined social realism of the streets with a realistic depiction of the criminal investigative process.

**Biography** • Israel Zangwill was born in the ghetto of London's East End. His father, an itinerant peddler, was an immigrant from Latvia; his mother, a refugee from Poland. Part of Zangwill's childhood was spent in Bristol, but by the time he was twelve, the family had returned to London, where young Israel attended the Jews' Free School in Whitechapel, becoming at the age of fourteen a "pupil-teacher" there.

By the time he was eighteen, Zangwill had manifested extraordinary talent for writing, winning first prize for a humorous tale brought out serially in *Society* and publishing a comic ballad. He showed, too, an early interest in social realism by collaborating on a pamphlet describing market days in the East End Jewish ghetto. In 1884, Zangwill was graduated from London University with honors in three areas: English, French, and mental and moral sciences. He continued teaching at the Jews' Free School until 1888, when he resigned to devote all of his considerable energy to a career in letters.

Subsequently, the writings of Israel Zangwill were indeed prolific: In addition to twenty-five collected volumes of drama and fiction, Zangwill wrote hundreds of essays for popular and esoteric journals and gave as many speeches.

He worked efficiently and rapidly and editors quickly recognized and rewarded his talent. Zangwill once observed that he had never written a line that had not been purchased before it was written. His plays were produced in London and New York; his final drama, staged on Broadway, provided Helen Hayes with one of her first starring roles.

Zangwill's range of interests was remarkably extensive: art, economics, pacifism, politics, racial assimilation, World War I, and Zionism and the Jewish homeland. Around these themes he composed romances and satires, entertainments and polemics. Though he continued his strenuous habits of composition right up to his death, Zangwill's most effective period of fiction writing came, so the consensus records, during the 1890's, the era he had ushered in with *The Big Bow Mystery*. Critics of fiction regard *Children of the Ghetto, Being Pictures of a Peculiar People* (1892), *The King of Schnorrers: Grotesques and Fantasies* (1894), and *Dreamers of the Ghetto* (1898) as his most provocative and enduring contributions to socioethnic literature. His most famous drama, *The Melting-Pot* (1908)—"That's a great play, Mr. Zangwill," declared President Theodore Roosevelt on opening night—presented for the first time the now-clichéd metaphor of America as a crucible for uniting into a single people the disinherited of the Old World.

Israel Zangwill soon focused his work on social and political issues, bringing to contemporary problems a sensibility at once idealistic in its hopes and realistic in its proposed solutions. His ideas were given wide publicity in both England and America; he was always a popular attraction as an orator. Late in his life, Zangwill suffered a nervous breakdown, brought on by the stresses of his work for the theater as dramatist and theater manager. He died in the summer of 1926 in Sussex.

**Analysis** • In the lore of mystery and detective fiction, Israel Zangwill's reputation, based on one classic work, is secure. He is the father of the locked-room mystery tale, a subgenre launched by Edgar Allan Poe in short-story format but made especially attractive by Zangwill's versatile, full-length rendering. Written in 1891, when Zangwill was at the virtual beginning of his career, *The Big Bow Mystery* was serialized in the *London Star*, published a year later in book form, and finally collected in *The Grey Wig: Stories and Novelettes* (1903). More than a whodunit cipher or a pure exercise in inductive reasoning, Poe's "ratiocination," Zangwill's novel brings together the intellectual acumen of the scientific sleuth with the inventive imagination of a poet. At the same time, the novel offers a perceptive and sociologically valid picture of working-class life in late Victorian England, replete with well-defined portraits of *fin de siècle* London characters. Many of the issues and ideas distinguishing the turbulent 1890's are mentioned or explored in the novel.

As a writer with roots in the ghetto, Zangwill theorized that it was essential to reveal the mystery, romance, and absurdity of everyday life. In *The Big Bow Mystery* he employs a photographic realism to render the human comedy. With vivid attention to detail, he depicts the truths inherent in class relationships, the tensions in political realities, and the passions in reformist clamor. Influenced himself by the pulp novels or "penny dreadfuls" of the time, Zangwill was perhaps paying homage to them through loving parody. In the main, however, the literary sources of the novel are Edgar Allan Poe, Charles Dickens, and Robert Louis Stevenson, whose romances of the modern and the bizarre, particularly *The Strange Case of Dr. Jekyll and Mr. Hyde* (1886), had caught Zangwill's attention.

The characters in *The Big Bow Mystery* are Dickensian in name as well as behavior: Mrs. Drabdump, a hysterical widowed landlady who, with retired Inspector Grodman, discovers the body of the victim; Edward Wimp, the highly visible inspector from Scotland Yard who undertakes the well-publicized investigation; Denzil Cantercot–poet, pre-Raphaelite devotee of The Beautiful, professional aesthete–who has ghostwritten Grodman's best-selling memoirs, *Criminals I Have Caught*; Tom Mortlake–union organizer, "hero of a hundred strikes," veritable saint to all workingmen of Bow–who is arrested for the murder of Arthur Constant–idealist, much-loved philanthropist, believer in The True. The ideas of the philosopher Arthur Schopenhauer, particularly those set forth in his essay on suicide, had become important to Constant; so, too, had the visions of Madame Helena Petrovna Blavatsky, one of the founders of Theosophy, who claimed power over superphysical forces and whose cult during the 1890's attracted serious thinkers, dabbling dilettantes, and crackpots. Fascinated by the confluence of these intellectual and spiritual forces, Zangwill juxtaposed esoteric discussions of astral bodies to pragmatic reviews of trade unionism. *The Big Bow Mystery* presents an almost encyclopedic view, sometimes satiric but always accurate, of polarized British thought patterns of the age.

Constant's dead body is discovered in a room sealed as effectively as a vault, with no instrument of death found on the premises. As Grodman and Wimp, experienced Scotland Yard detectives, endeavor to solve the mystery, the popular *Pell Mell Gazette* prints numerous ingenious theories mailed in by interested amateurs. With a sly twist, Zangwill even brings Poe directly into the story by having a newspaper correspondent assert that Nature, like the monkey she is, has been plagiarizing from "The Murders in the Rue Morgue" and that Poe's publisher should apply for an injunction. Another would-be investigator suggests that a small organ-grinder's monkey might have slid down the chimney and with its master's razor slit poor Constant's throat. Thus Zangwill pays his debt to Poe and serves notice that he intends to embellish the genre.

As the true and the useful, the aesthetic and the utilitarian collide, as the tenets of Oscar Wilde and Algernon Charles Swinburne challenge the ideas of John Stuart Mill and Jeremy Bentham, Zangwill graphically sustains the brooding, gaslit Victorian atmosphere. His characters trudge through London mists, take tea in musty, gray boardinghouses, and slink through bleak working-class neighborhoods. Zangwill possessed a strong awareness of environmental factors and their effect on people's lives. Before he begins to unravel the complexities of this tale, however, even Prime Minister William Ewart Gladstone and the home secretary appear as actors in the drama. The ultimate revelations come as a shocking series of twists, yet no clues have been denied the reader; the solution is honest, intricate, and logical. Zangwill has remained in total control of his material.

*The King of Schnorrers* contains two mystery tales: "The Memory Clearing House" and "Cheating the Gallows." Again, Poe is the inspiration behind both. "The Memory Clearing House" has as its basis a theory of supernatural thought transference, with people selling unwanted and superfluous memories to a memory broker, who catalogs these unique materials and sells them. He runs a "pathological institution." When an author purchases a murderer's memory for use in a realistic novel he has in progress, the complications begin. The climax occurs when the published novel is damned for its tameness and improbability. Zangwill's inventiveness is again evident in "Cheating the Gallows." In this story, an odd pair who happen to live together—a respectable bank manager and a seedy, pipe-smoking journalist—become involved with the same woman. A murder, a suicide, and a phantasmic dream bring about several stunning revelations. A few other grotesques and fantasies from the volume—"A Double-Barrelled Ghost," "Vagaries of a Viscount," and "An Odd Life"—also capture Zangwill's art in the area of mystery; each has a balanced dose of humor and pathos.

As much an interpreter of life's vicissitudes and problems as he was an entertainer in his mystery writings, Israel Zangwill—and his famed locked room in Bow—will continue to occupy a prestigious position in the annals of detective fiction.

### Principal mystery and detective fiction

NOVEL: *The Big Bow Mystery*, 1891.

SHORT FICTION: *The King of Schnorrers: Grotesques and Fantasies*, 1894; *The Grey Wig: Stories and Novelettes*, 1903.

### Other major works

NOVELS: *The Premier and the Painter: A Fantastic Romance*, 1888 (with Louis Cowen); *The Bachelors' Club*, 1891; *The Old Maids' Club*, 1892; *Merely Mary Ann*, 1893; *Joseph the Dreamer*, 1895; *The Master*, 1895; *The Mantle of Elijah*, 1900; *Jinny the Carrier: A Folk Comedy of Rural England*, 1919.

SHORT FICTION: *Children of the Ghetto, Being Pictures of a Peculiar People*, 1892; *Ghetto Tragedies*, 1893; *Dreamers of the Ghetto*, 1898; *They That Walk in Darkness: Ghetto Tragedies*, 1899; *Ghetto Comedies*, 1907.

PLAYS: *The Great Demonstration*, 1892 (with Cowen); *Aladdin at Sea*, 1893; *The Lady Journalist*, 1893; *Six Persons*, 1893; *Threepenny Bits*, 1895; *Children of the Ghetto*, 1899; *The Moment of Death: Or, The Never Never Land*, 1900; *The Revolted Daughter*, 1901; *Merely Mary Ann*, 1903; *The Serio-Comic Governess*, 1904; *The Mantle of Elijah*, 1904; *The King of Schnorrers*, 1905; *Jinny the Carrier*, 1905; *Nurse Marjorie*, 1906; *Melting-Pot*, 1908, revised 1914; *The War God*, 1911; *The Next Religion*,

1912; *Plaster Saints: A High Comedy*, 1914; *The Moment Before: A Psychical Melodrama*, 1916; *Too Much Money*, 1918; *The Cockpit*, 1921; *We Moderns*, 1922; *The Forcing House: Or, The Cockpit Continued*, 1926.

POETRY: *Blind Children*, 1903.

NONFICTION: *Motza Kleis*, 1882 (with Cowen); *"A Doll's House" Repaired*, 1891 (with Eleanor Marx Aveling); *Hebrew, Jew, Israelite*, 1892; *The Position of Judaism*, 1895; *Without Prejudice*, 1896; *The People's Saviour*, 1898; *The East African Question: Zionism and England's Offer*, 1904; *What Is the ITO?*, 1905; *A Land of Refuge*, 1907; *Talked Out!*, 1907; *One and One Are Two*, 1907; *Old Fogeys and Old Bogeys*, 1909; *The Lock on the Ladies*, 1909; *Report on the Purpose of Jewish Settlement in Cyrenaica*, 1909; *Be Fruitful and Multiply*, 1909; *Italian Fantasies*, 1910; *Sword and Spirit*, 1910; *The Hithertos*, 1912; *The Problem of the Jewish Race*, 1912; *Report of the Commission for Jewish Settlement in Angora*, 1913; *The War and the Women*, 1915; *The Principle of Nationalities*, 1917; *The Service of the Synagogue*, 1917 (with Nina Davis Salaman and Elsie Davis); *Chosen Peoples: The Hebraic Ideal Versus the Teutonic*, 1918; *Hands off Russia*, 1919; *The Jewish Pogroms in the Ukraine*, 1919 (with others); *The Voice of Jerusalem*, 1920; *Watchman, What of the Night?*, 1923; *Is the Ku Klux Klan Constructive or Destructive? A Debate Between Imperial Wizard Evans, Israel Zangwill, and Others*, 1924; *Now and Forever: A Conversation with Mr. Israel Zangwill on the Jew and the Future*, 1925 (with Samuel Roth); *Our Own*, 1926; *Speeches, Articles, and Letters*, 1937; *Zangwill in the Melting-Pot: Selections*, n.d.

TRANSLATION: *Selected Religious Poems of Ibn Gabirol, Solomon ben Judah, Known as Avicebron, 1020?-1070?*, 1923.

MISCELLANEOUS: *The War for the World*, 1916.

## Bibliography

Adams, Elsie Bonita. *Israel Zangwill*. New York: Twayne, 1971.

Leftwich, Joseph. *Israel Zangwill*. New York: T. Yoseloff, 1957.

Oliphant, James. *Victorian Novelists*. London: Blackie & Son, 1899.

Udelson, Joseph H. *Dreamer of the Ghetto: The Life and Works of Israel Zangwill*. Tuscaloosa: University of Alabama Press, 1990.

Wohlgelernter, Maurice. *Israel Zangwill: A Study*. New York: Columbia University Press, 1964.

*Abe C. Ravitz*

# GLOSSARY

**Above-the-line:** Espionage jargon for an agent who operates in a foreign country using as cover a position in an organization or institution.

**Access:** Espionage term describing a convenient job which is close to sources of information.

**Alimony:** Espionage term for wages held for an agent while he is operating in hostile territory.

**Amateur sleuth:** Person who is neither a private investigator nor a policeman and who, either through accident or invitation, finds himself in a position to solve a crime. Bird watchers, gardeners, and clergy most often find themselves with the opportunity or the equipment to accomplish the task.

**Analytic school**. See **Whodunit**.

**Angels:** Espionage term for local security services.

**Angle:** Selfish motive or an unethical plan by which a person hopes to advance his or her own interests.

**Antecedents (British):** Criminal's history.

**Armchair detection:** Method of detection in which the detective solves a crime solely through analysis and deduction of the facts with which he has been provided.

**Babe:** Sexually desirable woman.

**Baby:** Man, especially a mean or intimidating one, a tough guy; a man's sweetheart.

**Baby-sit:** Protect an agent while he is involved in an espionage operation.

**Back door:** Agent's emergency escape route, usually prepared in advance of an espionage operation.

**Bag:** Unattractive girl or woman.

**Barkeep:** Bartender.

**Bat phone (British):** Policeman's radio.

**Below-the-line:** Espionage term for an agent who operates in a foreign country without an official cover.

**Ben Franklin:** One-hundred-dollar bill.

**Big wheel:** Important man.

**Bird:** Gentleman.

**Black-bag job:** Espionage term for an illegal break-in, usually by the Central Intelligence Agency or the Federal Bureau of Investigation.

**Blake:** Become a double agent and jeopardize one's espionage network.

**Blown:** Espionage term for the situation in which an agent's cover has been penetrated.

**Book off (British):** Go off duty.

**Book on (British):** Report for duty.

**Bookie:** Bookmaker.

**Booking:** Recording of an arrest.

**Box:** Espionage jargon for a group tailing an agent, each individual positioned at a different place.

**Boys in blue:** Police.

**Brain:** Detective.

**Branch lines:** Agent's espionage contacts.

**Break (British):** Breakthrough in a case; a burglary.

**Broad:** Young woman or girl; a prostitute.

**Brothel creepers:** Boots with soft soles.

**Brush over the traces:** Hide the signs of espionage.

**Bug:** Listening device.

**Bump off:** Kill.

**Bunco:** Swindle or cheat.

**Bunco artist:** Confidence man.

**Burn:** Espionage term meaning to blackmail.

**Burrower:** Espionage jargon for a researcher.

**Button man:** Espionage jargon for an agent.


**C-note:** One-hundred-dollar bill.

**Cabbage:** Money.

**Cabbie:** Cabdriver.

**Camel:** Espionage term for an agent who transports secret material.

**Car coper:** Espionage term for an agent skilled in car engines.

**Case:** Examine a location with a view to robbing it.

**Catch:** Take on an assignment.

**Chamber of horrors:** Trial room at headquarters.

**Charge room:** Police processing room.

**Cheap:** Stingy; unrefined; promiscuous; having a bad reputation.

**Chicago lightning:** Bullets.

**Chisel:** Cheat or acquire something using petty means.

**Chiseler:** Petty crook; a schemer.

**Clams:** Money.

**Clean:** Innocent; usually referring to the lack of a gun on a person.

**Climber (British):** Cat burglar.

**Clink:** Prison.

**Coat trailer:** Espionage term for an agent who shows interest in being recruited by the enemy.

**Cobbler:** Espionage jargon for a passport maker.

**Collar:** Arrest.

**Collator (British):** Policeman who keeps records.

**Company, the:** Espionage term for the U.S. federal government's Central Intelligence Agency.

**Con man:** Confidence man or swindler; any charming, persuasive man.

**Conjuring tricks:** Set of basic espionage techniques.

**Conscious:** Espionage term describing one who is informed on matters of operational intelligence.

**Cooks:** Espionage term for narcotics chemists.

**Cooping:** Time out, as for a nap, for a policeman, on police time.

**Cop, or copper:** Policeman.

**Cover:** Lie for a person who is suspected of a crime; in espionage jargon, a false identity assumed by an agent during an operation.

**Crash:** Espionage jargon for an emergency or urgent situation.

**Creep:** Undesirable person.

**Croak:** Die.

**Crook:** Thief.

**Crusher:** Espionage term for a guard.

**Curtains:** Death.

**Cut-out:** Espionage term for an agent who serves as a mediator between two other agents, thereby keeping each unknown to the other.

**Dame:** Woman.

**Dead:** Espionage term indicating that an agent is retired.

**Dead letter box:** Espionage jargon for a place used to hide secret messages.

**Deduction:** Logical technique used by Sherlock Holmes. (See also **ratiocination.**)

**Deep six:** Destroy evidence.

**Defective detective:** Term from the 1930's pulp writers, who created detectives with physical disabilities in order to make them unique.

**Deskman:** Espionage jargon for an agent who works at headquarters rather than in the field.

**Detail:** Temporary assignment (police).

**Dick:** Detective.

**Dimmer:** Dime.

**Dispatch:** Kill.

**Divisional sleuth (British):** Detective.

**Do time:** Serve a sentence in prison.

**Dope:** Information.

**Double agent:** Espionage term referring to an agent who turns and begins operating for the enemy.

**Double-double game:** Espionage jargon for the turning of agents against their own side.

**Dough:** Money.

**Downtown:** Police headquarters.

**Dropper:** Messenger.

**Duchess:** Girl, especially a sophisticated one.

**Duck-dive:** Espionage term for a sudden disappearance.

**English tea cozy.** See **Whodunit.**

**Equalizer:** Pistol or other gun.

**Espionage:** Type of fiction which has as its subject the clandestine machinations of government agents, usually regarding the discovery, theft, or recovery of secret documents. This subgenre is also characterized by the use of a distinct and often colorful vocabulary.

**Fair-play cluing:** Convention in which the mystery writer abides by certain rules in writing his works: among others, that the reader will have access to the same clues as the fictional detective and at the same time, and that there will be no coincidences or supernatural solutions to the crime.

**Fallback:** Espionage jargon for a cover story; a secondary or spare clandestine meeting place.

**False-flag operation:** Espionage term for an operation in which agents pretend to belong to another service in order to protect their own service from scandal or embarrassment.

**Family man:** Clean-living police officer.

**Fence:** Person who buys and sells stolen goods.

**Ferret:** Espionage term for a person whose specialty is uncovering electronic listening devices.

**Fieldman:** Espionage jargon for an agent who works in enemy territory.

**Filter:** espionage term meaning to elude a tail.

**Finger:** Identify; in espionage jargon, to set up a rival or double agent for capture.

**Finger man:** Espionage term for an assassin.

**Fireman:** Espionage term for an agent.

**Fireproof:** Espionage term meaning invulnerable.

**Flaking:** Planting evidence on a suspect to facilitate arrest.

**Flash:** Espionage jargon term for the most urgent level of cable message to an agent in the field.

**Flasher:** Person (usually a man) who exposes his genitals.

**Flatfoot:** Policeman.

**Float:** Espionage term meaning to work for a time solely on one's cover job to establish one's false identity.

**Flute:** Whiskey-filled soft-drink bottle.

**Flying:** Temporarily assigned to another command.

**Follow-up:** Espionage term meaning to execute a compromised figure.

**Foot-in-the-door operation:** Espionage jargon for a situation in which an agent must use some force or intimidation to contact a target.

**Footpad:** Espionage jargon for an agent.

**Footwork:** Espionage technique.

**Fragged:** Espionage term meaning emotionally fragmented.

**Frame:** Contrive evidence against an innocent person.

**Frighten the game:** Alert the target of an espionage operation by accident.

**Fry:** Be executed, especially by electrocution.

**Fun toy:** Listening device.

**Gentleman:** Fair superior (police term).

**Germs:** Pimps, prostitutes, junkies, and other unsavory characters.

**Give a ticket:** Espionage term meaning to kill.

**Going equipped:** Being in possession of tools for crime.

**Going to the mattress:** Disappearing, leaving town.

**Gold seam:** Espionage jargon for the route of laundered money from one bank to another.

**Golden age:** Period beginning roughly in the 1920's in Great Britain and continuing into the late 1930's, primarily in the United States, when the mystery/detective genre went through its most profound changes. Beginning with an emphasis on rules (see **Knox's Decalogue**), with the puzzle being the most important element in the story (see **Whodunit**), the genre gradually moved into more complex forms (see **Locked-room mystery**) and eventually into the hard-boiled form in the United States. It was during the Golden Age that mystery writers consciously set the limits and conceived of a philosophy by which the genre would be defined.

**Gong (British):** Medal.

**Goods:** Information.

**Goon:** Hoodlum or thug; one lacking in brains or imagination.

**Gopher:** Young thief or hoodlum; a safecracker; a dupe.

**Gorilla:** Hoodlum or thug, particularly one with more muscle than brain.

**Gothic:** Subgenre characterized by a vulnerable female who finds herself in an isolated, mysterious setting populated by strange and sinister people who are driven by some secret. The characteristic setting is an ancient mansion. There is often an evil uncle and a vindictive housekeeper—and perhaps an insane wife in the attic.

**Grand:** One thousand dollars.

**Grand Dames:** Dorothy L. Sayers, Agatha Christie, Margery Allingham, and Ngaio Marsh, the four female mystery writers who developed and perfected the classic English whodunit.

**Greasy spoon:** Inferior or cheap restaurant or lunch counter.

**Great Detective:** See **Master sleuth**.

**Gumheel:** Work as a detective.

**Gumshoe:** Private detective; to walk quietly; to walk a beat; to work as a police detective.

**Gunsel:** Boyish assistant; a thieving or untrustworthy person.

**Guts:** Intestinal (or other) fortitude.

**Had-I-But-Known school:** Phrase (coined by Ogden Nash) referring to a type of plot and narration in which the story is artificially stalled and prolonged by odd coincidences, senseless acts which upset the sleuth's plans, accidents which cause a character to forget to relate something of importance, and so on. The narrator (usually female) laments that "had I but known what was going to happen, we might have stopped it."

**Handler (British):** Person who buys and sells stolen goods.

**Handwriting:** Espionage jargon for an agent's own unique operating style.

**Hard-boiled:** Unsentimental, mean, cynical, unconcerned about the feelings or opinions of others; a type of detective fiction whose protagonist is a tough guy, a man of action who uses his fists and his mind to solve a crime. He is sometimes dishonest and not always chivalrous with women. His displacement of the more cerebral master sleuth reflects the 1920's American recognition that irrationality is the rule rather than the exception. The most representative writers in the genre are Raymond Chandler, Dashiell Hammett, and Ross Macdonald.

**Hard-guy/soft-guy interrogation technique:** Two-man method in which one officer is intimidating and rough while the other is more reasonable toward the suspect. The two together can often bring about a confession or obtain information.

**Hardwire:** Espionage jargon for electronic equipment.

**Hat:** Five-dollar bribe ("Go buy yourself a hat").

**Heat:** Police; a handgun, as in "packing heat."

**Heat on, put the:** Demand payment or information, specifically with the use of threats.

**Heat's on, the:** Condition of being energetically pursued or sought, usually by the police.

**Heat-packer:** Gunman.

**Heeltap:** Espionage jargon for an agent's technique for avoiding possible tails.

**Heist:** Steal (verb); a robbery (noun).

**Hit-and-run job:** Espionage term for a particularly dangerous and violent mission.

**Hold the bag:** Be double-crossed or left to take the blame for others.

**Honey-trap:** Espionage jargon for making an enemy agent vulnerable to blackmail by luring him into a sexually compromising situation.

**Hood:** Gangster; in espionage jargon, an agent.

**Hook:** Influential friend.

**Horror comics (British):** Police circulars.

**Hot:** Stolen.

**House:** Espionage term meaning to capture.

**Ice:** Diamond, or, collectively, diamonds.

**Ice, put on:** Kill.

**Iceman:** Jewel thief.

**Illegal resident.** See **Below-the-line**.

**Illegals:** Foreign agents.

**In grays:** Still in the police academy.

**In the bag:** In uniform.

**In the heave:** Time out.

**Inside job:** Crime committed against an organization by someone within it.

**Interrogation:** Espionage jargon for torture.

**Inverted story:** Crime story told from the point of view of the criminal. In this case the emphasis is not on "whodunit," since this is already obvious, but on how. The reader is often able to sympathize with the protagonist, in spite of his criminal nature.

**Jake:** All right, satisfactory.
**Jane:** Girl or young woman; a man's sweetheart.
**Job:** Robbery.
**Joint:** Prison.
**Ju ju man:** Espionage jargon for an agent who plans, rather than carries out, missions.
**Jug:** Prison or jail, usually a local one.
**Jug day:** Celebration for promotion or retirement.
**Jumper:** Actual or potential suicide victim.
**Junkie:** Drug addict.

**Keep on ice:** Keep an agent inactive for a time until a better espionage opportunity arises.
**Key-holder:** Espionage jargon for a person who provides a place for a secret meeting.
**Kite:** Complaint to the police received through the mail.
**Knock off:** Kill.
**Knock-off (British):** Arrest.
**Knockout drops:** Drug, often chloral hydrate, put into a drink to render the drinker unconscious.
**Knox's Decalogue:** Ten rules for writers of detective fiction composed by Ronald Knox in 1928. Intended to allow the reader a fair chance at solving the mystery, it holds that the criminal must be mentioned early in the story; there will be no use of the supernatural; there will be no more than one secret room or passage; no new poisons or new appliances necessitating long explanations at the end of the story will be introduced; no "Chinaman" can figure in the story; no accident or intuition can aid the detective; the detective may not himself be the culprit; the reader must receive the same clues as the detective and must get them around the same time; the sidekick, or Watson character, must not conceal any thoughts which pass through his mind, and he must be slightly less bright than the average reader; and twin brothers or doubles may not be used without ample preparation by the writer.

**Lace-curtain job:** Espionage operation calling for very discreet observation.
**Lag (British):** Ex-convict.
**Launder:** Espionage jargon for preparing secret funds for legitimate use.
**Leash dog:** Espionage jargon for an agent who works under immediate supervision.
**Leave on one's socks:** Espionage term meaning to beat a hasty retreat.

**Legal resident.** See **Above-the-line.**

**Legend:** Espionage term for a fabricated history of an individual or an event. (See also **Cover.**)

**Legman:** Espionage jargon for an agent who carries secret messages between two other agents.

**Lettuce:** Money.

**Line-up:** Group of five persons (one suspect and four policemen) lined up for identification of a perpetrator.

**Lip:** Attorney.

**Liquidate:** Kill, often in large numbers.

**Locked-room mystery:** Type of "miracle crime" in which a person is found murdered in a locked room which it appears impossible for a murderer to have entered or exited. Story emphasis is on "howdunit" as much as on "whodunit." (See also **Miracle crimes.**)

**Lock-ups (British):** Arrested persons in custody

**Loid:** Item used to open locks, often a credit card (from celluloid).

**Lolly (British):** Loot.

**Looker:** Pretty woman.

**Loser's corner:** Espionage jargon for the predicament of an interrogatee who is unaware of how much his interrogators already know.


**MacGuffin:** Term used by Alfred Hitchcock to refer to the plans, papers, secrets, or documents that must be found, stolen, discovered, and so on, and which are vital to the characters of espionage stories. The formula of most stories of this kind have at their center this entity.

**Mailfist job:** Espionage term meaning an operation with the objective of assassination.

**Mainline operation:** Major espionage enterprise.

**Make a pass:** Approach an enemy agent in order to gather intelligence.

**Maltese Duck:** Wild-goose chase.

**Manor (British):** Policeman's beat; a criminal's territory.

**Mark:** Easy victim, a sucker, the victim of a confidence man.

**Master sleuth:** Larger-than-life figure capable of a supreme level of detecting, who uses his powers of observation and reason, rather than his muscles, to unravel a puzzle. He rarely works for money; rather, he works for the sheer pleasure of finding a crime puzzling enough to challenge his superior intelligence. Sherlock Holmes is the quintessential example of this kind of fiction and character.

**Mean streets:** Term coined by Raymond Chandler to describe, in a narrow sense, the squalid, crime-ridden milieu of the private investigator and his quarry and, in a broader sense, a world marked by disorder, uncertainty, and violence.

**Mickey Finn:** Strong hypnotic or barbiturate dose given to an unsuspecting person to render him unconscious.

**Minder:** Strong-arm man.

**Miracle crimes:** Crimes which seemingly have no rational explanation but which are ultimately demonstrated to have occurred through natural rather than supernatural means.

**Mole:** Foreign national recruited and prepared for later use as a double agent.

**Moniker:** Name.

**Moola:** Money.

**Mouthpiece:** Attorney.

**Mug shot:** Police photograph.

**Murphy man:** Confidence man.

**Nail:** Catch.

**Necktie party:** Hanging.

**Network:** Espionage ring.

**Newgate novels:** Kind of literature popular in the eighteenth century, characterized by semifictional colorful accounts of highwaymen and other criminals, often with implied admiration for these outlaws. Based on the lives of English criminals who ended up in Newgate Prison.

**Nick (British):** Police station.

**Nicked (British):** Be arrested for a minor offense.

**Nip (British):** Pickpocket.

**Nutter (British):** Crazy person.

**On the lam:** On the run.

**On the skids:** On the decline from one's previous position.

**On the tin:** Free.

**Operational intelligence:** Usable information, in espionage jargon.

**Operative:** Espionage term for an agent.

**Pack a heater:** Carry a gun.

**Panda car (British):** Local beat patrol car.

**Paraphernalia:** Innocent objects used for murder.

**Patient:** Espionage jargon for an interrogatee.

**Pavement artist:** Espionage jargon for an agent who specializes in surveillance.

**Pawn:** Espionage term for an agent.

**P.I.:** Private investigator.

**Pick man:** Lock picker.

**Pickings (British):** Loot.

**Pin on:** Cause blame to fall on.

**Pinks, the:** Pinkerton detectives.

**Play back:** Return enemy agents to their own countries after they have been turned.

**Play for a sucker (or sap):** Take advantage of.

**Play it long:** Espionage jargon for to act with extreme caution.

**Plug:** Wound a person by shooting him.

**Pointman:** Espionage term for an agent who forms one of several tails on a quarry.

**Poker face:** Private investigator.

**Pokey:** Jail.

**Police procedural:** Type of crime story in which the police and their methods in solving a crime are of primary importance. The reader follows the police, seeing the methods they employ in tracking a criminal. Realism is an important characteristic of this type of story.

**Postman:** Case officer who handles the daily needs of an intelligence network.

**Potsie:** Shield.

**Previous (British):** Criminal's earlier convictions.

**Private dick:** Private investigator.

**Private eye:** Private investigator; taken from the logo used by the Pinkertons, which was a wide-open eye with the legend "We never sleep."

**Psychological:** Kind of crime fiction that focuses primarily on the internal or mental causes for crime. The emphasis of the story is on "whydunit," rather than "whodunit."

**Pulps:** Early mystery magazines, such as **Black Mask**, so called for their use of grainy paper made from wood pulp. Characterized by garish covers which were often the best part of the magazine, they measured seven by ten inches, and their pages were short-fibered, fragile, and difficult to preserve.

**Put out smoke:** Espionage jargon for to reinforce one's cover by behaving in accordance with one's false identity.

**Put the screws on:** Make things difficult.

**Put the squeeze on:** Force, harass, or embarrass someone into doing something.

**Queen bee (British):** Senior female officer.

**Quentin quail:** Teenage girl below the age of sexual consent.

**Rabbi:** Influential friend.

**Racket:** Illegal enterprise.

**Railroad:** Convict falsely.

**Rap:** Charge.

**Rat:** Inform.

**Ratiocination:** Edgar Allan Poe's term for the rational, deductive method used to solve a mystery. This method presupposes a benevolent and orderly universe which is ultimately knowable.

**Recycle:** Return defecting agents to their own countries for use as double agents.

**Red herring:** Extraneous clue that distracts the reader's attention from the real solution.

**Reptile fund:** Secret government fund for intelligence operations.

**Rings (British):** Officer's calls to the police station to receive updates on new developments.

**Ripper:** Safe-cracker.

**Rock:** Diamond. (See also **Ice**.)

**Roman policier:** French police novel. Émile Gaboriau's works featuring Monsieur Lecoq and involving painstaking reconstruction of the crime and analysis of detail are characteristic works in this subgenre.

**Rub out:** Kill.

**Run:** Espionage jargon meaning to control an agent; a mission into enemy territory.

**Safe house:** Espionage term for a secure location in which it is safe to conduct secret meetings.

**Safety paper:** Passport paper.

**Safety signals:** Espionage jargon for a sign system between agents to indicate when it is safe to meet.

**Sanction:** Espionage term for a counter-assassination.

**Sap:** Fool; to hit a person on the head, as with a blackjack, to render him unconscious.

**Scarper (British):** Flee.

**Sensation novels:** Genre that became popular in the 1860's. Characterized by a paradoxical combination of luridness and convention, romance and realism, these works focused on crime, villainy, and evil. The term was a derogatory one, meant to condemn the works of writers such as Charles Dickens, Nathaniel Hawthorne, and Wilkie Collins, as well as many lesser figures, for their preoccupation with crime.

**Series character:** Character who appears in a number of books by an author.

**Shake the tree:** Espionage jargon for doing things that will cause a target to panic and thus accelerate the operation.

**Shakedown:** Act of extortion.

**Shamus:** Private investigator.

**Shiv:** Knife.

**Shoemaker:** Espionage jargon for a forger.

**Shoes:** Espionage jargon for Western passports.

**Shoo-fly:** Plainclothes policeman, usually assigned to investigate the honesty of uniformed police.

**Shopsoiled:** Espionage term for an agent whose cover is no longer effective.

**Silence:** Kill.

**Sing:** Inform.

**Sister:** Woman.

**Sitting-duck position:** Espionage term for an exposed, vulnerable position during a fight.

**Skip:** Leave town after being told by authorities to remain.

**Slammer:** Prison.

**Sleep:** Wait for a long time before commencing espionage activity.

**Slug:** Bullet.

**Smacker:** One dollar.

**Snow:** Cocaine.

**Snuff out:** Kill.

**Sob story:** Very sad account of personal misfortunes, usually calculated to arouse sympathy in the hearer.

**Sound thief:** Espionage jargon for a hidden microphone.

**Spring:** Aid in an escape from prison.

**Sprung:** Released.

**Spy:** Espionage jargon for an incompetent agent.

**Squeal:** Complain or protest; to inform to the police.

**Squealer:** Informer.

**Squeeze:** Extortion, graft.

**Squirt:** Espionage jargon for a radio transmission.

**Stash:** Hide something; a hiding place; a cache.

**Static post:** Espionage jargon for a fixed surveillance position.

**Stick-and-carrot job:** Espionage term for the use of bribes and threats together to obtain information.

**Stick-up:** Robbery.

**Stiff:** Be drunk; a dead body; a stupid or drunk person; an average man.

**Stir:** Prison.

**Stooge:** Underling, especially one who is a puppet of another.

**Stool:** Inform.

**Stool pigeon:** Informer, usually a police informer.

**Sucker:** Easily deceived person, an easy victim.

**Sûreté Generale, the:** The first modern police force, established in France in the early nineteenth century.

**Sussed (British):** Suspected.

**Swag (British):** Loot.

**Sweat:** Espionage jargon meaning to interrogate using some physical force.

**Swing one's legs at:** Espionage term meaning to blackmail.

**Tag:** Espionage jargon for a single tail or follower.

**Tail:** Follow; one who follows; in espionage jargon, to follow an agent from his clandestine meeting.

**Take a powder:** Disappear.

**Take for a ride:** Kill or cheat.

**Talent spotter:** Espionage jargon for one skilled at spotting potential recruits for the espionage line.

**Tap:** Listening device.

**Telephone monitor:** Listening device.

**Ten-spot:** Ten-dollar bill.

**Ten-thirteen:** Call to assist a police officer.

**Tenner:** Ten-dollar bill.

**Thin one:** Dime.

**Third degree:** Prolonged, sometimes rough, questioning to acquire information or a confession.

**Thriller:** Broad category of fiction which involves a battle between good and evil, represented by a hero and one or more villains and with reader suspense as to the outcome.

**Tiger's claw:** Espionage jargon for a self-defense technique involving a blow to the windpipe.

**Tin star:** Private investigator.

**Tip off:** Warn of something impending, to inform; a clue or hint.

**Tip the wink (British):** Let in on a secret.

**Tomato:** Very attractive girl or young woman.

**Tonsil varnish (British):** Tea or coffee in police canteens.

**Torpedo:** Espionage jargon meaning to eliminate a fellow agent who is suspected of turning.

**Tough guy:** Private investigator.

**Tough-guy school:** Outgrowth of the hard-boiled school of mystery/detective fiction whose distinctive characteristics include the private investigator as the central character, the whodunit plot emphasizing deduction over violence, and little or no emphasis on sociological insights.

**Tradecraft:** Espionage techniques.

**Tradesman:** Espionage jargon for a specialist who is not an agent but who can be called on to provide certain services.

**Trail:** Espionage term meaning to set up a situation of personal advantage.

**Traveling salesman:** Espionage jargon for an agent.

**Trawl:** Espionage term meaning to seek out.

**Treff:** Espionage jargon for a meeting with a contact or fellow agent.

**Turn:** Persuade an enemy agent to betray his country; to change allegiance and betray one's country.

**Two-bit:** Cheap, inferior, second-rate, small-time.

**Unbutton:** Espionage jargon for decoding a secret message.

**Undesirables:** Pimps, prostitutes, junkies, and other unsavory types.

**Unpack:** Espionage term meaning to provide information.

**Varnish remover:** Strong coffee.

**Verbal (British):** Confession made orally.

**Vicar:** Controller of an espionage network.

**Voluntary (British):** Freely given statement.

**Walk in the park:** Espionage jargon for a clandestine meeting.

**Walk-in:** Espionage term meaning to approach an enemy embassy with the intention of turning.

**Walking papers:** Passport.

**Waste:** Kill.

**Watch:** Espionage jargon meaning to keep an enemy agent under surveillance.

**Watch my back:** Request a fellow agent to provide protection during an espionage operation.

**Water games:** Training in techniques for espionage activities on water.

**Water-testing:** Espionage jargon for techniques to be sure that an agent is not being watched.

**Whiz kid (British):** Rapidly promoted officer.

**Whodunin:** Type of plot in which the killer's identity is known from the beginning, but that of the victim is unknown until the end.

**Whodunit:** Classic English mystery; characterized by many clues, faintly comedic overtones, several suspects, usually aristocratic and stereotypical, and at least one corpse. Often set in an English country house or some other idyllic setting; emphasis is placed on the hierarchical nature of society.

**Wireless intercom:** Listening device.

**Wooden kimono:** Coffin.

**Wooden overcoat:** Coffin.

**Wopsie (British):** Woman police constable.

**Work over:** Beat up.

**Working a beat:** Patrolling on duty.

**Workname:** Espionage jargon for an alias used by an agent within his own service.

**Wrangler:** Espionage jargon for a code-breaker.

**Yard, the:** Scotland Yard.

**Yellow:** Cowardly.

**Yellow perils (British):** Traffic wardens.

**Yellow sheet:** Record of previous arrests.

**Yob (British):** Thug.

*Rochelle Bogartz*

# Time Line of Authors

| Date and place of birth | Name |
|---|---|
| May 20, 1799; Tours, France | Honoré de Balzac |
| January 19, 1809; Boston, Massachusetts | Edgar Allan Poe |
| November 11, 1821; Moscow, Russia | Fyodor Dostoevski |
| January 8, 1824; London, England | Wilkie Collins |
| November 13, 1850; Edinburgh, Scotland | Robert Louis Stevenson |
| May 22, 1859; Edinburgh, Scotland | Arthur Conan Doyle |
| April 11, 1862; London, England | R. Austin Freeman |
| September 11, 1862; Greensboro, North Carolina | O. Henry |
| January 21, 1864; Whitechapel, London, England | Israel Zangwill |
| September 23, 1865; Tarna-Örs, Hungary | Baroness Orczy |
| June 7, 1866; Middlesbrough, Yorkshire, England | E. W. Hornung |
| October 22, 1866; London, England | E. Phillips Oppenheim |
| 1868; Marylebone, London, England | Marie Belloc Lowndes |
| May 6, 1868; Paris, France | Gaston Leroux |
| June 25, 1870; London, England | Erskine Childers |
| May 29, 1874; London, England | G. K. Chesterton |
| April 1, 1875; Greenwich, England | Edgar Wallace |
| July 10, 1875; London, England | E. C. Bentley |
| August 26, 1875; Perth, Scotland | John Buchan |
| August 12, 1876; Pittsburgh, Pennsylvania | Mary Roberts Rinehart |
| 1878; Mussoorie, India | Patricia Wentworth |
| August 26, 1884; Warren, Ohio | Earl Derr Biggers |
| December 1, 1886; Noblesville, Indiana | Rex Stout |
| July 23, 1888; Chicago, Illinois | Raymond Chandler |
| October 15, 1888; Charlottesville, Virginia | S. S. Van Dine |
| July 17, 1889; Malden, Massachusetts | Erle Stanley Gardner |
| September 15, 1890; Torquay, England | Agatha Christie |
| July 1, 1892; Annapolis, Maryland | James M. Cain |

| Date and place of birth | Name |
|---|---|
| June 13, 1893; Oxford, England | Dorothy L. Sayers |
| July 5, 1893; Watford, Hertfordshire, England | Anthony Berkeley |
| April 8, 1894; Philadelphia, Pennsylvania | Baynard H. Kendrick |
| May 27, 1894; St. Mary's County, Maryland | Dashiell Hammett |
| April 23, 1895; Christchurch, New Zealand | Ngaio Marsh |
| 1896 or 1897; Inverness, Scotland | Josephine Tey |
| January 10, 1896; Kansas City, Missouri | Frances Lockridge |
| September 25, 1898; St. Joseph, Missouri | Richard Lockridge |
| July 6, 1899; University Place, Nebraska | Mignon G. Eberhart |
| November 13, 1899; Chicago, Illinois | Vera Caspary |
| November 25, 1899; Springfield, Ohio | W. R. Burnett |
| February 13, 1903; Liège, Belgium | Georges Simenon |
| December 4, 1903; New York, New York | Cornell Woolrich |
| December 21, 1903; New York, New York | Lawrence Treat |
| May 20, 1904; London, England | Margery Allingham |
| October 2, 1904; Berkhamsted, England | Graham Greene |
| January 11, 1905; Brooklyn, New York | Manfred B. Lee (Ellery Queen) |
| October 20, 1905; Brooklyn, New York | Federic Dannay (Ellery Queen) |
| 1906; Anadarko, Oklahoma Territory | Jim Thompson |
| September 30, 1906; Edinburgh, Scotland | Michael Innes |
| November 30, 1906; Uniontown, Pennsylvania | John Dickson Carr |
| December 24, 1906; London, England | James Hadley Chase |
| May 12, 1907; Singapore | Leslie Charteris |
| May 13, 1907; London, England | Daphne du Maurier |
| October 7, 1907; Glasgow, Scotland | Helen MacInnes |
| December 17, 1907; Malaya | Christianna Brand |
| May 28, 1908; London, England | Ian Fleming |
| September 17, 1908; Southfields, Surrey, England | John Creasey |
| November 24, 1908; Boston, Massachusetts | Harry Kemelman |
| June 28, 1909; London, England | Eric Ambler |
| July 29, 1909; Jefferson City, Missouri | Chester Himes |
| August 9, 1910; Zutphen, Netherlands | Robert H. van Gulik |

| Date and place of birth | Name |
| --- | --- |
| August 21, 1911; Oakland, California | Anthony Boucher |
| May 30, 1912; London, England | Julian Symons |
| July 17, 1912; Billinghay, Lincolnshire, England | Michael Gilbert |
| August 21, 1912; Cleveland, Ohio | Robert L. Fish |
| September 28, 1913; Horsehay, Shropshire, England | Ellis Peters |
| December 13, 1915; Los Gatos, California | Ross MacDonald |
| February 5, 1915; Kitchener, Ontario, Canada | Margaret Millar |
| July 24, 1916; Sharon, Pennsylvania | John D. Macdonald |
| September 17, 1916; Sunderland, Durham, England | Mary Stewart |
| October 6, 1916; Brooklyn, New York | Stanley Ellin |
| April 5, 1917; Chicago, Illinois | Robert Bloch |
| March 9, 1918; Brooklyn, New York | Mickey Spillane |
| 1920; Brooklyn, New York | Lawrence Sanders |
| June 22, 1920; New Haven, Connecticut | Hillary Waugh |
| August 3, 1920; Oxford, England | P. D. James |
| October 31, 1920; Near Tenby, Pembrokeshire, Wales | Dick Francis |
| January 19, 1921; Fort Worth, Texas | Patricia Highsmith |
| December 6, 1922; Chicago, Illinois | William P. McGivern |
| May 27, 1925; Sacred Heart, Oklahoma | Tony Hillerman |
| October 11, 1925; New Orleans, Louisiana | Elmore Leonard |
| January 13, 1926; East Orange, New Jersey | Amanda Cross |
| February 19, 1926; Oklahoma City, Oklahoma | Ross Thomas |
| August 5, 1926; Göteberg, Sweden | Per Wahlöö |
| October 15, 1926; New York, New York | Ed McBain |
| March 3, 1927; London, England | Nicolas Freeling |
| May 25, 1927; New York, New York | Robert Ludlum |
| September 29, 1927; Canton, Illinois | Elizabeth Peters |
| February 18, 1929; London, England | Len Deighton |
| February 17, 1930; London, England | Ruth Rendell |
| February 22, 1930; Rochester, New York | Edward D. Hoch |
| October 19, 1931; Poole, Dorset, England | John Le Carré |
| September 17, 1932; Springfield, Massachusetts | Robert B. Parker |

| Date and place of birth | Name |
| --- | --- |
| July 12, 1933; Brooklyn, New York | Donald E. Westlake |
| September 25, 1935; Stockholm, Sweden | Maj Sjöwall |
| January 22, 1937; East Pittsburgh, Pennsylvania | Joseph Wambaugh |
| June 24, 1938; Buffalo, New York | Lawrence Block |
| August 25, 1938; Ashford, Kent, England | Frederick Forsyth |
| October 9, 1939; Johannesburg, South Africa | James McClure |
| November 3, 1942; Reading, Pennsylvania | Martin Cruz Smith |
| April 13, 1943; Petaluma, California | Bill Pronzini |
| June 8, 1947; Ames, Iowa | Sara Paretsky |
| date unknown; Pittsburgh, Pennsylvania | Martha Grimes |

# Index of Series Characters

# List of Authors by Plot Type

AMATEUR SLEUTH
Allingham, Margery
Bentley, E. C.
Berkeley, Anthony
Block, Lawrence
Boucher, Anthony
Carr, John Dickson
Chesterton, G. K.
Christie, Agatha
Collins, Wilkie
Creasey, John
Cross, Amanda
Eberhart, Mignon G.
Ellin, Stanley
Francis, Dick
Gilbert, Michael
Grimes, Martha
Henry, O.
Hoch, Edward D.
Innes, Michael
Kemelman, Harry
Leroux, Gaston
Lockridge, Richard, and Frances
    Lockridge
MacInnes, Helen
Orczy, Baroness
Peters, Elizabeth
Peters, Ellis
Poe, Edgar Allan
Queen, Ellery
Rendell, Ruth
Rinehart, Mary Roberts
Sanders, Lawrence
Smith, Martin Cruz
Thomas, Ross

COMEDY CAPER
Westlake, Donald E.

COURTROOM DRAMA
Gilbert, Michael

COZY
Allingham, Margery
Brand, Christianna
Christie, Agatha
Gilbert, Michael
Lockridge, Richard, and Frances
    Lockridge
Sayers, Dorothy L.

ESPIONAGE
Allingham, Margery
Ambler, Eric
Balzac, Honoré de
Block, Lawrence
Buchan, John
Carré, John le
Carter, Nick
Childers, Erskine
Creasey, John
Deighton, Len
Fleming, Ian
Gilbert, Michael
Greene, Graham
Hoch, Edward D.
Ludlum, Robert
MacInnes, Helen
Oppenheim, E. Phillips
Sanders, Lawrence
Smith, Martin Cruz
Thomas, Ross

HARD-BOILED
Burnett, W. R.
Cain, James M.
Carter, Nick
Chandler, Raymond
Gardner, Erle Stanley
Hammett, Dashiell

Himes, Chester
MacDonald, John D.
Paretsky, Sara
Parker, Robert B.
Sanders, Lawrence
Spillane, Mickey
Thompson, Jim
Waugh, Hillary
Westlake, Donald E.

HISTORICAL
Carr, John Dickson
Du Maurier, Daphne
Forsyth, Frederick
Gilbert, Michael
Lowndes, Marie Belloc
Peters, Ellis
Stevenson, Robert Louis
Van Gulik, Robert H.
Wambaugh, Joseph
Woolrich, Cornell

HORROR
Du Maurier, Daphne
Leroux, Gaston
Stevenson, Robert Louis

INVERTED
Balzac, Honoré de
Berkeley, Anthony
Bloch, Robert
Block, Lawrence
Burnett, W. R.
Cain, James M.
Dostoevski, Fyodor
Freeman, R. Austin
Greene, Graham
Henry, O.
Highsmith, Patricia
Hornung, E. W.
Innes, Michael
Millar, Margaret
Symons, Julian
Thompson, Jim
Westlake, Donald E.
Woolrich, Cornell

MASTER SLEUTH
Biggers, Earl Derr
Brand, Christianna
Doyle, Arthur Conan
Gardner, Erle Stanley
Sayers, Dorothy L.
Stout, Rex
Van Dine, S. S.

POLICE PROCEDURAL
Allingham, Margery
Balzac, Honoré de
Biggers, Earl Derr
Boucher, Anthony
Brand, Christianna
Burnett, W. R.
Creasey, John
Fish, Robert L.
Freeling, Nicolas
Gilbert, Michael
Grimes, Martha
Henry, O.
Hillerman, Tony
Hoch, Edward D.
Innes, Michael
James, P. D.
Kendrick, Baynard H.
Lockridge, Richard, and Frances
    Lockridge
McBain, Ed
McClure, James
McGivern, William P.
Marsh, Ngaio
Oppenheim, E. Phillips
Peters, Ellis
Rendell, Ruth
Sanders, Lawrence
Simenon, Georges
Smith, Martin Cruz
Sjöwall, Maj, and Per Wahlöö
Tey, Josephine
Treat, Lawrence
Wahlöö, Per, and Maj Sjöwall
Wallace, Edgar
Wambaugh, Joseph

Waugh, Hillary
Woolrich, Cornell
Zangwill, Israel

PRIVATE INVESTIGATOR
Block, Lawrence
Boucher, Anthony
Carter, Nick
Chandler, Raymond
Christie, Agatha
Ellin, Stanley
Francis, Dick
Freeman, R. Austin
Gardner, Erle Stanley
Hammett, Dashiell
Henry, O.
Hoch, Edward D.
James, P. D.
Kendrick, Baynard H.
Macdonald, Ross
Paretsky, Sara
Parker, Robert B.
Pronzini, Bill
Sanders, Lawrence
Spillane, Mickey
Stout, Rex
Treat, Lawrence
Wallace, Edgar
Waugh, Hillary
Wentworth, Patricia
Westlake, Donald E.

PSYCHOLOGICAL
Balzac, Honoré de
Berkeley, Anthony
Bloch, Robert
Dostoevski, Fyodor
Du Maurier, Daphne
Ellin, Stanley
Grimes, Martha
Highsmith, Patricia
Hillerman, Tony
Lowndes, Marie Belloc
Millar, Margaret
Poe, Edgar Allan

Rendell, Ruth
Simenon, Georges
Stevenson, Robert Louis
Symons, Julian
Thompson, Jim
Woolrich, Cornell

THRILLER
Allingham, Margery
Balzac, Honoré de
Berkeley, Anthony
Block, Lawrence
Buchan, John
Caspary, Vera
Charteris, Leslie
Chase, James hadley
Childers, Erskine
Christie, Agatha
Creasey, John
Dostoevski, Fyodor
Ellin, Stanley
Fish, Robert L.
Forsyth, Frederick
Freeling, Nicolas
Gilbert, Michael
Greene, Graham
Highsmith, Patricia
Innes, Michael
Leonard, Elmore
Leroux, Gaston
Ludlum, Robert
McBain, Ed
McGivern, William P.
Marsh, Ngaio
Oppenheim, E. Phillips
Peters, Ellis
Rendell, Ruth
Spillane, Mickey
Stevenson, Robert Louis
Stewart, Mary
Thomas, Ross
Wallace, Edgar
Waugh, Hillary
Westlake, Donald E.
Woolrich, Cornell